Without Fear or Favor

Other books by Harrison E. Salisbury

―――――

"To Give the News Impartially without
Fear or Favor Regardless of any Party,
Sect or Interest Involved."
Adolph S. Ochs
1896

Harrison E. Salisbury

WITHOUT FEAR OR FAVOR

The New York Times
AND ITS TIMES

Times
BOOKS

Published by TIMES BOOKS, a division of
Quadrangle/The New York Times Book Co., Inc.
Three Park Avenue, New York, N.Y. 10016

Published simultaneously in Canada by Fitzhenry & Whiteside, Ltd., Toronto

Library of Congress Cataloging in Publication Data

Salisbury, Harrison Evans, 1908–
    Without fear or favor.

    Bibliography: p. 593
    Includes index.
    1. New York Times. I. Title.
PN4899.N42T567   071'.47'1   79-66866
ISBN 0-8129-0885-6

Manufactured in the United States of America

Remarkably the lifetime of one woman, Iphigene Ochs Sulzberger, the only child of Adolph S. Ochs, spans the entire period of *The* New *New York Times,* conceived and published by her father.

It is to this extraordinary woman, daughter of the founder, wife of Arthur Hays Sulzberger, Mr. Ochs' successor as publisher; mother-in-law of Orvil Dryfoos, Mr. Sulzberger's successor, and mother of Dryfoos' successor, Arthur Ochs Sulzberger, that this book is dedicated.

Contents

A Word to the Reader

*I*N THE PAST QUARTER OF a century the American Establishment has been shaken to its foundations by what amounts to a new American Revolution. Power has flowed into different and not always steady hands. The country has been passing through (there is no sign that the process is yet complete) an epoch of change which begins to rival those surrealist dramas, Russia in 1917 and China in 1949.

The totality of this metamorphosis lies beyond the scope of this book, but what I try here to document is the role of *The New York Times,* how it has participated in these new currents, affecting them and being, in turn, profoundly changed itself.

We think of a newspaper, even a great newspaper like *The Times,* as holding up a looking glass to history. For many years *The Times* described itself as "a newspaper of record." It is my thesis, to paraphrase McLuhan, that, in a sense, the mirror has become the message; that in showing us what we are and what we are doing; in reflecting the bloat, the complexity, the contradictions of the post-World War II society, *The Times* has come to fulfill a new function; it has quite literally become that Fourth Estate, that fourth coequal branch of government of which men like Thomas Carlyle spoke.

I have centered my attention on a half-dozen events, mileposts, if you will, of this process. The great confrontation over the Pentagon Papers takes a central place because it stands as a metaphor of the emergence of *The Times* into its new social role and, moreover, is in every respect an exciting, a cautionary and an until-now untold tale, one which reveals to us in their many aspects the principal actors in the press, the government, the White House in a dynamic scenario which inevitably leads to Watergate, as surely as Dred Scott led to Fort Sumpter.

One can imagine the Watergate break-in without the Pentagon Papers affair; one cannot imagine the Watergate exposé, the whole debacle of the Nixon presidency without Pentagon.

And yet, it is wrong to see Pentagon and Watergate in isolation. Without the trauma of the Civil Rights struggle, without *The Times'* legal battles in the Sullivan and Connor cases, the victory of Pentagon in the U.S. courts might not have been won.

These acts in the American drama flow out of the continuity of *The Times,* of its rebirth under Adolph S. Ochs, its slow, insistent strengthening of tradition and principle, as these pages make plain. A newspaper is not born whole, fully formed, ready to go out and report the world. It is fashioned by time, by mistakes, by achievement, by learning. It is always learning.

My emphasis has been placed on the modern *Times* and *its times,* and particularly upon the American experience, the experience of the last twenty or twenty-five years, the experience of change in the American Establishment and the American charter.

One cannot say that *The Times* has always been at the center of these happenings because there has been no *center;* no single source; no charismatic leader; no political movement in the old style; no manifesto; no blinding personification of Good or Evil. It has been *vox populi* in a classic sense.

The parameters are domestic. The matter does not revolve on world balance, the cold war or détente, although these, of course, are affected. It is concerned with Vietnam at home not in Asia; the consequences of *Brown* v. *The Board of Education;* with the CIA as a metaphor of homegrown, secret and out-of-control bureaucracy.

Only segments of this story can be presented here but they are segments that have shaped the world around us, the manner in which we perceive ourselves, our relationship to our society. They have changed the men, the institutions and, supremely, the balance of forces within the American Establishment. It is the story of how *The Times* has affected the country and its power structure; a story of publishers, editors, reporters and of the men, in government and out, whom they have confronted.

Quintessentially it is the story of an unending and imperfect search for truth; of a struggle against what the poet Robert Bly once called the "American system of hypocrisy," the seamless belt of lies (as Bly put it "the ministers lie, the professors lie, the television lies, the priests lie.")

A revolution, even an unperceived revolution, is not a time of ease. Nor is this an easy story. The men around whom it is told are not easy men. They are not characters of black and white. They do not always make the right decisions, understand events with perfect clarity, stand totally tall at high noon. They are, to be certain, real people with the faults and the virtues of real people and they and hundreds like them make up the skeletal structure of *The Times.*

Amid it *The Times* reaches out with its reporting skills, identifies the new thrusts, the new players, and tries, sometimes with clumsiness, to act as surrogate for the people, seeking to strengthen the First Amendment powers which enable it to examine, as the people no longer can, the BIGS, Big Government, Big Bureaucracy, Big Spying, Big Interests, Big Labor, Big Business, all the multiplicands that have transformed our Jeffersonian society into something quite different, quite frightening at times, seldom understood, carrying on the task, as Mr. Ochs promised, "without fear or favor."

Without Fear or Favor

I

"Let it be four-thirty!"

THE OPEN-FACED CLOCK AT the Gaiety Delicatessen on Forty-seventh Street west of Broadway showed 1:25 P.M. when the telephone at the cash register rang. Annie Gabel, ex-showgirl, blond and bosomy, reached for it lazily, putting an order pad in front of her and answered, "Deli." An excited voice said, "Will you tell Mr. Rosenthal of *The New York Times* to return to the office immediately. It's urgent."

Annie Gabel walked back to the booth where Abe Rosenthal, managing editor of *The Times,* was sitting with James Greenfield, his foreign editor, eating a corned-beef-on-rye.

"Mr. Rosenthal," she said, "your office called. They want you back. Something urgent."

Rosenthal looked at his companion. "My God!" he said. "Maybe this is it."

He didn't say *what* was it. He didn't have to. The men scrambled from the booth, left a ten-dollar bill for their half-eaten lunch and hurried out onto Broadway. It was a lazy Saturday afternoon. The thermometer stood at eighty-seven and the usual throng sauntered along the tawdry street, some headed for matinées, some window-shopping and crowd-staring. Rosenthal and Greenfield noticed none of this. They walked briskly past the Forum Theater, where a movie called *The Cop* was showing, past the Victoria, whose marquee offered *Doctor No* and past *Escape from Planet of the Apes* at the Astor (later transmogrified into the "World's Largest Flea Market"). If they saw the Winston man rhythmically puffing smoke rings above Bond's Clothing Store they gave no sign. The electric bulletin on what was then the Allied Chemical Tower (and had once been the Times Tower) stuttered along, spelling out a dull day's news. No hint of crisis anywhere.

The men turned into West Forty-third, the narrow street already choked with trucks and transporters that soon would roar away with the Sunday papers, and headed for No. 229, entering the revolving door. The clock above the entrance showed 1:32. The two men nodded to

3

a brown-uniformed guard and rode the elevator to the third floor.

It was Saturday, June 12, 1971. Abe Rosenthal was forty-nine years old and had been managing editor of *The New York Times* not quite two years. He had worked for the paper all his professional life. The question beating at his mind as he headed toward *The Times'* city room was: What has gone wrong? What has gone wrong with the secret and exclusive story *The Times* is preparing to print in the Sunday paper?

Earlier there had been other questions—and they would persist: Where would the trail of events unfolding from this story lead? Where, if he had to, would Rosenthal get another job?

At the moment neither personal concern nor philosophical concept entered Rosenthal's thought. His total attention focused on the problem at hand. Was there trouble from Washington? Had the publisher changed his mind?

On this summer afternoon *The New York Times* was approaching the 120th anniversary of its founding. For seventy-five years it had been published by the Ochs family, the first forty by Adolph S. Ochs himself and the last thirty-five by his heirs. The present publisher was Arthur Ochs Sulzberger, forty-five, "Punch" as he was universally known except by his wife, Carol, who called him Arthur, deeming the nickname "Punch" *dégagé* for the publisher of *The New York Times.* He had held his post for eight years, having unexpectedly succeeded to it on the premature death of his brother-in-law, Orvil Dryfoos, in 1963.

The Times was a large enterprise, a very large enterprise, indeed. It ranked 407 on *Fortune* magazine's list of the 500 largest American corporations. It numbered 6,793 employees and embraced a variety of operations in addition to *The Times* newspaper—newsprint mills, radio and TV stations, magazines and smaller newspapers. But *The Times* was its core and heart. By careful enhancement the newspaper that had been so brilliantly conceived at the turn of the century (within the framework of the faltering original *Times*) by Adolph Ochs had grown and grown under strong family direction. It was no accident that of a baker's dozen newspapers published in New York City when Mr. Ochs came up from Chattanooga in 1896 *The Times* was the only real survivor, a robust survivor with a daily circulation of 815,000. The press run for Sunday, June 13, had been ordered at 1,500,000. In the first half of 1971 the paper had been selling about 1,456,000 copies each Sunday and over 850,000 daily. The year of 1971 would not be the greatest in *Times'* history in terms of profit, but it would not be a bad one. In the first six months *The Times* would report earnings of $4,-627,000 on a volume of $124,236,000. More important than this (*The Times* never measured itself primarily against an economic yardstick), the newspaper stood alone in the United States and in the world. It was universally recognized as *the* leading newspaper. No other paper in America and no other paper anywhere possessed comparable resources, esteem and influence. When *The Times* spoke, the chancelleries of Europe listened and the Kremlin took notice. Most Presidents of the United States (although not, by his own insistence, the incumbent of the moment, Richard Milhous Nixon) looked at page one of *The New York Times* even before their morning coffee.* *The Times* was by every objective criterion the most thorough, most complete, most responsible newspaper that time, money, talent and technology in the second half of the twentieth century had been able to produce.

Rosenthal pushed through the low swinging gate that gave access to the city room and headed across a sprawl of writers and editors, circular copy desks and busy typewriters to a clot of battleship-gray steel desks —installed in the city room in his apprentice days by Punch Sulzberger himself—halfway down the room on the Forty-third Street side. This complex constituted the bullpen, locus of the operating editors of the paper, and at this hour a gray, thick-bodied, easy-speaking man named Larry Hauck was in charge.

The Times' city room was the wonder of the world of journalism, a block long from Forty-third to Forty-fourth Street and a half block wide, a two-acre industrial setting in which the noise level of typewriters created a zone of privacy in which each person worked in total visibility and instant communication with his fellows. It drew gasps from Soviet visitors for it was the epitome of the industrial commune, a monument to egalitarianism, a totally efficient working space.†

Hauck handed Rosenthal a sheaf of copy. The first page bore the headline "The McNamara Papers" and the signature of James Reston, *The Times'* senior editor and famous Washington columnist. It was Reston's column for Sunday, commenting on the great *Times* scoop being printed June 13, 1971, dictated by its author from his mountain

---

*Actually, this public contention of Mr. Nixon's was empty bravado. His associates said that like all Presidents he turned to page one of *The New York Times* and the *Washington Post* as soon as he awakened. (Personal interview, Lyndon K. Allin, 9/15/78)

†The city room was destroyed in 1978–79 by *The Times'* in-house office designers who lined the walls with cubicles, filled the room with dividers and "cluster islands," laid wall-to-wall acrylic carpeting (for the benefit, it was said, of the new electronic editing terminals). They replaced the functional entrance hall, installing vertical head-to-foot letters spelling out "News Department" and Ramada Inn globe lights with open filaments. As *Times* architectural critic Ada Louise Huxtable commented on the editorial page, "Gild not the lily, perfume not the air; when the designer comes in, let the worker beware." (*The New York Times,* 1/31/79)

retreat at Fiery Run, Virginia, near Washington, to *The Times'* New York dictation bank about twenty minutes earlier.

The opening lines read:

> Washington, June 12. The official documents on the origins and development of America's involvement in the Vietnam War are now being quietly circulated in Washington. They have not been released or "leaked" by the Nixon Administration but they are now in the hands of some congressmen and Presidential candidates and they are now being published by The New York Times.

Rosenthal, a short energetic man with quick, almost addictive, mannerisms, shook his head as if to clear his vision while his eyes scurried down Reston's column. "I just can't believe it," he said. "Scotty dictated that to the wire room without any embargo, open and clear?"

"That's right," Hauck responded in his slow drawl. "But everything's okay. We have collected all the copies of the column. None of them got out. I have the newsroom copies right here on this desk. The syndicate is holding theirs until we give the order for release."

Rosenthal lifted his shoulders, then dropped them as if freeing himself of a heavy burden and wandered back toward his office at the southwest corner of the floor. For a time he paced nervously into the newsroom and then back inside his office. Finally, he sat at his desk, put his head down on the cradle of his hands and uttered what sounded to one colleague like a prayer: "Let it be four-thirty. Just let it be four-thirty."

Four-thirty was the magic hour. At that moment the flow of copy would cease from the third-floor desks to the composing room on the fourth floor where thousands and thousands of words set into hot lead type and placed in steel forms for stereotyping and casting into plates to be locked onto the twelve trains of Goss and Wood presses in the subbasement of the Forty-third Street building.* A little more than fifty minutes later the composing room would close and at 6 P.M. the presses would rumble into action like enchained giants and there would be no turning back, no new decisions, no dramatic changes.

By 6 P.M. the Sunday edition would begin to flow from the presses at the rate of 200,000 papers per hour. The huge transporters would lumber out of the Forty-third and Forty-fourth Street loading platforms and hustle across the country to Washington and Boston, to Philadelphia and Pittsburgh, to the waiting planes at La Guardia and JFK, to Paris, to Moscow, Rome and Peking, to San Francisco and Atlanta. The papers would be dumped in mountains at waiting news-

---

The Times completed conversion to cold-type, photographic reproduction and computerization on July 1, 1978.

stands in Times Square, the East Side, the Upper West Side and in suburban depots a hundred miles away. Out in the Midwest, university professors would rise at 6 or 7 A.M. on Sunday morning and drive fifty miles to local airports to pick up the "pool papers" for their friends and colleagues.

And even before *The Times* arrived at these distant destinations AP, UPI, Reuters, Agence France-Presse, Tass and *The Times'* own news service would transmit the chief dispatches by wireless and satellite to the most distant parts of the world.

Within minutes, in other words, the first installment of the "Vietnam Archive," as Rosenthal called the great *Times'* scoop, would become public property. History, in fact. (Several days and many crises later this story would acquire the name under which it would enter public annals: the Pentagon Papers.)

Now as Rosenthal alternately paced the floor or waited nervously in his office the city room of *The Times* looked like the most peaceful of places. Hardly a third of the desks were manned—the Saturday staff was always a short one—and the pace of work seemed languid. Office boys and girls sat toying with typewriters and dreaming that an emergency might arise that would compel the city editor to send them out on a big story.

Punch Sulzberger spent that afternoon quietly at his pleasant house on Rockrimmon Road in Stamford, Connecticut. It was a relaxing afternoon after the argument and tension of the past few days. He puttered about his lawn (he was, as one of his sisters said, never so happy as when engaged with the tools and engines of the suburban householder) and thought occasionally of the trip abroad he was going to start on Monday morning with one of his *Times* associates, Ivan Veit. His wife and daughter were going along, and after his business was finished in London the family planned a little vacation.

Later Punch was to concede that he had not thought that this Saturday afternoon might mark a watershed in his life as publisher of *The New York Times,* that the Vietnam Archive would create a new dimension in American journalism which ultimately would profoundly affect American policy, American politics and even, as many came to believe, the shape of American life. Puzzling over this, he would feel that he had not, perhaps, ever gotten a wholly defined idea of the story's implications, possibly because his associates themselves did not grasp the total sweep of the event in which all were caught up. Each man, quite naturally, tended to evaluate it in terms of his own involvement. Certainly, Punch recalled, in the early phases nothing had been said that would cause him to conclude that *The Times* was about to set off an earthquake whose shock might affect the future of the paper itself.

And when he had been told about the story in considerable detail the full impact did not strike him although by this Saturday afternoon he well understood that the matter was considerably more grave than he had first supposed. But, as he freely acknowledged, he did not imagine that *The Times* might be moving out onto ground which his grandfather would have avoided as he would avoid quicksand.

At the opposite pole was Neil Sheehan, thirty-four, the author of the story. Sheehan was not at *The New York Times* on Forty-third Street that afternoon. He was holed up in Room 1106 of the New York Hilton hotel, still banging away on the Vietnam series. This last afternoon as he waited for the first section to appear in print was the most tense of the hundreds of hours Neil had spent on what he knew was to be the great story of his career. An Irishman with intense brown eyes, looking more like a rangy football end than a sensitive, thoughtful correspondent, Neil was all nerves, hunched over his standard Remington typewriter, battering it like a boxer hitting a punching bag.

To Neil his story was "like a thermonuclear vial." He hoped that it would rock the country and rock the world. That was what he *wanted* to happen. But would it? Might not something at the last moment abort the enterprise to which his life had been devoted for many, many months? There was no way of being certain until the presses actually started to roll. He had a fatalistic feeling. If the story was not published on this precise weekend it probably would not be published at all. And even if later on it should be published the "vial" would not explode.

Max Frankel, just turned forty-one, *The Times'* bureau chief in Washington, was far from sharing Sheehan's apocalyptic views and, in fact, the two men held sharply differing philosophies of life. But as Frankel sat in his Washington office on the eighth floor of the black-slate Railroad Building on L Street Northwest smoke puffed from his briar pipe like bursts from an old switch engine. He had told his colleagues that he was staying in the office because of the White House wedding —Tricia Nixon was marrying Edward Cox that afternoon. Actually, Frankel felt he must be on hand in the event of a last-minute crisis.

The day was an oppressive one in Washington, overcast, high humidity, high temperature and periodic drenching rain. Not a pleasant day, nor was it a pleasant season for President Nixon despite the excitement of the White House wedding, the first ever held in the Rose Garden. There was a sour mood in Washington, a sour taste in Washington mouths. Tempers were edgy. The hysteria of Cambodian spring and the Kent State massacre a year ago had gradually faded but the scar tissue was ugly and there was no sense of ease, particularly between the President and the press.

But today it was not the press that worried Mr. Nixon. It was the rain and the stubbornness of his daughter. He had tried to persuade Tricia to move the ceremony inside but, as he told reporters in the press tent, rain still dribbling on the canvas, she was adamant. The guests assembled, protecting themselves as well as they were able—Henry Kissinger making jokes about being the next White House bridegroom (he was already deeply involved in arranging his July trip to Peking, which was to give Mr. Nixon his spectacular China gambit but only the President was aware of this); John Ehrlichman and Harry Robbins Haldeman, stalwart, silent and a little aloof from the others; Attorney General Mitchell, accompanied by the irrepressible Martha (alone among the guests she clung to her umbrella); Herbert Brownell, Eisenhower's Attorney General and head of the powerful New York law firm of Lord, Day and Lord, among whose important clients was *The New York Times;* Alice Roosevelt Longworth, who had herself been a White House bride sixty-five years before. J. Edgar Hoover was there, looking like an aged mastiff. What might have been on his mind no one could guess. Almost alone among those present he *could* have known what was about to happen in New York. His FBI agents had displayed an on-again off-again interest in Daniel Ellsberg, a defense analyst, formerly of the National Security Council, formerly of the Rand Corporation think tank in Santa Monica, California, and now at Massachusetts Institute of Technology in Cambridge, Massachusetts, and (it later turned out) in some other individuals involved in the case of the Vietnam Archive. But there never was to be any evidence that Mr. Hoover's omnipresent bureaucrats managed to splice it all together or brought what they found to the attention of the Grand Inquisitor himself. The only shock J. Edgar suffered that day was when Luci Johnson sneaked up from behind and kissed him on the cheek. He seemed quite startled and not altogether pleased.

All in all it can be concluded that there was no sense among the wedding assemblage that crisis lay at hand. It was a Nixon day like any other Nixon day. Not as good as some but a lot better than others that lay ahead. William Safire, one of the President's speech writers, was among a small group of White House intimates who was not invited. He sat at home and watched the proceedings on television, a little sorry for himself at being cast out of the inner circle. He wasn't exactly sure why he hadn't got an invitation. But he knew the paranoia in the White House and he knew, too, that there were some, including Henry Kissinger, who considered him a security risk. What he didn't know then was that he had been numbered among quite a few individuals who had been wiretapped at the orders of Kissinger and/or the President, suspected, as Safire later put it, of "association with known journalists."

Tricia's was not the only wedding in the capital that day. There was another at Scotty Reston's nearby mountain retreat at Fiery Run, Virginia. Scotty's son, James, Jr., was being married that afternoon to Denise Leary and the Restons were plagued by much the same worries as the Nixons. The young couple wanted their ceremony held on the tip-top of the mountain. But the downpour was so heavy that not even a jeep could master the ascent. Finally, with last-minute scurry as the guests crowded into the old cabin, a tent was thrown up in the yard outside.

At midafternoon the telephone rang. In the steaming cabin Reston had been chatting with Kay Graham, publisher of the *Washington Post*, archrival of *The Times*. Now he picked up the telephone. It was New York gently chiding him about sending his column in the clear with no embargo. Reston explained he hadn't intended to tip anyone's hand but what with the wedding, the early deadline, the publication of the big scoop the next morning he had felt there was no other way of handling it if he was to get his comment into the Sunday morning paper. New York was afraid he might have given the scoop away. Reston apologized. There was nothing to be done now. A bit later, talking to Donald Graham, Kay Graham's son, he told the young man that *The Times* would be publishing a story, based on classified government documents, on Sunday about the origins of the Vietnam war. Reston didn't put any special emphasis on his remarks and they didn't mean much to Donald, then working in the *Post*'s auditing department, but on the way back to Washington he mentioned it to his mother and when he got home he called the *Post*'s national desk, which had been frantic for several days over rumors that *The Times* was about to break a "super-story."* By the time he called the *Post* editors *The Times* had hit the street and they knew what the story was. As Mrs. Graham put it the editor, Ben Bradlee, "went ape!"

Max Frankel did not leave his office on L Street until after he had word that *The Times'* presses had started to roll. Then he went home. His wife, Tobi, wanted to go to the movies but Max insisted on staying

---

*Donald Graham became publisher of the *Washington Post* on January 10, 1979. Rumors of *The Times'* story were general in Washington. Tom Wicker had played tennis that Saturday with David Kraslow, of the *Los Angeles Times*. "I hear you guys are going to drop a blockbuster on us tomorrow," Kraslow said. Wicker grinned but didn't say anything. Several other newspapermen were present, none from the *Washington Post*. (Personal interview, Wicker, 1/7/75)

home—just in case. Nothing happened. His phone didn't ring all evening.

Frankel was puzzled by the lack of immediate reaction. He had not minimized the uproar which would follow publication of the Vietnam Archive but to him the enterprise stood in the mainstream of *Times* tradition. *The Times* had made its name by obtaining important documentary materials from the day it printed the records exposing the Tweed ring in New York City in 1871. *The Times* had published scoops on the British and German White Papers in World War I. It did the same with the text of the Treaty of Versailles in 1919 and the German Reparations Agreement in 1921. It had published inside position papers of the Washington Naval Conference in 1922 and of the Locarno Conference in 1925. Its scoops on the Dumbarton Oaks Conference in 1944 and on the text of the Yalta papers in 1954, both obtained by James Reston, had resounded around the world.* So did the text of Nikita Khrushchev's "Secret Speech," revealing the crimes of Josef Stalin, which was leaked to me by the State Department and the CIA in June 1956. When Sydney Gruson in Bonn exclusively obtained for *The Times* the text of the U.S. plan for Germany, President Kennedy grumbled, "Why should a Jew act as a spokesman for the German Government?"

Whatever might happen Frankel felt secure in his conviction that publication of the Vietnam Archive was fully justified by *Times* tradition.

Rosenthal, sweating out the last hour before press-start in New York, did not share Frankel's view. He had, of course, a clear vision of the historical nature of the Vietnam Archive but he talked in what some of his colleagues thought were Dantean tones of the decision to publish. It involved, Rosenthal thought, almost everything that was important— patriotism (and as a Canadian-born American citizen whose roots were in Russia's Pale of Jewish Settlement he took his patriotism more seriously than many), the future of the country, the future of *The New York Times,* the future lives of everyone involved in the enterprise, including his own. He had even toted up what his severance pay would be if he lost his job, how much money he had in savings and insurance and whether he would still be able to send his three sons to college.

*Iphigene Sulzberger went to college with Hollington Tong, who was for many years Chiang Kai-shek's chief adviser on American affairs, she at Barnard, Tong at Columbia. Tong's son-in-law was a member of China's delegation to Dumbarton Oaks and Iphigene Sulzberger introduced him to Scotty Reston. Mrs. Sulzberger felt she had at least a minor hand in Reston's Dumbarton Oaks exclusives because the source was Tong's son-in-law. (Personal interviews, Iphigene Ochs Sulzberger, 1/13/75; Reston, 11/17/78; 11/15/78)

To Rosenthal it was make-or-break. *The Times* had not done any-thing like this before. Ever. Not in its 120 years of existence. Nor had any newspaper. It was a first and Rosenthal did not believe that any-thing—*anything*—would be quite the same again after the Sunday *Times* of June 13, 1971, hit the streets.

It was an enterprise—and all agreed on this—which might have unusual legal consequences. The lawyers had made that perfectly clear. Rosenthal and some of his colleagues joked about the possibility of going to jail but possibly no one but Rosenthal took this seriously.

Yet not even Rosenthal, with his sense of drama, could have under-stood where the powder train about to be set off on this hot June afternoon would lead.

It seemed like an endless wait for the presses to start as Rosenthal paced the worn floors of the city room, blinking owlishly when the proofs of the story, drawn in a secret locked-door mini-composing room on the ninth floor, were furtively spread out on his desk, nervously warning his associates "not to take any telephone calls, not any calls at all, before the presses start," retreating into his office once again and cushioning his head in his hands as he muttered his mutilated prayer: "Let it be four-thirty. Let it be four-thirty."

The presses finally started—late—at 6:13 and the first papers came up to the city room at 6:16 P.M. They bore a neat headline in 24-point type on page one over columns four, five, six and seven. It read:

Vietnam Archive: Pentagon Study Traces
Three Decades of Growing U.S. Involvement

Joe Harrington, the lanky dark-haired slot man of the metropolitan desk, glanced at the modest display and the quiet headline and said with a calculated yawn, "Well, there's one quarter-of-a-million-dollar story I don't have to read."

2

A Question of Trust

*L*ooking back on June 12, 1971, it is hard to find anyone on *The Times* except Rosenthal who had a real concept of the historic consequences of *The Times'* publication of the Vietnam Archive, and even Rosenthal, quite naturally, focused largely on potential effects upon *The Times*, its editor and staff, its publisher.

Rosenthal, when he saw the page proofs from the special secret mini-composing room spread out on his desk, was overwhelmed with an emotion which he could not quite verbalize.

"Seeing all those documents from the government files!" he pondered later. "You can't imagine the feeling it gave you. It was strange. I just walked around looking at them. I could hardly believe it. This hadn't been done before. *The Times* wasn't used to publishing secret documents."

Rosenthal's inarticulateness was matched by that of James Reston, despite his long years in Washington and skill in diplomatic reporting, author of more scoops than anyone could count and winner of two Pulitzer Prizes.

No more than Rosenthal did Reston articulate the nature of the Rubicon which was crossed with publication of what Reston called the "McNamara Papers." And in his sedate column, which caused so much concern when it landed in *The Times'* wire room, unembargoed and technically free to be distributed immediately to the 360-odd newspapers then taking *The Times'* wire service, he did not even address the consequences of publication.

Reston discussed the documents in what some of his colleagues thought was a perfunctory manner and arrived at a downbeat conclusion. He quoted the historian Gibbon as saying that "history is little more than the register of the crimes, faults and frailties of mankind" and observed that the "McNamara Papers" presented "compelling new evidence of this melancholy conclusion." From one as addicted to Scotch Presbyterianism as was Reston this seemed a rather narrow finding. There was not a word to suggest that Reston felt American public opinion would be or should be profoundly shaken by publication of the documents or that *The Times* was taking a quantum leap toward a new role in history.

Two questions, the central one of the morality (the immorality, rather) of the American Government as exposed in the documents on the origin and conduct of the Vietnam war, and the other issue of the appropriate function in our society of the American press and, specifically, of *The New York Times,* escaped Reston.

The indistinct edges of these questions were brushed by the intense and analytic mind of James Goodale, the not-quite-thirty-eight-year-old general counsel of *The Times,* but he had been so immersed in pragmatic concerns, in studying possible Government actions against *The Times* and in the legal defense of the newspaper in the courts that the larger issues tended to be submerged. He possessed, moreover, an aggressive rather than a reflective personality, with a penchant for sharp words, decisive acts, quick and clear-cut decisions and he had invested all of these talents in the arguments, debates, deliberations, steps forward, steps backward and steps sidewise which accompanied the editing, presentation and decision to publish the Vietnam Archive.

Yet it was Goodale who most clearly perceived the implications of the giant—and to him inevitable—step. The issue ultimately was squarely joined in argument between Goodale and Louis M. Loeb, at seventy-two a senior member of Herbert Brownell's law firm of Lord, Day and Lord whose association with *The Times* went back to the days of Adolph S. Ochs. *The Times,* said Loeb, cannot publish if the Government asks it not to publish; *The Times* is part of the Establishment and the Establishment press does not go against the Government. This is the tradition of *The Times.* To which Goodale responded that *The Times* not only could but must publish the Archive. It had the obligation under the First Amendment of the Constitution to publish and must take the consequences, come what may. As an institution, Goodale declared, *The Times* would never be the same again if it gave in to the Government and *The Times* should not and must not give in.

But this climactic exchange, which, like a laser beam, illuminated the difference between the old *Times* of Mr. Ochs and the new *Times* of his grandson Punch, this extraordinary acknowledgment that *The Times* no longer was handmaiden, supporter, crony, adherent, bondsman, counselor or confidant to "government" but was itself an independent power with independent rights, independent judgment and an independent responsibility, was not to occur until the publication of the Vietnam Archive had gotten under way. Even then it was to come in the context of events so rapid-fire, so tension-filled that it was only afterward that the participants began slowly to comprehend what, in fact, were the implications of publication of documents from and details of the study of the origins and conduct of the Vietnam war which a troubled Secretary of Defense Robert McNamara had ordered undertaken on June 17, 1967, in order, if possible, to leave a record for his successors and the American public of how we got involved in the Vietnam war, and what had gone wrong. As McNamara was later to say, he thought that at the least the people deserved a chance to profit by the mistakes of the past so that they might avoid making similar errors in the future.

The Ochs Tradition

When Mr. Ochs came up to a sultry New York in the summer of 1896 to negotiate for taking over the bankrupt *New-York Times* (its circulation was down to 9,000; it was losing $2,500 a day) he himself was, for practical purposes, also a bankrupt. He was the publisher of an enormously successful small newspaper, the *Chattanooga Times,* but he had plunged over his head in Chattanooga real estate. Members of his family thought he should declare receivership and pay off his debts at a few cents on the dollar. When he opened negotiations to buy *The Times* they literally believed he had lost his mind and his mother thought of taking legal steps to restrain him. But the New York bankers and financiers with whom Mr. Ochs dealt trusted him. J. P. Morgan trusted him. Jacob Schiff trusted him. August Belmont trusted him. Spencer Trask and Charles Flint and Charles Miller, the putative owners of *The Times,* trusted him.

One of the legacies that Mr. Ochs bequeathed to the successful *Times,* which was his creation, was the concept of trust. You hired the best man you could find for the job. Having hired him you trusted him to do his work. You did not look over his shoulder by day or spend your nights worrying whether he had done his job capably. Mr. Ochs had a simple principle. If you could not trust a man—don't hire him.

The principle worked for Mr. Ochs and it was still working for *The Times* in 1971—particularly in the area of news and editorial responsibility. On the afternoon of June 12, 1971, Punch Sulzberger had never asked Abe Rosenthal the source of Sheehan's story. Nor had Rosenthal ever asked Sheehan. He had asked Sheehan to be certain the "Archive" was genuine, that it hadn't been forged or perpetrated by some band of antiwar people. And when he saw the material he had asked his foreign editor, James Greenfield, if on the basis of Greenfield's experience in the State Department (where he had served for a while as public relations officer) the material seemed authentic. Greenfield said it was without question authentic. That was that. Max Frankel, Sheehan's chief in Washington, had never asked him how he got the Archive. Nor did James Reston, nor James Goodale, whose responsibility it would be to defend *The Times* from legal consequences of publication of the Archive. Nor, of course, had any of Sheehan's colleagues who helped in preparing the material for publication. It was an unwritten rule on *The Times* that if a man did not feel it appropriate to reveal the source of a story, he was not pressed for it. The Ochs rule held: If you hire a man trust him; if you don't trust him don't hire him.

Thus it was with some bewilderment, three days after publication of the Archive, that Dan Ellsberg received a telephone call from a reporter on *The Times'* rewrite bank, calling to check whether he was, as a New York radio station had reported, the source of *The Times'* story. He was even more surprised to receive a call from James Reston asking the same question. Reston also asked whether there was a chance of getting a look at the diplomatic volumes of the Archive which Ellsberg had held back from releasing.

Years later, long after the Supreme Court verdicts, long after the Watergate revelations, long after Ellsberg's personal vindication in the federal courts, after a half dozen books and hundreds of newspaper and magazine articles had been written about the Vietnam Archive, Ellsberg's puzzlement remained. *The Times* still had not officially declared what the source of Sheehan's material had been; the compact of trust invoked by Mr. Ochs before the turn of the century had not been broken.

Because it was so important an American institution, *The New York Times* received as guests many visitors, often distinguished, often foreigners—statesmen, publishers of newspapers, delegations from Communist countries, groups of educators and academicians. It was traditional that the visitors were given a tour of the newspaper, dinner in a private dining room and then taken to the board room on the fourteenth floor, a suitably impressive Edwardian chamber whose darkpaneled walls had changed only in minor detail from the days of Adolph Ochs. There they were given a chance to ask the editors any questions that came to their minds.

Again and again, of course, the visitors would ask about the process of publishing the paper—how was it organized, how did, in fact, *The New York Times* get out every day. It was a question to which successive *Times* publishers and editors responded with a modest smile. Often they began by saying, "Well, you know, that is a question we often ask ourselves." There would be a ripple of polite laughter and then various editors would be called upon to describe their role in the process.

The visitors did not always accept the deprecatory remarks about "how the daily miracle occurred." Sometimes they would probe with vigor trying but never quite penetrating to the heart of the secret. The fact was, of course, that there was more truth than the visitors imagined in the self-effacing answer. No single editor on *The Times*, and certainly not the publisher or the managing editor, knew exactly how the paper managed to be published on a single day. True, they knew the general parameters. But the countless details of fitting the millions of words available into a news space of 90 or 100 columns—these were a mystery to which no single person held the key.

Nothing was less believable to the visitors. They were convinced there must be a master plan or a program for coordination. No visitor from Moscow, no correspondent for *Pravda,* and possibly no foreign minister from Bonn or premier from Japan would have believed that there was not one single editor, correspondent or executive on *The New York Times* on June 12 who could have told him how the Vietnam Archive had come to be published, how *The Times* on this particular day in this particular month in this particular year had arrived at this great divide in its long and illustrious career—certainly not the publisher, certainly not the managing editor, certainly not the correspondent who brought the story in and least of all the source.

Neil Sheehan

The correspondent who brought in the story was Neil Sheehan. Not many persons on *The Times* really knew Sheehan. They may have thought they knew him but it was the outer Sheehan, the public man, whom they knew. To really know this complex and troubling man you had first of all to know Tralee and the classic Irish paraphernalia: the green, the cold fog of the Atlantic, the peat fire on the hearth, Ireland's western tip where the names trill from Irish lips like the silver notes of a harp—Ballybunion, Castlegregory, Dunkerran, Caragh, Carntual, Dunlee, Kilarney, Ballinskellig, Dingle, Kilconey, Stradbally and Castlemaine.

Nineteen miles past Tralee in a white stone cottage precisely like a hundred other white stone cottages set against emerald grass and a sky of sunshine and showers, Patrick Joseph Sheehan lived in the village of Killorglin on Dingle Bay until he picked up his chattels, set them over his shoulder in a leather bag and followed his neighbors to America in 1901. A half century had passed since the potato famine but the population of County Kerry was still dropping at the rate of 10 percent every decade.

Patrick Joseph Sheehan was the grandfather of Cornelius Mahoney Sheehan, born October 27, 1936, at Holyoke, Massachusetts. On June 12, 1971, Cornelius Mahoney Sheehan, now known as Neil Sheehan, a correspondent for *The New York Times,* was busily engaged in Room 1106 at the New York Hilton hotel, one of a specially engaged suite of rooms where for reasons of security *The New York Times* had installed its Archives task force. Sheehan was working on Installment Three of *The Times'* account of the Pentagon Papers.

It is not likely that Sheehan's colleagues at *The Times* that afternoon spent much time pondering Neil's Irish ancestry. Yet later on, in trying to assess the forces which led to the publication of the Papers and all that followed, attention naturally centered on Sheehan for, of course, without Sheehan, the Papers would not have been published. And in thinking about Sheehan and his role more than one person was brought up short by the Irishness of the man.

Perhaps, they thought, it could have happened regardless. But studying Neil as he evolved from hard-hitting wire service reporter to engagé critic of the Vietnam war it was difficult not to hear echoes of Parnell and O'Connell, men who would not rest until "the Truth is out and Justice done."

Neil Sheehan was a complicated, driven man. As a reporter he possessed limitless energy and doggedness. No detail was too small to resist his curiosity. Once when faced with a libel suit over a book he had written he took nearly a year to footnote every sentence, every paragraph, every question, direct and indirect, in a 250,000-word volume, to provide his lawyers with evidence with which to defend the action. They did not *need* this apparatus, no one *asked* that he verify every word and every comma. But once launched on the task nothing could deter Sheehan.*

It was these characteristics of devotion to detail, bulldog tenacity, of an almost perfect nose for news coupled with that fire in the belly which for centuries kept the Irish cause aglow in which was rooted Sheehan's great project.

In fact, it was the chance or, as a deterministic thinker might put it, the ordained conjunction of Sheehan and another remarkably different but equally driven personality that produced the revelation of the Vietnam Archive, or, as we have come to know it, the Pentagon Papers.

The second personality was Daniel Ellsberg, five years older than Sheehan, six years ahead of him at Harvard and three years behind him in getting to the killing ground of Vietnam. The two men differed profoundly but they met at a point and place in time where their contrasting characteristics fused with the kind of shock which occurs when a lightning bolt hits a high-voltage transmission line. Sheehan was a farm boy, Ellsberg a city boy. At the age of thirteen Sheehan was running the pasteurizing plant of the dairy farm his father operated on the outskirts of Holyoke. It was a small farm, forty to fifty cows on three hundred acres of scruffy New England pasture, but it turned a profit until the mid-1950s when big homogenizing plants killed off the small milk producers. (In those years Ellsberg, born in Chicago, child of

---

*Neil's memo to his publisher ran 343 typewritten pages. (Susan Sheehan, *The New Yorker*, 9/25/78)

Depression as he grew up in Springfield, Illinois, and Detroit, his father a sometimes unemployed engineer, was spending six or more hours a day practicing on the piano at the edict of a strong-willed mother. At six he could recite the Gettysburg Address.)

Neil's family was pure Irish, his grandfather an emigrant from County Kerry and his mother from Kerry, too, at the age of sixteen. To Neil's regret neither his father nor mother spoke Gaelic. (Ellsberg's background was Russian Jewish—his grandfather emigrated to the U.S.A. to escape the Czar's military service, twenty-five years of conscription at that time, but Ellsberg's parents left the Jewish faith and converted to Christian Science.)

Farming was not Neil's thing. He learned to run the dairy but never to milk a cow. He enjoyed the $21 a week he earned but he resented not playing baseball and football like the other kids. A bit later he developed a passion for the drums. He combed his hair back in a pompadour, wore a cardigan sweater and thought he looked like Gene Krupa. He got $5 a night playing Polish polkas in beer joints. (Ellsberg played concertos with amateur orchestras. He also played tennis, soccer, became a not-bad boxer, dabbled in amateur sleight of hand, wrote poetry and a humor column for his school paper. He ultimately abandoned the piano after his mother was killed in an automobile accident and he went on to college.)

After ten grades in the Holyoke public schools Neil won a scholarship to Mount Herman, spent his last two years there and won another scholarship that took him to Harvard. (Ellsberg, too, won a full scholarship to Harvard, courtesy of Pepsi-Cola, after attending on a scholarship the elite Cranbrook School for Boys at Bloomfield, Michigan, where his classmates, many of them children of the automobile aristocracy, picked him as most likely to make a contribution to human progress. The headmaster recorded that Ellsberg's attitude was inclined to be superior.)

Neil's father saw no point to Harvard. Why didn't Neil go to the University of Massachusetts like his cousin? His father, Neil thought, had the Irish attitude toward education: no need for it except to improve your chances for a job. Neil's mother had acquired quite a few books from a woman she had worked for and Neil read them all, beginning with *All Quiet on the Western Front.* Years later, Remarque's picture of the pointlessness of war, the random killing, the certainty of death, the futility and stupidity was vivid in Sheehan's mind and gave him a frame of reference within which to evaluate Vietnam. (About the time Neil was reading *All Quiet on the Western Front* Dan Ellsberg was reading James Jones' *From Here to Eternity* and writing an enthusiastic review of it for the *Harvard Crimson.* The review was headlined "Soldiers and

Whores," and Dan's father was upset at that language.)

Neil got on none too well with his father but respected him. He worked hard and gave Neil a decent upbringing. He didn't drink and he loved farming. He was no hypocrite—he would not eat veal because he sold his calves for butchering. All his life he drove a school bus because the farm's profits—shared with two brothers—were not enough to support Neil, his two younger brothers and his older sister. After Neil got into Harvard his father was proud of the fact.

Cornelius Mahoney Sheehan was a month shy of eighteen when he matriculated at Harvard, thin, dark-haired, handsome, with an attachment, his friends remembered, to country ways. He was so Irish it was hard to believe. All he talked about was the Irish, the Irish poets, particularly Oliver St. John Gogarty. Sheehan knew Dublin better than he knew Cambridge and listening to him was like reading Joyce. His roommates called him "Gogarty" Sheehan. After two or three drinks Sheehan seemed to take off across the gray Atlantic and land in a Dublin tavern. It was not always easy for his friends to hold his flights to a figurative plane.

There was no hint of politics in Neil's world. All was literature and poetry. He joined the *Harvard Advocate* and expressed contempt for "scribblers," as he called them, the would-be journalists of the *Crimson*. To him they were illiterates. He became addicted to the new criticism and, successively, to Yeats, T. S. Eliot and Ezra Pound.

(Five years earlier the president of the *Advocate* had been Dan Ellsberg but an eon separated the two men; Ellsberg's name was hardly known to Sheehan's generation. For the *Advocate* Ellsberg had written two sketches, one an account of a visit to his mother's grave after the car accident in which she was killed, Ellsberg and a sister injured, their father driving the machine at the time, uninjured, and the other of terror-haunted dreams and marijuana.)

The great problem, Neil's friends found, was to get him to bed and after getting him to bed to keep him there. Once after he had been safely tucked in he got up, donned a raincoat, a pair of shoes and nothing else and ran down to the Hay-Bix for coffee and a hamburger.

Sheehan's best-remembered college adventure started on a May night in 1956 at an *Advocate* dinner at the Harvard Club in downtown Boston. One of those present recalled passing out with the mashed potatoes. Neil did not pass out. He returned with his companions to the *Advocate* office on Bow Street in Cambridge where it was hoped he might sleep it off on the *Advocate* board-room table. By chance, a boisterous riot was under way just outside, a typical Harvard spring riot long before the days of "protest." The ostensible target of the students was a Cambridge city councilman named Alfred Vellacci who had recently suggested that Harvard be "turned into one large parking lot."

Sheehan had been left asleep on the *Advocate* table. Now he was roused by the shouting and appeared in his shorts in the Bow Street window exhorting the crowd and managing to toss a typewriter out the window.

The crowd stormed off and to its delight Vellacci appeared in his Cadillac. The students surrounded the car, rocked it back and forth and refused to let Vellacci emerge.

The next day Sheehan found himself about to be suspended as the instigator of a riot of which he had no recollection. With some difficulty the authorities were persuaded to put Neil on probation. But the details were enticing enough to be written up by *Time* magazine. It was Sheehan's initial appearance on the national stage.

As with so many young Americans the direction of Neil's life was taken out of his hands. In late summer, 1958, a friend bumped into Neil at Fort Devens, Massachusetts. College days were over. After graduating *cum laude* Neil found himself number eleven on the draft list at Holyoke and enlisted for three years in the Army. By the winter of 1959 he was serving with a Seventh Division battle group in Korea —no fighting, of course, the war was long over, but cold, miserable weather, boredom, routine, futility. The banality if not the tragedy of the soldier's life which Neil had absorbed from Remarque was now the fabric of his own. He was a pay clerk, adding up endless columns of meaningless figures, punching and stamping forms, a gray unit in the thousands of gray units which comprised the clerical corps of the military occupation force. It was the low spot of his life. A friend remembered him rolling in of a night roaring, "Mother of God!" The friend would turn to a barracks mate and mutter, "Oh Christ, Sheehan has been at it again." One New Year's Eve he went out on a bender. Only chance spared him from a dreadful fracas, something he hinted later that might have sent him to Army prison for years. He woke up next morning determined never to take another drink so long as he lived. Nor did he.

Gradually, Neil lifted himself out of the rut. He got a job in the information section at Seoul and was transferred to the division newspaper in Tokyo. Now he could wear civilian clothes. He met some *New York Times* men—Bernie Weinraub, then an Army Pfc, and Abe Rosenthal, then *New York Times* correspondent in Tokyo.

Soon Neil, the Irish fantaseur who had looked upon reporters as "scribblers," "ink-stained wretches," in Samuel Johnson's full contempt of the term, was working eighteen to twenty hours a day as a newsman himself, by day for the Army, by night for United Press International.

On the promise of a staff job from UPI, Neil took his Army discharge in Tokyo in April 1962. Two weeks later UPI's Saigon correspondent,

Mert Perry, quit, sending "Asia Ernie" Hoberecht, the UPI Asian chief, a telegram which read simply, "Fuck you." In May of 1962 Sheehan was in Saigon. Bureau chief of UPI. Director of the UPI Vietnam staff—one Vietnamese reporter and one Vietnamese assistant. He held the job for two years and then, with difficulty, managed to get on *The New York Times*.

Neil Sheehan met two men in Vietnam who were to prove remarkably important in his career—Homer Bigart, the best and most professional war correspondent of his generation, and David Halberstam, just moving toward maturity as an eloquent and critical observer and writer. Both worked for *The New York Times*. A third man who was to loom even larger in Sheehan's life followed him into Vietnam in the summer of 1965, but the two, so far as they later could recall, never met in Southeast Asia.

Daniel Ellsberg

The third man was Daniel Ellsberg. On the afternoon of June 12, 1971, Ellsberg was two months and five days past his fortieth birthday, a lean wiry man who made a fetish of physical fitness, intense, intellectual, possessor of one of the finest analytic minds in the country. He was living with his second wife, Patricia Marx, on the third floor of a large old house at Number 10 Hilliard Street in Cambridge, a few steps off Harvard Square. The floor had been converted into a $350-a-month apartment, one very large room that served as living room and study, a tiny kitchen and a small bedroom. Soundproofing had been unknown in the Victorian days when the house was built and when Ellsberg pounded on his typewriter all night (as he frequently did) the noise reverberated through the building and caused his second-floor neighbors to complain. Ellsberg gave them short shrift. There was nothing he could do about the noise, they would just have to lump it. Once Patricia Ellsberg invited the neighbors up to look at the apartment, to show them how difficult it was to muffle the sounds. The living room-study was sparsely furnished. On the walls were enlarged photographs of Pat and pictures of camping trips—Ellsberg was an amateur photographer—and a signed Picasso print. Before Patricia took the visitors into the bedroom she apologized with a chuckle for the mirrors on the ceiling and on the walls. "Pay no attention to them," she said. "It's just a fantasy that Dan has had since childhood."

No one in the circle of friends and acquaintances Ellsberg had made since moving to Cambridge and joining the staff of MIT as a $20,000-a-year senior research associate in late summer, 1970, had to ask in June of 1971 with what Ellsberg was preoccupied. All knew that it was the war in Vietnam. Ellsberg's every waking hour was dedicated to this cause. He participated in demonstrations and antiwar meetings. He spent hours on the telephone. He met with dozens of people. He traveled to New York, to Washington, to the Coast. He wrote articles. He had written two that spring, causing his typewriter to reverberate alarmingly in his neighbors' ears. The first elaborated on a thesis which he had presented at the American Political Science Association meeting in Los Angeles the previous September. Now he published it in the quarterly *Public Policy* for Spring, 1971, and effectively demolished Halberstam's "quagmire theory" of American involvement in Vietnam. Ellsberg advanced a new and startling explanation of United States policy.

The problem was not, Ellsberg insisted, that the U.S.A. was being inexorably drawn against its will deeper and deeper into an Asian quagmire. The problem was that the last four Presidents and now the fifth (Nixon) were acting on what Ellsberg called Rule I of Indochina policy for an American President: "Do not lose the rest of Vietnam to communism before the next election." He applied the same logic (and stated knowledge of the inner decision-making of the Government) to a searing critique of Nixon's invasion of Laos in an article which appeared in the *New York Review of Books,* March 11, 1971.

In a word, Ellsberg lived, breathed and slept with Vietnam and, thus, it would have surprised none of his friends to learn that on this lazy June afternoon he had received yet another telephone call dealing with his obsession.

The call came from a *New York Times* editor named Anthony Austin and it was a message of high distress. Austin had written a book on the Tonkin Gulf affair of 1964, a book that revealed there had been trickery and "calculated misunderstanding," to put it politely, in the administration's presentation of the Tonkin evidence.

Austin had consulted Ellsberg on some delicate points in his reconstruction of Tonkin Gulf and now the *Times* man was in despair. He had just heard from a colleague that *The Times* on Sunday, the next day, was publishing something called the "McNamara papers" and he had a queasy feeling that this was going to scoop his book and render his work and research valueless.

Ellsberg spent some time trying to buck up Austin. At the same time, Austin recalled, Ellsberg seemed to be extraordinarily excited about the publication of the McNamara Papers. "Are you sure?" he asked. "Are they really publishing those papers Sunday?"

Austin reiterated that indeed *The Times* was publishing the papers —publication time was only a few hours distant.

"Well," said Ellsberg, "I'm glad you told me."

Within a minute Ellsberg had placed his own call to *The Times.* He was calling Neil Sheehan. Richard Mooney, an assistant foreign editor, got the call. He took Ellsberg's number and promised to relay the message.

Mooney called Sheehan in Room 1106 at the New York Hilton.

"Some fellow named Ellsberg is trying to get ahold of you," Mooney told him.

"Okay," Sheehan said. "Give me the number and I'll call him back later. Let me know when 100,000 papers are off the presses."

"Fine," said Mooney.

No one at that hour on *The New York Times* except for Sheehan knew who Ellsberg was or the significance of the telephone call.* Even Austin had no idea that Ellsberg had any connection with the imminent publication of the McNamara Papers. A few *New York Times* men had met Ellsberg at one time or another. But not one person on *The New York Times* outside of Neil Sheehan knew of a connection between Ellsberg and the "Vietnam Archive." And, in fact, until Austin's frantic telephone call Ellsberg had no knowledge that the archive to which he had devoted his existence for the past two years was about to appear in public.

---

*Some of the editors working on the project had noted the name Ellsberg written on several of the sheets. They did not know who Ellsberg was but thought he must have some connection.

3

An "old fog-ist" Newspaper

*T*HE IDEA OF A NEWSPAPER as a "fourth branch of government" has honorable roots in rhetoric but only the wispiest of underpinnings in law, or even in public concept. The notion that newspapers occupied a special and powerful place in the social order had its origin in the debates over the French Revolution. (Actually at that time they were largely political leaflets or pamphlets.) It was then that the reporters in England's parliamentary gallery were first referred to as a Fourth Estate, more powerful than the other estates, the nobility, the clergy and the burghers. The idea was advanced by Thomas Burke and Thomas Carlyle put it into popular currency without anyone trying to define exactly how the press or the media, as we would now say, occupied such a special position.

There is not a scintilla of evidence to indicate that Adolph Ochs came up to New York from Chattanooga in 1896 with any intention of establishing an organ whose power some ultimately were to compare with that of one of the three constituent branches of the American Government. Mr. Ochs was the son of Julius Ochs, an intelligent and educated emigrant who had made his way to Tennessee from Furth in Bavaria in 1845 at the age of nineteen and, starting out as a peddler, served in the Second Ohio Volunteers during the Civil War (his wife was to die forty-three years after the war a still unreconstructed Rebel) and supported a large and growing family with energy and ingenuity. Adolph Ochs not unnaturally went to work at a very early age, learning the printer's trade as a "devil," or assistant, to the hand compositors of the country papers of the 1870s, demonstrated a flair for business (he started the *Chattanooga Times* in 1878 with actual cash in hand of $37.50 of borrowed money of which he had to pay out $25 to keep his AP wire going) and came to New York to show that he could establish, as he said, "a decent, dignified and independent" (and prosperous) paper against the competition of some of the most spectacularly sensational entrepreneurs who ever entered the ring—men like William Randolph Hearst, who was accused of starting the Spanish-American War in order to boost the circulation of his *New York*

Journal, Frank Munsey, known as the "murderer" of newspaper row, James Gordon Bennett, the younger, who once demonstrated his contempt for social opinion by publicly urinating on his fiancée's grand piano, and Joseph Pulitzer, whom many believe invented "yellow journalism."*

In contrast with these individualists Mr. Ochs had a flair for what now would be described as understated public relations. He ran a contest to select a slogan for his newspaper and declared as winner the one he had fancied from the start: "All the News That's Fit to Print." He took the slogan seriously.† His newspaper did not print sensational or pornographic or gaudily spiced reports of crime, sex or bloodshed. It refrained from the cartoons and comics which brought so much circulation to his competitors. His headlines were discreet. There was nothing in his business and financial columns (by which he set great store) which would give offense to the great bankers, merchants and entrepreneurs of the day. His editorial page was bland and wholesome. He did not believe in shrillness or strong statements. In fact, there were those who felt he would have been happier had there been no editorial page.

Mr. Ochs' formula was successful. Within six years his *New York Times* was earning more than $200,000 a year and within the decade he had it all in hand, safe and secure, the ownership his, no great obligations outstanding, and never again in his life would he face the threat of bankruptcy or financial debacle.‡

This does not mean that Mr. Ochs was not interested in making his newspaper influential. He was. He knew that a successful newspaper must be influential. But if he had the kind of gambler's touch that led him to move his newspaper out of "newspaper row" on Park Place and up to Longacre Square on the edge of the new theatrical section (and persuade the city fathers to rechristen it Times Square); if he was shrewd enough to finance Perry in his exploration of the North Pole or Marconi in his development of the wireless rather than following Hearst and Pulitzer in backing freebooter incursions of Cuba, he also believed in a low profile; of being the confidant of Presidents and

---

*"How Do You Like the Journal's War?" Hearst asked in a banner headline. Mr. Ochs predicted that "in less than five years Mr. Dana will die of old age, Pulitzer of nervous prostration and Bennett of riotous living." (*Times'* archives, Ochs to C. H. Rowe, 5/19/95)

†Mr. Ochs invented the slogan himself and began running it within two months of his purchase of *The Times.* Then he ran a contest and hired the distinguished editor Richard Watson Gilder to see if anyone could suggest a better one. On November 24, 1896, a $100 prize was awarded to D. M. Redfield, 39 Lynwood St., New Haven, Conn., for his slogan "All the World News but Not a School for Scandal," but Mr. Ochs liked his own slogan better and kept it. (*Times'* archives, Ochs Mss., 1896)

‡So it appeared publicly, but there was an important qualification which was not to be revealed until many years later.

Secretaries of State; of having quiet entrée to Whitehall or No. 10 Downing Street rather than bringing down cabinets or putting his own man in the White House. He very quickly became part of the Establishment and was proud of that fact. He was a Democrat because he had been raised south of the Mason-Dixon line but this did not mean that he was a "silver Democrat" or that he could stomach a man like William Jennings Bryan. He was for gold and fiscal conservatism.

Mr. Ochs knew the value of a dollar because he had had to know its value from childhood. He never forgot the worn leather purse of his father, the two-bit pieces, thin dimes, Liberty cap dollars and worn, worn dollar bills that went through hundreds of calloused hands before they came to rest within the nickel clasps of the peddler's wallet. In the first years of his *Times* ownership Mr. Ochs' Washington correspondent, W. C. Dunnell, solicited advertisements on the side, and when in July of 1897 Mr. Dunnell managed to obtain free from the Bureau of Rolls a reproduction of the Declaration of Independence instead of paying the usual twenty-seven cents, Mr. Ochs was delighted. He ran the reproduction as a full page in *The New York Times* and his heirs and successors continued the custom each July 4th at a cost which came to be five times more in hundreds of dollars (that is to say an ad rate of $15,440 a page) than Mr. Ochs would have shelled out in pennies had not Mr. Dunnell wangled a free copy.

Mr. Ochs highly valued his association with and his support by the eminent Wall Street men who assisted him in the purchase of *The New York Times*. To the end of his life he recalled with pleasure and surprise his first meeting with J. P. Morgan, the elder, in Morgan's portentous offices at No. 23 Wall Street, a young southern country entrepreneur of thirty-eight, expecting Jovian thunder. Instead, Mr. Morgan rose pleasantly from his desk, shook hands and said, "So you're the young man I have heard about. Now, where do I sign the papers?" Mr. Morgan's reception was duplicated by the response of all the others, August Belmont, George Peabody and Marcellus Hartley, director of the Equitable Life Assurance Society (an association that was to plague Mr. Ochs during the great Equitable scandal culminating in Charles Evans Hughes' investigation). The truth was that for many, many years *The Times* was haunted by rumors that Mr. Morgan was its real owner, a rumor that bothered Mr. Ochs considerably in later life but which may have served the paper in good stead in its shaky beginnings. There was another rumor, believed by many during World War I, that the British Government or Lord Northcliffe somehow was behind the paper, a rumor which may have been nourished by *The Times'* ardent Anglophilism and an association much prized by Mr. Ochs with his older and then more luminous English counterpart, *The Times* of London, owned by Northcliffe.

But as August Belmont said in 1904 when he helped Mr. Ochs get New York City to change the name of Longacre Square to Times Square:

"I never owned a share of stock but even if I had everyone knows you and your independence and the words of your paper have all the strength necessary in consequence."

And it was true that Mr. Ochs had made independence of *The Times* a given although this was, perhaps, defined in somewhat narrower terms than his son-in-law, his son-in-law's son-in-law or his grandson would come to use. To Mr. Ochs, independence meant that no businessman, no advertiser, no "interest" and no politician could buy *The Times* or its influence. He did not permit his news pages to be used to curry favor with the great New York department stores or Tammany Hall. His editorial columns were not for sale and this meant a good deal more seventy-five or eighty years ago than it would later. There *were* newspapers in New York City then which did not mind printing a "puff" in return for an advertisement or, more serious, writing an editorial at the dictation of a banker or politician.

The Jewish Question

This did not mean that Mr. Ochs believed in crusades or setting himself and his newspaper against the Establishment. After all it had not been easy for him to become part of the Establishment and he relished his position. There were not many sons of Jewish peddlers from the troubled Germany of the 1840s who occupied Mr. Ochs' position in New York and he did not propose to jeopardize the economic health of *The New York Times* with unconventional attitudes. And he was sensitive to the fact that he was the Jewish owner of what he intended to be *the* paper of the Establishment. There were rivals to this position. Not, of course, Mr. Hearst with his *Journal,* Mr. Munsey with his *Sun* or Mr. Pulitzer with his hell-raising *World.* But there was Mr. Bennett's *Herald* (granted that it had seen its best days) and the towering presence of that safe, secure, Republican monument to Horace Greeley, the *New York Tribune,* now owned (at last free of the piratical influence of Jay Gould) by the epigone of WASP society, Whitelaw Reid. Mr. Ochs was a sophisticated man. He was married to the remarkably charming Effie Wise, daughter of Rabbi Isaac Wise, founder of the Hebrew Union College in Cincinnati and the most prominent rabbi in the United States (some would say in the world). Mr. Ochs did not, could not and would not have thought of hiding his Jewishness but he did not push it in *The Times.* He did not wish to burden his remarkable creation with the weight of being known not only as the "Morgan" paper, the "British" paper but also the "Jewish" paper. It was no accident that in his lifetime and those of his first two successor publishers *The Times* never had a Jewish managing editor. Nor were Jews to be found in prominent positions among the editors and leading correspondents until the emergence at the time of the 1929 Depression of Arthur Krock (a very proper converted Episcopalian) as *The Times'* Washington chief and Lester Markel in what was for many years an almost invisible "house" position as Sunday editor.

Mr. Ochs—and he was to bequeath this philosophy to his successors until his grandson, Punch, took over—was not a Zionist. He did not admire the idea of the Jewish homeland nor did he have much use for Theodore Herzl. He considered himself an American whose religion happened to be Jewish and he thought the whole movement for a special homeland was impractical, dangerous and illusory.

"I know Judaism only upon one question," he said in laying a corner-stone of the Temple Beth El at Glen Falls, New York, August 3, 1925. "I have nothing of Judaism in me that does not spell religion. Religion is all that I stand for as a Jew. I know nothing else, no other definition for a Jew except religion."

Mr. Ochs had a sharp eye and a sharp pen for his co-religionists. He wrote his wife July 17, 1896, that he had visited a seaside hotel where his Aunt Addie was staying. "It struck me as cheap and uninviting and as a mammoth Jewish boardinghouse. I do not believe that there are any but Jews there and they are of all classes, the ordinary predominating."

On November 15, 1896, he wrote his wife about a dinner he had attended at Delmonico's at which "there were only thirty-two plates and the party was made up of the *crème de la crème* of New York Jewish culture and refinement." Among the guests were Oscar Straus, Isidor Strauss, Senator Cantor, Judges Isaac, Lachman and Newburger; Kohler, Grossman, Silverman, Harris, and Wise of the clergy; Schiff and May of the banking community; B. Altman and Sulzberger among the merchants and Henry Rice and A. S. Solomon, whom he classed as philanthropists. It was a kosher dinner and Mr. Ochs quoted his brother George as saying "that now we have been accorded the highest position that can be accorded an American Jew." Mr. Ochs spoke at the dinner saying he hoped "not only to achieve a success for my own sake but for the sake of Judaism" and added that he would do all he could "to promote the general welfare."

"The whole affair," Mr. Ochs wrote his wife, "was a grand success —not a coarse joke; nothing boisterous, not too much drinking— nothing that would not have taken place in the very best society. We sat down at seven o'clock and arose at eleven o'clock."

Just because many Jews read his newspaper he felt no reason for making any concession to their viewpoint. He carried this philosophy to an extreme, some would now say beyond the extreme, and even the rise of Adolf Hitler did not sway him. When a woman wrote him a month or two after Hitler had taken over, asking him to open *The Times'* letter columns to comments on the Nazis and the plight of the Jews in Germany, Mr. Ochs replied that he considered Hitler's conduct "the worst attack on humanity and civilization that has occurred during our lifetime." But he firmly refused to open up the subject for discussion in *The Times* because of the volume of mail that would pour in and because under *The Times'* rules he would have to devote equal space to the other side. He did, however, dispatch his trusted managing editor, Frederick Birchall (Birchall was always called "acting" managing editor because he was a British citizen and Mr. Ochs feared the full title would be grist for the mills of those who thought *The Times* a British organ), now serving as European correspondent-at-large, to Germany to report on Hitler and the Jews.*

The Good Gray *Times*

If by Mr. Ochs' policies he contributed to the image of what later came to be called "the good gray Times" he could not have cared less. As he remarked in a letter to a correspondent in 1933, "I do not take umbrage, as you do, with the prominent New Yorker who called *The Times* an 'old fog-ist' newspaper. An 'old fogy' sometimes contributes a good deal in preventing too sudden a transition from old and established methods to new, untried or dangerous experiments."

His words were written in the fifth month of Franklin D. Roosevelt's New Deal, a political administration with which Mr. Ochs found little to sympathize. He was a good friend of Herbert Hoover, whom he considered "courageous, wise, sagacious," and a frank admirer of Calvin Coolidge.

There was an admirable consistency in Mr. Ochs' philosophy. He did not say one thing and do another; he did not believe one thing and permit his newspaper to take an opposite position. So far as government was concerned, and this he felt was due even those administrations like Roosevelt's, which made him uncomfortable, *The Times* (as he wrote a complaining subscriber in 1931) "so far as possible consistent with honest journalism attempts to act and support those who are charged with responsibility for Government."

Mr. Ochs died in 1935. In the last eight or nine years of his life he had often been inactive because of illness—through much of his later life he had been subject to traumatic spells of depression. But he left

---

*When Hitler came to power in Germany the Ochs and Sulzbergers got all their surviving relatives (not many were still left) out of Germany. Most of them were fairly distant connections. Iphigene Sulzberger recalled two families who were brought out and established themselves very successfully. She could not recall any relative who had not made the transition successfully and each in the end repaid his passage money. (Personal interview, Iphigene Ochs Sulzberger, 2/13/70)

The Times substantially as he created it and his concept of the newspaper and of its role would dominate the conduct and thinking of his heirs even long after they had modified, abandoned or totally reconstituted (often only dimly aware of the fact) many of the practices which guided him from his appearance on the New York scene in 1896 to his death of a stroke on a visit to Chattanooga thirty-nine years later.

Mr. Ochs had been dead for thirty-six years on June 12, 1971. The newspaper still carried in its "left ear," the little box beside the flag, or nameplate of *The New York Times* on page one, Mr. Ochs' slogan "All the News That's Fit to Print." There were some who thought the slogan had become a little dowdy with the passage of time; there had been too many jokes about "fitting the news into print," but no one on *The Times* would seriously have suggested that it be dropped even though a great deal of the kind of news which now appeared in *The Times*—news of women's liberation, homosexuality, frank and open discussion of sexual and physical topics—would have been considered by Mr. Ochs unfit for polite dinner-table conversation and in consequence equally unfit for *his Times.*

And he would assuredly have been deeply troubled with much of the dissent which filled *The Times*—reports of flagburnings (Mr. Ochs was strong for the flag; had considered running a miniature reproduction in color on his page one during World War I), draft-card burnings, violence around the White House and Capitol, barnyard epithets like "pig" for the police and considerably stronger for the President (although here *The Times,* under Abe Rosenthal, staunchly held the line and regardless of the practice of other publications kept words like "fuck," "shit," "piss," "ass" and "motherfucker" out of the paper until, with great reluctance, Rosenthal permitted publication of some of them in transcriptions of the White House tapes because these were the verbatim words of President Nixon).

By this time, of course, Mr. Ochs' newspaper had moved far beyond the position held by its founder toward the end of his second decade of ownership when he assured a friend that "we have almost a prohibition against the employment of women in our editorial staff." No Nellie Blys for Mr. Ochs, and until his son-in-law approved the addition of the talented Anne O'Hare McCormick as editorial writer, and later columnist, just before World War II there was no prominent woman employee of any kind. In fact, the problem of female employment on *The Times* was to persist into the seventies and assume the form of a massive class action suit charging *The Times* with consistent discrimination against women, a suit which was settled in 1978 with an agreement by *The Times* to place $233,500 in an annuity fund for its 584 women employees and to prosecute with vigor a program for adding more women to its staff.

Nor could it be said that *The Times* of Mr. Ochs had been out front in the field of race relations. As late as 1930 Mr. Ochs was being compelled to insist firmly that his founding newspaper, the *Chattanooga Times,* come into line with practice on *The New York Times* and capitalize the word "Negro." The only black employees of Mr. Ochs' *Times* were porters and elevator operators, many of whom had come up from the South and been given employment at *The Times* because of Mr. Ochs' southern background. He enjoyed the company of blacks and felt comfortable with them in the tradition of the society in which he grew up in the South but it would not have occurred to him (any more than it would have occurred to any of his fellow publishers) to hire a *black* reporter or a *black* bookkeeper or a *black* advertising solicitor, and, of course, all of the printing trades unions, including the typographical union in which Mr. Ochs held his card until he died, were lily white.*

In none of this was Mr. Ochs or his *Times* in any way unique and the facts are worth reciting only as a yardstick by which to measure the social and economic torrent which swept *The Times* and the country forward into a world of largely changed values. The fact that the black elevator operators at *The Times* vanished with the automation of building elevators in the late 1950s (some of Mr. Ochs' blacks continued on for a few years as maintenance employees or receptionists) and that a steady stream of young black, Hispanic and other ethnic men and women moved onto *The Times* was merely testimony to that end. The bust of Mr. Ochs still stood in the entrance hall of *The Times* with the quotation from his opening 1896 issue spelled out on the wall behind him—"To give the news impartially without fear or favor regardless of any party, sect or interest involved"—but the world that passed through that lobby and the world beyond that lobby on Forty-third Street, with its pimps and prostitutes, drunks and drug-takers, guzzling Thunderbird from brown paper bags or spaced-out in unconscious heaps against the graffiti-mutilated walls of the once lovely Lyric Theatre,† had changed rather more than a casual comparison of the front pages of *The Times* of 1896 and those of 1971 would indicate.

---

*It was not until 1955, at Arthur Sulzberger's insistence, that the *Chattanooga Times* ceased to segregate its obituary columns. Until then black deaths had been listed under the heading "Colored." When death was desegregated at the *Chattanooga Times* the paper lost 8,000 circulation, which it took several years to regain. (*Times'* archives, Arthur Hays Sulzberger memo, 4/1/57)

†Miraculously restored with its sister theater, the New Apollo, with their original entrances on Forty-third Street after years of service as Forty-second Street "grind houses."

Punch Sulzberger

Punch Sulzberger never really knew his grandfather. He was only nine years old when Mr. Ochs died and he retained no recollection of ever having been given any advice by Mr. Ochs. He never sat in his grandfather's lap, possibly, he mused, because the old gentleman may have been afraid he would pee. He was much closer to his grandmother and he remembered having made a present for her birthday in 1936, a small wooden bowl which he turned on a lathe. But she died before he could give it to her. So it was probably natural enough that when the issue of publishing the Pentagon Papers arose it never occurred to Punch to wonder what his grandfather might have done. After the event—not before—he did wonder whether his father would have published the documents and decided that he would have done so in his prime years of the 1930s and 1940s. Possibly, Punch conceded, his father would not have published the papers in his later years because he had become quite conservative, plagued as he was by ill health.§In this Punch Sulzberger disagreed with his mother, the remarkable Iphigene, only child of Mr. Ochs. She was firm in the conviction that her father would not have published the papers. Nor, she felt, would have her husband or his successor as publisher, Orvil Dryfoos, husband of the eldest Sulzberger daughter, Marian.

No, said Iphigene Ochs Sulzberger, pursing her lips a bit, her eyes sparkling with the life spirit which grew stronger and stronger as she entered her eighth decade, no one of them would have done what her son had done. Punch did not consult his mother or his family beforehand. But he did inform his sisters at a private session before the regular monthly board meeting on Wednesday, June 9. The sisters were not unanimously in favor of publication. Ruth, in particular, had reservations although years later she said wryly, "I hope I wasn't too opposed."* Had Punch consulted his mother there is no doubt what her

§See Notes section.
*These meetings were the outgrowth of a custom begun not long after Mr. Ochs' death. Every year Edward S. Greenbaum, friend and counsel, met with the Sulzbergers to review the position of the family, the Ochs Trust and the paper. As the children grew old enough they were brought into the meetings. Then, they developed into a kind of younger generation family council in which only the four Sulzberger children participated. "We used to talk about what we would do if we didn't have Mother to tell us," Marian Heiskell recalled. (Personal interview, Marian Heiskell, 1/23/78) The first meeting of this kind was held in 1961 in Chattanooga; everyone went down by train and came back by train. It was a great sentimental outing. For a time after Punch became publisher Turner Catledge joined the sessions. There was no regular schedule for the meetings. In 1977, for the first time, the thirteen Ochs grandchildren joined the meeting with their four parents. (Personal interviews, Arthur Ochs Sulzberger, 3/8/79; Greenbaum, 2/13/70)

advice would have been: Publish! However, Iphigene Sulzberger was quick to note that in the days of her father and her husband and her son-in-law people didn't have the same attitude toward government. They thought that the paper should support the government. To do something like publish the Pentagon Papers was to publish stolen documents—so they would have thought. That, her son conceded, was very close to his own initial attitude. His instinct, he recalled, told him to stay away, stay away from the whole project. He had been taught and the teaching had been reinforced by his years of service in the U.S. Marines that you were not supposed to publish classified documents and things marked "Top Secret."

But, in the end, Punch's mind had been clear. He had no alternative. The Papers *had* to be published. In this he was one with all of his editors. He had learned to respect their opinion and their judgment. The man who had educated, taught, guided him in a perception of the role which responsible editors and a responsible publisher must play in the direction of an institution like *The New York Times* had been Turner Catledge, no longer active on the paper but its managing editor when Punch so unexpectedly landed in the publisher's chair and the man upon whom Iphigene and Arthur Sulzberger had relied to nurture their son's instincts and train him in the complicated role of directing the world's leading newspaper.

Turner, Punch said several years after the Pentagon Papers had been published and the Pentagon controversy had inexorably given way to newer ones—Watergate, the CIA and all, was the man responsible for his running the Pentagon Papers. Catledge had been like a second father to Punch and it was Catledge's counsel which had taught him what *The Times* expected of him and what he must expect of *The Times*.

There was no question but that Punch's analysis was correct. Everyone close to *The Times* understood that it was the throw-away wizardry of Catledge, the "good ol' boy" from Mississippi, which had prepared the paper for its transition from "good gray Times," repository of moral enlightenment, historical record and beyond-the-need-of-duty loyalty to the Establishment, to its new but still unacknowledged role of guardian of public interest, of living embodiment of the First Amendment principles bestowed upon the press by the founding fathers, of modern fulfillment of the rhetorical statement of Thomas Burke in 1790 that in Parliament sat three estates—the peers, the bishops and the commons but that "in the Reporter's Gallery, yonder, there sits a Fourth Estate more important than they all."

4

"Mr. and Mrs. Thompson"

ON THE AFTERNOON of Friday, March 19, 1971, a good-looking young couple, the man tall, dark and faintly military in appearance, the woman several inches shorter, with blue eyes and long auburn hair, the kind the French call *châtain*, signed the register of the Treadway Motor Inn in Cambridge, Massachusetts, a few blocks from Harvard Yard, as "Mr. and Mrs. Thompson."

In fact, they were Neil Sheehan and his wife, Susan, a stunningly frank, gifted writer for *The New Yorker* magazine, a refugee from Austrian Anschluss at the age of three who had grown up on Seventy-ninth Street in New York. Susan was a strongly built woman, a fact not without significance in light of the mission of Mr. and Mrs. Thompson. The reason for their arrival in Cambridge was simple. They had come to steal the Pentagon Papers. That sounds melodramatic and they certainly would not have so described their enterprise but the term is not far off the mark. The Sheehans would have said that they had come to *copy* the Pentagon Papers, which is what they proceeded to do, to copy them so, as Neil once expressed it, they would have them in their hands and never again would the government be able to lock them back into the safe.

But this project, which took three nerve-racked days, a good deal of muscularity on Susan's part, lugging sixty pounds of papers back and forth in shopping bags, ultimately costing $1500 in fees to all-night copying agencies, was in every way as clandestine as the registration of "The Thompsons" at the Treadway Inn would indicate. No one knew in advance that they had come to town. No one knew what they were copying. *The New York Times* did not know although it provided the $1500 after a rather ill-tempered bureaucratic squabble. Nor did Daniel Ellsberg, the "trustee" of the Papers, who had himself clandestinely copied them seventeen months earlier in Santa Monica, California. Later on, their mysterious activities in Cambridge provided the FBI with grounds for a report which it sent to the White House that "a band of antiwar activitists" had been engaged in copying secret war documents.

The first that Bill Kovach, the saturnine, extremely professional *New York Times* resident correspondent in Boston, knew of this undertaking was when Neil called him from a telephone booth. Sheehan didn't want his name mentioned or any talk on the phone and the men arranged to meet in the Treadway lobby. Over a cup of coffee Sheehan explained that he needed Kovach's help. Where could he get some high-speed xerography done—a place that would work all night and all weekend? Also he needed money to pay for the job.

By good fortune Kovach knew a shop that had just opened in Bedford, Massachusetts. He got in touch with the proprietor, explained that he had a manuscript that had to be turned in to the publisher on Monday morning and persuaded the man to bring in some extra help and work day and night until the job was done. Kovach passed the word to Neil, and Susan loaded the heavy documents, four or five shopping bags full, into a taxi and hurried out to Bedford. Meantime, Kovach telephoned New York and arranged for the money to be wired in his name. This caused a row among junior news executives at *The Times,* none of whom on that weekend had any more idea than Kovach what Neil was about, but, amid grumbling, the money was dispatched and Kovach paid the bill. All Neil told him was that he had gotten some very important documents "out of M.I.T." and they had to be back in place on Monday. The copying did not go easily. The reproduction machines at Bedford broke down under the strain and another shop had to be found. But by Monday the job was done and the original documents were returned to where Neil had gotten them in a flat which belonged to the stepmother of Ellsberg's wife, Patricia.§

Kovach had nothing more to do with the affair until one morning later in the summer his apartment bell rang at about 7 A.M. and he found two FBI men on the doorstep. They wanted to interrogate him about the "McNamara Report." Kovach politely declined to answer any questions but invited them in for fried apples and a cup of coffee. They refused to cross his doorstep and finally left, having learned nothing.

A couple of years later Father Drinan, the antiwar congressman from Massachusetts, sent Kovach a copy of a document that had turned up in the Watergate inquiry. It was a memorandum from J. Edgar Hoover to H. R. Haldeman saying the FBI was on the trail of a "Bill Kowitch who might be William Kovich of *The New York Times.*" Kowitch was said to have represented himself as a colonel in the Air Force in arranging with the Bedford company for the copying of the Pentagon documents. This touched off alarms in the jittery White House, which

§See Notes section.

leaped to the conclusion that new and possibly more sensational revelations might be forthcoming. In fact, the FBI report was so suggestive that seven years later, John Ehrlichman, ruminating on the case of the Pentagon Papers, recalled the report and said that he had long suspected that Ellsberg was not the source of *The New York Times* documents and, instead, that they had been provided by this "other group of antiwar activists in Cambridge"—proof, if proof were needed, that in real life people as well as cats sometimes chase their own tails.

Later Kovach learned from an FBI friend that the two agents who appeared at his door had been terrified of entering for fear he would tape the conversation. He also deduced from the phonetic spelling of his name as "Bill Kowitch" that the FBI had picked up its tip by tapping his phone, a tap probably installed because Kovach met many antiwar people in his newsgathering, particularly in his coverage of a Media, Pennsylvania, raid on an FBI office which had produced a considerable number of embarrassing FBI documents.

Homer Bigart

A long, long trail lay behind the arrival of the attractive young "Thompson" couple at the Treadway Inn.

Neil Sheehan had not returned to the United States in 1966 as an opponent of the war. He had gone originally to Saigon in 1962 as a gung-ho reporter in the old stop-the-press tradition. If he had any bias against war or any conviction against killing it was not visible to his comrades in Vietnam, men like Homer Bigart, whose acquaintance with war had begun in London in 1943 and who had since seldom been able to get its stench out of his nostrils, and David Halberstam, new to Saigon after a stint in the dark and murderous Congo wars and like Sheehan more interested in getting a "good story" and getting it first than in attempting to assess the morality of the American experience in Southeast Asia. The fact is that, difficult as it was to recall later, not many Americans in Vietnam or out of it had moral objections to what the U.S. was doing there in the early sixties. That was to come later.

A friend of those times remembered Neil before he left the Army and went to Vietnam as "very right-wing, very conservative, a real believer, a strong Taft man." Taft, he said, was very important to Neil. Sheehan in these days liked to argue politics, hazing his friend (who was Jewish) about Israel. He seemed to believe in the Army and soldiering and he was good at it, took his guard duty and drill without complaint.

There can be no question that Vietnam itself, the tedious resemblance which it bore to Remarque (blasted jungles instead of bottomless mud, buzzards instead of rats devouring corpses, napalm instead of poison gas, grass-cutter bombs instead of the ceaseless '75's but the same death, death, death) caused Sheehan, like many Americans, to begin to revise his thinking. But it is equally true that the worn and worldly cynicism of Homer Bigart played a role. Bigart could hardly bear Vietnam. He could not bear war. Any war. He had been at it since the days of the late Ernie Pyle in World War II, that poet of the GI who came to hate the debasement of the men of whom he wrote, saying "If I hear one more GI saying 'Fuck my shit' I will blow my brains out. 'Fuck my shit.' That is what war adds up to."

Homer Bigart did not agonize as did Pyle. He simply spat out a casual word that pierced the balloons of Army rhetoric, Army casuistry, Army hyperbole, Army hypocrisy like a hot needle. He had seen Vietnam from the beginning. He had come into Saigon in 1945 just after Colonel Peter Dewey, an OSS officer who was the first American casualty in Saigon, was shot down in the street by hysterical Vietnamese excited by a blimpish British commander named General Douglas Grasey. From the moment of arrival Bigart felt (as had Colonel Dewey and there are those who still suspect this was why Dewey was killed) that the only sensible American role was to support Ho Chi Minh and his Viet Minh nationalists. That was September 1945. Homer was to go back again and again and in between he covered the Korean war. December 1950 found him in Hanoi visiting the French outposts, which were finally to fall with Dien Bien Phu on May 5, 1954. He was back after the French fell, after Geneva and the creeping intervention of the Americans. He was in Saigon when the redoubtable American Colonel Edward Lansdale was building up Ngo Dinh Diem and he was there in the early 1960s when the Americans were beginning to let Diem drift off, as the CIA would have put it, toward termination with extreme prejudice. Bigart covered Vietnam first for the New York *Herald Tribune* and then for *The Times*. It was in 1962 that he met Sheehan, new to Vietnam, a raw young correspondent, and Bigart thought him very, very good for a young reporter. Once he brought Sheehan down a peg or two, an incident Sheehan remembered for years. Only two weeks in Saigon, Sheehan had gotten from a U.S. Army major the story of a victory by the Seventh ARVN Division. They had killed two hundred Vietcong in an engagement in the Delta, flown to the scene by U.S. Army helicopters. He filed his urgent dispatch to UPI's Tokyo bureau and dropped off to sleep about 4 A.M.

At 8 A.M. Sheehan's telephone rang. A husky voice said, "This is Bigart. Sh-hee-han, y-you wiped me off the f-f-front page. Y-y-you shirt-tailed me, you s-s-son-of-a-bitch." Bigart's stutter always became pronounced when he was angry. Sheehan, the most junior correspondent in Saigon, felt a cold chill.

Bigart continued on the telephone:

"I-I-I h-h-have this rocket from New York. It says U-P-I has two hundred Vietcong killed in the D-D-Delta by waves of attacking Vietnamese troops. Sheehan, there better be two hundred bodies there because you and I are going down to have a look. I have a car and I'll pick you up in five minutes."

Of course there were not two hundred bodies. There were twelve. It had been a big engagement fought under the direction of Colonel Frank Clay, son of General Lucius Clay and American "adviser" to the Seventh ARVN, but Sheehan's source had enhanced the casualties by twenty times.

It was a grim Sheehan who started back to Saigon with Bigart. He was going to have to "row back," as the agencies put it. He was sure UPI would fire him.

"D-d-don't worry about it, kid," Bigart suddenly said. "They're not going to fire you. I've done it many times myself. But—just don't do it again."

That was Sheehan's first lesson in the Bigart school of journalism. Sheehan began to tag after Bigart like a dog and to learn from him the elements of the war correspondent's trade—skepticism, accuracy, checking and rechecking, seeing with your own eyes, never staying far from the front, learning to discriminate between go-go boys on the make to build up an operation or a general and the reality of war, the same war Remarque had written about—tedious, small, dull, everlastingly unsuccessful, frightening, painful, confused, dirty, meaningless.

Sheehan once went out with Bigart on three successive operations. Nothing happened on any of them. No story. Then they went on a fourth. Same thing. Yet each time Bigart conscientiously questioned the officers and men before they went into action and after they returned, question after question, a tiresome interrogatory. On the way back Sheehan was in despair. He told Bigart, "Jesus—all that time and no story."

"Really?" Bigart replied. "There's no story?"

"Well, what story is there?" Sheehan asked in surprise.

"It-t doesn't work, kid," Bigart said. "It doesn't work anymore."

Suddenly, Sheehan realized what Bigart had been about in his painstaking, time-consuming fashion. He was establishing that the operations against the Vietcong no longer were successful. Once they had been. Now: "It doesn't work anymore." The year was 1962. It took General Westmoreland, General Taylor, Presidents Kennedy, Johnson and Nixon twelve more years, tens of billions of dollars and tens of thousands of lives to come to Bigart's laconic conclusion: "It doesn't work." Sheehan went back to Saigon and wrote one of the best stories of his career. He called it "A Long Hot Day in the Sun."

David Halberstam liked to tell the story of the first encounter of Bigart and Sheehan. As he told it Bigart awakened Sheehan in the

night, saying a bit ominously, "Mr. Sheehan? This is Homer Bigart."
That was wrong, Bigart said. "I didn't go about calling people 'mister.'
I probably said, 'Hey, you!' " But Neil remembered the conversation
precisely. Bigart addressed him bluntly as "Sheehan." Later on, Neil
recalled, "he used to call me 'Sonny.' "

Charles Mohr, a big brave man who went to Vietnam for *Time* magazine and switched to *The New York Times,* went through the classic
transition. He did not become antiwar, no one was antiwar in this
period, but he became a pessimist.

"Of course, the military knew nothing about this kind of war, a
people's war, a guerrilla war," he recalled. "Their whole experience had
been with conventional positional war. They knew nothing about revolutionary war. Neither did the new generation of reporters—fortunately—so they stayed away from the old hands and went down into
the countryside to see for themselves."

He remembered going to a prototype of a strategic hamlet, called
"Operation Sunrise." It was being shown to Robert McNamara on his
first trip to Vietnam—McNamara, as described by Mohr "in his Sears
Roebuck chino pants, his farmer baseball hat and his Matterhorn
boots."

There were lots of children, lots of old men and women in the village.

"Homer said to me," Mohr recalled, " 'Notice there are no men,
only old men and children and women.' " Mohr asked a conducting officer about this. "The men are all with the VC," the officer
said.

McNamara noticed a strongpoint, with two pillboxes, protected by
concertina wire, barbed wire and sandbags.

"What's all this?" he asked.

He was told it was the final strongpoint. If the hamlet was overrun
the officials would hold out here till help came. McNamara was troubled. "What about the people?" he asked. "Oh," said an official, "the
VC won't hurt the people. Most of them have relatives in the VC."

McNamara was still troubled. It was obvious there was no way to
protect the five hundred villagers. Finally a bright Vietnamese officer
spoke up. "We can't afford to put up pillboxes for everybody," he said,
"but we can put slit trenches in front of their huts."

McNamara smiled. He jotted in his notebook, "slit trenches." Everyone took out their notebooks and jotted, "slit trenches."

Bigart simply said, "Shit."

Mohr had only a month overlap with Bigart but later on he was to
conclude that as years passed "people just repeated what Homer had
done. He was so perceptive. Such a good feeling. He knew the enemy

looked weak. He knew the enemy wasn't weak. Go back and read his stuff."

Malcolm Browne, Sheehan's chief competitor in Vietnam, was also to join *The New York Times*. In Vietnam he reported for AP, Sheehan for UPI. AP and UPI were the Gimbels and Macy's of the news business. Browne got to Vietnam a year ahead of Neil. He had been brought up a Quaker and went to Swarthmore, but, like Sheehan, he had served in the Army in Korea and had dropped his Quaker faith.

Bigart was Browne's hero just as he was Sheehan's and Halberstam's.

"Everyone looked up to Bigart," Browne recalled. "He was the beau ideal of younger correspondents like myself and Sheehan. He was our only link with World War II and the Korean war. He hated Vietnam, hated the war, hated the bureaucracy and hated the American cant."

And, said Browne, he too came to hate it. He had arrived in Vietnam with no ideological bias against the war. He did not think Sheehan had a bias either. Browne did not believe in killing people but, sometimes, he thought it was necessary. What began to turn the correspondents off was the hypocrisy of the Americans, their lordly assumption that they knew the answers better than anyone else, that their answers were the right answers and their insistence that the war was being won when anyone with eyes could see that it was not. This was what came first. It was only later that the correspondents began to question the whole philosophy and rationale of the war, what the U.S. was doing in Vietnam and in Asia, the nature of the Saigon regime and the fact that the United States was taking sides in what was essentially an Asian civil war, the racism, the bigotry.

Both sides, Browne thought, did terrible things. Browne married a Vietnamese girl and his father-in-law was brutally murdered by the Vietcong. The Americans claimed that it was only the other side that was evil. But Browne and Sheehan and the other correspondents went to the war every day. They could see that it was a bad war and that there were no good guys. The Americans turned the correspondents against themselves by clumsy tactics, silly propaganda and lies. It was the lies that did it.

Halberstam's picture of Neil Sheehan, of the Vietnam correspondents and the war did not differ basically from Browne's. Neil had been a freshman at Harvard when David was a senior, class of '58 against class of '55. The two men had not known each other as undergraduates; three years is a gap as wide as the Atlantic in undergraduate Harvard. But the two got on quickly in Saigon. Halberstam thought Sheehan was an intuitive reporter without equal—fast, quick, marvelous at leg work but a little clumsy at first—he hadn't yet mastered the carpenter's tricks. But certainly Sheehan was not antiwar. He was just pessimistic, a pragmatist who believed in at least limited American involvement but who could not see how it would work.

"We didn't have doves and hawks in Vietnam," Halberstam later said. "The war was a given. We were there to cover it. If there was a debate it wasn't about winning or losing—it was about the lies. It was lies, lies, lies."

It was, Halberstam thought, the Battle of Ap Bac that did it, as far as the reporters were concerned. At Ap Bac in January 1963 the crack ARVN Seventh Division, now directed ("advised" was the ritual word) by the legendary Colonel John Vann (whom many correspondents came to believe was the only American military man who really understood Indochina) refused to move into attack when the Vietcong stood and fought. Ap Bac opened the eyes of the correspondents; it showed them the reality of Vietnam. Admiral Harry Felt, commander of the Navy's Sixth Fleet, flew in to Saigon airport at that time and berated the newsmen for their negative reports. Ap Bac, he insisted, had been a victory for the Vietnamese. He turned to Sheehan and said, "So you're Sheehan. You ought to go down and talk to some of the people who've got the facts."

Sheehan responded, "You're right, Admiral. That's why I went down to Ap Bac every day during the fighting."

The Home Office

It was in this reality of 1961, 1962, 1963, and 1964 that the views of Sheehan and the other reporters began to be forged. There was no American antiwar movement at this time. No bands in the streets. No sit-ins. No colleges ablaze with indignation. No SDS. No Tom Hayden and no Mark Rudd. Congress was approving "defense" budgets ritually. President Kennedy and then President Johnson had no trouble mustering public opinion for their tidy escalations. The shuttle trips of the generals and high Pentagon men between Washington and Saigon were beginning and were taken with total seriousness. There was no major editorial opinion against the war. *The New York Times* supported Administration policy in Southeast Asia as it had doggedly—some later were to say blindly—supported it since 1945. *The Times* had been as appalled in 1954 as John Foster Dulles at Dien Bien Phu, as convinced as the Joint Chiefs of Staff, of the necessity for standing firm against the Communist presence in Southeast Asia. It had not raised a whisper against the domino theory. It believed in containment (Dulles' military version of George Kennan's theory, not the author's original thesis of military power as a lever for diplomatic resolution). As late as August 1964 *Times* editorials said of the Tonkin Gulf affair (which Tony Austin's book in 1971 revealed to be almost totally contrived) that it offered "an ominous perspective . . . the beginning of a mad adventure by the North Vietnam Communists." If *The Times* editorial writers were paying any heed to the splendidly realistic correspondence which *Times* and other American correspondents in the field had been transmitting since the end of World War II—the informed dispatches of Robert Trumbull,* the déjà vu reports of Tillman Durdin, the hard-eyed realism of Homer Bigart—there was no evidence that it had affected the stream of editorials, each one as like the latest government pronouncement as one sausage resembles another.

The Times' editors were proud of, and always emphasized, one of Mr. Ochs' firm principles—the total separation of news and editorial functions. Not only were the two departments physically separate, news on the third floor and editorial on the tenth floor, but the psychological separation was even broader. Charles Merz, when editor in chief, would no more have attended the daily conferences at which the news executives reported to managing editor Turner Catledge than he would have considered dancing in his BVD's in Macy's Thirty-fourth Street display window. John Oakes took the same position. Nor would Catledge have thought of sending a memo to Merz or Oakes or telephoning them about a striking new development in Southeast Asia, Europe or even in Brooklyn—which might be the basis for an editorial. In fact, the editorial writers largely depended for their news upon the daily AP wire. The first they usually saw of *Times* reports was when they picked up the paper the next day. Presumably they looked at page one before turning to read the editorial page although there were those in the news department who swore that the editorial writers didn't know there *was* a page one. It was equally true that few correspondents or news editors could have sworn on a particular day exactly what *The Times'* position was on a given issue beyond a conviction that it probably hadn't changed much in the past year, or the past decade.

If, as occasionally happened, there was a concordance of editorial

---

*The name of Robert Trumbull is seldom mentioned in lists of correspondents who illuminated Indochina on the pages of *The New York Times*. But on January 27, 1947, he reported from Saigon, "It is difficult to see how France can achieve a military victory in Indochina in a reasonable length of time. . . . France faces a clever foe. It is a foe that employs elusive guerrilla tactics over a vast area and fights to the last man when occasionally pinned down. . . . The Vietnamese in defense of their ideals, however gently these may be expressed, fight like savages. . . . In any stand-up fight in which artillery could be employed the French, with what armament they have, would undoubtedly be victorious every time. But the Vietnamese do not fight that way. Against superior odds they retreat, leaving nothing behind but ashes and ruins. By night they return in small bands again and again, making life uncomfortable for the foe." Trumbull's low-key words write an epitaph *in advance* to the three decades that were to follow.

comment and a correspondent's dispatch, the chances were that it was accidental and that neither of the great and powerful fiefdoms of *The Times*, the news department or the editorial, was aware of it. If they were aware they probably were made vaguely uneasy.

It was this total lack of correlation or coordination of news and editorial operations that was, perhaps, hardest for foreign observers to understand about the paper, conditioned as they were to the European press where news and editorials were integrated and where correspondents frequently wrote editorials as well as dispatches and often wrote dispatches to support the editorial line of their newspaper. For Soviet correspondents, for example, the situation of *The Times* was not only confusing—it was unbelievable. They might listen politely to the explanations but they really didn't understand why the editors of *The Times* told such fairy stories. There were not a few readers (especially critics of *The Times*) who took the same position.

When a correspondent like Sheehan returned from an overseas assignment it was the custom for the publisher to invite him to lunch with the chief editors, including, of course, the editor in chief, the Sunday editor and some of the editorial writers. There he would talk about the situation as seen in the field, be subjected (quite often) to skeptical questioning from editors who had never been within two thousand miles of the area and then would be released to take his home leave, return to his assignment or go to another post, whatever his fate might be.

Thus, it would be difficult to adduce any evidence that Sheehan's reporting from Vietnam, or that of Browne, or Bigart, or Charles Mohr, or Halberstam or any of the field correspondents affected the editorial course of *The New York Times* in these years.

But their experience in Vietnam did affect their own thinking, their own point of view, their own philosophy. They were sensitive men. Had they not been they could not have held the posts that they did and filled them so capably. So, regardless of the ideology or views that they carried out to Vietnam they returned with something quite different. And this change occurred uniformly and well ahead of substantial change in public opinion in the United States about the war.

The case of Sheehan was not untypical. What is revealing, however, is that unlike some of the others Sheehan put down his views on paper and they were published in the autumn of 1966 by *The New York Times Magazine* under the title "Not a Dove but No Longer a Hawk."

It was an article of unusual candor and self-revelation in which Neil sought to convey his concern at what we were doing to ourselves in prosecuting the war in Vietnam. He distinguished the Vietnam war from that in Korea in which he felt Americans fought with clear moral justification for "human freedom and dignity."

But in Vietnam, he sadly wrote, "moral superiority has given way to the amorality of great power politics." By this time there were 317,000 American troops in Vietnam, Lyndon Johnson was well into his program of escalation and bombing and privately seemed ready to put as big a force into Vietnam as necessary to win. It was a time when many Americans, including, it later would become clear, Mr. Johnson's Secretary of Defense Robert McNamara, were beginning to have second thoughts about the war.

Neil perceived the hard outlines of the American dilemma clearly. The United States was headed for the creation of what he called a "killing machine" powerful enough, it was hoped, to force Hanoi's collapse through exhaustion and despair.

Despite his misgivings he still saw no alternative to continued prosecution of the war. Yet, in this process he felt that the nation was corrupting itself and he asked whether the United States or any nation had the right to inflict such suffering and degradation on another people for its own ends.

He was not, as he insisted, a dove but he was no longer the hawk who had flown into Saigon in March of 1962. Nor was *The Times* the same newspaper, deeply and consistently supportive of the Southeast Asian war effort it had been in 1962. It, too, increasingly was raising questions in its editorials and had been doing so since early in 1965.

The first serious editorial challenge by *The Times* to President Johnson's undeclared policy of escalating the war came on February 9, 1965, coincident with the spectacular Vietnamese attack on Pleiku airfield and the U.S. bombing of North Vietnam.

The issue was rapidly developed. In a series of editorials written by Herbert Matthews in collaboration with editorial page director John Oakes, *The Times* warned February 21 against the strategy advocated by the hawkish military correspondent of *The Times*, Hanson W. Baldwin, of saturation bombing and sending in one million Americans, if necessary, to win the war. Four days later *The Times* warned that time was working against the United States and called for exploration of a negotiated end to the conflict.

These themes were struck again and again by *The Times*. Oakes coined the word "descalation." He was to use it repeatedly in the next year or two but neither the word nor the policy caught on. However, the editorials were the first by a major newspaper to challenge Mr. Johnson's conduct of the war and *The Times'* increasingly strong stand heartened those voices across the country (very few at first and largely confined to academic circles) that began to speak out against Vietnam. *Times* men began to hear in scattered places a remark that was to become more and more common: "Thank God for *The Times!* At least *The Times* makes it respectable to be against the war."

Oakes, a strongly patriotic man, a wartime member of the OSS, did not come easily to his antiwar position nor did his conviction arise overnight. But the steady growth of U.S. forces in Vietnam and his emerging conclusion that there was no way in which the United States could win a land war in Asia caused him as early as April 22, 1965, to warn that the President's policies could lead "to a catastrophe."*

The Times stood almost alone in this position in 1965. By 1973, when the war finally stumbled to a conclusion, *The Times'* view had become commonplace.

*Oakes later was to feel that *The Times'* opposition to Vietnam could be traced as far back as 1964. However, examination of 1964 editorials does not support this view. There were occasional suggestions for a diplomatic approach but *The Times* was as strong as anyone in its support of Mr. Johnson on the critical Gulf of Tonkin resolution. (Personal memo, Oakes, 3/23/70)

5

The Madman Theory

*I*T HAD NOT BEEN Dan Ellsberg's original intention to utilize *The New York Times* as a medium for publicizing the Pentagon Papers. Like many intellectuals, he read *The New York Times,* depended on *The New York Times,* took an extraordinarily proprietary and critical interest in *The New York Times* but simultaneously was ignorant of its ways, suspicious of its motives and intimidated by its image.

Ellsberg did not understand how *The New York Times* worked. He couldn't get the *feel* of it and this was frustrating because he had a knowing touch for the bureaucracy of government, of the defense establishment and for the academic world, the great universities, institutes and research centers like the Rand Corporation. He knew which buttons to press and which assistants to the powerful men could ensure him access—"access" was the word that was always used. Access was power.

Ellsberg was by no means alone in his difficulties with *The New York Times.* His feeling was shared by many intellectuals. They often came to *The Times* with projects for investigating, for instance, its "decision-making process." They were endlessly interested in learning how *The Times* determined which candidates to support for public office, particularly for the presidency. The editors carefully explained the procedures: first, a careful study of the candidates' records, an analysis of backgrounds and positions on major issues. For important offices like mayor of New York, governor, senator or the presidency the candidates were invited to *The Times* for firsthand appraisal. They met with the editors, particularly the editorial and political writers, over lunch with the publisher or, sometimes, for a working, taped, question and answer session. These were not cream-puff affairs. The questions were tough and even mean, so much so that when he ran in 1968 Richard Nixon at first flatly refused to come to *The Times.* "Why should I?" he said, speaking through his competent and long-suffering press aide, Herbert Klein. "Why should I go to *The Times* and subject myself to those sarcastic questions from Markel [the Sunday editor] and Oakes [John Oakes, then director of the editorial page]. What's in it for me?" Nixon finally yielded and lunched with the editors September 23, 1968. It was his fourth luncheon at *The Times* and he handled himself very well. However, Clifton Daniel noted that he ate not a bite of his lunch. Years later Klein attributed Mr. Nixon's initial refusal to meet with *The Times* to two sharply worded editorials published by *The Times* June 16 and 19, 1968, calling for a Nixon–Rockefeller debate. *The Times* was equally critical of Humphrey. It said, "It is time for Mr. Humphrey and Mr. Nixon, as the overcomplacent frontrunners, to stop playing cheap little games. . . . They have no right to glide into the nominations with silence and platitudes."* Later on it seemed to some that Mr. Nixon's antagonism to his country's leading newspaper was a portent of what was to come, but that was hindsight.

After studying the candidates and their records *The Times'* editorial writers met, discussed them and made a recommendation to the editor in chief. He conveyed the recommendation to the publisher and the choice was ratified. It sounded neat, precise and suitably bureaucratic but when theory was compared with process it turned out that there was no necessary concordance between what the editors said (and perhaps thought) had happened and what really did happen.

Eisenhower

There was, for example, the occasion when *The Times* came out for General Eisenhower not only in advance of the Republican National Convention of 1952 but before it had any idea of the Democratic candidate. There had been nothing systematic about this choice, no consultation, no discussion. It was the decision of the publisher, Arthur Hays Sulzberger (heartily concurred in by his alter ego, editor in chief Charles Merz). Mr. Sulzberger strongly favored General Eisenhower, had used his personal influence to get him to run and was concerned lest Robert Taft, whom Sulzberger regarded as a dangerous isolationist, win the nomination. It was true that this arbitrary decision caused most of *The Times'* editorial board, many on its staff and members of Mr. Sulzberger's family, particularly his wife, Iphigene, enormous distress when the Democrats nominated Adlai Stevenson, but in spite of an unprecedented, formal effort to induce Mr. Sulzberger to change his mind, *The Times'* decision held and Iphigene Sulzberger even bowed

---

*Nixon felt *The Times'* comment was totally unfair and he wanted nothing to do with the paper. Klein had hoped to arrange for meetings between Mr. Nixon and *The Times* after Mr. Nixon's inauguration but these never took place. After Mr. Nixon's first two months Klein's own influence with Mr. Nixon took a radical plunge. (Personal interview, Klein, 1/16/78) Mr. Nixon recalled that he was not invited to meet *The Times'* editorial board in 1972. He did not want anyone on his staff to urge such a meeting and said, "Thank God we had not done so." (Richard M. Nixon, *Memoirs,* New York City, 1976, p. 684)

to her husband and *voted* for Eisenhower. When they went to the polls together Iphigene said, "You know, Arthur, it's only for love of you that I am casting my vote for Eisenhower." The second time around in 1956, when the paper again supported Eisenhower over Stevenson, she bolted and voted for her choice, having by that time become fed up with Eisenhower.

Iphigene's first doubts about Eisenhower had been aroused when she called on him in his president's office at Columbia University to invite him to speak at a meeting of the Federation of Jewish Charities. Eisenhower agreed to talk but in his conversation managed to say that he had no prejudices against the Jews, adding that he had no prejudices against the Catholics either. Her second and more serious question arose on the McCarthy issue. Arthur Sulzberger had suggested to Eisenhower that when he went to Wisconsin he make a statement supporting General Marshall, then under attack by McCarthy. Sulzberger wrote a paragraph which Eisenhower agreed to include in a speech. But when Eisenhower delivered the talk in Milwaukee he deleted the Marshall defense. "There's your man for you!" Iphigene told her husband.

Not that it should be supposed that Iphigene Sulzberger was prickly on the Jewish question. Her own spirit was ecumenical. Ordinarily she went to the synagogue only on the anniversary of her father's death. As she once told the rabbi, she simply could not stand the prayers—God as the Great Protector of the Jews. If He was—why did He let all those Jews die in the concentration camps? The rabbi said she was too literal. To which she replied, "Well, I'm not and I can't stand those prayers. They should be rewritten." When in 1974 she visited China and dined with Premier Chou En-lai he asked about her family, "probably just to make conversation," as she recalled. She told Chou she had everything in her family—Jews, Catholics, Protestants and a black (the husband of Ruth Sulzberger Holmberg's stepdaughter) but no Chinese. What should she do about it—put an ad in the *Peking Daily?* No, Chou said, our papers don't carry ads. Maybe then, she suggested, I should put up a great character poster in Tien an-mien Square. "Oh no," Chou replied, "that would cause a riot."

Moynihan

The Eisenhower example was not the first nor was it the last in which the procedures described by *Times'* editors had little connection with reality as a later-day example was to demonstrate—the imposition by Punch Sulzberger of the endorsement of Daniel Patrick Moynihan over Bella Abzug in the Democratic primary election of 1976 for the U.S. Senate, an event so shattering, so lacking in the amenities with which *Times'* decisions were normally cloaked that it produced from editorial director John Oakes a violent outburst, deep permanent wounds and a published disclaimer (but even his disclaimer, Oakes bitterly noted, was cut to mute the force of his protest).

It was probably not surprising that Oakes and Sulzberger disagreed over Moynihan and Abzug. Sulzberger was an essentially conservative man and had grown uncomfortable with some of Oakes' views. Under a complex and controversial arrangement Oakes was retiring as director of the editorial page December 31, 1976, to be replaced by Max Frankel.

The change had been handled untidily and much bad feeling had been generated. Now Oakes and Sulzberger disagreed over the question of U.S. senator. Punch was not taken with Bella Abzug. He had met Moynihan and found him quite intriguing. He remembered going to a cocktail party at Moynihan's suite in the Waldorf Towers. Pat told Punch that he was considering running for the Senate. "Of course," Moynihan said, "I would never get any support from *The New York Times.*" Punch remembered responding, "Well, you never know— why don't you try?" Later on, as Moynihan began to campaign, Punch thought he would make a really good senator. When Moynihan got up to talk, people listened.

There had never been serious disagreements between Oakes and Sulzberger on candidates and not too many arguments of any sort. From the beginning they had agreed, Punch believed, that on candidates he as publisher had the last and deciding word.

The two men argued over Abzug and Moynihan amicably enough and when Oakes left for a month's vacation on Martha's Vineyard he thought the decision was still open. He had pointed out to Sulzberger that *The Times* did not have to endorse a candidate in the primaries and in any event did not have to endorse one immediately.

Sulzberger agreed but, as he remembered it, told Oakes, "Well, if you don't want to do it I'll try my hand at putting something down on paper." Punch later was to say, "Never in a million years did I think this was going to cause trouble."

Trouble, however, did follow. Oakes did not take Punch's remarks to mean he had decided to endorse Moynihan but he did take them seriously enough to telephone his assistant, Fred Hechinger, and ask him to draft a memo on why Moynihan should not be endorsed. He would have it handy if the question arose. (Oakes' feelings about Moynihan were simple: He didn't trust him.)

Nothing further was heard until the day Oakes was leaving the Vineyard when Hechinger telephoned that he had been given a pro-Moynihan editorial, drafted by Punch and considerably revised by Max Frankel with instructions to run it the next day. Oakes telephoned his cousin (the men are first cousins once removed) and protested. Punch was adamant. At least, Oakes said, wait till I get back. No, said Punch, it must run tomorrow (Friday) because the primary is Tuesday. If it doesn't run tomorrow it won't influence the election.

The men argued back and forth, Oakes more disturbed than he had been in the thirty years he had spent on the paper. He suggested that Punch run the editorial over his own name. No, Punch said, that wouldn't do. Oakes said that since he had responsibility for the page he must be permitted to publish a disclaimer. Punch agreed and Oakes wrote a letter on the ferry making a powerful case against Moynihan and for Abzug. He telephoned it to New York from Wood's Hole. Sulzberger refused to print it. "It's too strong," Punch told Oakes. As Oakes later said, had he not been retiring December 31 he would have submitted his resignation. Now he insisted that *The Times* publish a disclaimer and finally he was permitted to run a three-line letter saying:

> As the editor of the editorial page of The New York Times I must express disagreement with the endorsement in today's editorial columns of Mr. Moynihan over other candidates in the New York Democratic primary contest for the U.S. Senate.
>
> John B. Oakes
Chilmark, Mass.
Sept. 10, 1976

This was not the end of the affair. Roger Wilkins, a black editorial writer, had prepared a column for the Monday paper taking issue with the Moynihan endorsement. *The Times* traditionally never interfered with expressions of opinion by its columnists, who often disagreed with the paper's editorial policy. Not this time. Again Punch exercised his veto. When asked why, he simply said, "I want Moynihan to win," which Moynihan proceeded to do.*

Of course from these incidents it might be deduced that whatever procedures *The Times* employed, whatever ritual it observed, in the end the publisher had, as might be expected, the first, last and final word.

But that would be a misleading simplification, too. *The Times* was institutionally quite subtle. Lines of command might or might not

---

*Moynihan, an inveterate controversialist, repaid *The Times* for its support with an attack on the paper's editorial columns and Oakes personally in a book which he published in 1978. With customary bombast he managed to echo the words of the not completely forgotten Spiro T. Agnew, who had accused *The Times* of being "an early and ardent advocate" of the Vietnam war. Moynihan revised Agnew slightly, saying "an early enthusiasm [of The Times] was the Vietnam war." He accused Oakes of running an "ethnic" editorial page bearing "the mark of German Reform Judaism." Moynihan's charges of advocacy of the Vietnam war and ethnicity fitted his own political philosophy more closely than that of Oakes and *The Times*. (Moynihan, *A Dangerous Place*, New York City, 1978, pp. 63–68)

exist. Often results were determined not by an individual's position but by his skill, understanding and ability to use the vast instrument of the newspaper. I once was decrying the state of the world to Clifton Daniel, then in training to become managing editor of *The Times.* "If I had the power," I said, "I would really do something about this."

Daniel smiled in a worldly way. "But," he said, "you do have the power. You are on *The Times.*"

But this was not always easy to see. One of the older men closely associated with Punch Sulzberger in his early days as publisher in 1963 said, "Punch was always hunting for a magician, for a magic formula that would enable him to run *The Times.* He hadn't been properly prepared for the job by the family because they didn't think he would ever be put in that position. So he had never really had an opportunity to familiarize himself with the whole paper. He didn't understand how *The Times* ran; that there was no magic formula and could not be one and that anybody who thought he had one was either a con man or stupid."

Punch had a tidy and orderly mind. He had spent years in the U.S. Marines and had become familiar with a chain of command and neat divisions of responsibility. He had a visual mind and he liked to see a chart of organization and run a pencil down the lines to see how decisions were made and how responsibility flowed from one man to the next.

This was to cause him considerable difficulty. He was for a long time greatly attached to a *Times* business executive named Andrew Fisher who liked to prepare four-color charts and big graphs showing how alternate decisions would affect costs and profits. Punch was painstaking but he hated nitty-gritty and when Fisher seemed to have done his homework and came up with solid, positive answers that could be displayed in the front of the room on an easel and spelled out with a pointer, Punch was impressed. It *looked* as though Fisher had found a short cut through the briarpaths of *The Times* and Punch respected that. But, said Punch's associate, the young publisher was not a fool. It finally dawned on him that the charts were really just camouflage for a power play; that in essence all they said was that if you raised the ad rates you made more money—so what else was new? What Fisher was really after was getting Punch to put the paper in *his* hands and letting him run it. At that point if Punch still hadn't found out how *The Times* ran at least he had found out what made Fisher run and soon Fisher was gone. This analysis was quite unfair to Fisher who possessed substantial abilities but it contained a nubbin of truth.

Madness

In these circumstances it was not surprising that Ellsberg found it difficult to get a grasp on the mechanics of power at *The Times* when circumstances finally compelled him to ponder the question of letting *The Times* present the Pentagon Papers to the world.

Ellsberg, like many of his generation, possessed a homing instinct for power. Power and its application was his specialty. His senior honors thesis* at Harvard was written on economic "game theory"—game theory had just come into the academic (and military) world as the newest and most chic way of quantifying and qualifying power and its application—and it was this intimate analysis and understanding of power which was to guide Ellsberg's life for many years into the era of the Pentagon Papers and beyond it in his perpetual, restless search for causes into which to channel his enormous energies and piercing intellect.

It was, in fact, these talents of Ellsberg's which first brought him into association with Henry Kissinger, an association which was to continue for years like a long-running Victorian courtship. There was an attraction–repulsion between the two men and its components were power (addiction for) and intellect (blade-sharp).

One of the early Kissinger–Ellsberg contacts occurred when the future Secretary of State was still conducting his famous seminars at Harvard. In March of 1959 Ellsberg had given the Lowell Institute lectures at the Boston Public Library under the title "The Act of Coercion: A Study of Threats in Economic Conflicts and War." Among Ellsberg's topics were "The Theory and Practice of Blackmail" and "The Political Uses of Madness" (an analysis of Hitler's strategy). Kissinger asked Ellsberg to present his ideas to his seminar and Ellsberg did so.

Ellsberg analyzed Hitler's strategy in terms of game theory. The young political scientist concluded that blackmail and threat lay at the heart of contemporary diplomacy and that Hitler had been its most daring and successful practitioner.

"The language of threat and ultimatum is today the language of diplomacy," Ellsberg said. "The ability to coerce is a form of power; perhaps the most important form underlying calculations of the 'balance of power.'

*The title of Ellsberg's thesis was "The Theory of Political Choice Under Uncertainty: The Contribution of Von Neuman and Morgenstern." A comment on Ellsberg by the faculty said, "If there is one principal shortcoming in his work it is an unfortunate tendency to be somewhat erratic in the pursuit of a single line of investigation which leads to a lack of depth and completeness."

"It is the *threat* to compel or punish, in short, coercion, which is the peace-time tool of diplomacy."

For effective blackmail, Ellsberg said, "it pays to be mad. For the man who is convincingly mad the risks may be peculiarly small; his claim to believe the risks are small or his willingness to take large risks will be credible against rational opponents. The madman in this world can win. More than that he can win safely."

Hitler, he pointed out, was "erratic, unpredictable, totally unbound by convention, honor, morality" and it was the belief of his opponents that he could act irrationally which gave strength to his blackmail.

Ellsberg concluded that unlimited evidence of rationality might be a handicap. To win you didn't have to be crazy but it helped.

"Just as Hitler was indispensable to the success of German threats in the Thirties not every man can wield effectively deterrent threats of mutual annihilation; a certain reputation, a public impression is required and it is not come by overnight.

"Madness," he told Kissinger's seminar, "is power—bargaining power."

While these words might seem balderdash to the ordinary citizen, Kissinger found Ellsberg's analysis possessed deep insight; an insight which he wanted his seminar to study and understand. As Ellsberg recalled Kissinger saying many years later in the presence of his friend Lloyd Shearer, "I've learned more from Dan Ellsberg about bargaining than anyone else."

Ellsberg's theory fell on fertile soil. In the negotiating tactics which Kissinger was about to unveil in dealing with Hanoi and Moscow, Ellsberg's 1959 concepts were reflected in the deliberate cultivation by Kissinger of an erratic and unreasonable personality, sudden and irrational shifts in diplomatic positions. In his writings Kissinger declared, as had Ellsberg, that a statesman must be free to act with "credible irrationality."

A fixation on "positive" irrationality was shared by Mr. Nixon, and, indeed, may have been implanted in the President's mind by Kissinger. Nixon once explained to H. R. Haldeman his basic negotiating tactic with Vietnam. "I call it the 'Madman Theory,' Bob. I want the North Vietnamese to believe I've reached the point where I might do *anything* to stop the war."

Nixon's "Madman Theory" was indistinguishable from Ellsberg's "Political Uses of Madness." In that lecture Ellsberg concluded, "Where a little madness or just the suspicion of madness could win the world—is it impossible that a madman might someday find authority? And might he not then—or others behind him—find the power of his madness?"

Kissinger and Nixon were to leave behind them the Cambodian

"incursion" of 1971 and the Christmas bombing of Hanoi in 1972 as grim monuments to Ellsberg's "Madness Theory."

Management and decision-making was Ellsberg's specialty, a useful talent for a young man who evolved during the Kennedy and Johnson years as one of the boldest of the new academic government breed known as crisis managers. Ellsberg's techniques were already so highly valued by the early 1960s that when two executives of *Parade* magazine, Jess Gorkin and Lloyd Shearer, conceived a proposal for a "hot line" between Nikita Khrushchev in the Kremlin and John F. Kennedy in the White House they consulted with Ellsberg, at the recommendation of the Rand Corporation, on the proper tactics to use in advancing their proposal. Kennedy was no problem. His acceptance was assured but they were worried about Khrushchev. Ellsberg concluded that Khrushchev would go for it and, in fact, that turned out to be the case. Ellsberg, thus, became midwife of the hot line which persists to this day as a means of reducing the risk of unexpected confrontations between Moscow and Washington.

None of his capabilities, however, served Ellsberg well in the situation in which he found himself in early 1971. Ellsberg had lagged substantially behind Sheehan in his metamorphosis from hawk into dove, possibly because it was not until 1965 that he reached Vietnam as a pistol-packing, carbine-carrying, certified military buff. The arc of Ellsberg's traverse to opponent of the war was close to 180 degrees. He had (after marrying, in his junior year at Harvard, Carol Cummings, a Radcliffe sophomore whose father was a chicken colonel in the Marine Corps) enlisted in the Marines for a two-year hitch, even extending his tour during the Lebanon crisis. He had a fetish about arms, learned to shoot both right-handed and left-handed and was proud of the fact he emerged from the corps in 1957 as the only lieutenant in command of a rifle company in the Second Marine Division. He plunged almost immediately into "crisis management" at Harvard, at Rand in Santa Monica and soon in the Pentagon* itself, working on topics like the missile gap (he badly overestimated Soviet capability), the U-2 crisis, Soviet nuclear potential and the Cuban missile crisis, spending, as he would recall in a fifteenth anniversary report to his Harvard classmates, "nine months in various sub-basement document saferooms, reading mostly about the Cuban crisis." From then on it had been Vietnam, Vietnam, Vietnam. He tried to go out with the Marines but had acquired along with his top security

*Walt Rostow claimed credit for a hand in getting Ellsberg his first government job in the Pentagon early in the Kennedy Administration. (Personal interview, Rostow, 9/28/78)

clearances a GS-18 classification, the equal of a lieutenant general, so he went, instead, as a gung-ho civilian, moving with Army units and Marines into the Delta, carrying a carbine (and getting his picture published in *Life* magazine), risking his life repeatedly in fire fights, and acquiring some perceptions of life in the Vietnamese countryside which he articulated in a touching vignette of a "pacified" village, a village, like so many others pacified only on paper, where an old man, a Cao Dai by faith, told him that he knew some Catholics who thought peace might come to Vietnam by the year 2000. Ellsberg, listening to gunfire in the nearby thickets, told him, "I hope it will come much sooner than that."

This was a hope which faded rapidly when Ellsberg returned to the United States and to Rand, to high-level analysis and decision-making, to a special assignment in Washington to participate in a Defense Department study of the war in Vietnam.

6

"It Doesn't Work"

BY LATE AUTUMN, 1966, Robert McNamara, Secretary of Defense, was deeply troubled. If American policy and tactics in Vietnam had any single architect he was that man. First for John Kennedy and then for Lyndon Johnson he and the glittering team he had assembled at the Pentagon had devised, invented and carried out the Vietnam war. Now he was beginning to realize in the dour words spoken more than four years earlier by Homer Bigart that "it doesn't work." Not only was Vietnam not working, it was eroding the American ethos. That autumn McNamara visited Harvard and there in November he encountered for the first time a massive rally of students who shouted him down when he tried to speak. He met privately with a group of faculty. This meeting was more decorous but the message was the same: morally, the war is criminal; pragmatically, it doesn't work. To a man whose whole career was founded on ingenious and profitable ways of making things work (McNamara had come out of the Air Force after World War II to join Henry Ford II's remarkable "whiz kids" who turned the corporation around and made it once again a vigorous competitor of General Motors) this was chilling news. Moreover, he himself had come to, or was coming to, realize that "it doesn't work." He was too hardheaded and analytic to fool himself longer about the results and now he was exposed personally to the agony the war was producing within the country, the extent to which the fabric of society, and particularly that of the younger generation, was being strained and torn.

One of the men present at McNamara's meeting with the Harvard faculty was Richard E. Neustadt, whose penetrating government studies had placed him close to John and Robert Kennedy and who was associated with the Kennedy Institute of Politics, which McNamara helped establish and which was his Harvard host.

Neustadt had done a postmortem of the crisis that arose between the United States and Britain in 1961–62 over U.S. cancellation of the Skybolt missile, which the British had expected to use as their nuclear deterrent. Kennedy wanted to know the administrative details that caused the sudden flare-up. Neustadt completed his study November

15, 1963. On November 20 the President, having read it, told Mac Bundy he wanted to see Neustadt "when I return from Texas." After Mr. Kennedy's assassination McNamara had examined the study in hope of avoiding such incidents in the future.

It was in this context that a discussion arose at McNamara's Harvard meeting about a similar study on Vietnam—how we had gotten in, what we had done, what we should have done, what we should not have done. One Harvard participant recalled that the idea was advanced by Neustadt but Neustadt himself was not certain whether he raised the question or whether it came from McNamara. What is certain is that the idea began to germinate within McNamara's mind.

General Robert Pursley, one of McNamara's two military aides, believed that McNamara already was possessed of considerable doubts about the war. Pursley recalled that in June of 1960 McNamara first showed concern about Vietnam operations. He was bothered by the June 27 bombing of Haiphong which had been strongly urged by Walt Rostow. McNamara felt this attack went against the conclusion of the post-World War II Strategic Bombing Survey which concluded that such attacks on secondary supply centers were nonproductive. On July 4, McNamara hobbled into his Pentagon office with a broken foot and instructed Pursley (deeply upset because his mother had died the night before) to find out what real intelligence existed to justify such operations. Pursley went to Defense intelligence specialists and found they had literally no information to respond to McNamara's sharp questions. McNamara went to Richard Helms, head of the CIA, and asked him for independent intelligence analyses, and when the CIA reports failed to bear out the optimistic calculations of the military, McNamara's worry about the war intensified. The meeting at Harvard had an impact on him and when he went to Amherst in February 1967 and again put himself at the disposal of the students and again was subjected to a critical barrage the effect was deep. The fact that his own son had turned angrily against the war also played a role.

Pursley recalled the Secretary talking to him after the Harvard and Amherst appearances. He was deeply disturbed and said he had been beset by very difficult questions. He wanted to put together what he called an "encyclopedia" of just how we had gotten involved in Southeast Asia. He did not, as Pursley recalled, intend the materials to be for general distribution but for use in the future as "a base for history." It would have narrow distribution and would draw on all sources, regardless of classification, across the board, every kind of source and every kind of documentation. No holds bared. Let the chips fall where they might (he was aware that some would be knocked off his own record and reputation).

McNamara's recollection supported this account of the study's origins. It didn't begin with the Harvard discussion. His own doubts had begun six months earlier but the discussion around the room that evening played a role in his own growing conviction that an examination should be made of the origins of the war; that it should be done within the present time frame rather than ten years later when memories were less sharp and that it should serve as a base from which scholarly study of the origins and conduct of the war could be pursued.

The Project

Sometime in the spring of 1967, probably in May, Neustadt got a telephone call from John McNaughton, McNamara's ruthlessly realistic right-hand man (soon to be killed in a plane crash in North Carolina with his wife and son). McNaughton asked whether Neustadt would be willing to do a Skybolt-type study of Vietnam for McNamara if they could get White House clearance for the idea. It would be a one-man show and must have President Johnson's approval and access to all the White House and State Department documents as well as those of the Pentagon. It was a huge assignment but Neustadt agreed to take it on and stood by to hear from McNaughton. Ten days later McNaughton called again. No one-man band. It wasn't going to work on that basis. They would have to do it in-house. Neustadt assumed McNamara could not get White House approval for the idea and therefore had determined to go forward using his own facilities.*

Liaison on the project was established through Colonel Robert G. Gard, McNamara's other military aide, and on June 7, 1967, the project formally got under way, headed by Leslie Gelb, a quiet man who belonged to the fraternity of academic government scholars, Harvard Ph.D., associate of Kissinger, friend of Morton Halperin, then head of the Defense Department's brain trust (called the International Security Affairs Section) who had been McNamara's first choice for the job.

The project started off with what Gelb later came to call "the 100 questions," handwritten questions put together by McNamara and McNaughton, to which Gelb was to seek the answer. They were questions like: Could Ho Chi Minh have become an Asian Tito? What have we accomplished in Vietnam? How do we know the body count is correct? Gelb was supposed to come up with answers in two or three months. To get the answers Gelb felt he had to put them into a historical framework. Memos flew back and forth to McNamara through the intermediary of Gard. McNamara preferred to work with

---

*Ellsberg recalled writing a memo to McNamara in May 1967 proposing a Skybolt-type study of Vietnam. He passed it on through Dr. Alain Einthoven (Assistant Defense Secretary for Systems Analysis), whom he often used for access, but never got a response from McNamara. (Personal interview, Ellsberg, 2/26/77)

memos—short, tight, one-sentence pieces of paper.

Gard cleared out McNamara's walk-in safe and gave all these materials to Gelb. Later McNamara spoke to Dean Rusk at the State Department and Rusk authorized Dave Reed, his assistant, to make available anything that was needed and promptly put the matter out of his mind. McNamara told President Johnson that he was doing the study but little material was obtained from the White House. Walt Rostow, LBJ's Security adviser, said later that he was "conscious" of the study but never heard any more about it. One reason why Rostow heard nothing was that, as one of the study's directors recalled, "we installed a special cut-off in the White House to try to be certain he didn't get the information that it was in progress because we were certain he would run to LBJ and try to get it stopped."

Gelb's first proposal was for sixteen separate studies to be done by a staff of six. Before it was over the staff had risen to thirty-six. Most of the men came aboard for a month or two, did a study and then dropped out. There was a constant struggle to get top-ranking men. One of those who was approached was Henry Kissinger, then associated with Governor Nelson Rockefeller as his foreign policy adviser. "We wanted him very much," Halperin recalled. At first Kissinger was going to participate but finally he said no for lack of time. He did, however, read some of the studies.

McNamara approved almost every proposal submitted to him by Gelb and Gard and later this caused some confusion over McNamara's motives. The participants said they didn't think McNamara knew exactly what he wanted. McNamara's explanation was that he didn't want to influence the study in any direction.∫

Ellsberg's Evolution

Ellsberg was back from Vietnam now, gradually recovering from hepatitis, his skin still tinged with yellow, his energy levels as low as they had ever dropped, back at Rand, living in a Malibu beach cottage, gradually moving out of his hawkish role, divorced from his wife (but she and the two children lived nearby), still not in tune with his wife-to-be, Patricia Marx, who had visited as a radio reporter in Saigon, arguing with him, she a dove, opposed to the war on principled grounds, he still a hawk, becoming more friendly with a fellow Rand Corporation employee, Anthony Russo, who had also been in Vietnam and was far more radicalized than Ellsberg (who was not at all at this point), not cutting his hair, however, letting it grow long as he had warned his '52 Harvard classmates he might in his fifteenth-anniversary letter, restless, dissatisfied, very much wanting to get his teeth into

∫See Notes section.

something—something new. It was at this point that Dan got a telephone call from Leslie Gelb, in need of more hands for the "encyclopedia of Vietnam." Would Dan come and join the project? He would and did, working through November and December 1967* and into January 1968 on leave from Rand, finally submitting a 350-page draft on JFK's 1961 policy in Vietnam.

However much his views of Vietnam had modified, Ellsberg was still very much a man of the system, a man inside the system. When Patricia Marx violently argued with him Ellsberg moved only halfway in her direction (they would not marry for four years after their Vietnam encounter) and he would talk a good deal about going to jail, the danger of jail if opposition was carried too far. He worried about that.

A lot was to happen before Ellsberg finally approached Neil Sheehan to talk, cautious as a cat, about the possibility that *The Times* might publish the Pentagon Papers.

Being a "systems" man, an "access" man, an "options" man, a "crisis manager"—being, in other words, very much the modern super-bureaucrat, Ellsberg had a fascination for techniques—"leaking," for instance. When he spoke of leaking he put it in capital letters, as it were, and it became a new governmental tool like an advanced computer program or games theory. He himself did not quite know how it worked. Once he happened to be in the office of a Pentagon man who was on the telephone to Joseph Kraft. The Pentagon man was leaking the contents of a top-secret document to Kraft. Ellsberg had never seen this done, Kraft on the telephone, taking notes on a top-secret document. Ellsberg was mightily impressed, and he decided to try it himself.

It was the spring of 1968. Tet had knocked American plans galley-west in February. Washington was filled with every kind of rumor. Ellsberg was, for the moment, a temporary consultant for the Defense Department (crisis managers were forever in transit from university to think tank to government and back again; at any moment they were apt to be wearing two, three or four, hats). The Administration was trying to play down Tet and claim it as an American victory but Westmoreland had privately sent LBJ the message: he needed 206,000 more American troops. Ellsberg went to Robert Kennedy with this information, thinking that Kennedy would go to the floor of the Senate and expose all. But, as Ellsberg was to remember, he did not understand

---

*Ellsberg took time off from work on the Pentagon Papers to go to Bermuda in December 1967 where he participated in a Carnegie conference on Vietnam. He talked, participants remembered, a good deal about the concentration of power in the hands of great men.

how a sophisticated politician works. Kennedy had no intention of being tagged with a claim that he had leaked confidential defense information. Instead, a member of his staff passed a tip along and, lo, the story appeared on page one of *The New York Times*. There was a hell of a ruckus, Congress got on its hind legs, although always previously LBJ had been able to spoon-feed it, to diddle it. When Westmoreland asked for 100,000 troops, LBJ would ask Congress for 50,000, then another 50,000 later on and then another, and Congress never seemed to catch on.

Now there was a tremendous splash and Ellsberg, who had been depressed about Congress and LBJ's ability to con it, decided to try to keep the pot boiling. For the first time he called Neil Sheehan directly and (just as he had seen it done with Kraft) leaked a story about the Vietnamese order of battle and how it had been phonied to justify the new troop escalation. It had, for practical purposes, simply been doubled. He leaked Westmoreland's pre-Tet report in which the general incautiously declared that "all major concentrations of enemy have been wiped out south of the DMZ." This leak, as Ellsberg had hoped, added gasoline to the fire and he decided to try again. He had in his hands (and still had years later) a remarkable sequence of cables between Washington and Saigon, between Westmoreland and the Pentagon, disclosing the mechanics of troop escalation. Westmoreland would propose a figure, the Pentagon would reject it as too high, Westmoreland would trim his proposal, back and forth the bargaining would go until agreement was reached on a figure that the traffic (that is, the American public and Congress) would bear. Then it would be put forward with appropriate fanfare.

Ellsberg again got in touch with Sheehan and arranged to meet with Tom Wicker, then chief of *The New York Times* bureau in Washington.

As Wicker recalled it Ellsberg told him, "These guys are putting you on. They've cooked the figures. They've been exchanging cables and deciding how to cook and submit the figures."

Ellsberg told Wicker that he could prove what he had said, that he had seen the classified cable traffic but did not offer to give Wicker the cables. Wicker recalled giving Ellsberg a lecture—his duty was to his country and not to some pedantic security classification. His duty was to the truth. Wicker told him he would have to get the cables and present them to *The Times;* he couldn't just take Ellsberg's word for it. Ellsberg was surprised—and shocked. This was a top-security matter and here was Wicker talking openly about it in a room that might be bugged. Ellsberg actually had the cables in his pocket but he kept them there and when he left the room he told Neil how shocked he was. Neil soothed his feelings and Ellsberg let him have the cables to be copied and returned.

Before *The Times* could do anything with the materials, Westmoreland resigned, LBJ made his March 31, 1968, speech, announcing he would not run for reelection and proposing peace to Hanoi, and Ellsberg decided against releasing the materials. Wicker (who, in fact, was of two minds about the story because Ellsberg did not have the entire cable sequence) gave them back to Ellsberg and that impressed him a lot.*

So it was that Ellsberg, after nearly a year of secret, frustrating effort to persuade some leading political figure (his first choice was William Fulbright, chairman of the Senate Foreign Relations Committee) to go public with the Pentagon Papers, finally and quite reluctantly (although he had been advised by at least two senators to take this course) turned to *The New York Times* and once again arranged to see a reporter whom he knew, had dealt with before and whom he trusted (insofar as he trusted anyone at this point). He met with Neil Sheehan on February 28, 1971, and outlined what was on his mind.

*LBJ was furious over the leak of the 206,000-troop escalation figure and ordered an FBI inquiry. At one point someone in the International Security Affairs Section of Defense had remarked, "Isn't it interesting how much access Ellsberg had to this material." But it was promptly noted that Ellsberg was properly cut in on the traffic because of the project on which he was engaged. W. Donald Stewart, the FBI agent assigned to investigate, felt he had enough evidence to make a case against Ellsberg. But the CIA and Defense Department advised Justice they had no interest in pursuing the matter further and the inquiry was signed off. (Personal interview, Ellsberg, 5/10/75; Jack Anderson, *Washington Post,* 9/28/75)

7

"The Daily Planet"

*T*HERE was no reason for any embarrassment on Daniel Ellsberg's part that he encountered difficulty in trying to conceptualize the power structure of *The Times.* By this time he knew a fair number of newspapermen and in the autumn of 1970 he would occasionally question them about *The Times.* Tom Oliphant of the *Boston Globe* remembered Ellsberg asking how you could get through to the top officers at *The New York Times.* Ellsberg asked Edwin Diamond, a former *Newsweek* editor, questions like: "Where is the power at *The Times?* Who runs what?" Diamond was helpful. He filled in Ellsberg on some of the rivalries—for instance, the conflicts between the editorial page and the news departments.

The questions were reasonable ones and Ellsberg, who had begun to undergo psychoanalysis in the spring of 1968 with Dr. Lewis Fielding of Beverley Hills (and would continue in the process for a couple of years), would have been remarkably heartened had he known that the institution which puzzled him so much was, for practical purposes, itself undergoing "psychoanalysis" at the hands of a Harvard professor, a man named Chris Argyris, who held an endowed chair in the Harvard Graduate School of Education and whose specialty was "organizational behavior."

Argyris' study was the product of Punch Sulzberger's continuing search for a magic formula. He brought in groups like McKinsey & Co. to make surveys of *The Times,* he held summit meetings to talk things out with his associates in fashionable executive watering spas, golfing and motel complexes within a two hundred-mile radius of New York City, far enough away so that the two- or three-day meetings would not be interrupted by routine business but close enough to get back to Forty-third Street in case of an emergency.

It was against this background that what some ribald *Times* men came to call the "argyrol" study got under way. Argyris had conducted examinations of management in such bureaucracies as IBM, Polaroid, General Electric and certain branches of the federal government. His psychological techniques were highly valued in the business circles that

Punch respected, and John Mortimer, a *Times* vice president, suggested his name to Punch.

Mr. Ochs' Management System

There is no record that any Harvard Business School graduate ever came to Adolph Ochs with a proposal to study his "management system." Nor did Mr. Ochs find it necessary to consult academic specialists for help in running his newspaper. Not that he scorned advice. Before purchasing *The New York Times* in 1896 he talked with other newspaper publishers and particularly with important money men like J. P. Morgan and Jacob Schiff. One person to whom he turned for advice was Herman Kohlsatt, publisher of the *Chicago Inter-American.* Mr. Ochs went to Kohlsatt in the midst of his negotiations to buy *The Times.* "What's bothering you?" Kohlsatt asked. "I'm afraid I'm not a big enough man for the job," Ochs replied. "Well," said Kohlsatt, "don't tell anyone that and maybe they won't find out."

In Mr. Ochs' day it was taken for granted that a business was run by its owner or a manager acting in the name of the owner. Mr. Ochs ran his newspapers in a direct one-on-one fashion. He attended to most business arrangements himself and they could be exceedingly complex because of his habit of operating largely on borrowed money. His bookkeepers, his advertising and circulation men were hired by him and they worked with him, for him and at his direction. On the mechanical side, as an old-time printer, he knew printing, printers and printing machinery inside out. No one had to tell him how a printer felt, whether he was working up to speed or soldiering on the job or whether a new press was worth buying. He himself knew. As an apprentice nicknamed "Muley," starting pay twenty-five cents a day, he had set type by hand at the age of fourteen on a struggling paper in Knoxville, Tennessee, called *The Chronicle.*

Mr. Ochs hired good editors and gave them their head. Of course he and his editor in chief consulted on every important question. It was unthinkable that an editorial would appear in *The Times* which did not represent his viewpoint (although one during World War I was to cause him some bad moments). As for news, he laid down the general line he wanted his paper to follow and, especially during the long reign of his greatest editor, Carr Van Anda, seldom interfered. The nature of his relationship was defined in a brief encounter he had with a new night city editor, Frederick T. Birchall.

One evening Mr. Ochs came into *The Times'* city room to talk with a reporter named Percy Bullock about a story that was of great concern to him, a story about Charles Evans Hughes' investigation of the Equitable Life Assurance scandal. Bullock was late with his copy and Birchall presently interrupted the conversation between Ochs (whom he had not met and did not recognize) and Bullock. Mr. Ochs promptly apologized to Birchall for holding up the story. "I didn't realize you were close to deadline," he said. *"You were looking after my business. It was the thing to do."* (Italics added.)

The New York Times was Mr. Ochs' business from stem to stern. He created it. He directed it. He managed it. If any questions were raised—they were asked by people who wanted to know the secret of his success. If there was profit—it went to him. If there was loss (and there never was) it was his loss. Outside of three or four close associates whom he rewarded with gifts of small amounts of stock (these small amounts grew to be very valuable over the years) the stock ownership was almost entirely in his hands.

Mr. Ochs set forth his principles of management succinctly in an early draft of his proposal for taking over *The New York Times:*

"Unless I am put in absolute control of the property and of all who are employed therewith, I would not undertake the management at any price, for I am certain I could not succeed as manager with any abridgement of almost autocratic power."

By 1971 this had all changed. Neither Arthur Hays Sulzberger, Mr. Ochs' son-in-law, nor Orvil Dryfoos, Mr. Sulzberger's son-in-law, nor even Punch Sulzberger was brought up in the newspaper business, as had been Mr. Ochs. Mr. Sulzberger started out in his family's textile business. Mr. Dryfoos had a Wall Street background. Punch had several jobs on the newspaper, a training bout as a reporter on the *Milwaukee Journal* and a spell in the Paris bureau of *The New York Times* but no experience in running any major *Times* department. Arthur Sulzberger, because of natural inclination, concentrated on editorials and news, letting his cousin-in-law, General Julius Adler, take the major role on the business side. Dryfoos was more interested in business and was the first to bring "management men" into *The Times,* men like Amory Bradford, Andrew Fisher and Harding Bancroft—men like himself from outside the newspaper field.

The fact was that even before Mr. Ochs died in 1935, and surely before Mr. Sulzberger gave way to Mr. Dryfoos as publisher in 1961, *The Times* had grown to a magnitude that would have outmoded Mr. Ochs' one-on-one management even if Mr. Ochs by that time had not been old and ill.

With size and numbers (*The Times* had 4,000 employees by its one hundredth anniversary in 1951) had come what could be described as institutional momentum and bureaucratic inertia, that is, those organic transformations diagnosed by Dr. Parkinson and formulated by him into Parkinson's law. Regardless of management *The Times* functioned according to its own internal rules, stresses and personalities. As Punch once said, "It is screamingly difficult to make any real change on this paper. It's equally hard to make a mistake. Whatever you do the paper comes out in the morning. I really think that I could take all the brass away and the paper would still come out the next day and no one would know how or why." There was no way in which Mr. Ochs could have directed the 1971 paper as he had that of 1907 or 1927 as a simple projection of his own personal predilections. It was this reality that confronted Punch Sulzberger when he took over in 1963 and tried to get a handle on what made *The Times* go.

The truth was that *The Times* had evolved characteristics that seemed to defy classification or systematization. No wonder Ellsberg was confused.

The Argyris Study

Argyris was first invited to give a talk to *Times* executives but refused. He proposed, instead, that he conduct in-depth interviews of *Times* executives, be permitted to sit in on business and editorial huddles, tape-record his sessions and follow through with in-house seminars in which he would apply the knowledge he had gained to improve management skills and procedures. He asked and received permission (under close conditions of *Times'* control) to write a book in which he would set forth his findings.

This survey went on over a three-year period and was in midstream at the time Ellsberg approached Sheehan. There is no evidence that Argyris, on the one hand, or Sheehan and Ellsberg on the other, had any mutual awareness or that their conduct would have been modified had they known. But it is possible that Ellsberg, so much a systems man himself, might have shied away from *The Times* had he been privy to the conclusions of Argyris, and it is possible that Argyris might never have undertaken his study if he had realized that probably the most significant decision in the history of *The Times,* and quite possibly of modern American journalism, would be taken during the period when he had the institution on his psychoanalytic couch and that he would be totally unaware of it or how it had come about.

It is true that the "argyrol" study more or less came apart in 1972 when its author and conductor bowed out, having finally concluded (as some friends had told him before he started) that *The Times* was a "lost case" and that nothing he discovered or recommended would ever affect *The Times.** And it is equally true that when it was over Sulzberger conceded that his own expectations had not been satisfied.

But even if this had not occurred, even if Argyris had not simply (and accurately) concluded that *Times* management and *Times* executives

*"To put it mildly," Argyris was told, "they would consider your views nonsense." (Chris Argyris, *Behind the Front Page,* San Francisco, 1974, p. x)

had little genuine interest in his concepts of orderly procedures, "open decision-making" and "self-renewal," it had been apparent to common-sense observers from the start that *The Times'* addiction to what might be called "creative anarchy" was (and undoubtedly rightly was) so strong that no psychoanalytic systems man could come up with solutions that would have reasonable meaning for the newspaper, no matter how well they might serve IBM or, say, the Defense Department's procurement section. For one thing, as Argyris sadly found, he could not convince *Times* executives that the bottom line was what counted, that profits were more important than editorial integrity. The news executives demonstrated what Argyris considered total inability to make "effective cost-efficient decisions"; in fact, they didn't even *want* to be more cost-efficient in decision-making.

Argyris considered *The Times'* executives hopelessly "conservative" in the sense of not being attracted to the latest discoveries of Harvard academics, unwilling to speak out frankly among themselves, emotionally resentful of the endless "encounter" sessions which he conducted.

Argyris was confident that unless he could introduce his psychocommercial techniques *The Times* was headed for disaster. His report on *The Times* was called *Behind the Front Page* and he disguised *The Times* as *The Daily Planet.* Participants in his awareness meets were named "Mr. P." (for publisher Sulzberger), "Mr. R." (for editor A. M. Rosenthal), "Mr. Q." and "Mr. T." (for John Oakes, editorial page director), etc. Oakes was so concerned lest his identity be disclosed that he insisted on two pseudonymous initials.

No one could fault Argyris for dedication to his task and concern for his subject. But few in the newspaper profession shared Argyris' conclusion that "affirmative feedback" was more important than the First Amendment to the U.S. Constitution, which guarantees the freedom of the press.*

To Argyris, after hundreds of hours of listening to the cross-talk, evasions, back scratching, eye gouging, emotionalism and intellectual put-downs of one of the most talented group of men and women ever collected in a publishing enterprise, the important thing was not what they did, not the newspaper they produced, not their service to the public, but their failure to respond positively to his professional categorizing. He concluded in *Behind the Front Page* that unless newspapermen were able to shape up as the corporate executives of Polaroid, GE and the National Institute of Health shaped up (under his guidance)

---

*Punch concluded that Argyris' chief failing was his attempt to introduce his theories into *The Times'* news and editorial operations where, in Sulzberger's opinion, they had no application. (Personal interview, Arthur Ochs Sulzberger, 8/29/78)

little reason existed for them to receive the special protection of the First Amendment.

As he said, "One question that I hope this book raises is whether newspapers should be protected if, by their own admission and behavior, they are not capable of creating an open learning system within their own boundaries."

To which Kenneth M. Pierce, editor of the Columbia *Journalism Review,* in a review of the Argyris book, simply exploded, "Hell, yes!"

8

Ellsberg Makes His Move

*I*T WOULD NOT BE correct to say that Ellsberg turned to Sheehan on
that mild spring day in 1971 out of desperation. But he was coming
to the end of his ideas for making public the Pentagon Papers with the
shock effect which he hoped would bring the Vietnam war to a close.

The Ellsberg of February 1971 was not the Ellsberg of 1966. He had
made the full turn from strongest of hawks to most hawkish of doves.
It was a change into which many factors fed—his personal experience
of the brutality of Vietnam and his own gradual and agonized perception of the unbridgeable gap between Washington theory and Indochina reality; his long talks with his friend Anthony Russo and with
Patricia Marx; his self-reappraisal stimulated by psychoanalysis; a sharp
break in life-style; the traumatic events of 1968, particularly the assassinations of Robert F. Kennedy and Martin Luther King; and his growing acquaintance with and attraction to the philosophy of Mohandas
Gandhi and nonviolent resistance.

The summer of 1968 was probably decisive in his transformation. On
the surface it seemed a drifting life on the Malibu beach, increasing
alienation from work at Rand (Rand was exclusively oriented toward
defense research and had, in fact, been set up through the Air Force,
primarily so that projects could be farmed out to scientists of all kinds,
some of whom might not meet Air Force security standards, and
projects on which the Air Force might like to have "deniability.")
Ellsberg's thinking was no longer compatible with that of many of his
associates, although, in fairness, it should be said that not a few occu-
pants of the dreary California warehouse, across the street from the
Santa Monica City Hall, that housed the Rand Corporation were
moving in Ellsberg's direction.

Looking back on the summer of 1968 Ellsberg thought of it as an
endless frieze of girls, one summer girl after another, girls, girls, girls.
No real interest in anything. No participation in the election campaign.
Even the war in Southeast Asia faded to a blur.

"I was," he later was to recall, "fighting an extreme case of powerlessness."

Options for Kissinger

Ellsberg's feeling of powerlessness, of drifting, of substituting random nights with random girls for confrontation of reality persisted until the November elections. With victory Richard Nixon quickly moved to take over Nelson Rockefeller's foreign policy brain truster, Henry Kissinger, and one of the first things Kissinger did was to visit Rand in Santa Monica and confer with his old friend Henry Rowen, the director, as to who would be a good man for an options paper on Vietnam. Kissinger had long talks with Ellsberg, whom he knew not only from Harvard but also from a visit to Vietnam when Ellsberg had spoken frankly and at length and Kissinger had been grateful for it. As he later was to say, "I profited a great deal by what I learned from Dan in Vietnam. I learned more from him than anyone else there."

Rowen recommended Ellsberg to Kissinger as an options man and both Rowen and Ellsberg were surprised when Kissinger raised a question as to Ellsberg's discretion. The question, it turned out, stemmed from Ellsberg's openness in Vietnam. Kissinger was afraid Ellsberg might talk with equal candor about his work for Nixon.

Despite doubts, however, Kissinger brought Ellsberg aboard and in the hectic six weeks that Nixon spent in the Hotel Pierre in New York before inauguration January 20, 1969, Ellsberg worked hard, preparing for Kissinger a comprehensive list of Vietnam options. They ran, Ellsberg said, from A to Z—from dropping the bomb on Hanoi to full withdrawal. Later, when Kissinger submitted Ellsberg's options to the National Security Council, he removed the proposal for total withdrawal.

Kissinger was pleased with Ellsberg's work, and Ellsberg, close to the hand of power again, was equally pleased. There were those among Ellsberg's friends who contended that it was not so important to Ellsberg what figure he was close to as that he was close to power. Be that as it may, Kissinger gave Ellsberg a second assignment. He was to prepare what came to be called NSSM-1, an extraordinary questionnaire drafted by Ellsberg and submitted to the Defense Department, State Department, CIA and U.S. Embassy in Saigon. NSSM-1 was an acronym meaning National Security Study Memorandum No. 1. In it Ellsberg listed all of the basic Vietnam problems, contradictions in policy, alternate viewpoints and conflicts and called upon the agencies to submit individual responses to each question. NSSM-1 was designed to produce a small handbook on war policy and it did—40,000 words of responses which Ellsberg spent the month of February 1969 analyzing and summarizing for Mr. Kissinger and Mr. Nixon.* Once again Ellsberg felt he was at the center of events. It did not seem impossible to him that his recommendations would move the Administration to end the war.

The Pentagon Papers

But it did not happen. Ellsberg, years later, still agonized over what went wrong; why Nixon and Kissinger opted for war rather than peace. Something happened. Ellsberg wanted to know what it was.†

With his failure to move the new Nixon Administration toward peace, the Pentagon Papers began to take over Ellsberg's life. In December 1968 the great study had been completed—forty-seven volumes, 3,000 pages of narrative, 4,000 pages of documents, each page stamped "Top Secret—Sensitive." Fifteen copies of the study were authorized. Copy number one went to McNamara, another to his successor, Clark Clifford, two to the State Department, designated for use by Nicholas Katzenbach, Undersecretary, and William Bundy, Assistant Secretary, two to National Archives, one for the Kennedy Library and one for LBJ's; one copy went to Laird, three copies were designated for McNamara's deputies, Paul Warnke, Cyrus Vance and Paul H. Nitze. Laird had only one copy, stored in his personal walk-in safe at the Pentagon, but there were, it later transpired, ten additional copies stored in another Pentagon vault. Some of these copies were ultimately sent up to Congress by President Nixon after the Supreme Court approved publication of the Papers by *The Times.* ‡

When Ellsberg flew back from Washington to Rand at Santa Monica he carried with him, as designated official courier, ten volumes of the papers. Later he was to bring eight more volumes to Rand and

---

*Winston Lord and Morton Halperin, both of whom joined Kissinger's permanent staff (and both of whom later were to be wiretapped) worked with Ellsberg on drafting the 4,000-word summary. Most of the writing was actually done by Lord. (Personal interview, Lord, 1/23/79)

†This question still eludes answer. Nixon told the writer before election in November 1968 that peace in Vietnam was number one on his agenda since without it he would be badly handicapped in achieving both domestic and foreign policy goals. If he did not make peace within six months it would become, he said in words later echoed by his Secretary of Defense, Laird, "Nixon's war." His memoir seems partially to reflect this view. However, soon after his collaboration with Kissinger began he moved away from this attitude and became, in private, an extreme hardliner. What role Kissinger played in this shift cannot be precisely documented.

‡Gelb insisted that only fifteen copies of the Papers were authorized but there has long been suspicion that a few more were printed. If Laird is correct in his recollection that ten copies were found in another Pentagon vault this would seem to bring the figure to about twenty. (John Ehrlichman, handwritten White House notes, 6/23/71, quoting Laird, House Judiciary Committee Impeachment Hearing, Appendix III, 1974, p. 105)

for much of the year all forty-seven volumes were at his disposal, officially and in accordance with Rand's rather flexible security rules.

Ellsberg devoted spring and summer of 1969 to two things—to reading the Pentagon report and to the study of Gandhi. He had begun his reading in nonviolence in April 1968. He read Joan Bondurant's *Conquest of Violence,* Barbara Deming's *Revolution and Equilibrium,* Thoreau's *Essay on Civil Disobedience.* He read Martin Luther King and in August of 1969 he attended a conference of the War Resisters League at Haverford College in Pennsylvania. Pastor Martin Niemuller was there and strongly impressed Ellsberg. So did many of the participants, some of whom had been arrested for demonstrating on the anniversary of the invasion of Czechoslovakia.

Before summer was over Ellsberg knew more about the Papers than anyone with the possible exception of Gelb, the project director. By October, Ellsberg, working night after night, until "I thought I would go blind from the green light of the Xerox machine," was copying the Pentagon Papers with the help of his children, Robert and Mary, thirteen and eleven respectively, Ellsberg's friend Russo and Russo's friend, Lynda Sinay, who had an advertising agency and who made her copying machine available for the project.

Ellsberg, a systems man, couched his decision in systems terms. Government, he said, had been transformed into a system that "from top to bottom had come to act reflexively, automatically, to conceal murder for political convenience by lying." He decided to "stop lying" and copy the Pentagon Papers. Like the correspondents in Vietnam years before, like Bigart, like Halberstam, like Sheehan, it was the lies, the seamless belt of lies, which finally turned Ellsberg around and compelled him to devote thought to the moral question of Vietnam and America.

By November, Ellsberg had embarked on what was to prove a year of frustrating, fruitless effort to persuade prominent American politicians to bring the Papers to public attention. He first tackled Senator Fulbright, chairman of the Foreign Relations Committee and a leading skeptic of the war. He gave Fulbright a sample of the documents and then later, in February 1970, some 3,000 pages.*

But Fulbright, while a powerful figure (and this was what attracted Ellsberg to him), was something of a Hamlet. Ellsberg wanted Fulbright to use the Papers for a full-scale Senate hearing on the war. The idea attracted Fulbright but he did not like to go out of channels. Instead of making the Papers public he entered into a protracted

*For months the papers lay in Fulbright's files, gathering dust.

correspondence with Laird trying to get the Secretary of Defense to release the documents officially.

Fulbright called Ellsberg to testify before his committee on May 13, 1970. The two men had a long public exchange about the Pentagon Papers, not calling the study by that name, but referring to it with great frankness, Fulbright angry that he had not been able to pry it loose and Ellsberg expressing his wish that President Nixon and the National Security Council (Kissinger) read the study and apply its lessons to the present.

Fulbright went even further. He denounced the "classification of historical incidents."

"Anything that might be embarrassing to a political leader is classified," he said. "I think there should be some reasonable limits to classification. I can't subscribe to this extension of the concept of classification to prevent our knowing about the past. It is difficult enough to make a judgment on it with information. Without it it is impossible."

The hearing neither budged Laird from his stand nor produced the faintest public ripple. No newspaper reported the remarks of Ellsberg and Kissinger. The situation remained static.

Fulbright made one more appeal to Laird and got another refusal in late July. In August, Fulbright went to the floor of the Senate, criticized Laird's refusal and added, "I hope the first enterprising reporter who obtains a copy of this history will share it with the committee."

He might as well have been speaking in the Sahara Desert. Not one reporter responded to the challenge. In fact, Fulbright spoke to an empty chamber and an empty press gallery. Later on there was not to be a reporter who could recall having heard Fulbright or heard about his speech.

Ellsberg's frustration mounted. He had made a selection of his documents, principally of the years 1962–64, available late in 1969 to the antiwar Institute for Policy Studies for use by Ralph Stavins, Richard J. Barnet and Marcus G. Raskin in a study of Vietnam war decision-making (which would not be published until after the Pentagon Papers). Yet he had not entirely given up on the Establishment. There was to be one more round between himself and Kissinger before it all went down the drain.

Ellsberg was now amid a major change in his personal life. He had severed official connection with Rand April 15, 1970, after a telephone call from his ex-wife on April 7. She had told her stepmother about the Ellsberg children's work in helping to copy the Pentagon Papers and the stepmother had gone to the FBI. Now the FBI had come to see Mrs. Ellsberg. It seemed obvious that the next call would be on Ellsberg at Rand. Ellsberg had just been offered a job as senior research associate of the Center for International Studies at MIT. He decided to get out of Rand to spare them embarrassment if the FBI came around. He submitted his resignation at Santa Monica and flew east on April 15 to take up the new job with MIT, carrying his copies of the Pentagon Papers with him. He arrived in Harvard Square just as a huge antiwar, anti-Cambodia demonstration was going on.

What Ellsberg was not to learn until much later was that on April 27 an FBI agent named William McDermott interviewed Richard Best, Rand's top security official, about a report that Ellsberg had removed classified documents and had them reproduced outside Rand. The FBI knew that these documents were the Pentagon Papers and apparently had been told that Ellsberg might turn them over to Senators Fulbright or Goodell. Nothing came of the FBI inquiry. Rand's head, Dr. Rowen, a close friend of Ellsberg's, told the FBI that an Air Force or Defense Department inquiry into the matter was going to be made and the FBI dropped its investigation. No other inquiry was ever made, Ellsberg did not lose his security clearance, Rand quietly checked the Pentagon volumes into its security system but Ellsberg retained access and, during the summer of 1970, continued to work intermittently at Rand and even copied some other classified documents relating to the war.* He was told nothing about the FBI inquiry and no Air Force or Defense Department investigation was undertaken.

Kissinger and Ellsberg

The sequence of events that was to lead Ellsberg to offer the Pentagon Papers to *The New York Times* moved forward through an increasingly complex quadrille with Kissinger. Ellsberg and Patricia Marx had finally decided to get married. The ceremony was performed August 8, a big affair, a hundred guests, a Presbyterian minister, on the Westchester estate of Patricia's brother, Louis, Jr. Their father was the wealthy Louis Marx, toymaker, long-time friend of J. Edgar Hoover, a warm, engaging man who collected friends among the high and mighty, especially the military.†

---

*Ellsberg had a lingering doubt whether the FBI inquiry was completely shut down but hard evidence that the case was kept open did not surface. Plain luck seems to have been with Ellsberg.
†Ellsberg's marriage to Patricia Marx and her father's connection with Mr. Hoover led the Nixon Administration to conclude, perhaps with some justification, that Mr. Hoover would never permit his FBI to make the kind of an "inquiry" into Ellsberg that they wanted, and, thus, in what proved a fateful move, they put the matter into the hands of the White House Plumbers. It was a fact that Hoover exiled to "Siberia" an FBI agent who ordered Marx questioned about his son-in-law. That is to say, he

Lloyd Shearer, who once had solicited Ellsberg's advice on the Washington–Moscow hot line, had become a good friend and just before Ellsberg was to leave the Coast for his wedding, Shearer, still editor of *Parade* magazine, a Sunday newspaper supplement, told Ellsberg he had a date to see Kissinger at San Clemente. Ellsberg asked if he could go along. Shearer had been running gossipy items about Kissinger in *Parade*, mostly about beauteous young ladies whom Kissinger had been escorting in New York and Washington, and that had led to the date for lunch. When Shearer suggested to Kissinger that he bring Ellsberg along Kissinger demurred. "He's a marvelous fellow," Kissinger said. "He has all the clearances." Still he didn't want him at San Clemente. Shearer teased Kissinger, "You sound as though you are afraid of him," adding that Ellsberg was getting married and "I think he kind of expects this as a wedding present." At that Kissinger gave in and Ellsberg went to San Clemente, meeting Kissinger on the patio of the President's bungalow.

It was, Ellsberg recalled, a perfunctory meeting. They traded small talk, then Kissinger sent Ellsberg to lunch with General Al Haig, his assistant, on Haig's patio, while Kissinger and Shearer lunched on Kissinger's. Ellsberg and Haig talked Vietnam and Ellsberg criticized administration policy.

After lunch Ellsberg gave Kissinger a copy of a paper he was going to deliver to the American Political Science Association in Los Angeles September 12 and Kissinger asked Ellsberg whether he knew anyone who was an expert on the Vietnamese Communist Party. Ellsberg recommended a specialist at Rand named Conrad Keller. Kissinger said he'd like to see Ellsberg when he returned from the honeymoon he and Patricia had planned in Hawaii. Ellsberg was pleased at Kissinger's suggestion. Perhaps he could still work within channels. The men agreed to meet at San Clemente September 3.

When Ellsberg and Patricia flew back into Los Angeles Airport from Hawaii August 23, they went to the Avis counter to pick up a rented car. Ellsberg left Patricia briefly to go to the toilet and when he returned his briefcase had vanished. It contained the text and notes of his talk to the Political Science Association, the proofs of a review he had written for the *Washington Post* on Robert Shaplen's Vietnam reportage, *The Road from War*, and some other notes. Ellsberg still did

---

first ordered the agent, Charles Brennan, assistant director for Domestic Intelligence, sent to the Cleveland FBI office. Later he was given the meaningless title of chief inspector of special investigations, censured (at his own request) and put on probation. Nixon and Attorney General Mitchell thought Hoover's action would touch off a wave of resignations and that "this will finish Hoover." It didn't. (John Ehrlichman, White House notes, 6/29/71; David Wise, *The American Police State*, Vintage Press, New York, 1976, p. 280)

not know that the FBI had showed up at Rand but decided he must be under surveillance.*

Whether or not Ellsberg was under surveillance it did not interfere with his meeting September 3 at San Clemente. He and Kissinger spent thirty-five minutes in a businesslike atmosphere. Once again Kissinger wanted from Ellsberg an options paper on Vietnam, the kind Ellsberg had done at the start of the Nixon Administration. Ellsberg gave Kissinger a brief outline of his views on Vietnam—the time had come to end the war, there was no possibility of a win policy, the bullet must be bit, etc. This did not bother Kissinger. He said he wanted Ellsberg and wanted him right away. This time Ellsberg would not be an official White House consultant but the White House would pay his air fare, hotel and expenses. This was fine with Ellsberg. What Ellsberg wanted, of course, was access and input. The technicalities did not matter. Kissinger asked Ellsberg to go to work immediately but since he and Patricia were just moving to Cambridge he could not put the whole burden on his wife. Kissinger said it was a very urgent matter. Ellsberg replied, "Well, you've been getting along without my advice for a year and a half."

Finally a date was agreed upon and that, for practical purposes, was the end of it. Kissinger and Ellsberg never did meet. Their first date was broken, a new date fixed. Then that was broken and a third was fixed. Finally, Ellsberg told Kissinger's secretary, "Look, when he is free —let him call me." The secretary said, "Really—he is very anxious to see you and have you do this."

But Kissinger never called. In the broad context the incident was trivial but as a measure of the symbiosis between Kissinger and Ellsberg it was not trivial. There had existed a push-pull attraction between the two men and later, much later, as the Pentagon Papers crisis unrolled, there were many who saw in this curious ambiance one source of the fuel which propelled that crisis to incandescence.

What happened? Why didn't Kissinger and Ellsberg meet for a new round of the options game? Possibly too much was going on that September. Perhaps Kissinger's secret schedule became too crowded. He was now resuming his clandestine meetings in Paris with Hanoi, meetings which had been broken off since the Cambodian bombing in the spring. There was the sudden flare-up in Jordan, which preoccupied

---

*Much later, when Ellsberg obtained his CIA file under the Freedom of Information Act, he found that in August and September the CIA was receiving information on Ellsberg from the FBI, the nature of which the files did not disclose, and that CIA had concluded, "This man under no circumstances is to be given clearance." (Personal interview, Ellsberg, 7/24/78)

him and the White House for a month. Certainly Kissinger was a busy man but he was always a busy man and this need not have prevented another round of dealings with Ellsberg. Did Kissinger get wind of Ellsberg's security problems at Rand? Had he learned of Ellsberg's implication in the Westmoreland troop affair under President Johnson? Had he noted the close connections between Ellsberg and Morton Halperin, Kissinger's own assistant who had been wiretapped since May 9, 1969, and would continue to be into the indefinite future?*

There seems no way now of knowing. Alert as Ellsberg was to the possibility of surveillance, neither he nor anyone then had a concept of the intensity of paranoia within the White House and the extent to which it was already wiretapping and subjecting to surveillance both its own officials and newsmen.

There was another possibility—that Kissinger simply wanted it to appear that he had consulted a broad range of opinion ("Look, I've talked to everyone. Even to Dan Ellsberg"). This was one of his frequent ploys. Clark Clifford recalled that he had four long meetings with Kissinger in the interregnum between Nixon's election and January 20, 1969. Once Clifford talked to Kissinger until after midnight. Kissinger gave most sympathetic attention as Clifford argued for a speedy U.S. withdrawal from Vietnam. Finally, Kissinger asked Clifford if he would be willing to make the same presentation to Mr. Nixon. Clifford said he would be delighted. But Kissinger never called. Later on Clifford heard from someone high in the Administration that Kissinger and Nixon had no intention of following Clifford's advice because they thought it would make the United States look like a "pitiful, helpless giant."†

Through the early winter of 1970–71 Ellsberg kept trying to get some prominent politician to take up the cause of the Pentagon Papers. He wrote a sharp letter to *The New York Times* in November 1970 in

---

*Ultimately it was revealed that Ellsberg had been overheard fifteen times during the tapping of Halperin's telephone. At least once Kissinger had been officially informed of this by J. Edgar Hoover, who gave him the text of a conversation in which Ellsberg talked with someone named "Harry" about a "trip." Hoover said it was obvious that the conversation concerned drugs. (David Wise, *The American Police State*, Vintage Press, New York, 1978, p. 79) These were the tappings which led to the dismissal of the government's attempt to prosecute Ellsberg for his role in copying the Pentagon Papers in Los Angeles, May 11, 1973, by Judge Byrne.

†Don Oberhofer of the *Washington Post* interviewed Kissinger in January 1971 on his first two years as White House adviser on foreign policy. Later Oberhofer telephoned Ellsberg to ask if he had ever worked for Kissinger. "Why do you ask?" Ellsberg said. "Because," Oberhofer said, "Kissinger said that some of those currently criticizing our foreign policy had a role in shaping it and cited you." (Personal interview, Ellsberg, 2/26/77)

which he called the war "immoral, illegal and unconstitutional." Then in January he had a critical series of talks with Senator George McGovern, the nation's leading congressional opponent of the Southeast Asian conflict. At first Ellsberg was enormously encouraged. He gave McGovern a sampling of the papers, but after reading them and consulting with Senator Gaylord Nelson of Wisconsin, McGovern turned down the proposal. He suggested that Ellsberg go to *The New York Times.* Ellsberg pondered giving the Papers to the United Nations. His friend Tony Russo suggested getting a helicopter and dropping them over Washington or New York. Russo had once hired a helicopter for an advertising project and the two men pondered showering the papers down on the Capitol. That would be one way to get them into circulation and permanently out of the government's security system. Ellsberg thought of hiring a printer to publish the Papers and he even thought he might get the *Harvard Crimson* to do it.*

Angered by the rebuff from McGovern, losing hope of Fulbright's cooperation, uncertain where next to go, Ellsberg decided—with reluctance and many reservations—to talk with a reporter whom he had respected for a long time and a man whose work and antagonism to the war in Vietnam had recently and forcibly been called to his attention. All this was in his mind when he finally telephoned Sheehan and the two men met on Sunday evening, February 28, 1971.

*Sometime in this period Ellsberg met Henry Grunwald, editor of *Time* magazine at dinner. Ellsberg sounded out Grunwald cryptically, thinking *Time* might publish the Papers. But Ellsberg judged Grunwald unsympathetic and the matter went no further. Later a legend grew up that Grunwald turned down a chance to carry the Papers. This was not correct.

9

"You Have Permission to Proceed, Young Man"

ONE MORNING IN the first week of March 1971, Neil Sheehan, more dour and gloomy than his wont, asked Robert Phelps, then news editor of the Washington bureau of *The New York Times*, to step out of the newsroom to the reception lobby by the elevators, a dim chamber with wall-to-wall carpeting, looking a bit like an undertaker's parlor.

Neil had come to believe that *The Times'* Washington bureau might be bugged and he didn't want to take any risk. He told Phelps that he had a chance to get a secret history of the war in Vietnam which had been done by the Pentagon but there was a condition that *The Times* publish the whole thing. What did Phelps think?

Phelps, a quiet man whose easy manner belied a sharp eye and fast mind, told Sheehan that *The Times* would never make a blind deal. How long was the history? Sheehan didn't know but he thought it was very, very long.

"You better go to Scotty Reston and Max Frankel," Phelps said. "We can't get into something like this without knowing what it involves."

Sheehan's next call was on Tom Wicker, now a columnist. Several weeks previously Wicker had written a column about the "vile" plot of Philip Berrigan and other peace advocates to kidnap Kissinger. Ellsberg, very upset, had telephoned Wicker. How could Wicker use the word "vile" when talking about persons opposed to Kissinger, the man who had been bombing Hanoi and prolonging the war? He reminded Wicker of their conversation two years earlier when Wicker told him that duty to the truth came ahead of security concerns. That had impressed him tremendously, Ellsberg said, and he now asked whether Wicker had ever called the actions of the government in Vietnam "vile." Wicker thought Ellsberg had a point and he wrote a couple of columns in which he criticized U.S. policy in sharp terms. In one article he mentioned Ellsberg and the critique of the United States which he had written for the *New York Review of Books*.

In the course of their talk Ellsberg spoke of a Pentagon study of the war but his words meant nothing to Wicker.

As he had with Phelps, Sheehan insisted that Wicker come out into the corridor for fear the office was bugged, and as they sauntered down the narrow hall from Wicker's office to the wire room and back Sheehan said, "What would you think if I told you that there is a complete history of the Vietnam war over at the Pentagon?"

"Oh," said Wicker, his mind clicking, "you're getting this from Dan."

Sheehan gave Wicker an equivocal answer and Wicker did not press the point.

"You must fill Scotty in," Wicker said. "He is the key. If he thinks it should be published—then it probably will be published. But if he is against it—then it won't be published."

Reston's O.K.

So it was that Sheehan took his problem to Reston. At the time of Sheehan's conversation Reston was the elder statesman of *The Times.* No one's career matched his. He had come to *The Times* at the start of World War II, a young reporter from Ohio, born in Clydebank, Scotland, a protégé of James Cox, publisher of the Dayton, Ohio, paper, a savvy, bright, poor young Scot, going through the University of Illinois with Cox's aid, marrying a classmate of rare intelligence and judgment, Sally Fulton, getting onto AP as a sports writer and marvelously positioning himself in London at the outbreak of the war when he joined *The Times.*

Reston's career had been magic from the start. He was the kind of young man whom important older men instinctively wanted to adopt, seeing in him a reflection of their own youth, bright-as-buttons and as ambitious and cunning a lad as Caledonia ever set loose on the world. Before World War II ended Reston was a super-nova in the *Times'* firmament, headed for certain success, recognized as the single most important asset on the paper by Arthur Hays Sulzberger, by his shrewd wife, Iphigene, and by Arthur Krock, the distinguished *Times* Washington chief. Krock was becoming restive with the routine of running the Washington bureau and failing to persuade Turner Catledge to take it over, suggested that Arthur Sulzberger offer it to Reston, who was dallying with an offer to join the *Washington Post.* This kept Reston on *The Times* but Krock later came to regret his loss of authority to a younger man.

Through the first two postwar decades Reston made himself the most powerful journalist in the world: his column in *The Times* was obligatory reading for all diplomats; he was the confidant of every American Secretary of State—Marshall, Acheson, Dulles, Rusk; he had exclusive interviews with presidents and kings; Stalin answered his questions; he became the darling of American academics and through skill and personal attraction he put together an amazing group of young men, the most brilliant Washington news corps ever assembled, and wielded a power within *The New York Times* matched by none.

In truth, by 1971 Reston had passed his peak, having emerged with his prestige tarnished from the bruising encounters of the late 1960s within *The Times'* bureaucracy over control of the Washington bureau and of *The Times'* news operation. These were the struggles and intrigues which provided Gay Talese with the drama of his study of *The Times* called *The Kingdom and the Power*.

Now, in 1971, Reston was tired, somewhat puzzled as to how all the changes that had put Abe Rosenthal at the head of *The Times'* news function had come about, and under his avuncular exterior quite hurt and disappointed. But he was a vice president of *The Times*, was headed for a seat on the board of directors and still possessed his column (although it was never to regain its lost eminence), and Wicker was undoubtedly correct when he told Sheehan that if Reston was for the story it would be published; if he was against it—it would not be.

Sheehan promptly went to Reston and told him he had a chance to get an archive of the war. To get it there must be a promise to publish the whole archive, possibly in book form, by *The New York Times'* book subsidiary, if not in the paper. It was top secret and sensitive. It would not make McNamara (a close friend of Reston's) look good. Nor would it be kind to Dean Rusk, former Secretary of State. It had been done by the government, commissioned within the Pentagon by McNamara, but it pulled no punches. Neil had little more to tell Scotty; in fact, he knew little more about it. Reston listened sympathetically and told Sheehan he'd find out New York's views.

A few days passed. Neil had specified that Reston not consult New York by telephone, but, in fact, he did use the telephone and in the typically oblique fashion of *The Times* he consulted neither the paper's publisher (who chanced to be out of town) nor its editor. He talked instead to Ivan Veit, a senior vice president, an extremely able, skillful in-house man who by this time had emerged as Punch's chief adviser. Scotty merely told Veit that the paper was onto what he called "the biggest story of the century" and he could not reveal to Veit what it was. Veit asked if Reston had informed Rosenthal and Reston said he had not. Veit asked if he could tell Rosenthal and Reston agreed that he might.

Later that day Sheehan was standing in the office lobby waiting for the elevator. Scotty came up, put out his arm and drew Sheehan back from the waiting elevator.

"You have permission to proceed, young man," said Reston. "If you get it you will win the Pulitzer Prize for it."*

Sheehan wasn't so sure about the Pulitzer (with good reason it turned out) but now he was off and running.

Sheehan in Washington

Sheehan was not on good terms with his immediate superior, Max Frankel, and later he was inclined to think it was fortuitous that Frankel chanced to be out of town, which made it possible for him to approach Reston first about the story.

In the winter of 1971 Sheehan had been five years back from Vietnam. He was unhappy and he had not been doing well professionally. Somehow he had never really hit his stride in Washington. He had gone back to Vietnam in 1965 with high hopes. It had not been easy to get onto *The Times* in spite of a strong recommendation from Halberstam. Reston had backed him and so had Seymour Topping, then foreign editor, but it was only when Reston told New York that it looked as though *The Times* was going to lose Neil to the *Washington Post* that Abe Rosenthal, then metropolitan editor, agreed to take Sheehan on the city staff for training while waiting for a foreign spot, presumably Vietnam, to open up. His first assignment was to go down to the subway at Times Square and interview people on how to get to Grant's tomb. Only one out of twenty-five people he asked had any idea where Grant's tomb was located. What this survey proved it was hard to say. It was in this time that Neil and Susan Black met and fell in love, a match he was later to describe in rococo fashion as having been "made by a public adulterer." Susan was working on *The New Yorker.* Her best friend was Nan Talese. Neil's best friend was Halberstam and Halberstam's best friend was Gay Talese. So it chanced that Gay introduced Susan and Neil on a blind date and when Neil was suddenly sent to Jakarta he cabled back for her and they were married there, living in a crumbling hotel, paying $1,200 a month for a hall bedroom and then moving on to Saigon, where they had a larger and more comfortable room in the Hotel Continental.

When Neil returned from Vietnam he was assigned to Washington to cover diplomatic and foreign policy stories, Pentagon assignments, special projects. He had an occasional good story, particularly in 1968, in LBJ's last year, but had never quite fitted into the convoluted politics of *The Times'* Washington bureau. He was no longer the lighthearted youngster of Harvard, nor the endlessly energetic correspondent of the Vietnam jungle. He had become a dour man, his friends felt, introspec-

---

*As far as the record shows the "permission to proceed" was given by Scotty himself. Neither Sulzberger nor Rosenthal knew what the story was at this point. Max Frankel was still absent from Washington.

tive, pessimistic, but, as always, driving himself to nail down the last tiny fact in a complicated story.

By autumn of 1970 Neil felt he had stumbled into a blind alley. His temperament didn't mesh with Frankel's. Sheehan was supposed to be doing long investigative stories. Sometimes he worked for months and there would be a long wait and endless wrangles before his copy was published. He was writing on domestic subjects but the best of his copy always seemed to have a bearing on the war.

Frankel, a compact, efficient man, felt that Neil was undisciplined. Frankel thought that if Neil tried shorter, less involved subjects it might work better but Neil resented suggestions. He was very much his own man, with a compulsion for working in his own way at his own pace.

This frustrating pattern was broken in late autumn 1970 when Roger Jellinek, an imaginative editor on *The New York Times Book Review,* gave to Sheehan for review a book called *Conversations with Americans* by Mark Lane, who had won fame for his cranky insistence that Lee Oswald's assassination of President Kennedy was part of a grandiose plot.

The Lane book was not worthy of the attention of a serious reporter but Sheehan approached it as though it were a buzz bomb in wartime London that had to be defused with extreme delicacy and then totally demolished. He accomplished his task in several weeks of work, going back over Lane's ground, interviewing the men Lane said he had talked to, correcting and filling out the record and then moving forward to his own powerful conclusion that:

> The country desperately needs a sane and honest inquiry into the question of war crimes and atrocities in Vietnam by a body of knowledgeable and responsible men not beholden to the current military establishment. . . .
> Anyone who spends much time in Vietnam sees acts that may constitute war crimes. One of the basic military tactics of the war, the air and artillery bombardments that have taken an untold number of civilian lives, is open to examination under the criteria established by the Nuremberg tribunal.
> Is it a war crime? We ought to know. And those professional soldiers who value their uniform would be wise to welcome such an inquiry.

These were strong words. The man who had returned from Vietnam nauseated by the lies had moved onto new ground. No longer was it lies and hypocrisy against which Sheehan inveighed. It was war crimes . . . Nuremberg . . . a quantum leap in the philosophy and thinking of this increasingly pessimistic moralist, this Irish fantaseur *manqué,* this dogged investigative reporter, so long entangled in the nimble and mawkish kind of stories that were being suggested to him—that he go around the country and examine the Presidential libraries, find out what was in them and with what they concerned themselves; or interview members of the Congressional Armed Services committees to see what manner of men they were, where their interests lay, what their philosophy was. There was no fire in these topics to stir Sheehan's chilled spirit. Like so many Americans, he was no longer in Vietnam but it was as though he had not left. As long as the agony persisted he was where the agony was, felt it in the marrow of his soul and endured its torment in an Old Testament conscience.

His angst cried out in the Mark Lane review. It was an eloquent piece of writing and in the polarized temper of the winter of 1970–71 Sheehan's essay was bound to attract attention. (It did not, however, find any echo in the editorial pages of *The Times*.)

Sheehan's review appeared in *The Times* of December 27, 1970, the Sunday after Christmas, the thinnest *Book Review* of the year, lost among holiday celebrations and surfeit. Ellsberg did not remember seeing it but early in January his antiwar friends Marc Raskin and Richard Barnet mentioned to him that Neil was "doing some very interesting work on Vietnam" and suggested that Ellsberg might want to talk to him.*

By this time Sheehan was engaged in another and more compelling project—a review-article based on a bibliography by Mark Saperof of thirty-three antiwar books. The bibliography had already aroused controversy on *The Times* before it was given to Sheehan by Roger Jellinek, the same editor who had suggested the Lane review. The bibliography had been submitted to *The New York Times Magazine* and rejected. The Sunday editor, Dan Schwartz, who had supervision over both *Magazine* and *Book Review*, was not taken by the idea. This did not deter Jellinek. John Leonard, newly in charge of the *Book Review*, a feisty editor on the lookout for ideas with which to make his mark, strongly backed Jellinek.

Neil's concern about the war had been sharpened by his work on the Lane article. He had had a call from some young Army officers—active serving officers—who were trying to start a Commission to Investigate the War Crimes of Americans in Vietnam. He met Raskin and Barnet and then Ellsberg looked him up, not to talk about the Pentagon Papers, but to talk about war crimes. Neil plunged deeply into this subject. He got the relevant Army manuals on conduct in war, copies

---

*Neither Raskin nor Barnet had met Sheehan prior to the publication of his *Book Review* article and they were startled to find that in his thinking about Vietnam he had come to many of the same conclusions that they had earlier reached about American war crimes. (Personal interview, Raskin, 9/9/78)

of the Geneva conventions on warfare, talked with Army men (and Ellsberg). He was supposed to spend a month writing a 3,500-word essay. He wound up taking three months and writing 10,000 words.

It was late March before Sheehan's massive article was published and not without a considerable row. Dan Schwartz didn't want to publish it. He hadn't liked the idea from the beginning; he thought the piece polemic, an example of advocacy and not a book review, was not sympathetic to Neil's views on the war and he was appalled at its length. But John Leonard was determined to see it in print. As he admitted later, "I kind of played fast and loose with it." He cut the piece and put it into page proofs, and Schwartz, angry and still opposed, finally and reluctantly permitted Leonard to go ahead. To make certain no one missed the significance of the article Leonard and his staff mailed advance copies (something which the *Book Review* had never done) to about a hundred persons in the media world with the result that there was a great publicity splash—columns by Nick Von Hoffman of the *Washington Post,* favorable mention on CBS by Mike Wallace, and Neil wound up getting one of the prizes awarded by *The Times* internally for the best work of the month.

Sheehan's words in *The New York Times Book Review* on March 28, 1971, were strong indeed:

> The cleansing of the nation's conscience and the future conduct of the most powerful country in the world towards the weaker peoples of the globe demand a national inquiry into the war crimes question. . . .
>
> History shows that men who decide for war, as the Japanese militarists did, cannot demand mercy for themselves. The resort to force is the ultimate act. It is playing God.

The question, said Sheehan, was whether or not U.S. intervention in Vietnam was itself a violation of the Nuremberg principles forbidding wars of aggression.

What Neil was saying here, in plain English, was that there should be a national inquiry into the origins of the war and that if it were determined that Presidents Kennedy and Johnson, men like Generals Maxwell Taylor and Westmoreland and their advisers, were responsible for instigating an "aggressive war" they should, like Goering and the other Nazis, be placed in the dock and made to stand trial for their lives. This was heavy stuff. Neil's position had moved light-years since his Vietnam days. It was as uncompromising as that of Ellsberg. Possibly more so. Sheehan had long parted company with the measured indignation and moral protest of *The Times'* editorial page conducted by John Oakes. (Yet, Arthur Krock, the grand old man of *The Times* Washington bureau, probably the most conservative man associated with the paper, a man who had turned on FDR at the time of Roosevelt's court-packing plan and played a major role in defeating it; a man who had little use for Truman; who supported John F. Kennedy only out of friendship for his father, Joseph Kennedy, and fondness for young Jack as he was growing up; a backer of Lyndon Johnson's most conservative strains and an advocate of tax and fiscal policy far to the right of Nixon was to congratulate Sheehan on his role in the Pentagon Papers and tell him with some emotion that if there should be a war crimes tribunal in Washington Joseph Alsop and Walt Rostow, LBJ's security adviser, would go to the dock. "They talked JFK into going to war," Krock said.)

Small wonder, then, that when Neil showed Ellsberg an early draft of his *Book Review* article some time in mid-February, Ellsberg was impressed. He had just had a final skirmish with Kissinger (the two men seemed as fated to meet-yet-never-meet as enchanted figures in a fairy tale). The confrontation came at a Boston weekend seminar under MIT auspices, Kissinger speaking and declaring there were no good choices left in Vietnam. Ellsberg pressed Kissinger on what the cost in Asian casualties might be of the Administration's policy of "Vietnamization." Kissinger spoke of options but Ellsberg interrupted, "I know the options game, Dr. Kissinger . . . can't you just give us an answer or tell us you don't have such estimates?" Kissinger did not respond.

On the last weekend in February 1971, Ellsberg went to Washington. He was participating on Monday, March 1, in a panel discussion at the National War College on Vietnam with General Richard Stilwell, then deputy chief of staff of military operations for the Army, and Professor Joseph Zasloff of the University of Pittsburgh, a specialist on Vietnam.

It was a lovely spring weekend, sunny and mild. The war was wearily winding on. President Nixon had presented an American disengagement plan to Congress a day or two before but warned that we would not be moving swiftly on it. American forces in Vietnam were attempting for the umpteenth time to seal off the Laos frontier and Senator Fulbright was still hoping he could force Mr. Nixon's high aides to testify on the war before the Senate Foreign Relations Committee. Everything, in a word, was normal. Ellsberg took advantage of his visit for a long and frank talk with Raskin, who strongly urged him to discuss with Sheehan the possibility of *The Times* publishing the papers.

Ellsberg made up his mind and called Sheehan and it was this talk that lay behind Sheehan's approach to Phelps, Wicker and Reston later that week.

Sheehan had already learned of the Pentagon study in earlier talks with Raskin, Barnet and Ralph Stavins, all associated with the Institute for Policy Studies to which Ellsberg had given a selection of the most important papers. Sheehan had seen some of the documents and the idea of publishing them was in his mind although he did not yet clearly know the scope of the Pentagon study.* Of course, the truth was that in the scholarly political Washington–Boston–New York axis the subject was fairly well known, and, in fact, while the remarks of Ellsberg and Fulbright in the Senate Foreign Relations Committee and Fulbright's appeal on the Senate floor for an enterprising newsman to obtain a copy of the documents had gone unnoticed by the professional press there had been fleeting mentions of the study in print. The first, probably, was a reference by Ward Just on the *Washington Post* editorial page early in 1969. The second was in *The New York Times* itself. In an article in *The New York Times Magazine,* November 9, 1969, Henry Brandon of the London *Sunday Times* (later to be wiretapped at J. Edgar Hoover's insistence and with Henry Kissinger's knowledge) wrote that McNamara before leaving the Pentagon had "ordered detailed historical records to be assembled and there are now thirty or forty volumes that will be the raw material for a definitive history of that war."

More than a year went by before another reference. This came in *Parade* magazine October 25, 1970. But not, Lloyd Shearer swore, because of the discussions he and Ellsberg had with Kissinger a month or so earlier. It was simply a response to a query from a reader named "B. T. Clancy of Washington" who had heard that Nixon had ordered an extensive study of the origins of the war. Shearer called McNamara and Leslie Gelb and found that the study had been authorized by McNamara, executed by Gelb, was extremely long and probably never would be published. He reported these simple facts, adding that the study ran to thirty volumes and 10,000 pages and that there were few copies in existence. The item produced no response whatever.†

At the moment he spoke to his colleagues at *The Times,* Sheehan had not yet seen any of the Pentagon Papers possessed by Ellsberg or even sample sheets from Ellsberg's store of duplicates.

•

*Sheehan was not aware that there had been a disagreement between Ellsberg and his friends at the Institute for Policy Studies because of what Ellsberg thought was their carelessness in allowing access to the papers that he had given them. Ellsberg was concerned lest the FBI get on the track and he finally compelled Raskin to return the documents. Ellsberg later conceded that he had suspected (correctly) that the institute had retained at least one copy for its use. Obviously, Ellsberg was not the only one who could play the copying game. (Personal interview, Ellsberg, 10/16/78)
†Shearer insisted that the item was evoked by a reader's inquiry but the reader's question related to Nixon. Shearer did not explain why he called McNamara and Gelb or who directed him to them. Ellsberg later declared he had not mentioned the papers to his friend.

The Times' High Command

As of March 1971 *The New York Times* had been reporting the Indochina war for twenty-eight years. It had published in those two and a half decades hundreds of editorials on the subject. In the decade ending with March 1971 *The Times* published 647 editorials on Vietnam, the number sharply escalating from twenty-eight and nineteen in 1961 and 1962, respectively, to a level of 130 a year in 1966–68, then gradually falling to sixty to seventy editorials in the years 1970–71. In 1945 a single correspondent covered the scene and even he was not permanently assigned. In those days there was only one Indochina. A correspondent could freely move from Hanoi to Saigon and back. Over the years, and especially since President Kennedy's decision in 1961 to assign American "advisers," gradually escalating in his unfinished term to more than 14,000 men, *The Times'* Vietnam staff had grown and grown. By March 1971 *The New York Times'* Saigon bureau numbered six or seven Americans (some rotating in from Hong Kong or Bangkok) and half a dozen Vietnamese. Vietnam was day-in day-out the leading foreign story in the paper, occupying more page-one space and more auxiliary space inside the paper than any other topic. Vietnam and its political repercussions often called for the services of eight to ten Washington correspondents on a given day, and the domestic flareback, the demonstrations, meetings, antiwar activities, speeches and endeavors throughout the country not infrequently required the assignment of another eight to ten men.

What had been a small peripheral interest, a tiny segment of the Pacific and Asian story at the end of World War II, had grown like a cancer. Just as it preoccupied the minds of American Presidents, American statesmen, the American military and American politicians so it preoccupied the resources and attention of the nation's leading newspaper.

It came to be widely believed by supporters of the war, by some of the U.S. military establishment and quite possibly by Presidents Johnson and Nixon and their foreign policy advisers, Dean Rusk and Walt Rostow for Johnson, and Henry Kissinger for Nixon, that the editors of *The Times* had become dangerous radicals possessed by an extreme antiwar fixation.* But this was as far from the truth as are most convictions that seize individuals caught up in violent conflict. The truth was much closer to the opposite.

---

*After publication of the Pentagon Papers in June 1971 Dean Rusk refused to write an article for the Op-Ed page of *The New York Times* criticizing their publication— to which he violently objected. Earlier he had said he would not permit an article under his signature to appear in a newspaper "which is engaged in starting World War III." (Personal conversation, Rusk, 6/17/71)

Turner Catledge, managing editor and executive editor of *The Times* during most of the Johnson period, would have described himself as a Mississippi Democrat, a breed not particularly notable for excessive liberalism and certainly devout in support of the nation's military honor. His Ole Miss classmate had been John Stennis, as stalwart a hawk and military proponent as was to be found in the U.S. Senate. Catledge's successor as managing editor, close friend and deputy from the late 1950s, was Clifton Daniel, another southerner, a North Carolina Democrat whose political persuasions were close to those of his father-in-law, President Truman, and his wife, Margaret Truman Daniel. Possibly Daniel was a smidgen more liberal than Catledge but neither was a radical nor even a progressive. They were firmly fixed in the centrist tradition of southern Democratic Party politics, that stratum which traditionally worked in close collaboration with the middle levels of the Republican Party. They were the kind of men who had no difficulty in supporting President Eisenhower but a good deal in relating to President Nixon. In President Johnson's early months no President in U.S. history had been as close to *The Times,* its publisher (these were Punch's first years) and its editor, Catledge. Johnson was often on the telephone to the paper an embarrassing three or four times daily.

If these men presided over a newspaper that published dispatches that were increasingly damning to U.S. Indochina policy it was clearly not out of ideological commitment. Nor could a case for radicalism be made against the Sulzberger family, which held ultimate responsibility for the conduct of *The Times.* Arthur Hays Sulzberger had approved the paper's support of Franklin D. Roosevelt in 1936, but with substantial reluctance, and gladly switched to Wendell Willkie in 1940. Sulzberger backed FDR in 1944, but only as a wartime measure. He supported Dewey in 1948 and warmly backed Eisenhower in 1952 and 1956. The paper's choice of John F. Kennedy in 1960 was as much out of distaste for Nixon as it was attraction to Kennedy. LBJ was backed wholeheartedly in 1964 but in 1968 there was no enthusiasm for Humphrey, rather, continued abhorrence of Nixon.

This was hardly the record of radicals, and while in 1971 there were still to be found diehard New Yorkers who referred to *The Times* as the "uptown edition of *The Daily Worker,*" a relic of McCarthy passions, there were not many around in 1971 who even knew what *The Worker* was, or had been.

True, Iphigene Sulzberger was more liberal than her husband. Her taste in politics had been formed in the days of Woodrow Wilson's New Freedom. She had been a college-girl admirer of the young Walter Lippmann (and a life-long admirer of his cool, cultured and analytic mind) but the man who was to epitomize her political taste was Adlai

Stevenson, hardly a credible threat to the status quo. There was no other member of the Sulzberger family as liberal as Iphigene.* None of her daughters, Marian, Ruth or Judith, were as liberal as she, and her son, Punch, was the most conservative member of the family. None was formed, as once was said of Lenin, of the dough out of which Robespierres are baked.

Nor could any of the editors of *The Times* have won a prize in a flaming liberal contest. Scotty Reston was an essentially conservative man who grew steadily more conservative as the years passed. True, he was the darling of liberal professors and do-good elements but careful analysis of his opinions showed that with rare exceptions he was a don't-rock-the-boat man. Not for him the role of consistent critic of the Establishment. For practical purposes Reston had been for nearly twenty years the amanuensis of the Establishment. Henry Kissinger was one of his most precious sources. Kissinger valued Reston equally highly. The same had been true of Dean Rusk, Walt Rostow, McGeorge Bundy and Dean Acheson. Reston was not only part of the Establishment, he was an integral part of it. It was to Reston that Cabinet ministers turned for a sympathetic column to explain away an error or a controversy, and it was Reston with his good-guy sympathy (sometimes flavored with a little Jimmy Cagney toughness) who jollied them into giving *The Times* just a bit more (or sometimes a great deal more) of the story than anyone else.

Max Frankel, like Reston, an emigrant (except that his milieu was pre-Hitler Berlin, not Clydebank's shipyards), consciously modeled himself on Reston. He'd done a memorable stint as a foreign correspondent in Moscow, had gotten in on the coverage of the Hungarian revolt from Vienna in 1956 and made foreign policy his special preserve. He didn't speak with Henry Kissinger's accent but the two men were cut from the same swath of the German–Jewish *Heimatland* and the last thing that would have entered Frankel's mind was to hassle the American Establishment, of which he was so proud to be a part.

The same could be said of managing editor Rosenthal, who had emerged as the most conservative editor on the paper, although he came from a typically radical Jewish emigrant family, suffused as were so many from Russia's Pale of Settlement with the ideals of social

---

*Iphigene Sulzberger was deeply touched when Richard Nixon, President-elect, attended her husband's memorial service at Temple Emanu-El, Sunday, December 15, 1968, three days after Arthur Hays Sulzberger's death at seventy-seven. Mr. Nixon came to her after the service and said, "Arthur was always very kind to me." She was glad to be able to tell him that each time Arthur had seen him he had liked him better. Tactfully, she did not voice her own opinion—that she did not like Mr. Nixon very much, and by the time she recalled this incident, in 1970, liked him even less. (Personal interview, Iphigene Ochs Sulzberger, 2/12/70)

progress, strong leanings toward the Jewish Bund, with its advanced socialist philosophy, beliefs in perfectionism and change. This was the radical strain which contributed strongly to the advancement of social causes in America and provided battalions for the defense of the cause of Bolshevism in Russia. Abe was brought up in these traditions. He studied at City College of New York when that institution was a vortex of struggle between the Young Communists and the Young Socialists, the mirror image of the violent quarrels of Europe, of Social Democracy, of Trotskyism, of Stalinism, of the Communists and Spain.

Rosenthal's background would seem to have pointed him toward a liberal or radical crusading spirit. But the reverse had occurred. Of all the paper's chiefs in March 1971 no one was postured more firmly against what he saw as shapeless anarchy swirling up from the streets, and particularly from turbulent young people, than Rosenthal. It was Rosenthal who confessed to Sheehan after he had learned what the Pentagon story was and had satisfied himself that it was authentic and after he had ordered all hands to go full speed ahead that the publishing of the Pentagon Papers would "hurt my views and hurt the views of my friends." He added honestly that "I don't want to see it published but it must be published."

There was one major *Times* editor who was outspoken and vigorous in his opposition to the Vietnam war and to American policy in Indochina as carried out by Presidents Johnson and Nixon. This was John Oakes, fifty-eight years old in March 1971, director of the editorial page, the man who had turned *The Times'* editorial policy against the war in 1965, first cousin (despite the disparity in ages) of Iphigene Sulzberger (his father was George Ochs, younger brother of Adolph Ochs, and had changed his name from Ochs to Oakes in World War I because of his anti-German feelings). John Oakes was very much one of the great Ochs family tribe. He and Cyrus L. Sulzberger, in sailor suits, had been pages at the wedding of Iphigene Ochs and Arthur Hays Sulzberger, uncle of Cy, but Cy and John never were to become close in their long years on *The Times.* John Oakes, loyal as he was to the great Ochs tradition, always harbored a feeling that his father, George, had not quite been appreciated by Adolph Ochs. When John Oakes was made chief of the editorial page by Orvil Dryfoos in 1961, displacing Charles Merz, he moved his father's great oaken desk into his office as a gesture of tribute and continuity.

John Oakes was second to none in his opposition to the war. An extremely intelligent man, he had an almost perfect record at Collegiate and Lawrenceville, graduated from Princeton in 1934, *magna cum laude,* went to Oxford as a Rhodes scholar and served with the OSS in World War II. Oakes was a member of X-2, the counterintelligence group of OSS, and among his colleagues was Ben Welles, son of Sumner Welles, also to have a distinguished career on *The New York Times*, and James Angleton, the eccentric genius who ultimately headed the counterintelligence branch of CIA until his removal amid fireworks by William Colby late in 1974. Oakes worked briefly on the *Washington Post* before joining OSS. He came to *The New York Times* May 1, 1946, a month before his formal discharge from the Army, as an editor and writer in the Sunday department, and joined the editorial board in 1949.

Oakes was a painfully honest, painfully principled man. There was no one more upright on *The Times* than Oakes but there was no one so totally lacking in humor. Oakes was dedicated in his opposition to the Vietnam war, dedicated in his general hostility to Richard Nixon but concerned (although this was hardly guessed even within *The Times*) over what he considered a developing tendency toward political advocacy on the part of *The Times'* news pages, a loss of the newspaper's long-standing tradition of objectivity.

Although critics of *The Times* would have popped their eyes in astonishment, Oakes had declared his total agreement, during one of the Argyris kiss-and-tell sessions, with Rosenthal's worry over what he perceived as the paper's trend to the left politically. Rosenthal was concerned with what he thought was a leftward leaning of the editorial page and editorial columnists and most of all by the fact that "many of the bright reporters have come out of an atmosphere of advocacy." Oakes, of course, disagreed as to the editorial page but responded that he fully agreed as to the reporters and added, "I would fire some of those bastards."

This, then, was the top echelon of *The Times,* which in March 1971 prepared to confront and cope with what Reston had called "the greatest story of the century."

10

The Ides of March

*T*HERE IS NO INSTITUTION in Washington so hallowed as the annual Gridiron dinner. The Gridiron Club is an assembly of troglodytes, the wise and stuffy Old Men of Washington journalism. Their names might or might not be known beyond the confines of that Chinese wall which Raymond Clapper insisted encircled the nation's capital but within the wall their names were golden. Young correspondents were expected to genuflect at the mention of the institution.

All during the year, members—membership was limited to fifty and seemed to confer an extraordinary life-span—wore in their lapels small golden replicas of a gridiron. It was in Washington a symbol more respected than, say, a Phi Beta Kappa key, the Medal of Honor or even cuff links presented by JFK, a tie clasp from Eisenhower or Mr. Nixon's enameled American-flag pins. Cuff links, tie clasps and enameled flags came and went but the Gridiron never changed. It *was* the core of Washington. So its members believed and they had convinced a good many others.

The Gridiron Club was eighty-six years old when it assembled at the Statler-Hilton hotel on the evening of March 13, 1971. The stated function of the white-tie dinner was to "roast" the President. For months distinguished journalists sweated over skits, jingles, parodies and dances designed to "take the hide off" the nation's leader, his associates and enemies. In reality the roasting had the burn power of a *Harvard Lampoon* cartoon and that same adolescent quality. Still, it was, the Gridiron's critics conceded, *something* to see staid sixty- and seventy-year-old pundits like Arthur Krock of *The New York Times*, David Lawrence of the *U.S. News & World Report*, Joseph Alsop and even Scotty Reston cavorting on a makeshift stage, sometimes dressed as milkmaids, trying to milk the udder of a long-suffering national cow (played by two other colleagues under a fake cowskin) or portraying French doxies, flipping their skirts, to get a handout from Lyndon Johnson. The pièce de résistance of the evening, of course, was a locker-room address by the President in which he laughed off his critics and gave them as good as he had gotten—an address that was often deliberately sprinkled with barnyard phraseology in keeping with the among-the-boys atmosphere.

In reality the occasion was a turnout for every lobbyist and power broker in the capital. By 1971 not even the Statler-Hilton could accommodate them all. It was an evening for the big defense contractors, the corporate chiefs of the aeronautic, steel, electronic and transport conglomerates, the full admirals and sometimes too full generals, particularly of the Air Force, for the wheeler dealers, the contract boys, the top administrators, the cabinet members, the Warren Burgers, the Henry Kissingers, and senators like Jackson and Tower and Stennis and Humphrey and Russell Long.

Although the club boasted only fifty members there were well over five hundred guests at the dinner and this was what it was all about. There were scores of suites for the private parties before the dinner and after the dinner and there was hardly a publisher in the country who was not proud and pleased to shell out thousands of dollars entertaining the guests he had rounded up through the magic of his correspondent's membership in the Gridiron.

There were not a few in Washington who had felt for years that the institution was a total anachronism. It had been a long, long time, probably not since the days of Herbert Hoover, since the Gridiron had actually taken the hide off a President, and the White House incumbents had learned how to turn the tables to their own advantage. The anomaly represented by the Gridiron was painfully apparent by 1971. Indeed, outside the Statler-Hilton, a hostelry whose total blandness was epitomized by its doubled name, a group of women journalists picketed the dinner because women were excluded from Gridiron membership (some critics of the Gridiron felt the women should have been celebrating not protesting their absence). Nonetheless they were present and a few of the five hundred guests had decided, for that reason, not to attend. The only ones, however, who were known to have stayed away were four politicians—Senators George McGovern and Muskie, both already running for the 1972 presidential nomination, Senator Mike Mansfield of Montana and Mayor Washington of Washington. Nixon Administration figures, led by Vice President Agnew, had no trouble with the picket line. They rode right through it in their long limousines. Senator Kennedy crossed it, too, but he stopped first to chat with the pickets.

There was one notable absentee at the dinner—President Nixon. Mr. Nixon was not an aficionado of the Gridiron although he had attended many of the affairs. He happened to be in Florida and didn't bother to come back for the party. Instead he was represented by Secretary of State Rogers.

It was at this dinner that James Goodale, general counsel of *The New*

York Times, first heard of the big story. He was sitting at *The Times'* table with Max Frankel, Scotty Reston and their guests, Senator Tunney of California and Roger Mudd of CBS. The dinner was over and as they started to walk out to a reception given by Mike Cowles, who was in the process of merging Cowles publications into *The New York Times,* Max Frankel told Goodale about the Sheehan story. He did not, however, tell Goodale what the story was—simply that it was a big story, it involved history, it was based on classified documents and Goodale might have a problem with it. Goodale was extraordinarily busy, fiendishly busy as he recalled it. The Cowles merger was in its final stages. Max had given him only a capsule idea of the story, but even so, he felt he better get some research under way and he asked an assistant at the Columbia Law School to look up the law. Even though he did not know what the story was he thought he could use some briefing in a field in which he was not too familiar.

All Systems Go

By this time all *Times'* systems were go on Neil's story—that is, as far as getting it was concerned. Max Frankel had returned to Washington and been filled in by Neil. Max was a little edgy at not having been brought in on the first round and wasn't going to make a commitment until he saw some of the actual documents but he agreed instantly that the story was worth pursuing and rejected totally the idea that it be relegated to an archival compilation to be issued by New York Times Books. He didn't want to discuss the matter with Rosenthal until he had documents in hand and a few days later Neil produced a sheaf, largely dealing with the Tonkin Gulf affair.* Frankel and Sheehan examined them behind the closed doors of Frankel's office. Frankel had no doubt of the genuineness and importance of the documents and immediately took them to New York where he met with Rosenthal, foreign editor Jimmy Greenfield and assistant managing editor Seymour Topping. All agreed that the material appeared bona fide and that the story was a major one. But there was one problem. At this point Sheehan did not have the Pentagon Papers. He had been offered them by Ellsberg, conditionally. But the condition was publication in toto and even on that there was a lot of nervousness. Ellsberg still had not really given up on his idea of the great Senate hearing, the television cameras, the total attention of Congress and the nation. Newspaper publication, even in *The New York Times,* clearly seemed second best

---

*The fact that these documents dealt with Tonkin Gulf suggests that Sheehan got them from what he called "my secondary source." That is, the Institute for Policy Studies, to whom Ellsberg had given precisely these documents. (Personal interviews, Neil Sheehan, 12/4/74; 6/5/75)

to him. He kept suggesting that the best plan would be Senate hearings *plus* publication in *The Times.* But Ellsberg did take Neil to the place in Boston where he kept the papers (for security reasons he never, or almost never, kept them in the Hilliard Street flat) and he gave permission to Neil to read the papers, familiarize himself with them, to take notes but not to copy or reproduce them. He let Neil keep the key and gave him free access to the flat—after all it would take Neil quite a while to make his way through the many volumes.

"I trust you with the key and documents," Ellsberg recalled telling Sheehan, "and what you do when I am gone I have no control over."

Sheehan didn't remember it quite that way. He recalled Ellsberg saying of the Archive, "If I give it to you then I lose control over it."

It was a touchy situation. Sheehan at one point thought he had persuaded Ellsberg to let him have the documents for *Times* publication but Ellsberg was nervous as a cat. He was afraid that in the end *The Times* wouldn't publish and one more opportunity would go down the drain. And he was continuing to negotiate with political figures. He gave a copy of the documents to the Republican Senator Charles Mathias of Maryland, who, like the others, had seemed enthusiastic and then cooled down. Soon Ellsberg would bring Republican Representative Paul McCloskey of California into the picture and he never entirely gave up on Fulbright. It was a nerve-racking time for both Sheehan and Ellsberg, neither quite trusting the other, Neil never feeling he could give an absolute guarantee of publication to Ellsberg, Ellsberg, the old pro of the options game, insistent that he play the game out to the last card, Sheehan haunted by fear that his great story, his "thermonuclear vial," would get away from him, Ellsberg obsessed with horror that he might not be able to bring off the *coup de théâtre* which he had convinced himself would end the war and agonized lest Nixon suddenly drop an H bomb on Hanoi. The atmosphere was paranoid, almost psychopathic, and in this it faithfully reflected the general mood that had come to grip the country. Sheehan knew, of course, that copies of the documents that Ellsberg had given to the Institute for Policy Studies had circulated into a good many hands; he knew the circle of the knowledgeable was steadily widening; he believed (and the editors of *The Times* soon came to share this conviction) that at any moment some other source might break the story. He was determined not to be frustrated. The documents must be published and must be published in proper form and there was no medium outside of *The New York Times* capable of doing this. After all, as Neil told himself, these documents did not belong to any one person: not Johnson, not McNamara, not Nixon and surely not Kissinger. And not Ellsberg, either. "They belonged," Neil felt, "to the people of America and of Indochina who had paid for them with their blood."

Sheehan's nightmare that the story might get out of hand was more realistic than he knew. During the winter of 1970–71 an informal institution had been sponsored in Boston by Tom Winship, editor of the *Boston Globe* and a staunch foe of the Vietnam war. Winship knew the Cambridge community well and the Cambridge community was a beehive of antiwar sentiment. Once a week, Winship, a *Globe* staff man or two and a coterie of antiwar people met for lunch at a Chinese restaurant called Joyce Chen's, not far from MIT. One regular at the round table was Noam Chomsky, the radical scholar and specialist in linguistics. One day he said, "There's a new guy you've got to meet, a convert and a fascinating character." The man was Ellsberg and in the course of January and February of 1971 Tom Oliphant of the *Globe* saw a lot of him. Again and again in discussing the war Ellsberg referred to the Pentagon Papers. Oliphant hadn't the foggiest as to what the Papers really were but they sounded important and when he got down to Washington he went around to Mort Halperin, then at Common Cause, and to Leslie Gelb and asked them about the Papers.

Halperin was delighted at Oliphant's inquiries and helped him with the story but Gelb was horrified and wanted no part in it. Oliphant got the impression that the Papers must be a kind of magical potion, something out of a story by the Brothers Grimm. If you read them you were instantly turned violently against the war. Out of that came his story. It was published on page one of the *Boston Globe* March 7, 1971, under the headline "Only Three Have Read Secret Indochina Report: All Urge Swift Pullout."

The dispatch was a factual three-column account, quoting Ellsberg at considerable length, giving his background and an outline of what the Pentagon study was about. It said all three men worked on it and now all three were opposed to the war. It quoted Ellsberg as saying that he had come to feel that "I was participating in a criminal conspiracy to wage aggressive war."

Oliphant did not give any details of the Pentagon Papers. He did not possess any. He never thought of asking Ellsberg for the Papers and, in fact, never imagined that Ellsberg had a copy. Nor did Ellsberg offer them.*

Oliphant learned later that his story made a great impression on Ellsberg and firmed his notion that if everyone would budget their time

---

*When the Pentagon Papers broke in *The New York Times* Ellsberg gave the *Globe* a copy of the Kennedy section and apologized to Oliphant, wanting to make certain Oliphant did not feel he had done something behind his back. (Personal interview, Tom Oliphant, 11/3/76)

so they read just an hour of the Papers a week it would change their lives. And, of course, end the war.

Sheehan, somehow, missed the Oliphant story and it was just as well that he did. His nerves, already close to break-point, would have been subjected to even greater stress. And, in the curious pattern which cast an aura over the Papers, the *Globe* story did not stir a whiff of national interest. No wire service picked it up. Neither *The Times* nor its Boston correspondent gave it any attention nor did any other national newspaper. *Time* and *Newsweek* and network television did not see it—or if they saw it they failed to react. Yet a competent editor reading the Oliphant story could easily see submerged behind it the clear outline of the much greater story. In fact, the Oliphant story was almost a blueprint for the kind of discovery mission undertaken by Sheehan. Once again his great story was safe—by default—but how much longer could these Perils of Pauline persist without a fatal slip over the cliff? In retrospect it was hard to resist the conclusion that Sheehan and *The Times* scooped the world not through remarkable initiative but by total failure of the rest of the media. Not to mention the supineness of a number of politicians who had made a reputation as vigorous opponents of the Vietnam war.

Times' Finances

If later on Punch Sulzberger was always to have difficulty in remembering exactly when he first heard of the Pentagon story, what he was told about it and the exact circumstances there was very good reason. The person who told him about the story was Reston, who did not go into details (as Punch recalled he said the Washington bureau had gotten onto a "very interesting story") because he was talking with Punch on the telephone and the fact was that the publisher's mind was preoccupied with something else in that March of 1971. This was the Cowles acquisition, the merger into *The Times* of the great magazine, newspaper and TV/radio complex controlled by Gardner Cowles, publisher of the ailing *Look* magazine, which was specifically excluded from the deal.

The inner business and finances of *The New York Times* from the time of Mr. Ochs until shortly before the Cowles acquisition could well have been described in Winston Churchill's classic phrase about the Kremlin—"a riddle, wrapped in a mystery inside an enigma." The truth was that *The Times*, in 1971, not without some pain, was just coming out of the closet. As long as he lived Mr. Ochs held the only key to the money secrets of *The Times*. To this day not all of the complicated details of his purchase of *The Times* and his operations in the early years are known to his descendants nor can they be entirely recaptured by the closest scrutiny of surviving records.* In measure this was due to the fact that growing up in the shaky financial structure of the post-bellum South, beset by money panics, real estate and other speculation, plagued by chronic shortage of silver and federally backed paper, Mr. Ochs became by necessity a genius in what was in those times the greatest of business arts—the art of kiting or floating checks or what is classically called borrowing from Peter to pay Paul.

When Mr. Ochs put through the deal which gave him control of *The Times* he was by every accounting standard a bankrupt. He owed far more money than he could pay and even the insignificant $75,000 which he personally put up to gain *The Times* (the rest of the money came from *Times'* owners and creditors) was beyond his means. He had to borrow *that* money on top of all his other debts. It had not been easy. He patched together about $25,000 of cash from one resource or another, some of it from relatives. He got Chattanooga banking friends to put $25,000 into his banking account, against security of bonds which he had printed for the *Chattanooga Times*. But he was still $25,000 short. This $25,000 he had expected to get from an old business associate but at the last moment the man did not show up. How he got that last $25,000, which he admitted "caused me some little concern," he promised in a letter, August 13, 1896, to his wife announcing the formal purchase of *The Times*, to tell her when they next met. He labeled this paragraph "For your private ear."†

The detail is significant because of the extraordinarily thin ice on which Ochs skated in his acquisition of *The Times*. He started his tenure with the shaky $75,000 for which he received 75 $1,000 *Times* bonds and 1,125 shares of *Times* stock (fifteen shares of stock were offered to each purchaser of a $1,000 bond as a sweetener). There was a total issue of 10,000 shares of stock, 2,000 of which went to the old owners, and 3,876 of these new shares were held in escrow to be turned over to Mr. Ochs when, as and if he had put the paper on a profit-making basis. This would give him a total of 5,001 shares, controlling interest in the enterprise.

Mr. Ochs did not leave himself room to turn around. He had hoped to have $200,000 in working capital through sale of *Times'* bonds but

---

*Mr. Ochs in a fit of depression in the early 1920s destroyed many of his early records. (Personal interview, Iphigene Ochs Sulzberger, 11/6/69)

†The last $25,000 probably came from Henry B. Hyde, founder and head of the Equitable Life Assurance Society. The Equitable had an investment of $85,000 in the pre-Ochs *Times*. On August 10, three days before the court sale of *The Times* to Mr. Ochs on August 13, 1896—to be effective August 18—Hyde agreed to put up another $26,000, taking $27,000 in bonds of the *Chattanooga Times* as security. (*Times'* archives, Ochs papers, Ochs memorandum of letter to Hartley 1/12/99; Ochs papers, sheet X100)

in the shakedown about half this money had to be used to cover unexpected debts. Mr. Ochs found himself with two critical problems: the transformation of *The Times* into a viable newspaper, economically and editorially, and keeping his financial boat afloat long enough to accomplish this task. The *Chattanooga Times* continued to produce a reliable income but Mr. Ochs' Chattanooga land speculations were bleeding him to death. And now he had the problem of keeping his costly New York property afloat until he could put it on a paying basis.

Mr. Ochs had far too much experience not to see almost immediately that he had to have more money. Fully 50 percent of his correspondence was devoted to writing excuses to his creditors, to begging a bit more time from one, to putting off another, to soliciting turnover after turnover of notes and bills, to placating this man and smothering the next in cheery assurances. *The Times* flourished from the start, just as the *Chattanooga Times* had and was continuing to do. But if Mr. Ochs had to spend his working day keeping the leaky financial boat afloat the whole enterprise might sink.

The businessmen who were associated with Ochs at *The Times* could see this too and by spring of 1897 they were casting about for ways to raise more capital. Their initial goal was a loan of $100,000 with a 6 percent interest rate and a two-year term so that Ochs wouldn't be constantly facing imminent maturity dates. An early proposal by Spencer Trask, one of the principal owners, was that Mr. Ochs' escrow stock of 3,876 shares plus the remainder of treasury shares and shares reserved for subscription, a total of 5,424 shares in all (well over a majority), and $60,000 in *Times* bonds be pledged as security for a $100,000 loan.

As an interim solution, funds, probably $100,000, were advanced to Ochs by stockholders of the company, including Henry B. Hyde, the head of Equitable, and Marcellus Hartley, founder of Equitable. Each man was a stockholder. Each was close to Ochs, both men were attracted to him and he to them, Hartley in particular.*

But the sum was insufficient and the arrangement temporary. Within the year the board of directors had authorized Mr. Ochs to borrow $150,000 at 6 percent, pledging as security any stock held in the treasury of the company. That stock, of course, was the control stock in the company, the shares held in escrow for Mr. Ochs and the other shares specified by Trask a year earlier.

---

*From the very beginning Mr. Hyde gave Mr. Ochs his warmest support. Mr. Ochs wrote his wife September 9, 1896, that Mr. Hyde had telephoned "telling me he was very pleased with the improvements in *The Times* and that he was prepared to do everything in his power to help make *The New-York Times* the London *Times* of America. I do not see how I can fall down with such men behind me. The problem is simply to get started; the future is certain." (*Times'* archives, 1896)

By the winter of 1898–99 the problem was still acute. The paper had begun to take off. Mr. Ochs had cut the price from three cents to a penny, circulation had quadrupled and it was obvious that his wild gamble was going to succeed. But still there was the stubborn and dangerous shortage of working capital, the ramshackle structure of notes, loans and borrowings of every conceivable description. Financially, *The Times* resembled the famous one-hoss shay. Any severe bump might cause the bottom to fall out.

By this time Henry B. Hyde had died, to be replaced by his high-flying but enormously attractive son, James Hazen Hyde, and by this time Ochs and Hartley had formed what Ochs later described as "an almost romantic" relation.

Mr. Ochs had not yet come into physical possession of the control stock in his paper but there was little doubt in anyone's mind that he was on the way to success. His purchase agreement provided that the stock would pass to him if in the three-year period July 1, 1897–July 1, 1900 the company earned and paid its fixed charges, met all operating expenses and had no interest outstanding on its bonds as of July 1, 1900.

The Equitable Loan

In the winter of 1899, Mr. Ochs went to work on his fiscal problem. There exist in his archives three draft proposals dated January 12, January 24 and February 17, 1899, the first addressed to his warm and "romantic" friend Marcellus Hartley, the second unaddressed but destined for Equitable and the third addressed to James W. Alexander, then vice president of Equitable but soon to become president.

The proposals varied a bit on details. The first was an application for a loan from Hartley, personally, to *The Times* for $250,000, secured by the control stock of 5,001 shares (due but not yet in the hands of Ochs) plus his personal endorsement. He offered Hartley an option to buy half the control interest and to share control jointly with himself. Hartley would have the right to name the treasurer and cashier of *The Times.* Either partner would have the right and option to buy out the other.

The second proposal, drafted twelve days later (presumably Hartley rejected the personal arrangement), was designed for Equitable. It called for a $250,000 loan on the note of The Times Company at 5 percent interest, personally endorsed by Ochs, secured by the control stock in the company. Ochs offered to insure his life for $100,000 in favor of Equitable or any other company they desired.*

*Mr. Ochs took out four life insurance policies with Equitable in 1899–1901. Their total face amount was $212,000. (*Times'* archives, Ochs papers, 1899–01)

The third proposal suggested a loan of $150,000 for five years at 5 percent, secured by the control stock in the company. Mr. Ochs offered to make himself personally responsible for the loan. He said the loan had been authorized by the board of directors and that "the stock making up the controlling interest has been loaned to the Company for this purpose by the largest stockholders." It was addressed to Mr. Alexander of Equitable.

It was summer before the terms of the loan were worked out fully but by July 13, 1899, Ochs wrote Alexander expressing his satisfaction at the arrangement and agreeing that Equitable should have the right at any time to send its auditors into *The Times* to examine his books. Alexander's letter outlining the terms of the loan does not seem to have been preserved but it was, in effect, a pleasant, convenient and sensible business arrangement between men who held each other in high esteem and who had a mutual interest in furthering the cause of *The New York Times.* As Ochs pointed out, Equitable had a substantial interest in *The New York Times* because of its investment, he had every hope to bring that investment home safe for them and by advancing him working capital all interests should be well served.

There can be no doubt that a sigh of relief was uttered on all sides once the Equitable loan had been confirmed. Certainly it took a monkey off the back of Mr. Ochs. Only a year later he got ownership of the escrow stock. He submitted his claim for it in July 1900 and after some bickering and a careful study of Ochs' profit and loss statement Mr. Ochs' claim was upheld and in August the stock became his.

Ochs wrote his wife in triumph, "The deed is done. The contract I made in 1896 is ended. My title is perfect. Now I am monarch of all I survey and none my right to dispute."

It was a glorious moment for the venturesome young man from Tennessee. There was only one fly in the ointment. The control stock of 5,001 shares, the 3,876 that had been in escrow and Ochs' own 1,125 shares were all in hock to the Equitable Life Assurance Society. Certainly they were his. Certainly Equitable had no intention of voting the shares against him. Certainly Mr. Ochs was not only boss—he was *The New York Times.* Certainly they were all friends together. But a hostile critic might well have challenged Mr. Ochs' view that he was "monarch of all I survey."

And, in fact, this was the exact conclusion Mr. Ochs himself was compelled to arrive at five years later.

By this time Mr. Ochs' remarkable friend Marcellus Hartley was dead and a specter haunted the publisher of *The New York Times,* the specter of public scandal.

The greatest American financial scandal of the turn of the century had erupted and at its center was the Equitable Life Assurance Company, which held the control stock of *The New York Times.*

James Hazen Hyde, who had inherited control of Equitable at the age of twenty-three, had once declared (not too inaccurately), "I have wealth, beauty, intellect: what more could I wish?" In January 1905 he gave the greatest party of the era at Sherry's new Fifth Avenue restaurant, five hundred plates, Madame Gabrielle Réjane, the star of Sardou's *Madame Sans-Gêne,* as honored guest, the ballroom decorated to resemble the gardens of Versailles, Chauncey M. Depew in attendance from Washington, at a cost estimated by Pulitzer's *World* at $100,000.

Immediately a violent struggle emerged between Hyde and Alexander for control of Equitable, which brought in most of the notable financiers of the time, Henry Clay Frick, E. H. Harriman, J. P. Morgan, Cornelius Bliss, Thomas Fortune Ryan. The *World* denounced Equitable and the giant insurance companies as "great agencies in high finance and trust exploitation." It declared there existed an alliance of "insurance executives and crooked politicians." Day by day the scandal grew. Day by day Equitable was the lead story in Mr. Ochs' *Times* with two, three, four and even five columns devoted to the charges and countercharges. Again and again *The Times* sought to stress the need for compromise, for understanding among men of good will (Mr. Ochs' original backers were ranged on all sides of the row) but the scandal roared ahead. On April 4, 1905, *The Times* sadly noted that "the root of the Equitable trouble is not far to seek. It is as old as human society and pretty much coexisted with it. We mean the love of money."

It became more and more apparent that the Equitable affair could not be contained, that it was headed for government investigation, and, indeed, by June, Charles Evans Hughes, later to become Chief Justice of the U.S. Supreme Court, was charged with what proved to be a watermark inquiry into the wild, high and fancy financial uses to which the insurance titans put the extraordinary sums which ten-cents-a-week policies for the working man generated.

To say that Mr. Ochs watched the evolution of the Equitable scandal with apprehension is an understatement. What would happen when, as inevitably it would, Charles Evans Hughes' auditors uncovered that small sheaf of papers dealing with Equitable's advances to *The Times* and found the control stock of what Mr. Ochs had already made the country's most solid, respectable, distinguished newspaper, founded like a rock on the principles of independence and immunity to any interest, a newspaper that was dedicated "without fear or favor" to publishing all the news that was fit to print? What would happen then? What would happen when the Hearsts, the Pulitzers and the rest uncovered this dirty little secret? What help then if, in fact, Mr. Ochs had never been beholden to Equitable, that his newspaper had covered the charges and allegations with meticulous care?* Enough trouble had already been caused *The Times* by false rumors of "secret" ownership, "hidden interests." What would happen now if the undeniable control stock of *The Times* was found in the possession of one of the most hideously venal corporate bodies which the high, wide and handsome entrepreneurs of the late nineteenth century had managed to concoct?

What indeed! Mr. Ochs acted quickly and decisively. He did not have the cash to take up the Equitable loan. He had gone much more into debt with mortgages (also held by Equitable) to build his new building on Times Square. He wasn't worried about the mortgages. Mortgage money was mortgage money. But control stock was a different kind of currency.

He went to Marcellus Hartley Dodge, an appealing young man, nephew of his great friend Marcellus Hartley, and in a few direct words spelled out his dilemma. He must take up the Equitable loan and he needed the money to do it. Would Dodge lend him $300,000? He would put up with Dodge the same control stock in *The Times* which then rested in Equitable's vault. Dodge agreed overnight and the next morning the deed was done. The whole matter was kept secret between the two men. Dodge was owner and controlling stockholder in what became the Remington Arms Company. Out of the Equitable vault leaped *The Times* control stock into the safe-deposit box of Dodge of Remington Arms, there to rest without a hint of its presence for years to come. The shares were still there in 1915 when *The Times* came under investigation in the U.S. Senate for its pro-British policy amid charges that it was controlled by "British gold."

A *Times* editorial on March 17, 1915, proclaimed:

---

*Close examination of *The New York Times* reporting on the Equitable scandal does not show favoritism but *Times* editorials tended to be sympathetic to Equitable's problems. However, there still rests in Mr. Ochs' personal archive an embarrassing earlier exchange of letters between himself and James H. Hyde. Hyde had asked if *The Times* couldn't be more helpful toward Equitable. Ochs responded Sept. 26, 1902, "My dear Mr. Hyde: I have your letter about giving a 'boost' to the Equitable Trust Co. As soon as possible I will respond to the call." To which Hyde replied Sept. 29, 1902, "Dear Mr. Ochs: Your note of 26th inst is received and I thank you for your promise to 'boost' the Equitable Trust Company. We are making strenuous efforts to push the company forward and I shall be grateful for whatever assistance you may be able to give." However, no "boost" for the Equitable Trust did appear. (*Times'* archives, 1902) On Sept. 27, 1902, the day after Mr. Ochs' letter to Mr. Hyde, *The Times* devoted the better part of a column to a speech by James W. Alexander, president of Equitable Life Assurance, opposing a proposed tax on life insurance. The coverage of the Alexander speech was consistent with the general pattern of *Times* coverage of insurance, banking and tax matters of that period. (*Times'* files, Sept.–Oct. 1902)

> Mr. Ochs . . . is in possession, free and unencumbered, of the controlling and majority interest of the stock of The New York Times Company and has no associate in that possession . . . nor has he ever been beholden or accountable in any form, shape or fashion, financial, or otherwise for the conduct of The New York Times, except to his own conscience and to the respect and confidence of the newspaper reading public, and particularly to the readers of The New York Times. . . .

There can be no doubt that Mr. Ochs believed every word of this statement. But in fact the stock still lay pledged to the Dodge loan. Just a year later Mr. Ochs paid it off. Dodge had become hard-pressed. The Remington Arms Company, undercapitalized, overextended by huge war orders, had gotten into a tight fix. The moment Mr. Ochs heard of Dodge's situation he sent the money back. In fact, he could have done so at many times in the intervening years. Money was no longer in short supply with *The New York Times* and its publisher. But the relationship with Dodge was a warm and sentimental one and when all was said and done Mr. Ochs had operated on borrowed money since the very beginning. He felt comfortable that way. In 1930, Mr. Ochs attended the funeral for Dodge's son, who had been killed in an automobile accident in France—the youngster had wanted to take up flying but his mother, fearful of aviation, persuaded him, instead, to go on a motor tour of France. The tragedy cost her her mind. Later Dodge wrote Ochs, "Our friendship has been an altogether lovely one. You knew when you entrusted me with what you did, your confidence would not be betrayed and it wasn't. You felt safe with me and I with you."

Nothing more typified *The Times* in the Ochs era than these private, confidential and long-enduring arrangements among friends. Never during Mr. Ochs' lifetime did anyone other than three or four trusted secretaries or bookkeepers know that in *de jure* as opposed to *de facto* terms Mr. Ochs did not throughout the first two decades of his direction of *The New York Times* hold, as he insisted, total control of the paper, free and clear. In those twenty years rumor after rumor had swept business circles and the public about the ownership of *The Times.* But they were the wrong rumors. No one stumbled on the facts, and even after Mr. Ochs' death they came to light only piecemeal. It is possible, even likely, that as the years passed it never occurred to Mr. Ochs after he had turned the paper around that it was not wholly his. But, in fact, it was not until 1916 that he came into possession of the control stock in his great enterprise. It had never mattered since these were men of exceptional trust in one another and this despite the fantastically disreputable procedures at Equitable. But this kind of financing, this kind of back-pocket, hand-clasp, personal-dealing had, to be certain, disappeared by 1971.

It had been a long, long time in going. And, in effect, it was not until the Cowles deal, which preoccupied Punch Sulzberger and the top brass of *The Times* in March 1971, that the paper as a business entity and a great corporation actually joined the twentieth century. This was the reason that within the executive echelon on *The Times* the month of March passed with only random attention to the Pentagon Papers story.

II

A Corporate Coming-Out Party

*T*UESDAY, APRIL 20, 1971, was so lovely a spring day, thermometer in the seventies, blue sky, little wind, that when the annual meeting of *The New York Times'* stockholders broke up at 1:12 P.M. at Town Hall, *Times* executives and editors sauntered down the short Forty-third Street block, reluctant to go back indoors for lunch.

There was a holiday mood in the air and as Max Frankel walked back with James Goodale he said, "We're having a meeting after lunch in Scotty's office on our big story. I'd like to have you come."

Goodale, who understood what the big story was without Max having to explain, said he would certainly be there.

In 1971 public stockholders' meetings were still an innovation at *The Times* but this session had, in a way, served as a kind of corporate coming-out party. *Times* editors were self-conscious about their presence at a meeting which, like so many corporate sessions, was dominated by what the *Times'* financial page called "corporate gadflies," persons like John Gilbert and Wilma Soss, offering Punch Sulzberger sharp-edged advice on how to run *The Times.* There were moments of confusion when Mrs. Soss asked Punch whether *The Times* was getting into the cassette business and Punch thought she asked if *The Times* was getting into the sex business. After the confusion was cleared up Mrs. Soss added a few words as to how *The Times* should cover news relating to sex (with propriety and caution).

This was the first stockholders' meeting since the Cowles deal had been approved at a special session March 24, and in this sense, too, the meeting had particular significance for it marked the full emergence of *The Times* from the world of Mr. Ochs' late-Victorian financial arrangements into mid-twentieth-century corporate practice with the implications this brought.

At the time of Mr. Ochs' death in 1935 *The New York Times* was a private fief. Comparatively few shares of stock were in the hands of outsiders; capitalization consisted of one million shares of common stock and four issues of preferred stock totaling $20 million. A little of this was held by heirs of Mr. Ochs' associates but most of it constituted Mr. Ochs' own estate and went directly into the Ochs Trust of which there were three trustees, Mr. Ochs' daughter, Iphigene, her husband, Arthur Sulzberger, and her first cousin Julius Adler.

Alfred A. Cook, partner of Leopold Wallach, Mr. Ochs' original New York lawyer, had devised the trust for minimizing estate and inheritance taxes. Iphigene Sulzberger was the beneficiary of the trust in her lifetime and the holdings automatically passed free of tax through to the next generation, the children of Iphigene and Arthur Sulzberger.

It was a clever plan but it had a dangerous drawback. Mr. Ochs had not accumulated cash or securities that could be used to pay the inheritance taxes although *The Times'* newspaper itself held an extraordinarily large cash surplus piled up by Mr. Ochs out of caution bred by his early years of hand-to-mouth financing.

The situation alarmed Arthur Sulzberger. He was fearful that upon Mr. Ochs' death the trust might be compelled to sell large quantities of securities or borrow from the banks, in either way losing or jeopardizing independence and control of *The Times.* He proposed to Mr. Cook that in the event of Mr. Ochs' death the trust sell its holdings of preferred stock back to The New York Times Company, which had ample cash to make the purchase. The cash could be used by the trust to pay the death duties.

Mr. Cook approved the plan and when Mr. Ochs died it was put into effect. *The Times* offered to purchase from stockholders their holdings of the four classes of preferred.

The Ochs Trust tendered $6 million worth of preferred stock, which at 8 percent had been earning $480,000. This was used to pay the duties and attorneys' fees.

As Arthur Sulzberger was later to say, "We were unwilling to have any bank, or group of banks, hold the control of *The New York Times* and we were prepared to make any sacrifice to avoid that."

FDR

There the matter might have rested, a private, economical and wise mechanism for securing the continuity and integrity of *The Times,* had it not been for Franklin D. Roosevelt.

One of the strings to Mr. Roosevelt's bow, almost now forgotten, was his effort by means of taxation to prevent or impede the piling up of huge fortunes. Another, after his reelection in 1936, was his ill-fated Supreme Court packing plan. The court plan came under severe attack by *The Times,* led by its Washington correspondent, Mr. Arthur Krock, who up to that moment had been something of an intimate of Mr. Roosevelt's.

Mr. Sulzberger chanced to see Mr. Roosevelt in 1936 not long after Mr. Ochs' death at a time when the President's Corporate Surplus tax bill had just been introduced into Congress. Mr. Sulzberger pointed out that such a tax would have prevented Mr. Ochs from building *The Times* since he had done it exclusively by plowing back into the business whatever money he made. He told the President this policy of Mr. Ochs' was going to provide the money to pay the taxes on Mr. Ochs' estate. The President offered no criticism.

A year later, with the Supreme Court fight on, the President invited Mr. Sulzberger to Hyde Park to lunch. He sat between the President's mother and the President's step-sister-in-law, Mrs. Roosevelt Roosevelt. The first question that the President's mother put to him was what he did on *The New York Times*. The first word from Mrs. Roosevelt Roosevelt was, "You can't believe anything you read in the papers."

After lunch Mr. Roosevelt took Sulzberger to his study where the conversation soon got around again to the Corporate Surplus tax. Mr. Sulzberger told the President that in his thirty-five years of ownership Mr. Ochs had put 74 percent of *The Times*' earnings back into the business. The President said he thought this was an "appropriate use" of corporate surplus. "The President talked like a capitalist and a Democrat," Mr. Sulzberger observed. The only difference between talking to him and the owner of some other great estate along the Hudson, he thought, was that Mr. Roosevelt did not criticize the Administration.

Mr. Sulzberger was quick to learn that FDR had been less than candid. Soon after the Hyde Park lunch Senator Pat Harrison of Mississippi asked Turner Catledge in Washington what FDR had against *The Times*. Harrison repeated Sulzberger's conversation with the President and said Mr. Roosevelt described it as "a dirty Jewish trick." "When Iphigene dies," said Mr. Roosevelt, "we [the government] will get it [meaning *The Times*]." Within a short period three more individuals, Thomas Lamont, Bernard Baruch and Richard Patterson, came to Mr. Sulzberger, each after a private talk with the President. Each said Mr. Roosevelt had it in for *The Times* and "would burn us at the stake if he could." One quoted the President as saying that Ochs had violated the law and that Sulzberger had confused his corporate and his trust personalities.

Word, inevitably, got back to Mr. Roosevelt and once again Mr. Sulzberger lunched with Mr. Roosevelt, this time in the White House, December 28, 1939, where the two men had a long rambling conversation, the kind that diplomats call a *tour de horizon*. It focused on the war and Europe, Russia's attack on Finland, Mr. Sulzberger's fear that the United States might get into the war "by the back door," by which he meant an attack by Japan.

Finally, Mr. Roosevelt got to the real subject of the meeting—his remarks about the Ochs settlement. He said that he had expressed himself as thinking that the Ochs surplus was too large but hastened to add that this was no reflection on *Times* management past or present, that it was all legal and proper and "I would have done the same thing myself."

To which, of course, Mr. Sulzberger replied that he was delighted. The question of the "dirty Jewish trick" did not arise but Mr. Sulzberger told the President that "now that we are confessing, let me confess one." He recalled that a rumor was going about that he was going to lead a delegation to the President to ask him not to appoint Felix Frankfurter to the Supreme Court because "it was dangerous for Jews to hold positions of importance during these days when anti-Semitism is rife." He assured FDR he had no such intention but that he did oppose the idea of a "Jewish" seat on the Court, or a "Catholic" seat. Mr. Sulzberger, in writing a minute of his talk, noted that soon thereafter Attorney General Frank Murphy was named to replace Pierce Butler, a Catholic, and, of course, Frankfurter did fill the Brandeis seat.

The memory of FDR's "dirty Jew" remark never left Mr. Sulzberger's mind. He never, of course, mentioned it publicly but after Mr. Roosevelt's death he did solicit Messrs. Lamont, Baruch and Patterson to make certain that their memories coincided with his. Baruch gave him an equivocal response, Lamont did not apparently reply but Patterson said the facts were as Mr. Sulzberger recalled. He carefully recorded all of this and preserved it in his papers, feeling that it was important evidence of one of the less attractive sides of Mr. Roosevelt's nature.*

Modernization

Mr. Cook, of course, had no way of knowing his "passing through" mechanism would succeed so brilliantly, in part due to the long life of Iphigene Sulzberger.

---

*There seems no question as to the accuracy of the remarks by Mr. Roosevelt. Senator Harrison was chairman of the Senate Finance Committee and extremely close to Roosevelt. He was on most intimate terms with his fellow Mississippian, Turner Catledge who more than forty years later vividly recalled being called in by Harrison and questioned closely about the "trouble" between FDR and *The Times*. Catledge did not know of the FDR–Sulzberger exchange. Harrison then told him the story as here recorded, expressing amazement at Roosevelt's anger and pettiness. Sulzberger, Catledge recalled, at first did not credit Roosevelt's remarks but when they were repeated to him by men like Lamont, Baruch and Patterson (a close personal friend of Sulzberger's) to whom FDR had repeated them, Sulzberger accepted them as being true. At the close of one of the discussions between FDR and Sulzberger, Roosevelt said: "All right, Arthur, you go on controlling the editorial page of *The Times* but I'll control your front page" (that is, by making the headlines). (Turner Catledge, personal interview, 11/9/79; Sulzberger, personal papers, *Times'* archives)

Only with her death was the Trust to end, then to be replaced with a new voting trust in which the four Ochs children, Punch, and his sisters Marian Dryfoos Heiskell, Ruth Golden Holmberg and Judith Cohen Levinson had co-equal interests. This trust would run for ten years after which the stock was to go to the four children. Each child had agreed, following the ten-year period, to transfer the stock into a common trust from which each could withdraw the shares any time he or she wished. Under this arrangement, it appeared entirely likely that ten years following Iphigene's death changes in family control would come about.

In 1976 these arrangements were revised and the four children and their children—Iphigene's grandchildren—entered into a new agreement. This provided for a trust for each of the four to last for each of their lifetimes unless terminated by a vote of three of The Four.

Following their deaths, the stock would go into successor trusts for the benefit of their children, The Thirteen. Again each of the 13 trusts could be terminated by three-fourths vote of The Thirteen.

The new arrangements could last as long as 21 years from the date of the death of the last of Iphigene's grandchildren—a date far into the twenty-first century.

In the late 1950s Arthur Sulzberger very shyly, one-step forward, one-step backward, unburdened himself of his concerns over the future of *The Times* to a close friend, George Woods. Woods was a charmer. So was his California-born wife, Louie. The Woods and the Sulzbergers first met at Hobe Sound. The Sulzbergers had started going there because it was run, essentially, by Mrs. Permelia Reed, daughter of Sam Pryor, a friend and business associate of Marcellus Hartley Dodge or "Marcey" as Iphigene called him, the man who had kept Mr. Ochs' control stock in his Remington safe. Some of their Jewish friends had raised an eyebrow at the Sulzberger's going to Hobe Sound but they themselves had not noticed any anti-Semitism.* The Woods didn't care for Hobe Sound and didn't visit it again.

The Sulzbergers and the Woods quickly became close friends. George, more liberal than Louie, was particularly fond of Iphigene Sulzberger. Louie hit it off with Arthur, more conservative than Iphigene. The quartet began to travel the world together—trips to India, with which George Woods had become fascinated and for which

---

*Later the Sulzbergers gave up Hobe Sound. At the time of the Korean war they invited Punch and his wife to come and stay but discovered that Hobe did indeed have rules against Jews which Mrs. Reed had deliberately waived for them. Years later Iphigene remembered with some asperity Averell Harriman telling her that he was shocked by all this and would have pulled out himself except that his friends enjoyed visiting him there so much. "So why did he mention it?" she asked. (Personal interview, Iphigene Ochs Sulzberger, 10/13/72)

Arthur Sulzberger didn't care much, vacations in Jamaica and other spots in the West Indies, long weekends at Hillandale, the Sulzberger estate in Stamford.

In addition to charm George Woods possessed a keen professional mind and was a skilled moneyman, head of First Boston Corporation and later of the World Bank, holding that job until he gave way to Robert McNamara in 1968.

The question on Arthur Sulzberger's mind in the fifties was what happened after the Ochs Trust expired. He was a man who had strong and not necessarily conventional ideas about money. He had never liked tax-savings devices, particularly the complicated inventions of accountants and lawyers to save the money of the wealthy. He had refused to permit General Greenbaum to set up a plan to donate his personal papers to a library and take a tax deduction. He thought such schemes cheap and unpatriotic. For many years he had inveighed against Mr. Cook's settlement of the Ochs estate and the Ochs Trust but by the time of his conversations with George Woods he had recognized the wisdom of Mr. Cook's work. However, he had never permitted himself (or the Ochs Trust) to invest in any outside business, contending that such investments might lead to a conflict of interest. He kept his personal funds in U.S. Treasury obligations and he insisted on the same rule for the Ochs Trust. He refused even to put the money into short-term government paper. George Woods argued, insisting that "money is worth its hire," but he couldn't budge Arthur Sulzberger. All of *The Times'* financing was in the hands of Morgan Guaranty.

There was another serious problem—the question of the *Chattanooga Times.* The Chattanooga paper was run by Ruth, the second Sulzberger daughter, and her then husband, Ben Golden. Mr. Ochs' founding creation was locked in to-the-death competition with the rival *Chattanooga Free Press* in a city which could support only one modern newspaper. The *Chattanooga Times* was 97 percent owned by the Ochs Trust. It took a million-dollar loss one year, another million the next year and so on. The Trust simply borrowed at the banks to meet Chattanooga's needs and the loans were up to $7 or $8 million.

In a sense the Trust was like a big umbrella that sheltered the whole family. At one time it owned the houses the Sulzbergers lived in, the cars they drove. *Times* common stock had paid no dividend since 1930 and under the intricate provisions of the Ochs Trust common dividends were, in effect, a charge against the Trust. It was from holdings of the preferred 8 percent stock that family income was largely derived, plus *Times'* salaries and coupons from U.S. Treasury bonds. Needs over and beyond that were likely to be met by the Trust.

Times' earnings were plowed back into the paper, and Godfrey

Nelson, *Times'* corporate secretary and an expert on tax law (he wrote a column for *The Times'* business pages), was extraordinarily skillful in tucking money away in a manner that was free from taxation.

The Times had a policy of buying up at low prices any stock which became available from minority holders. Some minority holders were beginning to get restive at the lack of information on the business, the low prices, the lack of dividends.

The situation was untidy, unhealthy by modern fiscal tests and if sudden or coincidental events were to bring the Trust to an end there would be major problems. In fact, the tax burden might be so heavy as to require forced sale of substantial *Times* stock and loss of control.

It was this situation to which Arthur Sulzberger tentatively directed the attention of George Woods. Woods conferred with General Edward S. Greenbaum, the oldest and best friend of the Sulzbergers and the man who served as their personal legal counsel, and had no difficulty in diagnosing *The Times'* problem. What was needed, Woods told Sulzberger, was to create a market for *Times* stock and to begin to move it into the hands of the public. This meant making stock available and it meant that *The Times* must issue public reports and conduct itself like a modern corporation.

Arthur Sulzberger didn't like that advice. *The Times'* affairs had never been public property. Mr. Ochs never made public reports and his private reports were so minimal that often his closest associates didn't know the status of the business. It was a family company and that was that.

Arthur Sulzberger had another concern. *The Times* had almost lost Scotty Reston in 1951 to the *Washington Post.* Two or three other able men had been lost. Sulzberger wanted to be in a position to offer key executives stock in the company, to enhance their financial rewards and tie them more closely to *The Times.* This wasn't possible under the archaic *Times'* makeup. Woods did what he had done a dozen times with privately held corporations. He brought in skilled people from First Boston Corporation, Sulzberger began to put some stock into the hands of his executives and First Boston began to make a market in it as an unlisted stock. Woods joined the board of directors of *The Times.*

Woods estimated it would take at least five years to create a public market for *Times* stock and while this was in progress he left *The Times'* board to head the World Bank. However, the fiscal modernization continued. In 1968 the Ochs Trust sold $34 million worth of *Times* A stock at $53 a share close to the top of the market. This money enabled the Trust to repay bank loans incurred by the needs of the *Chattanooga Times,* provided reserves against future Chattanooga needs and a cushion for eventualities which might arise before termination of the Ochs Trust. The proceeds were invested, as George Woods recommended, in securities other than government bonds.

In 1957, at Woods' insistence, Sulzberger had agreed to change the stock basis of *The Times.* Stock was divided into two classes, A and B, nine shares of A for every share of B. Only B had voting rights.

However, when it came time for the next move on the Woods program—public listing of stock—the New York Stock Exchange refused to list the A stock because it had no voting rights. To obtain American Stock Exchange listing a compromise was adopted—A stockholders elect three directors, B stockholders elect six. The B stock, of course, was almost entirely in the hands of the Ochs Trust and therefore continued to control the board of directors.*

Modernization went forward inexorably. More and more detailed financial statements were issued. *The Times* adopted the glossy-paper, four-color annual report formula of its fellow corporations. More stock was gotten into public hands when the Adler Trust, created by General Julius Adler, Iphigene's cousin and business manager of *The Times* until his death in 1955, sold 301,000 shares in 1971, not long before the Cowles transaction. Then, in the Cowles acquisition, 2,600,000 shares of A stock were issued, creating for the first time a substantial minority outside interest in *The Times.* The deal gave Cowles roughly 25 percent of the outstanding A stock. The Ochs Trust held 3,860,900 shares of A stock. The Cowles acquisition reduced the trust ownership from a shade under 50 percent to about 37 percent.

These were the far-ranging transactions so much in the minds of Punch Sulzberger and his associates as March of 1971 drew into April. No longer was *The Times* a private enterprise, run by its owner, as Mr. Ochs had described himself, wielding "almost autocratic power." Now it was a great corporation, publicly responsible, its financial transactions monitored like those of all Fortune 500 corporations by the Securities and Exchange Commission and other government regulatory agencies, paying a regular dividend (and this obligation had come to weigh more and more on Punch) to stockholders, who were quick to complain over corporate policies that they did not think favored the bottom line.

From the moment Mr. Ochs took over the paper a remarkable number of people had felt they had an ex-officio right to make plain their opinions about its deeds and misdeeds. Now each year more owners of *Times* stock felt they had acquired the privilege of participating in *The Times'* editorial councils. This was something new and *The Times* had by no means gotten used to its uncomfortable implications.

The great virtue of the Cowles acquisition, the architect of which

---

*The arrangement ultimately provided that "A" shareholders elected 30 percent of the directors, regardless of the size of the board.

was Ivan Veit, the intelligent and business-wise vice president who had emerged as Punch's closest counselor with the resignation of the previous favorite, Andrew Fisher, was that it gave *The Times* a major stake in other communication enterprises—magazines, TV, radio stations and the like.* Many of these enterprises (except for a string of medical publications which eventually was sold off) were largely lossproof. They churned in revenues that rose year by year like an upward-sloping plateau. They gave The New York Times Corporation a solid core of increasing earnings and, perhaps most important of all, gave the paper immunity from the kind of crushing fiscal losses imposed by the 114-day New York newspaper strike of 1962–63 which cost the paper fearsome sums and contributed to the collapse and death of the then publisher, Orvil Dryfoos. Never again would the enterprise be so nakedly exposed. If it had to close down—as it did in the protracted newspaper strike of 1978—the revenues of operating subsidiaries poured steadily in. These did not make up for the enormous cash flow of *The New York Times* newspaper but they did much more than merely keep the ship afloat.

Not that the Cowles transaction was without its critics. A few months later *New York* magazine, in one of a sequence of carping articles on *The Times,* which then editor Clay Felker thought (correctly) were sure-fire circulation builders, found nothing but fault with the Cowles acquisition, with Punch Sulzberger's management, with the whole *Times'* mystique, which it insisted was still firmly lodged in Mr. Ochs' nineteenth-century practices and characterized by "the torpidity typical of family-run firms." The writer, Chris Welles, suggested that unless *The Times* changed its ways it might find itself snatched up by "new entrepreneurs like Marty Ackerman who grabbed up the Curtis Publishing Co., and Saul Steinberg who tried to snatch the Chemical Bank," an analogy which subsequent events demonstrated could hardly have been more badly chosen.

The last piece of business transacted at *The Times'* annual meeting in 1971 was to introduce to the stockholders a new corporate symbol. During Mr. Ochs' years, and through most of his son-in-law's stewardship, *The Times* had managed to exist without a symbol. It was, in effect, its own symbol. This had remained unchanged until 1958 when Arthur Hays Sulzberger fell in love with an eagle, a magnificent carved wooden eagle which he found in a London antique shop, promptly purchased and brought back to New York. So enamored was he of his

---

*Ben Handleman, later a *Times* senior vice president, saw the Cowles annual report on *The Times'* financial page and brought it to Veit's attention. (Personal interview, Veit, 1/7/75)

eagle that he had Joe Schultz of *The Times'* art department incorporate it in a symbol for *The New York Times,* which he placed on the editorial page. It was also used as *The Times'* corporate seal and on a medal given to fifty-year employees. The Sulzberger eagle was not universally admired. Now after a life of only thirteen years the eagle went into the discard. It was replaced by a device which faithfully reflected the corporate faddism of the early 1970s—the letters NYT in sans-serif type set against three slim boxes shown in relief, looking a little like three coffins cheek-by-jowl. It was hardly a thing of beauty but it resembled the symbols adopted by dozens of other corporations and in the words of its designer was supposed to cause people "to associate The New York Times Company with more than the publication of a newspaper." In other words, it was part of the new Wall Street gimickry which so attracted some *Times* executives.

12

Neil Presents His Story

A DOZEN *TIMES* editors and executives gathered a little before 3 P.M. on April 20, 1971, in the somewhat self-consciously cluttered New York office of Scotty Reston, dominated by a fine rolltop desk, suitably teetering heaps of papers, magazines and books, an old-fashioned green-shaded lamp and enough couches and chairs to accommodate most of the group. Reston presided, leaning back in his swivel chair, window behind him, cluttered rolltop at his elbow. In the available chairs, benches and on the wall-to-wall taupe carpeting were managing editor Abe Rosenthal, assistant managing editor Seymour Topping, foreign editor Jimmy Greenfield, columnist Tom Wicker, general counsel Jim Goodale, Sydney Gruson, then special assistant to Punch Sulzberger, Peter Millones, assistant to Rosenthal, Jerry Gold, a senior copy editor who had been working for two weeks with Sheehan and, of course, Sheehan himself. Turner Catledge, in town for the stockholders' meeting, dropped by and was invited in, to the horror of some, who mistakenly thought Catledge, with his easy manner and love of gossip, would betray the great secret. He listened silently to the discussion, then wished his colleagues luck on their "great story."

None of those present remembered, nor did Catledge remind them of, the declaration he had made before the American Society of Newspaper Editors' meeting in San Francisco in 1957 in response to the proposal of a Los Angeles lawyer named Loyd Wright to make it a crime for a newsman to communicate information classified as secret.

"I could not resist this question," Catledge said with fire in his eyes. "It concerns the frightful assumption that we are in danger of perishing. I, too, have children and grandchildren but I don't seem to have the same fears that you seem to have about what is in store for us.

"I will ask you, don't you think we should look to our strength as well as our weakness? Shouldn't we look to our courage as well as our fears? Are we planning some sort of retreat from the things in which we believe? It seems to me we are. I don't say dangers do not exist but we don't have to burn down the whole barn to get a few rats."

The Editors Agree

The floor was given to Sheehan. Later on Goodale was to say that he never could figure out what the meeting was about. But this was disingenuous. For the past two weeks Sheehan and Jerry Gold had been holed up in the Jefferson Hotel in Washington reading through and sorting out the five cartons of papers which Neil had copied in Cambridge. (In the process he and Susan had copied some documents which were related to the Pentagon Papers but not part of them— command studies and things of that kind.)

Sheehan and Gold started their work at Neil's Washington home where Neil had arranged the materials in filing cabinets. Then Gold began to lug the documents, section by section, to his hotel room, locking them into his closet at night and carting them with him when he went out for meals. As he got through the sections he made several trips to New York where in the privacy of *The Times'* fourteenth-floor executive offices the documents were copied. The publisher didn't know who was using his copying machine and expressed puzzlement as to why it was so continuously tied up.

Once Gold sent a batch of documents to New York with his neighbors, Jerry and Dorothy Duel, who happened to be in Washington. They didn't know what was in Sheehan's B-4 bag but they were impressed with the need for care and secrecy. After the Papers had been published the Duels confessed to Gold that they'd had a flat tire on the way to New York and had to dump the bag out on the road in order to get at their spare. But they had their two kids sit on the bag while the tire was changed—just as a precaution.

Gold had never dealt with anything like these materials. There was chronology, analysis, footnotes, texts of cables, military reports, everything jumbled together. Gradually, however, the picture began to come clear. Gold and Sheehan made lists of what they thought were the main points and one night at Neil's house they put their lists together. The two were almost identical. Both men assumed that *The Times* would publish the full text of the documents since this was basic to the understanding by which Neil had access to the Papers. Moreover, after going through the material, both were convinced that the full text should and must be published. Neil suggested to Gold that the Papers be published in three installments. Gold favored at least a twelve-part publication. Perhaps even a twenty-part series.

At the end of the second week Gold and Sheehan telephoned New York and, in Gold's recollection, announced, "The moment of truth has arrived. Everybody should know now what we have here."

This then was the genesis of the meeting in Reston's office.

Sheehan, serious, earnest, now totally in command of the scope of the documents, presented a concise summary. He cited a few high spots, the revelations about Tonkin Gulf, the mechanisms of troop escalation, the CIA estimates, which invariably were more pessimistic (and accurate) than pronouncements by Westmoreland and the politicians. He did not state his sources but made it plain that he did not have a final "go," although he was confident of getting it. He emphasized that others knew of the Papers and that others had possession of copies and that there was a real chance *The Times* would be scooped unless it worked swiftly to prepare for publication even in advance of formal approval to publish from what he always referred to as "the sources"—plural.

All the materials were classified, Neil said, all top secret, although the copies which *The Times* had did not actually bear the "Top Secret" stamp. Somewhere along the copying chain someone had blanked out the classification marks.

No one asked Sheehan what his source was, although the question of authenticity was raised by Reston. Sheehan responded that he knew of the study before he obtained the documents, that he knew many of the men who had worked on it; he knew the project had been authorized by McNamara and he knew the documents were authentic from their contents.

Abe Rosenthal asked Sheehan how he could be certain the materials were genuine—why couldn't they have been faked by some antiwar group? Neil replied that he knew many of the actual incidents described and the Papers rang true. But Rosenthal wasn't entirely satisfied and later he asked Greenfield, the foreign editor who had worked in the State Department, to read the whole file because he felt that Greenfield, with his State Department expertise, could tell if the Papers were genuine or forgeries.

"Now that we have the documents," Neil remembered saying, "you can read them and see for yourselves."

He went on to describe the background of the study. It had been done because McNamara had turned against the war. Sheehan said McNamara had asked for the study not realizing, perhaps, that it would show him in a bad light. McNamara had a copy of the study, Neil said, and he, Neil, knew who had been involved in putting the study together and what their orders were.

"I told them," Neil recalled, "that it was going to turn most of the easternized Establishment against us because it would ruin the Bundys, the McNamaras and turn the wrath of the gods against us. By publishing the secret history of the war—these men didn't know how bad it was going to make them look."

Sheehan emphasized the sensitivity of his "sources," the risks of the enterprise and his conviction that once the materials were published "there were so many tracks, so many fingerprints on it that the FBI would have no trouble in finding the track."

Assistant managing editor Topping could not understand why the "sources" felt so sensitive about revealing their identity. "If this stuff is so explosive," he said, "why are these people so worried? They would not be getting into trouble. They haven't done anything wrong."

Goodale was sitting next to Sheehan. As the discussion went forward he sank lower and lower in his chair. Finally he interjected to Neil, "Can't you eliminate all that detail? Why do you have to tell them that?"

Sheehan responded that he had to set the facts before his editors. They had to know all the background before they made a decision.

But that decision was apparent long before the discussion was over. Not an editor expressed doubt. If the materials were authentic, and despite the questions of Reston and Rosenthal everyone assumed that they were, then of course *The Times* had to publish the story.

Sheehan told the group that he did not have and was not going to get four Pentagon volumes dealing with the diplomatic history of the war. U.S.–Vietnamese negotiations were still going on in Paris to end the war and his "sources" had made clear that the volumes would not be released for fear their revelation might in some manner jeopardize the peace talks. This, in a way, Neil thought, made the task of *The Times* much simpler since he and Gold thus far had found nothing in the Papers that breached military security.

The documents, Reston observed, were, in fact, history—a history of the war written by the government itself. There could therefore be no question of national security. The situation, he felt, was very similar to that when he obtained the so-called Yalta Papers from Secretary of State Dulles and presented them in *The Times.* The Yalta Papers also had been classified Top Secret. They had been the government's own conclusions and the government's own record of the Yalta Conference. The Pentagon Papers were the same kind of historic record.

But the parallel with the Yalta Papers was far from exact. Yalta had been a Republican partisan issue as early as 1948 and in 1952 the Republicans pledged themselves to publish the Yalta "secrets." Despite violent agitation by Senator McCarthy and other isolationists the documents were not made public by John Foster Dulles. In March 1955, Reston suggested to Dulles that he let *The Times* publish the Papers. A week later Carl McCardle, Dulles' press secretary, told Reston the Papers were being released and he could have an advance copy so *The Times* could publish the text, thirty-two whole newspaper pages, as it turned out. Reston leapt at the offer. The *Chicago Tribune,* which had led the campaign for exposure of the Yalta "secrets," discovered what was happening and under pressure from Republican right-wingers like Senators Knowland, McCarthy, Everett Dirksen and Styles Bridges, the State Department turned a copy of the Papers over to the *Chicago Tribune* as well. *The Times* and the *Tribune* published the text simultaneously March 17, 1955.§

This history, however, was not recalled by the editors as they discussed the Pentagon Papers. To them it seemed that the parallel was direct and very close.

Frankel then put the key question to his colleagues—journalistically, did the story warrant defying the government and possible government legal action; did the documents, in fact, betray a pattern of deception, of consistent and repeated deception by the American Government of the American people.

There was agreement in the room that this was precisely what the documents showed. Reston added, "These are the government's own conclusions. This is not only what our article is about—this is its basic concept."

And, thus, the editors meeting in Reston's office had swiftly come to the same conclusion reached so much earlier by Bigart, by Halberstam, by Browne, by Mohr, by Sheehan and all the other reporters in the field and then, later, by Ellsberg. It was the lies, the government's lies, continuing one administration after the other, which lay at the heart of the matter.

So, added Rosenthal, this would be the manner in which *The Times* would present the material—it would be *history*. The government's own version of history. The documents would not be carted around Washington and discussed. *The Times* would not interview people on their role in the study, nor would it solicit views on the accuracy of the conclusions presented. *The Times* would present the Pentagon Papers as they had been prepared by the government. But now they would be presented to the American people for their own information and judgment.

Sheehan was content. After all that was what the Pentagon history was and its particular interest lay in the fact that the historians, in many cases, had been the assistants to the men who made the war decisions themselves. The documentation told that story.

If the editors were of a mind on the decision to go forward with the Pentagon Papers there was an individual in the room who saw trouble ahead. This was Goodale. But one thing reassured him from the outset —if the Pentagon Papers were history, O.K.

"As soon as I heard it was history," Goodale recalled, "I thought of an article Alsop had published in the *Saturday Evening Post* some years earlier about the Bay of Pigs. I knew that somebody in the government

§See Notes section.

had told the story to him and that it was all based on classified information and that Alsop had published it. If Alsop could do it we could do it too."*

But just because Alsop had done it and gotten away with it didn't mean that *The Times* was in the clear. There was a real possibility, Goodale felt, that the government would try to halt the publication by injunction—couldn't the editors either drop the documents or agree to publish it all in one lump?

And Goodale was worried about the size of the meeting in Reston's office. He did not think so many *Times* people could keep the secret —and he had good reason for that fear since newspapermen are notorious gossips, even against their own best interests.

"There are too many people in this room," Goodale said nervously. "Somebody will talk. I just know they will."

As the meeting finally broke up, Goodale, white-faced, warned, "Everyone has to remember. Be quiet! Because everyone in this room may have participated in a felony."

Goodale was probably the only one present who could have defined a felony but the conferees were suitably impressed.

By the time the meeting was over there were no skeptics in Reston's office. The framework for publication of the story had been determined. It was decided to shift operations to New York, to security-guarded quarters in the New York Hilton hotel in order to assign additional manpower. An enormous amount of work had to be done and the danger of the story breaking elsewhere was recognized as acute. It was true that the final shape of the story was yet to be determined just as was the final commitment from Neil's "sources" but, as Max Frankel recalled, the meeting "came pretty close to deciding that while we didn't know what form, we didn't know when, we didn't know how —this was a helluva story and we were going to print it."

After the meeting Sheehan sat a while in Rosenthal's office.

"How can you be sure," Rosenthal asked again, "that this isn't something made up by fifty radical kids in some cellar, putting the whole thing together?"

Neil recapitulated the evidence once more.

"Well," Rosenthal said, "it still bothers me. Will you please keep

---

*The article was written by Stewart Alsop and Charles Bartlett and appeared in June 1961. *The Times* editorialized, "The secrecy of one of the highest organs of the United States has been seriously breached. What kind of advice can the President expect to get under such circumstances? . . . Does no one in Washington recall the McCarthy era and the McCarthy technique? . . . The integrity of the National Security Council and of the advice received by the President is at stake." What *The Times* did not know was that President Kennedy helped Alsop and Bartlett get their classified material and read the article before publication. (Alsop, *Newsweek,* 6/23/71)

asking yourself that question as you work on it?"

Neil said that he would.

"O.K.," Rosenthal said. "We've got to figure out a way to publish it. But you go to work and leave that question to us."

As they talked the telephone rang. It was Goodale. He wanted copies of some of Sheehan's materials for a conference with *The Times'* counsel, Louis Loeb of Lord, Day and Lord.

"That scared me shitless," Sheehan recalled. He regarded Lord, Day and Lord as an ultraconservative firm. Herbert Brownell, Mr. Nixon's close friend, was its head. The next thing Neil could see happening was the FBI knocking on his hotel door.

Rosenthal reassured him. "Don't worry," Rosenthal said. "Let me take care of this. I'll handle this side of it and you write the story."

13

The Times
Suppresses a Scoop

*W*HEN LOUIS LOEB heard about the Pentagon Papers April 21, the day after *The Times'* editors decided to go forward with the project, he exploded. There was no way, in his opinion, that the papers could be published.

Louis Loeb's professional life had been dedicated to *The New York Times.* He had, in a sense, inherited *The Times* as his principal law client, having joined the firm of Alfred Cook, Mr. Ochs' lawyer, in 1922 and then nailed it down, as it were, by marrying Mr. Cook's daughter.*

Louis Loeb in the spring of 1971 was seventy-two years old, a genial figure known to every executive of *The Times,* a member of Turner Catledge's branch-water and bourbon club which met about 6 P.M. in a hideaway adjacent to Catledge's office almost every day during Catledge's tenure as managing editor of *The Times.*

He was a handsome, tweedy man with a rangy stride and thick glasses that gave him a slightly myopic appearance. Loeb had met Mr. Cook in 1919 at a summer house on Saranac lake in the Adirondacks and Mr. Cook was very encouraging to him when he decided to take up law. But Mr. Cook was a Harvard Law graduate and he thought Harvard was the only institution in the country in which to study law. Mr. Loeb had gone to Yale and studied law at Columbia, which seemed to bar him from Mr. Cook's firm but to Loeb's surprise Mr. Cook hired him. "I thought you took only Harvard graduates," Mr. Loeb said. "Well," Mr. Cook replied. "That's so. But I was at the Columbia dinner last night and I thought your [graduation] skit was very good. I think if you'd like to come to this office we could find a place for you."

Mr. Cook took care of all problems at *The Times* himself, but one day in 1929 Mr. Loeb appeared for the first time at a *Times* stockholders' meeting. "There's not much going on at our meeting today," Mr.

---

*Theda Bara was present at the Cook–Loeb wedding. So was Mr. Ochs. The two took an immediate interest in each other and, as Mr. Loeb later recalled, paid little or no attention to the bride and groom. (*Times'* archives, Loeb, Oral History, p. 405)

Ochs assured the group, "so Mr. Cook has sent his young man, Mr. Loeb."

By the time Mr. Cook died Loeb was handling most of *The Times'* affairs. He got on well with Arthur Hays Sulzberger, working closely with him in complicated and difficult negotiations in the late 1930s with the American Newspaper Guild, and helped to sustain Mr. Sulzberger's position that the Guild, which then was under strong American Communist Party influence in New York, should not win control of the editorial staff of *The Times.*

Mr. Loeb had joined Lord, Day and Lord in 1947, bringing *The Times* with him as a client, and for many years spent half of every day in his office in Wall Street and the other half in *The Times'* offices at 229 West Forty-third Street. There was hardly a detail about *The Times* with which Louis Loeb had not been familiar. It was true, however, that he never became as close to Punch Sulzberger, a child when Loeb's association with *The Times* began, as he had been with Arthur Hays Sulzberger. Being a man of the older generation, Loeb had a tendency to measure events by the standards of an earlier day. He always thought of himself as a reasonable man, certainly more liberal than conservative (there were some who thought of Loeb in the 1930s as being "to the left"), but Punch and others at *The Times* had noticed that, with the coming to office of Richard Nixon, Loeb had taken to wearing a small, enameled American flag in his lapel.

James Goodale had graduated from the University of Chicago Law School in 1968 and knocked on Wall Street doors until he got a job at Lord, Day and Lord. He specialized in corporate law and made a good record. At the time of the 114-day New York newspaper strike of 1962–63 Amory Bradford, himself a lawyer and general manager of *The Times,* and Harding Bancroft, also a lawyer and a vice president of *The Times,* decided *The Times* should have its own legal department and staff it with a bright young lawyer. Loeb's colleagues thought Goodale extremely able and Loeb had no hesitation in recommending him to *The Times.*

Goodale went to work the day the long strike ended and in the nine following years had built a solid base of confidence. *The Times* had wanted a young man of independence and integrity and these were qualities which Goodale possessed. Although he and Loeb were divided by thirty-five years in age they got along well, liked and respected each other and continued to do so even after their differences over the Pentagon Papers.

When Bancroft, now *The Times'* executive vice president, telephoned Loeb on the morning of April 21 and told him briefly about the Pentagon Papers, Loeb became, in Goodale's words, "very angry."

The Times, Loeb said, did not do this kind of thing. It was a matter of patriotism. *The Times* must go, first, to the government. That was what Mr. Sulzberger had always done. And Mr. Ochs before him. There was no way, in Loeb's instant opinion, in which *The Times* could publish such material. Later on, when the Pentagon crisis was over, when passions had died down and *Times* men could take a more objective view, some were inclined to blame not Mr. Loeb but the temper of the times for his instant and hostile reaction. These were not normal days. Not for the country which all of them loved, each in his way, nor for the government and its head, Richard Nixon, nor for the paper to which they were devoted. In one respect, they were agreed, Mr. Loeb had certainly been right. Publication of the Pentagon Papers was not in Mr. Ochs' tradition nor in that of Arthur Hays Sulzberger.

Kaiser Wilhelm II

Few *Times* men in 1971 had ever seen or heard of a three-paragraph item which appeared on page one of the paper on July 21, 1908, reporting that William Bayard Hale of *The Times* had been "cordially received" by Kaiser Wilhelm II on his yacht, the *Hohenzollern,* at Bergen, Norway, on the evening of the nineteenth. The Kaiser, it was said, had spent nearly two hours in private conversation with Dr. Hale. From that day until July 16, 1939, *The Times* remained silent on the contents of Dr. Hale's conversation. Then in a magazine article written by Hal Borland, later famous as the author of *The Times'* Sunday nature editorials, *The Times* published a summary of Wilhelm's words on that pleasant summer evening as the imperial yacht, all white paint, polished brass and gleaming mahogany, lay at anchor in Bergensfjord.

Of the many circumspect acts of Mr. Ochs' *Times* the handling of Dr. Hale's exclusive interview with the Kaiser was a classic for this was no simple over-the-cigars-and-brandy discussion. It was a conversation which Dr. Hale thought so incendiary that had the Kaiser's words been published war might break out between England and Germany "within twenty-four hours."

This sounds like an excitable judgment but it was shared by experienced European journalists and diplomats. The Europe of 1908 was by no means as safe as it seemed to the American traveler, even, say, to Adolph S. Ochs, who had taken his wife and his teen-age daughter, Iphigene, abroad that summer. Although few American sightseers were aware of the fact Germany had feverishly built a navy which, some experts thought, was already powerful enough to challenge England, and Wilhelm had emerged as a venturesome, ambitious troublemaker hoping to promote a winning alliance against the British.

The United States was outside these maneuvers, although with the defeat of Spain and President T. R. Roosevelt's display of "the Great

White Fleet," as the American Navy was called, in distant oceans it was clear that the U.S.A. was about to burst the cocoon of isolation.

In a word, the scene was being set for World War I. Nowhere was this better known than in Germany. In Paris and London a growing body of opinion favored a preemptive strike against Germany before it grew stronger.

It was into these dangerous waters that Dr. Hale, a rather handsome, scholarly man, an ordained Episcopalian minister from Massachusetts and an experienced free-lance journalist and editor, strayed in the summer of 1908. He was now editor of the literary supplement of *The Times* and earlier in the year he had spent a week in the White House, writing for *The Times* a series of chatty, intimate pieces about T.R.

Now July found him in Berlin, trying to repeat his feat with the Kaiser.

On the evening of July 18, Dr. Hale cabled William C. Reick, general manager of *The Times*:

"Just had two hours audience with Emperor. Result so startling that I hesitate to report it without censorship of Berlin."§

Reick was both exhilarated and disturbed—exhilarated at the prospect of an exclusive interview with the Kaiser but disturbed that he might lose it through censorship. He sent Dr. Hale a cable suggesting he consult the American ambassador in Berlin but instructed him to "avoid even the appearance [of] betrayal [of] confidence."

Then Reick wrote Mr. Ochs in Europe a letter of self-congratulation, seemingly certain that the interview would be forthcoming. Dr. Hale sent Reick a letter giving the substance of his talk, declaring that "no restrictions of any kind were laid on me" and that "the Emperor was eager to talk for publication and to be talked to." Then he hurried to Berlin.

Here American Ambassador Hill assured Dr. Hale that he was certain the Kaiser intended his remarks to be published. Frederick Wile, *The Times'* string correspondent in Berlin, said the same thing. However, Dr. Hale insisted on taking his story to the German Foreign Office, which, appalled at the Kaiser's indiscretions, declined to clear it.

In New York, general manager Reick, at the instructions of Mr. Ochs, took the matter to President Roosevelt. He, too, counseled against publication, a judgment he reinforced when Dr. Hale hurried back from Europe and met with him at Sagamore Hill on August 12.

The Times published not a word of the Kaiser's interview and that was that—but not quite. The German Foreign Office had indicated to Dr. Hale that it would not object if "noncontroversial" parts of the

§See Notes section.

interview were published by an American magazine. Dr. Hale cast this material in the form of an article which *Century* magazine in New York announced for its December issue. An advance notice described it as containing the Kaiser's "impressions of President Theodore Roosevelt," "War and Christianity," "The Roman Catholic Church"—a "delightful, sympathetic appreciation of a Christian King who has learned to restrain his arm, though he exults in its strength."

But even this was to perish when the Foreign Office instructed a visiting German cruiser to pick up the type-cast plates of the *Century* article, the text and proofs and take them to sea where they were destroyed. They paid *Century* its out-of-pocket costs of about $8,000.

For all these precautions the essence of the Hale interview did become known in a spectacular spread which covered the entire top half of William Randolph Hearst's *New York American* on November 20, 1908. The article described the Kaiser as attacking the "yellow peril," characterizing England as "a traitor to the White Man's Cause," warning that she would lose India, South Africa and even Australia and New Zealand as a result of the Anglo-Japanese treaty and predicting a common front between Germany and the United States. The Kaiser called England "the renegade mother country."

Hearst's competitor, Pulitzer's *World,* carried another version the following day, November 21, offering the suggestion that the Kaiser might have been drunk when he talked to Dr. Hale.

None of this drew affirmation or denial from *The Times.* Nor from Dr. Hale. The fact that Mr. Ochs had in his safe a 5,000-word summary by Dr. Hale of his talk was never mentioned, nor was there a word in *The Times* to indicate its existence. After a few days' sensation the story faded away.

But not entirely. It emerged Phoenix-like in December 1917. Now the United States was at war with Germany. The *New York Tribune* published a summary of the Kaiser's interview revealing that, in fact, the Kaiser had predicted World War I and had made no secret of his hostility toward England and Germany's efforts to align the powers, including the United States, against her.

As the *Tribune* concluded:

> Wilhelm II, as far back as 1908, had revealed himself as the character in the role of which he now stands convicted—the world's troublemaker. As such England and the rest of the world might have appraised him with more or less accuracy immediately after the Hale interview appeared in print. But the interview did not appear. The Emperor had talked for publication but it was suppressed nonetheless.

The *Tribune* added that while both the *American* and the *World* had quoted the Kaiser rather loosely the essence of their reports was correct, a conclusion which Dr. Hale's original notes substantiated.

In his first report to Mr. Reick Dr. Hale had declared, "Germany is expecting to fight England and in my judgment the Emperor doesn't care how quickly. He poured a steady stream of insult on the English for two hours."

Wilhelm, said Dr. Hale, "is exceedingly bitter against England and full of the yellow peril."

He quoted the Kaiser as saying, "England is a traitor to the White Man's cause. She will lose her colonies through her treaty with Japan. The invitation to our [American] fleet to go to New Zealand and Australia was to serve notice on the British that these colonies were with the White man and not with a renegade 'mother country.' The solution of the Eastern question [China] is about to be made by Germany and the United States. It has been agreed between himself and President Roosevelt to divide the East against itself by becoming the recognized friends of China."

The Kaiser said he was providing arms to the Moslem world to make them allies in the coming battle against Japan. He swathed his talk in verbiage which made clear that Hitler was a direct ideological descendant of the Kaiser.

"The future," the Kaiser assured Dr. Hale, "belongs to the White Race. It does not belong to the Yellow or the Black nor the Olive colored—it belongs to the Blonde Man and it belongs to Christianity and to Protestantism. We are the only people who can save it. There is no power in any other civilization or any other religion that can save humanity, and the future belongs to us—the Anglo Teuton, the man who came from Northern Europe."

At other moments the Kaiser praised the Maximum Leader:

"There must always be one man willing to assume responsibility," he said, "to do things. Parliaments consider—they do not act. . . . The strong upright personality rules."

Christianity, he averred, was the faith for the military:

"The greatest soldiers have been Christians. The greatest degree of fortitude and of courage are inculcated by Christianity. Christianity inimical to war? Why, the early Christians had no scruple about propagating the faith by the sword. We are ourselves Christian by reason of forcible conversion."

The Kaiser attacked Roman Catholicism, particularly Roman veneration of Mary:

"There can be no compromise within the Catholic Church," he declared. "It is ultramontane or nothing. . . . The day of Catholicism, of course, is past."

England's leaders, he sneered, were a bunch of "ninnies." "The ninnies there," he said, "have got that Government in an absolutely impossible position."

This then was the essence of *The Times'* great scoop. What would have happened had it been published? Despite the judgment of Dr. Hale that it might have brought war "within twenty-four hours" this seems improbable. Certainly, it would have sharpened relations between England and Germany. It would have put powerful ammunition into the hands of the war parties of England and France by betraying the Kaiser's naked hatred, ambitions and intrigues. It would have supported the Anglo-French (and Russian) military who felt that the Kaiser must be dealt with immediately before the Reich grew stronger.

Perhaps more importantly the publication would have critically weakened the Kaiser within Germany. His indiscretions already were notorious.

That this would have damaged him and his militaristic supporters is clear in the light of a scandal he stirred up a few weeks later during a visit to England. On this occasion the Kaiser criticized the English for supposing him to be antagonistic to them.

"You English," he said, "are mad, mad—mad as March hares. What has come over you that you are so completely given over to suspicion? It is quite unworthy of a great nation."

He said he had devoted his life to trying to be friends with England.

"Have I ever been false to my word?" he exclaimed. "Falsehood and prevarication are alien to my nature. To be forever misjudged, to have my repeated offers of friendship weighed and scrutinized with jealous and mistrustful eyes, taxes my patience severely.

"How can I convince a nation against its will?"

The remarks caused a storm in England—but more of a storm in Berlin. The Reichstag insisted that foreign questions must be left to the German Cabinet subject to Reichstag approval. The Kaiser must be kept out of it all. Finally, Chancellor von Buelow consulted the Kaiser and assured the Reichstag that the Emperor had promised to be circumspect.

Had *The Times* interview been printed the political storm within Germany would have been so great that the Kaiser might have been removed from influence on German foreign policy and the adventurist clique in Germany badly wounded.

Would or could World War I have been averted? Perhaps not, but the fact that such a question could be posed was testimony to the importance of Dr. Hale's interview and the consequences of the action of *The Times* suppressing it for more than thirty years. The author of that policy was Mr. Ochs. It was not until four years after his death and the verge of World War II that the Kaiser's interview was exhumed when one day Arthur Hays Sulzberger found it in rummaging through Mr. Ochs papers.

Louis Loeb's Position

It is not likely that Louis Loeb remembered Mr. Ochs' suppression of the Kaiser's interview when he got Harding Bancroft's telephone call about the Pentagon Papers. But the philosophy of Mr. Ochs existed lively and decisive in the mind of Louis Loeb. Mr. Ochs never explained his suppression of the Kaiser's declaration. "He ran the paper like a czar," Arthur Hays Sulzberger once said. Mr. Ochs was not in the habit of explaining his acts and in this case no explanation was really needed. *The Times,* as Mr. Ochs conceived his newspaper, was a *responsible* newspaper. It went along with the American Government and felt that this was its natural and proper posture. To be sure Mr. Ochs did on occasion challenge policies in Washington but these were editorial arguments, they did not spill over to the news pages. He did not extend that same policy to foreign governments, of course, but here, too, he tended to go with the official side.

Since Mr. Ochs was in Europe he was not privy to the original decision on the Kaiser's interview, but later, when he was apprised of the circumstance, he instructed his New York editors to obtain the opinion of President Roosevelt. When TR said the interview should not be printed—well, that was that. Mr. Ochs never budged, not when his New York competitors, the *American* and the *World,* in November 1908, printed their summaries, nor later in 1917 when the *New York Tribune* and other newspapers published more comprehensive and accurate reports. (How the Hale report leaked to other papers was never explained: some suspected Frederick Wile in Berlin; others thought Mr. Hale may have talked a bit too freely.)

True, Arthur Sulzberger finally published a story but not until the interview had a largely historical frame of reference and when, in reality, it served the editorial policy of *The New York Times,* which in 1939 was attempting to alert and prepare the United States for the war in Europe which Arthur Sulzberger was convinced would soon break out. Belatedly, three decades belatedly, Arthur Sulzberger's publication of a feature story about the Kaiser's interview simply showed that Adolf Hitler's roots were firmly anchored in the soil of Wilhelmian Germany. World War I had been fought with all its consequences and World War II was about to begin. But there was nothing in the Hal Borland résumé of Dr. Hale's interview to indicate that *The New York Times* had learned an editorial lesson as a consequence of its suppression of this remarkable document.

Nor, it might be said, was there in 1971 any among *The Times'* executives who had more than the dimmest recollection that in 1908 *The Times* had suppressed a document which might have changed the direction of the world. The discussion within the upper echelons of the paper over the Pentagon Papers touched off by Louis Loeb's instantly negative response went forward with no reference to the historical record, which, if remembered at all, was seen merely as a quirk which occurred early in *The Times'* career. It was not seen as an action that symbolized the journalistic era about to come to an end on June 13, 1971.

The argument that Louis Loeb opened on the morning of April 21, 1971, was to go forward with occasional intermissions until the evening of June 14, 1971, as the third article in *The Times'* Pentagon series was about to roll off the press.

Louis Loeb was never to change his position against publication; *The Times'* editors were never to change their position for publication and in the end the forty-year association of Louis Loeb and *The New York Times* simply tore apart. "There were terrible arguments," Goodale recalled years later, his mouth tightening and his face grim in the recollection. "Just terrible arguments."

14

A Question of Responsibility

FOR DAN ELLSBERG, April 1971 was another month of frustration, of frustration and hope. He celebrated his fortieth birthday April 7 at the apartment at 10 Hilliard Street in Cambridge, where he and Pat were living. Birthdays and anniversaries were important to him and this was a particularly important birthday, the boundary between youth and the advent of middle age. To Ellsberg his birthday was like the toll of a bell which showed that time was running out, that despite the nervous effort and ingenuity which he had poured into his great mission, the making public of the Pentagon Papers and, as he felt, by so doing causing the almost certain ending of the Vietnam war, he had fallen short. The Pentagon Papers still rested unknown, tucked away in saferooms and secret hiding places. Possibly, as his friend Neil Sheehan had said, they were "a thermonuclear vial" but up to the present they lacked a detonating fuse.

Ellsberg could not assess what the prospects might be of publication in *The New York Times.* He knew that Sheehan was bending every effort toward this end but, as far as Ellsberg knew, there had yet been no binding decision by *The Times.* He was right in this, although preparations for publication were more advanced than he could have imagined. While Ellsberg had not entirely given up on Fulbright and the Senate Foreign Relations Committee and while Fulbright was still struggling to obtain the documents through channels—as late as April 30, 1971, he was to address another letter to Secretary of Defense Laird appealing for release of the papers, command studies and information on the Tonkin Gulf incident—Ellsberg had no reason to believe that his effort with Fulbright would be crowned with success.

He was, with some reluctance, seeking another channel for possible publicity. In principle he had always hoped to get the papers presented by a U.S. senator, a prominent senator with an important antiwar record, a man like Fulbright or McGovern or Mathias, but now he was beginning to think he might have to look elsewhere.

At the time of his birthday party on April 7 Ellsberg saw no reason for optimism over his protracted negotiations with Fulbright and his staff, and only generalized hopes for *The New York Times.*

Among the guests at the party were K. Dun Gifford, his wife and daughter. Gifford, an attractive, gregarious man, had worked for a time with Senator Edward Kennedy as a legislative assistant and was a friend of Sheehan's. Another guest was a young woman named Cynthia Fredricks, a member of the Concerned Asian Scholars, who was doing a thesis on the Tonkin Gulf affair. She had gotten some Tonkin information from Ellsberg and fell into conversation with Gifford about her thesis. Gifford told her to forget it because *The Times* soon would be coming out with a big exposé of the affair.

The next day Cynthia telephoned Ellsberg, worried about her thesis and the conversation, and asked how she could get in touch with Gifford. Ellsberg was upset. He liked Gifford, knew he was a good friend of Sheehan's but was angry that he should be talking publicly. Late that afternoon Ellsberg stormed over to Gifford's house, a block or two distant, sat down on the hall settee and demanded an explanation. Gifford said that he had been in naval intelligence and that Neil had consulted him on some questions about the Papers. "I think Ellsberg thought this was in reference to Operation 34A [the Tonkin Gulf affair]," Gifford said later. In any event Ellsberg accepted Gifford's explanation but told him it was absolutely essential to keep strict secrecy, particularly since it wasn't yet certain that *The Times* would print the Papers.

"Here you are talking," Ellsberg said, "and who knows when the FBI will come down on me."

Gifford apologized and promised he would say nothing more. But he added that he didn't think Ellsberg should underestimate Neil.

"When he gets his teeth into something nothing will stop him," Gifford said. "He is a newspaperman and I'd assume if I were you that Neil is going to use that material."

Ellsberg continued to be concerned about loose talk and he spoke a bit later to Sheehan, who confirmed that he had shown some materials to Gifford, giving the same explanation—that he wanted an independent opinion on their authenticity.*

Sheehan did not tell Ellsberg what was happening at *The Times* but even had he been more candid his report would hardly have been totally encouraging. *The Times* had assembled a staff of half a dozen persons

---

*In reality Sheehan had called Gifford late one cold March night. Gifford was already asleep. Sheehan said he had some materials that had to be copied immediately, could Gifford help. "I knew from Neil's tone that this was something which had to be done," Gifford recalled. "I got up and met him. It was very late and the streets were absolutely deserted. I had a copying source which he could use. That's how I came to know about the Papers. I knew they were important but I didn't want to know very much." (Personal interview, Gifford, 1/11/79)

in specially rented suites at the New York Hilton hotel where operations got under way April 22. But, in fact, as late as May 5 not one line of copy had been produced. The writers and editors were still poring over the materials, dividing them into piles, trying to absorb the contents and arguing about a logical and effective way of handling the mountain of paper. As Jerry Gold, the rotund, pragmatic and able editor assigned to work with Sheehan, remarked, "We started at cherry-blossom time in Washington and it is now May 5 in New York and we are still working and not a line has yet been written."

In fact, there had been no final decision to publish the Papers despite a long and sometimes angry discussion with Louis Loeb on April 29.

Loeb had the law looked up and came to *The Times* April 29 with a couple of assistants. He met with Punch Sulzberger, Scotty Reston, Bancroft, Goodale, Rosenthal, Topping and Greenfield. Loeb's mind was clear. He said publication by *The Times* would constitute a violation of the statute on classified documents and that those responsible could be (would be, was his belief) prosecuted and sent to jail. That was that. He recommended that *The Times*—if it still felt it should publish—consult the government and follow the wishes of the government.

What this discussion made clear, although the participants did not seem to be aware of it, was the fundamental philosophical change that now separated the old *Times* of Mr. Ochs and the new *Times* of his grandson. Louis Loeb's words would have been controlling on Ochs' *Times*. They were not on *The Times* of the grandson.

James Reston responded to Loeb with panache. He said that if *The Times* did not publish the Papers he would publish them in his own newspaper, the *Vineyard Gazette*, the Martha's Vineyard paper that he had purchased in 1968 just before assuming his post as executive editor of *The Times*.

Later he was to explain that he had not meant literally that he would publish the Papers in the *Vineyard Gazette* but that he did mean it when he added that he would "be delighted to go to jail" on the issue.

The discussion of the legal issues and precedents was notably defective. Loeb had concentrated almost entirely on the classification statute and the criminal penalties for its violation and had not touched the deeper constitutional questions. He read out the penalties for publishing military secrets, sentences of up to ten years, but the memorandum of law prepared by Lord, Day and Lord was hardly comprehensive; it did not examine legislative history nor distinguish between bureaucratic regulations and statutory law.

The core of Loeb's argument remained his conviction that *The Times* could not go against the government, could not publish in defiance of the government, could not "Publish and be damned" as he was inclined to think some of the editors wanted.

The Bay of Pigs

One of the editors cited the precedent of *The Times'* conduct at the time of the Bay of Pigs in 1961. In what way, it was asked, did the question of publication by *The Times* in 1961 of plans for the CIA-sponsored invasion of Cuba differ from the proposal to publish the historic archive on Vietnam?

Loeb said the case of the Bay of Pigs was different. In the Bay of Pigs the government knew that *The Times* had the material and was going to publish and it requested that *The Times* not publish and *The Times* respected the government's wishes. In the present case, the case of the Pentagon Papers, the government did not know *The Times* had the material, and he, as counsel, did not know how the materials (which he had not examined at this point and refused to examine because he did not want to become party to their "security secrets") had come into *The Times'* possession but it was pretty clear from the discussion that it was material that had been "stolen out of the government files."

To Loeb's assertions concerning the Bay of Pigs the editors made no rejoinder although they did deny that the Pentagon Papers "had been stolen."

The reference by the editors to the Bay of Pigs was a fully appropriate one for, in fact, *Times* reporting on the Bay of Pigs was a landmark in the progress of the paper from its Ochs-age role of defender-support-er-upholder of government to its contemporary status as an independent entity, exercising independent but responsible judgment in carrying out its First Amendment function of serving as the eyes, ears and interpreter of the world to its readers.

And, contrary to the declarations of Loeb, which amazingly were not challenged by those gathered in Sulzberger's fourteenth-floor office, the Bay of Pigs provided a direct and complete parallel to what *The Times* proposed to do with the Pentagon Papers.

The truth was that by this time the Bay of Pigs story had been so encrusted by myth, legend and distortion that even the editors of *The Times* no longer had clear in their minds what actually happened.

The Bay of Pigs fiasco had deep roots. The Eisenhower Administration attempted to deal with Fidel Castro by rather half-hearted diplomacy but by March 17, 1960, concluded that this would not succeed. On that day President Eisenhower gave permission to the CIA to go forward with a plan to recruit and train Cuban émigrés for an effort to overthrow Castro. The idea had been advocated by Vice President

Nixon as early as the spring of 1959. In August 1960, Eisenhower approved $13 million for the project and training camps were secretly established in Florida and Guatemala, hundreds of men were recruited, particularly from the anti-Castro émigré colony in Miami, anti-Castro political leaders were brought into the picture and a German refugee named Droller was named chief liaison officer and paymaster to the Cuban group. Droller went under the name of Frank Bender. He had served in the U.S. Army before being recruited by the CIA and knew virtually no Spanish. Another man who had been assigned a role was a CIA employee named Howard Hunt, of whom more was to be heard in the future.

Rumors quickly circulated through the Miami Cuban colony and much of Latin America. They first reached print in *La Hora,* the leading newspaper of Guatemala, where the training bases were common knowledge. Later it was to become certain that Fidel Castro (who had hundreds of supporters and clandestine operatives amid the Cuban colony) heard of the CIA plans as soon as they began to become operational or before. His agents got places among the CIA "volunteers" and he monitored the CIA's operation with ease.

Word of the CIA scheme was carefully concealed from the American public and from ordinary officialdom in Washington. In the autumn of 1960 the presidential campaign of John F. Kennedy and Richard Nixon was at its height. Both candidates were receiving intelligence briefings from Allen Dulles, head of the CIA. Nixon was wholly "witting" in the CIA term, having been in on the operation from the start, but word of the plan was withheld from Kennedy even when Cuba became a splashy issue in late October.

The first public reference to the CIA project in the United States occurred in the October issue of a scholarly journal called *Hispanic American Report,* published by Dr. Ronald Hilton, a specialist in Latin American affairs at Stanford University. Hilton chanced to visit Guatemala City at the moment when Clemente Marroquin Rojas, editor of *La Hora,* published a front-page editorial in which he declared that an invasion of Cuba was "well underway, prepared not by our country, which is so poor and so disorganized, but implicitly by the U.S.A." It was this information which Hilton published in his journal. Word quickly spread among Latin American specialists in the United States and even more swiftly in Cuban circles.

In late October the news was breaking out in many places. *The Times* on October 26 and again on October 29 published small stories, well inside the paper, quoting Guatemalan authorities as denying that training camps for Cuban guerrilla invasion forces had been established on their territory and on November 1 *The Times* published on page one a declaration by Foreign Minister Rao of Cuba at the United

Nations warning that the United States had plans for invading Cuba "within a few days." Rao said the attack would come from guerrilla camps established in Guatemala and the United States. He privately told Herbert Matthews,* the *Times* correspondent and editor, that he knew the precise location in Florida and Guatemala of these camps.

Thus, six months before the ill-fated compañeros of La Brigada 2506 were to land at Bahia de Cochinos, Castro had an accurate grasp of American intentions. The Cuban community knew that *something* was up and many in the community knew *what* was up and well-informed persons in Latin America had a good picture of what was being proposed.

The only persons who were ignorant were the American people. This pattern had occurred before; it was to occur again and again and again as the 1960s moved forward, as the Bay of Pigs gave way to successive national and international adventures, culminating in the accelerating Vietnam tragedy and finally coming to embrace the core of the American political structure, the White House itself, in Watergate.

This scenario had two themes and they were those which had been identified by American correspondents in Indochina in the mid-1960s —one was the seamless tissue of lies, of government lies, and the other was the Aeschylean chorus, the chant, the Greek chant: "It doesn't work!" It would not work at the Bay of Pigs, as most sophisticated outsiders knew it would not; it was not to work ten years and hundreds of billions of dollars later in Vietnam, as many sophisticated outsiders knew that it would not.

Running through this compulsively repetitive saga was the urgent debate on the role of the reporter, the correspondent, the editor and, specifically, the role of *The New York Times*, the role of the nation's watchmen, as specified by the First Amendment, in apprising the American people of what was *really* happening within the stolid and ever more massive steel and concrete bunkers of the Washington Establishment.

All of this, of course, was to become obvious much later. In the glorious autumn of 1960, as John F. Kennedy carried forward his almost joyous crusade for the presidency against the dogged efforts of Richard Nixon, only the barest fringes of the question that was to dominate the next decade and the decade beyond that had begun to emerge. Thus far it had not yet begun to trouble the editors and

*Matthews had "discovered" Castro in his Sierra Madre hideout in eastern Cuba in 1957, interviewing and photographing the legendary Cuban guerrilla at a moment when the Cuban dictator Batista, whom Castro shortly would overthrow, had declared he was dead.

correspondents of *The New York Times*. No editorials were being written about the dangers of the "invisible government." No *Times* men had begun to grasp the pervasive consequences of totally irresponsible government. No one was now talking of the "Imperial Presidency." No one was thinking about the alienation of the American voter. No one was considering—not for a minute—that the system might be synergically in trouble. All of this, the horror of the war, the agony of the streets, the deadly centrifugal violence, the assassinations, the murders in cold blood at the very apogee of the American dream, all of this lay ahead (but far closer than anyone on *The Times* would guess).

The Nation's Report

Now in these late October and early November moments when the quest for the grail of Camelot moved toward climax all that had appeared was the faintest cloud on the horizon—the reports and rumors of U.S. plans to do away with Castro.

Soon these reports gathered momentum and higher visibility. In its issue of November 19, 1960, *The Nation* took note of Professor Hilton's bulletin. *The Nation* had a small circulation, less than 50,000, but it was widely read in Washington, in New York and particularly by persons interested in world affairs, by correspondents and editors. A report in *The Nation* was not automatically accepted by the other media but it was respected. If the information was new it was checked out by important newspapers and news agencies.*

The Nation's article was published under the heading "Are We Training Cuban Guerrillas?"

It said:

> Fidel Castro may have a sounder basis for his expressed fears of a U.S.-financed "Guatemala-type" invasion than most of us realize. On a recent visit to Guatemala, Dr. Ronald Hilton, Director of the Institute of Hispanic-American Studies at Stanford University, was told:
>
> 1. The United States Central Intelligence Agency has a large tract of land, at an outlay in excess of $1 million, which is stoutly fenced and heavily guarded. It is "common knowledge" in Guatemala that the tract is being used as a training ground for Cuban counter-revolutionaries who are preparing for an eventual landing in Cuba. United States personnel and equipment are being used at the base. . . .
>
> 2. Substantially all of the above was reported by a well-known Guatemala journalist in La Hora, a Guatemalan newspaper. . . .

*Seventy-five copies of *The Nation* article were distributed in advance to major news media in New York but as far as *The Nation* could determine only one paper, *The Gazette and Daily* of York, Pennsylvania, picked it up. (James Aronson, *The Press and the Cold War*, Indianapolis, 1970, p. 155)

3. More recently, the President of Guatemala, forced to take cognizance of the persistent reports concerning the base, went on TV and admitted its existence but refused to discuss its purpose or any other facts about it.

The American press has apparently remained unaware of the public commotion the subject has aroused in Guatemala. . . . We ourselves, of course, pretend no firsthand knowledge of the facts; nevertheless, we feel an obligation to bring the subject to public attention. If the reports as heard by Dr. Hilton are true, then public pressure should be brought to bear upon the Administration to abandon this dangerous and harebrained project.

There is a second reason why we believe the reports merit publication: They can, and should be, checked immediately by all U.S. news media with correspondents in Guatemala.

The Nation's editorial appeared simultaneously with the first briefing to the new President-elect on the Cuban invasion project. On November 17, Kennedy, at Palm Beach, Florida, was told by Allen Dulles, the CIA director, and Richard Bissell, operations director, about the plans.* Kennedy was, as Theodore Sorenson later was to recall, "astonished by its magnitude and daring." A few days later, November 29, he was given a more comprehensive briefing. His response was sufficiently affirmative for Dulles to take it as permission to proceed at an expedited pace.

If the newly elected President or his staff noticed the question posed by *The Nation* it left no impression on their minds when later they tried to recapitulate what had happened.

Nor did *The Nation's* call spur the American press into a flurry of action. However, Herbert Matthews did bring the Hilton article to the attention of Emanuel Freedman, the rather phlegmatic but conscientious foreign editor of *The Times,* and after *The Nation* reprinted it Freedman had a staff man telephone Hilton to see if he had anything more, as Freedman later reported to Clifton Daniel, assistant managing editor, "than the hearsay evidence attributed to him in *The Nation.*" Hilton said he had nothing to add. Freedman then asked *The Times'* Washington bureau to check out the report and got a blank. He cabled his string correspondent in Guatemala who said there had been some rumors about U.S.-organized training bases but nothing more.

At this time an insurrection broke out in Guatemala and President Eisenhower sent U.S. naval forces to patrol the coasts of Guatemala

*On Friday, November 18, in San Francisco, Inspector General Lyman B. Kirkpatrick of the CIA spoke at the Commonwealth Club and was asked about Professor Hilton's report and Hilton's comment that "it will be a black day for Latin America and the U.S. if this takes place." Kirkpatrick was silent for a time then responded, "It will be a black day if we are found out." (Aronson, *The Press and the Cold War,* p. 156).

and Nicaragua to protect against a supposed threat of Cuban intervention. Paul Kennedy, *The Times'* Central American staff man based in
Mexico City, was sent to Guatemala. While there, at instructions from
Freedman, he interviewed President Ydigoras about the reported U.S.
training base. His story was published November 20. The President
told Paul Kennedy that Guatemalan forces were being trained in guerrilla tactics at a ranch near Retalhuleu near Helvetia, about ninety miles
from Guatemala City. Ydigoras said reports that it was a U.S. operation
"were a lot of lies." He conceded that the United States was giving him
help but pooh-poohed the idea that an operation against Cuba was in
contemplation. Paul Kennedy said that Ydigoras' political opponents
had raised questions and that there had been parliamentary debate over
the issue. And that was that. A major takeout on Cuba, the supposed
threat to Guatemala and Nicaragua and President Eisenhower's dispatch of naval forces occupied most of page one of *The Times* Sunday
editorial section, Sunday, November 20. It did not mention the bases
nor did Paul Kennedy refer to them or the CIA in a three-column
analysis.

No one reading this layout was likely to have an idea that unknown
to the American public its government was already waist deep in an
operation based in Florida and Guatemala and directed against Castro.
Paul Kennedy's reports from Guatemala strongly suggested that rumors
about a U.S. plot were Cuban propaganda. His investigation could not
be described as more than "once-over-lightly."

The Times Takes a Look

Only one other American correspondent made a pass at checking out
the situation, and he, quite by accident.

This was Richard Dudman, the small, wiry, infinitely tenacious correspondent of the *St. Louis Post-Dispatch,* a newspaper which sought
to carry on the tradition of iconoclastic investigative reporting bequeathed by Pulitzer.

Just before Thanksgiving, Dudman's editors in St. Louis instructed
him to fly to Guatemala to investigate the uprising there. As Dudman
was leaving the office, his colleague the veteran liberal columnist Mar-
quis Childs called to him, "Take this along. If you get a chance you
might look into it."

Childs handed Dudman a page he had torn out of *The Nation.* It
was *The Nation*'s call for American newspapers to investigate what the
CIA was up to in Guatemala.

Dudman stuffed it into his pocket and after he had checked out the
coup he got a taxi outside his hotel in Guatemala City and asked the
driver if he could take him to Retalhuleu. The driver knew the place
and they started out in the warm morning sunshine, a 125-mile drive

to Retalhuleu, then fifteen miles up and up, twisting and turning along a rocky mountain road. They went the last mile in a borrowed jeep. Dudman had only a quick look. He saw what appeared to be an airstrip under construction, some bulldozers at work and several buildings that looked like barracks. Before he could explore further several soldiers in battle fatigues, one carrying a submachine gun, told him to get out of there. He got out. One of the soldiers told Dudman in good English that there were no Americans there. On the way back Dudman's driver told him the other men had spoken what he called "Cuban Spanish."

What Dudman had gotten was a quick glimpse of part of the enormous coffee *finca* of Roberto Alejos, brother of Carlos Alejos, Guatemalan ambassador to the United States. Roberto Alejos had made his property available to the CIA under an agreement, the terms of which have never been revealed, with Miguiel Ydigoras, president of Guatemala. The plantation employed more than 2,000 Indian workers and was totally self-contained. It had its own hydroelectric power plant, manufacturing and shipping facilities. By this time there were several hundred Cuban recruits and CIA personnel on the Alejos estate but Dudman got no clue of that. Although Dudman did not know it the Alejos estate had been used before by the CIA—as an air base during its successful overthrow of the regime of Colonel Jacob Arbenz in 1954.

When he went on to El Salvador to file his dispatches, one on the unrealized coup, and one on the base, Dudman was rather contemptuous of the guerrilla effort. He wrote that it didn't look to him like a million-dollar air base, as *The Nation* had suggested. His editors weren't impressed with the story. They combined his two dispatches and subordinated the guerrilla piece to that on the coup. However, the Dudman dispatch contained the essential elements, the training base, the guerrillas, the rumors of CIA sponsorship. It appeared in the *St. Louis Post-Dispatch* November 23, 1960, and created no national interest. Later on in the winter of 1960–61 Dudman was to write a continuing series of dispatches which illuminated U.S. preparations. Their impact on the country was nil.

With the curious compartmentalization that renders the national press blind to the reports of even such distinguished regional papers as the *St. Louis Post-Dispatch,* Dudman's story produced no answering echo in the media. Certainly it escaped the attention of John F. Kennedy and his associates, now immersed in the fever of preparing to take over the administration January 20, 1961.

On December 1 a reader, John G. Katecht of Northbrook, Pennsylvania, wrote *The New York Times* asking whether the assertions of *The Nation* were true and if so why they had not been reported by *The New York Times*. The letter landed on the desk of Clifton Daniel.

Daniel thought the reader's question was legitimate and suggested to foreign editor Freedman that he look further into the matter.

The Times moved with something less than promptitude. It was not until the first week of January 1961 that Paul Kennedy was sent to Guatemala to have another look.

By this time a great deal more had happened. There had been snippets about the guerrillas in the *Washington Post, The Wall Street Journal,* the Spanish-language New York newspaper, *Diario de las Américas,* and the *U.S. News & World Report.* The *Los Angeles Times* sent its aviation editor, Donald Dwiggins, to Guatemala. Like Dudman, he poked about and discovered the training camps. On December 22, 1960, his story appeared in the *Los Angeles Times* and was reprinted in *The Nation*'s issue of January 7, 1961.* Word of what was going on was now so widespread that even *Time* magazine ran a spread in its issue of January 6, 1961, a very knowledgeable piece, outlining the plans and reporting that "Mr. B is the CIA agent in charge." Mr. B, of course, was Frank Bender.

It is fair to say, thus, that by January 1961 the scope and detail of the operation had been about as widely disseminated as possible, short of an official announcement by the CIA. As far as conspiratorial technique was concerned the CIA had demonstrated the same degree of amateurism which had been shown by Lenin and his Bolsheviks when they were plotting their coup d'état of November 7, 1917, in Petrograd. One had to be blind and deaf not to know what was going on.

By this time there was not the slightest reason to suppose that the Castro Cubans were not privy to the "secret" plans. Indeed, in a New Year's address by Foreign Minister Rao to the United Nations Security Council December 31, 1960, he publicly denounced the forthcoming invasion and said that the State Department had circulated a document "to all chancelleries" (presumably of the Organization of American States) declaring that the Cubans were preparing "seventeen launching pads for Soviet missiles." The document said that construction on the missile pads had been temporarily halted but that the U.S. was prepared to intervene if the construction work was resumed.†

This then was the situation when Paul Kennedy returned to Guatemala. Kennedy now, like Dudman and Dwiggins before him, had a look at the incredibly beautiful Alejos coffee plantation. He penetrated a couple of miles into the staging area before he was thrown out.

---

*Dwiggins reported that U.S. pilots were being recruited at $25,000 a head to fly "in a fantastic air-raid operation scheduled for some time early in 1961." (Aronson, *The Press and the Cold War,* p. 158)

†Rao's allegation December 31, 1960 of an *Eisenhower* plan to invade Cuba because of the construction of missile pads casts a curious and so-far unexplained shadow ahead to the Cuban missile crisis of autumn 1962.

He reported that intensive air practice was going on daily; he saw commando forces in combat training directed by "foreign personnel mostly from the United States," which, he said, was supporting the operation with material, construction and improvement of air facilities. He said that opponents of President Ydigoras had contended the preparations were offensive and that they were paid for and directed in large measure by the United States. However, he once again interviewed President Ydigoras, who described it as Guatemala's effort to protect herself against Cuban attack. There was much local detail to support the Ydigoras version. Paul Kennedy said that the United States had turned down requests for material requested by the Guatemalans because these requests went beyond defensive needs. He said the Guatemalan "guerrillas" had been drawn from each of the Guatemalan military districts and had been flown back to their posts during the abortive November revolt and then returned to the Alejos plantation. He added the curious detail that some trainers were Russian-speaking and shouted their orders in Russian so that the commandos would become familiar with Russian. There was no explanation what this meant.

Kennedy's dispatch was low key but it was published on page one of *The Times* together with a map of Central America. There was only one thing wrong with it. Had the story been dictated by the CIA as a cover it could hardly have done better. The first paragraph, under a Retalhuleu dateline, said, "This area is the focal point of Guatemala's military preparation for what Guatemalans consider will be an almost inevitable clash with Cuba."

True, at the end of the article *The Times* tacked on what is called a shirttail, quoting Cuba's Foreign Minister Rao in New York as saying the United States was training mercenaries in Florida and Guatemala for an invasion of Cuba. But, as the state of public consciousness clearly was to disclose, this was not enough to alert readers. Freedman received half a dozen complaints about the story, half criticizing *The Times* for suggesting the U.S. was involved, half complaining *The Times* hadn't exposed the U.S. role.

There is no way now of discovering why an experienced correspondent like Paul Kennedy went out of his way to stress the "Guatemalan" aspect of the story.* Paul Kennedy has been dead for several years. Freedman commended him for his Retalhuleu story and added, "Let's keep ball rolling. Have tip Yucatan might be fruitful after you complete present visit." For whatever reason Paul Kennedy wrote no more on

---

*Paul Kennedy was never regarded by his editors as a top-flight correspondent. However, his performance on this story fell so far below par as to raise questions of motivation.

the subject until April 1961 despite several prods from Freedman.

The Paul Kennedy dispatch was published ten days before John F. Kennedy's inauguration in Washington. There is no sign that it was read at the time by the incoming President or his associates. One can only speculate on the effect on future history had Paul Kennedy presented the reality of the operations under way at the Alejos coffee *finca*. Had Paul Kennedy attributed it all to a CIA-sponsored scheme to invade Cuba one can imagine the sensation this would have produced on the eve of John Kennedy's swearing-in. It is possible, of course, that the operation would have stayed on the rails laid down by Allen Dulles. But it would have given the new President and the public an opportunity to know what was happening and to make a judgment at an early and convenient time.

The defective and generally misleading Kennedy dispatch from Retalhuleu provided a classic example of the damage inflicted on public perceptions by inadequate reportage. It is symptomatic of the shallowness of most discussions of the role of the press that in the thousands of words written later about *The New York Times'* coverage of the Bay of Pigs not one critic, inside or outside the journalistic profession, zeroed in on this defective reportage by Paul Kennedy.

To be certain, the planners and the movers in the CIA had noticed the spreading stories about their operation but they said nothing to anyone in a position to influence the course of events. Allen Dulles and General Lemnitzer gave a detailed briefing January 22 to a group which included the President, Secretary of State Dean Rusk, Robert McNamara and Robert Kennedy. They failed to point out that secrecy had long since been stripped from the scheme, that Castro was aware on what may have been a day-by-day basis of what was happening and that a dozen reports had already appeared in the American and Latin press.

The flurry of individual stories made no impact on public perception or knowledge. The great television and radio networks, which served as the source of information for so many Americans, said no word about it. The number of Americans outside a small circle in Washington who had an idea of what was going on probably numbered at most a thousand or two.

In what was to become a familiar pattern the American public knew nothing; the man against whom the plot was directed, Fidel Castro, knew almost everything.

Ten years later as the editors of *The New York Times* discussed with their lawyers the morals, principles and precedents which should underlie their decision on the Pentagon Papers these details had long since become fuzzy in their minds if, indeed, they had ever lodged there, and in the discussions the editors were guided more by instinct and an overwhelming feeling for what was right and just and where their duty lay than by the wisdom which comes from precise knowledge of the past and close analysis of the consequences.

15

A Critical Mass

*T*AD SZULC LOOKS like a secret agent. He acts like one. He talks like one, and not a few young reporters, seeing him in action, classical tan trenchcoat and all, an accent that perfectly fits The Third Man, a weary arrogance that suits a spy who can't come in from the cold, have imagined that he might be a secret CIA agent.

In fact, Tad Szulc was in 1961, as he had been for eight years in the past and would be for eleven years into the future, an experienced and energetic correspondent for *The New York Times.* His background was Polish (Szulc was born in Warsaw; his name is the Polish transliteration of Schultz) and much of his professional career had been spent in Latin America. In March of 1961 he had completed a six-year tour of duty and had left Rio de Janeiro to travel by leisurely stages to Washington, where he had been reassigned.

Szulc had reported from Cuba before and after the rise of Castro. He knew the Cuban underground and numbered among his friends not only leaders of anti-Castro movements but CIA, State Department and American military specialists in Cuban and Latin affairs. He was, in Turner Catledge's phrase, the kind of reporter who is "news-prone," by which Catledge meant that almost as soon as Szulc arrived in a city or a country something happened that made the headlines. Later, *The Times* assigned Szulc to Spain in hope this would put him on hand for the death of Generalissimo Franco and the exciting events which were bound to follow. On this occasion Szulc's magic failed. He waited three years in Madrid and left in frustration for another assignment, the venerable Franco still in good health.

It was literally true, as the younger reporters noted, that Szulc *looked* the role of a secret operative. He liked to whisper from the corner of his mouth and this habit, overlaid by his accent, made his observations seem even more mysterious than they were. He had a passion for meeting odd strangers in ill-lighted bars in ill-frequented parts of town —any town. It was rare when he would pinpoint a source but his reporting was often exclusive and there were few men as good at digging into cryptic goings-on in romantic settings like Budapest,

Havana, Vientiane or, as was to transpire, Miami. His specialty was scoops. Sometimes, his enthusiasm for scoops misled him (as was later to be the case on the Watergate story) but this did not happen often.*

Now, in late March 1961, on his way to Washington he paused in Panama to see friends and came on to Miami on March 31 intending to spend a leisurely Easter weekend with someone whom he would never describe more precisely than to say he was a U.S. Government official who had formerly been stationed in Cuba and now was in Miami for professional reasons—obviously a CIA man.

Szulc had read *The Nation*'s account of the Guatemalan training camps and his friend Paul Kennedy's January 10, 1961, report but he had not come to Miami on a reporting assignment. He had come to relax and in the late afternoon of Friday, March 31, he was sitting with his old friend and the friend's wife in the bar of the MacAllister Hotel having a drink. As Szulc sipped his first martini his friend began to tell him about the Cuban project. As they talked a young Cuban Szulc had known as active in the Havana underground against Castro came up. In no time he was talking about the invasion plans and arranging to meet Szulc the next morning to give him more details. Soon an old naval friend of Szulc's from Cuba sauntered by. It took no more for Szulc to know he had stumbled onto something hot.

Within twenty-four hours Szulc possessed the major details of the operation. He knew of its CIA sponsorship and direction; he knew about Frank Bender and had his phone number (when he called Bender refused to talk); he knew how the recruitment and training were being conducted; he had the details of the Guatemalan camps; he had located an old airfield at Opa-Locka, Florida, which the CIA was using (the same field had been used by the CIA in its Guatemalan operation for the overthrow of President Arbenz in 1954); he had spotted young recruits moving off to training; he knew that physicians and nurses had been signed on for battle duty. He had been able to accomplish this swiftly because he had done a lot of reporting from Cuba, knew the Cubans, had good contact among the émigrés and American personnel who dealt with Cuba. If Szulc could gather such detail in forty-eight hours, Castro agents in place could do the same or better.

---

*During Szulc's career in the Washington bureau of *The New York Times* his fellow correspondents noted in awe, envy and amazement that every Wednesday he received a plain brown envelope, delivered by a special messenger. The CIA Executive Committee, which approved all operations, met every week on Tuesday morning. The plain brown envelope, it was whispered breathlessly, contained the *minutes* of that weekly meeting, specially provided to Szulc by one of his high sources. No one ever knew whether this was true for Szulc was not one to deny or confirm such a report. But the fact that the story was widely believed in *The Times* office is a measure of the legends which surrounded Szulc.

The Plot

By the time Szulc arrived in Miami the anti-Castro plot had vanished from the pages of the principal American newspapers although it continued to glimmer now and again in secondary papers, including some in Florida.

The disappearance of news stories did not mean that the CIA had abandoned its plans. In fact they rapidly matured. The U.S. Chiefs of Staff had given an O.K. somewhat grudgingly. President Kennedy was going forward although some advisers, notably Arthur Schlesinger and Dean Rusk, had no stomach for it. There were the inevitable delays. The first target date was April 5, 1961, but as late as March 16 Kennedy was saying that while the CIA could go ahead the operation might be called off on twenty-four hours' notice. An insurrection had broken out among the guerrillas in Guatemala but the CIA concealed this from the White House. President Ydigoras of Guatemala came to Washington in February and begged the President to get his adventurers out of the country, and Allen Dulles was beginning to talk about the "disposal problem," by which he meant what would they do with the guerrillas if the invasion was canceled. At one point CIA advisers told the guerrillas to go ahead with the operation even if Washington called it off.

Finally on April 5 President Kennedy signed off a "go" after a meeting of his advisers at which only Senator Fulbright and Arthur Schlesinger openly opposed the coup. D-Day was again advanced, this time to April 10 and then to April 17.

These complex discussions went on out of sight of the public. Not an echo appeared in the press. Not a line was printed in *The New York Times* or the *Washington Post.* While no President had entered the White House with closer press friends than Kennedy none of this coterie, not William H. Lawrence of *The New York Times,* not Charles Bartlett of the *Chattanooga Times,* not Ben Bradlee then of *Newsweek,* wrote a line about Castro or the CIA. If they knew anything they kept it to themselves. The national newspapers paid no notice to the drumfire of accusations coming out of Havana. The defective Paul Kennedy story seemed to have laid the subject to rest.

One day in late March an old Carolina friend of Clifton Daniel's, Don Shoemaker, editor of the *Miami Herald,* happened to be in New York. Daniel took him to lunch at Sardi's. Shoemaker regaled Daniel with stories about the coming invasion of Cuba. He said the commandos were drilling on the Florida beaches in full public view.* Everyone

---

*A photograph of the Cubans training in Florida was published on the front page of the Spanish-language newspaper *El Avance* of Miami March 3. It subsequently appeared in *Time* magazine with a UPI credit line and a caption pinpointing it as having been taken in Florida. (Clifton Daniel in memo to Turner Catledge, 4/26/61)

in Miami, including Castro's agents, knew what was coming off. The Miami papers had written a little about this, although gingerly. They were fearful of treading on national security interests.∫

By the end of March there were signs that the story was coming to life again. Arthur Schlesinger recalled being told March 31 by Howard Handleman of *U.S. News & World Report*, just back from Florida, that Cuban exiles were saying to anyone who would listen that they were about to invade Cuba with everything by way of U.S. support that they wanted. A few days later Gilbert Harrison, editor of *The New Republic*, sent to Schlesinger at the White House a comprehensive report on "Our Men in Miami," written by Karl Meyer. Schlesinger showed it to President Kennedy, who asked that it not be published and it wasn't.

The Times on the Story

Szulc telephoned New York and asked permission to come up and talk about the story and on Monday afternoon April 3 he presented his findings to foreign editor Freedman, managing editor Catledge and publisher Orvil Dryfoos, whom Catledge invited to sit in because of the importance of Szulc's information. Catledge immediately authorized Szulc to return to Miami and dig out the whole story. At the same time he put *The Times'* machinery into gear. Max Frankel was alerted to go to Guantanamo, the U.S. naval base in Cuba. Paul Kennedy was ordered back to Guatemala as fast as he could make it and Reston in Washington was told what was up.

Szulc stopped by Washington on his way to Miami. He had no trouble in getting confirmation of what he had already heard in Miami. Scotty Reston talked to Allen Dulles, who did not deny something was afoot but said the CIA was not involved.

Wallace Carroll, Reston's deputy in Washington, a man with extraordinary intelligence contacts (he had left newspaper jobs several times to undertake important psychological warfare and intelligence-related assignments) went to work on the story. He talked first to Arthur Schlesinger, a World War II associate in London, now in the White House. Schlesinger told him that the Cuban operation was "the hottest thing in government and is gathering momentum." However, he said that it was still being debated and that "if I know Jack Kennedy he will not allow this to happen."

Carroll then went to Richard Helms, an old and close friend. They had worked together in UPI in Europe before the war. Helms was deputy to Richard Bissell in CIA who was in charge of the operation. However, Helms told Carroll he had disassociated himself from the Cuban project. Helms told Carroll, as Carroll recalled, "You have to

∫See Notes section.

understand the lead-time on this. If you are going to stop it you will have to act damn quick."

Carroll telephoned his information to Catledge, warning that the final decision had not been taken and that unless care was taken *The Times* "could be caught holding the bag."*

While Szulc rushed back to Miami, Paul Kennedy checked in to Guatemala again. He called on President Ydigoras' secretary, who said, "What! You back? Did they let you back into Guatemala?"

Kennedy jokingly said he had come back to "know something about plans to invade Cuba from Guatemala." The secretary told him he would be put in jail if he talked like that. Kennedy poked around a day and a half, then cabled Freedman "nothing apparent here" and proposed going on. Freedman told him with some asperity to stay in Guatemala until further notice.

In New York the legendary Peter Kihss, whom many newspapermen of his generation revered as the founder of contemporary investigative reporting and a man who at his prime had no peer in its practice, went to see Foreign Minister Raul Rao at the United Nations and on April 6 *The Times* published Rao's assertion that a "so-called liberation army" of counter-revolutionaries, mercenaries and adventurers, including ex-Nazis, had been rounded up by the United States and was being trained for invasion of Cuba at bases in Guatemala and Florida. He was prepared to give the United Nations specific information on the location of the bases and displayed to Kihss photocopies of U.S. checks which he said had been paid to dependents of the guerrillas.

The operation, Rao said, was under the direction of "United States experts" and had the active cooperation of U.S. officials. It was, as events were to show, an excellent outline of exactly what was in progress.†

The news that Szulc had stumbled upon a major story involving Cuba did not remain a secret in the *Times* newsroom. From the moment of his meeting with Catledge there were whispered rumors that he was

---

*This was Carroll's recollection in a personal conversation June 7, 1979.
†Kihss had specialized in Cuban affairs, among many other things. He had heard for months rumors that the United States was backing an attempt by the refugees to overthrow Castro but he personally doubted Castro could be overthrown because he was so well entrenched. The plot, he felt, was almost certain to fail. City editor Frank Adams suggested that Kihss interview Rao to see what he knew of U.S. plans with the idea that *The Times* would publish such material as seemed to be solidly based, sloughing off Cuban propaganda. Kihss hoped this might cause President Kennedy to take a second look at plans for an invasion. When Kihss talked with Rao he knew Szulc was working on a Cuban story but knew none of the details. (Personal interview, Kihss, 11/22/78)

"onto something big" that involved Cuba. There were even reports that it had to do with the CIA.

By the time Szulc got back to Miami he was not alone. At least three more national correspondents had checked in at the MacAllister Hotel. They were Stuart Novins of CBS, Hal Levine of *Newsweek* and Howard Handleman of *U.S. News & World Report,* who had come back after telling Schlesinger about his findings on March 31. These men were professionals. Their presence ensured that within a short span of time they would have the basic facts of the invasion project.

Szulc and Novins began to work as a team. They were not in a competitive situation, one reporting for a newspaper and the other for radio, and they were able to intensify their efforts by exchanging impressions and reports.

By noon of April 6 Szulc felt he had his story in hand and sat down to write a dispatch which said the invasion was imminent (Szulc had been told that all Caribbean wireless transmissions for April 18 had been suspended and believed this indicated the invasion would be on that date); that it was organized and led by the CIA; and outlined in detail the roles assigned to the Cubans and the general shape of the intended operation. Szulc and Novins agreed to file their stories for what amounted to simultaneous release. Szulc would appear in the first edition of *The New York Times,* hitting the street at about 9:45 P.M. and Novins' broadcast tape would be played at 11 P.M.*

Szulc's story arrived in New York, two columns long. A good many telephone conversations followed between Szulc and Freedman. Freedman, a careful, cautious and conservative man, was concerned lest Szulc in his enthusiasm go overboard. Finally all Freedman's questions were met and answered and the Szulc story was edited and prepared for publication.

The Times bullpen, that is, the major news editors, Theodore Bernstein and Lewis Jordan, two skilled professionals who approached the daily task of "laying out" page one of *The Times* with the solemnity of open-heart surgeons, placed the Szulc story in column eight of page one and assigned it a four-column headline. This meant that the story led the paper and the four-column headline signified in the typographical symbolism of *The Times* that it was a story of exceptional importance—not, perhaps, as important as Congress overriding a presidential veto of a tax bill; certainly not as important as the death of a pope or the election of a new governor of New York State but decidedly more important than a presidential press conference or a speech by the Secretary of State on a "new Soviet threat." The headline and the play were designed to bring the story forcefully to

---

*Actually the Novins' broadcast was used in the 8 P.M. CBS "World News Roundup."

the attention of the ordinary readers of *The Times* and perhaps even more important, in the minds of Bernstein and Jordan, to the attention of the key figures of the media, the editors, for example, of *Time* and *Newsweek*, of the *Washington Post* and *The Wall Street Journal*, to Walter Cronkite of CBS and, of course, to that special elite of readers, the President of the United States, the Secretary of State, the Prime Minister of England, the Soviet Communist Party Secretary, the powerful committee chairmen of the Senate and the House and the heads of great banks like Chase and Morgan and Rothschild.

When Bernstein and Jordan assigned a headline and play position on page one of *The New York Times* they felt (and they were not far from being right) that this was a judgment akin to that of the Joint Chiefs of Staff in assessing a degree of military alert.

The layout of page one was a ritual performed in Bernstein's monastic cubicle at the southeast corner of the third-floor newsroom, a room devoid of decor except for a map of the world painted on the wall in front of which Bernstein sat and a rather poorly executed self-portrait in oil, Bernstein seated at his desk, Jordan leaning over his shoulder and a satanic Daniel in profile, witnessing the sacred rite. Bernstein and Jordan sat down to their task after the general news conference held by managing editor Catledge. They worked swiftly and in virtual silence, their minds and news judgment so finely attuned that rarely was there disagreement, and in these rare cases Jordan, a tall, quiet, studious, intense man who suffered a slight impairment of hearing, quickly deferred to Bernstein, his senior, his mentor, his idol, a man of high nervous tensions, heavy cigarette consumption and extremely conscious (and jealous of) his genuinely unique talent and position. Catledge was, in theory, of course, free to attend and participate in the process but almost never did. It went forward in what some witnesses felt was the holy hush of the communion with a subaltern editor or two sitting silently at the table, never uttering a word, drinking in what the participants felt was the ultimate ecstasy of the news process, ready to rush to the duplicating machine the completed draft of the page-one layout as soon as it was done. It was not unusual when important news was breaking for Bernstein to autograph copies of the page-one layout for his colleagues to preserve among their important memorabilia.

After the dummy for this page had been drawn, Orvil Dryfoos, the publisher, did an unusual thing. He came down to the office of Turner Catledge and said that he had been talking to Reston in Washington and that Reston had advised against saying that the invasion was "imminent." Reston did not believe *The Times* should be so precise and noted that the plan might change and *The Times* would be left holding the bag; he felt that if the affair went sour *The Times* could be blamed for tipping off Castro.* Dryfoos told Catledge he wondered whether *The Times* should carry the story at all. Catledge said *The Times* had to carry a story. It was obvious that something was brewing in Florida and this was major news. Catledge proposed removing the reference to the imminence of the invasion and the specific references to the CIA since, as he later contended, *The Times* couldn't prove it was a CIA project and the U.S. had so many secret organizations it might be another that was involved. Catledge proceeded to reduce the play of the story from a four-column headline to a one-column headline. Catledge never offered an explanation of why he cut the size of the headline but presumably this was an outcome of his conversation with Dryfoos.†

After he finished talking with Dryfoos he called the bullpen and ordered the changes in the story and in its page-one play. Bernstein and Jordan were stunned. Never had Catledge intervened or counter-manded a layout.‡ The two men made the ordered changes but they were badly shaken. Bernstein, following his ritual, left for Sardi's for his one-martini and rather spartan dinner, a meal he always took at the same table, crammed into the hour or so between the final layout of page one and the closing of the paper and beginning of the makeup process about 8 P.M. Jordan remained behind. Bernstein and Jordan believed the changes had been made for political reasons and Jordan was more upset than he had been since starting work for *The Times* before World War II.

Finally he could not contain himself. He went to Catledge and told him that never since he had been on *The Times* had such a thing

---

*Dryfoos' telephone log shows he talked to Reston Monday, Tuesday and Wednesday. If he spoke again to Reston on Thursday he did not make a note of it. It seems almost certain that Reston's warning to Dryfoos was based on Carroll's information from Schlesinger and Helms which Carroll had already conveyed to Catledge (Personal interview, Carroll, 6/7/79)

†The nonreality of all this was emphasized when the first edition of *The Times* appeared. The reference to CIA and imminent invasion had been removed from Szulc's story but a "shirttail" had been attached which quoted Stuart Novins' broadcast to CBS reporting unmistakable signs that plans for the invasion of Cuba were in the "final stages." Novins said that the Miami guerrilla bases were "calm," the guerrillas having left by boat and plane for their final staging areas. From the beginning Szulc had made plain his knowledge that it was a CIA operation, not one conducted, say, by a secret army group.

‡The headline on the Szulc story read:

Anti-Castro Units
Trained to Fight
at Florida Bases
Force There and in Central
America Is Reported to
Total 5,000 to 6,000

occurred and he would like the publisher "to tell me in person the reasons for these changes before the first edition." Catledge flushed with anger. It was an unprecedented moment for him as well. His personal authority was challenged. Nonetheless, he telephoned Dryfoos to come down. The publisher spoke with Jordan and said he believed the changes must be made in the interests of national security. The matter rested there. The publisher, of course, had the authority to do anything he pleased with the story but in the experience of Bernstein and Jordan no such power had been exercised. The incident left a mark on Bernstein (who talked the next day with Dryfoos) and Jordan and it told a great deal about the manner in which *The Times* was run and the enormous responsibility which was placed in the hands of line editors. The fact that their judgment was overridden in this case still burned when the men discussed it fifteen years later. To them the news evaluation ritual was sacred and they were its high priests. This process had been contaminated by infidels and they never really got over this.

The incident left a sense of guilt with both Catledge and Dryfoos. They knew that the reputation of *The Times* was dependent upon the objective functioning of the news process and they were always to be most defensive in discussing their actions on the Szulc story.

This was not a question which was to be understood outside *The Times*. Not then; not later.

Kennedy's Response

What happened outside *The Times* was something very different. Although *The Times* (and other newspapers) now began to report daily on the guerrillas and the invasion plans, no reaction was evident in the White House. It was later contended (by President Kennedy among others) that the invasion was in too advanced a stage to be called off when the Szulc story appeared although by this time there was not a shred of secrecy cloaking it. Despite the editing of *The Times* story and the reduction in play the cat was out of the bag and everyone in and out of Washington knew it. As for the claim that the interval between April 7 and the invasion date of April 17 was too short a period in which to cancel—this, of course, was nonsense. The invasion had been on and off since mid-March with the date constantly being advanced because Kennedy couldn't make up his mind. Ten days was more than ample time for Kennedy to cancel had he wanted to; he had told Arthur Schlesinger, Jr., "You know, I've reserved the right to stop this thing up to twenty-four hours before the landing"; there was ample time for Congress to have reared on its hind legs if it had wanted to; for Fulbright and others to denounce the plans; for other American newspapers and media to have weighed in with major coverage; for the American public to have shouted disapproval.

It did not happen. Steadily, inevitably, with the sureness of the Greek tragedy which it resembled, the actors played their parts; pitiful wisps of CIA imagery were cast about the oh-so-public plans; pseudo-guerrilla radio stations (Radio Swan and others) made their propaganda broadcasts; the generals tinkered with the plan; Kennedy sweated; imitation dissident Cuban fliers carried out strikes on Cuba although they flew them from Guatemala (the CIA didn't even get the right model aircraft to maintain the deception); Castro moved his forces about with the coolness of an old revolutionary; Cuba was put on alert; everything was nailed down and the ambiguous and stupid operation crashed forward to inevitable disaster.

Predictably, *The Times'* coverage of the Cuban adventure was accurate and informed—how could it have been otherwise with Szulc and a battery of knowledgeable reporters on the scene? *The Times'* editorial page, however, did not distinguish itself. Although the editors knew as much as they needed to know about what lay ahead they published nothing of consequence, nothing that might give a lead to public or to government. The only illumination was contained in two dramatic columns by Reston that raised the question of how far the United States could legitimately go in secretly arming and assisting a group of Cubans to overthrow Castro without placing in doubt its commitment to international law and order and, specifically, its commitments under the charters of the United Nations and the Organization of American States.

"The moral dilemma," said Reston, "of backing an invasion of a country to which we are treaty bound . . . remains."

And, he added, in what was the essence of it all:

"If we have reached that point [of invasion] over the deteriorating military situation in Cuba a Government of laws should at least let the people know."

Reston had arrived at the core issue and stated it fair and clear in his column on the editorial page of *The New York Times* on April 12. Five more days lay ahead before the CIA launched its pitiful puppets on the doomed adventure. Reston's question was not answered. It was not picked up by any other newspaper. It was not echoed in the editorials of his own newspaper. Nor did the President of the United States bother to respond. The question still stares out, shimmering with the true aura of reality from the yellowed files of *The Times.*

Once the dreary debacle had run its course the quick, instinctive response of the bureaucrats was to look for a scapegoat and the first that came to hand was the press, particularly *The New York Times.*

At a State Department briefing two days after the failure Allen Dulles told newsmen that the Bay of Pigs proved there should be an "official secrets act." He admitted that other lawyers thought this unconstitutional but added that he was a lawyer, too, and he knew what the country needed. Roger Tubby, the State Department press officer, chimed in, saying that newsmen must be concerned not only whether a matter was newsworthy but whether it was in the public interest to print it.

To which Richard Dudman, the straight-arrow correspondent of the *St. Louis Post-Dispatch,* angrily responded that "the problem is not too much information but too little information. If there had been enough information the American people would have risen up and stopped it."

President Kennedy continued in the Dulles theme at a talk to the Bureau of Advertising of the American Newspaper Publishers Association April 27 in which he called upon newspapers to impose self-censorship. "Every newspaper now asks itself with respect to every story, 'Is it news?' All I suggest is that you add the question, 'Is it in the interest of national security?' "

This tactic disturbed many editors and they went to the White House a couple of weeks later, led by Turner Catledge, and asked the President what he meant.

The President complained about the Paul Kennedy story of January 10 (of all things) and when Catledge pointed out that the essential details of the invasion had been reported by a number of publications the President smiled and said, "But it was not news until it appeared in *The Times.*"

Yet at the moment of saying this he called Catledge aside and said, "Maybe if you had printed more about the operation you would have saved us from a colossal mistake."

But this was an ex post facto opinion and it was by no means shared by the sponsors of the disaster. Allen Dulles came to the board room of *The Times* Friday afternoon, May 12, accompanied by Tracy Barnes, a close CIA associate. He met with Dryfoos, editorial page editor John Oakes, Punch and Clifton Daniel.

By this time there was widespread feeling in Washington that President Kennedy might dismember the CIA. He had said in his first anger that he would "sunder the CIA into a thousand pieces." There were rumors of further and more damaging disclosures. These had been touched on by Walter Lippmann in a column in the *Herald-Tribune* and he was so disturbed that he telephoned Reston to suggest that the crimes of the CIA were so vast that only a great news organization like *The New York Times* could properly undertake the task of investigating them. He did not believe the inquiry was within the competence of his own newspaper, the *Herald-Tribune.* As so often, Lippmann proved remarkably prescient although it was to be five years before the first *New York Times* inquiry into the CIA was to get under way.

Dulles' presentation to *The Times* on that May afternoon was not effective. He stressed the danger of the CIA being dismembered and of its losing the confidence of the American people. (It had already lost Kennedy's confidence.) He felt the press had been responsible for the CIA's troubles by printing "untrue information" and he particularly singled out *The New York Times.* Among the assertions which *The Times* and other newspapers had printed which he said were untrue were allegations that the CIA had been poorly informed about the possibility of an uprising in Cuba, that it had favored right-wing Cuban elements and that it had imprisoned left-wingers in the émigré army.

"My honest opinion," Daniel wrote in a memorandum to Catledge, "was that Mr. Dulles made a very poor case. He did not effectively, to my mind, disprove the allegations against the CIA."

Dryfoos thanked Dulles for his presentation and asked him what he proposed that *The Times* do. Dulles had no answer to that and the meeting ended on this inconclusive note.

All the meeting had done was to make clear that the crime to Dulles' mind was not the stupidity of the operation and his operators but the revelation of that stupidity. In this there was no facing up to the underlying implications of the Bay of Pigs.

The Times, in an editorial of May 10 entitled "The Right Not to Be Lied To," made an effort to close this gap. "Neither prudence nor ethics," it said, "can justify any administration in telling the public things that are not so. . . . A democracy—our democracy—cannot be lied to. . . . The basic principle involved is that of confidence." Here it was again. Lies. . . . The government lies. In a column, published on the same day, Reston touched on a problem much closer to home— the role of the press, including that of *The New York Times.* The press, he observed, had known what was going on. It knew that the United States was breaking its treaty commitments. It knew we were putting our reputation in the hands of a "squabbling band of refugees."

But, said Reston, the American press, which had "roared with indignation when Britain and France broke their treaty commitments to invade Suez," had "very little to say about the morality, legality or practicality of the Cuban adventure when there was time to stop it."

If, Reston concluded, "the press had used its freedom during this period to protest it might have been influential even in the White House."

Reston's words could have been a lecture to his own editors. Perhaps they were so intended, but even this wisdom was quickly obscured in the scapegoating and wry efforts of President Kennedy to put the affair behind him.

The editors of *The Times* were somewhat flattered at Kennedy's suggestion that they should have published more on the Bay of Pigs but knew that had the operation been canceled, the press, and specifically *The Times,* would have been made sacrificial lambs. They understood as well as Kennedy that one reason why he did not cancel the Bay of Pigs was that it had been concocted by a Republican administration. Had he washed it out he would have been charged with partisanship and cowardice. For the press it was a no-win situation. But this was not unusual. Rare was the politician who would give the press credit for saving his shirt, or the country's for that matter.

The Missile Crisis

Of course Kennedy learned a lesson from the Bay of Pigs, as far as *The Times* and the press were concerned, and it was to serve him in good stead the next time a "national security" crisis arose.

Dryfoos emerged from the episode with a nagging concern for the proper role of the press vis-á-vis national security. He was convinced that *The Times* had acted correctly in the Bay of Pigs but he realized that the issue might arise in different form in the future.

He met with President Kennedy in the White House September 13, 1962, for a serious discussion of these issues.

Before going into the talk he had been carefully briefed by Catledge on the importance, as publisher of *The New York Times,* of insisting that the paper fulfill its obligation to its readers.

This, Catledge noted, was essential if the readers were intelligently to exercise their functions as citizens and voters.

"National security," Catledge said, "must not be confused with political security."

Catledge urged Dryfoos to stress that the press must be aggressive in seeking out information and bold in presenting it.

"No government official, from the President down," Catledge advised Dryfoos, "can possibly have any greater awareness of the public interest than you have as the publisher of one of the world's most influential newspapers. Furthermore, we do not believe that there is any more disinterested group of citizens in the country than the editors of this newspaper."

Catledge concluded by insisting that "a free press in a free society cannot accept an absolute veto by any public official, except in times of war."*

Catledge was frank in his presentation to Dryfoos as was Dryfoos, in his quiet way, in talking to Kennedy. It was on this occasion that Kennedy told Dryfoos, "I wish you had run everything on Cuba. I am just sorry you didn't tell it at the time."

---

*Catledge's memo was not cited by *The Times* in the Pentagon Papers case. It lay forgotten in *The Times'* archives.

Neither man could have realized that a month later the issue of *The Times* and national security would arise once again; once again the question would be Cuba; once again the issue would be joined in dramatic form.

On Sunday, October 21, 1962, Scotty Reston learned that the Russians had placed missiles in Cuba.* The President telephoned and asked him to hold up the news. He said he was going on television Monday evening to inform the American public and he needed twenty-four hours to complete preparations to meet the Russian threat—otherwise Khrushchev might give him an ultimatum. Reston advised the President he could do nothing about the story; he would report the facts to his office in New York and, if his advice was asked, would recommend that the story not be published but it was not his responsibility to make the decision. Mr. Kennedy instantly telephoned Dryfoos, who agreed to withhold the news until the President completed his arrangements.

In fact, Dryfoos in his conversation at the White House September 13 had invited the President to do exactly what he did—to telephone him directly if a major matter of security arose in the future.†

In the aftermath it was impossible to determine whether the withholding played any significant role in the management of the crisis but it signaled an advance in the President's sophistication in dealing with the press.

Lessons

What was notable about the Bay of Pigs was the evolution of *The Times* in its role of responsible newspaper, publishing the news without "fear or favor" as Mr. Ochs would have said, even in a case where a President later questioned the propriety of the action.

The Times did publish the Szulc story and the deletions were not so material and the play was big enough to make clear to everyone what was going on.

---

*Many years later Reston confessed that "I probably faked it a little" in getting his scoop on the fact that the Soviets had implanted missiles in Cuba. In fact, he had called McGeorge Bundy, President Kennedy's security adviser, and, talking knowingly of what he had learned about preparations for the naval blockade of Cuba, had gotten from Bundy confirmation of what he suspected but did not actually know until Bundy said it—that the Soviet missiles were actually in place. Bundy telephoned Kennedy and the President almost immediately called Reston back. (Personal interview, Reston, 11/15/78)

†Kennedy wrote Dryfoos October 25, "I wish to express my appreciation to you and *The New York Times* for your cooperation last weekend. Events since then have reinforced my view that an important service to the national interest was performed by your agreement to withhold information that was available to you on Sunday afternoon. (*Times'* archives, John F. Kennedy to Orvil Dryfoos, 10/25/62)

But there were lessons that *The Times* did not learn. It did not look back to the Paul Kennedy story as a disaster, an act of misfeasance. In fact, when Turner Catledge wrote about the experience ten years later he cited it with pride. So did Daniel in his extended comment of June 1, 1966. Yet, this was clearly the point at which *The Times* went wrong and Daniel, at least, understood that *The Times* should not have dropped the matter with Paul Kennedy's report. It should have gone forward, followed up the story, checked again in Guatemala, followed matters in Florida and in Washington. This was not done and to this day there is no real explanation of why beyond the short attention span of editors.

But short attention span was to play a continuing role and when the editors assembled to argue about how to handle the Pentagon Papers with their lawyers not one of them remembered the sequence of events in the Bay of Pigs clearly enough to challenge the thesis which Loeb put forward. The government in April 1961 did not (as Loeb contended) know that *The Times* was going to publish the Szulc story although it was aware that *The Times* and other newsmen were probing in Miami. Nor did President Kennedy telephone publisher Dryfoos, Scotty Reston or Turner Catledge about the story as Loeb implied. The action which *The Times* took was on its own responsibility as a result of conversations between Reston and Dryfoos and Dryfoos and Catledge and Carroll and Catledge.

Most important, *The Times* had not killed Szulc's story. It had published it prominently on page one of its issue of April 7, 1961. A curious blackout of memory first affected Arthur Schlesinger, who wrote in his classic, *A Thousand Days,* in 1965, that the Szulc story had been suppressed as "another patriotic act." He added that he had often wondered if "the press had behaved irresponsibly, it would not have spared the country a disaster."

Schlesinger's memory misled him. But so did that of Louis Loeb, counsel of *The Times,* in the discussions of April 29. He repeated what Schlesinger had said, that *The Times* responded to presidential intervention—and not a *Times* man present challenged him.*

---

*William Colby, ex-chief of the CIA, as late as 1978 was following Schlesinger's lead and reporting of the Bay of Pigs that *The New York Times* at John F. Kennedy's request "suppressed" its story. (William Colby, *Honorable Men,* New York, 1978, pp. 181–82) Sanford J. Ungar, in *The Papers and The Papers* (New York, 1975) reported that the Szulc story was "buried deep inside the paper with a drab headline." (P. 99) Edwin Diamond, *Good News, Bad News* (Cambridge, 1978) followed the same mistaken pattern, writing that "the symbolic journalistic event of the 1960's was *The New York Times* decision not to print the story its reporters had obtained about the prospective Bay of Pigs invasion. Its editors, in consultation with the White House, feared publication would harm the operation." (*Nieman Reports,* Winter 1978, p. 13)

It was, as circumstances were to demonstrate, a tragic misremembrance by Loeb; an almost incomprehensible misremembrance by the editors of *The Times.*

The momentous decisions on Szulc were made by *The Times* on its own, acting in what the editors considered to be the broadest national interest. They slightly modified but did not suppress a story, even though it was a story of an *ongoing* military operation, one which they had reason to believe might be starting momentarily. Despite those factors (and, again and again through the years the argument later would echo: "Would you print the news of the departure of a troop ship?") *The Times* believed it was more important to publish than to withhold. Publish it did.

Regardless of what he thought at the first moment, an intelligent and bold President of the United States had finally said and repeated it a year later that *The Times* had been right and he had been wrong; that the public interest and *his* interest would have been better served with *more* published facts, not less.

This was the lesson of the Bay of Pigs, but it would take the country and future Presidents and even *The Times* a good many years before it got that lesson firmly tucked into its memory bank.

There was another aspect underlying all of this which neither *The Times* nor the world had become aware of and one which years later would not be really understood. *The Times* had now reached a critical mass, not a mass in terms of readers and advertisers, although this was inextricably linked to it. No, it had reached a critical mass of reporting and expertise. It now genuinely covered the world, covered Washington, covered the nation and the city with its own staff men and women, and these were not merely journeymen. They were the best reporters and editors who could be obtained. They had gathered on *The Times* not because of monetary rewards—*The Times*' pay scale was good but had never been spectacular. They had gathered because *The Times* offered a unique outlet for reporting and editing. Nowhere were standards of professionalism so high. This critical mass of reporters and editors now was of such size and quality that it functioned almost without conscious direction. All over the world *Times* men were ranging, news tentacles acutely inclined, probing and digging and asking questions.

Even David Halberstam presented a breathless account of an agitated President Kennedy on the telephone to James Reston, warning that the "blood of dead men" would be on the hands of *Times* editors and of Dryfoos ordering the story "sanitized." Dramatic stuff but it didn't happen. (David Halberstam, *The Powers That Be*, New York, 1979, pp. 447–48) Peter Wyden in his authoritative *Bay of Pigs*, New York, 1979, reported that "Dryfoos was in touch with the President." (P. 154) He wasn't. (Personal interviews, Reston, 8/5/79; Catledge, 3/8/79)

This was what led to the great story on the Bay of Pigs. No one assigned Szulc. No one directed him to go to Miami and find out what the CIA was up to. Nor was Szulc a genius. He simply passed through the city and within an hour or two was onto the story because he had the right contacts and the instinct to use them. All New York had to do after that was to let him go on doing what he did naturally. It was the same with Sheehan and the Pentagon Papers. A decade and a half later social scientists and political observers were still trying to find out what the *plan* was behind all this, how *The Times'* editors directed their men to get onto such stories and what the motivation was. They did not perceive the simplest truth of all—that the institution which Mr. Ochs had created to function without "fear or favor" had now begun to do precisely that.

So it was not so unusual perhaps that about the time preparations for the Bay of Pigs went into high gear a *Times'* correspondent, touching briefly in Honolulu, encountered a request. He was sought out by the Chief of Intelligence for CINCPAC, the American proconsul of the vast Pacific reaches. The intelligence officer had a problem. His duty was each day to prepare the world intelligence assessment for his chief. That he could do. But his chief had another requirement: that alongside the intelligence assessment on his desk there must also lie the latest copy of *The New York Times*. The intelligence man had subscribed for the airmail edition of *The Times* but *The Times* was sending him its international edition, then printed in Paris. This often took four days to arrive. How could he arrange to get the New York edition airmail in Honolulu each day? The delay in delivering the Paris edition was delaying his reports to the admiral.

The correspondent arranged the matter with ease, advising the circulation director in New York of the problem and a copy of the late city edition was daily flown to Honolulu at a cost to the U.S. Navy of about $300 a year.

Why, however, asked the correspondent, did the admiral insist on having *The New York Times* alongside the estimate which was made up on the basis of the U.S. intelligence establishment into which possibly $20 billion a year was being poured.

"Oh," said the naval intelligence man, "the admiral wants to check up on the intelligence and see what is really going on in the world. He can't do that without *The New York Times.*"

16

A Matter of Patriotism

THE PACE OF WORK on the Pentagon Papers rapidly quickened. A miniature staff was assembled at the New York Hilton. Sheehan worked on "the yellow floor" in Room 1106, the others on the "blue floor," the thirteenth. Sheehan's work habits were different. He rose late in the morning, spent the afternoon poring over documents and caught his stride as the evening wore on, hitting a peak between 1 A.M. and 4 A.M., long after the others had gone to bed. He found his hotel chair uncomfortable so the Washington bureau sent up his battered green straight-back steel Remington-Rand model by bus and it was taken to the Hilton suite.

Neil needed a special lamp for his desk and when his secretary, Muriel Stokes, went to buy it she ran into a boy friend who had been complaining because she was tied up every evening. "What are you doing?" he demanded. "Buying a lamp for the boss," she replied. "Oh, yeah!" he said. After the Papers were published he apologized. Most of the Hilton team became paranoid. Every time a waiter arrived with a ham sandwich they expected the FBI. Editor Jerry Gold ran into Flora Lewis, then a syndicated columnist. He was sure she suspected what he was up to. One Saturday morning he encountered Juan De Onis, a *Times* foreign correspondent. De Onis knew that Gold lived in New Jersey. "What are you doing in New York on a Saturday?" De Onis asked. Gold winked. "I wanted him to think I had a mistress in New York," Gold said. De Onis laughed and said, "Okay, don't worry. I won't tell."

The staff grew until there were fifteen or sixteen, including three editors, four reporters, five secretaries, one researcher, a makeup editor and several *Times* security guards who did not know what the staff was working on but who maintained twenty-four-hour vigilance. Three large safes were delivered to the suite in which to store the papers. Rough drafts and scrap paper were lugged back to *The Times* in shopping bags, "classified garbage" as the reporters called it, to be put through a shredder. After the government brought action to halt *The Times'* publication the shredder was used to destroy all copies of duplicated material that bore initials and notations. The shredded materials were taken to the eleventh-floor *Times* cafeteria and put into garbage disposals after the cafeteria closed at midnight.

There was constant fear that *The Times'* telephone lines had been tapped. Eugene Zaccor, *Times* security chief, brought in specialists early one Sunday when the building was almost empty and conducted a sweep of lines on the third, tenth and fourteenth floors, that is, the news floor, the editorial floor and the top executive floor. They made a physical check, searching for bugs or illegal connections and found none. They tested selected lines for possible pickups by microtransmission, that is microtransmitters attached to the lines and received by a nearby interceptor. It was very time-consuming but gave no indication of interceptions. No sweep of the Washington bureau was ever conducted.* *Times* reporters spotted the telephone security check and rumors spread that some "unclean" lines had been found and that a special lock had been installed on the junction box in the third-floor reception room. The staff at the Hilton frightened themselves with melodramatic fantasies. Someone had heard that the FBI once surrounded the house of Drew Pearson, the Washington columnist, with riflemen and seized confidential documents he had obtained. They worried that President Nixon might go on television, accuse the paper of treason and try to destroy it.† One afternoon Gold bumped into Ben Welles, son of the late Undersecretary of State, a *Times* diplomatic correspondent known to be extraordinarily close to the CIA. Gold exchanged the briefest of greetings and skulked away, certain that Welles had caught on to the story and would tell the agency. In reality the operation went forward in the Hilton as though it were invisible. Maids came in and out of the rooms, waiters brought meals, clerks and secretaries hauled mailbags of documents through the lobby but, as Al Siegal, an editor, concluded, "You could lead a camel through that hotel and nobody would notice it."

This did not apply to *The New York Times* staff on Forty-third Street. Nothing was more difficult than to keep a secret there. It did not take the reporters long to note which members of the staff had vanished and to conclude that a big project concerning the Vietnam war must be going on.

The inevitable occurred. On May 20 Nat Hentoff published an item in the *Village Voice* saying that a task force of *The New York Times*

---

*At one point *after* the Pentagon Papers it was rumored in the Washington bureau that Reston had had a warning from a high FBI official to be careful because *The Times* had been tapped. But Reston had no recollection of such a warning.
†Rosenthal had a private nightmare which he never told to anyone that Nixon would line up all the ex-Presidents, Truman, Eisenhower and Johnson, and go on national television together to blast *The Times*. (Personal interview, Rosenthal, 2/27/79)

was at work on a major exclusive which he described as a "breakthrough unpublished story concerning the White House, Pentagon and Southeast Asia." Hentoff noted that there was internal debate on the story and asked "Is this story going to be published? Or are there still *Times* executives and editors who might hold back such a story 'in the national interest'?"*

This sent a tremor through the reporting staff. It reinforced their paranoiac visions. Now, certainly, the police, the FBI, the CIA and Nixon would swoop down on them.

But this was melodrama of the imagination. Not a shred of evidence turned up to indicate that any agency of any kind got around to investigating what *The Times* was up to.

Behind the Scenes

Behind the James Bond fabric that had been woven in the minds of impressionable reporters, dramas of real significance were being played out. That of Neil Sheehan for example. Sheehan was obsessed with fear that the FBI might descend or that the Papers might suddenly be publicized on the Senate floor or in another medium while he was still struggling to write the first draft of his first story (it was not to be completed until May 18). And he was torn by the complexity of his relationship with Ellsberg. He had not told Ellsberg that he and Susan had copied the Papers; he had not told him that work on publication was so well advanced because, as he was later to explain, he continued to fear that despite everything *The Times* might not, in the end, publish the documents. He was like a small boy who is afraid to speak for fear his luck will change. It was a ticklish position and when it was over Sheehan agonized whether he had done the right thing, whether he should have brought Ellsberg into the picture earlier and was not at all certain that his conduct had been correct although experienced investigative journalists, men like David Halberstam, Wallace Turner and myself, assured him that he had no course but this under the tricky and unpredictable conditions in which he was working. At mid-May, Sheehan asked Ellsberg whether he might have a set of the Papers that Ellsberg had in a New York apartment. Ellsberg gave him permission to take the Papers for use in his story. Sheehan did not need this extra set of the Papers but he now had open and above board, with Dan's full knowledge, the basic tool for writing the story. The action had an important symbolic meaning for both men and was intended by Shee-

---

*Hentoff never disclosed his source, but years later he confirmed that he suspected it represented a leak from an editor who feared the story might not, after all, be published and wished to build a backfire against such an outcome. (*Village Voice*, 5/20/71; Hentoff, 12/28/79)

han as a signal to Dan that he was now proceeding to prepare the story although he again told Ellsberg (accurately) that no final decision to publish had been made by *The Times.*

Whatever significance the extra copy of the Papers had for Neil it did not cause Ellsberg to relax his efforts at obtaining publication by other means. On April 19, 1971, he attended an antiwar meeting at Princeton at which Senator Vance Hartke of Indiana and Representative Paul McCloskey, the antiwar Republican from California, appeared. McCloskey was testing the waters for a possible presidential challenge of Mr. Nixon. McCloskey knew of Ellsberg from his writings in the *New York Review of Books* and the men arranged to meet. McCloskey was so busy that the only opportunity he and Ellsberg had of talking was on a transcontinental flight to the Pacific Coast. Ellsberg bought a ticket, accompanied McCloskey to California and had a long discussion of the war and the Papers. He gave McCloskey documents concerning Johnson's 1965 decision to send the Marines into Vietnam and a selection of other papers, some six volumes in all, and told McCloskey he could have the rest when he wanted them. McCloskey stored the papers in his safe and had a member of his staff sleep nights in the office to keep watch over them.

Ellsberg was hoping that McCloskey could use the Papers in a filibuster against the Defense Appropriations Bill but, of course, filibusters can only be conducted in the Senate and McCloskey was a member of the House.

It was not long after this that Ellsberg made contact with Senator Gravel of Alaska. By this time Ellsberg was convinced that he must not put his eggs in one basket. Only by pursuing a selection of channels, he believed, would he be able to achieve his aim.

This was what Sheehan feared—that the story might break in Congress before he published it. He heard that McCloskey had the Papers, and late one night he telephoned Bob Phelps, the Washington editor whom he had first consulted in March. Phelps had already gone to bed.

"You know," he told Phelps, "how they are hounding me to get the story out. Now I've heard a rumor that McCloskey has the Papers. It would destroy us if he put the Papers out first. Could you sound out McCloskey? Don't let him know what we have."

Phelps invited McCloskey to lunch with some *Times* reporters to discuss reports that he was thinking of running for the presidency. In the course of the lunch Phelps took McCloskey aside and said, "I hear you have copies of some secret history of the Vietnam war."

McCloskey looked surprised. "That would be against the law."

Phelps pressed him. "Do you plan to give them to the *Los Angeles Times?*"

"Oh," said McCloskey, "that would be breaking the law. I learned in the Marine Corps that you don't break the law."

Phelps concluded that McCloskey was not going to give the Papers to a rival newspaper.*

This was true but McCloskey was a stubborn, determined man and he had by no means given up his effort to force the government to make public the papers. He now joined forces with Senator Fulbright, who was equally stubborn.†

Once again there was a dramatic colloquy in public before the Senate Foreign Relations Committee about the Pentagon Papers and the government's secrecy. It was the most open of all the discussions before the Papers were published by *The New York Times.*

McCloskey, testifying before the committee, offered a brief and accurate summary and description of the study telling how and why McNamara had ordered it. He said the Papers revealed the "deception of Congress" by the Executive branch and demanded that they be made public. Fulbright supported McCloskey and read into the record his latest request to Laird (made on April 30) noting that the Defense Department had taken the position that release of the documents "would be contrary to the national interest."

"We have had many instances," Fulbright observed, "going back to my first effort of looking into the validity of the allegations made at the time of the Gulf of Tonkin, of great difficulty in obtaining information."

Fulbright said that "the most difficult of all the questions that have confronted the committee since I have been in the Congress is how do you force cooperation of the Executive branch."

"We all are brought up to believe in this Constitution," Fulbright said. "I do believe in it, I think, if we can live up to it and if it can be made effective. How do you propose to force an unwilling Executive to respond to these requests for information?"

Without this information, he said, it was almost impossible to legislate intelligently.

McCloskey responded that "constitutionally and historically the

---

*Phelps kept close watch on the *Washington Post* but never saw any indication that they had the Papers. He also talked to Marc Raskin at the Institute for Policy Studies and concluded they were not going to make the Papers public and, in fact, only had a few volumes. (Personal interview, Phelps, 2/10/77)

†Seven years later Fulbright was to say that he felt it would have been counterproductive for him to make public the Papers given him by Ellsberg and conduct hearings on that basis. This would have confused the issue and caused the administration and prowar advocates to attack the release of the Papers, diverting attention from the issue of the war. This was why he insisted again and again that Laird turn the Papers over to the Foreign Relations Committee in accordance with normal governmental practice. (Personal interview, Fulbright, 9/9/78)

Congress was intended to be the dominant branch of the government. We enact the laws and the President carries them out."

McCloskey proposed that if the Executive branch continued to deny to the Congress information needed on which to form judgments then "we ought to go to the Supreme Court and have it ultimately determined whether the Chief Executive can extend this claim of Executive privilege to decisions that were made several years ago or facts which today exist."

Fulbright asked whether, in fact, the courts were not inclined to consider these questions as political and, thus, to refuse jurisdiction. To which McCloskey said with a certain eloquence:

"The nature of the despair that so many people feel that this government cannot be responsive justifies testing some of the more outrageous statements of this administration as to what is necessarily withheld by Executive privilege in a court."

Fulbright gently indicated skepticism of the judicial route. He thought it was a political question and that, if the war was to be halted or Congress was to carry out its responsibilities, "we have to generate in the Congress a sense that the Congress is important and that we are not sycophants or errand boys for the Executive."

McCloskey and Fulbright concluded by agreeing that regardless of political attitudes there should and must exist in House and Senate a majority against employment of the claim of Executive privilege for "denying us information, particularly deceiving us or willfully trying to conceal facts that would cause us to act differently."

The discussion reached the heart of the case for publication of the Pentagon Papers—did the government possess the right to withhold information from the public, Congress or the press which was crucial to the decision-making process? Did it have, in fact, the right to deceive, to lie, to distort and to prevent the facts from going to the people?

This was what the Pentagon Papers affair was about. Did the McCloskey-Fulbright exchange electrify Congress? Did it sweep the country, touching off public debate, newspaper editorials, television commentaries? It did not. Like the other cries of alarm it went unnoticed. A small story was carried on the *Los Angeles Times* news wire, simply because McCloskey was a California congressman. It was printed briefly in one edition of the *New York Post* but never made the home paper, the *Los Angeles Times. The New York Times* did not print the discussion. Nor did the *Washington Post.* Once again it was as if it had not been said and later on when the debate over the Pentagon Papers went forward no one remembered that the issues had been laid out before Congress three weeks before *The Times* published the Pentagon texts Sunday morning June 13.

Lawyers

It cannot be said that the debate that was conducted in the board room on the fourteenth floor of *The Times* building on May 12 reached the principled level of the Fulbright-McCloskey discussion although this was the full-dress presentation by *The New York Times'* counsel, Lord, Day and Lord, on the Pentagon Papers matter. Herbert Brownell, Attorney General under Eisenhower, leading behind-the-scenes man in the Republican Party, close friend of Thomas Dewey and Richard Nixon, head of Lord, Day and Lord, was the spokesman. Louis Loeb, *The Times'* old attorney spoke beside him. No member of the news department of *The Times* was present. *The Times* was represented by Punch Sulzberger, his assistant, Sydney Gruson, vice president Harding Bancroft, vice president Ivan Veit and *Times'* counsel, James Goodale.

The position of Lord, Day and Lord was clear and simple. Publication of classified documents—and there was no question but that the Papers bore or had originally borne classification stamps—was prohibited under Section 793 of the Espionage Act.

"You cannot publish it," Brownell said. "It's a matter of patriotism," said Loeb.

Goodale argued like a terrier. He called it the duty of *The Times* to publish. He stressed the First Amendment. He said it is a question of history. It is not, Brownell responded, it is a matter of national security. Brownell was quiet-spoken, firm. It was not, he said, the kind of thing to which *The Times* should lend itself. Loeb spoke of tradition, Goodale of responsibility.

Loeb spoke of the classification system. This was the key. The government had classified the documents. That fact could not be challenged.

But the classification argument did not weigh heavily with Goodale. It happened that he had had experience with classified documents and had held a security clearance. Before coming to *The Times* he belonged to a reserve Army intelligence unit called the Strategic International Research and Analysis unit and there were thirty-one members of it including four enlisted men of whom he was one. Among the other members were Steven Rockefeller, son of Nelson, and Mel Gussow, a *Times* reporter. This unit conducted research and analysis studies and their chief source was *The New York Times.* They would go to the New York Public Library, look up *The Times'* files, put together intelligence reports and stamp them "Top Secret." But, of course, there was nothing top secret about them. Nothing secret, in fact. So the classification system didn't seem sacrosanct to Goodale. Harding Bancroft had held a security clearance when he was working at the State Department and the two men had had arguments about classification procedures. Bancroft was willing to concede that "Top Secret" didn't mean much but what about the higher classifications? Goodale couldn't answer because he hadn't been cleared for anything higher than Top Secret and Harding had.

Actually, although none of the participants understood this, the classification system had proliferated so as to defy description. There were three basic security classifications: Confidential, Secret and Top Secret. Possibly 1,200,000 persons were cleared for Top Secret. But this was made meaningless by the existence of a dozen higher classifications, totally unofficial, the categories of which were classified and known only to individuals specifically cleared to see each category of information.

Punch, too, had been cleared for Top Secret. He was, moreover the only one in the room who had actually engaged in combat under fire. He liked the military and his response to "Top Secret" was not the same as that of Goodale. As he said later he never, never would have given a Top Secret document to anyone but, he mused, he had never really been put to the test. If someone had given him a document showing that the Marines had slaughtered a million people—what would he have done? He didn't know but his bias was the other way.

Loeb and Brownell pressed the matter of the classification stamps but, in Goodale's view, the argument was not important. Classification was only a set of rules promulgated by the government bureaucracy and it had no force of law.

Even at this point neither Loeb nor Brownell nor anyone in the firm of Lord, Day and Lord had read any Pentagon Papers documents. With what some *Times* executives felt was rather histrionic emphasis Brownell declared that he and his colleagues must respectfully decline to examine the materials lest by doing so they feel a compulsion to inform the government that *The Times* had them in its possession. Otherwise, he said, Lord, Day and Lord itself could be prosecuted as collaborating in violation of the Espionage Act.* He did not attempt to distinguish between the position of Lord, Day and Lord which *knew*

---

*The reaction of Loeb and Brownell was not unique. Ellsberg consulted a friend in the Washington firm of Arnold and Porter after giving the Papers to Fulbright. His friend said informally he saw nothing wrong with that. Then Marc Raskin consulted his lawyer, Mitchell Rogovin, also of Arnold and Porter, after Ellsberg gave the Institute for Policy Studies some of the Papers. Rogovin brought the matter to the attention of the partners and one member exploded. He said that if the firm were to defend Ellsberg and Raskin it would be guilty of treason. He wanted to get on the telephone to the government immediately. Finally the matter was resolved by a decision that because of conflict of interest the firm could not represent both Ellsberg and Raskin so they would represent neither. Later Rogovin represented Sheehan and still later he represented the CIA, causing Ellsberg to fear that the CIA might have had inside knowledge all along. (Personal interview, Ellsberg, 10/16/78)

The Times had the documents and the position of Lord, Day and Lord if it *saw* the documents. Perhaps, in the minds of the lawyers, it was a case of being only "a little pregnant."

Again and again Loeb insisted that if Arthur Sulzberger were alive he would not publish the Pentagon Papers against the government's wishes. No one could answer that question since Arthur Sulzberger was dead but, in fact, the issue had been argued out with him more than twenty-five years previously at the time Scotty Reston obtained his great scoop on proposals submitted at Dumbarton Oaks for the future United Nations. Sulzberger approved Reston's reporting but confessed that some of his associates felt it was wrong to publish confidential documents in the middle of a diplomatic conference.

Reston responded with a carefully argued brief. He conceded that the government must have the right of private negotiation but insisted that "the people in a democracy have the right to know the broad outlines of the policy its administration proposes to follow" and said his objective was "to clarify rather than confuse the issue."

He pointed out that the government had been negligent in releasing information, that the vacuum had been filled by rumor and that the administration had "clamped down complete secrecy on the conversations, threatened everyone on the delegation with an FBI investigation if anything leaked."

In Reston's view *The Times* had "performed a considerable service on a fundamental issue by publishing the correct facts and at least contributing some truth to the discussion . . . of the difficult security problem rather than a lot of inaccurate speculation and an exaggerated account of secret discussions."

Arthur Sulzberger accepted Reston's reasoning. Reston's case provided a powerful analogy to the Pentagon case; it involved an ongoing diplomatic discussion; it violated the strictest government security impositions; it put out into public view the precise positions of the United States, the British and the Russians. It was in every way a "hotter," more current story than the Pentagon Papers.

No one present at the discussion remembered these facts and they were not presented.

No decision was arrived at during this meeting. Punch listened quietly. He tried not to come down on either side. He assured Loeb and Brownell that he would take into careful account their arguments, including an impassioned oration by Loeb on the dire consequences for the paper. And he made plain to Goodale that he understood Goodale's position, which he knew reflected that of his news executives.

17

At the Foot of Bank Street

*T*HE MOST IMPORTANT individual in the *Times* board room on May 12 was Punch Sulzberger. He had now been running *The New York Times* for eight years but he was still thought of by his associates as young, relatively untested, something of an uncertain factor. He was genial, easy, marvelously self-assured and self-deprecating. No one had the slightest difficulty in talking with him. He had a warm smile and a pleasant word for people he met in the elevators and when the going got hot at meetings he could be depended on to make a bad pun or crack a silly joke that broke the tension. He was the love (and sometimes the despair) of his family as he had been through his life. As his favorite sister, Ruth, said in a profile of her brother for the house organ, *Times Talk,* when he became publisher in 1963, he had managed to get acquainted with almost all the good schools in the New York vicinity, each of them delighted to have such a charming young man and each in turn sadly confessing they were "not getting through" to him.

But this provided little clue to what Punch was about. When her son was eight years old his mother sent his father a little note:

"Punch the other day said he would like to be king of the world. 'What would you do then?' I asked. 'Well,' said he, 'I would first make all the countries stop fighting and be friends and then I would fix up Germany.' 'How would you do that?' 'I would make Hitler into a plain man and make them get a good man as President (he thinks Hitler is President of Germany) and then I would go to Africa and kill all the bugs that make people sick.'"

Iphigene Sulzberger believed that Punch had displayed a good deal of thought for an eight-year-old. She was pleased to note he hadn't said a word about himself and felt he possessed an unusual sense of social responsibility.

This letter was the first item which his father put into his son's office file. In fact, until he got this note he had no file folder for the youngster.

Punch's early school reports were preserved by his parents and they revealed no precosity but he sent his Marine exam scores to his father and they showed him in the highest percentiles in interpretation of social studies, natural sciences, literary materials and mathematical ability.*

But he displayed neither enthusiasm nor aptitude when he began to work in the New York office of *The New York Times* and his position of assistant treasurer in 1963 indicated little confidence by his family that he would follow in the footsteps of his remarkable grandfather, and, in fact, Punch later conceded that in the early days it never occurred to him that he might one day become publisher of *The Times.*

His leap into his grandfather's shoes was made under conditions that might have served as the first act of a modern Götterdämmerung.§ Orvil Dryfoos had been publisher for a little more than two years before his sudden death in 1963. He had been carefully trained into the position and it was assumed that his tenure would span the "generation of the children" and that his successor would be drawn from the grandchildren or even, possibly, from outside family ranks. As Punch once said of his days as assistant treasurer, "My career didn't look very promising. I'd go up to Orv occasionally and ask him to give me something to do. I was in charge of the cafeteria and purchasing. Nobody wanted to give me anything to do—no honest-to-God job. But then all the proverbial shit hit the fan and overnight there was the change."

What Punch referred to was the death of Orvil Dryfoos, what went before and what came immediately afterward.

Amory Bradford

One star-lit July night in 1972, Amory Bradford, three months shy of his sixtieth birthday, son of a Congregational minister and a minister's daughter, face carved out of New England flint, tall with a Gary Cooper handsomeness, one-time general manager of *The New York Times,* sat at the edge of a rotting pier at the foot of Bank Street bracing himself to plunge into the dirty waters of the North River and end his life. He was jobless, an alcoholic, quarreling with his third wife, his remarkable career in broken shards, his nerve gone, his sense of being lost, no logical reason to live, spending his days in a blur of alcohol and inchoate rage.

Ten years earlier Bradford was within grasp of his wildest ambition,

*Punch's mother and sisters believed he suffered from dyslexia, a childhood learning disability in which words and letters seem to be transposed. Punch's grandfather was said to have had the malfunction, which may be hereditary and more prevalent among males. Iphigene Sulzberger and her daughter, Ruth, both insisted they were plagued by the difficulty. Nelson Rockefeller had the same trouble. (Personal interviews, Iphigene Sulzberger, 11/4/69; Ruth Holmberg, 11/28/78; Jane Brody 4/18/79)
§See Notes section.

the control levers of *The New York Times.* He was right-hand man and closest friend of Dryfoos, whom he had known for years (Orvil had been a suitor of Bradford's wife, Carol Warburg, daughter of an owner of the Federated Department Stores chain, before Amory and Carol had married).

The two men liked each other enormously and when Orvil in 1947 asked Amory whether he would care to leave his Wall Street law firm, Davis, Polk and Wardwell and join *The Times* he leaped at the chance. His first job was special assistant to Arthur Hays Sulzberger, taking the place of Nicholas Roosevelt, who had just resigned. Soon he became secretary of *The Times* and by the early 1950s he was the key man in the little group Orvil Dryfoos was forming to take over management when he replaced his father-in-law as he did in 1961. Bradford had some hand in modernizing the financial structure of *The Times,* working with George Woods and General Greenbaum, and tried to balance off the influence of General Adler, the blimpish business manager who in the opinion of the Dryfoos group knew little about modern corporate practice. Bradford went onto *The Times'* board of directors in 1955, became business manager in 1957 and general manager in 1960.

As Bradford saw it he and Dryfoos were a perfect team. Orvil, in Bradford's words, was warm, loving, with enormous human insight. He understood people and instinctively got on with them. Bradford saw himself as a highly trained expert, an executive who knew business and knew what the shape of the corporation should be. They had worked side by side as assistants to Arthur Hays Sulzberger; they knew *The Times,* knew its skeletal structure; knew where the power lay and thought they knew what was needed to ensure its survival and future growth.

Bradford felt the key weakness was an ambiguous relationship with the dozen craft unions which dominated the newspaper field and he arrived at the conviction that two things were needed: strong, unified union representation and a strong publishers' organization. The two would be able to bargain as equals, keep the weak in line and prevent the field from being chewed up by wildcat strikes, aberrant union ambitions and cussedness. It was a neat, cool analysis from what his associates more and more came to consider Bradford's cold-steel mind.

Bradford set out to establish a relationship with the brightest star of the newspaper unions, a young chief named Bert Powers, of the Typographical Union. He and Powers met regularly for lunch. They liked each other, at least Bradford liked Powers, and he thought they were laying a groundwork of understanding and collaboration. In this he was woefully mistaken. On December 8, 1962, what proved to be the longest strike in New York newspaper history, a 114-day walkout, began. Bradford was chief negotiator and spokesman for the publishers and *The Times,* Powers for the unions.

When it was over the name of Bradford had become one of hate among newspapermen and newspaper workers in New York, he had lost public sympathy for his cause, he had turned Arthur and Iphigene Sulzberger against him, he had, as he would come to think, killed his best friend, Orvil Dryfoos, he had broken his own career, he had destroyed his marriage and he had set in train a total personality destruction that took him to the Bank Street wharfside.

The tragedy of Bradford came straight out of Eugene O'Neill. Bradford was not, despite his name, a Brahmin although he acted Brahmin-born in the Long Strike. He came of poor parents, a line of Congregational clergymen (he was the first male in four generations who did not choose the cloth). When he was asked once why he had not become a minister he told a story of pulling his sister's hair one Sunday morning at the age of three. His mother told him that his father was in church where he would preach a sermon saying "Be good, boys. Be good, girls. Be good, people. Brothers don't pull sisters' hair." She asked if he would like to preach that sermon, too. He remembered getting up, turning a small chair around, putting both hands on the back, just as his father seized the lectern in the pulpit, and reciting the words as his mother spoke them. Often his mother would ask him to repeat the sermon and each time he would do it. "Perhaps," he said, "that's why I never became a minister." He was a left-handed child (as was Punch Sulzberger) and he worked his way through Andover with scholarships and waiting on table, won the headmaster's prize with the highest grades in a class of two hundred, went to Yale as an undergraduate and finished Yale Law School in 1937. It was as New England a success story as one could find.

What happened to Bradford in the days of the Long Strike? Never had such an arrogant figure been seen. He sneered at Turner Catledge when Catledge tried to question him about some detail of the strike negotiations. "Oh, you couldn't understand that!" he once said, turning his back on the managing editor.* Once Punch was witness to an argument between Orvil and Amory on the street. Amory snapped, "I quit," and strode off on his long New England legs. Dryfoos, a head shorter, ran behind, begging him to come back. "I made up my mind," Punch later said, "never to have anything to do with him."

Only a handful of people knew it, but Dryfoos was not a well man. He suffered from a valvular defect in his heart. He himself had only learned of the ailment accidentally when he was rejected for a naval officers' training program in 1940. He called up an old chum, a Dartmouth classmate and long-time friend of his wife Marian, Armand

---

*Catledge later said that if Bradford had stayed on the paper he would have resigned.

Deutsch, of the Philadelphia Rosenwald family, and told him of his rejection in amazement. He told Marian as well and they agreed they would not let it affect their life.

Bradford knew nothing of this although he realized that Dryfoos avoided violent exercise, preferring golf to tennis. One day during the Long Strike, toward the end of January 1963, Bradford ran into George Cardin, Dryfoos' personal physician, at the Century Club. Cardin asked Bradford how long the strike was going to last. Bradford said he didn't know. Cardin said that Dryfoos had a serious heart condition, an enlarged heart valve which was being aggravated by stress. It got bigger and bigger and would not close properly.

Bradford said he hadn't known that. Why didn't Dryfoos take a vacation, go away and relax? That wouldn't work, Cardin said. Dryfoos would worry even more if he knew his condition was so critical.

"So it is really a question of how long the strike is going to last," Cardin said. "Is it going to be a matter of weeks?"

"No," said Bradford. "It's going to be a matter of months."

"Isn't there anything you can do?" Cardin asked.

"No," said Bradford and turned on his heel. That, he later was to say, was part of the guilt that suffused him. At the time, he remembered thinking, well, there is nothing to do about it. If Orv is going to die he is going to die. It is just like death in a war. It was part of the price you pay. He did nothing to speed settlement of the strike and, in fact, put the conversation out of his mind. Cardin did all he could do. He insisted on Dryfoos seeing him often and finally at 8 A.M. every morning. He used what medical magic he could conjure. But he felt from the moment of the talk that his patient was doomed.

"I think Amory kind of went crazy during the Long Strike," one of his oldest friends said later. Bradford came to share that conclusion. "I was destroying myself, destroying my job, destroying my best friend, destroying my marriage. I was not acting in any reasonable way," he said.

When the Long Strike ended in April 1963, Orvil Dryfoos and Marian went to Puerto Rico for a rest. But it was too late. Dryfoos collapsed on the second hole of the golf course at the Dorado Beach Hotel. Marian had so firmly put his heart condition out of her mind that she didn't at first connect it with his inability to get a breath. Punch met the plane when Orvil and Marian arrived and drove them directly to the Harkness Pavilion. Marian asked the doctor, expecting a positive and reassuring reply, "Is he going to make it?" Cardin said, "I don't know." It was a total shock. Characteristically Punch immediately got a catalogue of home elevators to pick one that could be installed in the Dryfoos house. But it was an unnecessary gesture. Dryfoos was dead in a little more than a month.

This put the question of a successor up to Iphigene and Arthur Sulzberger. By this time Arthur Hays Sulzberger was adamant that Bradford not be given the post. He had not thought much about the possibility of his son becoming publisher and had, in fact, been an unconscionable nit-picker about what he regarded as Punch's inattention to detail since he had been working at 229 West Forty-third Street, but now he wanted him in the number one position.

To be honest, few of the top *Times* personnel regarded Punch's abilities highly. Various combinations were proposed and lobbied in the fortnight of fevered discussions that began even before the Dryfoos funeral (which was preached by Reston). Reston himself was a candidate. He and Bradford discussed the situation before Dryfoos' funeral and Bradford recalled Reston saying that what Bradford had done on the business side must be done on the news side. It would require, in Bradford's memory of Reston's words, a tough son of a bitch to do it. Bradford told Arthur Hays Sulzberger that he would be happy and willing to serve as number two to Scotty. Bradford's account may not be totally accurate but it is certain that the idea of a Reston-Bradford combination was not the only one that was advanced. George Woods knew from the start that the family intended to put Punch in as publisher. He did not oppose that, but he did believe there was danger in casting a young man (Punch was thirty-seven) who had never had top management or editorial experience in such a demanding role. Woods proposed a team of Punch and Scotty, Punch to be publisher and Scotty to be president. He felt this gave the balance necessary to enable Punch to cope with the major problems that lay ahead.

Whether this idea was seriously considered by the Sulzbergers is uncertain. Iphigene Sulzberger said many years later that she didn't believe much thought was given to such a combination. "We had to take a chance on Punch," she said. "Maybe because he was the youngest he hadn't been considered so much. But he turned out so well. He was better than anyone could have expected."

The idea of "a package" did not die until the last moment and it was killed only by the decisiveness of Punch. The plan of having Bradford as number two to Punch persisted in spite of the reservations the family felt. However, once it became apparent he was not to be number one, Bradford retired to his house in Peru, Vermont, and when he was approached by Louis Loeb, *The Times'* counsel, with a proposal from the Sulzbergers to become number two to Punch, he rejected it. He said he was willing to be number two to Bancroft or number two to Reston but not number two to Punch. Bradford's wife, Carol, urged him to take the second spot and so, apparently, did Arthur Sulzberger, conquering his dislikes and objections.

But Bradford had set out to destroy himself and he came close to succeeding. Having, as he thought, killed his best friend and ruined himself with *The Times,* he took a newspaper job in New York that (after a lengthy lawsuit) cost him very substantial retirement benefits from *The Times.* His marriage broke up and so did two successive remarriages. He began to drink heavily and by July of 1972 was ready to end his life. He did not do so for a wholly aberrant reason. He suddenly realized he could not bear to choke to death. Obviously he did not want to end his life. The next day he called a psychiatrist who agreed to treat him if he would stop drinking. He did it cold turkey and started six years of therapy to emerge a person so different his old friends could not recognize him. One day he sat down at the long table of the Century Club, full-bearded, hair to his shoulders. The members were startled. They heard something familiar in the voice but they did not know the man behind the hair. Finally, he laughed and said, "It's all right. It's Amory Bradford speaking behind all this." He had worked in Oakland, California, on a major jobs-and-housing program about which he eventually wrote a novel, published in 1968, called *Oakland's Not for Burning.* It wasn't a bad book and got quite good reviews around the country but *The New York Times* ignored it. For a while Bradford became a sort of a guru and then went to work on environmental problems for the Nixon Administration. His life-style had radically changed. The last time he attended a reunion in the Thousand Islands with his fellow Yale Skull and Bones members one remembered Amory lounging in the nude while they sat on the beach in their trunks. In fact, he went nude for most of the day.

By 1978 he had given up his house in Vermont and was traveling slowly along the Pacific Coast in his camper, stopping as the spirit moved him, beginning to write the story of his life and contemplating becoming a Gestalt practitioner.

"The best way to describe myself," he said, "is to say that I have died and been reborn. My life is more exciting than ever before. I sit in my camper with my hair down to my shoulders, a couple of joints in my pocket and I look at my face and it has an ease and gentleness it never had before. I don't drink and I don't smoke and I'm happy."

Punch Takes Charge

Need all that have been? Not by reason and logic, as Bradford is the first to concede.

In fact, despite Bradford's expressed refusal to work with Punch, the family had decided to name him president of *The Times,* serving with Punch, who would be publisher. Turner Catledge chanced to be in Punch's office when his mother entered and said, "Darling, I'm sorry but that's the way your father wants it."

"I won't take it then," Punch recalled saying. "I'm going to see him."

"I went back to Dad and said it wouldn't work," Punch recalled. "I couldn't work with Bradford." He came back a few minutes later, smiling: "It's all settled."

And it was. When Punch flatly refused to serve with Bradford his father, with no great reluctance, acceded to his son's will.

"Well, I guess you're right," Punch remembered his father saying. "I couldn't get along with the S.O.B. so why should you?"

This was the boldness and decisiveness that Punch had shown in the moment of getting his job and it was characteristic of the decisiveness he was to display as publisher. He might not always make the right decision but he did not mind putting his chips on the line. He did it over and over again, gradually weeding out dead wood and older executives at *The Times* and replacing them with younger, more vigorous men. If he made a mistake—and it happened not infrequently in his early days—he would cheerfully try again.

All of Punch's sisters loved him, but none with more perceptive devotion than Ruth. Ruth was a newspaperwoman herself. She had cubbed in the great city room of *The Times* and gone on to become publisher of her grandfather's first creation, the *Chattanooga Times*. Punch's success as a publisher, she felt, stemmed from his ability to look at problems objectively without engaging his emotions. He was not cold, not at all cold, she felt, but he was self-sufficient. As a child he had always been happy. If you told him "yes" he was happy; if you told him "no" he was happy. He had an inner security that set him apart. Mothers of other little boys were constantly telling Punch's mother that their little boy was Punch's best friend. But often Iphigene had not even heard of the little boy. Punch never had more than one friend at a time when he was a child; he didn't need them.

"If I had been made publisher," Ruth reflected some fifteen years after her brother had taken over the job, "the paper would be down the drain by now. Punch was the only one who had the toughness to do what was needed."

She contrasted her brother with Dryfoos. Dryfoos had been a warm person. He had many friends and felt strongly about them. This made it hard for him to make decisions but it was easier for Punch because he wasn't personally involved.

Not that anyone had foreseen Punch's ability. Everyone in the family, she conceded, had thought he was too young. They thought of him as being younger than he really was. Her father thought that he didn't have a serious attitude. No one was in a hurry to train him. Perhaps if Orvil hadn't died he never would have gotten his chance.

Ruth believed the person who had the strongest influence on Punch was his mother. After that Turner Catledge and Scotty Reston. Once Punch's short attention span had worried her. Later she came to realize that this was a positive factor. It enabled him to organize his work and not agonize over decisions.

One characteristic he inherited clearly from his father. This was a sense of neatness. It had not come from his training in the Marines although perhaps that strengthened it. Arthur Hays Sulzberger had always been meticulous about his dresser, his clothes, his desk. Marian had the same fetish. Ruth called herself the family slob. The inside of Punch's garage was neater than her living room.

This then was the character of the young man who sat listening in the board room as Brownell, Loeb and Goodale spoke their lines and laid the issues of the Pentagon Papers before him. He was cool, non-committal, and his instructions to his associates were very clear. They were to read the material with the greatest care. They were not to go overboard. But in the belief of Sydney Gruson, who was his executive assistant and who was closer to him in this period than anyone else, there never was real doubt in Punch's mind about publishing the Papers even when he angrily exclaimed, "Goddamn it! We don't have to publish all this stuff."

His decision was not based on deep philosophical understanding of the issues. No such analysis had been presented to him. Up to this moment the legal arguments had been based on the narrow ground of a dubious and unstudied statute and a set of untested government regulations. The editors' arguments had been based more on the emotional appeal of a "great story" than careful consideration of the role of the newspaper under the First Amendment and its expanded role in contemporary society.

But, whatever the arguments and whatever the principles, it was clear to Gruson that the publisher was headed toward the correct decision.

18

"Playing God"

ON JUNE 6, 1971, James Goodale returned to his office after taking a week off, in frustration and anger. He had turned his back on *The Times,* having, as he said, dusted off "my annual resignation." His daughter, Ashley, had been born May 21. He took his wife and family up to their pleasant country house on Lake Waramaug in New Preston, Connecticut, and devoted himself to domestic pleasures, leaving the Pentagon Papers behind him.

It had seemed to Goodale that the arguments at *The Times* were escalating, that whatever control he had over the situation had been lost and that, in the end, *The Times* would not publish the Papers. By this time Goodale confessed "a terrific desire" to see them published.

"It was a point of principle," he recalled. "But it seemed to me I was going to lose somehow. I was strongly considering an alternative choice of career."

Goodale thought that the logic of Lord, Day and Lord had won; that Punch Sulzberger was prepared to follow the reasoning of Herbert Brownell and Louis Loeb, not that of himself, and that it was a lost cause.

Goodale was wrong. But there had been enough argument in the higher echelons to cause a trickle of rumors that finally reached the secret editing suite at the New York Hilton and sent a chill of fear through the reporters and writers there. The editors made efforts to keep this away from the hypersensitive Neil Sheehan but, inevitably, he, too, heard that a "debate" was under way and saw visions of his "thermonuclear vial" drowning in a swamp of editorial negativism. This possibility, of course, had been faced by many of the editors even earlier. Seymour Topping, assistant managing editor, reached China in late May to join his wife, Audrey, and his father-in-law, Chester Ronning, China-born former Canadian ambassador, in Peking. Topping whispered to Audrey on the roof of the Hsin Chiao Hotel that he might have to resign if *The Times* did not publish the Pentagon Papers. And this, of course, was what caused Rosenthal to check on his bank account, his insurance policies and his severance possibilities. The commitment of the editors to the story was total and as early as the April 29 meeting Topping had told Rosenthal "our jobs may be on the line."

What actually was in progress by the time Goodale returned from sulking at Lake Waramaug was a disorderly debate about nuts and bolts, about mechanics, about parameters, about quantities and qualities, about what to put in and what to take out, about publishing the whole of the Papers or only part, about publishing one huge installment or radically reducing the required space by eliminating all or most of the documents.

But this was not the way it was perceived in the rapidly overheating circles of editors. The group at the Hilton was the last to realize that there was a debate in progress and assumed the worst.

One day James Greenfield, the foreign editor, came to the Hilton suite (as he did every day and sometimes two or three times a day), and Jerry Gold, acting as spokesman, said, "We've all agreed that if it is not going to be published—we are going to take it somewhere else and publish it."

Greenfield, depressed by the wrangles going forward on Forty-third Street, said gloomily, "It's very good of you to tell me about it but I don't think it will come to that."

The editors and writers at the Hilton did not know that the editors and executives at Forty-third Street were arguing about cutting down the wordage and dropping the documents. Publication in toto had been a condition of Ellsberg's from the start and Sheehan had emphasized this to his editors. To Reston, Rosenthal, Frankel, Topping and the news personnel full publication was a basic. From the beginning they had acted on the assumption that the entire Archive was to be published. The editing team at the Hilton proceeded on this basis and had carefully keyed the documents to the mass of individual stories and dispatches being written.

Debate

What was not known to the writing team and what was only partially known to editors like Rosenthal and Greenfield was that Sulzberger had quietly and secretly broadened the base of his consultation.

Sheehan completed his first draft May 18. As might be expected from the number of cooks with spoons in his soup, it was not a very stylish job. After two or three rewrites Rosenthal took Sheehan's story, all the other copy that had been produced, and a set of documents edited for publication, put them in a big shopping cart and wheeled the whole to Sulzberger's fourteenth-floor office.

"I never really saw it," Punch recalled, "until Abe came up with those damn cartons from the A&P and dumped them in my lap. I confess for the record that I didn't read it all. I don't know who did read it all."

From the beginning the story had never seemed to Punch to possess the dynamics his editors claimed for it and now he began to grumble. He thought Sheehan's draft was jumbled and hardly sensational and he could not see allotting such an enormous volume of space. He was thinking about costs and newsprint consumption. It was just too much. Maybe it didn't have to be published after all.

Sydney Gruson, sitting with Punch that first afternoon in the publisher's back-office alcove, said, "Don't kid yourself. It's not a question of not going to publish this but of how we are going to publish."

Wearily, the publisher agreed that Gruson was probably right. But he wanted the material read and he wanted as many opinions as he could get. Because of the emotions and jealousies among the editors the reading process now became a kind of Chinese puzzle, secrets locked within secrets. What happened on the fourteenth floor was not necessarily known on the third floor. What was known on the third floor was not necessarily known at the Hilton workroom and what was known at the Hilton was not necessarily known in the Washington bureau.

The first readers to plunge into the fiberboard boxes of materials were Harding Bancroft and Gruson. Gruson's instant reaction was that the story was not publishable in the form in which the Hilton editors had presented it. Since at this time Gruson and Rosenthal were barely on speaking terms (because of previous quarrels),* this opinion was presented to Rosenthal not as Gruson's but as Sulzberger's, which was fair enough because Sulzberger, too, found the materials disorganized and lacking focus.

This provoked further problems because Sheehan was already edgy over what seemed to him excessive interference and editing of his copy.

"I want to remind you," Sulzberger had said in turning the copy back to Rosenthal, "that I haven't yet given permission for this story. I must see every word of the copy."

These words shocked Rosenthal and raised the specter in his mind

---

*When Reston and Punch were contemplating the changes which brought Rosenthal in as Managing Editor Rosenthal got his wind up; he was convinced he would be passed over. Gruson strongly backed Rosenthal and promised that if Rosenthal was not named he would resign. In return Rosenthal, as Gruson recollected, promised to back Gruson's appointment as executive editor. But in the showdown Gruson learned that Rosenthal had not really supported him for the executive editorship. Despite this Gruson offered to become Rosenthal's deputy but the job went to Seymour Topping. On this occasion Punch presented Gruson with a black hand, all the fingers except the forefinger retracted. "I told Punch that it was appropriate," Gruson said. He and Rosenthal did not talk for a year after this and were still barely on speaking terms at the time of the Papers.

that the story might not be published. This was probably more responsible than anything else for the rumors that *The Times* might not publish the story. Reston now took a copy of the Sheehan story down to Washington, where he showed it to Frankel, who agreed that the copy needed work, particularly when you were asking the publisher for fifty to a hundred pages of space. He decided to see whether he could do a general introduction of 1,000 to 1,500 words, which would get the story off to a fast start.

It was at this point that Goodale returned from his sulk and was greeted with relief by Bancroft. Goodale found that instead of the Pentagon Papers being dead (as he had feared) the project was going ahead at full speed. Bancroft and Gruson were plowing through the copy. Bancroft immediately asked Goodale to take a hand. "Really, I'm glad to have you back," Harding said. "You're the only one the news department will listen to."

Goodale plunged into it. He read half the material the first day and the remainder on the second. He had not—from the beginning—been on what he called "the documents team." That is, he was certain publication of all the textual material would cause problems. He, like several editors, thought it better to duck the documents problem by quoting from them, just as Alsop had quoted from top-secret documents in his report on the Bay of Pigs.

"I knew that all those texts would or could cause problems," Goodale recalled. "But when I read the documents I told Harding, 'You just have got to print this. I suppose it would be better if the documents weren't printed but I don't care.' "

Gruson, Bancroft and Goodale were not the only executives who made their way into the cramped back room on the fourteenth floor where the Pentagon Papers stories and documents were piled. Ivan Veit read some material. Dan Schwartz, the conservatively inclined Sunday editor, took off a day and a half and carefully went through the mass. He was not impressed, thought the story overrated and recommended that the documents be dropped and the stories be radically curtailed. John Oakes, who never on principle participated in or was consulted on news questions, was, in this extraordinary situation, asked by Punch to read the copy and provide another opinion and he, too, took a negative attitude to the textual materials. Lester Markel, Sunday editor emeritus but still an important adviser to Sulzberger, was brought in and offered an opinion not much different from that of Oakes but expressed more violently. Clifton Daniel was consulted and, while strong for the story, was lukewarm toward the documents. My views were sought and I, too, was hesitant about the documents but for a somewhat different reason. I felt, perhaps more strongly than some, that there was real danger of the Nixon Administration seizing upon the Pentagon Papers and trying to use the issue to destroy *The Times.* My opinion was influenced by intimate knowledge of the extraordinary hostility felt toward *The Times* by Mr. Nixon. In a memo to the publisher I cited the parallels of Nixon's use of documents in the Hiss case and the earlier use of documents in the Amerasia case. "I think we should be sophisticated enough to recognize that not everyone in Washington wishes us well and only too many would delight in a vendetta," I wrote. I took the view that publication of the series by *The Times,* citing the documents and quoting from them, would have the effect of forcing out the texts themselves through privileged congressional sources.

One other proposal was strongly advanced at this time by Reston. Goodale had urged that the material be presented in a single issue of *The Times.* This would eliminate possibility that the government might halt publication by injunction or prior restraint. Reston now picked up this idea and proposed that the Papers be presented in *The New York Times Magazine,* the whole of a single issue being devoted to them. He was dissuaded from this notion by Gruson, who felt it would never be accepted by Rosenthal, who would see it as taking away "his" story and giving it to the Sunday department. Because the daily department, headed by Rosenthal, and the Sunday department, headed by Schwartz, were strong competitors this was not so absurd as it might sound to someone outside *The Times.** It was also true that when Goodale originally suggested one-shot publication Max Frankel had strongly objected, saying that it was offensive to act as though "we were running with one eye on the sheriff." *The Times'* editors believed what they were doing was correct, eminently right and entirely justified. They did not think they should guide their presentation, in Frankel's phrase, "to beat a rap or prevent an injunction."

These were the arguments as *The Times* moved into the final week before publication, a deadline artificially set by the chance that Punch Sulzberger was flying to London June 14 with Ivan Veit for negotiations concerning the British edition of *Family Circle.* Sulzberger announced that the question of publication must be determined before he left.

It was to be a week of intense excitement, thrills and alarms, false rumors, continuous discussion, crisis after crisis, and Neil Sheehan later on was to say:

"We were playing God like the Pentagon had been playing God. It was like a war room at the Hilton. I wanted it to be like a barrage. Bang. Bang. Bang. One after another. Day after day. Not all in one package."

---

*This kind of internal division led Sulzberger in 1976 to consolidate the two departments under Rosenthal.

The roles had shifted in Neil's analogy. No longer was it the government playing God. Now it was Neil and his companions of the typewriter constructing their printed version of a "thermonuclear vial."

The Issues

Despite the intensity of discussion which preceded publication of the Pentagon Papers no one who reads the record can fail to be impressed by what was lacking in the argument. These were not arguments of men who possessed fundamental philosophical differences, nor the arguments of men whose concern was moral decadence, the pernicious tendencies of government, the gap between the word and the deed. These were pragmatic arguments by pragmatic men—mechanics not visionaries; journeymen not preachers. Despite Sheehan's flamboyant rhetoric, this was no band of crusaders.

There was not, so far as the record can be recaptured, so far as collective memory reflects, so far as memoranda reveal, or controversy illuminates, a single discussion that drew upon the lessons of history, comparisons with the past nor analogies to the equivalent experiences of other men, other institutions or other eras.

But this circumstance was deceptive. The discussion of the underlying factors which the Pentagon documents so admirably illustrated had already taken place in other forums. The conclusions had long since been hammered out in the minds of the editors and correspondents. These were givens. They did not have to be stated all over again. From the time of Homer Bigart in the early 1960s the editors and writers had gradually been learning the basics: the seamless tissue of lies and the lesson, as Bigart had put it, that "It doesn't work." Gradually, they had come to share a coherent view of the world in which code words sufficed to convey a whole range of meanings. If one of them said "hasty withdrawal from Vietnam" the other knew almost certainly how he felt about Women's Lib, about Kent State, about Norman Mailer.

Basic discussion of the issues had been going forward, among other places, within the Council on Foreign Relations of New York, regarded by radical left-wing (and right-wing) circles as the board of directors of the Establishment. *Times* editors and correspondents took a major role in these discussions.

In the winter and spring of 1970 a seminar was conducted into government decision-making in East Asia by James C. Thomson, Jr., who had worked in the White House for the Kennedy and Johnson National Security Councils and was now at Harvard. Thomson, born in China of missionary stock, was one of the country's leading young China hands and had a remarkable grasp of the inner workings of Washington bureaucracy.

The score of participants in the seminar included half a dozen men like Thomson who had sat at the elbow of power in Washington, assistants to secretaries and undersecretaries, specialists who knew how and where the paper traffic led, who communicated laterally among themselves about the matters which their principals deliberated, men who knew the motivations behind decisions and knew how to push a policy paper to the top of an in-basket and what hour of the day was favorable for getting a "yes" or a "no" from the man they worked for and the man their man worked for. Knowledgeable, power-conditioned, intelligent men like Daniel Ellsberg. In fact, Ellsberg was one of the number and no one around the table seemed more at ease in this company, more quick in his judgments, more lucid in his comments. How many around that table had, like himself, worked on the Pentagon Papers is uncertain. But probably half the participants knew of the Papers and several (it would seem in retrospect) had intimate knowledge of them.

Perhaps that is why the discussion seemed to me to cast so penetrating a light into the Washington process, its distorted results, its drift so far from the democratic ideal.

It was in the context of this discussion that I heard, for the first time, that President Johnson's aides had drawn up a "blank check" resolution to be put through Congress at an appropriate moment—the resolution, in fact, which was passed with only the most minor of changes at the time of the Tonkin Gulf incident in August 1964; of the elaborate planning that went forward from August 1964 for massive air bombardment of North Vietnam, an "option" not to be exercised, LBJ made clear, until after he had won the November 1964 election on a "peace" plank against Goldwater's "hawk" program; the mechanism of the "options game," as Ellsberg was to call it in his final dialogue with Kissinger, the submission of three alternatives to the President, carefully loading two of them so that he would be bound to pick the "middle ground" favored by the bureaucrats.

The greatest revelations to a man who had thought himself knowledgeable about the American Government were declarations by the bright young men of the Security Council, the Defense Department, the CIA and the White House, these trained crisis managers, that in arriving at such decisions as the bombing of North Vietnam almost none of the fundamentals were factored in. For example, no specialist could remember a call for testimony by an expert on the country that was to be bombed; no testimony on the nature of Vietnam; the history of Indochina; the kind of society and temperament of its people; of its social and economic organization. None of this was ground into the picture. Why?

After much head scratching the consensus was that belief in U.S. air power was so total that to no one did it occur that peculiarly Vietnamese facts need be taken into account.

Nor, so far as recollection testified, had there been reference in this context to the well-known studies on the effects of strategic bombing that had been carried out at the end of World War II, studies which conclusively showed that in the case of Germany bombing *raised* rather than *lowered* civilian morale and so spurred the economy that at war's end the Germans had increased production of critical material rather than diminished it. This finding was particularly striking since several participants in the White House decisions, George Ball for one and Mr. Johnson's security adviser Walt Rostow for another, had participated in the study. There was, the witnesses said, intense dislike for French diplomats and specialists who knew something about Vietnam and whose opinion was shunned because it might negate the basis on which White House decisions were being made. Any French initiative was automatically branded as coming from "bad people." Memos by Ball, the official "devil's advocate," were closely held and not permitted distribution to administrative assistants (that is, persons like the participants in the council discussions). It was conceded that the most certain way to keep a memo from influencing action was to restrict its reading to Cabinet members and keep it away from the administrative assistants who conducted most of their chiefs' business.

What, someone asked, was it thought would be the result of the heavy bombing? There was consensus that the decision-makers believed it would produce such extreme pressure that Hanoi would sue for peace. Rather than lose its industries Hanoi would bow to the United States. That was why the military were so eager to bomb Vietnam's power plants and steel mills. So, asked one participant, what would they do if after six weeks of bombing Hanoi still held out? Well, someone said, in this case they would bomb for another six weeks. No option was considered after that. American bombing power was thought to be so great that no one could survive beyond twelve weeks. No one suggested in 1964 that if the bombs didn't work we would have to send in ground troops.

There was a great deal of talk among the executive assistants of what they called the "security phobia" within the government. It was not just the matter of classifying every document "Top Secret." It went much further. Again and again these men would remind each other to type their memos themselves on their own paper, not using government secretaries or government paper because the memo might leak not to Vietnam, not to some foreign spy, but to an enemy within the bureaucracy, an agent of the NSC might get hold of a State Department recommendation or vice versa or the Joint Chiefs of Staff might find out what the Defense Department was up to. (Not an unrealistic fear; in the Nixon White House a naval yeoman was uncovered who was secretly copying Kissinger's documents and providing them to the Joint Chiefs.)

Ellsberg made many contributions to this discussion. One of the most pertinent was his observation that he knew of no decision in the government that got as much staff work as the bombing question and yet the results of the bombing policy (stiffening of Hanoi's resistance) were not predicted.

At one point there was a reference to a McNamara memo of 1967 declaring bluntly that bombing did not work and could not work. It was a tough memo (and was revealed in the Pentagon Papers). It was honest and accurate—if very, very late. The young men at the council table agreed it probably led to LBJ's decision to ease McNamara out and into the World Bank. Truth was not a commodity in high demand in the government's inner councils.

Harold Isaacs, who had witnessed China's revolution and gone on to a Harvard academic career, observed that you had to be unbelievably ignorant of Vietnamese history to suppose that the American policy would work. "The ignorance that was required was available," one discussant replied.

In the end the seminar concluded that the decisions on Vietnam were made by men who knew nothing about Vietnam, nothing about the Vietnamese people, almost nothing about the real situation which they confronted, men who were armed with such arrogance in the totality of American power that they marched forward blindly into disaster. David Halberstam pointed out, as he was to emphasize in his early study *The Best and the Brightest,* that participating in the decisions of both Kennedy and Johnson were some of the most articulate, intelligent and public-spirited public servants the nation had ever commanded. What went wrong? The answer, of course, had been given years earlier by Bigart. It did not work and it would not work, it was morally wrong. But anyone, even a man like McNamara who finally came to understand this, was pushed aside and the tissue of lies went on. As Ellsberg was later to articulate—it was never a good year for an American President to lose the war in Vietnam.

Just a year later the Council on Foreign Relations sponsored three lectures by McGeorge Bundy that might have been entitled "Vietnam Revisited." Many *Times* editors and writers participated in these discussions. Bundy went back over the traumatic years when he served Kennedy and Johnson as security adviser and tried to put the decisions into context. Bundy's talks reflected his own agonizing reappraisal. They did not go down well with some of the younger council members and some young academics.

Bundy's first talk was given in the late afternoon of May 3, 1971, a few hours after one of the biggest of antiwar demonstrations in Washington, one in which 7,000 demonstrators were arrested and confined in holding pens around RFK stadium. Daniel Ellsberg and his friend, the MIT radical and language theorist, Noam Chomsky, had been clubbed and maced. That afternoon Ellsberg took the shuttle for New York. He changed his clothes and came to Bundy's talk at the council. Ellsberg was angered by Bundy's presentation. No questions were permitted from the floor and he felt that Bundy had made no basic changes in his position.*

After the talk Ellsberg went to dinner at the West Side apartment of Robert Kleiman, a wartime OSS officer in Burma who was now an editorial writer for *The New York Times.* Another guest was Carl Kaysen, the famous MIT economist. Ellsberg and Kaysen had not met for ten years.

Once again and inevitably the conversation turned to the Vietnam war. Kleiman was a critic of the war but a moderate critic. He had maintained good relations with Bundy and while he challenged, in part, some of Bundy's conclusions he did not take Ellsberg's radical view. But like Ellsberg he thought that Bundy had not fully confronted the issues of the war and the judgments made, including President Johnson's 1964 decision to bomb North Vietnam. He felt Bundy had not properly emphasized the fact that Johnson received contrary advice on bombing, specifically in editorials by *The New York Times.* Quintessentially, Kleiman was interested in what for many was the most basic question: Had all this been the error of one man or was it the fault of the system or systems through which Johnson and other Presidents received advice and took their decisions?

This question, the basic question of whether the American system itself had begun to malfunction on a colossal scale or whether the problem was the intractability of successive presidents, lay at the heart of what troubled so many Americans. If it was an individual malfunction it could be corrected by getting rid of a Kennedy, a Johnson, a Nixon. But if it was systemic—another and more fearsome issue was raised.

The conversation revolved around these questions and there was an exchange between Ellsberg and Kaysen which was to remain long in Ellsberg's mind and which, in a way, epitomized the philosophical differences that had already been worked out in the minds of *The*

---

*Bill Bundy remembered Ellsberg coming back to Cambridge after listening to his brother's talk. "He was sore at Mac," Bundy recalled. "He felt he hadn't recanted. He wasn't wearing sackcloth and ashes. Dan had that Old Testament thing about him." (Personal interview, William Bundy, 1/4/79)

Times' editors who argued through those early June days about how to present the Pentagon Papers to their readers.

Ellsberg stated with heat and eloquence his feelings about the war, about the Nixon Administration and about the flagrant abuse of the executive power over a long period of time.

Kaysen rejected Ellsberg's thesis. "The difference between us," Kaysen said in Ellsberg's remembrance of the conversation, "is that you judge these things morally. I don't."

To which Ellsberg responded that the path which the United States was pursuing led to the support of dictatorships in many foreign countries and might lead to dictatorship in the United States.

As Ellsberg remembered Kaysen's reply it was, "I don't like any dictatorship but I like a right-wing dictatorship better than a left-wing one. A left-wing dictatorship is forever."

This, Ellsberg thought, summed up the differences between himself and others who lacked confidence in the American position and those who continued to support it. His was not necessarily a view shared by the editors and correspondents of *The Times.* There were almost as many shades of opinion among them as there were individuals (which was one reason for the wildly confusing arguments about the handling of the Pentagon Papers) but most had arrived at a point at which they were highly skeptical of government policy, of what government said and of what government thought it was doing.

Others within and without government had come to this conviction long since. Jerry Wiesner, president of MIT, the institution to which Ellsberg was attached when the Papers were published,* had long since concluded that modern society, and particularly a modern democracy like the United States, simply could not stand secrecy. Secrecy was not compatible with the American psyche and any effort to maintain secrecy was certain to be violently thrown off. He felt this to be one of the most important underlying lessons of the Pentagon Papers affair.

Wiesner had reached this view as early as 1960 when he and Walt Rostow were sent to Moscow to negotiate for the release of American RB-47 pilots who had been shot down on reconnaissance flights inside the Soviet Union. The mission was successful, but in agreeing to the release of the Americans, Vasily M. Kuznetsov, the Soviet deputy foreign minister, told the two to look into the overflights and penetra-

---

*William Bundy, brother of McGeorge, one-time CIA official and Dean Rusk's right-hand man during much of the Vietnam war, had gone to MIT in 1969 as a fellow. He later said it was at his recommendation that Ellsberg was invited there. Ellsberg and Bundy had adjacent offices but their relations were cool. (Personal interview, William Bundy, 1/4/79)

tions of the Soviet frontier which had been consistently carried out by the U.S. Navy. Wiesner lent himself to this task when he returned to Washington.

"The Navy had been carrying on an enormous overflight program to flush out Soviet radar and air defenses," Wiesner recalled. "There was continuous intrusion over the Soviet borders of a kind that had it been done to us by the Soviets probably would have led to war."

But neither the higher levels of government nor the people knew anything about it. Maybe, he mused, if the people had known they would have approved it. But they hardly could have been indignant when the Soviets finally retaliated and shot down a U.S. plane.

"Once in a while," Wiesner said, "I see the cost of not having secrecy and yet the big problem remains. Toward the end of the war Mao Tse-tung tried to establish relations with Roosevelt. But it was all kept secret in the State Department. Nobody knew about it. You can not calculate what this secrecy cost us over the years."

The RB-47 incident brought Wiesner to the conclusion that it was impossible to fight the "security system" from within the government and that it must be done from the outside. He severed his relations with the government although without making public his basic ideas.

On the evening of Sunday, June 13, 1971, after the first installment of the Pentagon Papers had been published, Robert Phelps, the Washington deskman whom Sheehan first consulted about the Papers, had dinner in New York in a little Italian restaurant with Sheehan, Hedrick Smith and Ned Kenworthy, a veteran *Times* correspondent. Smith and Kenworthy had been part of the staff recruited to assist Neil.

Over a glass of chianti Phelps asked his friends, "Well, what have we learned from all this?"

To which Smith replied, "I've learned that never again will I trust any source in the government."

Neil and Kenworthy nodded and the four raised their glasses in acknowledgment. The toast was, no doubt, an overstatement but a natural one at that moment.

19

Mollie Parnis Gives a Party

Mollie Parnis was nervous. She had invited Henry Kissinger to dinner, it was almost five and she just couldn't get Lyndon Johnson out of her dress shop. He had come before three, curious about every detail of the establishment at 530 Seventh Avenue, but how are you going to tell an ex-President that you've got company for dinner, that you have to get home, put the flowers on the table, check the place cards and get yourself ready?

Mollie Parnis was not Mollie Parnis for nothing. It was divine having Lyndon come to the shop. He had telephoned that morning, said he was in town with Lady Bird, that he had always wanted to see her establishment and was going to drop in that afternoon.

"Here?" exclaimed Mollie.

"Yes," said the President. "I'd like to see what goes on there."

And so he had arrived a little after 2:30 and had poked his nose into everything, asking questions, making jokes with the girls. He was, Mollie thought, like a little boy in a candy shop. Or the last of the big spenders. He had a long list of presents to get and he was enjoying himself. But she looked at the clock. It was five all right and she had to get away.

She made her move. "Mr. President," she said, "I know that you are going to the theater tonight and I know Mrs. Johnson wants to have dinner before the theater and I'm afraid it's time to go."

Mr. Johnson looked at his watch. It was time to go. Mollie didn't have her car so she got in with the President and rode uptown. As they moved through the heavy traffic she told Lyndon Johnson, who was, of course, an old, old friend, that she was having a dinner party, and there was an early curtain for the theater, he and Lady Bird would be out by 9:30, so why didn't they drop by after the play. She showed him the list of guests arranged in alphabetical order. She was having two tables of eight. The first names on the list were those of Tom and Jo Braden, the Washington columnist and his wife, former CIA, very much of the Georgetown circuit. "Isn't that the guy from Oceanside?" Johnson asked. Braden had for a time been publisher of the paper in

Oceanside, California. Mollie said yes. He ran on down the names, Walter and Betsy Cronkite, Fred de Cordova, producer of NBC's "Tonight Show," Arlene Francis and Martin Gabel, Henry Kissinger, Mollie's son, Bob Livingston, Sally and Pete Peterson, Alan and Paula Schwartz, Arthur and Carol Sulzberger, Jean Vanderbilt and Barbara Walters. He paused at the name of the Sulzbergers. "Is that Punch?" he asked. Mollie said it was and the President said, "Gee, I don't know why I shouldn't come in after the theater."

So his car dropped him at the Pierre, where he and Mrs. Johnson were staying, and took Mollie on to her duplex on Park Avenue.

Mollie was an old friend of Henry Kissinger just as she was an old friend of the Johnsons and of almost everyone worth knowing in the New York-Washington political-journalistic axis. Her party for Kissinger had come up unexpectedly the way so many of her evenings did. She had bumped into Henry in Washington a couple of weeks before and invited him to dine with her when he was in New York. He telephoned a few days later, said he had to be in New York on business and so the dinner was arranged. Mollie seated Henry on her right and Punch on her left. Paula Schwartz sat next to Punch. The date was Thursday, June 10, 1971.

It was a gay party. Everyone knew each other. It was the kind of occasion Kissinger enjoyed, the kind of occasion all of them enjoyed. Sitting in the Park Avenue apartment, nine floors above the traffic flow, in that company—Kissinger, *The New York Times,* CBS, NBC and all. Well, it was the inner sanctum of power.

Kissinger was relaxed. He was in the middle of his complex and secret arrangements for going to China. That was *his* big secret. He talked a good deal about Mr. Nixon. No one, he said, knew what a hard job the presidency was, how human Mr. Nixon really was, what it meant to him to get personal letters from people who had faith in him. (This was, of course, a full year before Watergate.)

During dinner Mollie told Punch (but not Kissinger) that she thought President Johnson would be dropping in after dinner.

"Here?" Punch asked.

"Yes, here," Mollie replied. She thought Punch seemed a little edgy, not quite as easy as he usually was.

At one point Martin Gabel got Kissinger to talking about Metternich (he denied that he had consciously modeled his career on that of the nineteenth-century statesman). There were toasts to Kissinger before they rose from the table, and Walter Cronkite remembered worrying whether he would be able to think of one as deft as Barbara Walters' (but later couldn't remember either hers or his).

Even for Mollie Parnis, whose New York parties were always remarkable, this was going to be an occasion. Henry Kissinger *and* the Johnsons. She had known Mrs. Johnson for years. Lady Bird liked the Parnis style, as did a great many important women in New York and Washington and Los Angeles, and Mollie, with her warmth and spirit, had a special place in the Johnson entourage. Mollie Parnis is a shrewd, intelligent designer who had come up in that hardest of market places, Seventh Avenue. She had made it to the top. She knew it and everyone at her parties knew it. And so it was perhaps not unusual that the guests at her parties had made it, too—in politics, in business, in the arts, particularly the theater, and in the media world, which was the world that Mollie most enjoyed.

After dinner the men and the women separated. As Mollie recalled years later, "In those days the men still got together and talked and smoked cigars and had a drink of brandy after dinner." She went upstairs with the ladies. At this point the telephone rang. It was the Secret Service reporting that the President and his wife were on their way and should arrive within a few minutes.

So, Mollie recalled, she went downstairs. She still hadn't told Henry that Mr. Johnson might come. Henry was surrounded by men, pontificating.

"Henry," said Mollie, "President Johnson is coming. He is on his way right now. What shall we do?"

"Well," said Henry, "I guess we all have to stand up."

At that moment the Johnsons came in, their Secret Service escort joining Henry's Secret Service escort in the outer hall. There was a great deal of clatter. Lyndon Johnson enjoyed nothing more than this kind of assemblage. He didn't care whether he talked to the men but he loved talking to attractive women and Mollie rotated the ladies so that all had a chance to talk to Lyndon and he had a chance to talk to them. It was more fun, the ladies thought, talking to the President than making conversation about the Highway Beautification Program with Lady Bird.

Mollie knew that Barbara Walters had to be in Washington early the next morning so she took Kissinger aside, not realizing that it wasn't protocol to offer someone a lift in a borrowed presidential plane, and asked if he would give Barbara a lift back to Washington. Kissinger fumbled a bit and said that he would. But in the end he didn't. Barbara and he talked about it and, as she recalled, "at first we decided it would be good for our reputations and then we decided it wouldn't and finally he didn't take me and I caught the early shuttle the next morning."

The talk bubbled on, centering now around Lyndon Johnson not Kissinger. Johnson was in good form. "He told one dirty story after another just like a stage comedian," one guest remembered.

Lady Bird sat off to one side and listened quietly.*

To Mollie it was obvious that Kissinger wanted to leave but couldn't because he could not go until after the Johnsons. He glanced at his watch and stared into space. But Lyndon was having a good time. Finally about eleven o'clock Lady Bird gave Lyndon the time-to-go-home look. Johnson got up and began shaking hands but when he got to Walter Cronkite he whispered, "Pretend that you want to talk to me. Ask me a question. I don't want to leave so early." So the President shook hands all around and then to Kissinger's distress sat down next to Cronkite, talking, and went at it for another twenty minutes before he finally let Lady Bird lead him away.

Once the Johnsons left Kissinger was gone in a twinkle. As the last couple disappeared, Bob Livingston turned to his mother and said, "That's the most exciting evening I ever spent."

Mollie thought it was pretty good too. Then Bob said with some curiosity, "Did you notice Punch? He hardly had a word with either Kissinger or the President. He spent all his time out in the other room talking to the Secret Service men about their walkie-talkies and I don't know what."

Mollie had not noticed this. But now it came to her. Indeed, the publisher of *The New York Times* had seemed to have no interest in talking foreign policy with the Secretary of State. He had done no more than exchange a polite greeting with President Johnson. While the other guests clustered about the two men, bombarding them with questions and soliciting their opinions, Punch had hardly ventured out of the circle of Secret Service men all evening long.

It was, Mollie thought, very odd and she reminded herself that the next time she talked to Punch she would ask him about it. She thought it had been a wonderfully amusing evening but Punch seemed to have something on his mind.

Washington

It was after 1 A.M. by the time the Kissinger plane landed in Washington, a quiet, sleeping Washington. The capital was still pretty much a ten o'clock town. The streets were empty, lights glowed around the Lincoln Memorial, softly mirrored in the long reflecting pool. The Washington Monument rose bravely chiseled. The White House was a scene of peace and quiet. Washington was at its best and most

---

*On another occasion when LBJ was a guest of Mollie Parnis, Martin Gabel persuaded Harold Rome to play the piano for the President. Rome, knowing LBJ was a great admirer of Franklin Roosevelt, started off with "Franklin D. Roosevelt Jones." Johnson listened for a few bars then turned away without comment. "That changed my opinion about LBJ radically," Rome recalled. (Personal interview, Rome, 12/20/78)

beautiful in the hush of a mid-June evening, the pavements black and shiny and the air fragrant with primrose, locust and bridal wreath.

It was a handsome capital, the dome of the Capitol haloed by lights, gleaming marble in the distances, the federal massif of Constitution Avenue and the Mall solid as the pyramids, permanent, enduring, something for the ages. This was America's capital in June of 1971, capital of the greatest country of its era, capital not only of the United States, but, in measure, of the world. It was a thing of awe and Henry Kissinger could not but have felt a thrill of pride as he passed through the silent streets—*his* capital, *his* land, the *greatest.*

But all was not pride and comfort in Washington on what was now the early morning of Friday, June 11. Washington was a troubled city. Not everyone rested at ease even in the White House. In fact not since the Depression of the 1930s and perhaps not since Lincoln's time had dark undercurrents run so powerfully in Washington, not since those times had trouble boiled over into the streets as it had since the later years of the Johnson Administration.

For the moment, true, Washington seemed to sleep in tranquility. But that had not been so a month ago when the violent demonstration of May Day had turned 200,000 protesters into the streets, bent on bringing the very process of government to a halt. Those in government who felt there was a revolutionary smell to the air sensed in this one more whiff of powder. As Attorney General Mitchell looked down from his great windows on Pennsylvania Avenue he saw revolution and an echo of the sans-culottes of Paris in 1790. Nor was he the only one.

Beyond the perfume of the wisteria on the old red-brick walls of Georgetown and from the Doric columns of government compounds oozed the sour stench of fear. This could not have been far from the mind of Henry Kissinger as he drove to his lovely but well-guarded old Victorian house on Dumbarton Avenue where for so many years had lived Mr. Justice Frankfurter and his wife.

There were levels below this troubled surface, unrevealed, only guessed at or suspected in the minds, for example, of reporters and editors of *The Times.* They had long talked, sometimes jokingly, sometimes seriously, about Big Brother keeping his eye and ear on them, that is, about the tapping of telephones, the bugging of homes and offices and surveillance in general. In plain words the methods Americans associated with police states.

Sometimes, evidence bubbled up to reinforce the suspicions. Ned Kenworthy, *The Times'* Washington correspondent who had been recruited for the Pentagon Papers team, had this kind of evidence, dating to the Johnson days. Kenworthy was covering Fulbright's Senate Foreign Relations hearings on Vietnam. One evening his son Tommy came to him in puzzlement. He had gone to call his girl friend and found "Bill Fulbright on the telephone talking to someone." Tommy knew the senator's voice because he had been a Senate page. A couple of days later Tommy heard Tom Wicker on the phone.

One evening Kenworthy had a call from an old friend while he was out. His wife said Kenworthy would call back. In the morning Kenworthy called his friend and apologized for not calling sooner. The friend said, "But you did. You called me last night."

The friend had gotten a call from someone who identified himself as Kenworthy. "I thought your voice sounded kind of funny," he said.

Ned concluded that his phone was tapped and asked the telephone company for a check. They found nothing, the crew head said, adding, "But then we never do."

What no one at *The Times* knew (although Henry Kissinger knew this very well) was that in the past two years at least two men then on the staff of *The New York Times* and another who was later to join *The Times* had been numbered among six newspapermen and eleven other individuals, including seven on his own staff and three on the White House staff, who had been tapped.

The *Times* men were William Beecher, who had scored a notable series of exclusive stories, including the revelation that American B-52's were bombing Cambodia, and Hedrick Smith, who was to go on to Moscow, win a Pulitzer, write a best-selling book and head *The Times'* Washington bureau. At this moment Smith was working in the New York Hilton hotel suite as a member of *The Times'* Pentagon Papers staff. Smith had been tapped because of an exclusive story on Vietnam but by the time of the Pentagon Papers the tap had been removed. The *Times* man-to-be who had been tapped was Bill Safire, then one of Mr. Nixon's speech writers. The other newsmen whose calls had been intercepted were Joseph Kraft, the columnist (tapped not only in Washington, D.C., but also in Paris), Marvin Kalb of CBS and Henry Brandon, an English correspondent.

But the matter hadn't ended there. Among those of Kissinger's staff and the White House who had been tapped were men with whom *Times* reporters were in frequent touch—Morton Halperin, one of Kissinger's chief assistants and the first to be tapped, Helmut Sonnenfeldt, another Kissinger aide, Daniel I. Davidson, a Kissinger man who had long worked for Averell Harriman, Colonel Robert Pursley, chief military aide to Secretary of Defense Melvin Laird (tapped twice), Anthony Lake and Winston Lord. Conversation after conversation of *Times* and other newsmen had been intercepted. Big Brother *was* listening. There were other mysteries, shadowy break-ins and burglaries which had never been cleared up but which knowledgeable *Times* men attributed to surveillance and attempts to uncover sources.

Much of this was to surface after Watergate. But many of those tapped and put under surveillance or believing themselves tapped and surveilled wondered later on whether everything had been brought to light. Daniel Ellsberg repeatedly raised the question of whether more secret and technologically advanced methods of interception were employed, things like the system for overhearing conversations in a room by pointing a laser beam at a windowpane and recording the microvibrations. David Wise, knowledgeable both of Washington and of international espionage, found at least one bit of evidence suggesting that the White House did go this route.

All of this lay under the surface of the seemingly placid, architecturally buoyant Washington to which Henry Kissinger returned early on the morning of Friday, June 11. For the most part the wiretaps placed on correspondents and foreign policy staffers at his suggestion had now been removed. In fact, Tom Charles Huston, the young White House assistant whom Watergate was to expose as the author of the "Huston plan" for national security, a conglomerate program for "bag jobs" (burglaries), wiretaps, surveillance, undercover agents, mass opening of mail, was getting ready to clean out his desk and leave Washington. Despite his authorship of and spectacular advocacy of this secret plan, which was approved by the President only to be (formally) disapproved because of objections by J. Edgar Hoover (who had been doing most of these things anyway for many years), Huston had resigned his job and was getting ready to return to his native Indiana and his legal career in Indianapolis. His termination date was June 21, eight days after the Pentagon Papers were published. He was to miss all the fun.

This was a Washington laced with fear and hatred. It closely resembled the fright fantasies that preoccupied the minds of correspondents working in the New York Hilton suites and of their chief, A. M. Rosenthal. It was a dangerous Washington, dangerous to itself and to others. It was in a classic sense a schizoid Washington—on the surface bureaucracy as usual, the papers passing by the tens of thousands in and out of offices, piling up in acres of files; the clerks with their coffee breaks and their efforts to leave work ahead of the 4:30 rush; the politicians plying their trade; the bouncy young men and women legislative assistants plying the trade of their principals and resolutely changing bed partners with every change of the weather; the flashy lawyers and influence peddlers with their big suites, their steak dinners, their call girls, their Carolina quail hunts, their yachts and their weekends in Puerto Rico; the cynical newsmen writing their cynical stories (but most of them more or less under the sway of the power and glory of the men and institutions of which they wrote)—all this on the surface. Washington as usual. Despite Nixon. Despite violence in the streets and a sullen mood in the country.

Below this surface lay the other Washington where men in tan raincoats pried open embassy doors and cut their way into secret safes; where other tan-coated men jimmied French doors and ransacked the papers of a diplomatic correspondent; where nondescript panel trucks parked obscurely on side streets, windows too silty to reveal the man inside with his headphones; where neat telephone trucks appeared in alleys and linemen climbed the poles and installed little devices; where cavernous basement suites concealed batteries of listeners, ears glued to receivers, tape machines winding or ready to wind; where grim men met with other grim men in the White House or the FBI to talk about ridding the government of "bad apples"; where plans were laid and sometimes carried out to violate every provision the founding fathers had written into the First Amendment.

It was a split-level Washington, one the surface and one the subsurface, and they met at the place where government and press intersected, government clutching the dirty secrets of a decade and the germs of future dirty secrets and the press probing, sometimes hard but often too gently, to find what lay beneath the façade of gleaming limestone and beyond the protective fringe of the holly hedges.

Last Arguments

The night of June 10–11 was one which Abe Rosenthal, Jimmy Greenfield and Max Frankel would remember as the longest of their lives.   .

It started about the time Mollie Parnis was wondering how to get Lyndon Johnson out of her dress shop. At 4:30 P.M. Punch Sulzberger saw Abe Rosenthal. Punch had just finished reading a new lead and summary on Neil Sheehan's story about the Pentagon Papers that had been painfully crafted by Frankel and Sheehan, improbable collaborators on what each now saw as *the* story of his time. Punch's verdict was rendered to the Hilton hotel crew by Jimmy Greenfield: "We got a go-ahead, I think." It was just that. A guarded go-ahead. A conditional go-ahead forty-eight hours to press time. Punch told Rosenthal, in essence, that he still did not think the story lived up to the great promises the editors made for it. The writing was better and he knew it would be better still before it was published. But he had not been won over to publishing the documents. He said that if Rosenthal insisted, *The Times* would go ahead with the documents. But he really did not want to.

On the basis of that, John Werner, *The Times* production man, activated his secret mini-composing room on the ninth floor of *The Times* building and type began to be set. There was no question but that the Pentagon Papers story was going to be published Sunday, June 13. But it was still not clear *what* was going to be published.

After the publisher talked with Rosenthal he had a drink with Gruson and told him he was not convinced that the magnitude of the story warranted the risks of publishing the documents in the full form the editors proposed. Gruson agreed to take the question up once more directly with Rosenthal, despite the ruptured state of their relations. They left it at that and Punch departed. He had to change his clothes for Mollie Parnis' dinner party.

Gruson called Rosenthal and offered him a ride uptown. He remembered that Rosenthal was going some place on the East Side, Madison and Seventy-second, somewhere like that.

"Drive uptown with me," he said, "I want to talk to you."

"Look," Gruson said, as he guided his car through the heavy traffic, "there is no question but we are going to publish. The only question is how. Why don't we consider doing it without the documents, publishing them in excerpt form in the stories?"

This was a serious conversation between serious men. As Gruson said, "We forgot our bitterness on this. It was tough, straight talk."

Rosenthal remembered it in the same terms. Sydney gave him a hard time, a very hard time. Did we really have to publish it all? How much of it was just Boy Scout stuff? To please our pride? Wasn't there any give? Rosenthal remembered telling Gruson there was no give. The story had to be published and there couldn't be any compromise. He recalled thinking that if he showed any softness Gruson would sense it. He was pushing as hard as he could, doing the job the publisher had set him. The publisher had to know the bottom line and Gruson was determined to find it.

Finally Gruson dropped Rosenthal off with his promise to consider the publisher's views very seriously and talk it over that night with Max Frankel.

Rosenthal remembered walking down the street and going to Jaeger House for a couple of drinks. He thought again and again over what Gruson had said and more and more became convinced that *The Times* had to publish the story and that if it didn't he would have to resign. He felt under terrific tension and later on he would look back to it as one of the most tense times in a life that had been almost all tension.

Max was dining with his father-in-law that night but promised to come to Jimmy Greenfield's apartment at Seventy-seventh and Park after dinner "for a drink and a celebration" in honor of the go-ahead order, milk-and-waterish as it seemed to be. Abe would be there, too. When Frankel arrived at Greenfield's about 9:30 P.M. Greenfield whispered, "It's off!"

Frankel smiled. He thought it was a joke.

"I'm not kidding," Greenfield said. "The publisher came back and said he wanted to reserve decision until tomorrow morning on the documents."

There was polite conversation at the Greenfield dinner party until the other guests left around midnight. Then Greenfield, Rosenthal and Frankel talked until 3:30 in the morning. (Kissinger was long since soundly sleeping in Washington.) Abe took the devil's advocate position. He tried to give all the arguments for not publishing the documents—the cost of newsprint, the danger of government interference, boredom of the readers, overplay of the story.

Frankel and Greenfield answered back, If we are not going to do it right we are not going to write this story. We can't say that we have this wonderful source material and we know our story is true and, yet, not print the documents.

"You're not going to call Presidents of the United States liars and all kinds of other things unless you have the evidence," Frankel said, "and if you have the evidence you have to produce it."

Abe played his role so well that they really didn't know where he stood. He kept saying, "Is this just an ego trip—that we gotta have the documents? Why can't we just write a decent story?"

By the time it was over and the three staggered away Frankel was so upset he started to write a memo which he proposed to send to Punch if his decision was "no."

By 9 A.M. Max and Abe were at *The Times* office, closeted in Seymour Topping's cubicle off the city-room floor. Gruson walked in. He had just seen the publisher, always an early bird, and had told him, "Don't be surprised if Rosenthal comes up and is willing to go with the narrative and not the documents."

Now Gruson sat with Frankel and Rosenthal, both red-eyed, both sipping hot black coffee in white plastic containers.

"Let's go through it again," said Gruson. "Before we see the publisher."

Abe suggested to Frankel, "You tell him, Max. You've got a new voice and whatever you say I fully endorse."

Frankel was hesitant.

"Just tell him what you told me for three hours last night," Abe added.

"Well," said Max, "you know, Abe, I just don't know how you came out of last night."

"Well," Rosenthal replied, "I came out more firm than when I went in. I'm now absolutely sure. No documents, I say, no story."

What worried him was that the publisher might say, "Yes, there will be a story but no documents." Then he would have to think about quitting.

Frankel swiftly outlined the position, stressing that the consequences of publication were minimal or not difficult. But the difficulties of not publishing would be almost unbearable. *The Times* would lose its constituency, its readers and every value it cared for. It would lose out journalistically to another paper because if *The Times* didn't publish another paper would. It was a question of morale, reputation, trust. The name of *The Times* would be mud.

Moreover, he emphasized, there were no military secrets in the Papers. It seemed to Frankel that no one had made this argument to the publisher. "You mean there is nothing in there?" Gruson asked.

"Well," said Frankel, "I haven't read every word of it but as far as I could see there are no live military secrets in it."

Gruson said grimly, "Well, you fellows are moving me again. You better let Punch hear these things."

Gruson went back upstairs. "I was wrong," Gruson told Punch. "You have to do it their way. They are united. We'd face a wholesale revolt if we didn't. That is the way it has to be."

An hour later the publisher asked the newsmen to come to his office. Rosenthal, Frankel and Greenfield went to the third-floor lobby. As they waited for the elevator, Abe said to Frankel, "You're a new voice. Take the lead. Be crisp."

The trio got off on the fourteenth floor, apprehensive, anxious, gloomy, do-or-die, together-we-stand, together-we-fall. In the corridor outside Punch's office they encountered Harding Bancroft, shirt-sleeved, pleasant, wishing them a hearty good morning. No clue there. Inside they found Punch standing behind his desk, Gruson already in the room. They sat down and Punch made a few remarks about the long hours they were working and then said very seriously and quietly to Abe, "I've decided you can use the documents—but not the story."

For a moment there was dead silence. The editorial trio, ready for combat, could not believe their ears. Then there was a great guffaw. There was, too, Frankel admitted, a tremendous letdown. They had come to do battle to the end and their victory had been handed them on a platter. In fact Punch had taken the trouble to put his thoughts down in a neat memo saying they would go ahead on the basis of his decision of the afternoon before, using documents and text, for a maximum of six pages a day and that Bancroft and Gruson would examine the material to make sure there were no military secrets. That was it.

Later on when Punch was recalling the events of that Thursday and Friday he explained why he finally came down on the side of publishing the documents:

"The only thing," he said, "that ever bothered me was that the stuff was stamped 'Top Secret.' But on the documents question I finally came down on the side of Abe. Damn it—if we were going to get into so much trouble anyway this would not make much difference."

Characteristically, he had forgotten his joke that they just publish the documents and no story. "Oh, yeah," he said, "I thought I'd lighten it with a joke."

Much later, when asked if he had had anything special on his mind at the Mollie Parnis party, he said, "Not really, the Pentagon Papers thing was all decided."

But that was after the fact. Mollie Parnis remembered that she called to congratulate Punch on the Pentagon Papers.

"Gee, Punch," she said, "I'm proud of you. I think the Pentagon Papers just had to be released."

"Thanks a lot," Punch said, "and that was a wonderful dinner party. But, God, Mollie, wasn't that timing bad!"

20

Washington Weekend: June 12-13, 1971

T HE WHITE HOUSE never looked more gay than for the reception after Tricia's Rose Garden wedding on Saturday, June 12. What with the delay because of the rain the ceremony did not end until 4:48 P.M. A few minutes later the bride and groom took their places with President and Mrs. Nixon and the Coxes in the reception line in the Blue Room, fragrant with roses, marguerites and anemones. The four hundred guests slowly passed through and into the East Room, where Bill Harrington's orchestra was playing Tricia's favorites, "Wunder-bar" and "Love Is a Many Splendored Thing." It was almost an hour before the new bride and groom swung into their first dance.

Everything was very homey and the White House seemed an island of calm in a storm-tossed world. Hundreds of police had sealed off a two-block zone and during the night a green wooden fence had been put up around the Ellipse, where the May Day tribe had called upon protesters to gather. There was, in fact, no protest worthy of the name, just a score of bedraggled young people who stood in the rain near the Washington Monument holding a Vietcong flag.

Sometime during the reception Ron Ziegler, the White House press secretary, was called over to the usher's office at the east entrance. Dan Henkin, public relations man for the Defense Department, told Ziegler that *The New York Times* was carrying a story about what it called the "Vietnam Archive." Henkin had been telephoned by Jerry Greene of the New York *Daily News* about the story.§

Henkin knew that such a study had been made but little more than that; Ziegler had never heard of it and was not impressed. So far as he understood, the story didn't relate to the Nixon Administration and required no response on their part.

Later Ziegler was not able to recall doing anything special about Henkin's information. He thought he had probably informed someone from the National Security Council, either Kissinger or his chief aide,

§See Notes section.

Colonel (later General) Al Haig. He did not remember whether he told the President.

If Ziegler told the President it left no impression on him, not one that he could recollect a few years later, nor one that caused any interference with the gaiety of the wedding reception. Nor did Mr. Nixon order any inquiry.

Of Mr. Nixon's mood there could be no doubt. The guests found him relaxed as he seldom had been in the past two years; enjoying himself; even enjoying his first dance with the bride despite trepidations he had voiced about his dancing. Steve Bull, the President's appointments secretary, was in a position to attest to Mr. Nixon's spirits. The President never hid his feelings from Bull. If he was upset "he would take my head off and that was perfectly O.K.," Bull remembered. But all through the wedding day the President was in good form and, looking back on it, Bull could not believe that he had a worry on his mind. He did not believe that the President could have known the Papers were about to be published or if he knew that it bothered him. That was Ziegler's judgment, too, and he had as good reason to know the President's moods as Bull.

The wedding cake, which in the temper of the times had become controversial when Craig Claiborne of *The New York Times* submitted the recipe of Heinz Bender, White House pastry chef, to other culinary experts who found the White House formula less than chic, had been cut, the bride's bouquet of lilies of the valley, sweetheart roses, baby's breath and Baker's fern had been thrown from the grand staircase of the White House front hall, the bride and groom had made their getaway in a long black limousine and gradually the guests began to leave. It had been as pleasant an interlude as the Nixon White House had seen for a long time, as pleasant and carefree a day as it would ever see again.

First Response

Later on there were many people in and around the White House who had a feeling that they had known in advance that *The New York Times* was going to publish the Pentagon Papers. John Ehrlichman had that feeling quite strongly but was never able to pin it to anything specific. He thought the White House had some notice that *The Times* was going to publish a big story about the Vietnam war. But he conceded there was no concern about it, not on the Saturday of Tricia's wedding and not until later. He thought Haldeman might have picked up word. Or Ziegler. But Haldeman could not recall any tip although he too retained a faint image of an advance warning. Mr. Nixon himself could recall nothing, nor could Ziegler. One man had a more positive recollection. This was Melvin Laird, Secretary of Defense. He firmly believed that word had come in earlier. Not from the White House, he felt sure. Possibly from congressional liaison sources. He recollected a meeting with Robert Pursley, his chief military aide, and Dan Henkin about it. Despite Laird's conviction it seems likely that he was wrong. Neither Pursley, a handsome, quiet, immaculately precise military man, nor Henkin, an experienced public relations officer, recalled hearing about the *Times* publication until Saturday afternoon. Pursley felt certain there was no advance warning. Otherwise, some precautions would have been taken. Unfortunately, his notes and records of the period were lost mysteriously by the Pentagon during the time he served as Far Eastern commander in Japan in 1972.*

Years later Kissinger insisted that he did not know about the impending publication in advance and circumstantial evidence supports his contention. Perhaps the strongest testimonial is the fact that no effort was launched by Kissinger or his aides prior to Saturday evening to determine what *The Times* was up to. That was the recollection of Al Haig as well.

Despite the security precautions of *The Times,* despite every effort to isolate the Pentagon project from prying eyes, despite the fact that (as far as could later be determined) no one in the Nixon Administration discovered what was up until late Saturday afternoon and as far as investigation has disclosed, none of the nation's secret agencies, the FBI, the CIA and the rest, had gotten onto what was happening, there were five men in Washington who knew.

They were Leslie Gelb, Morton Halperin, Paul Warnke, former Undersecretary of Defense, Robert McNamara and his successor, Clark Clifford.

They had not been told by *The Times* or by Neil Sheehan or by any of the Hilton hotel team. But one member of the team, Hedrick Smith, had called Gelb for information about the mechanics of the Pentagon study. Smith thought his inquiry had been so masked that Gelb would not realize its purport and he did not recall telephoning until the very last minute, Friday or Saturday. But, in fact, the call was made a day or two earlier and Gelb drew the accurate conclusion that Smith was working on a story about the Pentagon Papers and that the article

*When Pursley was sent to Tokyo his personal records were transferred from his Pentagon office to a saferoom about 100 feet down the corridor. When he decided to retire from the Army he returned to Washington for routine hearings before the Senate Armed Services Committee and sent for his files. They were not in the saferoom and no trace of them was ever found. So far as Pursley was aware no documents had ever before been "lost" in this manner and when the wiretapping and activity of the Plumbers became known he wondered whether there wasn't a link between all this and the missing files. (Personal interview, Pursley, 6/8/79)

would appear in Sunday's paper. He guessed instantly that the source
was Daniel Ellsberg. Gelb quickly passed the word to Halperin and
Warnke. Warnke, in turn, relayed the information to Clark Clifford
(Warnke was by now a member of the Clifford law firm) and Robert
McNamara. No evidence has turned up to indicate that any of the five
passed the information to the Nixon Administration. Neither
McNamara nor Clifford had a recollection of doing so.

Whatever was known or wasn't known within the government on
Saturday evening one man went into action immediately—Al Haig.
Kissinger did not recall knowing about the Papers until Sunday morning when he picked up *The New York Times* before boarding a plane
for California. His memory may have misled him because Saturday
evening Haig was already hard at work trying to track down everything
he could find out about the Papers. It is not likely that Haig would have
launched this effort without consultation with Kissinger.

However, Kissinger betrayed no sign of special concern. His trip to
California, as he later explained, was "personal," not official, but he
apparently gave no thought to canceling it because of alarm over the
Pentagon Papers. Kissinger was, as his friend Lloyd Shearer, editor of
Parade magazine, pointed out, "between marriages." He had several
attractive young female friends in Southern California and often visited
them, sometimes staying at the Shearers', although not, apparently, on
this particular occasion. "He used our place as a hideaway," Shearer
recalled. "Sometimes he stayed with Pat Shriver. I remember that one
of Henry's girls kept a diary and later on, I heard, the FBI came around
and threatened her."*

One of the first persons Haig telephoned was Walt Rostow, President Johnson's security adviser, the man who held the same position
vis-à-vis Johnson that Kissinger held with Nixon.

"What is this Vietnam study which is going to be in *The New York
Times* tomorrow?" Haig asked Rostow.

"Who leaked it?" Rostow replied.

"We think it is a guy named Ellsberg," Haig said.

"The son of a bitch!" Rostow said. "He still owes me a term paper."

The "term paper" to which Rostow referred was a study of decision-

---

*Kissinger had many reasons for being grateful to Shearer. In the early months of the
administration, Haldeman imposed a rule that Kissinger was not to appear on TV or
speak on radio because of his heavy German accent. He told Shearer about this and
after Shearer published an item, Haldeman, in embarrassment, lifted the rule in order
to show that it didn't exist and Kissinger found himself free to appear on TV talk
shows, a freedom which he utilized effectively to build up his national image. (Personal
interview, Shearer, 1/19/79)

making in the Cuban missile crisis of 1962 which Ellsberg had done for Rostow. Ellsberg had presented an oral report but never submitted a written "term paper."

Rostow was not in a position to inform Haig about the study because, as he later said, he was only vaguely aware that McNamara had commissioned a history of the war in Vietnam. Rostow had never been approached for documents nor had he been cut into the paper flow (actually, he had been cut *out* of the paper flow in fear he might torpedo the project) and the whole thing had gone out of his mind until Haig called him on the night of June 12, 1971, reaching him in Austin, Texas, where Rostow had accompanied Lyndon Johnson after the President left the White House. Who else Haig reached that weekend is unclear. He did not reach William Bundy, who was in London; nor Mac Bundy, who was in the countryside. He did not call Leslie Gelb or Mort Halperin. Why he did not talk to any of them was puzzling because Haig was thoroughly aware of the Pentagon study; who authorized it; who worked on it; in fact, like Kissinger, Haig had been asked to participate by Halperin and Gelb.* As to why he had called Rostow he simply remembered that "at that time we were in very close contact with Rostow."

Ellsberg

In Cambridge, Ellsberg was in a state of excitement. After getting the telephone call from Tony Austin tipping him that *The Times* was publishing the Pentagon Papers on Sunday, he tried to reach Sheehan without success. He tried to call Anthony Russo, the associate at Rand who had helped him copy the Papers but had no better luck and he had called Neil's friend in Cambridge, Dun Gifford.

Lately Ellsberg had been in touch with Senator Mike Gravel of Alaska. Gravel was planning a filibuster on the draft bill and Ellsberg thought he might persuade Gravel to read the Papers into the record as part of the filibuster. On Thursday, June 10, the date of the Parnis party, Ellsberg had telephoned Congressman McCloskey to see if he might be ready to go ahead with releasing the Papers. McCloskey said no, he wanted to wait at least until the end of June. Dan then told McCloskey that he hoped to get Gravel to make the Papers public. McCloskey offered no objection.

---

*"We asked Haig to work on it when he came back from Vietnam," Halperin recalled. "He said he would think about it and then went in to see [Deputy Secretary of Defense John] McNaughton. He was hoping McNaughton would urge him to work on the project but when he didn't Haig said he wasn't interested." (Personal interview, Halperin, 1/23/79)

Normally Ellsberg never kept a copy of the Papers in the Hilliard Street apartment but he had broken this rule since he intended to deliver a set to Gravel on Monday. The Ellsbergs were dining Saturday night with Howard Zinn and his wife. Zinn was a professor at Boston University and the Zinns were active in the antiwar movement. They knew about the Pentagon Papers and when Dan and Pat arrived Dan said he had heard *The Times* was publishing them in the morning. Zinn was surprised that Dan was not elated by this fact—he was glad the Papers were coming out but irritated that he had not been told earlier. The two couples smoked some pot, then went over to Harvard Square and saw *Butch Cassidy and the Sundance Kid.* It was the third time Ellsberg had seen the picture and years later it was still a favorite. He was, and continued to be, enchanted by the free style of Cassidy and the Kid, of the danger that flowed through their lives as they rode carefree toward whatever destiny fate might provide. He was reminded of the days when he and John Vann, the nonpareil leader of Vietnamese troops, raced off on Vann's motorbike on jungle trails deep into the back country.

When they came back to the apartment the Zinns' son was there. He looked at them and said, "What's coming off here?" The smell of pot was heavy in the apartment. The last pot experience the Zinns had had was when their youngster was in high school and they had come home to ask *him* what the funny smell was.

Before the evening was over Ellsberg told the Zinns he had something he wanted them to keep for him for a couple of days and, no questions asked, sight-unseen, the Zinns agreed.

"Of course," Zinn recalled later, "we did know what they were and were glad to do it. It gave us a chance to read the Papers."

The Ellsbergs' apartment was on the third floor. Their downstairs neighbors later remembered being awakened on what they concluded was the night before the Pentagon story broke by the noise of boxes thumping down the stairs, and when they looked out they saw the Ellsbergs loading them into a car. Half an hour later they heard the Ellsbergs coming back. They were laughing and as they climbed the staircase they sang reveille. Later on the neighbors thought they must have been moving the Papers out of the flat.*

*Soon after the Pentagon Papers broke, the neighbors got a phone call from the Ellsbergs, who had fled their apartment and gone underground. Would the neighbors please get the key from the landlord and do something about the mirrors in the bedroom in case the FBI raided the flat? The neighbors got some Indian cloth prints and covered the mirrors on the walls and ceiling. Whether the FBI broke into the apartment is not certain but the Ellsbergs assumed that they did. (Personal interviews, Priscilla McMillan, 3/14/77; Ellsberg, 1/15/79)

At *The Times*

All of *The Times* reporters working on the Pentagon story (except Sheehan, who stayed at his typewriter) came over to the Forty-third Street building to see the first papers emerge from the subbasement pressroom. None were happy about the headline and the play. The desk editors had been unhappy since Friday afternoon when they had been informed that there was to be a four-column two-line head over the story. They had looked up Reston's scoop on the Yalta papers and knew that this had carried a five-column headline. Word that they were to have a smaller headline than Yalta jolted them. They already had been jolted by the cutback in space which the publisher had ordered. They had expected at least ten pages a day and it had been difficult to cut back to six at the last moment. They were exhausted and now they felt the story was not receiving the prominence it deserved.

Al Segal, one of the editors, remembered saying, "This is impossible!" He went to foreign editor Greenfield and was told the play had been ordered by Rosenthal.

There had been great discussion over what to call the story. On Friday Siegal had suggested "Pentagon Papers" but Rosenthal didn't care for that. He said it reminded him too much of the "Penkovsky Papers" and of Whittaker Chambers' "Pumpkin Papers." Segal suggested "Vietnam Archive" and this suited Rosenthal's mood of avoidance of excess. There was a technical argument for "Vietnam Archive." It fitted a one-column headline and therefore was useful for "jump headlines," that is, for the segment of the story that was continued on inside pages.

When Rosenthal saw the story in the paper, the four-column headline, the sedate play, the catchword "Vietnam Archive," he thought it looked just right. He congratulated the editors for their careful work and particularly for the manner in which they had been able to reduce the volume, eliminating practically all photographic display, yet still providing an attractive presentation. Looking back, Rosenthal was inclined to think that he underplayed the story. Still, at the time, it struck him as being just about right.

What caused Rosenthal second thoughts was the reaction that the story drew. Or rather the lack of reaction. In truth that had been apparent the moment the newspapers arrived in the city room on Saturday evening. Not a few editors and reporters, looking at the story with its modest headline and carefully qualified language, exclaimed, "Is this what they were all so excited about? Is this what they spent $250,000 on?"

It was not until Paul Montgomery, a general assignment reporter, came up to the cluster of editors and reporters, his face aglow, and exclaimed, "My God! This is dynamite! Absolute dynamite!" that the mood in the city room began to shift.

Montgomery was captured by the story. He ran up to one editor and reporter after another, saying again and again, "Dynamite!" Slowly the mood of the city room began to shift and presently it was accepted throughout the room that the story was, in fact, dynamite.

Once the city room settled down a bit the Hilton group went back to work, taking with them reinforcements. There was no longer need for secrecy. They could use as many men and women as they needed and there was plenty to do. There were more texts to edit and a mass of copy. Neil Sheehan was still working on his third dispatch. Bob Rosenthal, the foreign-desk copy boy, brought a stack of *Times* over to the Hilton. Sheehan was sitting at his desk, back to the door, typing. Rosenthal tossed three copies on his desk. Neil leaped up, clasped the papers to his chest and yelled in joy. He jumped up and down, shouting, "We'll all be jailed when this gets to Pedernales! It'll all be bullshit!"

Sheehan remembered Fox Butterfield, later to be *Times* correspondent in China, saying, "Christ! It's terrible. What a strange headline! It looks like just another Pentagon story."

That made Sheehan angry. "Get the hell out of here!" he shouted. "Look. We're into the wire. It's moving. We're going to take this position before they even wake up."

It was like a battle to Sheehan and the analogy to tanks moving forward through barbed wire seemed entirely appropriate to him.

After the first 100,000 copies of *The Times* had run off the presses Sheehan tried to reach Dan Ellsberg by telephone in Cambridge but did not succeed. "I owe him this!" Sheehan exclaimed. He did not get through that evening or the next day. And out of that failure a long coolness was to ensue between the two men most responsible for the story.* About that same time Neil's wife, Susan, called David Halberstam and told him the story was breaking in the Sunday paper. Halberstam, who was more than three-fourths of the way through his book *The Best and the Brightest,* dealing with the Kennedy-Johnson elite and the war, was angered. He thought Neil should have given him a hint. The Pentagon publication radically affected his book and at first he thought it might even sink his project (as Tony Austin thought— correctly—that the Papers had sunk his book on Tonkin Gulf). However, Halberstam recast sections of his book and, if anything, publica-

*They were not to meet again until May 9–10, 1975, when Neil went to Mill Valley, California, to interview Dan for his book on John Vann and the American involvement in Vietnam. I found the two, each with his own tape recorder, reliving the Vietnam experience across a broad redwood table at Ellsberg's mountaintop house. They talked for fifteen hours one day and six the next.

tion of the Pentagon Papers and the somber light it cast on the presidential advisers contributed to its success.*

John Vann, the American Vietnamese specialist, once told Halberstam that he believed Ellsberg "has the most brilliant mind ever exposed to these layers of Vietnamese society." Halberstam was a little miffed, he recalled, because "I thought I had the most brilliant mind."

The White House

The silence of Sunday, June 13, was palpable. It was an incredible June day, a day for golf, for sailing on Long Island Sound, for early treks to the beach, for sprawling on lounge chairs and slowly riffling through *The New York Times*, letting one fat section after another slip onto the flagstone terrace. It was a day when telephones did not ring. Not a call for Abe Rosenthal. Not a call for Neil Sheehan. Not a call all day long from the office to Punch Sulzberger's cool green acres in Stamford. No one called Max Frankel in Washington, not even to congratulate him on the big story. I spent the weekend at my house in the Berkshires, went to lunch with a company of addicted *Times* readers, in late afternoon met another group for cocktails and yet a third at dinner. With difficulty I kept my tongue reined in. Every kind of topic was discussed. The usual invective against Nixon and the Vietnam war. Not one mention of the Pentagon Papers. My God, I said to myself, the story is a bust!

In Washington calm enveloped the White House. The President and his wife relaxed. Mr. Nixon skipped church. Instead he and Mrs. Nixon had thirty of their closest friends and relatives in for Sunday morning coffee. After coffee, orange juice and danish, the Nixons took the group to the Executive Office Building and showed them the wedding gifts of Tricia and Eddie Cox on display in the Indian Treaty Room. The white wrought-iron pavilion where the wedding had taken place in the Rose Garden already had been dismantled and the white carpet and white ribbons removed. Everything was in apple-pie order.

The President spent a quiet day. He worked a bit at his office, looking over plans for the week ahead—a big meeting on the drug question, a visit by Chancellor Willy Brandt of Germany, a trip to Rochester, New York, to drum up support for his domestic policies.

When Mr. Nixon rose that Sunday morning one of the first things he did was to turn to the front page of *The New York Times* to read

---

*The first person Halberstam interviewed when he began work on *The Best and the Brightest* was Ellsberg. The two men talked for three successive days and Halberstam wound up with thirty-six pages of notes. Ellsberg later said he would have given Halberstam a copy of the Papers but the two did not hit it off and he decided against it. However, he made no secret to Halberstam of the fact he had the Papers and was working on them. (Personal interview, Ellsberg, 2/26/77)

the story about his daughter's wedding.* The story took the left-hand play in *The Times* with the headline "Tricia Nixon Takes Vows." There was a large picture of the wedding in the Rose Garden with Mr. Nixon standing beside his daughter. This story balanced off against the story of the Pentagon Papers on the right-hand side of page one.

Mr. Nixon did not record his immediate reaction to the Pentagon story, either in his *Memoirs* or in private consultation after publication of the *Memoirs.* However, there was nothing in the pattern of his actions or those of his aides to suggest concern. He spoke, as was his custom, with his press aide, Ron Ziegler, after breakfast for about ten minutes. A bit later he talked with Haldeman. At 12:18 he put in a call for Kissinger but was unable to reach him as Kissinger was en route to the Coast. Kissinger returned his call shortly after 3 P.M. after arriving on the Coast.†

For both Haldeman and Ehrlichman, Sunday, June 13, was a delightful day. The President had been in marvelous fettle for the wedding and the aura persisted. They gathered up their families and boarded the presidential yacht *Sequoia* for a cruise down the Potomac. They had their wives and children with them, Jody Ann and Bob Ehrlichman, then fourteen and twelve years old, and Ann and Peter Haldeman, then fourteen and sixteen.

An interesting discussion arose between Ehrlichman and the children. They had seen the story of the Pentagon Papers in *The Times* and wanted to know why this kind of information hadn't been made public by the government itself. Ehrlichman was not particularly aroused by the publication. It seemed to him (as to many others in the administration) that the Papers dealt largely with the Johnson years. Nothing to get excited about. But when the children raised the question he began to talk about the President's general concern about leaks and the difficulties which flowed from them. He mentioned that in the case of one particular leak an important intelligence informant was exposed and compromised and he explained that sometimes when information was leaked a foreign intelligence service could deduce the

---

*Ordinarily a daily news summary was prepared by the White House staff. However, the summary was not issued on Sundays. The Saturday-Sunday news was covered in the Monday A.M. summary. The summary treated very lightly stories contained in *The Times* and the *Post* since the President preferred to read them in the newspapers themselves. Only on one occasion during the Nixon presidency was there a Sunday news summary. That was on the occasion in October 1973 of the "Saturday night massacre." (Personal interview, Lyndon K. Allin, 9/15/78)

†The Nixon tapes and records presumably would cast more light on this subject but they are not at present available to outside researchers. Kissinger has said he has no record of conversations with Mr. Nixon not made from his office. (Personal interview, Kissinger, 10/26/78)

source from which it derived and this might destroy the usefulness of an undercover agent. He had been told, he later recalled, about some instances of this by Henry Kissinger or Richard Helms, head of the CIA. But, he agreed with the children, there wasn't this problem with the Pentagon Papers because they dealt with past history—still, Ehrlichman told the youngsters, Mr. Nixon was worried each time something like this happened because he felt that the U.S. position was further eroded.

It was an interesting theoretical discussion and years later its essence still lingered in the minds of the Ehrlichmans and the Haldemans.

21

Henry Kissinger

A N IDYLLIC ATMOSPHERE did not prevail in all of Washington. Henry Kissinger was not amused by *The Times* publication. Leaks —any kind of leaks—drove him wild. There is no other word for it. In fact, in the first and possibly best-documented instance of Kissinger's response to a "leak," the publication May 9, 1969, by William Beecher of *The New York Times* of news that U.S. B-52's were bombing Cambodia, the late J. Edgar Hoover quoted Kissinger as saying he hoped "I would follow it up as far as we can take it and they will destroy whoever did this, if we can find him, no matter where he is."

Kissinger's response to that leak was to move for FBI wiretaps of four men: three on his assistants, Morton Halperin, Helmut Sonnenfeldt and David Davidson, and a fourth on Colonel Pursley. The tap on Pursley was the equivalent, for practical purposes, of taping Laird himself since he was constantly on the phone to Pursley.

During the 1968 Nixon election campaign Laird, a clever, experienced congressman from Wisconsin, had developed a well-articulated antagonism toward Mr. Nixon's Golddust twins, Ehrlichman and Haldeman. Laird's hostility quickly extended to Kissinger. In an effort (successful) to keep the White House and, specifically Ehrlichman, Haldeman or Kissinger, from undercutting him in the Pentagon, Laird established an airtight set of rules. All White House calls to his Army, Navy, Air Force secretaries were filtered through his personal military and political aides. He permitted no one, no officer, no associate in the Pentagon, to take direct White House calls without clearance from his own closest personal aides. At his regular Monday morning staff meeting violators of this procedure were personally chewed out by Laird. They were not likely to violate the rule again. Nor would Laird himself take direct White House calls except from the President or from Henry Kissinger. If Al Haig called he had to talk to Pursley. "I had that all set up," Laird recalled. "I never took a call from

Al Haig, for example, he had to talk to Bob Pursley."*

Conflict between Laird and Kissinger had errupted with the beginning of Nixon's term. Laird came into office a staunch advocate of pull-out from Vietnam. He told *The New York Times* before the end of January that if Nixon did not get out of Vietnam in six months it would become "Nixon's war." Nixon had said much the same. Laird set up a schedule for U.S. troop withdrawals from Vietnam and sent the White House a memo on the program. The first withdrawal would be ordered March 15, 1969, unless countermanded by the President. The order was sent to Mr. Nixon at San Clemente and apparently got buried in a pile of papers. Since no contrary word came from Nixon, Laird announced the withdrawal March 15. There was an angry rocket from the White House, initiated by Kissinger, March 18, claiming that the Pentagon was whittling down the President's options.

Less than a month later another row erupted, this one over the shooting down of a U.S. Navy EC-121 reconnaissance plane off Korea.

Laird (and Pursley) thought the EC-121 mission was stupid. There was no need for the plane to have overflown North Korean waters. There were far better and more modern means of intelligence.

The White House (Nixon and Kissinger) wanted to retaliate with a B-52 strike on North Korea. Laird strongly opposed this as did Secretary of State Rogers. Laird counseled that if North Korea responded to the proposed strike with an invasion of South Korea the United States would have to order full mobilization since we did not have the military power in the Pacific to meet a North Korean thrust.†

Kissinger finally had a personal confrontation with Laird in the Pentagon in which, as one witness said, "he threw a first-class tan-

---

*Later Laird and Pursley were to credit these strict rules with preventing the Pentagon from being drawn in, as was the CIA, to the Watergate scandal. Twice, Laird said, "they tried to come down here on Watergate but they didn't get in." (Personal interviews, Laird 1/12/78; Pursley 9/19/78) One of these efforts may have involved a cloudy plan which Mr. Nixon discussed with Haldeman and Ehrlichman on July 7, 1971, to utilize the International Security section of the Defense Department headed by the extremely conservative Warren Nutter as a clearing house for a weekly direct report to the President on an "eyes only" basis of progress in uncovering the Pentagon Papers "conspiracy." (House Judiciary Committee Impeachment Hearings, Appendix III, p. 131)

†Mr. Nixon contended he had two options—number one, a B-52 strike on North Korea; number two, continuance of reconnaissance flights under armed protection. Later, he said, option three, a new strike at Cambodia(!), called Operation Lunch, was ordered. (*Memoirs*, p. 384) Haldeman recollected that Kissinger proposed nuclear strikes against North Korea if they responded to U.S. reprisals by attacking South Korea. (H.R. Haldeman, *The Ends of Power*. New York, 1978, p. 85.) Kissinger in his memoirs makes no mention of this and leaves it unclear exactly what advice he gave to Mr. Nixon. (Henry Kissinger, *White House Years*. New York, 1979, pp. 316–321.)

trum." He claimed the Pentagon was thwarting the wishes of the President. Haig contended that Pursley, a holdover from the Democratic McNamara and Clifford administrations, was feeding negative advice to Laird. But, of course, as Pursley later pointed out, this was ridiculous. Laird was his own man. It was Laird, not Pursley, who was opposing the Kissinger and/or Nixon initiatives.

The fact was that Laird and Kissinger not only were strongly opposed in their views on Vietnam, Laird wanting to get the U.S. out, Kissinger (and Nixon) all for staying in, but were personally incompatible. "Mel Laird was an enigma to Henry," Pursley recalled. "He never could figure him out. He never did trust Laird and, of course, the moment something happened he suspected him."

Leaks

It was against this background and well before the publication of the Beecher story on May 9, 1969, that Kissinger participated in a meeting on the subject of wiretapping and leaks. According to Kissinger the first meeting was held at the White House April 25 with the President, J. Edgar Hoover and Attorney General Mitchell participating. The names of four men who might be tapped—Halperin, Davidson and Sonnenfeldt of Kissinger's staff, and Henry Brandon, London *Sunday Times* correspondent in Washington—were said by Kissinger to have been mentioned. There were some, including former Deputy Attorney General William Ruckelshaus, who wondered whether this meeting ever occurred. However, there is no doubt that Kissinger did meet with Hoover in Hoover's FBI office on May 5, four days *before* the publication of Beecher's B-52 Cambodia bombing story, which ostensibly triggered the wiretap program.

It is significant that three of the four whose wiretapping was ordered after the Beecher story had already been named either April 25 or May 5 as possible tapees. It is even more significant that in the list of tapees submitted to Hoover by Haig on May 10 the name of Pursley, the key link to Laird, was substituted for Mr. Hoover's favorite "spy," Henry Brandon. Pursley was tapped for only fifteen days. But this was just a warm-up. On the night of May 2, 1970, when the White House heard that another William Beecher exclusive would be published the next day by *The New York Times,* reporting heavy new U.S. bombing raids in North Vietnam, Haig got in touch with the FBI and requested that the tap on Pursley be renewed and that taps be placed on Beecher himself, for the first time, and upon Richard Petersen and Ambassador William Sullivan, two high State Department employees. Shortly thereafter Kissinger had two more of his own employees, Anthony Lake and Winston Lord, tapped. The tap on Pursley this time would remain until February 10, 1971, when all taps were removed at Hoover's request so that he could claim to Congress that the FBI was tapping only the barest minimum of critical security risks.

Of course neither Melvin Laird nor Bob Pursley knew on the weekend of June 12–13, 1971, that Pursley had twice been wiretapped at Kissinger's and/or White House request. They had no knowledge that the second tap on Pursley had specified that both his home and his office telephones be covered.*

However, both Laird and Pursley were under no illusions. They knew that Kissinger blamed Laird, specifically, for the leak on the Cambodian bombing story because Laird had argued in the National Security Council that it would be impossible to keep the bombing secret with 10,000 American personnel (not counting the Cambodians and North Vietnamese) knowing about it. "It was because I had argued so hard on that," Laird recalled. "I said it just wouldn't stay secret and I offered to go to Congress and get approval of the bombing. I could have done it easily. But they didn't want that."

In a word, Laird well knew that he had no allies at the White House with the partial exception of Mr. Nixon himself, who, being a professional politician unlike Haldeman, Ehrlichman, Kissinger and most of the White House staff, had known Mel Laird for a long, long time and understood that he was a fox of the first water; that he not only knew how to take care of himself but knew his way around Congress as well or better than anyone in Washington and had a canny instinct for politics. In other words, whatever emotions Laird might generate in the breasts of the White House staff or even in Nixon, Nixon knew he had to move warily with him.

Laird's Role

Unlike the men in the White House, Laird and Pursley knew what the Pentagon Papers were about. Neither man had read them but Pursley had, of course, followed the study from its inception under McNamara and its completion under Clifford. He had briefed Laird, in general, about the project and periodically he inventoried Laird's walk-in safe and checked to see that the documents were still there. They occupied the whole top row of one side of the safe, a shelf so high that Laird, a fairly short man, would have needed a stepladder to reach them.

---

*Laird had his office periodically "swept" by the extremely sophisticated specialists of the National Security Agency and therefore was reasonably confident that his own phones were secure. However, he conceded this did not protect the telephone of Pursley from the technicians of the FBI. (David Wise, *The American Police State*, New York, 1978, p. 45) To this day Pursley is convinced that it was the EC-121 incident and the widening disagreement between Laird and the White House that led to his tapping—not the leaks. (Personal interview, Pursley, 7/19/78)

Laird's knowledge of the Pentagon study was nudged from time to time by the requests of Senator Fulbright that he turn the documents over to the Senate Foreign Relations Committee but Fulbright's requests had not sufficiently stirred Laird's interest to cause him to look at the documents personally.

"Pursley got into them occasionally," Laird recalled, "and gave me historical stuff that I needed. I got some historian to prepare the response to Fulbright. My contact with them was always through Pursley."

He had put the task of preparing a memorandum rejecting Fulbright's request into the hands of Dennis J. Doolin, Deputy Assistant Secretary for International Security Affairs, the department where the study had originated in McNamara's day.

In the spring of 1971 it occurred to Pursley that there was a potential for trouble about the Papers. He didn't have anything special in mind although his concern may have been triggered by Fulbright's persistent requests and the new requests that had started to come in from Congressman McCloskey.

In any event, he went to J. Fred Buzhardt, counsel to the Defense Department, and told him that "there were in Mr. Laird's vault some documents which had a potential for creating a stir." He thought Buzhardt at least ought to know of the existence of the study. Neither he nor Buzhardt did anything further.

The first thing Pursley did after hearing from Dan Henkin late Saturday that *The Times* was publishing the Pentagon story was to go to Laird's vault and make certain that all the volumes were there. They were. While he was at it he checked the inventory to see who else had copies. On Sunday he called McNamara, Clifford, Warnke and Gelb, checking to find out where their copies were. While others might be oblivious to the implications of *The Times'* story Pursley had no doubts from the start. There would be, he was certain, "a sizable investigation."

Undoubtedly, Pursley believed, Haig called him on Saturday evening. "He was calling all the time," Pursley said. "But I have no specific recollection of the Saturday night call."*

Melvin Laird was scheduled to appear on CBS' *Face the Nation* at noon Sunday. Laird had a routine on these occasions. He met at the

---

*Pursley's relations with Haig then and later were tinged with acid. He felt Haig had more than a little to do with having him tapped and that Haig was more than a little responsible for the extraordinary bitterness which characterized Pentagon-White House relations. In fact, he informed Haig in spring, 1972, that if such conditions continued "I would have no alternative but to turn in my suit." (Personal interview, Pursley, 7/19/78)

Mayflower Hotel coffee shop for breakfast with several colleagues and on the pleasant Sunday, June 13, he did this as usual. Pursley and Dan Henkin joined him for a leisurely breakfast. There was no tension. Henkin said to his chief, "Look, you can forget all about the things we expected they would ask. It will be the Pentagon Papers all the way."

Laird laughed. He thought the same thing. He made two or three telephone calls, one of them to Attorney General John Mitchell. Laird didn't think it was such a big story. Neither did Mitchell. If Laird was asked he could say they were looking into the matter, just fudge it some way. After all, as Henkin said, "it hadn't happened on his watch."

Laird was a skilled performer on television. Ordinarily he had two or three things he wanted to talk about and no matter what was asked he turned the subject to what he wanted to say. He was very good at this kind of thing and by the time he was ready to go on the air he was primed. He got up half a dozen times to shake hands with people in the Mayflower and then left for the CBS studio.

To Laird's amazement—and that of his staff—he didn't get a single question about the Papers. Not even from John Finney, a senior *New York Times* Washington correspondent. Years later Finney was asked why he hadn't raised the subject. He was as puzzled about it then as Laird was on Sunday, June 13.§

Kissinger's Role

Henry Kissinger recollected years later that his initial reaction on hearing about the Pentagon Papers was to assume they had been "selectively leaked by Laird in an effort to embarrass the previous Administration." He had, he said, a firm belief that the classification system should not be utilized for political purposes and ordered Haig to make every effort to discover what had happened.* It was not, he said, until late Sunday evening that he obtained from Haig a report indicating "the full scope of what was involved." He did not think he had talked about the Papers with Mr. Nixon in his Sunday afternoon conversation because at that time he did not yet know all the circumstances. As he recollected not much could possibly have been done about the Papers on Sunday because he spent so much of the day in travel.

§See Notes section

*"Of course he thought I leaked the Pentagon Papers," Laird later commented. "They always thought I leaked everything. They thought I leaked the Cambodian bombing, the bombing of the sanctuaries, because I argued so hard that you couldn't keep it secret." (Personal interview, Laird, 1/12/78) Pursley thought Kissinger's comment about Laird leaking the Pentagon Papers was probably half-serious, half-facetious but he found nothing amusing about Kissinger's remark. (Personal interview, Pursley, 10/31/78)

Looking back at the weekend there would be endless conjecture as to what caused the somnolent attitude toward the Papers by the administration to change and most of the speculation gave Kissinger the major role in this, partly because of his reactions in the past toward leaks and partly because of the explosions he would soon set off. But having traced the origin of the explosion to Kissinger the analysts would remain at a loss to understand the reactions of this brilliant, emotional man.

Some, however, found an explanation in the complex and many-sided nature of his relationship with Nixon and with the Nixon White House.*

Kissinger had not been on the Nixon team. He had in the not distant past declared that Nixon was "unfit to be President." He had made his entry into the Nixon circle in a most curious manner. He had, after all, been a Rockefeller protégé, not a Nixon backer. His roots were in the Cambridge-New York-Washington intellectual community, the community of the crisis managers so many of whom gravitated to his staff from the staffs of Johnson and Kennedy. He himself was on close terms with men like Ellsberg, Halperin and Gelb. Halperin had wound up on Kissinger's staff until he was wiretapped and gradually eased out. Kissinger had personally engaged Ellsberg to do contingency studies for him.

Kissinger was a strange bird in the Nixon establishment. He had had no prior role in White House politics or professional politics of any kind; he had no prior association with Nixon; no prior association with the Nixon staff. Yet, in the spring of 1971 he was a rising star in the palisaded executive offices. Alone among the White House intimates, he was getting good publicity. He had a wide range of acquaintances and contacts in the press, especially in the "eastern liberal establishment," which had been blasted and damned by Vice President Agnew and by Mr. Nixon himself.

In the Harvard days Kissinger had possessed no "public" character. He was gifted, he worked hard, he had a good mind, but most people

*There are many, many unresolved curiosities about Kissinger's relation to the Pentagon Papers. A distribution list of the Papers compiled by David Young, of Kissinger's staff and by this time a White House "Plumber," submitted by him to Ehrlichman July 22, 1971, showed the whereabouts of eleven of the original copies of the Pentagon Papers. Copy "I.," that is the ninth copy, was in the possession of Kissinger. This was the only copy outside of the archive copies in Laird's vault and in other Defense Department vaults that was in the hands of a member of the Nixon Administration. Kissinger had been consulted about the study; had pondered working on it himself; knew more than any other individual in the administration what it was all about. The copy in his office may not have been provided until Wednesday, June 16. These facts make his suggestion that he did not know "the full scope" of what was involved when he saw the story in *The New York Times* appear less than candid.

thought him something of a drag. Certainly he was not famed for histrionic or dramatic technique.

But in Washington this changed. A very old friend of his, an actress who had known him through the Rockefeller years, had lunch with him one fine day in the spring of 1971. It was an ugly moment of the war when the bombing had been escalated and demonstrators were shouting at the White House gates. Henry, she remembered, showed her around, took her into the President's office, which she had not seen before, and then they walked over to the Sans Souci restaurant. What with the angry demonstrators the friend couldn't help thinking—wouldn't it be something to be walking with Henry and have one of them shoot me. The four Secret Service men who plodded on behind didn't reassure her very much. Henry didn't seem to notice. They walked into the Sans Souci and sat down at a prominent table, Henry, talking away, greeting his friends right and left. Finally she couldn't restrain herself. She said, "Henry, how can you be so bright and gay with all these terrible things happening in Vietnam?" He replied, "Oh, darling, you don't understand. This is the time when *you* feel sad about these things that are happening. *My* time to be sad is before—when I know what is going to happen and no one else knows. Now I must be gay. What would the world think if they saw me downcast? I must put on a brave face no matter what I feel inside. And you, my dear, must understand this. It is like when you are in a play, starting a new one, and you put on a happy face no matter what you feel inside."

Later Henry's friend said she had been deeply shocked because she suddenly realized that to Henry the world was a stage and he was an actor, front and center. It was not a world of people, not to Henry. It was a world of actors in which he was playing his part, the star role.

Outside the White House, Kissinger appeared in a stellar role; inside the White House, his associates were to recall, he was extremely defensive, constantly the object of not always pleasant sarcasm because of his "liberal" contacts. And he was already the object of scarcely concealed antagonism and, in fact, in December 1972 would come close to being dislodged from the administration entirely, perhaps being saved only by the rapid evolution of the Watergate scandals, in which he would assume the role of a pearl among the swine.

The details of the supposed White House plot against Kissinger in December 1972 were confused. At that time Kissinger intimated to media friends that he was the target of a coup by Haldeman and Ehrlichman. He telephoned correspondents and commentators who wrote about him in late December and early January saying there was nothing to the rumors of his resignation but managing to convey that there *was* something to it. He lunched almost every day at the Sans Souci, obviously eager to be seen in public, but now he affected a mood of gloom and despond. This was at the time of the saturation bombing of Hanoi and the disruption of the Paris talks and he managed to persuade many in the press corps that he had broken with Nixon on the issue—without, however, ever quite saying it. Sydney Gruson of *The Times* lunched with him December 19 at Sans Souci, offering him a million dollars-plus in a complex deal for his memoirs. Kissinger gave Gruson the impression he was considering his options and well might leave the government. He confirmed a report published by John Osborne in *The New Republic* that on two occasions, once at Bay Biscayne and once at the White House, he conferred with Mr. Nixon only by telephone even though they occupied adjoining offices. He dined with Scotty and Sally Reston January 4, 1973, presenting a picture of total melancholy, talking of the past, of the tragedy of his times, of the futility of his life. He insisted that only the smallest company be present and only those whom he knew well.

It was a curious little group, not really satisfying Kissinger's specifications at all: Russell Baker, *The Times* columnist, and his wife, Mimi, neither of whom knew Kissinger more than casually, and Punch Sulzberger, who happened to be in town. Kissinger didn't actually come until after dinner. Baker recalled that he seemed deeply depressed, particularly about the bombing but never really said anything disloyal to Mr. Nixon. He was upset at parallels which had been drawn between U.S. mass bombing of Hanoi and Hitler's genocide of the Jews. Baker recalled Kissinger saying he had come to Reston's "at some risk." He was being "followed" wherever he went and "they" (whom he did not identify but whom Baker took to mean Haldeman and Ehrlichman) were out to get him. Of course, he was accompanied at all times by the Secret Service so it was difficult to know whether Kissinger meant that another "secret" detail had been assigned to keep track of him. Baker began to feel sorry for Kissinger but later concluded Kissinger was being duplicitous and was telling the company what he thought they wanted to hear. Reston had no remembrance of the evening.

What was really going on in those days? Both Ehrlichman and Haldeman later were to deny that they were involved in any scheme to oust Kissinger. Haldeman was particularly strong on this point; doubted that Kissinger had ever said this at the time; insisted there was no foundation for it and was confident Kissinger's memoirs would support his view.

Ehrlichman agreed as to himself and Haldeman. "No," he said, "it wasn't us. It is true that each of us, Haldeman and myself, were called in separately and asked by Nixon, 'Do you think Kissinger is all right?' Nixon was concerned about his stability and his ability to carry out his duties."

In Ehrlichman's view the idea arose in Mr. Nixon's mind during the late November and early December negotiations in Paris between Kissinger and Le Duc Tho which failed to follow the optimistic path to peace that Kissinger predicted before the November election. As Ehrlichman remembered it, Kissinger was sending back cables every day (Mr. Nixon reproduced some of them in his *Memoirs*). One Sunday Kissinger's Security Council aide, Colonel Richard Kennedy, brought a very pessimistic cable up to Camp David.

"It was very conciliatory to the Vietnamese," Ehrlichman recalled, "and the President was upset and started at once to compose a cable, as he said, to 'give Henry a little backbone and prop him up.'"

After that Ehrlichman remembered Nixon went out and swam in the outdoor pool. It was cold, and the pool, he thought, must have been heated to about 95 degrees.

Ehrlichman insisted he had no desire to drop Kissinger and thought rumors of this reflected Mr. Nixon using him as a surrogate. "Nixon was the person who entertained the idea of dropping him," Ehrlichman said. "But it was one of those things which was on his mind for several weeks in December and then it just sort of faded away."

Ehrlichman believed the President had in mind replacing Kissinger with Al Haig. "Haig had undertaken a lot of the burden," Ehrlichman said. "Nixon had been going around Kissinger and having Haig do things."

Haldeman's recollection was different. He said there was no effort at all to replace Kissinger. True, Kissinger several times threatened to resign, sometimes in a fit of pique, sometimes as a maneuver and sometimes in "a reaction of despair." There were differences between Nixon and Kissinger at this time—Kissinger was insistent that the President go on TV and "rally the American people" behind a tough line against Hanoi but Mr. Nixon, in Haldeman's view, was much more realistic than Kissinger and "knew you could only go to the people so many times." Nixon, Haldeman said, was deeply disturbed by this problem but he did not think Nixon's feeling went to the point of getting rid of Kissinger. As for the bombing—there was no difference of opinion whatever between Nixon and Kissinger on that, Haldeman said. Kissinger was for the saturation bombing, no question about it, just as strong for it as Mr. Nixon regardless of what insinuations he made to Scotty Reston.*

---

*Kissinger's account in his *Memoirs* of the December days is too confused to follow. He seems to be saying that he was in trouble with Nixon, in part, because Nixon thought Kissinger was beginning to up-stage him in public prominence (they were sharing *Time*'s cover as Men-of-the-Year) and, in part, because they were out of synchronization on dealing with Vietnam peace negotiations although not, Kissinger emphasizes, on the Christmas bombing which he suggests was Haig's idea but which

John Dean was not very close to these matters but he remembered hearing a lot of grumbling about Kissinger because he was a star and was building himself up. Dean was positive that Haig had won Nixon's respect because he "acted like a good military man and when he was given an order he carried it out, no questions asked."

It was to seem to some White House insiders like Ehrlichman that Kissinger's response to the Pentagon Papers was at least in part a preemptive strike, a violent offensive designed to obscure the fact that he had a connection with the Papers and that they had been "leaked" by a man with whom he had long and intimate professional and personal dealings. The Kissinger-Ellsberg relationship possessed so many tortuous interconnections that the permutations could hardly be followed. To what extent was Kissinger's diplomatic strategy a stepchild of Ellsberg's brilliant 1959 study of the "Political Uses of Madness"? To what extent did Mr. Nixon's "Madman Theory" derive—through Kissinger—from Ellsberg? Did, in fact, these questions zoom around Kissinger's quick mind like pinballs in a machine? Did Ellsberg suddenly appear on Kissinger's scanning screen as the kind of unpredictable, unstable and irrational political figure whom Ellsberg described in his talks before Kissinger's Harvard seminar and, even more dangerous, a man directly linked to Kissinger by a skein of intellectual and scholarly ties?

And, after all, in the view of Paul Warnke, who knew both Kissinger and Ellsberg well, the men *were* bound by a very special bond. Each conceived of the Pentagon Papers in exactly the same terms. Ellsberg had long been convinced that the Papers were a tremendous force— a force which would stop the war. Kissinger, Warnke came to believe, regarded the documents in exactly the same way. Possibly they were the only two men in the country, and Sheehan was a third, who saw them in precisely that context.

The Kissinger Leaks

There were those who thought that there might be another factor involved in Kissinger's complex psychology. They wondered whether the answer, in part, might lie in the way his association with Nixon sprang into being. It came about through Kissinger's "tips" to the Nixon camp on the highly secret, highly complicated negotiations then in progress between Johnson and his aides with Hanoi in Paris.

According to Nixon the first "tip" from Kissinger came to him through John Mitchell on September 12, 1968. Two weeks later Kiss-

---

he emphasizes he strongly supported. He also says he was in a state of personal depression. (Kissinger, pp. 1446–1457)

inger sent through a second report. Another report came a few days later and a fourth about October 12. Nixon used Kissinger again about October 22, 1968, to check on the Johnson camp. It is plain from Mr. Nixon's account that the information provided by Kissinger through his access to the highest levels of the Johnson foreign policy apparatus was of extraordinary importance. Nixon was obsessed with the thought (with some reason) that Johnson hoped to manipulate the Paris talks to ensure Humphrey's election. Access through Kissinger to inside private information on what was going on was extremely valuable.

There is no way of describing what Kissinger did in the closing weeks of the 1968 campaign except as "leaking," leaking information from one political camp to another. True, Mr. Nixon called Kissinger's information "tips." But tips about Nixon's foreign policy moves were classified by Nixon and by Kissinger as "leaks."

Kissinger and Nixon had no personal relationship during the period of the "tips" or before that period. But they did meet November 25, 1968, for the first time, with John Mitchell acting as go-between. Mitchell might seem an unusual matchmaker between Nixon and Kissinger but, in fact, Mitchell and Kissinger had gotten to know each other through Nelson Rockefeller. Kissinger was on Rockefeller's payroll for years as a foreign policy adviser, and Mitchell had a close relationship with Rockefeller on government fiscal questions. Nixon respected Mitchell's judgment on foreign policy and almost invariably consulted him on important decisions.

"I was responsible for bringing Kissinger and Nixon together," Mitchell was to recall. "I had put together financing packages for Nelson and I got to know Henry. Of course, he was gung ho for Nelson until after the 1968 convention."

After the convention, Mitchell said, Rockefeller called and said he thought Kissinger could be useful to Nixon.

"And he was," Mitchell said. "He was very useful. I used to meet him and he had access to knowledge about the Paris talks and what was going on there and he gave it to me and I passed it on to Nixon."

After Nixon had won the election, Mitchell recalled, the President-to-be "was looking for someone to handle all the stuff that was coming up from Washington." Mitchell thought of Kissinger, brought him up to the Pierre hotel, where Nixon had his headquarters, and put the two men together. "That was quite an accomplishment," he said. "And I'm proud of it."

Nixon, already predisposed toward Kissinger, took an instant liking to him and two days after the first meeting asked him to become his security adviser.

A man who paved his entry into the confidence of a President by passing inside information from the opposition camp might well be sensitive on the subject of leaks. Kissinger, some felt, was not only sensitive. He was close to paranoid on the subject.*

These were the powerful undercurrents which surged through Washington on that limpid Sunday of June 13, 1971, belying the surface calm, a calm so pervasive that Punch Sulzberger, breathing a sigh of relief, saw no reason to cancel his early Monday departure with his family and Ivan Veit for London. It seemed to him that his judgment about the Pentagon Papers had been vindicated. It was not after all the cataclysmic story which his associates had believed it to be.

As Sulzberger checked over his carefully packed bags he had not the slightest premonition that publication of the Pentagon Papers story that morning was triggering a sequence of events which would lead inexorably, step by step, to the greatest disaster ever to befall an American President, a disaster so profound, so far-reaching in implication that by the time it was over basic relationships in the American power apparatus would be changed; the very system would quiver; a President would fall; the balance of the tripartite American constitutional structure would shift; and the role of the press in America, the role of *The New York Times*, and even the function of the press in other great nations of the world would be transformed.

---

*Kissinger's own account of joining the Nixon Administration is disingenuous: he omits his prior friendship with Mitchell, touches ever-so-lightly on his pre-election contacts with Mitchell and brings the Attorney-General-to-be into the picture only to quote him as saying: "Oh, Jesus Christ, he [Nixon] has screwed it up again" (because Nixon supposedly had not made clear to Kissinger that he was being offered the post of National Security adviser (Kissinger, *The White House Years*, p. 14). Of Kissinger's account of how he got his job with Nixon, Mitchell snorted: "He's got it all mixed up. He's all ass-backward. He says it was all Nelson that did it. Maybe it's time to start getting some of this right." (Personal interview, Mitchell, 11/30/79) It is possible that Kissinger's chronic over-reaction on leaks may be related to an earlier period of his life, to the time when as a young Harvard teaching fellow he offered his services to the FBI in July, 1935, to pass on information about participants in an international seminar which he was conducting. (Prof. Sigmund Diamond, FOIA documents, *The Nation*, Nov. 10, 1979.)

22

The Times
Must Respectfully Decline...

THE WHITE HOUSE day begins early. In fact the White House never sleeps. All night long security officers make their rounds and guards tend duty, code clerks hover over mysterious machines in the communications room and duty officers drowse at their basement desks, ready to leap to alertness at any emergency. Marine details man their posts and before 7 A.M. the early shift begins to appear, showing plastic ID tags to the men at the watch posts, stopping at basement vending machines for containers of black coffee on their way to desks and typewriters.

Lyndon K. (Mort) Allin was an early bird. He and Pat Buchanan had the task of preparing the daily news summary for President Nixon. Allin was a newspaper buff who had grown up in Wisconsin reading the *Chicago Tribune* and Buchanan was the sophisticated and ideologically conservative former correspondent of the *St. Louis Globe-Democrat.* They made a good team. Pat was so fast on the typewriter they seldom bothered with a secretary to type up the sheets.

On Monday, June 14, 1971, Allin got to his office, Room 127 of the Executive Office Building, the General Grant pile next to the White House, before seven. The wire reports and network news summaries had been handled by the late staff, which went off duty around 2 A.M. Allin's task was to do "a new top," summarizing the materials and particularly the half-dozen morning newspapers that were checked for the President.

The Monday morning summary was always heavy since it covered both Saturday and Sunday. This Monday's was particularly heavy because of Tricia's wedding. There was no question in Allin's mind as to the lead story—it was the wedding. He summarized this coverage, including the hour and hour-and-a-half specials the networks had presented, mentioning the leading newspapers, quoting bits from their stories and editorials. The coverage had been up-beat all the way and he noted that even Dan Rather, not a White House favorite, had been very positive.

There were twelve pages of wedding materials. The Pentagon story made page thirteen. Allin gave it a perfunctory rundown. Number two in the series, published that morning, led with a dispatch by Neil Sheehan headlined "Vietnam Archive: A Consensus to Bomb Developed Before '64 Election, Study Shows."

Allin reported that David Brinkley had mentioned the story on NBC Sunday night, quoted briefly from James Reston's Sunday column and noted Senator Stuart Symington's comment that the people must be told the truth. That was it. The news bulletin went on to report the rest of the world's news.*

The news summary was completed a bit before 8 A.M. and Allin personally took it to the White House and, as was customary, placed it directly on Mr. Nixon's desk. The summary, unlike almost every other scrap of paper that reached the President, did not go through Ehrlichman, Haldeman or any aide. Before Mr. Nixon reached his office he would already have scanned *The New York Times* and the *Washington Post,* both of which went to his bedroom with breakfast.

By the time Allin made his trip from the Executive Office Building to the Oval Office the first scheduled White House event of the day was in progress, the meeting of the President's closest aides, who assembled in the Roosevelt Room between 7:30 A.M. and 7:45 A.M.

The participants varied but the core was Haldeman, Ehrlichman and Kissinger. Ron Ziegler, the press secretary, usually attended as did Charles Colson, economic adviser Herb Stein, Jeb Stuart Magruder, George Schultz, Don Rumsfeld, Peter Flanigan, Herb Klein and occasionally others. It was not a fixed group. Usually there were ten or twelve persons in the room.

Kissinger was often the first to arrive. He and Haldeman had a dog and pony routine. Kissinger would say, *"Guten Morgen,* Herr Haldeman."* Haldeman would respond, "And a *guten Morgen* to you, Heinz." When Kissinger was not in town his place was taken by Al Haig. Later Kissinger was to call the early morning meetings "a joke" but at the time he seemed to take them very seriously.

There is no evidence that the Pentagon Papers stirred much discussion at this meeting.† Neither Haldeman nor Ehrlichman recalled any

---

*By Tuesday morning what was now called *"The New York Times* controversy" led the White House news summary. A week later the summary began to call them "The McNamara Papers." (Personal interview, Allin, 9/15/78)

†A number of published accounts, including that of Charles Colson, describe this meeting in melodramatic terms with Kissinger beating his breast and demanding action against "the leaks." Nothing like this happened. Kissinger was in California. His representative, Al Haig, always spoke in cold precise bureaucratic terms and no one remembered what he said, if anything. (Charles Colson, *Born Again,* New York, 1975, p. 56; personal interview, Klein, 1/12/78)

excitement. Both thought the Papers no big issue. If they were an issue it was one which would cut against the Democrats since it was the Democratic Presidents, Johnson and Kennedy, who were exposed. Mitchell had not indicated particular concern in his talk with Laird on Sunday, and Laird, as he was later to say, didn't think the Pentagon Papers were such a big story. His only worry was the possibility that National Security Agency materials might have been exposed and he came to think that "it was a damn good thing the Pentagon Papers came out. . . . It didn't hurt us," he said. "It wasn't our stuff." He added, some years later, *"they* made it a big story. *They* did. It was always that way." By *they* he meant the White House, Mr. Nixon, of course, Henry Kissinger and, as the process got going, Haldeman, Ehrlichman and the rest.

Nor, at that point on Monday morning, did Ron Ziegler appraise the Pentagon story highly. On Capitol Hill Senator Robert Dole of Kansas, chairman of the Republican National Committee and vice presidential running-mate-to-be of Gerald W. Ford, thought the Pentagon Papers a bonanza for the Republicans. He looked at the situation in simple party terms. The Papers were embarrassing to the Democrats and particularly to President Johnson. Since the study had been completed in 1968 it could not hurt the Republicans and Mr. Nixon. This was probably Attorney General Mitchell's attitude. Later the rush of events tended to obscure the positions taken in the early phase of the Pentagon affair but those close to Mr. Mitchell believed that he seriously tried—but failed—to keep the lid on. Certainly his equanimity on Sunday and Monday morning supported this view. Laird talked to Mitchell again Monday morning because Laird was testifying before the Senate Foreign Relations Committee and expected questions from the senators or from reporters. Again Mitchell told him just to say that the Justice Department was looking into the matter.

Mr. Nixon

Mr. Nixon's attitude at this point cannot be established. He was, of course, and had shown himself repeatedly to be, extremely concerned about "leaks." Ehrlichman's résumé of Mr. Nixon's views in his discussion with the young people on the *Sequoia* on Sunday faithfully reflected this attitude and, in fact, Nixon had gone considerably further than this in private discussions.

During the campaign of 1968 Mr. Nixon had demonstrated an extraordinary sensitivity toward leaks and security. He had hired one of the country's best clandestine electronics specialists, John J. Ragen, long the FBI's top wiretapper, to sweep his convention and campaign facilities, making certain that no one put a bug in the Nixon suites or tapped his telephones. He had hired John J. Caulfield, of later Watergate fame, as his security chief in the spring of 1968. Hardly had Mr. Nixon taken office in the White House than Ehrlichman was secretly putting together a small investigative unit to work directly under himself at Mr. Nixon's specific orders, carrying out intelligence and covert assignments. Caulfield was signed onto the White House payroll April 8, 1969, and by May 1969 Ehrlichman and Caulfield were surreptitiously meeting in the VIP lounge of La Guardia Airport interviewing the ineffable Anthony T. Ulasewicz, also of Watergate fame, for the post of chief White House undercover sleuth, paid from surplus campaign funds channeled through the President's private counsel, Herbert Kalmbach, and the President's best friend, Bebe Rebozo. Their first big assignment in June 1969 was to tap the telephone at the Georgetown home of Joseph Kraft, the Washington columnist. The little group was not yet the White House Plumbers but it was its beginning. The Plumbers lay ahead, but the technique, the habit of turning to clandestine and illegal methods of investigating individuals and organizations perceived as hostile or politically dangerous to the President and the White House was well established long before June 14, 1971, or Watergate. It had come into the White House with Mr. Nixon. It comprised a routine, almost a reflexive response. At times Mr. Nixon would turn to the established agencies of the government—the FBI to tap and tail White House, State Department and Pentagon employees and journalists; the Secret Service to surveil his brother Donald; the CIA for tools of the espionage trade (red-haired ill-fitting wigs and voice changers for Howard Hunt) and other chores. At other times he would rely on his own privately organized, secretly directed, obscurely financed operatives.

Mr. Nixon had demonstrated no qualms about wiretapping his associates.* He had initially approved the Huston plan for secret surveillance, tapping, bugging and burglary. He had shown again and again his antipathy to anything he regarded as a "leak" and he had been sulphurous for years toward the press and specifically toward *The New York Times.*

In a word Mr. Nixon already possessed conditioned reflexes which could be expected to dictate prompt, violent, legal (and extralegal) response toward the Pentagon Papers publication and this had been anticipated by some *New York Times* editors. To be certain, no one outside the narrowest circle of Nixon intimates knew the President had

*Suspicion still exists that the tapping and surveillance of Joseph Kraft may have been triggered by Kraft's connections with Kissinger and thus been directed, in reality, against Kissinger; a classic example of the pot and the kettle. Kissinger suggested this to Kraft. (Wise, *The American Police State*, p. 28) In his memoirs, Kissinger hints his conversations may have been taped by the White House in December 1972–January 1973. (*The White House Years*, p. 1456)

already embarked on illegal use of government and nongovernment clandestine agencies. But his habits of thought were not exactly terra incognita.

There was, therefore, every reason to anticipate Mr. Nixon's reactions to the Pentagon Papers. As one of his colleagues (who later was to discover that he himself had been wiretapped with Mr. Nixon's knowledge) expressed it:

"He didn't give a damn about exposing LBJ's actions but the massive leak was a challenge, he felt, to the whole government concept. The press was arrogating to itself the right to decide what was national security."

Despite all this there is persuasive evidence that Mr. Nixon did not immediately plunge into the Pentagon battle like an avenging angel. He was, after all, one of the skilled politicians of his generation. He had his hang-ups and those concerning the press and leaks were oversize but he was by no means naïve and, looking back on it in 1978, he observed:

"From a political standpoint I recognized that the Ellsberg study and the classified documents which he illegally released to the press, far from being harmful to our administration, might even prove to be helpful. It was a critique of the actions of previous administrations which got the United States involved in the war in Vietnam and of their conduct of the war."*

Like all days, Monday, June 14, was a busy one for President Nixon. He spent the morning in a two-hour meeting on drug control and other domestic matters. Not until just before lunch did he have thirty-five minutes with Secretary of State Rogers and Al Haig. This may have been his first talk about the Pentagon Papers but neither he nor Haig nor Rogers later was to have a firm recollection of this. It was not until the end of the day that he had a chance for serious discussion of the matter. Kissinger spent the day flying back from California and did not meet with the President until after 6 P.M. when he went to the Oval Office with Ambassador Kenneth Rush.

At exactly what point Mr. Nixon decided to give the Pentagon Papers a "full court" presentation may never be determined. But certainly it could not have been until late Monday. Even Tuesday morning he did not seem very aroused—or did not wish to convey the impression of being upset.

That morning he met in the cabinet room of the White House with the Republican congressional leaders for the usual weekly session. Discussion of the Pentagon Papers was low key. He was angry at *The Times* but when several leaders, including Senator Hugh Scott of Pennsyl-

---

*Mr. Nixon to myself, letter of July 13, 1978.

vania, pointed out that "it wasn't our ball game" he did not challenge this view.

Mr. Nixon said that a negotiated end of the Vietnam war was the best outcome from the American standpoint and he was doing his best toward this end but couldn't tell the leaders any more because some things had to be kept secret. (Kissinger, of course, was holding periodic secret meetings in Paris with Hanoi.) Then Mr. Nixon switched to what he called *"The New York Times* story." It was, he said "an intraparty fight within the other party."

Scott commented that they should let the Democrats fight it out. Two or three others chimed in along the same lines. The President said the Pentagon Papers had damaged the integrity of the government and the trust of other governments in dealing with the United States. He asked his associates not to bring up the matter of whether codes had been violated. "The damage to the country could be lethal," Mr. Scott recorded him as saying in the careful notes he always took. The discussion took no more than ten minutes and when Scott went back to Capitol Hill he told his Republican colleagues that there were no "hot dogs" on the Papers and that they could take it as the party line that this was a Democratic not a Republican problem.*

Already, however, this attitude had been contradicted by administration actions and, judging from the private White House discussions of Mr. Nixon and his intimates late Tuesday afternoon, the die had been cast for battle—total, no-holds-barred, every resource to be committed.

Whatever was going on in Mr. Nixon's mind there was no doubt about the views and activities of Robert C. Mardian of the Justice Department, an extremely conservative and excitable man from Arizona and Southern California. Mardian had gone to Los Angeles to give a speech very critical of the U.S. media to a woman's group. He spent the weekend there, flying back on the red-eye special to Washington, arriving at 7 A.M. Monday. He knew nothing about the Pentagon Papers. Not a word had appeared on the Coast as far as he was aware. When he reached his office at the Justice Department a little before 8 A.M. he found *The New York Times* on his desk with Neil Sheehan's second Pentagon story prominently displayed. He was instantly aroused and got his secretary to find a Sunday *Times* in order to read the first installment. Before 9 A.M. he had talked to Mitchell on the telephone and a little later was in the Attorney General's office conferring on what should be done. Mardian was the deputy for Internal Security matters and the Pentagon Papers case fell within his jurisdiction. No one in Justice, Mitchell included, knew a thing about the Papers. Mardian

*Senator Scott took careful notes of this meeting and preserved them. (Personal interview, Scott, 11/9/78, quotations from his "Leadership Notes" of June 15, 1971)

called Secretary of State Rogers, Henry Kissinger and Laird. Laird ordered a memorandum prepared, outlining the nature of the study, who had authorized it, what it covered and a nonspecific statement that publication would harm national security. The fact was there was no one left in the Defense Department who was familiar with the study. Doolin, the Deputy Secretary of International Affairs, had not been in the department when the study was done. Colonel Robert Hixon, who had been, in Pursley's words, the "keeper of the keys," the administrative officer mostly concerned with overseeing the copies of the Papers kept in the Defense Department, had been transferred to Southeast Asia and was beyond range of consultation. The specialists involved in the project had left the government. Pursley, in fact, was the most knowledgeable man on hand. The memo for Mardian was drafted by Fred Buzhardt with a little help from Pursley.

A Quiet Monday

To the surprise of the editors of *The Times* Monday started like any other day, no thrills or alarms. Punch had taken off for London at 9:30 A.M. on Qantas flight 530, arriving in London at 9:15 P.M. The crew at the Hilton reported for duty as usual but about 10 A.M. there was a knock at the door—a girl reporter from *Newsweek,* asking how the great scoop had been organized. A bit later CBS broke the story that *The Times* crew was working in the Hilton and said they would have coverage of it on the evening news. TV cameras appeared in the lobby. The secret was out and the staff was told to leave immediately. Staff men took taxis pell-mell back to *The Times.* Copy boys and porters were dispatched to load up typewriters and equipment. Bob Rosenthal of the foreign desk put all the papers—two hundred pounds or more —into a suitcase. He was given $20 and told to get out the back door of the Hilton. If there were FBI men outside *The Times* building he was to just keep going. Two secretaries, Muriel Stokes and Eileen Butler, sat amid the debris, eating a sandwich. Suddenly Muriel exclaimed, "My God, if the police come we'll be arrested." Neil Sheehan, who was still gathering up his papers, said, "Don't worry. I'm the only one who will go to jail." Spare copies of the Pentagon Papers were piled in *The Times'* treasurer's safe on the seventh floor. But of course by this time everyone had a set stashed away somewhere, at home under the bed, in the luggage compartment of a car or behind the books in the living room. Susan Sheehan put one set in Fred Graham's deep freeze.

James Goodale spent the morning at the National Broadcasting Company executive offices at 30 Rockefeller Plaza. *The Times* was defending one of its reporters, Earl Caldwell, in an action in which the Justice Department was seeking to compel him to testify on his sources in connection with articles he had written about the Black Panthers in Oakland, California. It was an extremely important First Amendment case and NBC, CBS and ABC proposed to file a friend-of-the-court brief. The Yale legal specialist, Alexander Bickel, had been brought in to write the *amicus curiae* brief by Floyd Abrams of Cahill, Gordon and Reindel, representing NBC. Gene Roberts, national editor of *The Times* under whose jurisdiction Caldwell worked, was present. So was Reuven Frank, NBC news executive, and Ike Pappas, a CBS correspondent. The meeting at NBC was largely to show Bickel how newsmen worked and to help him get a feel of the practical considerations involved in the Caldwell action.

Just before the lawyers and newspapermen adjourned for lunch at the University Club a news bulletin came in from Washington quoting Laird as saying Mitchell had the Pentagon Papers affair under study. Goodale thought, Well, they've finally begun. Over lunch Bickel and Roberts talked. Bickel congratulated *The Times* and said "if Justice tries to clamp down on you I hope the hell you fight it to the hilt." Abrams, a vigorous man of middle height, very articulate, had been a student of Bickel's at Yale and he had proposed Bickel to write the *amicus curiae* brief because of his leadership in the field of First Amendment law. When he suggested the idea Bickel replied, "Do you know my views? I am not a First Amendment voluptuary." He meant he was not one of those who believed that the First Amendment was the be-all and end-all of the Constitution. He was, he was suggesting, a supporter of the First Amendment but not a mad and passionate lover of the law.

Now he and Abrams joined in saying "playfully but seriously" to Goodale that the Caldwell case was "very difficult legally," there were many new legal points which had to be established. But the Pentagon Papers was another thing, this was an old-fashioned freedom of the press case with a body of law to turn to. "That's one," Bickel said, "that you can't lose. But the Caldwell case is really hard."*

Goodale felt pretty good. "By this time I was ready to fight anyone," he recalled. "By evening I was cool as an iceberg."

But nothing happened. There was plenty of interest in the Pentagon Papers. The news agencies were onto it. The rest of the press, particularly the *Washington Post,* which after two days was still playing catch-up while managing editor Ben Bradlee rapidly went out of his mind, was trying to get a handle on the story. TV networks were interviewing *Times* editors and correspondents. Finally after two long

---

*The Bickel-Abrams assessment of the Caldwell case was prescient. It was soon to be lost in the U.S. Supreme Court.

days the Pentagon Papers were beginning to have an impact but still there was no sign of government action. A little before 7 P.M. Harding Bancroft left his fourteenth-floor office at *The Times* and went home. Sydney Gruson left about the same time. He had telephoned Punch in London after the publisher's arrival at the Savoy hotel and told him that nothing unusual was afoot. Rosenthal left the office about 7 P.M. and went to La Caravelle on Fifty-fifth Street, a smart restaurant which by a kind of reverse snobbery he never frequented. He was dining there with his old friends Dick and Shirley Clurman. Dick was a *Time* magazine executive and the Clurmans were good friends of Kay Graham of the *Washington Post* who often had dinner with them when she was in town as she was that Monday. Shirley knew that Ann Rosenthal was in Connecticut and invited Abe to join them. Mrs. Graham was complimentary to Abe about the Pentagon Papers and Abe suggested that she cable her congratulations to Punch in London, which she promised to do. They were having a glass of wine when a message came for Abe that the government was asking *The Times* to suspend publication of the Pentagon Papers. He left almost immediately. Mrs. Graham looked a bit concerned. She was debating whether or not to call the *Washington Post.* After a moment's deliberation she decided she had better call despite the embarrassment of having to use the head waiter's telephone since there was no phone booth in the Caravelle.

In Washington Robert McNamara had called Scotty Reston and his wife, Sally. McNamara's wife was in the hospital—could they keep him company at dinner. The Restons said yes.

The last person Goodale spoke with before leaving *The New York Times* office was Bancroft. As Goodale walked into his apartment on the Upper East Side the telephone stopped ringing before he could answer it.

"It was Harding," Goodale said. "It had to be. I called him back. He said we had a request from the government to stop publication."

"We can't stop," Goodale said instantly.

"I'm not so sure," Bancroft replied.

Goodale hurried back to the office. Bancroft telephoned Gruson, Rosenthal and Greenfield and they came back too.

Gruson stopped by the third floor. He found Rosenthal pacing in his office.

"Now we have no alternative except to go on publishing," Rosenthal said.

"Yes, we do have an alternative," Gruson said quietly. "We have the alternative of not publishing."

Gruson was not suggesting that he favored not publishing—he was trying to make plain to Rosenthal the context of the discussion, the alternatives that were bound to be considered. He himself had always favored publication and later Frankel was to give him great credit for steering the project to success.

But Rosenthal was in no mood for alternatives. He blew up. When Goodale walked in the two men were shouting at each other. Goodale was amazed. Gruson and Rosenthal were, he recalled, "fantastically excited." After a moment the three took the elevator up to the fourteenth floor.

The Government Moves

President Nixon spent forty-five minutes with Kissinger and it was precisely four minutes of seven when their meeting concluded. During the conversation Ehrlichman had called but the President did not pick up the phone. Now at 7 P.M. he returned Ehrlichman's call, talked very briefly and immediately telephoned John Mitchell at his apartment in the Watergate complex. Mardian had arrived at Mitchell's apartment a bit earlier and the two men had approved a message to be sent to *The New York Times* over Mitchell's signature. In the telephone call Mitchell informed the President of the message and the President approved its dispatch.

As received at *The Times* it read:

> NYK Times NY
> Arthur Ochs Sulzberger
> President and Publisher
> The New York Times
> New York New York.

> I have been advised by the Secretary of Defense that the material published in The New York Times on June 13, 14, 1971 captioned "Key Texts from Pentagon's Vietnam Study" contains information relating to the national defense of the United States and bears a top secret classification.

> As such, publication of this information is directly prohibited by the provisions of the Espionage law, Title 18, United States code, Section 793.

> Moreover further publication of information of this character will cause irreparable injury to the defense interests of the United States.

> Accordingly, I respectfully request that you publish no further information of this character and advise me that you have made arrangements for the return of these documents to the Department of Defense.

> John W. Mitchell
> Attorney General

After transmission the following exchange occurred:
Ack pls
New York Times reced Well thanks
FBI Washn DC

This was an exchange between the wire room of *The New York Times* in New York and a transmission operator in the FBI in Washington, D.C. It meant that the message, although drafted at Mitchell's apartment, had been returned to the FBI office on Pennsylvania Avenue for transmission. By mistake, as Mardian recalled, the FBI operator got the wrong telex number for *The Times* and the message was first transmitted to a fish company on the Brooklyn waterfront. Only after this error was straightened out was the message retransmitted to *The Times.*

After sending the telegram Mardian used Mitchell's White House line to telephone *The Times* about 7:30 P.M. Mardian asked for Sulzberger but *The Times* operator told him the publisher was in London. He then asked who was in charge. The operator rang Larry Hauck in *The Times'* bullpen and told him someone named "Margerine" was calling from the White House. Hauck had the call shifted to Bancroft and Mardian read him the message. While Mitchell made no specific mention of legal action Mardian said that if *The Times* did not comply the government would seek an injunction.

"Publication is injurious to the United States," Mardian said. "I want to put this in the strongest terms."

Bancroft told Mardian that *The Times* was preparing for publication of installment three of the story but would review the decision. He would try to reply within the hour.

Some time prior to this exchange John Mitchell telephoned his old friend Herbert Brownell in New York. The two men were fellow members of the New York Bar. Brownell was a senior statesman in the Republican Party, a king-maker. He had been close to Thomas Dewey, to John Lindsay and to Richard Nixon. He was the head of the law firm of Lord, Day and Lord.

Mitchell and Brownell had seen each other as recently as Saturday afternoon at Tricia's wedding. Despite their common Republicanism and the fact that Brownell, too, had been an Attorney General, serving under Eisenhower, the men were in no sense cronies. Brownell was already critical of Mitchell's conduct of the Justice Department and was to be more critical in the future.

Exactly when Mitchell telephoned Brownell about the Pentagon Papers case is not certain. Mitchell's recollection was infirm. He thought he had called Brownell Saturday morning from his home in Washington, having heard in advance that *The Times* was publishing the Papers. This is most unlikely. It is possible that he telephoned Brownell on Sunday, not long after the first *Times* installment appeared.

Brownell's memory was not precise either. He felt certain the conversation occurred during the weekend and most probably on Sunday.

He remembered being at home when the call came in and then calling Louis Loeb at Loeb's home in Mount Kisco, New York.

It was Mitchell's recollection that he telephoned Brownell "for the purpose of having him let *The Times* know of the Administration's concern with respect to the proposed publication." He did not think he heard back from Brownell because of "the initiation of litigation" against *The Times* soon after the call.

Brownell's memory was that Mitchell told him the government was going to sue *The Times* if it continued publication of the Papers and that Mitchell reminded him that he was the author of the executive order setting up the procedures for classification of documents. Brownell had drafted them for President Eisenhower when he was Attorney General. Mitchell warned Brownell that "we may have to call you up as a witness and that would be very embarrassing."

"Thanks a lot," Brownell recalled telling the Attorney General.

It was Brownell's impression that he had the law researched and found that what Mitchell said was true, that the government might, indeed, call him as a witness. He then telephoned Louis Loeb at his country house and said he believed that Lord, Day and Lord would have to get out of the case because the government might serve them with a subpoena to compel his testimony and if they failed to comply with the subpoena they could go to jail.

"This was a real shocker to me," Brownell said. He conceded that earlier in discussing the Pentagon Papers with Loeb and with *The Times* it had not occurred to him that the government might bring an action to enjoin. The fact that he had been the author of the classification procedures, important though they were, had not entered his mind. "What had concerned us," he said, "was the possibility of criminal prosecution of *The Times* after publication; not prior restraint."

As Brownell recollected it Loeb agreed that under the circumstances it was not possible for Lord, Day and Lord to handle the case and so informed *The Times*.

Despite the memory of both Mitchell and Brownell that their conversation occurred on the weekend, perhaps on Sunday, all other evidence points to the conversation being held on Monday evening, immediately after Mitchell's telegram was dispatched to *The Times*, probably initiated by Mitchell to try to reinforce the effect of the telegram and cause Lord, Day and Lord to use their influence to persuade *The Times* to desist in publishing the Papers.* Had Brownell gotten the call on Sunday, initiated the search of the law which he

---

*A tendency emerged in interviews conducted several years after the events for participants to relate their actions and reactions to *earlier* periods than was the fact.

recollected and then informed Loeb it is not conceivable that Loeb would not have warned *The Times* in advance. That Brownell and Loeb would have delayed for more than twenty-four hours in conveying so significant a piece of information to their client does not fit the character of the client relationship or that of the two lawyers.§

Nonetheless the matter cannot be resolved on the basis of the recollections of the two principals, and this question, critical not merely for chronological reasons in the drama that was about to unfold on the fourteenth floor of *The New York Times* Monday evening, June 14, 1971, must remain open.

Decision

It was extremely hot in New York that evening and there was no air conditioning on the fourteenth floor of *The Times* building. It was turned off at 7 P.M. because there was never anyone in the executive floor after that hour. The atmosphere was sweltering when Goodale, Gruson and Rosenthal entered Bancroft's office, pulling at their ties and loosening their collars. Bob Rosenthal, the office boy who carted the Pentagon Papers back from the Hilton hotel earlier in the day, was now at the secretary's desk outside Bancroft's office. The foreign desk was trying to reach *The Times'* correspondent in London, Anthony Lewis, in order to locate Punch Sulzberger and it was Bob Rosenthal's job to patch the call through to Bancroft when and if it was completed.

Bancroft was on the telephone to Louis Loeb when Goodale, Gruson and Rosenthal entered. He switched the call onto the loudspeaker so they could listen. Loeb had been totally surprised when Bancroft told him of the telegram from Mitchell. "Oh, my God!" he said. He hadn't expected it and had had no inkling of government action. As Bancroft's associates came into the room Loeb was, as he had so often before, declaring that *The Times* could not publish, could not ignore the government's request, that any other action would not be in the public interest. He urged Bancroft to put this to Punch Sulzberger in the strongest terms.

Rosenthal looked at his watch. The hour was moving toward press time. He had to call Larry Hauck, the editor in charge of the bullpen. He thought to himself, My God, it's just like the movies. I'll have to say, Stop the presses! He had never said that in his life. But when he got Hauck on the telephone he couldn't utter the cliché. It was too melodramatic. Instead he said, "Larry, slow things down a bit, will you?" Larry understood and said he'd keep the situation under control.

Now the call to Punch was patched through on the loudspeaker and

§See Notes section.

Bancroft hung up on Loeb. Punch had been asleep in his Savoy suite. It was about 2 A.M. in London.

Bancroft gave Punch a résumé of the Mitchell telegram. To some in the room it seemed that he was talking on and on in an inconclusive way.

Punch asked, "What does Louis say?"

"He's opposed to further publication," Bancroft replied. As Harding continued Rosenthal could contain himself no longer. He shoved Goodale forward, saying, "For God's sake say something!" Rosenthal shouted into the loudspeaker, "Punch! This is Abe. I think you should talk to Goodale."

Goodale said, "Everybody here agrees we have to publish."

Rosenthal interrupted, "Not everybody is in agreement." He was referring to the statements by Bancroft and Gruson that there was an alternative to publishing—not publishing.

Goodale went on talking. He said he felt strongly that as an institution *The Times* would never be the same if it gave in to the government and that *The Times* "should not do it and must not do it."

Punch asked if going ahead with publication would increase the paper's liability. Goodale answered, "Not by five percent."

"O.K.," Punch said. "Go ahead."

The paper had been held up awaiting the decision. Rosenthal, Greenfield and Gruson made for the elevator. Bob Rosenthal rode down with them. There was great tension, he remembered, great tension and emotion. These were powerful men and the air throbbed with their vibrations. Goodale and Rosenthal, he thought, were the heroes of the evening. Suddenly Abe Rosenthal noticed his young namesake. He tapped him on the chest and said solemnly, "Don't repeat a word you have heard tonight to any living soul—ever."

They got off at the third floor and entered the city room. A hundred and fifty people crowded around the foreign desk. People from all over the building. Printers with their tricornered folded-paper hats, makeup men. Everyone knew the paper had been held up and why. They were waiting for word.

"Go ahead!" Rosenthal said. There was a cheer and within minutes the huge presses in the sub-subbasement were roaring.

The Lawyers

But on the fourteenth floor the action was far from over.

Goodale immediately telephoned Loeb and told him of the publisher's decision to defy the government. He asked him to have a lawyer from Lord, Day and Lord in court in the morning to defend *The Times.* Loeb was taken aback. "I think you had better call Herb Brownell," he said.

Loeb had already talked with Brownell, who told him Mitchell had telephoned saying he could not believe Lord, Day and Lord supported the idea of *The Times* continuing to publish this material and assuring him the government would do everything possible to halt publication. Brownell told Loeb that his memorandum on the classification orders was still in the Justice Department files.

"Of course," Brownell told Loeb, "if the government goes after *The Times* and *The Times* refuses to comply, this will be brought out and it will be not only embarrassing to Lord, Day and Lord, but even more so, very embarrassing to *The New York Times.* I don't think we ought to put *The Times* in that position."

Goodale put through a call to Brownell, who courteously but firmly said that Lord, Day and Lord could not undertake the defense of *The Times* because of what he called a "conflict of interest." He told Goodale of the telephone call from Mitchell reminding him that he, Brownell, had been the author of Executive Order 10501 of November 5, 1953, establishing the regulations for the classification of government security materials and that the Justice Department had a memo in Brownell's name saying that the order was "valid, legally binding and enforceable." Brownell expressed his "shock" that *The Times* would defy Mitchell. It was a brief, cold conversation. Goodale felt a certain respect for Brownell's "courage" in taking so principled a stand. After all *The Times* had rejected his advice. Later Goodale wondered whether principles or politics had played the main role.*

While this conversation was in progress a formal reply to Mitchell's telex was being hammered out. Bancroft read a proposed text to Reston at McNamara's house in Washington. Reston took it down word by word and went over it with McNamara. There was a sentence in it saying *The Times* would abide by the "decisions of the courts." "No, no," McNamara interjected, "not the courts—the *highest* court." The statement was changed to read, "We will of course abide by the final decision of the court." This did not quite meet McNamara's point nor did it entirely satisfy Goodale. If anyone found any incongruity in McNamara offering advice to *The Times* in its defense against the government's effort to halt unauthorized publication of what the Nixon Administration would try to tag as the "McNamara Papers" it was not recorded.

The full version of *The Times'* rejoinder to Mitchell said:

> We have received the telegram from the Attorney General asking *The Times* to cease further publication of the Pentagon's Vietnam study.

---

*The decision not to defend *The Times* caused substantial inner tension within Lord, Day and Lord. Many young lawyers were shocked. Some quietly left the firm in ensuing months and the decision for a while affected recruiting.

The Times must respectfully decline the request of the Attorney General, believing that it is in the interest of the people of this country to be informed of the material contained in this series of articles. We have also been informed of the Attorney General's intention to seek an injunction to restrict further publication. We believe that it is properly a matter for the courts to decide. The Times will oppose any request for an injunction for the same reason that led us to publish the articles in the first place. We will of course abide by the final decision of the court.

Bancroft telephoned Mardian some time after 9 P.M. and gave him the answer. But *The Times* had an unprecedented problem to resolve. With court confrontation little more than twelve hours distant it had been abandoned by the law firm that (with permutations) had defended it for seventy-five years, since, in fact, Mr. Ochs had taken over the paper. In Goodale's words, "The situation woke you up a little."

Goodale thought he might have to go into court in the morning and argue the case, although, as he later admitted, his previous courtroom experience was limited to two uncontested divorce cases. But at least he had researched the law and he did not see why he could not make the argument as well as anyone—as anyone except Alexander Bickel, with whom he had lunched. He knew Bickel was sympathetic to *The Times* and he felt sure he would take the case if he could get Floyd Abrams of Cahill Gordon as litigator.

He proposed the idea to Harding Bancroft but Bancroft had another suggestion, that they try to get Herbert Wechsler, who had prepared the Supreme Court brief and argument that had won the day for *The Times* a few years earlier in the famous Sullivan case. Wechsler was not at his New York apartment but Bancroft got him on Cape Cod. He was enthusiastic but had another commitment.

Now the way was clear for Bickel—but Bickel could not be located. Goodale knew he was in New York—after all, he had lunched with him, but at midnight he was unable to find him. Meantime he called Floyd Abrams.

"I was living then at 1136 Fifth Avenue, in fact we had just moved in a month before," Abrams recalled. "I had gone to bed early and I was awakened by this call from Goodale. He told me it looked as though there was going to be a judicial proceeding over the Pentagon Papers, that Mitchell had sent a telegram asking *The Times* to stop publication and *The Times* had refused."

Abrams at first couldn't understand why Goodale was calling him. "I just couldn't accept the proposition that he was calling me to work on this case," Abrams said, "yet I knew he wasn't just calling to fill me in on it."

Goodale didn't tell Abrams that night that Lord, Day and Lord had refused to defend *The Times* but he said that *The Times* would not be represented by regular counsel and would like Abrams to work on it with Alexander Bickel.

Abrams immediately agreed if Bickel could be located. But he said he would have to have formal approval of his partners. Meantime, he would be glad to take a hand through the night in preparing for the proceedings Tuesday morning.

It was after midnight when Goodale finally went home, having asked the national desk of *The Times* to try to locate Bickel. Before he got back to his apartment *The Times* night rewrite battery had succeeded. It had taken twelve minutes and a series of phone calls from New Haven to Palo Alto to find Bickel at his mother's apartment on Riverside Drive.*

Goodale gave Bickel his citations and told him to call Abrams. In bringing in Cahill Gordon, Goodale had moved from one of the most starched-collar firms in New York (Lord, Day and Lord) to a brass-tough firm known as Irish gut-fighters. "They never ask you for anything and they never give you anything," one lawyer said. "You really bust your chops when you go up against Cahill Gordon."

Long since, *The Times'* Tuesday papers had been rolling off the presses by the hundreds of thousands. No longer was the Pentagon series the lead. Now the lead went to a five-column headline over a Washington story by Max Frankel: "Mitchell Seeks to Halt Series on Vietnam but *Times* Refuses."

For the first time in the three quarters of a century since Mr. Ochs had taken over *The Times* the institution was irreversibly headed toward full confrontation with the U.S. Government. There had been rows before but never of this magnitude. Only once in his long and successful stewardship had Mr. Ochs found himself embroiled in serious conflict involving government policy, but that was a totally inadvertent collision.

The message that *The Times* carried to its readers on the morning of June 15 was clear and bold. It was *The New York Times* versus the President and his government. The arena was the courts. No one reading *The Times* that morning could doubt that this was a confrontation of vast portent. No one on *The Times*, in the White House, the Justice Department or in official Washington doubted this although it was not yet plain that whatever the outcome the U.S. Establishment would never again be the same.

*On Tuesday morning, June 15, Abe Rosenthal posted a note on the city room bulletin board, "Thank God for night rewrite."

23

"There's Never Been a Case Like This"

THE CRISIS THAT WAS taking shape on June 15, 1971, around *The New York Times* and its publication of the Pentagon Papers was, of course, not the first conflict of national scope that had engaged the newspaper. *The Times* even before its acquisition by Adolph S. Ochs had been a powerful force and under Mr. Ochs its national and international prestige geometrically expanded.

There had been inevitable collisions but none approaching the scale of the Pentagon Papers. The greatest crisis of Arthur Hays Sulzberger's years had been his struggle against the know-nothing forces symbolized by the late Senator Joseph McCarthy of Wisconsin, climaxed by an effort of Senator Eastland of Mississippi to implant a "red" smear on *The Times*.

But the McCarthy-Eastland fight differed sharply from that over the Pentagon Papers. Then *The Times* was fighting a powerful body of congressional and public opinion, led by ruthless demagogues. The struggle did not pit *The Times* directly against the U.S. Government and an implacably hostile U.S. President.

Nor did Adolph S. Ochs ever find himself in chips-down combat with the American Government. He had his troubles with the U.S. Senate during World War I when isolationist senators attacked *The Times* for supporting the Allies against Germany and favoring American intervention. This was, as was well known, the policy of *The Times*, which had placed itself squarely in the Allied corner in an editorial by Charles Miller December 15, 1914.§

Abenia

The Times had easily brushed off the senatorial inquiry but the crisis of September 1918 was another matter. On Sunday, September 15, 1918, Mr. Ochs, his family and guests were enjoying the September weather in the Adirondacks at Abenia, a classic summer house on Lake

§See Notes section.

George which Mr. Ochs bought in late 1915 from George Foster Peabody,* a partner of Spencer Trask, one of the group from whom Mr. Ochs had purchased *The Times.* George Peabody, tall, handsome, bearded, then a man of about seventy, was a girlhood hero of Iphigene Sulzberger's. He was a supporter of Tuskegee Institute, a believer in education for the blacks, an opponent of racial discrimination. His story was a romantic one. All his adult life he had been in love with Katina, the wife of his best friend and partner, Spencer Trask, having fallen in love at first sight, seeing her sitting on the front stoop of her Brooklyn home, not knowing that she was already engaged to marry Trask. A few years after Trask's death, she, now an invalid, married Peabody. They lived a year or so in a great house at Yaddo, New York; ultimately the three, Trask, Katina and Peabody, being buried side by side and the house and grounds being left as a retreat for writers and artists.

In 1918 Abenia (the name means "house of rest" in Algonquin) was at its apogee.† It had been built in 1876 in the generous Adirondacks style, the house with innumerable rooms, surrounded by broad verandas. There was a garage with living quarters, a laundry with living quarters, a separate house used by Ochs' relatives in the summer, a summerhouse on the hill, greenhouses with a gardener's house attached and another house used by Mr. Ochs' secretary, who was "superintendent" of the establishment. A household of this magnitude was no small order, as can be seen by the rules and regulations promulgated as late as August 23, 1930, by the superintendent "by order of Mr. and Mrs. Adolph S. Ochs."

They came straight out of Mrs. Beaton:

"The staff at present will consist of a Parlor Maid, Waitress, Houseman, Cook, Second Cook, Kitchen Maid, Head Chambermaid, Head Laundress, Second Laundress, Mrs. Ochs' Personal Maid and Mr. Ochs' Valet."

Nor did this list exhaust the roster of employees. There was a night watchman, who was admonished to "keep a keen look out for fires, prowlers or other disturbances," as well as to turn off the oil burner under the hot-water heater in the basement at 10 P.M. and turn it on again "without fail" at 5 A.M. There were additional chambermaids and chauffeurs for "the motor department." Every Thursday if the weather was fair the chauffeurs were to take the help to Glens Falls for shop-

---

*His will left the funds for the establishment of the George Foster Peabody Awards for radio.

†After the death of Adolph Ochs and his wife the Sulzbergers tried to sell Abenia. They got a lone bid of $35,000 and finally had to get rid of it by auction. It has long since been torn down. (Iphigene Ochs Sulzberger, letter to author, 4/25/74)

ping. If the weather was foul the trip was made on Friday afternoon. On Tuesday evenings the chauffeurs took the staff to the movies at 8 P.M. and whenever possible they were to take them to Lake George Village (six miles away) for concerts or movies, or just for a drive in the open air. They were to be home by ten thirty or eleven. "Late hours," the rules said, "will not be tolerated." Transportation to 6 A.M. mass and church on Sunday was also provided.

The duties of each member of the staff were specified with care and employees were assured that "we have ever been most solicitous of the welfare and health of our employees and ready to aid them in the time of sickness or distress. . . ."

In return "we feel we are entitled to and we expect to receive loyalty, cheerful, harmonious service and cooperation."

The Austrian Crisis

This exquisitely Victorian establishment was Mr. Ochs' delight and on the weekend of September 15, 1918, it was, as always, filled to overflowing with young people, in whom Mr. Ochs took a special pleasure, relatives of his vast family, connections of various sorts, old friends and neighbors. Mr. Ochs loved such assemblages and it was rare that the house was not filled. He played rather poor poker with the young people, took them to the races at Saratoga (financing their bets but refusing to share any winnings), leading expeditions to the golf courses, swimming in the lake or dancing in the evening to the new red-label Victor records.

The war was on, the U.S. was fully engaged, and Mr. Ochs was now intimately concerned because his only daughter was married to handsome young Lieutenant Arthur Hays Sulzberger, who was awaiting orders to go overseas while Iphigene expected their first child in a couple of months.* But there was optimism in the air. It seemed apparent that the Central Powers would not be able much longer to resist the crushing offensives of the British and French and their powerful American comrades-at-arms, regardless of the debacle which Russian revolution had left on the Eastern front.

Mr. Ochs kept closely in touch with *The Times* from Abenia. His remarkable managing editor, Carr Van Anda, telephoned him every evening and he usually spoke with Charles Miller, the editor in chief, as well. On this occasion, it being a weekend, Miller was at his country house at Great Neck, Long Island.

At Abenia the Van Anda call was the event of the day. Each evening Mr. Ochs invited his neighbors over. Van Anda telephoned about 10 P.M. and the line was held open sometimes until 11 P.M. Van Anda read

*Marian, born Dec. 31, 1918.

the latest bulletins to Mr. Ochs (this was, of course, before the days of radio) and, in turn, Mr. Ochs read them out to the assembled crowd. In midevening on September 15 Van Anda telephoned Mr. Ochs. He had exciting news. The Austrian Government had issued an invitation to all belligerent governments to join in a nonbinding conference on terms for peace. "It is," said Van Anda, "the beginning of the end."

Mr. Ochs read out the news to his neighbors. Iphigene was in the group and long afterward she remembered her father saying to Van Anda, "Now, go easy on that." Van Anda told Mr. Ochs that the news had been telephoned to Miller and he was writing an editorial for the next morning's issue. "That's fine," Mr. Ochs said. He knew the views of Miller and Van Anda very well. They were 100 percent backers of the war and had been long before the United States had become involved. It didn't occur to Mr. Ochs to worry over what Miller was writing.* It was sure to be a good resounding thump for the enemy and he had total confidence in Van Anda, regarded him as a genius, was a bit in awe of him, a little sensitive because he felt Van Anda's knowledge was broader and more arcane than his own, a bit ashamed at what he regarded as his own inadequate education and very inclined to give him his head. He did not have exactly the same feeling toward Miller but considered him a competent man. (Iphigene always thought Miller was rather vain and pompous, not worth half her father, and she was probably right.)

The next day the roof fell in. By the time Mr. Ochs got to *The Times* there were on his desk more than 3,000 letters and telegrams denouncing him, *The Times* and *The Times'* editorial on the Austrian peace feeler. A friend who walked into Mr. Ochs' office found him sitting, his eyes staring into space, silent, dazed, with the look of a man who "had been hit on the head with a club." He staggered up and wandered down to the composing room. Later he asked a friend if he should not retire from the management of *The Times* and put the paper in the hands of a trustee. Old friends cut him on the street. The Union League Club called a meeting to carry out a public denunciation of *The Times*—the Union League Club, citadel of the men who helped Mr. Ochs acquire *The Times*, citadel of that rich conservative New York for which Mr. Ochs felt he had created his *Times*. President Wilson stormed in the White House. The other New York newspapers piled onto *The Times*, burying it in spleen and spite, particularly the

---

*Van Anda sent Mr. Ochs a telegram Sunday morning summarizing the Austrian peace initiative and characterizing it as "the beginning of the end." Van Anda reiterated this view on the telephone to Ochs Sunday night. Ochs telephoned Miller Sunday night but the connection was so poor all he heard from Miller was that he shared Van Anda's interpretation that the note "was a surrender and was the beginning of the end." (*Times'* archives, Van Anda telegram to Ochs, 9/15/18)

Hearst papers, the Pulitzer papers and the *New York Herald,* which advertised "Read an American paper." Only the eccentric and unloved Frank Munsey came to Mr. Ochs' defense in his *Sun.*

There were those who suggested that Mr. Ochs disavow the editorial since he had not seen it prior to publication. This he steadfastly refused. "I could not do such a thing," he said. "I have always accepted public praise and public approval of the many great editorials Mr. Miller has written for *The Times.* Where there is blame instead of praise I must share that, too."*

In 1916 Mr. Ochs had suffered his first clinical depression but rallied to become once more his ebullient self. The crisis of September 16, 1918, did not produce a new depression although a very serious attack was to follow in a couple of years but it brought to Mr. Ochs a sense of bewilderment, a feeling that all he had created had been lost in one unexpected throw of the dice.

What had *The Times* done? What whipped up this public and governmental fury? Looking back at the words Mr. Miller dictated to *The Times* from Great Neck it is impossible to fathom how they touched off such violence. His editorial, written with the faintly Spencerian grace of the era, recognized the Austrian initiative for what it was, the sign that a war-weary and defeated nation was prepared to sue for peace. Mr. Miller noted that Austria was not Germany, but that Austria could hardly have floated the feeler without Germany's acquiescence. He argued sensibly that the invitation be picked up.

"All the belligerents desire the end of the war," he wrote. "The stricken world longs for peace. While no armistice precedes the proposed conference, we are justified in entertaining the hope, the belief, even, that fighting will cease this year."

Miller called for no abatement in prosecuting the war but said "reason and humanity demand that the Austrian invitation be accepted."

How these sensible, reasoned words could have unleashed the crisis they did unleash is difficult to conceive at this remove. *The Times* was called a traitor and Mr. Miller's words treason. One hostile editorial said *The Times* had "run up the white flag," another hinted it had taken "Austrian gold." Mr. Ochs genuinely believed (as did some

---

*On September 28 Mr. Ochs wrote his nephew, Julius Ochs Adler, then a lieutenant in France, "How Mr. Van Anda, who is ever on the alert, let it [the editorial] pass without advising me is one of the mysteries and can only be credited to cruel fate." By the date of this letter, Mr. Ochs had regained his self-confidence and even pointed out that while the paper lost a little circulation from indignant readers it had gained more because of the stir. He reported daily circulation over 375,000 and Sunday over 525,000. *The Times,* he said, "is the lead daily and the *American* [Hearst] only now exceeds our Sunday." (*Times'* archives, Ochs to Julius Ochs Adler, 9/18/18)

associates and members of the family) that *The Times* might be destroyed.

Then, as quickly as it had flared, the fire died out with the end of the war less than two months distant. But the effects were traumatic. Mr. Ochs was powerfully reinforced in his long-standing conviction that eloquent editorial opinion was not for *The Times,* that "on the one hand" and "on the other hand" was a more prudent philosophy. From this he was not to deviate the rest of his life.

Whether the incident played a role in his serious depression at the end of the war cannot now be ascertained. Iphigene believed it did not but it may have played a role in an unpleasant incident associated with that depression. This was the curious joint demand of Mr. Ochs' three closest collaborators, Mr. Miller, Mr. Van Anda, and Louis Wiley, the genius of Mr. Ochs' business office, for $25,000 post-war bonuses. The demands, coming at a time when Mr. Ochs thought (in his depressed state) that he was losing all his money; that his tax statements had been falsified; that he was going to have to pay huge sums to the government did, in Iphigene Sulzberger's belief, deepen Mr. Ochs' illness.*

The difference between the crisis which struck Mr. Ochs' *Times* September 16, 1918, and that which caught up *The Times* of his grandson on the morning of June 15, 1971, is a measure not only of the distance between two epochs; the difference between two contrasted personalities but between two societies so transformed in value and power relationships that they seem to represent not stages in evolution but different worlds.

When the fire storm struck Mr. Ochs' *Times* in the penultimate weeks of the war; when President Wilson, the government, the general public, newspaper rivals and even some of the *Times* staff denounced *The Times* for what amounted to treason, Mr. Ochs was savagely shaken. He felt his brilliant creation stood at the brink of destruction, that *The Times* might not survive. He was prepared to sacrifice himself, if necessary, so that the institution might go on. Thankfully, the dangers vanished as quickly as they appeared, although their effects on Mr. Ochs endured.

It is not entirely fair to compare 1918 directly with 1971. The crisis of 1918 was unforseen; that of 1971 was entered into with some prevision. But if it is fair to say that Mr. Ochs would not have contemplated publication of the Pentagon Papers so it is fair to say that his

---

*Iphigene Sulzberger never forgave the three for pressing their demands on her father. She particularly blamed Miller: "After all he [Mr. Ochs] made Mr. Miller's fortune for him." (Personal interview, Iphigene Ochs Sulzberger, 1/14/69) Mr. Miller's stock in *The New York Times* was appraised for inheritance taxes after his death in 1921 at $1,270,784. (F. Fraser Bond, *Mr. Miller of The Times,* New York, 1931, p. 69)

response to the government's challenge would not have been that of his grandson. From the historical standpoint, the threat to *The Times* was far more genuine in 1971 than it could possibly have been in 1918. That of 1971 rocked the American structure of power, shifting the underpinnings, and the change would be felt into the indefinite future. As Whitney North Seymour, Jr., the thoughtful U.S. Attorney for the Southern District of New York who initiated the prosecution against *The Times* on Tuesday, June 16, 1971, later was to comment, the case "was not only to mark a milestone in First Amendment litigation but it was also to unleash a chain of events in the name of 'national security' which contributed to the collapse of the Presidency . . . and the unmasking of the reckless misuse of executive power."

Preparations

Seymour was asleep in a motel in Arlington, Virginia, across the Potomac from Washington, when his telephone rang at 7:15 A.M. on Tuesday, June 15, 1971. Seymour, a Republican of independent mind and a distinguished member of the New York Bar (as was his father), a tall man, six feet six, rather reserved and patrician in bearing, was, some thought, a curious choice by the Nixon Administration to fill the post of U.S. Attorney for the Southern District of New York, the most important single prosecutor's post in the federal establishment.* He had gotten his post almost by chance. Nixon had decided to replace the equally independent and stubborn Robert J. Morgenthau, Jr., a Democrat who had refused (against custom) to submit his resignation. Some of Seymour's friends sent in letters in his behalf, he was summoned to Washington by Deputy Attorney General Richard Kleindienst (whom Seymour had never met, just as he had never met John Mitchell or Richard Nixon) and given the job. He took over from Morgenthau January 16, 1970.

Seymour drove to Washington with his wife and children on Sunday June 13 and checked into the motel. He had come for the annual conference of U.S. attorneys at the Justice Department.

When his telephone rang at 7:15 Seymour sleepily lifted it to hear a brusque voice demand, "Where have you been? We have been calling your room every half hour since midnight." The voice was that of Robert C. Mardian, head of the Internal Security Division of the Justice Department, the man who since Monday had been in charge of the Pentagon Papers case, the man who, as Seymour was to say, came to be regarded "both inside and outside" the Justice Department as "a

---

*Mr. Nixon came to share this view. In the spring of 1973 a White House tape recorded his description of Seymour as "a soft-headed do-gooder." (Personal interview, Seymour, 1/10/79)

dangerous man," a man whose activities directed against so-called subversives came in Seymour's mind to be "a source of genuine concern," a man who played what Seymour described as a "chilling" role in the Pentagon case and who was ultimately indicted and convicted along with John Mitchell, H. R. Haldeman and John Erhlichman in the Watergate cover-up. (But the conviction was to be reversed.)

Mardian had been up all night. He had been unable to get Seymour because the motel kept ringing the children's room. The children half-awoke but didn't realize what the noise was. Mardian had, however, reached Silvio J. Mollo, chief assistant U.S. attorney in New York, a veteran of more than thirty years service, at about 6:45 A.M.

Mardian told Seymour of Mitchell's telex to *The Times, The Times'* refusal to halt publication, and the government's decision to institute proceedings. The Papers, Mardian said, had been unlawfully obtained and contained many extremely sensitive documents very damaging to national security. He instructed Seymour to seek a court order to halt publication and to compel *The Times* to return the Papers. He said a crew of lawyers had worked all night preparing the case. Seymour conferred by telephone with Mollo and with his chief of civil cases, Michael D. Hess, slim, bright, dark-haired, then just thirty, who had been roused at 7 A.M. They were preparing to go into court that morning.

"It wasn't until I hung up the phone and got over my early morning drowsiness," Hess recalled, "that I realized the magnitude of the case. I called Mollo, got dressed and hurried down to meet with Fred Buzhardt and his group from Washington. I got the complaint from Buzhardt, made a few minor alterations and signed it. Then I called the court to see who was in charge of emergency applications. There was always one judge. This day it was going to be Judge Gurfein, new to the bench. I didn't know him."

Seymour, later in the morning, went to the Justice Department where he listened to Deputy Attorney General Richard G. Kleindienst (later to plead nolo contendere to charges of perjury) tell the assembled U.S. attorneys, "It is of utmost importance to keep this administration in power and you men must do everything you can to ensure that result."

It was 1:15 A.M. Tuesday morning when Floyd Abrams, in a cab, had picked up Alexander Bickel at his mother's apartment on Riverside Drive and drove with him down to 80 Pine Street. Wall Street was deserted at that hour. The cleaning crews had long since gone home. Only an occasional lighted window showed in the fifty-, sixty- and seventy-story skyscrapers. There was no one on the streets. No one. But the lights still burned in Cahill Gordon, which occupied floors seventeen, eighteen, nineteen and half of sixteen. Secretaries, stenographers and proofreaders worked all night at Cahill Gordon, preparing briefs, transcribing notes, collating records. Abrams and Bickel went to the library and picked up an annotated version of the Espionage Act, which lists relevant decisions and statutes. Neither Abrams nor Bickel had read it before but they presumed from Mitchell's telegram that this would be the grounds for the government action. Abrams commandeered a night-duty typist, sent a proofreader out to find a copy of Tuesday morning's *Times,* got some coffee from the urn that was kept going night-long and he and Bickel began to draft their notes. As early dawn broke over New York Harbor, Bickel dictated a brief memo on the applicable sections of the Espionage Act. Both men had concluded by this time that there actually was nothing in the act which dealt with such matters as the Pentagon Papers publication.

Abrams still did not have formal approval from his firm to handle the case. At this point he was the junior partner. There were forty-two names ahead of his on the letterhead. (Now with 180 partners the names are listed alphabetically.)

At about 8:30 Lawrence McKay, senior litigating partner, came in. Abrams, rumpled and unshaven, went to his office. "You look like hell," McKay said, "what's going on here?" "I've been up all night preparing a case for a new client," Abrams responded. "What's that?" McKay asked. "Well," said Abrams, "you may have read about it in *The New York Times.*"

Abrams brought Bickel in, introduced him to McKay and said he needed clearance from the firm to take the case. McKay said he would call another partner just so the formalities were fulfilled and there would be no difficulties.*

About 9:30 A.M. Abrams and Bickel, bleary from lack of sleep, appeared at *The Times.* They had drafted a memorandum about ten pages long. Michael Hess had already called *The Times* saying that he was going into court that morning to ask for a temporary restraining order against further publication of the Pentagon Papers and for an injunction. Abrams telephoned Hess, who said he would be in court at noon. Abrams tried to get a little more time but Hess said the decision to be in court by noon had been made in Washington. So somewhat before noon Goodale, Bickel, Abrams and William E. Hegarty and McKay of Cahill Gordon arrived at the Federal Court Building in Foley Square, a stone's throw from City Hall and Brooklyn Bridge. By

---

*Years later Goodale joked to Abrams, "You never got back to me on whether Cahill Gordon would let you take the case." (Personal interview, Abrams, 1/31/79)

random process of assignment the case went to Federal District Judge Murray I. Gurfein.

The government's complaint named as defendants The New York Times Company and twenty-two executives and employees chosen from the paper's masthead and those who had worked on the Pentagon Papers. It sought a temporary restraining order to prohibit "further dissemination, disclosure or divulgence" of information in the Pentagon volumes and a Command study of the Tonkin Gulf incident and thereafter permanent injunctions to the same effect. It asked the court to order the defendants to return all relevant materials in their possession to the government.

Attached to the complaint were a copy of the Mitchell telex and an affidavit from Mardian asserting that he had read it to *The Times* and received a negative response. Mardian drafted his affidavit in the early morning hours and drove to the Alexandria, Virginia, police station to have it notarized, just in time to send it up to New York with one of his aides, George Calhoun. When he had finished the affidavit Mardian had found that none of his Justice Department employees was a notary public, the only notaries were FBI secretaries. He later was to say that he asked William Sullivan, deputy FBI director, to send one over. "Somehow J. Edgar Hoover found out about it and wouldn't let any of their notaries come over," Mardian recalled. "We almost missed the plane."

Mardian attached to the papers an affidavit from J. Fred Buzhardt, counsel of the Defense Department, asserting that he had "reviewed" the Pentagon study; that it was classified "Top Secret—Sensitive" and that publication of the contents "has prejudiced the defense interests of the United States" and that publication of further materials will result "in irreparable injury to the national defense." He deposed that *The Times* was not authorized to have in its possession the Pentagon study, the Command study of the Gulf of Tonkin incident or any internal documents relating thereto.

Buzhardt's affidavit was notarized in New York City. The fact was, although no one at *The Times,* no one in the U.S. district attorney's office, had any way of knowing it, Buzhardt had in no sense "reviewed" the estimated 2,500,000 words in the Pentagon study. He had only the vaguest idea of the contents except for what was published in *The New York Times* nor, at that moment, did anyone then on duty in the upper echelons of the Defense Department. As Pursley recollected, all Buzhardt knew about the Papers was the description given a couple of months earlier when Pursley warned Buzhardt that the Papers had a potential for causing trouble. Neither Pursley nor Buzhardt actually examined the Papers.

In Court

It was Gurfein's second day on the bench. He had been sworn in Thursday and had agreed with his friend District Judge Walter Mansfield (the two had served together in the OSS in World War II) to take over Mansfield's schedule, subject to the approval of the chief judge, which was readily given. Mansfield was moving up to the U.S. Court of Appeals. Judge Gurfein had spent Monday hearing the periodic roll of naturalization cases and had given the new American citizens a talk about the Bill of Rights and the First Amendment, which he suggested was one of the chief differences between the United States and some other systems.

Now on Tuesday morning he had been listening to routine motions. He had heard nothing of the Pentagon Papers case until Silvio Mollo, Seymour's permanent civil service assistant, came up in great excitement and told him the lawyers were bringing the case before him almost immediately. Word got around that the case was headed for Gurfein and before he finished talking with Mollo the room had begun to fill up. It was a high-ceiling courtroom, number 318, the largest in the building. By the time the case was called, as Goodale recalled, "the room was crackling. If you had lighted a match it would have exploded."

The first moves were the inevitable non sequiturs. None of the lawyers knew each other nor had Gurfein met any of them. Hess, of course, had had no opportunity to examine the Pentagon Papers except for a cursory look at the first two installments published by *The Times* (he hadn't had time to look at the third installment in Tuesday's paper) and he knew that would be a handicap. He questioned Buzhardt, who assured him that it was a very serious matter involving stolen papers, national defense and strategy. "At that point," Hess recalled, "I surely had no reason to question that. I was personally sure that this was a very serious matter. You don't question cabinet and sub-cabinet officers in a time of war on things like this."

When the case was called Hess started to address the court but a clerk immediately popped up and said the case could not be heard until the government went to the sixth floor, filed its complaint with the clerk there and the case was assigned a number.

None of the lawyers quite understood why this was necessary. In fact, the chief judge was conducting an experiment to streamline district court procedures. Cases were being assigned on a random basis to six judges engaging in the experiment, including Gurfein. If one of these judges drew a case he would keep it throughout its life, handling all motions, procedural matters and the trial (prior to this motions were handled at random, any number of judges might act on individual pieces of a court action). So the government had to go to the sixth floor, file its complaint with the clerk and draw a number. It was number 2665 and fortuitously this number fell in Gurfein's box and the case was returned to him.

Hess now directed himself to the court, declaring that national security would be severely compromised unless he issued a temporary restraining order. But there was another hitch. The complaint that had been drafted in Washington based the government's request on Section 893D of the statute. This section had to do with persons who were *authorized* to have certain materials. Judge Gurfein mildly observed that this section "doesn't seem to fit." Goodale and Abrams hoped that the judge would throw out the case then and there but he didn't. Instead, he directed Hess's attention to Section 893E, which related to *unauthorized* possessors. Hess took a moment to consult Buzhardt. He realized that the materials prepared by Buzhardt and Mardian were faulty and asked permission to amend and correct his application.

Hess told the court that on the basis of what had been published "serious injuries are being inflicted on our foreign relations, to the benefit of other nations opposed to our form of government." He contended that *The Times* would be delayed only briefly if it halted publication of the series until the case was tried. He suggested that *The Times* do so voluntarily.

The court broke for lunch. Goodale, Bickel and Abrams talked about the argument Bickel would present. They were, in Goodale's recollection, "all fired up." Goodale's final comment was, "Well, it has never happened before."

Bickel's argument was later described by those who heard it as "the most brilliant argument of the whole case." Unfortunately it was not transcribed.

He emphasized the very heavy burden that rested on the government. There had never before been a request for a temporary order of this character, for a prior restraint on publication. The government, he said, had not met its burden. All they had presented was an affidavit couched in the most general terms by Buzhardt and this did not satisfy the conditions. There were no specifics. Again and again he asked Judge Gurfein whether he wished to be the first judge in the history of the nation to impose prior restraint upon a newspaper. Abrams and Hess saw that this argument made Gurfein wince. "This argument bothered us a lot," Hess recalled. "We could see that it bothered Gurfein." He did not, indeed, wish to be the first American jurist to impose a strait jacket upon the press. But he was impressed with the government's arguments and he picked up the suggestion for voluntary restraint by *The Times*.

Finally he called the attorneys into his chambers and pressed a request that *The Times* exercise voluntary restraint while the case was adjudicated.

Bickel said *The Times*, of course, would consider this. The hearing was suspended while Goodale and Abrams telephoned Bancroft from a booth in the corridor, surrounded by eyes and noses pressing on the glass and ears straining to hear the conversation. "What's the company policy?" Goodale asked. Bancroft said he would have to consult. After fifteen minutes Gurfein became restive. Goodale pressed Bancroft, who replied, "Do we have to make up our mind right now?" "Yes," Goodale replied. "What do you think?" Bancroft asked. "We have to say no," Goodale replied. "O.K.," said Bancroft and the reply was relayed to Gurfein.

Gurfein promptly granted the government a temporary restraining order and set the hearing for Friday morning.

"The questions raised by this action are serious and fundamental," Gurfein said. "I believe that the matter is so important and so involved with the history of the relationship between the security of the government and a free press that a more thorough briefing than the parties have had an opportunity to do is required.

"There's never been a case like this," Gurfein added, echoing what Goodale had said to his colleagues at lunch. "So we knew the question," Goodale recalled, "but we didn't know the answer."

One thing concerned Goodale as he and his weary colleagues left Foley Square. He felt that Gurfein was angry, angry with *The Times* for not acting more "reasonably," for not responding to his appeal for voluntary restraint. He simply could not understand *The Times*. After all, as he kept saying, "we are all patriotic Americans." Neither he, the attorneys for *The Times* nor the prosecutors had a notion at this time of the depth of paranoia and political passion which underlay the government's action. In the courtroom before the case had been called some newspapermen had suggested that "the Nixon Administration is going to throw this one," that is, they thought that the action had been filed more or less pro forma. Why should Nixon want to suppress the Pentagon Papers, the argument ran? They dealt with Kennedy and Johnson. They could hurt only the Democrats. Nixon stood to gain from their publication.

One thing on which the lawyers agreed, however, was that the case had come before a judge who was a first-class lawyer, a man who knew the law and who knew his responsibilities. Whatever happened Judge Gurfein was going to give this action the attention and care which its importance justified. There would be no backing away from the hard rock of judicial consideration.

Mr. Nixon's Thoughts

What was happening in the White House?

Certainly something explosive had to be going on. It had already produced the first order of prior restraint, prohibiting an American newspaper from publishing a specific article, in the history of the republic. Obviously there had to be concern at the highest level. Whatever Mardian's personal input had been he was no rogue elephant. He was operating on instructions which had come to him through his superiors in Justice and their instructions had come from the White House.

Evidence to the mood within the White House, and, specifically, to Mr. Nixon's state of mind, is difficult to come by. Impressions change with time. So much happened so swiftly that participants later found it difficult to recall sequences and nuances. Mr. Nixon himself recalled his mounting concern over the Papers but without his tapes and logs had no recollection of when and with whom he talked nor details of conversations.

Happily, the clear-hand, precise, faintly symbolized notes written on long yellow legal pads by John Ehrlichman during this period provide remarkable insights into the thinking and actions of Mr. Nixon and his associates. Mr. Ehrlichman took the notes as he participated in the White House discussions and they covered a whole series of presidential deliberations devoted to the Pentagon Papers. The Ehrlichman notes may lack the expletive vividness of the presidential tapes but they provide a clear chart to the moves contemplated and made by Mr Nixon and the others.

Ehrlichman's notes offer a succinct record of discussions in which he participated with Mr. Nixon. They are neat, orderly and organized, presenting the essentials of what often were verbose and wandering conversations. Ehrlichman was the usual record-keeper of these sessions. Haldeman also took notes but ordinarily his were "action notes," a record of things which he was to do. The Ehrlichman notes attempted to cover the whole discussion. Unfortunately, only a slim selection of Ehrlichman notes are available, the bulk being tied up as are the presidential tapes and most White House papers by legal action of Mr. Nixon, seeking to prevent their release and to compel that they be turned over to him. Ehrlichman's notes on the Pentagon Papers were turned over to him in response to a subpoena for their use in his defense.*

---

*These notes, with the addition of Ehrlichman notes held by the Watergate Special Prosecution Force, were given to the House Judiciary Committee for use in the Nixon impeachment proceedings and published in Appendix III of the Judiciary Hearings (Supplementary Documents) May–June 1974. Several Ehrlichman minutes (in some

The first meeting of this kind recorded by Ehrlichman occurred at 3:45 P.M. on the afternoon of Tuesday, June 15. The President, John Mitchell and Ehrlichman were present. The discussion began while the attorneys for *The Times* and the government were awaiting Judge Gurfein's decision. Mr. Nixon's philosophy and intent were vividly exposed.

The subject of the discussion was a follow-up campaign against *The Times* and Ellsberg.

"No cause," said the President, "justifies breaking the law. It's treasonable."

Ehrlichman faithfully put down the President's words.

As for Ellsberg, the President said they would "get him," possibly through a congressional committee. Or, interjected Mitchell, through a grand jury in New York City.

There is, said Mr. Nixon, no higher morality than the law. And, he added, no one, no one in the White House was to talk to *The New York Times* in the future except for himself and Press Secretary Ziegler. (Ehrlichman, in his vivid note-taking style, jotted a memo to himself to inform Ziegler of this.) Dramatically, at that moment Ziegler himself walked in to announce that Gurfein had granted a temporary injunction against *The Times*.

Mitchell quickly said that he would have a grand jury convened by Thursday to seek indictments in the case, presumably against *The Times*, Ellsberg and others.

Ehrlichman turned to what he called "the PR of this," that is, the public relations stance the White House would take. Why, after all, was publication of the Papers such an issue? It was so important, the President said, because it breached national security. There was something which Ehrlichman called "colloquy re leaks," then the talk turned to implementing the "PR of this."

Mr. Nixon thought that the Defense Department or State Department, possibly through Press Officer McCloskey, should put out a statement. He wasn't sure who should write it but he wanted to see it before it was issued and he recollected that "I went through all this in the Hiss case and we won that." Evocation of the Hiss case by Mr. Nixon, its techniques, its difficulties was an analogy which Mr. Nixon was to repeat again and again as the Pentagon Papers case began its swift escalation over the high ledges of policy onto the rhetorical mountain trails that led to Plumbers-Break-ins-Watergate.

There was the question of what to call the case. In the Tuesday morning presidential news summary Allin had dubbed it *"The New*

---

cases more complete than the Judiciary Committee versions) were turned over to Morton Halperin, in response to a Freedom of Information action.

York Times controversy." Now Ehrlichman had a bright idea—why not call them "The Kennedy-Johnson Papers." This would neatly disassociate the Nixon Administration from the documents and the woes of Vietnam and pin the onus on the Democrats.*

Finally the three men talked about who might have leaked the Papers. The President suggested that Ellsberg, (Mort) Halperin and Stein possibly did it. To which "Stein" he had reference was not indicated. No one of that name was ever mentioned again nor did Mr. Nixon revert to such a suspect. It hardly seemed likely that he had in mind his Economic Adviser Herbert Stein.†

In the conversation of Mr. Nixon, Attorney General Mitchell and Ehrlichman there were only faint traces of the hysteria which soon was to characterize White House discussions, strategy and tactics in the Pentagon case.

Talking about these events much later, Pat Buchanan, one of the President's ablest and most pragmatic speech writers, said he had felt a bit divorced from it all in his office in the Executive Office Building, but thought this was one of "those things where the old man got all stirred up and then a week later he forgot all about it." Or as John Dean was to describe it much, much later the kind of "over-reaction that was very typical of the administration." Dean said he was amazed at the fanfare. But in time it came to seem typical—the kind of reaction which fed on itself, as had happened in the My Lai affair and the White House response to the Peers report on Lieutenant Calley.

But perhaps Marc Raskin, the radical critic of the war and of the Nixon Administration, sensed most perceptively the nature of the process which had gotten under way within the White House. In his view any small circle at the top (of government or other big organiza-

---

*Eventually, the White House began to call them "The McNamara Papers." Some of Mr. Nixon's associates later wondered whether Lyndon Johnson might have poured gasoline on the fires already burning in Mr. Nixon's mind to cause him to escalate the Pentagon controversy. (Personal interview, Patrick Buchanan, 1/12/78) Mr. Johnson's records at Austin show no telephone call between Mr. Nixon and LBJ in this period. Ehrlichman's notes of June 17 contain the notation "Check Johnson" and, in fact, the next day Bryce Harlow, Mr. Nixon's trusted political liaison man, telephoned Mr. Johnson at his Texas ranch and held a lengthy conversation. Harlow tried unsuccessfully to get Mr. Johnson to issue a statement criticizing *The Times* but LBJ refused on grounds that *The Times* and the *Washington Post* were just trying to "re-execute him" and that any statement he made would be turned against him. In the weeks ahead Mr. Nixon frequently discussed political strategies flowing from the Pentagon Papers that might be employed to split the Democrats, bringing Mr. Johnson to his side as against what he regarded as the Kennedy wing of the party. (Personal interviews Harry Middleton, LBJ Library, 2/22/79; Harlow, 3/15/79; Nixon, *Memoirs*, p. 510)

†John Ehrlichman had no idea who Stein was either then or later. The name never surfaced again. Ehrlichman was certain the President was not referring to Herbert Stein. (Personal interview, Ehrlichman, 3/22/79)

tion) was prone to overheat. A problem arose. Key people gathered to discuss it. Ideas spilled out. Each sought to outdo the other, to be more macho, to present a more daring scenario. The level of rhetoric inexorably rose. Each must prove his manhood. Each must prove his leadership.

The result—action *must* be taken. To the actors it seemed that they had the power to do *anything* and the response was bigger and broader and bolder than otherwise could possibly occur. It simply took off out of the real world.

He thought that happened in the Pentagon case. No one stopped to think where it would lead; no one looked behind; they raced off like hounds in pursuit of an imaginary rabbit. The same thing was to happen later when the White House tried to cope with Watergate.

And, as Raskin came to believe, the catalyst in this psychodrama was Henry Kissinger.

24

"Double Standard"

W HEN PRESIDENT NIXON sat down in the Oval Office of the White House at 5:20 P.M. on Thursday, June 17, with Henry Kissinger, H. R. Haldeman and John Ehrlichman it is not likely that any of the four believed this discussion was destined to play a fateful role in the Nixon presidency.

It seemed like a moment of pause in the Pentagon affair. *The Times* had been halted in publication of the Papers since Tuesday by the government's temporary injunction. No other papers had yet begun to publish the documents despite much scrambling around. Tomorrow, on Friday, in New York the government would present before Judge Gurfein its arguments for the issuance of a permanent injunction. There was no reason to believe that the government did not have a reasonable chance of persuading the courts of the validity of its viewpoint.

This late Thursday afternoon then was a suitable moment for reflection, for looking back at what had happened, for looking ahead, for considering the consequences of the Pentagon crisis, the lessons to be learned, the conclusions to be drawn. It was a moment, perhaps, in which the President might reasonably assess the legal and constitutional implications of the affair; in which he and his lieutenants might ponder whether the events of the past few days might dictate some changes of policy and procedure; an appropriate moment, it might be thought, for damage assessment and the drawing up of plans for the future.

All of these things might well have occupied the attention of Mr. Nixon and his companions. It is illuminating and a little frightening that almost none of them did.

Historians like to single out a turning point which later can be seen as that moment from which flowed a sequence of events, sometimes heroic, sometimes tragic.

This White House meeting on a late June afternoon would seem to fit such a definition. Surely there were to be many, many occasions thereafter when Mr. Nixon could have turned away from his Homeric destiny. Looking in on the discussion, the four men seated comfortably in their armchairs, Ehrlichman with his long yellow pad on his knees and a set of sharp-pointed No. 2 Eberhard Faber pencils in hand; Haldeman with his brush-cut hair and *his* yellow pad; Kissinger with his; the President, making somewhat more scanty notations—nothing signaled that a climactic moment had been reached.

But today, staring at those flat, clearly penciled notes of Ehrlichman's, it is plain that the embryo of almost all that was later to follow was present in that discussion—the institutionalization of paranoia, the creation of extralegal subversive units (the Plumbers), the organization of massive secret reprisals (in this case, against *The New York Times,* designed to cripple its reporting on the government—*"The New York Times* is finished in the White House"), a campaign for the "discipline of leaks," which would be carried forward (and already had been) by criminal means; the groundwork for an elaborate conspiracy against liberals, intellectuals and antiwar forces with Ellsberg as its focus; the stirrings of a political scheme to smear the Johnson-Kennedy administrations as architects of failure in Vietnam and (what ultimately was to prove suicidal) what Ehrlichman meticulously recorded as "The Diehm file," that is, an enterprise which finally was to involve bogus and fraudulent means to establish the complicity of President Kennedy in the overthrow and assassination of Ngo Dinh Diem in the Saigon coup of November 1, 1963.

There was to be found in the random and sometimes aimless discourse of the four men traces of the psychology and thinking that ultimately flowered into cancerlike perversion of great arms of government—the Justice Department, the FBI, the CIA and, of course, the presidency itself.

All of this, discussed within the general framework, as Mr. Nixon put it, of "Win PR, not just court case."

What was most significant about this White House discussion, perhaps, was not what was discussed but what was *not* discussed. No legal or constitutional issues were raised. You will search in vain through Ehrlichman's careful notes (and this applies to other recorded White House discussions of the Pentagon Papers, as well) for detailed examination of such matters as the purported danger which the revelations presented to U.S. intelligence operations and military and diplomatic codes. Not a word was spoken by Mr. Nixon or by Dr. Kissinger of the transcendentally delicate diplomatic negotiations in progress, the secret exchanges through Pakistan and Rumania that produced Kissinger's July trip to Peking;* the critical talks going forward between Washing-

*The first mention of the China talks as a rationale for action on the Pentagon Papers did not come until a discussion August 8, nearly two months after publication of the

ton and Moscow on SALT and the totally secret meetings that Kissinger was conducting with representatives of Hanoi in Paris.

Later on, these diplomatic transactions were to figure greatly in public charges of irresponsibility by the press and specifically *The New York Times*. The charge was to be repeated again and again by Mr. Nixon, by Dr. Kissinger and by administration spokesmen that this was the reason for their alarm over the Pentagon publication and echoes of this contention are still to be heard. But in the cozy talks in the Oval Office the subjects mentioned by Mr. Nixon and his Big Three were entirely different. They related to politics, to reprisals, "PR" and counterplots. Nor is there much reflection of Kissinger's hysteria, which was so often recalled by his White House associates.

Kissinger's explosions did take place. They had already rumbled through the early morning White House staff meetings as everyone remembered years later. Herb Klein, once the President's press secretary, and at that time coordinator for special media efforts, recalled that, sometimes, Henry would just sit through the morning meetings reading intelligence reports, saying nothing.

"This time he was mad as hell," Klein recalled. "He was jumping up and down," expressing concern not only over what had been published but over what would be published and over what might happen to undercover agents whose cover might be blown.

"There can be no foreign policy in this government," Charles Colson recalled Kissinger as saying. "No foreign policy, I tell you! We might just as well turn it all over to the Soviets and get it over with. These leaks are slowly and systematically destroying us."

Colson retained an image of Kissinger pounding on an antique Chippendale table, rattling the coffee cups.

"I tell you, Bob," Colson quoted Kissinger telling Haldeman, "the President must act—today. There is wholesale subversion of this government under way."

Kissinger pulled out a sheaf of papers and dramatically threw them on the table—cables, he said, from Australia, England and Canada protesting the security leaks.

"If our allies can't trust us," he asked, "how will we ever be able to negotiate with our enemies?"*

Papers and a full month after Kissinger's Peking trip. (House Judiciary Committee, Appendix III, pp. 166–169.)

*Haldeman had Kissinger making essentially the same argument to Nixon. The release of the Pentagon Papers, Haldeman quoted Kissinger as telling the President, "shows you are a weakling. The fact that some idiot can publish all of the diplomatic secrets of this country on his own is damaging to your image, as far as the Soviets are concerned, and it could destroy our ability to conduct foreign policy. If the other powers feel that we can't control internal leaks, they will never agree to secret negotia-

Colson first thought (and wrote) that the Kissinger explosion occurred Monday. Later he decided it must have been Tuesday or Wednesday. By this time he himself was energetically involved in the affair. He had talked with Mr. Nixon at least four times by Wednesday evening. In Ehrlichman's opinion it was Colson who was greatly responsible for firing up Mr. Nixon's feelings.

"It was Kissinger who got excited all right," Ehrlichman recalled, "but it was only after Colson talked to Nixon that things began to jell. Colson was responsible for that. Then the President talked to Mitchell and everything began to get going. For about a week there was a meeting every day about the Papers—all kinds of talk about legal measures—and other measures."

"Kissinger heated it up," John Dean recalled. "He pounded his fists on the table. And he talked to Colson. He was livid about it. Colson told me that."* (Colson recalled Nixon heating *him* up, shouting, "I want him [Ellsberg] exposed, Chuck. I don't care how you do it. But get it done. We're going to let the country know what kind of a 'hero' Mr. Ellsberg is. . . . I want those leaks stopped. Don't give me any excuses. I want results. I want them now.")

Haldeman agreed that Kissinger was the prime factor in stirring up Mr. Nixon. The President's first reaction, he insisted, was "muted." "But the Pentagon Papers affair," he added, "so often regarded by the press as a classic example of Nixon's paranoia was Kissinger's premier performance."

Members of Kissinger's staff like Winston Lord (wiretapped by Kissinger but the two somehow continued in mutual respect) agreed that the descriptions of Kissinger's temper tantrums were accurate. "With all my affection for Henry," Lord said, "he could get very excited."

The Kissinger Strategy

The meeting of Thursday, June 17, began with Kissinger offering to his colleagues a sketch of Ellsberg in which he emphasized bizarre and distorted detail likely to capture his listeners' interest and underplayed and misstated his own long friendship and collaboration with Ellsberg.

Kissinger described Ellsberg (there never was a question in his mind that Ellsberg was the source of the Papers) as a genius, "the brightest student [I] ever had." (Ellsberg had not, in fact, been a student of

tions." Possibly Kissinger repeated himself. (Haldeman, *The Ends of Power,* New York, 1978, p. 110)

*Despite Kissinger's collaboration with Colson in arousing Mr. Nixon's concerns about the Pentagon Papers there was no love lost between the two. Kissinger's private code word for Colson was "Mr. Slime." Few, indeed, of the White House intimates had a good word for each other in private. (Personal interview, Lloyd Shearer, 1/19/79)

Kissinger's. Kissinger was eight years older than Ellsberg but they were undergraduates at Harvard together, Henry two years ahead of Dan, and later Ellsberg had been a guest lecturer at Kissinger's seminars.)

Ellsberg had, Kissinger went on, "shot at peasants" in Vietnam and was "always a little unbalanced." Then Kissinger raised the subject of "Drugs." (Ehrlichman capitalized this and marked it with a special star for emphasis.) Ellsberg "flipped from hawk to peacenik," Kissinger said, and, except for an occasion at MIT when Ellsberg had heckled him (this was the encounter of January 1971), he had not seen him for a year and a half. (Conveniently, Kissinger overlooked his meetings of the previous August and September at San Clemente when he tried to recruit Ellsberg once again to do position papers on Vietnam and he did not recall his many other associations with Ellsberg.)

The next notation by Ehrlichman reads, "Murder in Laos . . . by Laos. . . ." Whether Kissinger suggested Ellsberg had committed murder in Laos or had been the victim of a murder plot could not later be deciphered.

(Haldeman recalled Kissinger making charges "that, in my opinion, go beyond belief. Ellsberg, according to Henry, had weird sex habits, used drugs and enjoyed helicopter flights in which he would take potshots at the Vietnamese below.")*

Two sets of the Pentagon Papers, said Kissinger, had been held at Rand. "Ellsberg stole one."

"Like Chambers," interjected the President, referring, of course, to Whittaker Chambers, Mr. Nixon's experiences with the Hiss case still resonating strongly in his mind as they would go on doing, the President often reminding his associates of Hiss and calling on them to read and reread the Hiss chapter in *Six Crises*, pointing out that in the Hiss affair he had managed to "win the PR" despite heavy odds.

Kissinger concluded his word picture with the information that Ellsberg was married to a wealthy girl.

The discussion became general, the President harking back to what he had said earlier and emphasizing that his objective was to "win PR not just court cases." In other words whatever the judicial outcome he wanted a propaganda victory. There was mention of what Ehrlichman called "the Discipline of leaks" in the National Security Council (Kissinger's own organization). The President spoke at a meeting of the council that day and warned that anyone

---

*Haldeman noted that Kissinger's remarks "unfortunately for Henry [were] recorded and may some day be played to standing room audiences." (Haldeman, p. 110) It is only fair to remember that Haldeman and Ehrlichman bore Kissinger little goodwill. This, however, hardly could have affected Ehrlichman's terse notes, jotted down as Kissinger spoke in the Oval Office.

responsible for leaking would be fired.

There was a long disquisition by Mr. Nixon on "PR." He himself would provide catchwords for the campaign and a list was made up of "things to be said."

Ehrlichman recorded Mr. Nixon as saying that he would not comment publicly on the Pentagon case while it was before the courts. He would talk only about the "responsibility of the President." He would point out that politically he was tempted to do nothing. The case involved none of "our decisions," all the actions were prior to the Nixon Administration and would only embarrass the opposition and he was not there to "judge them." But "any President must defend" the right to security in order to preserve freedom of government contacts and the ability to draw freely on advice. Thus, "our policy is and will be in the future," as regards security, "defending the law of the land and the reason for the law."

The President offered the remarkable suggestion that he might argue the case personally before the Supreme Court. He then said, *"The New York Times* is finished in the White House. No pools, etcetera." Here he was referring to the custom of rotating correspondents on "pool assignments," stories in which one or a limited number of correspondents was permitted to accompany the President, sharing reports with their colleagues. No more *Times* men were to get such plums.

Kissinger reentered the conversation to speak of McNamara. He described him as being "in tears" and swearing he "won't betray President Johnson." ("No, no, no," McNamara recalled years later. "Nothing like that happened.")

Kissinger added that "[McGeorge] Bundy wants to come clean." (Bundy later observed, "Henry's comment is typical of the way he sees things through inch-thick plateglass, as I later discovered. I didn't know how melodramatic they were in the White House when this story first broke." Bundy, despite obvious ideological differences with Ellsberg, was to testify as a defense witness at his Los Angeles trial.)

Ehrlichman put a note beside Kissinger's comments on McNamara and Bundy: "Check Johnson."

Ehrlichman ran down the cabinet list and major government offices, the Joint Chiefs, the OMB, the CEA, Secretary of Commerce Maurice Stans (later to be indicted and convicted), Mitchell (ditto), the Treasury and others, noting the President's comment: "Re *N.Y. Times*—cut them off case-by-case, cut them off."

Haldeman mentioned Secretary of State Rogers and the National Security Council but Mr. Nixon interjected sharply, "Forget it!" Apparently the President felt there was no keeping *The Times* out of the State Department and Kissinger's office. Haldeman proposed to add to the boycott list the names of Senator Dole, head of the Republican

National Committee, and Lynn Nofziger, his aide. Here the President's comment was, "Absolutely—RNC [Republican National Committee]. No one talk re politics."

At the bottom of the long list Ehrlichman wrote the President's conclusion: "Return no calls. Don't explain it."

Point No. 21 (Ehrlichman numbered each topic heading) was the flip side of the boycott. It read, "Play Hearst vs. Times." This expressed a simple directive to the administration to favor the Hearst press to the disadvantage of *The New York Times.*

Now Kissinger reentered the conversation with the observation that former Defense Secretary Clark Clifford "had no info" (about the Pentagon Papers) and had gotten what he knew "second-hand via a Congressman."

It was at this point that the question was raised of what Ehrlichman called "The Diehm file," by which, of course, he meant Ngo Dinh Diem, the file on the one-time dictator of South Vietnam, assassinated in the November 1, 1963, coup with, it had long been rumored (a rumor, as was to become apparent, in which Mr. Nixon had profound belief), the complicity of President Kennedy.

Ehrlichman's notes suggest that the question of the Diem affair was raised by the President.

The notation, No. 23, reads:

JFK back channels to Lodge—
Most damaging—
Not in this file—(N.Y. Times)

What this shorthand means in translation is that Mr. Nixon believed President Kennedy had communicated regarding the Diem coup with Henry Cabot Lodge, then ambassador to Saigon, using the so-called back channel, or CIA communications route, so that his messages would not show up in the State Department and White House files. The note "most damaging" implied that the "back channel" traffic would reveal Kennedy's complicity. "Not in this file—(N.Y. Times)" meant that the back-channel traffic was not to be found in the documents of the Pentagon Papers, which had been obtained by *The New York Times.*

How Mr. Nixon or Dr. Kissinger could have known at this point that the back-channel messages were not contained in the 2,500,000 words of Pentagon Papers is difficult to understand. It could, of course, have been an educated guess—if such messages had been included in the Papers *The Times* surely would have played them up. The plain fact was that even at this point, four days after *The Times* had begun to publish the Papers, the government was only beginning, in a haphazard and time-consuming way, to paw through the documents, to find out what was there, what *The Times* had published, and whether there were, in actual fact, any sensitive materials included in the collection.*

Of course Kissinger might have been aware of the absence of the back traffic from his own prior knowledge of the Papers and his close acquaintance with the men who prepared them, men like Ellsberg and Gelb and Halperin.

But most revealing of all was the interest of Mr. Nixon and Dr. Kissinger not in what *The Times* had published, not in what the Pentagon Papers had revealed—but *in what they had not revealed!*

Kissinger's response to the problem of "The Diehm file" and the question of the back-channel traffic to Lodge was spectacularly pragmatic.

"Tell Lodge," he said, "the President needs it—*say* The Times *has it.*" [italics added]†

That ended item No. 23. The next item, No. 24, read: "Double Standard."

Nothing was listed by Ehrlichman under this heading. Or if it was listed it was blanked out by the White House censors before the notes were turned over to the House Judiciary Committee.

Nixon's Obsession

Ehrlichman's yellow sheets revealed many things: that the White House battlewagon was rapidly accelerating into open and unknown territory; that Kissinger had sketched caricatures which the President would utilize in his "PR"; that Ellsberg had been established as the central villain; that a secret program of reprisal against *The New York Times* had been activated.

Most important, however, the Pandora's box of "The Diehm file" had been opened and Kissinger had proposed blackmailing Henry Cabot Lodge to turn over to Mr. Nixon any materials which would

---

*George Wilson, *Washington Post* Pentagon correspondent, by court permission, began to examine the government's master copy of the Pentagon Papers together with J. Fred Buzhardt, Defense Department general counsel, on Monday, June 21. Buzhardt even at this time had only the vaguest notion of what was in the Papers. The dozen or so military researchers who had started going through them were bogged down in the endless detail of trying to match references in *The Times* and the *Post* to the master copy. (Personal interview, Wilson, 1/19/79)

†When years later Lodge was told of the Nixon-Kissinger suggestion to come to him for the back-channel cables he exploded, "I don't think they did it. I never saw anything of them. I saw Haldeman maybe once in his office. I never saw Ehrlichman in his office. And I wouldn't have told them if they had asked me. I never took any classified papers with me when I left office in my life and a good thing, too." (Personal interview, Lodge, 1/9/79; 2/10/79) Charles Colson and Herbert Klein did visit Lodge on one occasion but that was in June 1970 to enlist his support in the ABM controversy. (Personal interview, Klein, 1/16/79; Lodge, 2/10/79)

show John Kennedy's complicity in the assassination on the false grounds that *"The Times* has it."

Amid a conversation ostensibly dedicated to leaks, Kissinger and the President had focused on a subject not dealt with in the Papers, a subject on which it was proposed to pry a different "leak" out of Lodge by means of threats.

Why the concern about Diem and Kennedy? How did this relate to the Pentagon Papers? Why had the topic arisen apparently out of the blue? Mr. Nixon's *Memoirs* offer no light on this question but to those within the White House the answer was easy. They well knew that President Nixon had several fixations. One was the Diem coup. He had long been convinced that President Kennedy had ordered it and was responsible for the assassination. He wanted the evidence which he thought would be a most effective weapon against Teddy Kennedy, whom he saw as his likely opponent in the 1972 election. (Kennedy was currently leading Muskie in the Gallup polls.) He had exhorted his aides about the Diem coup in the past. This was not the first time Mr. Nixon and Dr. Kissinger had discussed the subject nor was it to be the last.

"Nixon had a fixation about the Diem affair," Ehrlichman was to recall. "He had it long before the Pentagon Papers. He came back to it again and again. He felt it was the Achilles' heel of the Kennedys. There was nothing more natural than for him to raise the question in this context. He had reverted to it many times in the past."

There were, in the educated opinion of Pat Buchanan four major foreign policy obsessions of Mr. Nixon. The biggest was that of the Diem coup. Next was the Bay of Pigs in which he had a personal stake, having been, as he described himself, White House "action officer" on the plan, and he harbored strong feelings that President Kennedy deliberately let the operation fail. Another was LBJ's bombing halt and the frantic negotiations with Hanoi in progress in the weeks and days before Mr. Nixon's victory over Hubert Humphrey in November 1972. Mr. Nixon believed (possibly encouraged by the leaks fed to him by Kissinger from the Johnson camp) that LBJ tried to manipulate Vietnamese events to prevent Nixon's election. (Buchanan never could understand why Nixon couldn't get all the information he wanted on the bombing halt from President Thieu of Vietnam with whom he was on excellent terms.)

The fourth obsession was over what Mr. Nixon had described as "a Big History of the Vietnam war," in other words, the Pentagon Papers! Mr. Nixon had a pickup task force at work trying to locate and obtain the Papers at the moment they were being published by *The New York Times.* One member of the force was Pat Buchanan. Mr. Nixon wanted the Papers because he wanted access to the information which they contained. Buchanan had heard that Robert McNamara "had walked out of office with a big history" but he didn't really know what it was. He didn't understand what President Nixon was talking about and he hadn't the foggiest as to where to get hold of it or who might have it in his possession.

Tom Huston, the imaginative author of the "Huston report" for government burglaries, bugging, and bag jobs knew about the Pentagon Papers. He had heard about the study when he was in the Pentagon before he joined Mr. Nixon's White House.

There had been discussion of the Papers with the President and at the moment of *The Times* publication, in his last days before leaving the White House, Huston was working on a report for Mr. Nixon on another of the President's obsessions—the bombing halt. Huston knew, he recalled, that Paul Warnke and some others had taken copies of the Papers with them when they left office but as far as he was aware no one then in government knew where the report was.

"At least I sure didn't," Huston recalled ruefully some years later. "And there was no real heat on getting ahold of it."

The President and Kissinger were not to let go of the Diem affair. They reverted to the subject in another discussion of the Pentagon Papers a few days later, June 23, at which Kissinger was urging the President to "Go on the attack."

Mr. Nixon immediately brought up Diem, this time recalling that the late Marguerite Higgins, war correspondent of the New York *Herald Tribune,* had devoted two chapters of a book to the "murder of Diem."*

Mr. Nixon's reference was to an account which Miss Higgins incorporated in her book *Our Vietnam Nightmare,* published in 1965. Miss Higgins, a partisan of Ngo Dinh Diem, was not in Saigon at the time of his fall, but interviewed a large number of the participants. She made no secret of her antagonism to Ambassador Lodge, State Department officials, including Undersecretary Roger Hilsman, and others whom she blamed for shifting American policy away from Diem. But in conclusion she said that "it was clear to me that [Lodge] had sincerely hoped that Diem's murder could be avoided. It had also been President Kennedy's hope." She quoted Lodge's last conversation with Diem in which he expressed concern for Diem's safety and offered to help get

---

*In the same conversation Mr. Nixon suggested that Willard Edwards or Walter Trohan, correspondents of the *Chicago Tribune,* be asked to request the government to release more "secret material"—on World War II and the Bay of Pigs, material, it was clear, that Mr. Nixon felt would be embarrassing to the Democrats. Unlike Dr. Kissinger, who as late as 1978 said he opposed "use of the classification system for political purposes," Mr. Nixon didn't mind. (House Judiciary Committee, Appendix III, p. 109; personal interview, Kissinger, 10/26/78)

him out of the country. Higgins' book, in a word, proved directly the opposite of what Mr. Nixon thought (and wished) it to prove.§

The President's fascination with the Diem coup accelerated week by week. On July 9 he was again talking about it, this time with Ehrlichman and Haldeman, his interest centering on Lieutenant Colonel Lucien Conein, a colorful officer who acted as CIA liaison with the Vietnam generals who plotted the overthrow of Diem. Mr. Nixon appeared to believe that Conein, like Miss Higgins, possessed special inside knowledge of a Kennedy hand in the Diem killing. Conein, as the President probably had been told, had already been extensively interviewed by a new White House undercover operative, taken on only July 6 by Charles Colson. This was Howard Hunt, a former CIA man, and his activities in the next weeks and months were to escalate into the sensational cloak-and-dagger operations central to Mr. Nixon's downfall—the break-in of the office of Ellsberg's psychiatrist in Los Angeles, the bizarre interrogation of Dita Beard in Denver with wig and voice-changer provided by the CIA, a sophomoric effort to fabricate the evidence which Mr. Nixon vainly had sought in the government files—evidence of John Kennedy's hand in the Diem death*— and finally Watergate itself.

The Kennedy Fixation

Mr. Nixon was to offer his most revealing philosophical exposition concerning the Pentagon Papers in a long discussion with Attorney General Mitchell, Haldeman and Ehrlichman on September 18. He wasted no words on security matters. He set the Papers in a pure political context, emphasizing how to use them to put the Democrats on the spot on the Vietnam war. The problem, as he saw it, was to keep the issue alive "front and center" and the method which he proposed was through "Leaks, columns," that is, while inveighing against leaking government information, he would utilize selective leaking in order to make his own political points. He realized that his administration had certain "vulnerabilities"—he cited both Kissinger and Richardson— but believed that he could get the Democrats squabbling about the origins of the war and this would play into his hands.

§See Notes section.
*Later there was to be public confusion as to whether and when Mr. Nixon knew about the employment of Howard Hunt. He obviously was "witting" from the start. At the White House meeting of July 9 there was some discussion over Hunt and "memoirs" which Colson apparently had told Mr. Nixon Hunt had written. Mr. Nixon suggested a "Look (magazine) series for Hunt's memoirs" but exactly how the Hunt material was to be placed with *Look* was not spelled out. At the same meeting Ehrlichman advised Mr. Nixon that he had in hand Tom Huston's final report on the LBJ bombing halt. (House Judiciary Committee, Appendix III, pp. 131–132.)

The way to do this, he said, was to get a senator to put out a revelation of the details of the coup which overthrew Diem. This, he said, was "A Kennedy target" and the coup was the best ground for attacking the Democrats because Averell Harriman, a Muskie supporter, was involved, and so was Teddy Kennedy. He had always been critical of the way the press covered the Diem coup. The press, in his words, had been "afraid of that affair. They wanted the killing."

In his opinion, it was the assassination of Diem that "triggered the whole war." (He didn't explain how.) He thought that "LBJ can be with us on this" because Mr. Johnson "keeps saying that JFK started the Vietnam war—he is right."*

The question was, How to get this story out? General Paul D. Harkins, American commander in Vietnam at the time of the coup, had been opposed to the coup. He might talk and evidence should be available through Conein and General Edward G. Lansdale, the counterinsurgency expert.

The President pointed out that he had set the stage for putting the story on page one with a remark two days earlier at his press conference. In answer to a question from Peter Lisagor of the *Chicago Daily News* he had said, "I would remind all concerned that the way we got into Vietnam was through overthrowing Diem and the complicity in the murder of Diem; and the way to get out of Vietnam, in my opinion, is not to overthrow Thieu."

The reporters hadn't known what to make of Mr. Nixon's remark. Not many of them attempted to deal with it and it had fallen like a dud.† Now, Mr. Nixon suggested, one way to get the story going would be for a senator (he suggested Brock or Taft) to pick up the statement and demand that "Conein be released from silence" and "let the CIA take a whipping on this."

The puzzling part of Mr. Nixon's suggestion was that he was now proposing to go back over the very ground which Howard Hunt had painstakingly explored in early July just after the Pentagon Papers came out. In fact, Hunt's first assignment was an interview with Lou Conein

---

*It is probable that Lyndon Johnson stimulated Nixon's belief that Kennedy ordered Diem killed. As early as the weekend of January 4–5, 1964, while on the LBJ ranch, Johnson told Tom Wicker of *The Times,* Doug Kiker of the *Herald Tribune* and Phil Potter of the *Baltimore Sun* that the CIA had a hand in killing Diem (and others). He put the remark off the record. Johnson made the same statement to others and very likely to Nixon. (Tom Wicker, *On Press,* New York, 1978, pp. 190–92)

†As late as May 1973 after Hunt's forged cables had finally been revealed reporters were still trying to figure out their connection, if any, with Mr. Nixon's remark of September 16, 1971. To anyone who had sat in on Mr. Nixon's many discussions of the Pentagon Papers from the beginning, Thursday, June 17 (and perhaps earlier), it was apparent that he had sought all along to turn the Pentagon affair into an anti-Kennedy affair, keyed to the Diem assassination.

about the Diem assassination. Hunt had known Conein in his CIA days. He invited him to the White House and the two men talked lengthily in Ehrlichman's office over a bottle or two of scotch. Hunt didn't bother to take notes because a recording device had been concealed under the cushions of the sofa where they sat. The next morning Hunt found that the tape recorder had been crushed by their weight and had malfunctioned. So had his memory under the influence of multiple potions of whiskey. He called Conein on the telephone and with Charles Colson listening on an extension went over the whole conversation again. It was a bust. Conein knew all about the coup, its support by Ambassador Lodge and by President Kennedy in Washington. But there was no "smoking pistol" to show a link to the assassination.§

Hunt next interviewed Lansdale. By this time he had his office equipped with microphones and a Sony recorder in the lower right-hand drawer of his desk. Technically, the interview went excellently. Hunt covered much of the same ground he had covered with Conein. But again—no smoking gun. Later he talked to General Harkins in Texas. Harkins had been close to Diem, had opposed the coup, had been at odds with Lodge but he, too, had no smoking gun.

The CIA

In view of Hunt's lack of success with Conein, Lansdale and Harkins the persistence of Mr. Nixon's hope that the trio would provide evidence for his theory that President Kennedy fingered Diem seemed odd. But Mr. Nixon did not propose to rely alone on these three witnesses. He initiated stronger measures. He told Ehrlichman and Haldeman that by next Friday, that is September 26, 1971, he wanted the CIA to turn over "the entire Diem file" because his remark about Diem in the press conference had been "questioned." Moreover, he insisted on having the "full file" (Ehrlichman double-underlined the word "full") on the Bay of Pigs "or else." Ehrlichman put a star beside this note. Nothing was to be withheld. As to why Mr. Nixon needed these materials the rationale to the CIA would be that he was "deeply involved in the Bay of Pigs and must know all the facts." Again the word "all" was underlined. Egil Krogh, now head of the Plumbers, was to be filled in on this.

Richard Helms, CIA director, was to be told that the President was on the CIA's side but that "as questions arise [he] must be armed." Moreover, the President observed they must speed up getting their own man, General Vernon A. Walters, then military attaché in Paris, into the CIA.

§See Notes section.

The President didn't want to be personally involved in this. Kissinger, for example, was to report to Ehrlichman. What he was to report upon is not clear because two paragraphs of the discussion were deleted at this point by the White House. When the CIA files were obtained they were to be turned over to Richard V. Allen, an operative on the President's security staff, Charles Huston, long since out of the White House,* Gordon Liddy of the Plumbers and, to be certain, Howard Hunt.

The State Department quickly responded to Mr. Nixon's demands and by September 20, at the request of David Young of the Plumbers, Howard Hunt was able to examine the files and photocopy 240 cables.

The CIA was more difficult. Ehrlichman approached Helms directly at Mr. Nixon's order but, as Ehrlichman remembered it, "Helms stonewalled me." Mr. Nixon recalled that Helms refused to give Ehrlichman copies of either the Diem or the Bay of Pigs files and expressed concern that Howard Hunt wanted to "run around in the agency's soiled linen," as Mr. Nixon put it.

Mr. Nixon intervened and on October 8 Helms went to the White House. "Mr. Nixon decided to top Helms," Ehrlichman recalled, "and so he had me present for the meeting."

The President told Helms that he must have these materials because he "must be fully advised in order to know what to duck" and for "upcoming meetings next year." When Mr. Nixon pledged that he would not "hurt the Agency or attack predecessors," Helms responded that "I only have one President at a time. I work only for you."

Helms told Mr. Nixon that he had "found a document and wanted the President to know that it is in fragments." He handed over to Mr. Nixon an envelope which the President placed in the drawer of his desk.

Ehrlichman believed that Helms wanted to be absolutely certain that Ehrlichman had the presidential writ in this matter and the President satisfied this doubt (if it existed) by saying to Helms, "Ehrlichman is my lawyer—deal with him on this as you would me." To which Ehrlichman added, "I'll be making requests for more material."

"Okay," Helms said. "Anything."

---

*Later Huston was to be puzzled by this reference. He did, in fact, come back to Washington for one weekend in October to finish up his report on the bombing halt, which had not, despite Ehrlichman's statement to the President on July 9 that he had it in hand, been completed. He was not brought in on the Diem affair, he said. As to the bombing halt that, too, proved a disappointment for Mr. Nixon. Huston said he did not find "anything very exciting." He concluded that, in fact, LBJ did not manipulate the talks in Paris in order to assist the election prospects of Humphrey and "that's why I took issue with Bill Safire," who claimed the contrary in his book. (Personal interview, Huston, 2/9/79)

Ehrlichman carefully marked his notes of this discussion NODIS. NODIS was the highest existing security classification. It meant no copies went to anyone. These were the only pages in the available Ehrlichman notes so marked.

Exactly what was in the envelope which Helms handed to Mr. Nixon has never been revealed. The President turned it over to Ehrlichman, whose recollection later, supported by that of Nixon, was that "Helms didn't give the President what he was looking for. It was rather inconsequential stuff."

Mr. Nixon exclaimed in his *Memoirs,* "The CIA was closed like a safe and we could find no one who would give us the combination to open it."

Years later Ehrlichman was still convinced that Helms never gave Mr. Nixon "all the inside dope."

Helms' recollection varied significantly from that of Mr. Nixon and Ehrlichman. The matter started with a telephone call from Ehrlichman, as Helms recalled. He asked Ehrlichman to join him at breakfast and at that meeting Ehrlichman asked for a full report on Diem, Trujillo and the Bay of Pigs. Helms said he would find out what was available. He said he had not been involved in the Bay of Pigs. He was assistant to Richard Bissell, who was in charge of the ill-fated operation but had had no taste for it from the beginning and had formally requested Allen Dulles to cut him out and this was done.

There were, of course, whole safes in the CIA filled with material on these matters. Since other Presidents than Nixon had been involved Helms felt that he "damn well better be certain that Mr. Nixon" actually wanted the materials.

When he had put together what he thought were the pertinent documents he called Ehrlichman and said he would like to see the President. He insisted on seeing him and handing the files to him personally.

Helms took the data, bound separately in three binders and enclosed in a large manila envelope, to his meeting with the President, handed it to Mr. Nixon, and the President, as Helms recalled, put the envelope into his drawer unopened.

The conversation with the President, Helms recalled (and his recollection was supported by Ehrlichman's notes), began with discussion of J. Edgar Hoover and whether he might be persuaded to resign. (This was recorded by Ehrlichman as "Cooperation of FBI with Intell. Commun . . . extremely delicate . . . H and when to quit.")

Neither Mr. Nixon nor Ehrlichman, in Helms' recollection, complained about the data which he submitted nor did Helms ever figure out what they wanted. "I still do not understand," he reflected in 1979. "Mr. Nixon was a very curious man. He was paranoid about some

things. Obviously, he thought there was something there on Kennedy."
To Helms' recollection Mr. Nixon never asked for anything more
although in his *Memoirs* he asserted that he had.*

But what was it that Mr. Nixon hoped to find?

Not, in Ehrlichman's estimation, information about CIA plots
against Castro, schemes for assassination and the like which surfaced
later as a result of the Rockefeller and Senate investigations. It was
something quite different, something that had to do with operational
judgments, orders given, decisions taken. Exactly what these might
have been Ehrlichman was not prepared to guess. He was certain that
Mr. Nixon's preoccupation with the Bay of Pigs, like his preoccupation
with the Diem affair, was linked to what he called Nixon's "JFK
syndrome." Mr. Nixon was firmly convinced that the threat of a candidacy by Teddy Kennedy was best met by discrediting the Kennedy
Administration and that there was evidence in the Bay of Pigs to
support this endeavor.

John Dean recollected that he had been puzzled about Mr. Nixon's
preoccupation with the Bay of Pigs. "It was always as big a mystery to
me as anything in the White House," he said later. He had heard many
theories, even including a rumor that Nixon knew that the Bay of Pigs
had been sabotaged and knew Helms was withholding evidence of that.
In his opinion Ehrlichman should be the best witness to all this and
if he did not know Mr. Nixon's secret probably no one knew.

Howard Hunt of all people should have been able to divine the
nature of Mr. Nixon's interest in the Bay of Pigs. Hunt not only was
a considerable figure in the CIA operation but was privy to the White
House concern over it. He, too, confessed in later years that he was
baffled. He suggested that perhaps Mr. Nixon's interest was whetted
because Helms did not promptly pass over the Bay of Pigs files. "You
know Mr. Nixon's personality," he said, "he was a rather peculiar man.
When his requests were turned down perhaps this made him certain
the CIA was hiding something. His thought didn't follow a logical
pattern."

Whatever it was it would appear that in the end Mr. Nixon was
never to be satisfied. He did not get what he wanted from Helms nor
was he to do any better with his fixation about the Diem coup.

The 240 State Department cables were carefully scanned by Howard
Hunt. Later, he was to say that he found some missing serial numbers
and suspected some cables had been extricated from the files by
Kennedy officials for the JFK library at Cambridge but he never was
to search the Cambridge files for the missing serials. He looked through
the back-channel files of the CIA. Nothing there. If Helms turned over

*Helms offered his version of this affair in a personal interview, July 19, 1979.

any tightly held CIA traffic on Diem to Nixon it was never passed on to Hunt. He got no real cooperation from the Department of Defense.

"I told Liddy [A. Gordon Liddy, to be convicted with Hunt in the Plumbers operation] that he had to get the military traffic," Hunt recalled. "He went to Buzhardt and Buzhardt gave him a hard time. Finally he got some kind of a half-assed response. 'We are unable to find anything in response to your inquiry.'"

Conein's story, Hunt recalled, fitted the picture presented by the cables. But there was still a missing link. Hunt felt (and felt years later) that anyone reading the whole file could be in little doubt of the complicity of the Kennedy Administration in the Diem affair but the evidence he had been seeking was not present.

"There was no smoking gun. It just wasn't there," said Hunt. "That's why I was told to make up the cables."

And make up two cables he did at Charles Colson's instruction. He couched them in State Departmentese. The important one he dated October 29, 1963, three days before the Diem coup, and placed in it the words he had not been able to find in the real message traffic:

"At highest level meeting today decision reluctantly made that neither you nor Harkins should intervene on behalf of Diem or Nhu [his brother] in event they seek asylum."

Colson and Hunt made every effort to foist the false cable onto investigative reporter Bill Lambert of *Life* magazine. But Lambert could not be persuaded of its genuineness. In the end the only person to be taken in by the forged document was Conein. Conein had given an interview to NBC for a not-yet-released documentary on Vietnam. Hunt showed his forged documents to Conein, who accepted them as genuine, saying, "Funny, the things you don't know about when you are working in the field." At the suggestion of White House aide John Scali NBC refilmed the Conein interview so that he could grind the forged cable into his comment. The doctored documentary (neither NBC nor Conein knew it was doctored) was shown December 22–23, 1971.

Thus, for all Mr. Nixon's effort, the attempt to employ the Pentagon affair as a springboard from which to launch a propaganda petard which would destroy his Democratic opponents with revelations, genuine or contrived, about President Kennedy misfired.

Instead the apparatus which Mr. Nixon called into being—the Plumbers, the freewheeling combination of Charles Colson, Howard Hunt, A. Gordon Liddy and the others, the assortment of illegal and clandestine activities which flourished in the White House around the Pentagon affair grew into a vehicle which was to carry Mr. Nixon faster and faster down slippery heights, from break-ins of the Ellsberg psychiatrist's office to bugging, wiretapping, dirty tricks, the whole chamber of what Attorney General Mitchell ultimately was to call the "White House horrors" which took on the form of Watergate and sank the White House and Mr. Nixon with it.

To the outside world there was no hint of such activities. In Washington and in New York all attention was focused on the trial of law, press *versus* government. Judge Gurfein had set argument on *The New York Times* case for Friday, June 18. The whole thrust of *The Times* had shifted away from the Pentagon story toward an endeavor which was possibly of greater significance, the task of sustaining in the federal courts the right of a newspaper, inviolate since the time of the First Amendment to the Constitution, to publish "without fear or favor," without prior restraint, to publish without halters around the necks of printers and pressmen, regardless of the contents of the newspaper, a right unchallenged for a century and three quarters.

The Times did not, of course, demand immunity for anything it published. It was prepared to publish and face the courts on the consequences. But it was not prepared to accept precensorship by a government which sought to impose the restriction before it saw the newspaper and its published contents.

There had been no such case in the history of *The Times,* either before Mr. Ochs' tenure or in the period of his ownership and that of his heirs.

This was not to say that carrying forward the banner of a newspaper's right to publish was unusual to *The Times.* True, in the years of Mr. Ochs' regime no legal actions more serious than libel cases had been brought (and Mr. Ochs had early on made a rule to fight every case and had a notable record of winning almost every one). The same had been true in the era of Arthur Hays Sulzberger and Orvil Dryfoos. Mr. Loeb had been extremely proud that in the years in which Lord, Day and Lord represented *The Times* the newspaper had never been compelled to pay one single dollar in settlement of a libel action.

But this had gradually changed. This was not the first time that *The Times* had been compelled to go to court to fight for its basic right of publication. It had already been confronted in 1960 with the great challenge of the Alabama cases, arising from its frank and vigorous coverage of the Civil Rights movement in the South. It had won these cases and by so doing had remarkably strengthened and broadened the legal rights of the newspapers and electronic media in their coverage of public issues, political figures and political affairs. The Montgomery and Birmingham cases had become a new magna carta for the press.

Now *The Times* moved forward to a new and far more implicit challenge. The preparations of the newspaper were being made accordingly.

25

Traffic in Secrets

T ELEPHONES RANG EARLY and late during the Pentagon Papers crisis. Max Frankel's started ringing again about 7 A.M. Tuesday morning, June 15. His wife, Tobi, answered and handed the receiver to her sleepy husband. It was Goodale calling from New York. Both men had been up half the night, Goodale putting together the team of Bickel and Abrams to defend *The Times* against the government's expected action, Frankel writing the story from Washington of Attorney General Mitchell's effort to halt *The Times'* publication of the Pentagon Papers.

Goodale's message was urgent: "Get out of town!"

It had suddenly occurred to Goodale that the government might serve *The Times* in Washington. This he didn't want. *The Times* was preparing to defend its action in New York and he didn't want Frankel, the responsible *Times* executive, unexpectedly faced with service in a suit in Washington.

Frankel and his deputy, Bob Phelps, caught the 9 A.M. shuttle for New York. Frankel's immediate task now became an effort to round up from distinguished government officials, former government officials for the most part, affidavits to be used in support of *The Times* in the injunction proceeding. He and other *Times* men went down the list. The first to be tackled was McNamara, who had, after all, commissioned the study and who had (although neither he nor *The Times* now remembered it) been publicly quoted in *The Times Magazine* of November 1969 as saying the Pentagon Papers had been prepared for the purpose of writing the "definitive history of the Vietnam war," a formulation which certainly would have lent strong support to *The Times'* position. McNamara did not now wish to come forward. He said he was glad that the Papers had been published (his enthusiasm was not exactly overwhelming) and that he had originally hoped to put the study out immediately on completion (indicating that he, at least, had no fears that this would violate security) but when he had gone to President Johnson the President refused to give his approval. Now he did not think an affidavit appropriate. He didn't actually know what was in the Papers, had never read them and had rather not do it.

When *The Times'* counsel heard that LBJ had opposed release of the Papers they decided that McNamara's was testimony they did not need. The search went forward. Mac Bundy was tackled but refused. Later he was to become more philosophical about the Papers but at this moment he was quite bitter. Frankel had no luck with Nicholas Katzenbach, who had been Undersecretary of State and also Attorney General under Johnson, nor with Cyrus Vance nor George Ball. No one thought of asking Senator Fulbright. No one on *The Times* knew of his speech on the Senate floor nearly a year earlier calling upon the press to find and publish the Papers or of his public attacks in recent weeks on the classification system and the government's action in withholding the Pentagon Papers. Affidavits were obtained from Theodore Sorensen, who had been counsel to President Kennedy and who had, as a matter of fact, used classified materials in his book about President Kennedy, and from Barbara Tuchman, the historian, who said that publication of the Pentagon Papers "far from harming the national interest would serve it."

It was just as well that echelons of government officials did not rush forward with sworn statements upholding *The New York Times.* Had they done so it is possible that Frankel would not have turned to his typewriter and written what was to become the classic statement of the real-time relationship between government and the press, between the official and the reporter, a chart to the symbiosis among their intertwined ganglia. The Frankel affidavit, like the pail of water thrown on the old witch, dissolved the whole hypocritical, self-serving declension of "official secrets" and "classification" into a pool of rather dirty water.

No one, no judge, no ordinary citizen, no official, no editor after reading Frankel's case-by-case analysis of how government really operated could longer hold the delusion that the classification system was designed to keep secrets from the press. They could not but accept Frankel's common-sensical view that the principal purpose of "classification" was to create a stock of "secrets" which could be traded to reporters for headlines just as the Dutch traded wampum to the Indians for Manhattan Island; to provide a peddler's bag of news trinkets which could be cashed in to support a bureaucratic position or enhance a bureaucrat's reputation; to enable backers of a big Navy to stick an elbow in the eye of their Air Force competitors for government funds; to shove an unwary cabinet officer onto the banana peel of a slippery statistic; to fudge a President's credibility problem; to score a debating point against an opposing politician, et cetera,
et cetera,
et cetera.

Max set out to compose a brief memo to the lawyers to explain how Washington worked. Before he was through he had written an eighteen-page affidavit to which were attached seventy-two pages of exhibits.§

Drawing on his experience as a diplomatic and foreign correspondent, Frankel wrote:

"Without the use of 'secrets' there could be no adequate diplomatic, military and political reporting of the kind our people takes for granted . . . there could be no mature system of communication between the Government and the people." The Government, said Frankel, "is our regular partner in the informal but customary traffic in secret information, without even the pretense of legal or formal 'declassification' . . .

"To promote a political, personal, bureaucratic or even commercial interest incumbent officials and officials who return to civilian life are constantly revealing the secrets entrusted to them. They use them to barter with Congress or the press, to curry favor with foreign governments, and officials from whom they seek information in return. They use them freely and with a startling record of impunity, in their memoirs and other writings."

He told how officials employed classification to conceal mistakes of judgment, to protect reputations, to cover up losses or mistakes. He conceded that there were a few genuine secrets in military and foreign affairs but insisted that the government process, in general, was inseparable from what he called "traffic in secrets."

He submitted a glorious compendium of ad hoc "declassifications" by public officials to serve their interests—President Johnson standing beside Frankel, waist-deep in his Texas swimming pool recounting the secret details of discussions with Premier Kosygin at Glassboro, New Jersey; a State Department official letting Frankel take verbatim notes of a Gromyko-Kennedy conversation to demonstrate "Gromyko's perfidy" in denying knowledge of the Cuban missiles; Secretary of State Rusk telling Frankel in 1961 that Laos wasn't worth the life of a single Kansas farm boy and that SEATO was useless; President Kennedy offering exact quotes of arguments with Gromyko over the Berlin Wall in order to demonstrate Kennedy's toughness and many, many more.

Frankel cited recent books, memoirs of President Johnson, reminiscences of the Kennedy era and studies of the Vietnam war which drew freely, extensively and routinely upon so-called classified materials.

In foreign affairs, Frankel declared, the government rarely gave the press the full information it needed for the purpose of informing the people. For the most part the press obtained significant facts by making itself "a party to confidential materials" and acting as a conduit of this

§See Notes section.

information to other government departments and to the public at large. Without this service the government would literally be unable to function.

"This is why," Frankel concluded, "the press has been wisely and correctly called the Fourth Branch of Government."

Frankel, of course, had no way of knowing the character of the discussions now going forward in the Oval Office between Messrs. Nixon, Kissinger, Haldeman and Ehrlichman, the talk of "leaking" special information in support of the campaign against leaks, the release of classified information (and eventually the "manufacture" of classified information) in support of the President's objectives, but had Frankel had access to the still-undisclosed White House taping system it would have fully supported his thesis. Indeed, government and diplomacy had been conducted in the manner he described since the days of Machiavelli and long before.

There is no way of measuring the impact of Frankel's affidavit on the courts, of relating its role to the thinking, for example, of Judge Gurfein. But Frankel recognized that his blunt and unadorned thesis might shock and surprise many, even including those privy to the procedures he outlined.

He described the manner in which "a small and specialized corps of reporters and a few hundred American officials" regularly made use of "so-called classified, secret and top secret information and documentation," a ritual which "mystifies even experienced professionals in many fields, including those with government experience and including the most astute politicians and attorneys."

It was because this exchange of "secrets" had become so routine that "the sudden complaint by one party to these regular dealings strikes us as monstrous and hypocritical—unless it is essentially perfunctory for the purpose of retaining some discipline over the federal bureaucracy."

Frankel conceded "how strange all this must sound" to a generation taught by spy scares and the cold war "to think of secrets as *secrets.*" But, he said, "by the standards of official Washington—government and press alike—this is an antiquated, quaint and romantic view" for the reason that almost everything "that our government does, plans, thinks, hears and contemplates in the realms of foreign policy is stamped and treated as secret—and then unraveled by that same government, by the Congress and by the press in one continuing round of professional and social contacts and cooperative and competitive exchanges of information."

Whatever their effect on the courts, Frankel's words profoundly influenced *The Times'* defense team. Even for attorneys like Goodale, Frankel's logic came like an icy plunge into shadowless truth. Instantly the lawyers (and everyone who read Frankel's words) knew that *this* was the way it really was; this was the heart of the matter and any other constructs were tendentious, self-serving or overblown.

The Line-up

The Times had assembled a powerful legal team. Its core was Goodale, Bickel, Abrams and two other Cahill Gordon partners, William E. Hegarty and Lawrence McKay, backed by seventeen Cahill associates. Goodale had never worked with such an aggregate. "Formidable" was the word most often used to describe it. Legal scholars who later examined the sixty-three-page brief which Cahill Gordon prepared for Judge Gurfein were to call it a dazzling exercise, a document which put the government's short and cursory statement to shame.

The government's presentation was in the hands of two extremely able lawyers, men of high skill, professional and personal reputation, Whitney North Seymour, Jr., the U.S. District Attorney for the Southern District of New York, and his number one aide, Michael Hess. Both were experienced men, widely respected. Back of them, however, was no such team as had been fielded by Cahill Gordon. Back of them was Robert C. Mardian and the Justice Department staff that he had assembled. Later, those who participated in the trial were to conclude that it was Mardian who gave the case its Kafka-like quality.

Mardian came from a large family of Armenian origin that had located in Phoenix, Arizona. His father was a successful and prosperous contractor and Mardian had participated in the family business. He was a close friend of Richard Kleindienst, a neighbor in Phoenix, in fact, and through Kleindienst had joined the Goldwater presidential campaign. Kleindienst brought him into the Justice Department where with William Rehnquist the three formed what was sometimes called the Arizona mafia. The men possessed radically differing temperaments. Rehnquist was a cool, analytic ultraconservative who soon was to be given a chance to preach his philosophy from the bench of the U.S. Supreme Court. Kleindienst was a puzzle to many, affable, warm, intelligent but ultimately caught up in the muddy currents of Watergate. Mardian was a man about whom people formed quick and strong opinions. Looking back on him, Haldeman, who himself had the reputation of abrasiveness, said, "Mardian was very abrasive. It may sound funny for me to say that—but it was so." Mardian ran with the ball, Haldeman felt, but he carried it the way Mitchell wanted it carried. John Dean recalled that he took a behind-the-scenes role in the Pentagon case because of Mardian. He telephoned Whitney North Seymour, offering the help of his office (he was then President Nixon's White House counsel) because, as he said, "Seymour had considerable dismay in dealing with Washington personalities, particularly Bob Mardian, who was very emotional." Dean assigned Fred Fielding from his office

to work with Seymour and heard later that Seymour found this cooperation helpful because "it was legal and not emotional."

Herb Klein, Nixon's press coordinator, liked Mardian, thought he
"was very strong" but conceded he was probably a factor in stirring
things up on the Pentagon Papers. Ehrlichman described him as "most
diligent and zealous," positively not freewheeling, not operating on his
own. Mardian was, Ehrlichman felt certain, doing precisely what
Mitchell and, most of all, what Nixon wanted him to do. Mardian was
an instrument not a prime mover. Be that as it may, Mardian won the
nickname around Justice Department corridors of "Crazy Bob." He
was not well liked by many associates; J. Edgar Hoover did not get on
with him, nor did he win the love of Seymour and Hess, both of whom
found him "difficult" at best and "dangerous" in his overall approach.

Judge Gurfein was largely an unknown quantity to everyone in the case.
He had begun his legal career in the district attorney's office under
Thomas E. Dewey before World War II. He was one of the bright
young lawyers whom Dewey gathered about him in his gang-buster
days of the 1930s. Gurfein was a native New Yorker, a Harvard Law
graduate, class of 1930, and one of Dewey's original assistants, becoming chief of Dewey's Rackets Investigating Bureau. Like so many energetic rising New York lawyers, he was tapped by William (Wild Bill)
Donovan for the OSS, serving first in New York with Allen Dulles.
When Dulles went to Switzerland, Gurfein went to London and
worked under David Bruce, sharing a flat for a time with Frederick
Oechsner, who had headed UPI's Berlin bureau in the days of Hitler's
rise. Gurfein became one of Eisenhower's top men in strategic intelligence and psychological warfare and was a close friend of Richard
Crossman, the great English labor diarist, cabinet member and editor.

This was no ordinary run-of-the-mill jurist. Gurfein knew intelligence and had worked on Robert Jackson's prosecution staff at the
Nuremberg war trials. He was, as he was later to describe himself, "an
old civil liberties buff" and had a deep feeling about freedom of the
press. Out of wartime experience he had a personal understanding of
security matters and, as he once said, "I would have cut off my right
arm rather than steal a classified document."

Gurfein had been named to the bench by Senator Jacob Javits with
the support of Senator James Buckley and was, as he described it, "a
Republican conservative in economics." His old friend Tom Dewey
had advanced his name for the post. Even before the Pentagon arguments opened Gurfein had an excellent grasp of the law. He had
followed First Amendment cases through the courts and knew that
only one case actually bore on the Pentagon matter, this being *Near*
v. *Minnesota,* in which the Supreme Court had many years ago out-

lawed a so-called Minnesota gag law. "That was as close as I was going to get," he recalled, "and that simplified the matter to some extent."

Gurfein was to the attorneys on both sides more or less of an enigma. There was a feeling that he must be of a conservative bent. He had not been identified with controversial public causes. The attorneys for *The Times* had no reason to suppose that he would be particularly support- ive. This was not suggested by his background or by the fact that he was a brand-new Nixon appointee. The gossip around Foley Square was that Gurfein probably would be cautious, conservative and, given his OSS background, quite strongly opposed to those who made public secret documents and intelligence assessments. In the event, as Mi- chael Hess said later, "Gurfein was a marvelous judge. We were lucky we had him."

Arguments

Before Judge Gurfein began to hear arguments in the Pentagon Papers case Friday two critical but hardly noticed events had occurred.

Michael Hess, on behalf of the government, filed a motion asking *The Times* to produce the Pentagon Papers and other documents which it held. Gurfein set argument on this motion for Thursday morning. Hess felt this was important because there was confusion over what documents *The Times* had. Some of those published did not seem to be part of the Pentagon Papers. (In fact *The Times* had a mishmash of papers including working papers, first drafts and auxiliary studies as well as the Pentagon documents themselves.)

Abrams and Bickel worked most of the night preparing for this and other challenges. Since Abrams had done most of the research and Bickel didn't get to bed until 5 A.M. it was decided that Abrams would argue the point before Gurfein.

The question was more important than it seemed. If, as Abrams believed was likely, Gurfein ordered the documents presented in court he knew that *The Times* would refuse. There was no question on this point. The documents carried handwritten notations, fingerprints and other detail which *The Times* believed would lead the government and the FBI to the source of the Papers and enable it to identify for possible criminal action those who participated in the project.

If the judge ordered production of the documents and *The Times* refused, the paper would be held in contempt of court, and this, to say the least, would change the psychological if not the legal atmosphere. The case would move forward to the Court of Appeals and the Su- preme Court as a contempt case rather than a freedom-of-the-press case and Abrams well knew that judges have a special sensitivity on contempt-of-court matters and are likely to support their lower judges or at least to examine with extreme care the reasons for the contempt.

But Abrams' first exchange with Gurfein gave him great hope. Gurfein immediately said, "The Caldwell case gives you a lot of protection. There is a tremendous privilege there." (This was the case of *Times* reporter Earl Caldwell, still standing on appeal from the Ninth Circuit Court of Appeals on the Pacific Coast to the U.S. Supreme Court.)

The Times' position was that it would not turn over the documents nor agree to a proposal by Hess that they be examined in front of the judge.

But Gurfein, trying to find reasonable compromises, came up with one which satisfied both government and *The Times.* He suggested that *The Times* submit a list of the documents that it held. Hess agreed to this, and Abrams, with a sigh of relief, accepted for *The Times.* Later Abrams was to say, "The case may have been saved that morning. A great danger had been avoided because Gurfein thought of a way around it."

The next crisis came a few hours later and was totally private. There was a meeting Thursday night in the board room of *The Times* attended by Sulzberger, Goodale, Reston, Bancroft, Rosenthal, Tom Wicker, Frankel, Larry McKay, Bickel and Abrams.

The question was put, What to do if the court rules against *The Times:* Obey? Defy?

It was an issue closely linked with that which Abrams had successfully navigated with Gurfein earlier in the day. Abrams and McKay spoke strongly along the lines of the thinking that had motivated Abrams' concern over producing the documents in court. The most important thing, they said, was to win the case. This was paramount and to that end they should not get the judges angry at *The Times.* They spoke on a simple basis of tactics.

But Bickel, who quickly emerged as the commanding figure, addressed the question of principle. He made the broad argument that whatever the outcome the case would be lost if *The Times* did not respect the order of the court. What was at issue was the use of the judicial system to correct an abuse of executive power. You could not seek that redress from the courts and at the same time defy due process of law in the manner you accused the government of doing. He granted that there could well be cases in which it was necessary and right to test an order of a court. But he did not believe this rule applied in the present case.

This critical discussion was to have great bearing on future conduct of the case. Abrams and Bickel knew that the question of defying the court was not merely theoretical. Abe Rosenthal had raised it already. He had strongly stated his objections in principle to permitting a court, any court, to dictate to *The Times* what it could or could not publish. He expressed this concern first on Tuesday when Gurfein handed down his temporary restraining order. Rosenthal said that he was going along with the temporary restraining order but he spoke of his extreme distress that *The Times* should be in a position in which it had promised to obey a court order. He had been opposed to the line in *The Times*' rejoinder to Mitchell which said the paper "will of course abide by the final decision of the court." He had told Abrams that he was not advocating defiance of the temporary restraining order but he was seriously disturbed about it and about future commitments which seemed to give the courts a hand in the editing of *The Times.*

The situation was critical from the legal viewpoint. If *The Times* was headed toward outright defiance and publication regardless of what the courts did the lawyers should know, must know in fact, in order to take into account that explosive possibility.

When Bickel made his presentation Punch quickly spoke up and said, "Well, I guess it's agreed. We will obey the order."

Tom Wicker, sitting at the end of the table responded, "I didn't hear any vote on that, Punch, is the discussion over?"

"No, indeed," Punch replied. "Is there anything you want to add?"

There was. Wicker spoke briefly of the dangerous precedent that might be set if *The Times* lost its case before Gurfein and then, as a result, any federal court that came along used this as a precedent for issuing a prior restraining order against one thing or another that the judges didn't want published. Wicker said he was not advocating that *The Times* defy the court. He simply wanted everyone to understand the possible consequences. In essentials Wicker's case was exactly that which Rosenthal had raised earlier.

After Wicker's statement Punch asked if anyone else had anything to say. No one did. There was a show of hands and unanimously it was agreed that *The Times* would obey the court's order whether positive or negative.

Later on some critics outside *The Times* (including Ellsberg) were to challenge this position; were to contend that by agreement to abide by the orders of the court *The Times* had compromised the freedom of the press. This was not the view of *The Times*' legal counsel. Bickel, Abrams and Goodale were as one on this point. *The Times* was not out to challenge the American system. It was not making a case against the historic division of powers under the Constitution. It was defending the right of the press under the First Amendment to operate within traditional guarantees of freedom to publish and, in particular, it was defending itself against an attack by one branch of the government, the Executive, by recourse to another, the Judicial. What *The Times* supported was the preservation and maintenance of the American system rather than its destruction and distortion through whimsical and extralegal manipulation by one of the triequal branches.

The *Washington Post*

Hearing of the case began at 10 A.M. Friday morning, June 18, once again in Room 353, Foley Square, with an unpleasant surprise for the government.

For nearly two weeks before Sunday, June 13, the *Washington Post* had heard rumors that *The Times* was coming out with a big Washington exposé, possibly about the Vietnam war, but had been unable to get a clue of what it was. When the story finally broke the top *Post* editors, Ben Bradlee, Phil Geyelin of the editorial page, Ben Bagdikian, national editor, Chalmers Roberts, veteran political and diplomatic reporter, and Murray Marder, another diplomatic reporter, assembled on Sunday to see what could be done to match, and if possible, more than match, *The Times*.

A couple of false passes quickly resulted. The *Post* was offered but refused the Raskin-Barnet-Stavins manuscript called "Washington Plans an Aggressive War," based in large measure on volumes of the Pentagon Papers made available by Ellsberg. On Monday, Geyelin received through an intermediary who was in touch with Ellsberg two hundred pages of Pentagon documents, including a McGeorge Bundy memo calling for escalation of the war. Before the *Post* could get it into print much of the material appeared in the third *Times'* Pentagon installment, Tuesday morning. Finally, after *The Times* was enjoined, Bagdikian made direct contact with Ellsberg, who was eager to ensure the continued publication of the Papers.*

After a cloak-and-dagger trip to Boston, Bagdikian flew back to Washington Thursday morning, June 17, with a large fiberboard box, paying for two first-class tickets Boston-to-Washington in order to keep the parcel on the seat beside him. After this hugger-mugger Bagdikian ran into Stanley Karnow, a former *Post* reporter and China specialist, on the plane. Karnow took one look at the box and exclaimed, "Oh, you've got it!" Bagdikian looked daggers at Karnow, who quietly slipped down the aisle of the plane.

Bagdikian took his box to Ben Bradlee's Georgetown house where Roberts, Marder and Don Oberdorfer, another top *Post* reporter, Geyelin and his deputy, Meg Greenfield, converged.

While editors and correspondents struggled to make sense of the jumble of documents, 4,200 pages, many unnumbered, in the library of Bradlee's house a fierce argument broke out in the living room, where Roger Clark and Anthony Essaye, of the firm of Royall, Koegell

---

*As Ellsberg recalled he got in touch with Bagdikian, whom he knew, and arranged to meet him in a Boston motel. While Ellsberg was with Bagdikian at the motel he got word that the FBI had staked out his apartment. He never went back, going underground for the next ten days or so. (Personal interview, Ellsberg, 10/16/78)

and Wells, the *Post*'s attorneys, and later, Frederick R. Beebe, chairman of the board of the *Post* company, assembled. Clark, Essaye and Beebe were adamant against running the Papers. Bradlee, Bagdikian, Geyelin and Meg Greenfield took the opposite side.

The argument roared on hour after hour. The publisher, Mrs. Graham, was consulted by telephone as was Paul Ignatius, the newspaper's new president, a former Secretary of the Navy. Ignatius was opposed to publication. The arguments took almost the identical form of those between *The Times* and its lawyers, Loeb and Brownell.* But the *Post* lacked an in-house counsel like James Goodale to carry the argument for the news side.

Finally the case was submitted to Mrs. Graham by Beebe and she said, "Okay, go ahead."

But this did not settle the matter. Clark found a new cause for concern—the possibility that the *Post* might be guilty of "collusion" with *The Times* because its source was Ellsberg, just as was *The Times*. Once again the battle was fought over, this time with intense anger. Once again the case was put to Mrs. Graham, and at 12:25 A.M., five minutes before the *Post*'s deadline for the late city edition, the air blue with profanity and threats by editors and reporters to resign, Mrs. Graham put her foot down and told the news side to go ahead and print the story. The *Post* did. That morning a four-column headline read, "Documents Reveal U.S. Effort in '54 to Delay Viet Election. . . . First of a series by Chalmers Roberts."

It was this story in the Friday morning edition of the *Washington Post* that caused the unpleasant surprise for government attorneys Seymour and Hess. The surprise stemmed from the fact that they did not know of its existence, had not been told of its publication by Mardian and his aides, who had flown up that morning from Washington and who carried copies of the *Washington Post* in their briefcases. They just hadn't thought it necessary to pass the word on that the Pentagon Papers had broken out all over again—in Washington.

Thus, the first the government lawyers heard of this turn came when *The Times'* lawyers presented a new affidavit in addition to the fifteen which had already been filed. This came from James Greenfield, foreign editor of *The Times*, who reported the publication of the Pentagon Papers in the *Washington Post* that morning, noted that the *Post*'s material was appearing in many papers around the country through

---

*There was a special complication for the *Washington Post*. It was about to become a public corporation with an offering of 1,354,000 shares of Class B common stock to be listed on the American Stock Exchange. The underwriting agreement did not take effect for five days and the *Post*'s lawyers were concerned that it might be affected by an injunction or criminal prosecution for publication of the Pentagon Papers. (Sanford J. Ungar, *The Papers and the Papers*, New York City, 1972, p. 140)

syndication and said this placed *The Times* at an unfair competitive advantage, causing it to lose all benefit from the "large sums of money, time and energy" expended in the Pentagon project.

Alexander Bickel told the court that the *Post*'s action had eliminated any possibility that national security would be preserved by restraint on *The Times*. The case, he said, was "moot." If there had ever been a national security consideration—which he did not concede—it had been blown to bits by the *Post*'s publication. "There is nothing for your honor to protect," he said, concluding with great force:

"The government's position in this court, your honor, was that grave danger to the national security would occur if another installment of a story that *The Times* had was published. Another installment of that story has been published. The republic stands. And it stood the first three days."

Seymour and Hess exchanged glances of bafflement and bewilderment. Gurfein indicated uneasiness at restraining *The Times* while other papers were free to publish.

Hess consulted Seymour. Mardian stepped to their side (he was seldom to leave it during the day) and hurriedly whispered to the pair. Hess then told the court that the Justice Department would examine the *Post*'s article and take action "if it appears necessary."§

The Prosecution

It was not to prove an easy day for government counsel. Mardian, whom Hess was to come to call "the sinister influence" behind the case, sat in the front row, leaning forward, taking many penciled notes. Again and again he would reach forward, poke Hess in the back and slip him a note. "It is very difficult," Hess explained, "to be facing the court, presenting a carefully articulated argument and constantly to be interrupted with pokes in the back and notes." Seymour had the same problem. When he arose to address the court Mardian rose, too, his head reaching only to Seymour's shoulder. Repeatedly Mardian would stand on tiptoe and whisper into Seymour's ear, trying to influence his argument or objecting to what he was saying.

The fixation in Mardian's mind and that of Buzhardt on "security" became, as Seymour later recalled, "at times a comic opera." But it did not seem funny to him that day in court, nor had it seemed funny when Hess was trying to prepare the case for trial. In fact, the phobia about security was to cling to the trial like a caul, obstructing the government's efforts to prepare its case, torturing the prosecutors in their dealings with witnesses and embarrassing them in their relations with the courts and judges.

§See Notes section.

The problem had emerged as early as Tuesday. Hess found that he was getting call after call from Washington and not only from the Justice Department. The White House was onto him through John Dean and later through Dean's assistant, Fred Fielding, who wanted to be advised of every development. Even more extraordinary to the hard-working deputy district attorney was the interest of Henry Kissinger. Kissinger's deputy, a "Colonel Haig" of whom Hess had never previously heard, telephoned two or three times a day stressing the extreme urgency of security and demanding reports on progress. Haig gave Hess his number to call instantly on all developments.

Hess had had little experience with the White House. In fact, his one previous contact had been a call from John Ehrlichman in March 1970 when there was threat of a national mail carriers' strike. Hess was seeking an injunction against the carriers. Ehrlichman telephoned and what Hess later called "a rather curious conversation" ensued. The White House was considering ordering out the National Guard to deliver the mail and Ehrlichman wanted to know whether Hess thought the guardsmen should carry side arms. Hess didn't think the question was one he could answer but Ehrlichman persisted, saying Hess was on the scene. Pressed in this manner, Hess said he didn't think side arms were appropriate. It struck him as strange but the deeper he got into the Pentagon Papers the less strange it seemed; it was consistent with the attitudes he began to encounter.

The first thing that Hess had done on Wednesday morning was to get a set of the forty seven volumes of the Pentagon Papers sent to the district attorney's office so he could find out what the case was all about. The big conference room, 101, outside Seymour's office was set aside and the documents in their paper cartons were kept there under protection of a guard of the National Security Agency, gun in holster.

As Hess familiarized himself with the volumes he found doubts arising in his mind, questions about the solidness of the underpinnings of his case. He discovered that some volumes were made up almost entirely of texts of LBJ's press conferences. There were quantities of similar materials which could hardly be considered confidential. Despite the fact that the forty-seven volumes had been marked "Top Secret—Sensitive" they contained much that needed no classification.

What, asked Hess and his associates, would happen if and when Judge Gurfein took a look at the documents? The credibility of the government was bound to suffer. Hess began to worry. He was working around the clock. He would leave his office in Lower Manhattan just before midnight, drive up East River Drive to his apartment at Eighty-third Street and East End Avenue, catch a couple of hours sleep, get up, shower and go back downtown. In two weeks he was to lose twelve pounds from a rather sparse frame.

Despite growing questions, Hess went forward with the most sweeping kind of claim. Washington made it "totally clear," he recalled, that the argument which he must present was that when the Executive wants something classified "Top Secret" there is a point beyond which this is not to be questioned—by anyone.

"So that," he recalled, a bit ruefully, "was the argument we prepared for the court."

Seymour returned from Washington on Thursday and began to participate in the preparations. From the beginning Hess had insisted to Washington that they must provide him with excellent witnesses and Mardian assured him he would do so.

It was not until Friday morning, only an hour or two before the trial, that Mardian and the witnesses came in from Washington. Hess took them to the library of the district attorney's office to brief them on the procedure.

The witnesses turned out to be Dennis J. Doolin, Deputy Secretary of Defense for International Security, Vice Admiral Francis J. Blouin, Deputy Chief of Naval Operations, William Butts Macomber, Deputy Undersecretary of State, and George MacClain, a classification specialist.

The first inkling Hess had of problems came when Macomber, an intelligent, experienced government official, handed him a copy of the statement that he proposed to make.

"It was just as though he was going before a congressional committee," Hess recalled. "I had to say, 'Mr. Macomber, this is not the way we are going to do it. I am going to ask you questions and then the other side will cross-examine you.' "

Macomber was disturbed, but no more than Hess, who found that Admiral Blouin also had not been prepared for what to expect in court. He was more disturbed to find that neither Macomber nor Blouin had read the Pentagon Papers.

"I had my two most important witnesses and neither had read the Papers. I knew we were going to have trouble," Hess said. "Of course, there was Doolin. He said he had read the Papers but unfortunately he wasn't a very good witness."

When Hess pressed Mardian about the witnesses Mardian expressed surprise. Both he and Buzhardt felt they had gotten the most knowledgeable persons available and that they had done a good job. They had turned up three good witnesses from three different departments.§

"But frankly," Hess recalled, "we wanted a lot more."

Buzhardt came up with a suggestion. There was a witness he could

§See Notes section.

produce who could explain just how crucial the Pentagon Papers were. But this witness was such a top-secret official that the only way in which he could present testimony was for him to go into a private room alone with the judge. Even his identity could not be disclosed, nor the agency he represented, but it was clear to Hess that Buzhardt was referring to someone from the National Security Agency, the huge ultrasecret U.S. agency which conducts the cracking of diplomatic and military codes, monitors all communications around the world, including the illegal recording of internal U.S. communications, and listens with satellites and supersensitive installations to almost every faint electronic tremor within the Soviet Union.*

"Frankly," Hess said, "I was embarrassed to have to remind a fellow attorney that the judge could receive testimony only when he was sitting on the bench and that *The Times* had the constitutional right to cross-examine this mystery witness."

"No, that's not possible," Buzhardt exclaimed. "He can't do this in open court."

Buzhardt had another idea. What if the Mystery Man were to write out his statement and pass it along in a sealed affidavit just for the eyes of the judge.

"I said this presented the same problem," Hess said. "We had to know and the defense had to know what the testimony was."

"Then we can't do anything," Buzhardt snapped. "It is such a secret matter that it must be given to the judge alone."

Now it was time to go into court and the government's troubles grew. All of the witnesses spoke in rotund generalities. When asked to point to a specific document in the Pentagon Papers that threatened national security, Buzhardt interjected, "They cannot tell you. The information is classified." He refused to permit the witness to speak to specifics unless "all others are cleared from the courtroom," including, of course, defense counsel.

Mardian's position, as had been earlier forecast by Hess, was simplicity itself. The government had classified the documents "Top Secret" and that ended the matter. Once the government acted, no one, no one, had the right to challenge that decision.

"He was very brash," Seymour recalled, "and he came on very strong."

The government insisted on an *in camera* proceeding. Hess had anticipated this and, after conferring with Hegarty, had negotiated security clearance for Abrams, Bickel, Hegarty and McKay. Both Hess and Hegarty overlooked the fact that *Times'* personnel would

---

*The witness to whom Buzhardt was referring was Admiral Noel Gayler, head of the NSA. (Personal interview, Mardian, 2/15/79)

be needed to assist counsel. There was a brief flurry, and Seymour, to his embarrassment, was compelled by Mardian to object to their presence but Gurfein took the responsibility of having Max Frankel and Harding Bancroft present *in camera,* sensibly pointing out that they had already seen and read the Pentagon Papers. Goodale never was cleared. He simply went along with the others and no one challenged him.

Before the secret hearing got under way there was one more outburst by Buzhardt. As lawyers, witnesses and *The Times'* experts gathered in the robing room off the courtroom Buzhardt excitedly denounced *The Times.* "Don't you realize," he demanded, "that your publication will compromise Signal One, Signal Two, Signal Three and even Norad?" Buzhardt's explosion caused great turmoil in the robing room. None of the lawyers from *The Times* (nor Seymour and Hess for that matter) knew what he was talking about, although they recognized the acronym Norad, standing for North American Defense Command. It suddenly occurred to Hegarty that the government might be about to raise a question of *The Times* exposing U.S. codes. If so, he had an expert witness, David Kahn, the leading nongovernment specialist on cryptography, whom he wanted to be present. Hegarty asked Seymour if codes were going to be involved in the case. No, said Seymour wearily. Not at all. And that was that.

Seymour's nerves were raw by this time. Mardian kept shouting, "Damn it, Judge, the Executive has classified this and that is the end of it!" Seymour knew this was hardly the way to convince Gurfein but there was no way to keep Mardian quiet. Mardian did not remember anything like that. He did remember an altercation with Max Frankel. Frankel had a copy of *The New York Times* open before him. Mardian noticed that *The Times* bore a copyright slug. "I said to Frankel," Mardian recalled, "suppose the *Baltimore Sun* started printing your story. I'll bet you'd get a temporary restraining order on them. He said they sure would. I said, 'Well, hell, we own this damn thing. You are copyrighting our property.' "* It was Mardian's recollection that Judge Gurfein was much interested in his remark and asked *The Times* how it justified this distinction. Mardian could not understand why this line of attack was not pursued against *The Times,* why the government had not filed a replevin action for "the return of the stolen papers." Later on the same idea was to occur to President Nixon. But it was, in fact, bad law. The courts have never established that the government has

---

*Mardian was the only person who recalled talking with Frankel. Frankel did not recall any talk with Mardian, nor did others in the robing room remember the exchange. "I remember Mardian rushing around, stage-managing things," Frankel said many years later. "But I don't think he and I spoke." (Personal interview, Frankel, 3/6/79)

a property right in its papers. "The use of replevin," Seymour later commented, "was preposterous under the law. That's the kind of thing you do if someone has your cow and you want to get it back. There wasn't any grounds for using it in this kind of case."

26

A Cantankerous Press

*W*ITH SECURITY GUARDS at each entrance of a small cleared court-room, Judge Gurfein on the bench, his clerk and the court stenographer seated below him, no one present but government witnesses, lawyers and experts, the tall, aristocratic Seymour, the thin, wiry Hess, his face showing the strain of day-and-night concentration, dark-visaged, superbly tanned Mardian, dogged Buzhardt, intense Abrams, scholarly Bickel, Irishly handsome Hegarty, businesslike Lawrence McKay, thin-lipped Goodale, tweedy Bancroft and keen-eyed Frankel, the first star chamber, the first secret hearing in an American newspaper case since the founding of the republic got under way.

Nothing like it had ever been conducted. Although the outcome was to affect the dynamics of American society, the course of American life, the relationship of state and press, not a word of what transpired within that chamber was made public. Six years would pass until on March 16, 1977, the transcript was unsealed at the order of the District Court for the Southern District of New York under a Freedom of Information action by Anthony Lewis, *The New York Times* columnist.

Nearly six full years elapsed between decision of the case and release of the record of what went on in Judge Gurfein's courtroom. Actually, even the 1977 transcript omits one paragraph and three two-word references to the paragraph. The paragraph is one which was published by *The New York Times* in the first installment of the Pentagon Papers, June 13, 1971, and deals with the so-called 34A program of clandestine raids and operations against North Vietnam in 1964. The account that follows here is the first ever published of these proceedings. Even more extraordinary is the fact that secret briefs filed with the U.S. Supreme Court in the appeal of the case, briefs which, in the opinion of the attorneys who drafted them, illuminated the frailty of the government's case and the weakness of the government's evidence, had still not been completely released for publication nearly ten years after being sealed.

As far as Abrams was aware these were the only secret briefs filed with the Supreme Court in history. In espionage cases secret information and secret briefs are not employed since this would give away the government's data to the supposed spy.

U.S. District Judge Gerhard Gesell, on July 22, 1976, ordered a substantial portion of the suppressed materials of the *Washington Post* hearings before his court released. He made public the full transcript of the *in camera* hearing but permitted several deletions from the testimony of Macomber and Doolin and continued to suppress in full an affidavit by Vice Admiral Noel Gayler of the National Security Agency.

He permitted to be made public William Glendon's secret brief to the Supreme Court but continued to suppress a twelve-page government list of "sensitive items" contained in the Pentagon Papers and kept the ban on several pages of the government's secret brief. Glendon's *in camera* analysis of the evidence was released except for a three-page segment. *The New York Times'* secret brief remained secret, possibly by mistake; possibly no one had thought to ask its clearance.

In this most critical challenge of the rights of the press the full record had not yet been disclosed ten years after the event even though careful examination makes clear the general nature of materials which are still suppressed and the lack of genuine considerations of national security.

Thus, while tens of thousands of words spewed forth in the American press, including *The New York Times,* and in television, radio and the periodical press, while articles were printed from London to Tokyo, the people of the United States and even the editors of *The Times* had not been informed of the cut and thrust of the government's argument, the perversity of the government's attitude and the Kabuki atmosphere thrown up around and even within the legal process by Mardian, Buzhardt and their principals. With all their resources the American press could not convey a whisper of the inner paranoia of the case. In fact, at the time only the attorneys and some of the judges sensed its depth.

Inexplicably, once the Pentagon case was finally won in the Supreme Court and publication of the original articles was completed, *The Times* seemed to lose interest in the subject. It did not, for example, file suit under the Freedom of Information Act for release of the *in camera* testimony and secret briefs for publication, nor did it make an effort to get the four "diplomatic" volumes of the study, which it had never possessed. The release of the Gurfein *in camera* proceedings and other secret materials was obtained by Anthony Lewis, *The Times* columnist, acting on his own initiative.

Secrecy, Secrecy, Secrecy

There were other impedimenta. Not everything that happened could be reported—not by newspapers engaged in what might be a fight for their existence. There was, for example, the case of Chief Justice Warren Burger of the Supreme Court.

On the night of Friday, June 18, Judge Gurfein was concluding his *in camera* hearing in New York of *The New York Times'* case and in Washington the U.S. Court of Appeals was considering the government's appeal against Judge Gesell's decision in favor of the *Washington Post*. The argument went on and on toward midnight. If the appeals court ruled in favor of the *Post* the government would have to apply to Chief Justice Burger for an appeal and a continuance of the temporary restraint on the *Post*'s publication of the Pentagon Papers.

Unable to reach Burger by telephone, the *Post* sent reporters Spencer Rich and Martin Weil to Burger's home on North Rochester Street in Arlington, Virginia. They arrived shortly after 11 P.M., walked up Burger's driveway and rang the bell. "After a minute or two," Weil reported in a memo to his editor, "the Chief Justice opened the door. He was wearing a bathrobe. He was carrying a gun. The gun was in his right hand, muzzle pointed down. It was a long-barreled steel weapon. [It was a long-barreled pistol, not a rifle, as Weil later noted.] The Chief Justice did not seem glad to see us. Spencer explained why we were there. There was a considerable amount of misdirected conversation. It seemed for a bit that people were talking past each other. Spencer, who held up his credentials, was explaining why we were there, but the judge seemed to be saying we shouldn't have come. . . . Finally, after a little more talk, everybody seemed to understand everybody. The Chief Justice said it would not be all right for us to wait for any possible Justice Department emissaries outside his door, but we could wait down at the street. He held his gun in his hand throughout a two or three minute talk. Sometimes it was not visible, held behind the doorpost. He never pointed it at us. He closed the door. We went down the street and waited for about three hours. Then we went home."

The incident provided a vignette of the highest judge of the United States at the apex of the confrontation of government and press. It was an unusual and in some respects an unnerving encounter.

The editors of the *Post* planned to report the incident in the newspaper of Sunday, June 20. But Ben Bradlee killed the story and ordered all copies destroyed. It was, he conceded, an interesting sidelight but with the fate of the *Post* headed toward the Supreme Court this was a story that the *Post* and its readers could do without. Except for a paragraph in a gossip column no report of the incident ever appeared in a newspaper or periodical.

Bradlee's decision was one of judgment. The *Post* could have published the story but he felt, on balance, it was better not to. There was no such choice for the editors of *The Times* with regard to the secret session before Judge Gurfein. Nor was the *Post* given any choice in a parallel secret session of Judge Gesell. The press and the public was not permitted to know what happened *in camera.*

Yet, it was *in camera* that the weakness of the government witnesses was exposed; it was *in camera* that the difficulty which the government had in presenting genuine evidence came to light; and it was *in camera* that the fear and suspicion, the total lack of understanding of the principles of American law and American justice by Nixon's Washington was made apparent. It was the secret session which turned Judge Gurfein irrevocably away from the government and toward the arguments presented by Bickel and Abrams and Hegarty.

Without the smell, the feel, the sight, the impression of the secret proceedings the essence of the affair could not be captured.

"There was something strange and sinister about it all," Hegarty recalled.

Bickel was affected in the same way. He had come to the United States as a youngster from Rumania. Mardian kept staring at Bickel. "When I looked at him," he told Abrams, "I could see him instituting deportation proceedings to send me back to Rumania. It was in his eyes." "Mardian wore these thin steel-rimmed glasses," Hess recalled. "I know it sounds odd. But they gave him an evil-type appearance."

Years earlier Hegarty had read Stephen Vincent Benét's *The Devil and Daniel Webster* and he had seen the movie version in which Walter Huston played the Devil, "Old Scratch," as Benét called him. Now as Hegarty sat in the small windowless courtroom the scene of Benét's classic came back to him: Jabez Stone, the flinty New Hampshire farmer who had mortgaged his soul to the Devil for ten years' freedom from back-breaking toil and the courtroom where Old Scratch sought to collect on his mortgage; Justice Hathorn, the Salem witch judge on the bench, and Webster defending his client, Stone. In the jury box sat Walter Butler, the Loyalist who spread fire and horror in the Mohawk Valley during Revolutionary days; Simon Guty, the renegade who helped the Indians burn white men at the stake; King Philip of the Indian wars; Teach, the bloody pirate, and the others. Hegarty remembered Benét's description of the jury as Webster rose to address the court: ". . . the glitter in their eyes was twice as strong as before and they all leaned forward. Like hounds just before they get the fox they looked and the blue mist of evil in the room thickened."

It was not Judge Gurfein on the bench who brought this image into Hegarty's mind—it was the jury box. There in the informality of *in camera* proceedings sat Mardian and Buzhardt and government witnesses. As Hegarty stared at Mardian and Buzhardt the picture came to him of the jury Daniel Webster faced and the murmur that filled

Justice Hathorn's courtroom: "Hang them . . . hang them all. . . ."

"I know my imagination ran away with me," Hegarty recalled. "But that was the vision I had when I looked at those eyes staring from the jury box."

These conceptions may seem bizarre but they reflect the moment. These were fantasies which entered the minds of serious counselors-at-law, men to whom flights of fancy were as alien as palmistry to Einstein.

The Witnesses

What then did happen in these long-secret proceedings?

There were four witnesses: Doolin of the Defense Department, Macomber of State, Admiral Blouin and Buzhardt himself. Doolin was pressed again and again by Judge Gurfein and Hegarty, cross-examining for *The Times,* to identify specific passages in the Pentagon Papers— either material published by *The Times* or that might be published— which would support the government's contention of grave danger to security. In the end he refused to identify a single passage. He contended that U.S. relations with Australia had been disturbed by excerpts in the Papers reflecting on the reasons why Australia had sent forces to Vietnam; that Thailand might stop helping the United States because of revelations that she already was doing so; that something which he called SEATO Plan 5 might be compromised and that it would not be possible to get Sweden to assist in contacting Hanoi because of the Pentagon publication.

However, he conceded that there were no documents in the Papers which related to Sweden, that the facts about Thailand had been extensively reported and, in the end, offered no citations whatever. This discomfited Judge Gurfein. Doolin did say that there was "one particular area that frankly is so sensitive that I can't mention it even within this room and I could only mention it on a personal basis." Gurfein told Doolin that he didn't need this kind of personal confidence. "I don't want to hear it and so that is the end of that," he snapped.

"Obviously," Hegarty told the court, "the witness is not prepared to respond to either your questions or mine as to specifics."

He asked Gurfein to strike all of Doolin's testimony "as not being probative of anything." Gurfein refused, telling Doolin "I will give you one more chance" to cite one specific instance of anything in the Papers from 1945 to 1968 which supported the thesis of "dangers to security."

Doolin said that he and Buzhardt had called the Pentagon and asked the experts there to find some such instance "but I didn't have time to come up with a list of—a lengthy list of specifics."

Doolin said that he could give the judge some evidence about U.S.

intercepts of North Vietnam communications but he had been forbidden to do it. Finally, the government withdrew Doolin on grounds that he was not permitted to testify about such material.

Mardian complained that the attorneys for *The Times* were taking notes. Hegarty offered to destroy his before he left the room "if the government feels easier." The judge thought that would be a good idea. Bickel had been taking notes, too, and he was not about to give them up. He needed them for his closing argument. The court said he could keep them but eventually better tear them up.

Admiral Blouin's testimony hardly improved the government's case. He inveighed against the dangers of publishing the Tonkin Gulf Command Study but, as it turned out, *The Times* possessed only a summary of the report and most of what concerned him had already been brought out in hearings before the Senate Foreign Relations Committee, although neither he nor *Times'* counsel seemed aware of this.

Gurfein's skepticism of the government case was growing. The admiral said that the Russians and/or the North Vietnamese (there seemed little distinction in his mind) could learn a great deal about how the government operated by reading the Pentagon Papers. Gurfein rejoined that "about six books have been written about the Cuban crisis, every word President Kennedy said to Sorensen and to Bobby Kennedy, that has all been written up."

"Your honor," the admiral replied wistfully, "I can tell you even though I am not in uniform today I don't like operating in a fishbowl but that is what we do today."

To which Gurfein responded, "I wonder in the times we live in whether you don't have to adjust to that."

"I deplore much of what I read," said the admiral.

"When I heard the admiral make that remark about the fishbowl," Hess recalled, "I remember thinking, 'Admiral Blooey—well, that's just where the case has gone—blooey!' You kind of feel these things in the tensions and dynamics of the courtroom. I felt that Blouin blew it."

Blouin objected that the Papers revealed the rules of engagement in Vietnam but conceded that these were not current, and, as it developed, they had already been made public in 1969 by a House investigating committee.

Macomber testified that there had been four cases of embarrassment to the government as a result of the Pentagon publications, the most severe being the revelation that J. Blair Seaborn, the Canadian member of the International Control Commission in Indochina, had held discussions with Premier Pham Van Dong of North Vietnam on behalf of the United States. This had caused a political storm in Canada.

Australia had been embarrassed because the Papers made it plain that she had supported the United States in Vietnam not because of the SEATO pact but because of U.S. maneuvering.

The third embarrassment was publication of an exchange between Prime Minister Harold Wilson of Great Britain and President Johnson.

This, said Macomber "is just an absolutely unacceptable way for nations to deal with each other."

The argument did not impress Gurfein, who asked if it wasn't true that Mr. Wilson was currently writing his memoirs.

Macomber conceded that Wilson was writing his memoirs but insisted (as Kissinger had so angrily said in Washington) that "I just don't see, your honor, how we can conduct diplomacy with this kind of business going on."

The fourth example of a "security disclosure" had to do with a 1968 cable from then U.S. Ambassador Llewellyn Thompson in Moscow assessing possible Soviet reaction to U.S. escalation in Vietnam. Because of Thompson's standing as a specialist in Soviet affairs Macomber felt publication of this document would give Moscow valuable clues to American attitudes.

Macomber argued for the most limited declassification of diplomatic traffic, insisting that only the State Department should be the judge, despite suggestions by Judge Gurfein that classification was employed to conceal error and even to mislead the public.

Macomber insisted that without confidential diplomatic communications "we have irreparably damaged the chance of free government to endure." Never had the government's authority been so challenged as in the case of the Pentagon Papers. And he stood by the principle that the State Department was the best judge of what information should be given to the public and said that when it gave out information confidentially on an unattributed basis to individual correspondents this was not "a leak," not so long as it was done by government officials. This point did not go over well with Judge Gurfein. He asked how articles about American intervention in the 1971 guerrilla crisis in Jordan had gotten out. "You don't think those are leaks?" asked Gurfein.

"No," replied Macomber, "that the Sixth Fleet is coming storming down the Mediterranean? That isn't."

"It isn't a leak?" repeated Gurfein.

"No, sir," said Macomber.

Nor was he willing to accept "on the spot" declassification of the Yalta Papers by Secretary of State John Foster Dulles as providing any parallel to the Pentagon case.

Doolin's testimony elucidated the fact that copies of the Pentagon Papers were in the hands of former Defense Secretaries McNamara and Clifford as well as the Rand Corporation and the LBJ Library.

Judge Gurfein was puzzled to learn that while refusing to provide Senator Fulbright with the Papers because of "security" considerations no effort had been made to retrieve the other copies, particularly the Clifford and McNamara copies. Doolin insisted they kept their copies for reference in case Secretary Laird should ask questions about past department dealings. This did not satisfy Gurfein, and Buzhardt was summoned to the witness stand. He said that former Defense Secretaries were often consulted and, therefore, were given clearance and access to classified information. Moreover, he said it was the custom for former Secretaries to retain classified materials. The discussion was not conclusive and the figures on distribution of copies of the Papers didn't quite jibe. Doolin insisted the White House had not had a copy originally. He didn't know why but a copy had been sent there two days ago. Whether this was Dr. Kissinger's copy there was no way of knowing. Kissinger's name was not mentioned.

The question of jeopardy to U.S. codes kept coming up even though Seymour had assured Hegarty this was not part of the government's case. Doolin kept suggesting that a trained cryptologist would garner pertinent detail from study of the Papers. Gurfein was not convinced.

"It is difficult for me," he said, "to take a statement that is so general, that communications intelligence can be picked up in a study by a trained eye. Are we to believe our codes are so inflexible that we don't change them enough to fool an enemy?"

Doolin then switched and said that the problem lay with the revelation that we had intercepted enemy communications in Vietnam. This did not impress Gurfein. "Everybody intercepts everybody else," he commented.

Admiral Blouin suggested that if an enemy had access to the command study of the Tonkin Gulf "it would make it relatively simple for them to sabotage communications at the right place or even destroy buildings."

But this was not persuasive to Gurfein. "I hope our communications are not that static, Admiral," he said. "We are dealing with a 1968 situation."

Having been in Army intelligence and the OSS during World War II, Gurfein knew a good deal about security, interceptions and communications. One thing puzzled him. Were not the cables paraphrased before being distributed? Were not the words transposed to prevent the enemy from using the text to break the encipherment? He was assured by Doolin that they were not; that the Pentagon Papers contained raw exact texts.

"Isn't it the rule in the Services now that there is always a transposition for distribution and that the original text is kept in a safe somewhere?" Gurfein asked.

Admiral Blouin interrupted: "Your honor, you and I are the only ones who remember those days. They don't do it anymore."*

No one listening to the convoluted explanations of the government witnesses could remain under the illusion that they were making a case. Counsel for *The Times* asked that the proceedings be thrown open on grounds that nothing of real security interest had been or was likely to be discussed. Gurfein was sympathetic yet reluctant. He clung to the belief that the government must have some genuine security concerns to present.

Bickel

After the government's presentation Bickel again moved to have the restraining order lifted. He reminded Gurfein that it ran only until 1 P.M. Saturday and that *The Times* hoped to resume publishing the Papers on Sunday.

Bickel made one concession in his argument, one limitation on the First Amendment right. He conceded that in the case of a newspaper publishing information of the sailing of a troopship there was a specific section of the Espionage Act which applied and that in wartime the penalty for such publication was death.

But he pointed out that nothing like this was involved in the Pentagon Papers. Doolin had testified to little more than that the government felt a general sense of insecurity when classified information came into the open. Bickel made a good deal of the fact that former President Johnson, hard at work on his memoirs, had available to him a set of the Papers in the LBJ Library. Bickel expressed certainty that Johnson would publish any information which suited his purpose from the Papers and recalled the incident in which LBJ had waved a classified document on national television to prove a point about the 1968 bombing halt.†

"How grave a danger can there be in the case of documents which are in people's law offices which are obviously there for use by memoirists who have written on the subject with great frequency, like Townsend Hoopes, Roger Hilsman and others," he asked. "What great

---

*The same point came up in the *Washington Post* case. Ben Bradlee served as a destroyer officer in World War II and had been taught, as he recalled, "that you should never reprint the first words and the last words of a message." He was told he was out-of-date and it didn't matter anymore. (Personal interview, Bradlee, 3/15/79)
†During a TV interview with Walter Cronkite, Feb. 6, 1970, in response to a question whether Defense Secretary Clark Clifford had initiated a reappraisal of Vietnam policy, Johnson said, "That's totally inaccurate. Now if you would like to, Walter [producing some classified memoranda from his pocket], I'll declassify them now for a moment." He then read to a national TV audience from his classified documents. (*Columbia Journalism Review*, Sept.–Oct. 1971, p. 41)

dangers to the national security can there be in that?"

Gurfein, Bickel said, had sat listening patiently for specific indications of grave dangers but none had been illuminated.

Gurfein expressed concern about publication by *The Times* of communications between the United States and other countries. Had this ever happened before, he asked.

Bickel cited the Yalta Papers and the Kennedy-Khrushchev exchanges at the time of the Cuban missile crisis as providing similar examples and added:

"That brings us to the fundamental question of whether we can tolerate a government, whether we can have a government with respect even to communications with foreign countries that survives entirely on handouts, that survives by the decision being made exclusively by the government."

The embarrassment that was caused to the government, he felt, was certainly exaggerated. He pointed out that in the serialization of Harold Wilson's memoirs, then in progress only a year and a half after he was out of office, he published the text of a letter to LBJ telling him how he ought to react to a visit made by Premier Kosygin to London.

The government, Bickel concluded, "has the heaviest kind of burden to find a grave, serious, specific danger to the national security because it is seeking a prior restraint on publication and nothing else in my judgment could constitutionally justify it."

The question of how *The Times* got the documents, he insisted, was not germane. It could be punished for doing unlawful things—for stealing, for breaking open a safe—but the only area in which prior restraint might be applied was "grave danger to the national defense."

Bickel reiterated that he had heard "precious little" of genuine security nature and urged that Gurfein make public the record of the *in camera* hearing.

Bickel had one more compelling point. Macomber, who had been a law school classmate of Bickel's, had referred to the "chilling effect" of *The Times'* disclosures upon the frankness of diplomats who would restrain their observations in fear that they might be revealed.

This, Bickel declared, was a "curious inversion" of the concept of the First Amendment. (The most frequent argument against measures of government pressure on the press was that they would have a "chilling effect" on publication.)

Macomber's concept, said Bickel, was "a curious, curious inversion of [the First Amendment concept] which may very well be the final characterization of this case."

In the end Gurfein made clear to Seymour how troubled he was by the government's case. *The Times* had argued that under the Supreme Court interpretation of the First Amendment practically no precensorship or restraint was possible except in "the direst case." The question simply was, Is this "the direst case"? Whether the documents were received legally or illegally did not matter. If they did not affect security in the most extreme manner (the troopship sailing date) they could be published and there was no constitutional prohibition to halt this.

As the *in camera* session was ending, word came that Judge Gesell in Washington had denied the government the restraining order it sought there against the *Post.* Bickel urged Gurfein to follow suit but he declined. He would render his decision on Saturday and *The Times* would not be more than a half day behind if he ruled in their favor.

No one left the *in camera* hearing in much doubt how Gurfein would rule. Later some would suggest that Gurfein was pushed toward *The Times* by the Gesell ruling in Washington. The record of the *in camera* session does not support that view. Gurfein was openly skeptical of the government case from the beginning and grew more and more skeptical as the government floundered about with broad-spectrum contentions of security violations and no specifics. This was revealed in the long-suppressed transcript. But even the transcript falls short in conveying the "blue mist of evil" which suffused the courtroom. Later both Seymour and Hess inveighed against Mardian and Buzhardt. Buzhardt died late in 1978 without leaving a memoir of his role in the proceedings. Mardian, having returned to the flourishing family construction business in Phoenix, looked back with dour dismay on the Pentagon case. He went through both Pentagon and Watergate. "I don't know which was worse," he said. He was bitter toward Mr. Nixon. The President, he said, had not complimented him for his Pentagon job and, indeed, had never patted him on the back for anything. The only feedback he received was through Attorney General Mitchell and it was not complimentary. He insisted that he had left to Seymour the argument of the case and that Seymour had been most reluctant to take it on.

"He resented me very much," said Mardian. "He resented being put in the position of handling this case. It was the last thing on earth that he wanted. He was thinking of running for higher office and he didn't like any part of bringing a case against *The New York Times.* It was an impossible case. It wasn't going to help him at all. You just don't take a case against someone who has a tubful of ink."

As for himself, he insisted, when he was ordered to file a lawsuit he filed a lawsuit. Period. "Granted," he said, "it was just like fighting motherhood or apple pie. Freedom of the press is one of those code-words."

As for complaints by Seymour and Hess about the witnesses—well, Mardian insisted, Seymour didn't like Macomber, didn't like Macomber's testimony. "He didn't like what he testified about the effect of the Papers on our dealing with other countries, the business about the Swedes whoring for us, the fact that Americans were flying over Thailand when the Thais had denied it and that the Canadians had been less than honest in dealing with Vietnam."

The passage of years had blurred Mardian's recollection a bit. It was Doolin who had testified about the Swedes and the point about the Thais was not that the Americans were flying over Thailand but that the Thais were flying in U.S. planes over Laos.

The Gurfein Opinion

Outside Judge Gurfein's chambers in Foley Square there is a small marble hall. Shortly after noon on Saturday, June 19, the room began to fill with reporters, photographers, curiosity seekers and, finally, counsel for *The New York Times* and the government. Judge Gurfein had promised his decision by 2 P.M. and he and his law clerk had been up most of the night preparing it.

No one in the assemblage and, indeed, no one in the course of the whole proceedings recalled that this was a moment in history as well as the present, just twenty days shy of the one hundreth anniversary of *The New York Times'* exposé of the Tweed Ring.

On July 8, 1871, *The Times* had published the first excerpts from a transcript that had fallen into its hands of the transactions whereby Boss Tweed of Tammany Hall had stolen no less than $90 million a year from the treasury of New York City.

The Tweed Ring story was a journalistic classic. Every young reporter had heard how two enemies of Boss Tweed had come to *The Times* and pressed into the hands of the editors the fateful Tweed accounts.

Times reporters had not copied off the books at City Hall themselves. *The Times* was the beneficiary of the unauthorized actions of the men who provided transcripts that proved Tweed's graft. The mechanism of the Tweed Ring exposé—government documents, unauthorized copying, unauthorized publication—the whole pattern was identical with that of the Pentagon Papers. The differences lay in time and geography. *The Times'* exposé of 1871 brought not a legal action by the Tweed Ring to suppress the revelations but the offer of a $5 million bribe from Tammany.

The Times' articles destroyed Tammany as it then existed and Boss Tweed and his Ring. It was in its way as devastating as the Pentagon Papers, which would in their ultimate effect destroy a President.

But with that curious lack of historicism which characterized *The Times* of 1971 no one thought to point out this parallel to Alexander Bickel and Floyd Abrams. Somehow it didn't occur to Bancroft, Rosenthal, Frankel, Reston or even Punch Sulzberger, steeped as he was in the traditions of *The Times,* to remember that the reputation of *The Times* had been founded on an enterprise which, given the differences between the 1870s and the 1970s, provided as close a parallel as one might seek.

As Floyd Abrams was to say much later, "What I would have given if someone had mentioned this to me! It was such a dramatic parallel. Of course, legally the two actions were different. But the historical analogy—God, what Bickel could have done with that!"

Why did the historical parallel escape the attention of *The Times?* None now can say. Perhaps with the changing of the guard that followed Punch Sulzberger's accession as publisher, continuity and tradition had worn thin. The "old Dukes," as Gay Talese would have called them, men like Lester Markel, the Sunday editor, Charles Merz, the editorial page editor, even Turner Catledge, the remarkable managing editor who had bridged the epoch between *The Times* of Mr. Ochs and that of his grandson, were no longer there. Now, as the favorite words of Arthur Hays Sulzberger, carved on the reception hall of *The Times* proclaimed, "Every day is a fresh beginning; every morn is a world made new."

It was 2:45 P.M. before Judge Gurfein's opinion, still bearing interlined corrections and revisions, was handed out. It was as eloquent an affirmation of the principles asserted by *The Times* as one could wish, and, as time and circumstance were to show, Gurfein's opinion was the most eloquent, most elegant, most precise of all the opinions that were to be written, including the nine individual opinions that would be submitted by the Supreme Court along with Burger's decision in behalf of the court as a whole.

Gurfein was not convinced by the government. The testimony of representatives of the State and Defense departments and the Joint Chiefs of Staff failed, as he said, to convince him that "the publication of these historical documents would seriously breach the national security."

To be sure, he conceded, "any breach of security will cause the jitters in the security agencies themselves and indeed in the foreign governments who deal with us." But "without revealing the content of the [secret] testimony," he said, "no cogent reasons" were advanced to demonstrate that anything other than "general embarrassment" might result.

He accepted the contention of *The Times* that in publishing the documents it had done no more than "to vindicate the right of the public to know." There was no evidence of intention to communicate vital secrets to a foreign government or to the detriment of the United States.

He conceded that First Amendment rights were not absolute and might well not protect the divulging of the sailing of troop transports or the numbers and locations of troops.

But the kinds of security that might be asserted against the First Amendment were, in his view, extremely limited. The concept of the amendment must be read in "the light of the struggle of free men against prior restraint of publication."

"From the time of Blackstone," he wrote, "it was a tenet of the founding fathers that precensorship was the primary evil to be dealt with in the First Amendment."

Fortunately, no sharp clash between security values and free-press values was in his view involved in the Pentagon Papers. The only question was one of embarrassment "and we must learn to live with it."

Then in a passage which was to be quoted again and again and would go down as one of the great statements of the role of the press in a free society he added:

"The security of the Nation is not at the ramparts alone. Security also lies in the value of our free institutions. A cantankerous press, an obstinate press, an ubiquitous press must be suffered by those in authority in order to preserve the even greater values of freedom of expression and the right of the people to know. . . .

"In the last analysis it is not merely the opinion of the editorial writer or of the columnist which is protected by the First Amendment. It is the free flow of information so that the public will be informed about the Government and its actions.

"These are troubled times. There is no greater safety valve for discontent and cynicism about the affairs of Government than freedom of expression in any form. This has been the genius of our institutions throughout our history. It has been the credo of all our Presidents. It is one of the marked traits of our national life that distinguish us from other nations under different forms of government."

He continued the temporary restraining order so that the government could seek a stay from the Court of Appeals. This the government attorneys promptly did by taking the elevator up to the chambers of Circuit Judge Irving R. Kaufman, who granted the government's application, to the amazement of Goodale, who, as he later admitted, had committed his "only mistake of the litigation" by telephoning *The Times* and telling them to prepare to resume publication of the Papers.

If *The Times* was cheered by Gurfein's ruling—as it was—this was not the case at the White House. John Ehrlichman was called in by Mr. Nixon at 4:30 P.M. to consider the situation posed by what the President called "the novel doctrine" of Judge Gurfein.

The President said he was now prepared to "forget the press' good opinion" and go full steam ahead on the offensive. It was important, he asserted, to win the cases but "the next best thing was to get the Public view right."

Toward that end he proposed to "hang it all on Johnson." It was, he said, a "Johnson Administration" affair and "we're on the higher ground." As Herb Klein, his press coordinator, put it, we have "no fear of *our* future." If the case was lost in the courts, well, Mr. Nixon said, it wasn't necessarily bad because "LBJ screwed up the war."

Mr. Nixon decided to send a copy of the Pentagon Papers to Congress and ordered this done over the weekend. He also ordered a grand jury investigation but this was to be of Ellsberg "not [the] paper," as he put a terse reference to *The Times*. The grand jury was to get to work "now" and was to approach the matter from the angle that Ellsberg "is a thief rather than an informer."

He made a series of telephone calls to Kissinger, Mitchell and others to rally the administration's biggest guns for his campaign and was particularly interested in getting the views of Admiral Noel Gayler, chief of the National Security Agency, whose name Ehrlichman spelled "Galer" in his notes. But Gayler, it appeared, was "not as involved" as the President supposed. In any event the Defense Department was to round up all its top experts for a special Sunday meeting "to dig out material for affidavits."

27

The "Top Spook" Episode

Y EARS AFTER the Pentagon Papers case had been decided, years after the great challenge had given way to Watergate, to the resignation of President Nixon and the new issues which lay ahead, those of the CIA, the FBI and the whole role of secrecy and ethics in American life, what came to be known to a narrow circle of *New York Times'* executives and lawyers as the "Top Spook" episode still haunted their minds. To some it had become a metaphor of the whole affair, of the banality of official secrecy, the paranoia of the clerks.

The Top Spook episode had its origins in the sweeping verdict in behalf of *The Times* rendered by Judge Gurfein on Saturday afternoon, June 19. Then for the first time it began to dawn on Mardian, Buzhardt and officials of the National Security Agency that their blind belief in the infallibility of Executive power might not be supported by the courts; that, in fact, *The Times,* the *Washington Post* and other newspapers that were beginning to get into the act might shortly be publishing the Pentagon Papers with impunity.

After Gurfein announced his decision Buzhardt told Seymour that a man—who came to be known as the Top Spook, a high official of the National Security Agency—wanted to talk with someone from *The Times,* possibly Sulzberger or Bancroft, about certain security problems involved in the Papers.

When Seymour relayed the request to Bickel it aroused apprehension, particularly on the part of Hegarty, who was concentrating on the area of codes and security. "We thought it might be a trap," he recalled. "Something might be unloaded on us and we would be unable to respond. They would tell us more than we wanted to know. It would all happen outside the litigating process. We would be unable to cross-examine or refer to it. It might increase our risk of criminal prosecution and we would be mouse-trapped."

There were so many unknowns that Hegarty was loath to have *The Times* meet the Top Spook. Goodale, McKay, Abrams and he talked with Seymour. They complained that the government was already planting stories in the press about *The Times* endangering codes. "We suggested that if we got in bed with the Top Spook we might be in dutch," Hegarty recalled.

Late Saturday afternoon, after assurances from Seymour, *The Times* agreed to meet the man from the NSA. The Top Spook was not permitted to talk with anyone who did not have the highest security clearances. Bancroft had these clearances from his State Department days; Sulzberger had only his out-dated Top Secret clearance from his Marine Corps service; Bancroft was selected to represent *The Times*.

A Sunday morning meeting at Seymour's office was proposed but that wasn't secure enough for the Top Spook. Seymour's apartment or Bancroft's apartment were suggested but it turned out after all that the Top Spook couldn't be in New York on Sunday.

Finally a rendezvous was fixed for 3 P.M. Monday. Seymour came up with an ingenious idea. He arranged for the use of a small room at the Bar Association of New York building located between Fifth and Sixth avenues midway in the block. It had the unusual advantage of entrances on both Forty-third and Forty-fourth streets. Seymour and the Top Spook would enter through Forty-fourth Street, Bancroft and Hegarty through Forty-third. The parties would meet in a little room off the library stacks without having spoken a word in public.

The Top Spook came to New York on Sunday night and shared a hotel room with his bodyguard (he was not permitted to sleep alone), making his appearance in Seymour's office in late morning. The bodyguard, who was introduced as "Joe," carried two holstered revolvers. The Top Spook carried two more, one prominently strapped to his chest. The pair looked as though they had been sent by Central Casting for a remake of *Gang Busters*. The Top Spook was not permitted to walk the streets without the bodyguard at his side. "My impression," Hegarty would say later, "was that the bodyguard had orders that in any attempt at kidnaping he was to shoot the Top Spook."

The strange trio, the tall aristocratic Seymour, the rather short, dark-haired Spook, with his faint *Mitteleuropa* air, and the gangster bodyguard arrived just at 3 P.M. at the Forty-fourth Street entrance to the Bar Association and went straight to the rendezvous, getting there simultaneously with Hegarty and Bancroft.

The five men sat down in the dumpy little room. "It was the damndest thing I was ever in," Bancroft, a tweedy, Ivy League man, recalled. "The fellow sat there right across the table from me with that damn pistol strapped to his chest."

Seymour opened the discussion with the statement that the meeting was "completely off-the-record." "It has never been held," said Hegarty, and Seymour concurred. Seymour said the Top Spook had come from Washington to outline possible problems concerning the Pentagon Papers and a possible way of "defusing them." He was going to disclose some highly classified information and since he, Seymour, was not cleared to hear such information he would leave the room. Bancroft said he must make plain that he was not authorized to make any decision. All matters would have to be referred to the publisher.

Hegarty, Seymour and "Joe" withdrew, leaving Bancroft alone with the Top Spook. Hegarty and Seymour had gone to Yale together and now they sat outside on the landing or paced back and forth, making "lawyer talk" while Harding and the Spook conferred. Bodyguard Joe, his guns plainly obvious, did not leave his post at the door. Hegarty could not help thinking that if anyone chanced by they would find it more than strange to see Seymour in a secret rendezvous with the lawyer for *The New York Times,* an armed bodyguard hovering nearby. But no one passed.

Within the wretched room the conversation of Bancroft and the Top Spook was hardly of a caliber to sustain a John Le Carré thriller. Bancroft asked the Spook whether the matter concerned a single isolated document, several such documents, a category of documents or the whole forty-seven volumes of the Papers. The Spook replied that he was afraid it was the latter, the whole forty-seven volumes. What he was interested in, he said, was to make certain that publication did not disabuse a foreign government in the security of its communications, that successes in this regard were not mentioned, that means employed in interceptions were not revealed and that no time frames of interceptions were disclosed.

This, the Top Spook said, could be avoided if in publishing the Papers *The Times* avoided revealing intelligence sources, anything identifying specific movement of North Vietnamese troops or supplies or reference to specific interceptions from foreign governments.

Bancroft said he understood what worried the Spook and assured him that *The Times,* as a responsible newspaper, did not wish to breach such considerations. He saw no reason why *The Times* could not operate with these factors in mind. However, he said, some *Times* editors might not be "A" students and might by inadvertence fail to spot something that should not be published.

The Spook said he knew this and was prepared to help as much as possible but he would have to clear this with his superiors and was not sure they would agree. If Bancroft called him he would try to respond and he gave Bancroft two Washington phone numbers, one of them his home number, which he said it was better to use. Only two or three persons, he said, all of them in the intelligence community, knew of this conversation.

Bancroft promised to report to the publisher and he thought there should be no trouble. He asked whether the Spook felt there was any hazard to U.S. codes. "Hell, no," the Spook replied. None whatever.

No hazard to American codes. No hazard to American or ARVN troops or their supplies.

Bancroft then showed the Spook his notes to see if they faithfully reflected the points which had been raised and the Spook said they did. The Spook asked if Bancroft would sign an oath that sensitive and classified information had been disclosed to him and swear not to divulge it. He showed Bancroft a standard security oath used by the CIA and the NSA, a document known as a "disclosure statement." Bancroft asked if the Spook was requesting him to sign. The Spook said no. Then, said Bancroft, if I do not sign it this will not be regarded as a refusal. No, the Spook said, it will not. Bancroft did not sign the document and the Spook put it back in his briefcase.

Several times the Spook emphasized that the NSA was totally apolitical. It had no interest whether the Pentagon Papers were published or not except for security concerns.

That ended that. The Top Spook vanished with Seymour and bodyguard Joe. Bancroft and Hegarty walked the block or so back to *The New York Times,* shaking their heads over this new lesson in "Top Secrets" and reported the talk to Punch Sulzberger, Abe Rosenthal and Jim Greenfield. Greenfield said he'd look the copy over again but had already edited it with these considerations in mind.

Years later all of the participants remembered the Top Spook episode vividly but not one could remember the Spook's name. "I think his first name was Milton," Hess recalled. "Milton Somebody. He was a top man on secrets and codes." "It was some very simple name," Seymour said. "Something like Jones, I think, if he used his right name."

Bancroft had no recollection at all. But he remembered he had jotted his notes on a long yellow legal pad. By this time he was retired from *The Times,* raising Angus beef cattle in Millbrook, New York. Perhaps, he thought, he still had the memo out in the barn stored with some of his old papers from *The Times.* He looked and emerged, much as Whittaker Chambers had emerged from the pumpkin field. The memo had survived. There in Bancroft's clear handwriting was the name of the Top Spook, just as he had given it so many years before—Milton Zaslow, deputy director of the Office of Production of the National Security Agency. Milty . . .

"Stolen Documents"

The Times lost the next Pentagon round despite the fact that the government attorneys, Seymour and Hess, had become more and more dubious of their case. Hess, having extensively sampled the forty-seven Pentagon volumes, concluded that there was little if anything outside the four diplomatic volumes which deserved security classification. Seymour largely shared his view.

"We took a strong stand on the four volumes," Hess recalled. "But we had concluded that in the end forty-three out of the forty-seven might be important to one degree or another but really did not rise to the level of Top Secret classification so far as the current time was concerned."

The four diplomatic volumes concerned negotiations about and with North Vietnam and efforts by the United States to line up support among neutral and allied nations.

"We saw the only real issue as being confined to these four volumes," Hess recalled. "But my understanding is that these four volumes were never given out."

His understanding was correct. *The Times* did not and had never possessed these volumes. Nor had the *Washington Post* or the other newspapers, the *Boston Globe,* the Knight newspapers, the *Los Angeles Times,* the *Chicago Sun-Times* or the *St. Louis Post-Dispatch,* which eventually got around to publishing segments of the Papers on their own. The four diplomatic volumes had been consistently reserved by Ellsberg for precisely the reasons stated by Hess.

The realistic appraisal by Hess and Seymour did not hamper their efforts to prosecute the case against *The Times.* They changed tactics somewhat and when Bickel permitted himself to be trapped into a bootless argument with the presiding and conservative Chief Judge Henry J. Friendly, of the Appeals Court, over whether *The Times* was in the possession of "stolen documents" the case got off to a ragged start from which it never recovered. Seymour's presentation was skilled and his tactics clever. He managed to submit to the court a "special appendix," which he described as a mere housekeeping matter. In fact, it turned out to be fresh affidavits from government officials supporting allegations of "security dangers." These were the fruit of the Sunday meeting that President Nixon had ordered held at the Pentagon to collect evidence and, in fact, the affidavits were those that had been submitted at an *in camera* hearing conducted by Judge Gesell in the *Washington Post* case on Monday, the windows and doors of his courtroom sealed with black plastic to enhance "security." The *Post* had its expert diplomatic and military reporters on hand and was able to cross-examine and devastate the government presentation. One government contention was that the Pentagon Papers revealed details of Operation Marigold, an ill-fated American peace initiative toward Hanoi late in 1966 involving a Polish diplomat. *Post* reporters demonstrated that Operation Marigold had been widely written about (President Johnson discussed it in detail in his memoirs) and the Pentagon Papers revealed nothing new. By submitting the information in a sealed affidavit, Seymour, over the objections of Bickel, presented the materials to the eight-judge court without giving *The New York Times* a chance to rebut them, as had been possible in Washington.

The wrangle about "stolen documents" pursued Bickel to the end of his presentation, Judge Friendly finally proposing sarcastically that they be called "embezzled documents." Friendly's colleagues picked up the question and elaborated on it. Judge Mansfield suggested that *The Times* was "arrogating to yourself the power to decide what is of vital national defense importance."

Later, Abrams and Goodale were to say that they had not expected to win in the Court of Appeals. They were convinced that Judge Friendly would have supported the government and opposed *The Times* even if the question of the "purloined papers" had not arisen. Given the composition of the court, they felt that a decision against *The Times* was almost certain. Hess and Seymour believed it was their superior arguments that had prevailed.

Actually, the Court of Appeals decision was not a verdict for the government. The court ordered the case back to Gurfein for further *in camera* hearings on the evidence and continued the restraining order. Gurfein was to rule within ten days. The vote was five to three, three judges voting to sustain Gurfein's decision. The decision came after what one of the judges later described as possibly the "most emotional" conference of his period of service on the Court of Appeals. Three judges, headed by Friendly, wanted to override Gurfein. Three other judges were equally determined to sustain Gurfein. Two took the middle ground. A violent argument ensued. Finally, the two middle-of-the-road jurists persuaded Friendly and his two associates to vote with them on a ruling that Gurfein hear more testimony in the case.

Solicitor General Griswold

In Washington the Court of Appeals for the District of Columbia simultaneously heard the case against the *Washington Post.* The government's argument was presented by Erwin N. Griswold, the Solicitor General. It is rare for a solicitor general to argue a case in the Court of Appeals. His talents are usually reserved for the U.S. Supreme Court. Griswold had not argued a case in the appeals court for forty years.

At no point had Griswold been consulted by Attorney General Mitchell in connection with the Pentagon cases. All he knew was what he read in the newspapers and privately he was none too happy about the government's tactics. At 10 A.M. Tuesday he was called to Mitchell's office and asked to argue the case at 2 P.M. that afternoon in the Court of Appeals. "I don't know why I was asked," Griswold said much later. "I suppose it was a sign of how seriously the government regarded the matter." He demurred to Mitchell at first, saying he really knew nothing about the case and hadn't been following it. Mitchell said,

"Well, if you had rather not I suppose we can get someone else." Griswold replied that if the Attorney General really wanted him to handle it he would do so. Later, he was to say that he was being a good soldier: "When the general says, 'Charge!'—well, you charge."*

Griswold had only a couple of hours to prepare himself. Moreover, he was not properly dressed (as he thought) for court appearance, wearing, as he was, brown shoes and what he called "a noisy tie." His wife hurried down to the Justice Department with a pair of black shoes, a neat dark tie and some sandwiches he could eat at his desk.

When Griswold arrived, properly garbed, at the U.S. Court of Appeals he was challenged by a clerk who asked who would move his special admission to the appellate bar for the purpose of appearing in the *Post* case. Griswold replied that if the records went back far enough they would find "I was admitted to practice here forty years ago."

Griswold's argument went as badly for the government as did that of Bickel for *The New York Times* in New York. Griswold started by arguing property rights, citing a very old legal chestnut, the case of unauthorized publication of photographs of Queen Victoria. Griswold said that the First Amendment was not absolute and noted that the *Washington Post* was copyrighting its Pentagon articles. If the *Post* had found a Hemingway manuscript on the sidewalk or obtained a stolen copy, he said, Hemingway's widow could enjoin its publication under the copyright law.

Griswold's argument bore a remarkable resemblance to the inter-

---

*Mardian had a violently differing recollection of this. He remembered Griswold telephoning him and saying that if Mardian wanted him to argue the case in appeals court he would be glad to do it because then he would be better prepared to handle the case before the Supreme Court. "If you want me to argue the case," Mardian remembered Griswold telling him, "just call me." Griswold had no recollection of any such talk. Mardian added that Griswold did not argue the case "very eloquently" and that Mitchell, presumably acting on behalf of Mr. Nixon, wanted to know why Griswold appeared in appeals court. Mardian insisted that it was "my job" to argue the case in appeals court and Griswold's to handle the case in Supreme Court but because of Griswold's offer "I let him do it." Perhaps, with the passage of years, Mardian's memory misled him. (Personal interview, Mardian, 2/15/79)

There is nothing in Ehrlichman's Pentagon notes to support Mardian's version. A note of June 25 makes clear that Mr. Nixon personally approved Griswold's appearance before the Supreme Court (Mr. Nixon had abandoned his early suggestion that he might personally argue the case). There is nothing to suggest Mr. Nixon was displeased by Griswold's presentation. He did, however, become disenchanted with Mardian's handling of Pentagon. When Mardian went to San Clemente to report to Mr. Nixon July 12 the President was not satisfied, Ehrlichman recalled, and asked for "early designation of a White House man-in-charge." In fact, the President's dissatisfaction must have been manifest earlier since on July 9 Ehrlichman reported the decision to establish the "special project" that became known as the Plumbers. (House Judiciary Committee, Appendix III, p. 137)

change which Mardian recalled with Max Frankel in Judge Gurfein's robing room about *The Times* copyrighting "government property." It reflected, as well, an expressed White House desire to "change the focus of attention" by emphasizing that the Papers were government property and, thus, that to use them was to steal them. "This is a thief as distinguished from an informer," Ehrlichman wrote in his notes of a talk with Mr. Nixon June 19. The President proposed the catchlines "Do you approve of the theft of government papers?"; "Should a thief be punished?"

Wherever the idea came from it earned Griswold nothing but trouble. Judge J. Skelly Wright broke him off and asked for First Amendment arguments. "You know the First Amendment as well as I do," Wright said. Chief Judge David L. Bazelon asked, "Does your case depend on these documents being the property of the United States and thus copyrighted?" Griswold said it did not but that the law of literary property was relevant.

On the facts of the case, said Griswold, "the integrity of the institution of the presidency" was at stake. The President must be able to discuss issues frankly with subordinates "without the chilling effect— and I use that word with real feeling in this case" of press disclosure.* Pointing out that more and more papers had begun to publish the Pentagon Papers, Judge Robb asked, "Would you be asking us to ride herd on a swarm of bees?"

In a one-hour *in camera* session Bradlee agreed not to publish "very limited quotations from two documents which the *Post* did not deem to be of reportorial significance." Whether the *Post* actually had the two documents was not made clear.

Theater of the Absurd

Next morning there was another *in camera* session. The government had claimed publication of the Papers might disclose American capability for intercepting other nations' secret messages. Now the judges reconvened in solemn ceremony to receive what the government declared was an extraordinary piece of evidence. Behind locked doors, all unauthorized persons cleared from the chamber, the court was declared in session. A top-ranking aide to Vice Admiral Noel Gayler, director of the National Security Agency, appeared before the bench and handed to Chief Judge David L. Bazelon a briefcase. The briefcase was secured with double locks. Within it, declared the aide, was a communication from Gayler giving an instance of a threat to the security of

---

*In a White House meeting that very afternoon Mr. Nixon reiterated his view of the Pentagon case: "It's a PR problem." (House Judiciary Committee, Appendix III, p. 103)

U.S. code-breaking capability. Bazelon, with some difficulty, managed to unlock the first lock, then the second. He drew out of the briefcase a large manila envelope and opened it. Inside there was a smaller manila envelope. He opened that. Within the smaller manila envelope was a third envelope, this one small, white, bearing a red seal and ribbons. Before the hushed room Bazelon pulled the ribbon, broke the seal and opened the white envelope. Silently he read it, then passed it to the prosecution. The prosecution read the message and handed it back to Bazelon. Now he handed it to the *Post* lawyers. They read it. The silence deepened. The communication was signed by Gayler himself. It cited a cable contained in the Pentagon Papers which he said would reveal that the NSA had the capability of intercepting North Vietnamese communications and breaking their code. It related to a specific intercept which was said by the Defense Department to prove that North Vietnamese ships had fired on the Americans in the Gulf of Tonkin incident in August 1964.

There was a hush as the *Post* lawyers handed the message to George Wilson, the *Post*'s defense correspondent and the *Post*'s principal technical adviser on the Pentagon Papers evidence.

"I looked at the cable," Wilson recalled. "I knew that I had seen it before in public print. It was a moment of unbelievable tension. Suddenly it came totally clear to me. I had seen it on page thirty-four of the 1968 Senate Foreign Relations Committee hearings on the Tonkin Gulf. It was on the left side of the page. I could close my eyes and see it there."

By a Walter Mitty chance Wilson had a copy of the hearings in his back pocket. He reached for the pocket, opened the document and pointed out the cable in the testimony of February 20, 1968, to the *Post* lawyers. The dazzled lawyers seized the Wilson copy of the hearings and read out the relevant cable to Bazelon and the assembled judges. The government lawyers were stunned, asked for a recess and consulted the NSA, which was unable to come up with anything except the lame argument that the cable as printed in the Pentagon Papers carried a time group, indicating the day, hour and minute of transmission. But since neither the *Post* nor *The Times* nor anyone else had printed this or any other time group the argument fell on its face.

In all of the Pentagon court sessions, the trials of *The Times* in District and U.S. Court of Appeals, the *Post* trials in District Court and Court of Appeals, and the joint case in the U.S. Supreme Court, this was the solitary example ever cited to indicate a threat to the U.S. code-breaking capability. The example had no validity.

The U.S. Court of Appeals in Washington held seven to two for the *Washington Post* and the twin cases headed for the U.S. Supreme Court. The court agreed on Friday morning, June 25, to hear arguments the next day, Saturday, June 26, at 11 A.M. Four of the Supreme Court members, Justices Black, Douglas, Brennan and Marshall would have approved the judgments of Gurfein and Gesell forthwith.

The Supreme Court freed *The Times* and the *Post* to resume publication of the Pentagon Papers if they desired, except for sensitive material which could be so designated by the government. Rosenthal immediately responded that, on principle, he did not desire to give the government the right to decide what could and what could not appear in print. "That would be publishing under conditions," he said. "We're not inclined to do that." Bradlee, at the *Post,* was prepared to resume publication but at 5 P.M. the government submitted its list of forbidden subjects—forty-two in all (at 9 P.M., long after the deadline, the State Department tried to add four more subjects)—and as far as Rosenthal and Bradlee were concerned the question became moot. They would not publish under these restrictions. Moreover, secrecy was getting worse and worse. The list of excluded items was stamped "Top Secret." Rosenthal and his editors (as well as Bradlee) were forbidden to see it. Only lawyers working on the case and men like Max Frankel and Harding Bancroft for *The Times* and George Wilson for the *Post* were permitted to see the list of prohibited subjects, which in some cases comprised whole volumes of the Papers. The four diplomatic volumes that *The Times* did not have, for example, were banned.

The closer the case came to final resolution the higher were the barriers with which the government sought to protect its "secrets."

The affair was being turned into a medieval charade. The more apparent it became that the government had, in fact, nothing to hide, the more elaborate were the curtains held up to conceal the fact that the Emperor wore no clothes. It reminded me of the extraordinary security precautions Soviet authorities once took with trains passing through the supposedly fortified area of Porkkala in Finland near Leningrad. Trains were halted, great wooden covers were clamped on all windows, passengers were forbidden to move from car to car, sentries with bayoneted rifles stood guard in each coach—all to conceal the fact that, in truth, no fortifications existed in Porkkala.

Now the government refused to permit its exhibits in *The Times* case in New York to be transported to Washington because of "security" dangers. It refused to let the exhibits be duplicated without special permission from the Secretary of Defense and there was not time to obtain this permission and forward it to New York before the Saturday hearing in the Supreme Court.

Finally it was agreed that the government could deliver another set of the forty-seven-volume Pentagon study to the Supreme Court in place of that which was used in New York. The *in camera* exhibits could be brought to Washington but not by commercial airliner for fear of hijacking. If *The New York Times* would provide a limousine the documents could be transported to Washington accompanied by Paul C. Kurland, a *New York Times* lawyer, and Daniel Kellerman, a National Security Agency security officer. The limousine left New York at 4:30 P.M., arrived at the Supreme Court Building in Washington at a little after 9 P.M. and the documents were turned over to the clerk of the court after an elaborate set of receipts was signed.

From the beginning security officers put on even more of a show in Washington than they had in New York, so much of a show that some judges later thought the administration was deliberately trying to awe the courts through a theatrical display into believing that *The Times* and the *Post* had put the nation in terrible peril.

The first indication of this appeared in Judge Gesell's courtroom where three or four uniformed National Security Agency guards turned up with pistols on their hips. When the judge asked what the guards were doing he was told they were to "guard the documents," that is the Pentagon Papers. The judge sent word that he didn't need them and compelled them to leave.

The *Washington Post*'s lawyer, William Glendon, asked to see the secret affidavits that the government was going to present to Judge Gesell, a normal privilege of the defense, but the government refused to turn them over. However, at Judge Gesell's order the Justice Department let Glendon read them at the Justice Building under the watchful eye of an FBI agent. Glendon examined the affidavits, showed them to his colleagues and took some notes. At this point Mardian came in and told Glendon that note-taking was forbidden. After an angry exchange Glendon said that he was going to take his notes. If Mardian and the FBI men tried to stop him "there's going to be a helluva fight and I know I'm going to lose; but when I stand up in court tomorrow and I've got a few bandages on me, I'm going to tell people exactly what happened, that I was beaten up by the Department of Justice."

That stopped Mardian and it was agreed Glendon could have his notes if he would be personally responsible for them. Security agents came to Glendon's office and kept him in view as he worked on the *Post*'s secret briefs. For whatever reason the security men never objected to Glendon's secretaries, none of whom were cleared for Top Secret.

When Gesell was ordered to take more evidence by the Court of Appeals he held his hearing at his house because there was no air conditioning at the courthouse over the weekend. Guards showed up and took stations around the house to "protect" it. The government, it turned out, had told the NSA that the evidence included "war plans" which might be seized "by the enemy." After the hearings the guards wanted to take away the Papers. Gesell refused. He needed them in writing his ruling. When the guards asked how he was going to protect the Papers he said he had a big pillow on the divan in his living room and would hide them under the pillow when he got through working.

Mardian tried to bar the *Washington Post* defendants from Gesell's hearing at his house. As in *The New York Times* case the government had named all the masthead executives of the *Post* as defendants. Mardian claimed that Gurfein had barred *The Times* defendants from attending the *in camera* hearing and insisted that Gesell do the same. (Gurfein had done no such thing; he had insisted that *Times* men be present over Mardian's objection.) Gesell told Mardian, "This is not Russia. If you insist on barring the defendants I am going to dismiss your complaint here and now." At that Mardian backed down.

Such Graustarkian antics were not confined to "the enemy," as one security man characterized the newspapers and their lawyers. The same treatment was given to the Solicitor General of the United States.

When Griswold was confronted on Friday with the necessity of appearing in the Supreme Court on Saturday he was, as he recalled, "in the same position as Alex Bickel," that is, he had no more seen the Pentagon Papers than had Bickel. His first act was to have the set of forty-seven volumes delivered to his office. It arrived accompanied by a security guard who turned to Griswold's secretary and said, "Who is she?" Griswold said she was his secretary and would be working with him. "Is she cleared?" asked the security agent. Griswold said he did not know and did not have time to check. "Well," said the guard, "she can't work on it unless she is cleared." Griswold told him politely but firmly to get out and report to anyone he wanted, the woman was his secretary and he was going to need her help.

He then brought in, successively, State's Macomber, Lieutenant General Melvin Zais, director of operations for the Joint Chiefs of Staff (who had been an expert witness in the *Washington Post* case) and Vice Admiral Noel Gayler of NSA. He spent an hour with each man, saying "Now you tell me what are these things in this which are really bad." Griswold calculated that there were seven million words in the forty-seven volumes and there was no other way to get to the heart of the matter. The three men selected forty-two items which they considered "security risks."

He quickly concluded that one reason the cases had been brought was that nobody in the Justice Department knew anything about the Papers, had no knowledge of what might be in them or had even heard of them. (He could with slight modifications have applied this observation to the Defense Department and the White House as well.) Griswold decided that the real objective of the suit was simply to say "For

God's sake, give us time to find out what this is all about." Had he been privy to the private discussions of President Nixon, Henry Kissinger, John Ehrlichman and H. R. Haldeman he would have been less charitable.

After going over the forty-two items, Griswold picked eleven and waived the others. Later he conceded that "actually I would have claimed rather less than the eleven myself but I had to take into account the wishes of other people in the department." This was a reference to Attorney General Mitchell, who was loath to narrow the case but finally agreed to Griswold's list of eleven, one of which was the four diplomatic volumes that the newspapers did not have.

Later a reporter specializing in defense subjects suggested that the military could have come up with other and possibly genuine security items but did not do so because "they didn't trust even the government lawyers." Lack of trust in the government lawyers seems to have existed; that genuine security items were concealed in the Papers seemed less and less likely with the passage of years and extensive scrutiny of the Papers. The reality of what the government was conducting became plain from what was later revealed about the calculations of the White House, the personalities of the actors—a kind of Grand Guignol.

Griswold began dictating his secret brief about 6 P.M. Friday evening and it was 3 A.M. before he was finished. FBI agents guarded his office through the night. He and his secretary met at 8 A.M. Saturday morning and he proofread what she had typed, ran it off on the duplicating machine himself, twelve copies in all, and headed for the Supreme Court. There he encountered the NSA security agent again, the man who had objected to his secretary. "What are you going to do with those briefs?" the man asked. Griswold said he was going to file them with the clerk of the court. "Is the clerk cleared?" he asked. Griswold said he did not know and handed them to the clerk. The agent saw Griswold had two more copies. "What are you going to do with these?" he asked. Griswold said he would give one to Alex Bickel for *The New York Times* and one to Glendon for the *Post.* "Well," said the agent, "that is giving it to the enemy." Griswold shrugged his shoulders and turned over the copies.

But that was not the end of it. Monday morning, after the Supreme Court argument had been held and while a decision was awaited, Griswold got down to his office about 9 A.M. He was surprised to find Glendon waiting there.

Griswold asked to what he owed the honor of the early morning call.

"Well," said Glendon, "I never got to read your secret brief."

"What in the world do you mean?" asked Griswold. "I personally handed you a copy in the Supreme Court on Saturday morning."

"Yes," said Glendon, "but as soon as the argument was over that security guard came up and took it away from me."

And it was a fact. The security men not only took Glendon's copy away. They took Bickel's copy. They took the copies of Bickel's secret brief as well as Glendon's just as they had taken away the secret briefs in the Court of Appeals and to this day parts of them are still held under lock and key although they do not now, nor ever have, included one fact which even an armchair general would rationally consider of security concern.

There was to be one more element of the theater of the absurd before the Supreme Court convened. Secretly, and with no notice to lawyers for either *The Times* or the *Post,* Griswold filed with the Supreme Court a motion to hold a part of the hearing *in camera.* * Just before the justices entered the chamber the clerk called Bickel aside and informally told him of the government's request so that he might be apprised of it when the matter came up. But, for the moment, said the clerk, the matter must be considered secret. A moment later the bailiff chanted his traditional "Oyez, oyez," and the nine black-robed justices took their places on the high bench. When there was silence Chief Justice Burger announced that the government's secret motion, of which to this day defense counsel has no *official* notice (in violation of all judicial precedent and rule), had been denied over the dissent of himself and Justices Harlan and Blackmun. The case was now ready for argument and the Chief Justice called upon Mr. Griswold to begin.

*Griswold also filed two new affidavits of the State and Defense departments alleging additional security risks contained in the Pentagon Papers. This was done despite the 5 p.m. Friday deadline the court had fixed for such materials. (Anthony Lewis, unpublished notes, p. 260)

28

"'No Law' Does Not Mean 'No Law'"

T HERE IS NO CEREMONIAL in the United States that exceeds in awe a session of the Supreme Court, the Ionic dignity of the pillared courtroom, the Italianate marble walls, the great curtains of red velvet velour, the dark mahogany bar of justice, the gleaming ceiling lights, the uniformed ushers, the frock coats and morning trousers of the lawyers, the nine leather chairs with tall backs, the unchanging ritual, the justices in their robes, the nine black beetles of the Temple of Karnak as a Washington correspondent once dubbed them.

The session of Saturday morning, June 26, was no exception. The queue began to assemble not long after daybreak and swelled to 1,500 by the time the court was called into session at 11 A.M. But only 174 seats were available for the public.

It was a harshly divided court which took its place at the high bench, Chief Justice Warren Burger, new to his role, a Nixon appointee who already had begun to change the activist court of his predecessor, Earl Warren; a phalanx (soon to suffer grievous losses) of the once liberal majority of Warren days—Justices Black, Douglas (who had flown back from his home at Goose Prairie, Washington, where he had already started his summer vacation), William J. Brennan, Jr., and Thurgood Marshall (these four would have thrown out the government's case forthwith); Justice Byron White (a John F. Kennedy appointee and friend, "Whizzer White" of football fame but no liberal on the bench); Justice John F. Harlan, a conservative pillar; Justice Harry Blackmun, a Nixon appointee who with Burger formed the "Minnesota twins," and finally Justice Potter Stewart, emerging "swing man," now with the liberals, now with the conservatives. It was the vote of Stewart and possibly that of White which would tell the tale.

To the eye of the beholder there was no hint in the austere scene of that cheap detective swagger which colored the underside of the great constitutional confrontation. To the spectator there was no hint of hidden drama in Burger's dry words refusing the government's motion for proceedings *in camera*. Secret briefs were mentioned by the lawyers and the justices but nothing suggested a psychodrama. No whiff of this found its way into the tens of thousands of words written and spoken about the litigation by newspapers and TV commentators. To the American public the scene was dramatic but the contours of hidden flummery cast no shadow on the visible image.

Nor did the courtly dignity with which Solicitor General Erwin Nathaniel Griswold—sixty-seven years old, bowed with honors, former dean of the Harvard Law School, first in the land; member of the United States Civil Rights Commission; holder of twenty-one honorary degrees; an appointee of the Johnson Administration—plead his case suggest that something more than a profound contest of the law was being played out before the high court.

The same could be said for the argument and demeanor of Alexander Bickel, the one-time Rumanian emigrant, forty-six, as brilliant a man as distinguished the American Bar, one-time law clerk to Felix Frankfurter, protégé of that great justice and inheritor of his philosophy of judicial restraint, author of a work on the court called *The Passive Virtues*, Chancellor Kent Professor of Law at Yale, often himself mentioned for a seat on the court before which he was for the first time appearing.

To these men, to their colleague William Glendon, representing the *Washington Post*, to the associates Floyd Abrams, James Goodale and William Hegarty, to the justices on the bench, to the distinguished audience in the chamber, to the note-taking reporters and correspondents there was not and could not have been presentiment of the White House deliberations which had produced this hour—the fact, for example, that in considering whether or not to appeal the cases to the Supreme Court Mr. Nixon laconically observed, "It's a PR problem." Or that he had stated with that elegance which often graced his Oval Office, "If the Appeals Courts skunk us—don't push it to the Supreme Court."

Attorney General Mitchell (with whom Mr. Nixon was conferring at the time) assured the President that he could count on five justices: Burger, White, Harlan, Stewart and Blackmun.

To which the President skeptically asked, "On freedom of the press?" And added a moment later, "It would be bad for our court to turn us down." Note-taker Ehrlichman carefully underlined the word "our."

Those who peopled the courtroom probably would have been startled to know that such a quarrel over the Pentagon affair had arisen between Mr. Nixon and Attorney General Mitchell on the one side and J. Edgar Hoover on the other on the eve of court argument, that Mitchell was proposing to supersede Hoover and warning that a number of top FBI men would probably resign because of Hoover's arbitrary actions. "This will finish Hoover," the President added with some satisfaction since he had been at odds with the doughty G-man for a considerable period. The row did not, of course, finish Hoover, but it did accelerate that of Mr. Nixon.

The quarrel arose over Mr. Hoover's bureaucratic objections to the investigation of Daniel Ellsberg. When Mr. Hoover balked it created a tremendous stir within the White House and strengthened Mr. Nixon's resolve to create his own investigative unit, which came to be known as the Plumbers with consequences long since familiar to all.§

The Supreme Court

But of this, of course, there was not a whisper as the notable proceedings got under way with Mr. Griswold, once again, launching into a spiel about the laws of literary copyright and the sad case of Ernest Hemingway's manuscript, found on the sidewalk, illegally sold or just plain purloined and published by *The New York Times.*

For all the tension and human emotions concentrated in the courtroom that morning it cannot be said, reading the stenographic transcript years later, that there emerged many moments of pure reason, eloquence, logic or philosophy which might convey a feeling that these were men in the vortex of argument which would change the balance of power in the greatest nation of the world.

There were niblets, not dramatic thrusts; hobby-horses of aging men not Periclean odes. The justices were impatient with Griswold and the law of literary copyright. They were more impatient as he went on to analogies from other fields in which injunctions had been imposed under the First Amendment. But they expressed their feelings by fidgeting in their large leather chairs, swinging from side to side, physical not mental signs of *ennui.* Justice Stewart was first to break into Griswold's flow and he would be the most persistent questioner of the day, a man plagued by doubts, not yet certain where his opinion lay, troubled as a justice and a citizen by the contention of conflicting rights, concerned over the First Amendment but concerned, too, about those large issues arising from the critical confrontations of nations, the lives of soldiers in wartime, the perils to a beleaguered country's security.

He was to crystallize this concern with the harshest, toughest of questions. If to publish would cost the lives of a hundred innocent soldiers, nineteen-year-olds whom fortune gave low numbers in the draft, where did the judgment lie? On this question Bickel—who from the beginning had warned that he was not a First Amendment "voluptuary"; who had before Gurfein and before the Court of Appeals

§See Notes section.

willingly and freely conceded that the First Amendment was not absolute; that there were cases when it must be put aside for some higher national interest (the troopship sailing date); that "if grave and immediate danger" could be adduced the First Amendment must yield (although he was careful to emphasize that such instances could be only the most few, the most far between and the government's proof must be overwhelming)—was brought to assert that "my inclinations to humanity overcome the somewhat more abstract devotion to the First Amendment in a case of that sort."

For this limitation on the First Amendment privilege Bickel was to draw upon himself a sharp rebuke from the great civil liberatarian Justice Douglas, who asked, "Do you read that [the First Amendment] to mean that Congress could make some laws abridging freedom of the Press? That is a very strange argument for *The Times* to be making." And Justice Hugo Black, making what was to be his last appearance on the high bench, said to Glendon that it seemed to him that Glendon and Bickel had argued the case "on the premise that the First Amendment, freedom of speech, can be abridged by Congress if it desires to do so."

Glendon denied that he had done so. Black reiterated his view.

"You were talking about standards," Black said. "I am not talking about standards. Under the First Amendment Congress shall make no law abridging freedom of the press."

Glendon repeated his denial. Black still seemed skeptical.

But, of course, they had done as Black suggested, both of them, both Glendon and Bickel, they were not arguing the First Amendment as an absolute. They were arguing as "reasonable men" and their arguments were intended to and did have powerful impact upon the most "reasonable" of the men on the court, the man who stood squarely in the middle, the man who was throughout the session openly and obviously searching for enlightenment, trying to illuminate the dark corners of the case in order to settle in his own mind where he was to stand, Mr. Justice Potter Stewart. It was in a sense his induction into the range and potentials of the First Amendment and its role in American life, and out of the argument of this case and his confrontation with its contradictions was to emerge his stature as a First Amendment scholar, his position on the Burger court as its strongest and most powerful advocate and defender.

For the Solicitor General his most difficult and delicate moment came in discussion with Justice Marshall, who suggested that if the government should prevail the courts themselves would become, in effect, censors decreeing that this item might be published and that item not. "Wouldn't we then—the federal courts—" asked Marshall, "be a censorship board?"

Griswold stumbled on an answer. He said he did not quite know what an alternative might be.

"The First Amendment might be," said Marshall tartly.

Griswold then entered a circuitous argument in which he contended that the government was supporting, not challenging, the First Amendment.

He conceded that he did not agree with Marshall's interpretation. "You say," Griswold suggested, "that 'no law' means 'no law' [in the sense that Congress shall enact no law to abridge freedom of the press] and that should be obvious. I can only say, Mr. Justice, that to me it is equally obvious that 'no law' does not mean 'no law' and I would seek to persuade the court that that is true."

If this remark by the Solicitor General sounds like a rule for playing croquet in *Alice in Wonderland* it is only because, in fact, that was the meaning which the Solicitor General sought to convey. He was saying, as eloquently as Lewis Carroll could ever have put it, that when the Constitution said that Congress shall enact no law abridging the freedom of the press the Constitution, in reality, was saying just the opposite—that Congress *could* enact such a law; that the Founding Fathers, in an eighteenth-century foretaste of George Orwell, said one thing but really meant the opposite.

Now it is a fact, as Ehrlichman's precise, unimposing, surgically accurate notes record, that this was what the White House was seeking to do; to impose upon the press in the name of upholding Constitutional verities the exact opposite of what it said it was trying to do. In the name of suppressing a "leak" it was seeking to establish a monopoly of leaks; in the name of "security" for the nation it was seeking to impose security for itself.

If there was in the Supreme Court proceeding a moment of truth it was this frank statement by the respected Solicitor General. He was there before the court to try to convince the judges that black was white; that war was peace; that truth was falsehood; that "no law" meant the right to impose a law.

He went on to argue strongly against the position of Justices Black and Douglas that the First Amendment was an absolute. But Justice Stewart intervened with the sensible declaration that counsel for the newspapers did not disagree with Griswold; they, too, felt that the First Amendment had its limits. To those who knew the personalities of the justices it seemed clear that the Solicitor General's efforts to win the swing man to the government's side had failed; that the reasonableness of the Bickel position had convinced Justice Stewart, and, in fact, this proved to be the case. The court adjourned at 1:13 P.M. after an argument of about two hours and ten minutes. Many thought the court would decide immediately with a brief *per curiam* opinion. That did not happen. The court waited four full days and only at 2:34 P.M. Wednesday, June 30, reconvened (without Douglas, who had gone back to Goose Prairie) and announced its opinion. The verdict was six to three in favor of *The Times* and the *Post.* It was the simplest of decisions and the most complex of decisions. The extraordinarily brief *per curiam* decision said (shorn of judicial citations):

> "Any system of prior restraints of expression comes to this court bearing a heavy presumption against its constitutional validity." The Government "thus carries a heavy burden of showing justification for the imposition of such a restraint." The District Court for the Southern District of New York in the New York Times case and the District Court for the District of Columbia and the Court of Appeals for the District of Columbia Circuit in the Washington Post case held that the Government had not met that burden. We agree.

Simple. Direct. Positive

But there were nine more opinions. One for each justice and some of the justices shared in whole or in part the opinions written by other justices.

Reaction

A victory for the press? A warning to the press? A confirmation of First Amendment rights? A restriction of First Amendment rights? There was something for everyone in the nine decisions. The opinions ranged from the stark absolutist views of Black and Douglas to that of Justice Blackmun, who seemed to accept the totality of the government's position that the court had decided for "the death of soldiers, the destruction of alliances, the greatly increased difficulty of negotiation with our enemies, the inability of our diplomats to negotiate," the prolongation of the war and delay in freeing prisoners of war.

Burger had sharp comments for the speed with which the case had been handled ("a parody of the judicial function"), although he had long been a critic of the court's delays, a sharper word for the failure of *The Times* to report stolen property or secret government documents to responsible public officers, a duty, he said, which "rests on taxi drivers, justices and *The New York Times,*" yet, while agreeing in large measure with the negative views of Justices Blackmun and Harlan, he had not, himself, been willing to decide the case on its merits.

There was and would continue to be wide argument over what the court had done. Had it widened or narrowed the powers of the press? Bickel, not unnaturally, felt that the press had strengthened its position; that government in the future could only come into court prepared to show "irreparable harm to the country." But he conceded that "law can never make us as secure as we are when we do not need it."

Never before, he said, had the government tried to restrain newspaper publication in peacetime and in that sense "the spell was broken and in a sense freedom was thus diminished."

"But," he added, "freedom was also extended in that the conditions in which government will not be allowed to restrain publication are now clearer and perhaps more stringent than they have been."

Griswold was philosophical. After all, he said, outside of one or two the eleven items which he had singled out as the most serious cases of "danger" had never been published.

A body of critical literature was to grow up around the Pentagon Papers case, the philosophical posture of Bickel, the meaning of the decision or decisions. There would be a major split among constitutional lawyers, a solid body of opinion forming on the liberal side that the Pentagon cases gave more ground than they gained. Years later the debate was still open. There were even those who seriously argued that the case had moved Burger himself to a position far more supportive of the First Amendment than was generally recognized. Burger, a week or so after the decision, startled an American Bar Association audience with the statement that the court had "actually been unanimous" on the basics of the case. Exactly what he meant was never quite understood. But close reading of all the opinions seemed to indicate that since each justice wrote his own (to save the time of agreeing on common language) the occasion afforded an unusual opportunity for each man to vent prejudice, frustration and spleen at a convenient and familiar target.

The sharpest critic of Bickel was Melvin L. Wulf of the American Civil Liberties Union. He felt the selection of Bickel to handle *The New York Times'* case was a mistake because Bickel had committed himself in his academic work to the thesis that the court should adopt a passive posture when confronted with Executive or Legislative action. Because of this Wulf argued, to bring in Bickel to try to convince the courts to deny the Executive Branch the right to ban the publishing "of state secrets" was to invite a conflict between Bickel the attorney and Bickel the scholar. He felt Bickel in his argument and briefs was defending his published writings rather than acting as a lawyer arguing a great constitutional principle. Thus, Wulf felt, it was no surprise that the court's decision was narrow and failed to uphold what Wulf regarded as the absolute principle guaranteed by the First Amendment.

But legal debate was not the heart of the question. The question was not what did the lawyers think but what did the editors think; what did the public think; what did the Government think. How had the Pentagon affair changed the world?

At *The New York Times* the enormous third-floor newsroom was cordoned off by guards a half hour before the decision—to keep it from overflowing with visitors, curiosity seekers and TV cameramen. The scene was tense. Rosenthal held an open phone to Washington. The news caused Rosenthal to shout, "We won it! We've all won it! We've won the right to print!" Arthur Sulzberger said he was "extremely ecstatic." Publication of the Pentagon series was resumed. The articles, carefully reexamined with an eye to the Top Spook's considerations (and reexamined in the light of Justice Stewart's opinion and some private advice from Judge Gurfein), without as far as anyone could recall any deletions except possibly one sequential set of cable designations, were published. The papers tumbled off the presses. Editors and reporters congratulated each other and themselves. It was, as far as anyone could see, a famous victory. Right and Justice had triumphed. Opinion polls showed that the country strongly supported the press. Louis Harris reported that a majority believed the government had lied about the war and tried to suppress the facts. Gallup found that only 24 percent thought Nixon was telling the people all they should know about Vietnam, 67 percent thought he was not. In February, Gallup had found 61 percent calling the war a mistake; in July, Harris reported a majority thought it was immoral. By August, 61 percent, according to Gallup, favored complete withdrawal and only 28 percent would leave the troops. In Congress the split ran on party lines and few Republicans seemed to think this was an issue to keep alive. Agnew was silent. The President was silent. Ron Ziegler told reporters that Mr. Nixon's views on the First Amendment "are well known." The war went ahead but casualty tolls were winding down as "Vietnamization" proceeded apace. Ellsberg was indicted in Los Angeles and surrendered in Boston. Ahead, of course, lay other issues, other tests. *The Times*, typically, took the larger view, seeing in the court decision not so much "a victory for the press as a striking confirmation of vitality of the American democratic form of government." It felt the Supreme Court had sent a message that "the American people have a presumptive right to be informed of the political decisions of their Government and that when the Government has been devious with the people, it will find no constitutional sanction for its efforts to enforce concealment by censorship."

In the future, *The Times* hoped, the administration would realize that major decisions "must be discussed frankly and openly and courageously" and that it would abide by Adlai Stevenson's maxim to "talk sense to the American people."

The administration must display more consideration than in the past for "freedom of speech, of the press, of assembly." *The Times* quoted with approval Mr. Justice Stewart's remark that "without an informed and free press there cannot be an enlightened people."

Mr. Nixon's Response

The President's focus was a bit different. Quite a bit. He did, indeed, meet with all promptitude to contemplate the situation in the wake of the ruling of "*our* court." To the customary complement of Ehrlichman and Haldeman he added Charles Colson, champion of devices, ringmaster-to-be of the Plumbers. The four men assembled in the Oval Office at 10:30 A.M., July 1. The subject was not the esoterics of the Constitution, not the strong stand of the Minnesota Twins, the middle-of-the-road judgment of Mr. Justice Stewart nor the hard-rock words of the First Amendment devotees, Black and Douglas. The subjects were Mr. Nixon's chapter on the Hiss case in that golden lexicon *Six Crises* and Mr. Nixon's famous speech to the House of Representatives. (Mr. Colson was later to say he read *Six Crises* a half-dozen times that summer; John Dean read it twice.)

The lesson Mr. Nixon wished to imprint on the minds of his colleagues was that the Hiss case had been "won in [the] press." He had had no help from others. Not from President Truman, not from (Attorney General) Clark, not from J. Edgar Hoover. They "wouldn't help me," Mr. Nixon recalled, but he won anyway. It was clear that he had put the court decision of yesterday firmly behind him and was going over to the offensive. The press, he declared, was on a bad wicket. The price of the First Amendment was loss of life. The press had "won the constitutional right to profit [by] the publication of stolen documents under the First Amendment. This right is superior to the right of our soldiers to live." This was the message he proposed to carry to the country, and the way to do it, he declared, is "leak stuff out. This is the way we win."*

While Mr. Nixon's associates tended to squirm a bit at his frequent references to the *Six Crises* and his homilies about the Hiss case, there was significance in this; it was not the mere reminiscence of a political war-horse recapturing memories of glories past. Mr. Nixon had fashioned a philosophy by which his political life was guided: it was to seize victory from defeat. Out of the agony of failure sprang Antaeus and tomorrow's triumph. It was from the depths of dark despair, so he thought, that he had been able to marshal the forces which led him

---

*Kissinger's attitude on his own "leaking" (as contrasted with leaks by others) was spelled out at a meeting with Mr. Nixon August 8. The President was trying to work out a system by which highly classified documents would not be reproduced or used in "off-the-record" briefings. Kissinger said that the documents simply "must be Xeroxed." The President said, "O.K.—eliminate it [the proposed ban]." Kissinger added that he could not conduct off-the-record briefings "without secret contents." In fact, he added, he "only used secret documents." The President conceded this point as well. (House Judiciary Committee, Appendix III, pp. 177–78)

on to the next goal. Thus, he saw his presidential victory of 1968 as rising from the ashes of the bitter California defeat of 1962; his success as Vice President was born in the agony of the Checkers speech. So now he wasted no time on an inquest into the Pentagon decision; no discussion of its legal implications; no thought of the role of the Bill of Rights; no damage assessment in diplomacy or national intelligence. The talk on the day after the Supreme Court verdict was on the game plan for a new political success. His eyes were on 1972.

First he proposed to cope with the charge that he sought repression of the press and "cover-up." This he would do by issuing a somewhat sanitized version of the Pentagon Papers and by a major declassification of government documents. The declassification had, in fact, been under way before the Pentagon Papers. Now it was to be accelerated by a group directed by Assistant Attorney General and future Supreme Court Justice Rehnquist. But access to security material would be radically narrowed. Out would go "Q" clearances for everyone not working for the government—Harriman, Bundy, scholars at Brookings and Rand, at the Council on Foreign Relations, Harvard and Berkeley, out would go everyone but government people and they would be cut back to the bone. Mr. Nixon recalled that when he left office after being Vice President the CIA refused to brief him when he was making trips abroad. "They were right," he said. "People outside the government don't need it."

Mr. Nixon estimated there were 100,000,000 World War II documents still classified. None needed to be. Actually it turned out that there were 505,750,000 pages of classified documents for the years 1945–63. Figures for the LBJ and Nixon periods were never adduced. Mr. Nixon wanted to declassify 90 percent of that total. He estimated that 1,200,000 persons in government had Top Secret clearance. He would cut that to 100,000. And he would create a new class of supersecret documents, documents relating to presidential decisions. Maybe 100 persons in the inner circle would have access to these.

"Top Secret," said Mr. Nixon in words which would have startled Assistant Attorney General Robert Mardian, Solicitor General Griswold and the justices of the Supreme Court, "is meaningless, e.g., the menu for the Velasco dinner [a White House state dinner menu which had been so classified]."

Mr. Nixon thought the British Official Secrets Act was a good model and the Canadian Royal Commission "set-up" as well under which, as he understood, "one can't take the Fifth Amendment and they are jailed if they refuse [to testify]."

There was, the President said, a new morality abroad in the land in which determination of what the public should know was being made by the individual. "Once you concede," said Mr. Nixon, "that one can place himself above the law the Society is finished." As an example he cited newspaper editors. Those who disobey the law, said Mr. Nixon, "are immoral though they disagree with the law. That I believe."

"If the cause is right," the President went on, "(school desegregation, demonstrations against the war) (or kick a cop in the————) they disobey. That's fascism."

Ellsberg, he said, had been quoted as saying ten years is a small price to pay. "Yes," he added, "and he'll pay it."

The President wanted to move away from the Espionage Act, which had "the smack of treason about it." Espionage wasn't involved in the Ellsberg case—that was what distinguished it from the Hiss case. (The Hiss case always was to be his measuring yardstick.) Ellsberg was an ideologue and it wouldn't do to think in terms of spies.

The Plumbers

These were Mr. Nixon's initial reactions to the great First Amendment rulings but within a day a new and fateful element entered his thinking. This was not, he became convinced, the simple case of one man, Ellsberg. It was a conspiracy. The way to handle it was to present the evidence before a congressional committee, possibly the same old reliable House Un-American Activities Committee, which had been his own first platform. A conspiracy, mused Mr. Nixon . . . a good case would reflect on the newspapers. . . . He turned to practical details—was Representative Ichord, the chairman of HUAC, the man to do it? Who were the Republicans on his committee? Call Jerry Ford and get his advice. Make up a list. Call people before the committee. Get in "guys to help" from CIA, USIA, Warren Nutter of the Defense Department, the FBI. "Our men [to] push HUAC and the bureaucracy."

By July 6 he was ruminating again that Ellsberg was not a lone operator. It was a conspiracy. "We must get at them," said the President, "the public supports this. The public is against a thief. . . ."

To do the job properly, the President felt they must have the cooperation of J. Edgar Hoover (after all, he had not been "finished," as Mr. Nixon had hoped only a week before). The conspirators must be tried in the papers. The thing to do, he said, was to "get the conspiracy smoked out through the papers. Hiss and Bently [were] cracked that way." He was referring apparently to Elizabeth Bentley, a frequent witness before HUAC, in Mr. Nixon's days.

At this meeting, not participated in by Kissinger, who was conveniently en route to China, Mr. Nixon observed that "we can't assume [Kissinger's] NSC staff are not participants" in the conspiracy. Attorney General Mitchell reported that the case against Ellsberg was going well. Mr. Nixon suggested it might be a good idea to put a "non-legal team" onto the conspiracy. This was the first mention in Ehrlichman's notes of the idea for the Plumbers. Mr. Nixon suggested as an initial assignment "domestic communist ties to Ellsberg—Minnesota meeting."

This apparently was a reference to the trial of the so-called Minnesota Eight, eight young people charged with disrupting draft procedures. They were tried in January 1971 in Minneapolis, defended by a well-known Civil Rights lawyer named Ken Tilsen. Ellsberg testified in their defense and briefly contemplated submitting the Pentagon Papers as evidence.

Mr. Mitchell reported that a grand jury had been convened in Boston to consider the case of Neil Sheehan but the President promptly said "better to convict him before a committee." The President said it had been necessary to go to court on the Pentagon Papers. That was exactly the right thing to do. But now "we must continue to protect our security" and he favored congressional committees and the press for this purpose.

Mr. Mitchell reinforced the President's concern by assuring him that there was, indeed, a conspiracy. "The documents [were] distributed by 'our' Massachusetts conspiracy group," he said.

The President responded that the administration would "leak the evidence of guilt." He instructed Mitchell to fill in Hoover and "push Laird—Buzhardt."

Mitchell's use of the phrase "our" Massachusetts conspiracy group was not accidental. It proved to be the entering wedge of a curious fallacy that was to blossom within the White House, a delusion that Ellsberg did not, in fact, give the Pentagon Papers to *The Times* and that this was the act of a second (and potentially much more dangerous) group in Cambridge that possessed other documents, documents which might contain revelations about the Nixon Administration.

This was the "other group of antiwar activists in Cambridge" in which Ehrlichman in 1979 still expressed belief. But it was a "group" which had no existence. It was summoned into imaginary life by a plethora of FBI reports about individuals in Cambridge who had a hand in, or were believed to have a hand in, the copying and distribution of the Pentagon Papers. As late as August 26, 1971, Egil Krogh and David Young, directors of the Plumbers, were reporting to Ehrlichman that what would have been called in the Moscow purge trials "an alternate conspiratorial center" had been located in Cambridge and that its directors were Leslie Gelb, Morton Halperin, Paul Warnke and "Rand executives," operating independently of Ellsberg. In fact, said Krogh and Young, Ellsberg might not even have possessed some of the materials that wound up in the hands of *The New York Times*. §

This aberration would have only ironic significance had not

§See Notes section.

this "second conspiracy" heightened Mr. Nixon's paranoia about the danger of leaks and the need for more and more urgent measures by the Plumbers. And it strengthened the belief of Egil Krogh that the dangers he had been called to face were real and serious.

An atmosphere had been created in the White House in which rumor and allegation were more easily accepted than truth. When an FBI report turned up asserting that a copy of the Papers had been delivered to the Soviet Embassy in Washington, possibly even before publication of the documents by *The Times,* apprehensions rose (except, curiously, on the part of Mr. Nixon, who never seemed to believe that Ellsberg was engaged in espionage). The report apparently came from a shadowy and controversial agent nicknamed "Fedora," a Soviet official believed by many CIA specialists to be a double agent and totally unreliable. As Krogh was later to say, the report about Ellsberg and the Soviet Embassy was never carefully examined.* Neither he nor David Young were intelligence specialists. They had no way of evaluating the information and it was simply accepted. "I think the wish was kind of the father to the thought in this case," he said. "It provided us with more of a rationale for what we were doing." One thing Krogh and Young did was to get the British M-4 or M-5, the counterintelligence branches of the British Secret Service, to check whether Ellsberg, during his year at Cambridge University as a Woodrow Wilson scholar in 1952–53, might have been contacted by Soviet agents. The check, of course, drew a blank but it was this kind of fear that set the stage for the break-in of the office of Dr. Lewis Fielding, Ellsberg's psychiatrist, the commissioning of a CIA "psychiatric profile" of Ellsberg and other White House operations of the summer of 1971 that led to the Watergate scandal and Nixon's downfall.

An aberration that vividly illuminated the eerie atmosphere within the White House was a proposal by Charles Colson revealed by John Dean in the Watergate inquiry to fire-bomb the Brookings Institution, the respected liberal "think tank" in Washington.

The stimulus for this was a brochure that fell into Colson's hands listing studies under way at the institution. One of these was called "U.S. Policy and Vietnam—the Lessons Learned." It was the project of Leslie Gelb and was being prepared with a panel of consultants, one of whom was Ellsberg. There were a number of distinguished consultants, including Charles Bohlen, Dean Acheson

---

*David Nisson, prosecutor in the Ellsberg trial, testified in the House Judiciary Committee hearings on impeachment that the reason no charge of foreign involvement or espionage was brought against Ellsberg was that the government could find no evidence to support it. (Personal interview, Ellsberg, 1/14/79)

and John J. McCloy.* When Colson saw the list he sent a memo to Ehrlichman on July 6 saying, "It looks to me like we may soon expect another installment in the Pentagon Papers written by the same authors but doubtless more up to date . . . we could expect something dropping on us this fall. In my opinion, this should be promptly investigated."

This report, John Dean recollected, had the whole White House "climbing the walls, especially Henry Kissinger." Colson, according to Dean, proposed fire-bombing the Brookings Institution and, under cover of the confusion, raiding Gelb's office to sequester the dangerous papers. Whatever the scheme (Colson denied in the Watergate inquiry that he was serious about the fire bomb), it was squelched by John Ehrlichman.

Three days after being briefed about "our Massachusetts conspiracy group" Mr. Nixon reminded his associates that he wanted General Walters put into the CIA as number two (an appointment which he did not get around to making until May 12, 1972, thereby plunging Walters into the thick of Watergate). Mr. Nixon also talked of Lieutenant Colonel Conein (who had just been interviewed by Howard Hunt regarding Diem) and of putting a new man into Defense's International Security Agency who would report directly to Mr. Nixon on an "eyes only" basis with a "weekly summary re conspiracy, documents." The President went on, inevitably, to talk of LBJ's bombing halt and observed that Kissinger's staff "must be cleaned out." Kissinger's aide, David Young, was brought into the Oval Office and given "specifics re NSC." Before the meeting ended Mr. Nixon determined to transfer "Dave Young to a special project." This project, of course, was the Plumbers.† Kissinger, being in Peking negotiating with Premier Chou En-lai, the President said that Al Haig was to be instructed, "Don't bother HAK." Young would be kept technically on Kissinger's staff but would be on "special duty." He would be working with Egil Krogh, Jr., a very clean-cut White House staff man from the West Coast who had already been named to the unit.‡

---

*The panel never met after the Pentagon Papers came out. "My God," Ellsberg remembered Gelb telling him, "we can't meet again." Ellsberg said, "That's your problem." (Personal interview, Ellsberg, 1/14/79)

†Pat Buchanan recalled later that he had been tapped to head the post-Pentagon inquiry, which was centered on Ellsberg. "Haldeman told me," he said, "the Old Man [Nixon] wanted me to be 'a sort of liaison' on the Ellsberg investigation." Buchanan agreed to talk with Mardian but couldn't understand it because "Ellsberg had already admitted he was the guy so why all the investigation." Buchanan was not sympathetic to this approach. He proposed that he write a speech for the Vice President attacking *The Times* for publishing the Papers but this was turned down. Somehow he managed to ease out of the "liaison role," which, as it turned out, was eventually given to Krogh and, in Buchanan's words, "he wasn't even the second choice." (Personal interview, Buchanan, 1/12/78)

‡Kissinger always insisted that he was not aware of the nature of Young's duties as the head of the Plumbers. It was Egil Krogh's recollection that liaison with Kissinger was

The next day Mr. Nixon spelled out what he was up to. It was crisply summarized by Ehrlichman:

> Goal
> Do to McNam, Bundy, JFK elites the same destructive job that was done on Herbert Hoover years ago.
> LBJ angle—The Kennedy people he inherited.

The President had two other observations. One was for Secretary of State Rogers. It was concise: "Should be tapping more."

The other concerned the grand jury investigating Ellsberg. It was: "Don't worry re taps on discovery re White House."

That is, the White House was not about to let the courts know, as it was obligated to do under the law, that Ellsberg and many possible defendants and witnesses had been wiretapped.

As the President had pointed out, there was a new morality abroad in the land. Some would call it a kind of fascism.

---

maintained through Young. His memory was that if he wished to communicate with Kissinger it would be through Ehrlichman and that Kissinger would communicate in the same way "or directly, Henry to David [Young]." Krogh said he believed Young welcomed the Plumbers assignment because this shook him loose from the National Security Council "which wasn't always the most pleasant place to work." (Personal interview, Krogh, 4/16/79) In a memo that Young prepared for himself at the time of Ehrlichman's resignation, April 30, 1973, Young noted that he had told Ehrlichman "It better be clear to HK [Kissinger] as to what acts are and President's determination in national security area. So he is not asked outside." Young appeared to be warning Ehrlichman to be certain that Kissinger understood the "security" ground rules as to activities of the Plumbers, a clear indication that Kissinger was witting, in the CIA term, as to what the Plumbers were up to. (*The New York Times*, 7/19/74)

29

Dollops of Sorghum Syrup

*I*T WOULD BE TOTALLY WRONG to suggest that in the weeks which followed the Supreme Court's Pentagon decision the White House was stirred by consciousness that Mr. Nixon's secret program to turn the case around, to pin the "convict's badge," as Lenin would have said, on *The New York Times,* the *Washington Post,* Daniel Ellsberg and the "elite" of the Kennedy and Johnson Administrations, encompassed devices so dangerous that they might eviscerate Mr. Nixon's own establishment.

As the President met with his aides to discuss policies and politics, as Howard Hunt's career as a less-than-skillful master of underground capers developed, as Charles Colson's imagination spun off cheap detective tricks, as David Young and Egil Krogh got the Plumbers going, not one member of the White House, even in retrospect, was to remember any qualms. Looking back at it, a man who stood well outside the plots that engaged Haldeman, Ehrlichman and Kissinger, the wiretapping and all—Secretary of State Rogers—could not recall a sense of foreboding. To him what was happening was an intensification of what had long been characteristic of the White House, a paranoia which permeated all of its dealings, those within the government and those outside it.

"What the Pentagon Papers did," Rogers later said, "was to accelerate things. The paranoia was already there. The embryo of the Plumbers had been conceived as early as 1969."

He could have told Mr. Nixon and Kissinger and the others where it would lead. Mr. Nixon was not the first President he had worked for. He recalled very well President Eisenhower, sore as hell, calling up when Rogers was Attorney General and demanding that he put the FBI onto some leak to the press. Rogers would firmly but gently point out that in the first place the FBI probably wouldn't find out who did it; if they did there was nothing the administration could do anyway and if someone discovered what the FBI was doing there would be hell to pay. Mr. Eisenhower would gradually cool off and say with resignation, well, Bill, if that's the way you feel just forget it.

But, said Rogers, of course no one in the Nixon White House ever asked his advice because they knew what he would say: He would say to stop it and they weren't about to stop it no matter what he said.

Post-mortem

Just as there was no perception within the government that the ground had been cleared for another and more fundamental confrontation between the Executive and the press (plus the gathering weight of the Legislative and Judicial branches) so it would be totally misleading to suggest that within the ranks of the press there was perception of how the Pentagon case had shifted the fulcrum of the American power structure.

You will read the commentary in that slow sweltering summer of 1971 in vain for clues to the real significance of the Pentagon case.

The American press had never been noted for an ability to interpret itself or the society in which it existed. One man whose mind could have penetrated the studied obscurity of the post-Pentagon situation was Walter Lippmann, the remarkable philosopher and social thinker whom Iphigene Sulzberger more than forty years earlier had tried to persuade her father to hire for *The Times.* * But by now Lippmann was old and enfeebled and his mind had lost its resiliency and sweep. He still wrote an occasional column for *Newsweek* and his style was as elegant as ever but illness had deprived him of the ability to cope with issues as sharp-edged as those of the Pentagon Papers.

There were many attempts at analysis, usually narrow and frequently carping, of the Pentagon affair. A frequent criticism, particularly from those associated with the Johnson and Kennedy administrations, was that the materials had been presented out of context. Walt Rostow felt that the claim of a "consensus" for bombing North Vietnam in 1964 was wrong. It was, he insisted, only a "contingency plan." William Bundy felt that Neil Sheehan had "much to answer for at the bar of history" and that the articles did not reflect the diversity of views within the administration. Nonetheless, he called for a Senate Foreign Relations Committee inquiry. McGeorge Bundy felt *The Times* had

---

*At Barnard, Iphigene Sulzberger fell under the influence of the historian James Harvey Robinson, who was very sarcastic about the conservatism of *The New York Times* and delighted in holding up a copy of its editorial page saying, "I am now going to show you a perfect example of the workings of the medieval mind." Iphigene kept nagging her father to bring a more liberal writer onto the page and suggested the name of Walter Lippmann, the progressive editor of *The New Republic* who had just published his famous *Preface to Politics.* However, Lippmann was not interested unless he could have full control of the editorial page, which, of course, Mr. Ochs was not prepared to give him. (Personal interviews, Iphigene Ochs Sulzberger, 1/14/69; 1/13/69)

been one-sided and that the documents for the most part were "just internal memoranda on things that had long since been made public." The very conservative journalism review *Seminar,* published by the Copley Press, called *The Times'* action "journalism by theft" and Copley's *San Diego Union* demanded criminal prosecution. The *Detroit News* said *The Times* was "irresponsible" (Punch Sulzberger retaliated by withholding a charitable contribution which the *News* solicited), the *Birmingham News* called the Pentagon Papers "a two-bit scoop" and the publisher, Clarence Hanson, reneged on a promise to Ruth Sulzberger Golden (as she then was) to testify in her behalf in a lawsuit involving the *Chattanooga Times* and its rival, the *Free Press,* saying he wouldn't testify for a paper that had done something "so unpatriotic."

None of these criticisms touched the real issues. Richard Harwood, ombudsman or self-critic of the *Washington Post,* made a more serious point. He noted that many "revelations" of the Pentagon Papers were not, in fact, revelations; they were repetitions, or in some cases confirmations, of what had been known and reported earlier. But despite the coverage in which the leading Vietnam reporters of *The Times,* Bigart, Mohr, Sheehan, Halberstam, Browne, Trumbull, Gloria Emerson, Hedrick Smith and Jack Langguth, had participated, the American public (and most of Congress) just hadn't listened. In May 1964, Harwood recalled, 63 percent of those polled by Gallup had no opinion about the war, were paying it no heed, reading nothing about it. Six months later another poll revealed that 25 percent of adult Americans did not even know a war was in progress in Southeast Asia. Harwood drew the conclusion that the impact of newspapers on public opinion was "tragically limited" but he did not address himself to the question of why, in 1971, the Pentagon Papers publication had roused the public dramatically. James Thomson, curator of the Neiman fellowships for journalists at Harvard, came closer to the point with his conclusion that the reason for the Rip Van Winkle state of the American public was that the press "was not doing its job, was simply responding to government, showing the herd instinct, and seldom staying long enough with one central story or issue."

Thomson's thesis, slightly oversimplified, was that the Washington press in large measure had become part of the Establishment, had absorbed the value system of the Establishment, worked hand-in-hand with the Establishment and, in fact, had been co-opted into what he called the "National Security State" with its phobia for classification and secrecy.

The rule, Thomson said, that was operative when he went to work for the Undersecretary of State in 1961 was that "anything you don't want to see on the front page of *The New York Times* tomorrow you should classify." He followed the instruction with verve, stamping the products of his typewriter CONFIDENTIAL, SECRET, TOP SECRET, EYES ONLY, LIMDIS, EXDIS, NODIS or NIACT.

He felt that the break in pattern symbolized by the Pentagon publication had come very late; that it had come only after almost total collapse of trust within the Executive Branch (and within the Establishment) but that the break should be productive of new and healthy relationships within the American power structure.

A troubling question was posed by Walter Pincus in *New York* magazine. He pointed out that once the Supreme Court liberated *The Times* to publish those Pentagon materials that it had originally prepared, the story dropped dead. No other paper undertook a second, searching inquiry to see what might have been overlooked; *The Times* did not follow the many, many leads into American policy which the Papers opened up; the story sank like a stone. Nor did Congress do any better. Only a handful of congressmen bothered to look at the Papers, which Secretary of Defense Laird sent up for their use; the Senate Foreign Relations Committee made no effective use of this treasure-trove; no one made an effort to pry the four diplomatic volumes out of the government and, most chilling, neither *The Times* nor any of the press seemed to have the ability to apply the Pentagon findings to daily coverage of news from Washington and Vietnam. Although they now possessed a frame of reference as to how the U.S. conducted its military business in Southeast Asia this knowledge was not integrated into the field reports, the characteristically bland statements of the government press agents in the Pentagon, the State Department or in the U.S. establishments in Vietnam.

This came through strongly to Dan Ellsberg, who felt that once the legal battle was over the press lost interest in the contents of the documents. There was substance to this criticism. The cause, although this was not perceived by many critics, was brought out by Nat Hentoff in the *Village Voice*. Much of the problem lay in the way in which editors and reporters defined "news." They tended to think of themselves as chefs in a crêperie, serving up a hot, delectable but very perishable product. It must come off the griddle, fresh and tender, and go right to the palate. There was no such thing as a reprocessed crêpe or a day-old or week-old crêpe. If you missed yours at lunchtime you'd had it. Of course, there could be a whole new platterful tomorrow. And a new one the day after and the day after that. The simile is not completely exact but it is apt enough to explain why editors now thought the Pentagon Papers "stale news."

For the most part the critics dealt with the mechanics of the press; with the whys and wherefores; why was not a certain story published; why should another be published; why didn't the press get onto the government's errors and misdeeds earlier; why didn't it present them in a broader context; why didn't it do more; why didn't it do it better.

But the critics suffered from the same handicap as that of the chef in the crêperie. They could not see the world beyond their kitchen. Only *The New Yorker*'s "Talk of the Town" perceived that what the press and public confronted was government by conspiracy. *The New Yorker* agreed that the "conspiracy theory of history was seldom of value."

"But what other word than 'conspiracy,' " it asked, "can you use when a small group of men seize virtual control of the nation's foreign policy, and take the country into war by devising and executing elaborate plans that are carefully concealed from the public, the press and Congress?"

Alone, *The New Yorker* suggested that the conspiracy had not ended with the end of Mr. Johnson's term. It had continued. "This Administration has not reduced the element of secrecy," said *The New Yorker*, "it has tried to make it respectable." For the time being, the magazine concluded, "the American system of government remains suspended."

Reston's Judgment

James Reston did not stay in Washington to ponder the Supreme Court's verdict. He was off with his wife, Sally, for Peking even before the ruling came down, one of the first of a long roster of journalists and public figures to make the pilgrimage. Thus, he was never to write a commentary on the Supreme Court decision. But he was very clear on the fundamental issues and explored them at length in his last columns before taking off for Asia.*

The press, said Reston, could expose but not correct. It could oppose the Executive (or the Judiciary, for that matter) but it was no substitute for Congress as an effective instrument of investigation. (Here he touched upon the circumstance which would shortly arise around the Watergate scandal, the press investigating brilliantly but again and

*Bob Woodward of the *Washington Post* in doing research for his book on the Supreme Court, *The Brethren,* was told by several sources that Chief Justice Burger had claimed that Reston called him for an appointment at the time of the Pentagon Papers case. Burger was quoted as suggesting that Reston wanted to lobby on behalf of *The New York Times.* (Personal interview, Woodward, 12/18/79) Reston had no recollection of asking to see the Chief Justice, and of course, would never have thought to "lobby" him. (Personal interview, Reston, 12/20/79) Actually reconstruction of events makes the incident highly dubious. The Court agreed to take the case Friday, June 25, and heard argument Saturday, June 26. Reston wrote his last column for *The Times* before departing for China on June 26 and it was published Sunday, June 27. He left the next day for China and was gone from the country by the time the Court rendered its decision June 30. The supposed episode would seem to be a product of the hysteria of the period.

again balked and halted until the superior powers of the courts or the Legislative committees pulled forth the evidence which the press knew existed but could not obtain through ingenuity, intuition and diligence.)

The case was clear, in Reston's mind, for a congressional investigation "going far deeper and far beyond anything the press has been able to do." (This was Ellsberg's original aspiration, of course, the full-court Senate Foreign Relations Committee hearings.)

As Reston saw it the integrity of government, the judgment and honor of public officials were at stake. He saw the conflict between government and press as a symptom of a much larger and serious problem—the problem of lies or, as Reston put it in more polite language, "a certain amount of deception," which he said "has been much worse under Presidents Johnson and Nixon."

"For years now," he recorded, "we have not had that feeling of honest differences openly faced and plainly discussed which is essential even in adversary proceedings."

The press, Reston said, was a "blunt but limited instrument of democracy." Now Congress or an extraordinary commission must take over and get to the bottom of the whole affair.

Reston had little use for those who challenged the right and duty of *The Times* to publish the documents. They, and especially those critics who cried "treason," he said, had come very close to accepting Vladimir Lenin's view (he made the common error of miscalling Lenin "Nikolai" and *The Times'* copyreaders did not correct him) that opposition to the government was unpatriotic or worse.

He quoted Walter Lippmann, upon whom he had consciously modeled his role as a commentator, as warning against the view that the "insider" or the "top men" know best.

Lippmann had said in his seventieth birthday address to the National Press Club in 1960 that those who upheld the "insiders" argument "will be denouncing the principle of democracy itself which asserts that the outsiders shall be sovereign over the insiders."

Lippmann had warned that "if the country is to be governed with the consent of the governed then the governed must arrive at opinions about what their governors want them to consent to."

Here, said Lippmann, was the role of the press—to "make it our business to find out what is going on under the surface and beyond the horizon. . . . This is our job. It is no mean calling."

In the last column that Reston was to write before taking off for China he sought to answer the questions of a "troubled friend" who was concerned whether the press was knowledgeable or responsible enough "to publish things the Attorney General wants suppressed."

(Of course, neither Reston nor his "troubled friend" had a notion of the reality of views within the White House; the President's insistence that the basic question of the Pentagon Papers was "PR"; his efforts to turn the Pentagon case on its own axis and use it as a political weapon against Teddy Kennedy; his blunt statement that "Top Secret is meaningless.")

"No doubt," Reston conceded, "the press is often poorly informed and clumsy in its efforts to expose the dangers of this system, but the greater the power in the hands of the Executive, the greater the need for information and skepticism on the part of the Congress and the Press."

The greater danger to the nation, Reston said, far greater than any involved in the publication of the Pentagon Papers, "is the system of Executive secrecy, and the greater danger to the security of the nation is the mistrust this system of secrecy and contrived television propaganda has caused. . . ."

Having thus set the issues clearly before government, press and public, Reston took off for China, where, after a bout of appendicitis, and a treatment by acupuncture which placed that ancient Chinese art on page one of *The New York Times* July 18, 1971, having been totally scooped on Henry Kissinger's secret trip to Peking July 9–11, he finally sat down with China's Chou En-lai in early August for a long conversation in the course of which Chou congratulated *The Times* for its courage in publishing the Pentagon Papers (he had already said much the same to Seymour Topping, another *Times* editor who saw him a month earlier) and Reston jokingly asked if there were not some secret Chinese Pentagon Papers which *The Times* might publish, a jest which Chou didn't seem to relish, possibly because there *was* so much secret Chinese politics then under way, the Cultural Revolution, the plottings of Marshal Lin Piao, the political maneuvers of Mao Tse-tung himself and those of his venturesome wife, Chiang Ching.

Had anyone tried seriously to analyze the position of the press in the summer of 1971 he could hardly have failed to note that while it was true, as Reston said, that *The New York Times*, for instance, was far from possessing the investigative powers of Congress or the courts, lacking the resources of subpoena, lacking the apparatus which gave congressional agents almost unlimited access to materials within the government documents chain, possessing only a handful of investigative reporters and editors as contrasted with the battalions which could be mustered for a full-scale congressional inquiry or, for example, for a broad investigation by the Securities and Exchange Commission or a grand jury working at the direction of the Attorney General, nonetheless the outreach and freedom which the American press now possessed was without parallel in the world and without parallel in its own history.

This was in large measure due to *The New York Times,* but, characteristically, it is doubtful that anyone on (or off) *The Times* thought of it in those terms. The fact was that beginning in the brief regime of Orvil Dryfoos and accelerating into that of Punch Sulzberger *The Times* had confronted a notable series of legal challenges and it had spectacularly broadened its rights and those of the rest of the Fourth Estate, as Mr. Ochs would have put it, to cover the news "without fear or favor."

It was characteristic that this had not been achieved by high-level planning or intent of management. *The Times* had not gone into the courts with the design of establishing a new charter of privilege. The legal challenge had been thrust upon *The Times* as a consequence of carrying out what it deemed to be its duties as a responsible newspaper. The challenge and response were imposed upon *The Times,* not sought by it. By the time the process was completed *The Times,* somewhat to its surprise, found that it had opened the field of government and politics to unrestricted investigative reporting; it had demolished for political figures or officeholders use of the criminal or civil libel laws as a protection against free and objective reporting, whether the government employee was the highest official in the land or the lowliest. This astonishing effect was accomplished in two parallel cases brought against *The Times* in the state of Alabama, *Sullivan* v. *The New York Times* and *Connor* v. *The New York Times.*

Not unlike the Pentagon case the Alabama suits were instituted as part of a calculated strategy to bind and hamper the press, to prevent it, in a word, from reporting the Civil Rights struggle in the South. But the Alabama strategy, like Mr. Nixon's in the Pentagon affair, boomeranged. Instead of driving the press out of the South it opened the doors and gave reporters safe conduct, wide and free, to report at will. The Alabama cases not only would remove the legal barriers to political and social reporting in the South, they would free the press from court harassment by officeholders and politicians in every state, city and township.

The decision of the Supreme Court in *Sullivan* changed the basic interpretation of the law concerning American newspapers. Together with the verdict in the Pentagon Papers the court gave the press the instruments with which it could fully carry out the First Amendment function as watchdog for the public. In a very real sense the decisions armed the press with the authority and privilege which enabled them, together with an alert Judiciary (Federal Judge Sirica and the Supreme Court) and an aroused Legislative Branch (Senator Ervin and Congressman Rodino) to bring about the denouement of Watergate, the resignation of President Nixon and the criminal conviction of so many of his associates.

John Popham

The road to *Sullivan* v. *The New York Times* was long and complex. The South had always held special significance for *The New York Times* because it was from the South, the Reconstruction South, that Mr. Ochs emerged. He never cut his roots, nor had his descendants. Chattanooga was always a second home and they clung to the *Chattanooga Times* with Mr. Ochs' granddaughter Ruth, as publisher, through thick and thin (and it grew very thin as the sixties passed into the seventies) and resisted every counsel that the paper should be merged or sold.

Iphigene Sulzberger never lost her love for Chattanooga or her dedication to the South. She felt a deep sense of responsibility and harbored a strong conviction that with patience, effort, goodwill, intelligence (and an occasional good shove) the problems of the South, its poverty, its race relations, its backwardness in education and in Civil Rights could be overcome. Her views were not exactly those of her father, who came of an older generation more inclined to rely on the ability of southern society to handle its problems without too much advice or intervention. He undoubtedly would have moved less forcefully than she on the question of the blacks.

In Mr. Ochs' day *The Times* paid serious attention to the South, sending staff men like Raymond Daniell, later to become a famous war correspondent in London during World War II, and Mike Berger, *The Times'* remarkable crime and trial reporter, south to cover the rise and assassination of Huey Long and the endless trials of the nine Scottsboro "boys."

But it was not until after World War II that *The Times* took an action of far-reaching consequence. At the initiative of Turner Catledge, *The Times* sent to the South, to be permanently based in Mr. Ochs' old home town of Chattanooga, a reporter named John N. Popham.

Many efforts have been made—none wholly successful—to capture on paper the essence of John Popham. Roy Reed, a talented young reporter for the *Arkansas Gazette,* later to join and still later to leave *The New York Times,* was covering the violence that broke out at North Little Rock High School in the autumn of 1957. Governor Orval Faubus had precipitated a national crisis by defying a federal court order to desegregate the schools. Reed and some other reporters were standing outside the school with Superintendent F. Bruce Wright, who was so shaken by the outbreak, so physically and emotionally wrought, that Reed feared he was about to have a heart attack.

"Suddenly," Reed was to remember, "there was this little man with his hat pushed back on the back of his head and his hands in his pockets talking this outlandish Virginia Tidewater talk and I didn't know who in the world this was. I'd never seen him, never even heard of him.

"He just walked up to Wright and began to talk to him. Later it occurred to me what he was doing. He might have been saving this man's life. He could tell that Wright was so wrought up and he set in to just calm him down. He talked to Wright for ten, fifteen, twenty minutes. Wright never opened his mouth as far as I can recall. He just stood there bug-eyed, fascinated by this little man. He finally got Wright back to normal, loosened up, and then we interviewed him and got a pretty good story out of him. That was my first exposure to Johnny Popham."

Claude Sitton, editor of the *Raleigh News,* and probably the most talented man *The Times* ever sent to the South, attended a gathering at the Velvet Cloak, a Raleigh watering place, in 1974 and later wrote:

> Eyes popping, eyebrows arching, knuckles cracking—all in furious concentration on the tale at hand—Popham launches into a soaring soliloquy.
>
> His delivery and Tidewater accent approximate nothing so much as dollops of sorghum syrup spat from a Gatling gun. This tidal wave of sound has been known to levitate a listener who, transfixed by the onrush of oratory, rises up on tip toes, wide-eyed and open-mouthed.
>
> The man comes as close as most to matching the legend, an elfin figure with a twinkle of Irish con in his eyes. . . . Popham knew the South's Negro leaders better than they knew each other. No reporter was surprised when a shadetree mechanic back in some Appalachian cove asked after Popham's health.

Late in 1978 Popham was sitting in the buffet of the Reed Hotel in Chattanooga. Two years before he had retired as editor of the *Chattanooga Times.* His eleven-year service for *The New York Times* in the South was twenty years behind him. His career as a U.S. Marine Corps officer was thirty-two years back but he still held himself with Marine straightness and the Gatling-gun dollops of his Tidewater accent spurted ceaselessly, turning "about" to "aboot" or "abaut," "house" into "hoose" "mother" to "motha" and "father" to "fawtha," talking, talking, talking about the days when he *was* (south of the Mason-Dixon line) *The New York Times,* when there was no one else in the country doing what he did, traveling 50,000 miles a year by car over the roads, long before the big interstates linked it all together, one day (or night) at Brennan's restaurant in New Orleans, the next at a Mississippi agricultural experiment station, the next talking after midnight with the editor of a scruffy black weekly in a Carolina city and, when he left, his hosts praying that he would get back home all right.

No one did what Popham did and no one would do it afterward. His assignment evidenced a singular perception of the South, its problems and their importance to the nation. It may have been an accident that three of the last four editors of *The Times* had been southerners, Edwin L. James from Irvington, Virginia, Turner Catledge from Philadelphia, Mississippi, and Clifton Daniel from Zebulon, North Carolina, but it was the kind of accident that affected history. Each of these men, and in particular Catledge and Daniel shared what might be called *The New York Times'* concept of the South—a society which was slowly but irreversibly changing, a society in which the forces of good, of "the right thing," of industrial progress, of political enlightenment ("The New South") was healing the warped and ugly wounds of the war which the North thought had been fought a hundred years ago but which still seemed only yesterday in Mississippi, Alabama, Georgia and the Carolinas.

This was Popham's vision of the South and he would have been the last person to have imagined that he and his reporting might become a stepping stone toward *Sullivan* v. *The New York Times* but that was because his dedication to the perfectibility of the South through good works and education was as devout as his belief in the Church and as noncorrosional as his Tidewater accent.

How Popham had managed to retain the accent no one ever understood. Though he had been born and spent much of his boyhood in Fredericksburg, Virginia, he had gone to China with his father, a Marine Corps officer, and spent a couple of years in Tientsin and Peking. When his father was posted to the Brooklyn Navy Yard, Popham went along, studied law at Fordham and found a job as a reporter for *The Times,* helping cover the disappearance of Justice Crater, the Lindbergh kidnap case, the courts, ethnic groups, whatever came along.

"I covered Brownsville, East New York," Popham remembered. "I drank slivovitz and picked up some Yiddish. I should have been a Cossack—I was a goy. But I sat in the back room and drank slivovitz with the Polish Jews. My people landed in Virginia in 1680, I was the son of a Marine officer and a Roman Catholic. But I was active in founding the American Newspaper Guild and I walked the picket line in the *Brooklyn Eagle* strike of 1937."

That, Popham always insisted, was why Turner Catledge "gave me the present of covering the South."

There was nothing he was better qualified to do. He had all the right connections. He was a Marine veteran (having served in China during World War II), and in every little town there was a fellow Marine he knew or a relative from Virginia or the friend of a relative.

Wherever Popham went the word went out, "The *Times* man is here." Soon enough word went out through the NAACP that the first thing for anyone going South to do was to talk to Popham. "We never had anyone like him," Walter White, secretary of the NAACP, once said.

These were the days long before SNCC, long before the Supreme Court's 1954 ruling in *Brown* v. *The Board of Education,* long before the sit-ins, long before the "Mississippi Summer." The South was not yet a story but Popham was covering it, covering it and, as he was later to say, "accumulating." Not for the day but for next year and the year after. Popham had gone to Catholic mass as a youngster and taught at a Methodist Sunday school because the young lady he was courting was a Methodist. His father was Episcopalian, his mother a Catholic, and he played basketball with the Baptists. Now he would sometimes spend a week at the Assembly grounds in Asheville, North Carolina, in the summer because he knew that "if there was a revolution in the South these were the kind of people who would be on the barricades, these young Methodist ministers."

Popham was getting to knew the country. He knew the trouble spots and he worked out his own rules of engagement. If he was going to a place where there was likely to be trouble he would call the governor or a senator and say, "Who's the honcho in this town?" It might be the druggist, or the hardware-and-feed man or maybe the banker. "And," Popham recalled, "I'd say I've gotta go down there—would you call him and tell him a friend of yours is coming down and wants to talk to him?"

"Okay, Pop," the governor would say. The next morning when Popham got to town the "honcho" would telephone and ask him to breakfast. "And, then," said Popham, "if hell started to break loose, well, I've been up and down the Main Street, and I'm a friend of Mr. Jones. And I always made it a point to call on the mayor. And I always used all my connections. And I'd see the blacks but I wouldn't just hit the town and ask the hotel clerk how I could get in touch with the editor of the black weekly."

"I covered all the bases," Popham recalled. "It's buying a little protection, it's being seen on the street with the local power figure, eating, drinking, being seen around."

It wasn't fail-safe. Popham had his run-ins, his moments of danger. He was locked up in Jackson, Mississippi, when he was attending a meeting at a black church by two plainclothesmen who asked, "Are you white?" But the governor of Mississippi telephoned the mayor of Jackson and Popham was let out.

"I never ran from anybody," Popham said. "But I never was in serious trouble. It's a sense of security. I knew who I was. The South has a lot of that—a closeness, a family thing—'I knew your daddy.' "

As Popham summed it up: "If I did anything useful it was discovering how many really good people there were in the South, people who had no other way to be known, to be heard, except through a story in *The Times.*"

Popham was (and remained) an optimist. Like Iphigene Sulzberger, her daughter Ruth, Turner Catledge, the great liberal southern editors who were Popham's friends and associates, Ralph McGill of the *Atlanta Constitution,* Harry Ashmore of the *Little Rock Gazette,* Hodding Carter of the Greenville, Mississippi, *Delta Democrat-Times* and Pete McKnight of the *Charlotte News,* Popham believed the South was on the march and that the forces for change and for an end to segregation would, in time, triumph. He lent great support to the cause of southern education, to its colleges, universities and schools, to the Southern Regional Education Board, to Dr. Charles S. Johnson, first black president of Fisk University at Nashville, Tennessee, to Harold Fleming and the Southern Regional Council and the Southern Educational Reporting Service. Popham's support was not merely journalistic. Quietly he lent his advice, his influence and sometimes his name. He was always available to help anyone who got in trouble. As the black movement gathered headway and an organization like that of Martin Luther King set up a twenty-four-hour switchboard Popham would make midnight calls to a sheriff or a mayor to ease a crisis, to get the blacks or organizers out of jail. He found no incompatibility between his journalistic responsibilities and his commitment as a decent, liberal citizen.

Brown v. *The Board of Education*

This was Popham, the only national reporter covering the South in 1954 when the Supreme Court ruling came down in *Brown* v. *The Board of Education,* the only reporter in the country deeply qualified to understand the impact of this decision, a man who represented a remarkable blend of the ethnicity of New York and the tradition of the South.

The unanimous decision of the Warren court was a surprise to Popham and to the editors of *The Times.* The first tremor, as Popham well knew, had hit the South in 1948–49 when President Truman set up his Civil Rights Commission. That was enough to get the Dixiecrats going and it set off what Popham called "all this southern rhetoric, all this southern bullshit" by the Bull Connor of Birmingham and the other shifty politicians who got elected, as it was said, by "hollering nigger." But, as Popham insisted, you had to understand them. They put it on when they spoke on TV or when they were being interviewed for *The Times* but when they checked into the local hotel and sent the bellhop out for whiskey and cigarettes they would say, "How are you, Willie, boy?" And maybe they would rub his head a bit and then when he left the room they would lean back and say, "Well, you know, if they wuz all like William I'd go to school with them tomorrow."

Now the Supreme Court had ruled unanimously. The fact that it was unanimous meant a great deal. Years later Popham readily admitted that he had not believed there was going to be a big confrontation.

Turner Catledge thought much the same thing. He paid a visit to his native Philadelphia, Mississippi, in 1955 and found his old friends and neighbors very calm. He came back to New York and reported that the reaction in the South had "not been bad at all." He decided to have *The Times* make a southwide survey to see how things were going.

A team of ten reporters studied the South under Popham's direction and produced a 50,000-word eight-page report published March 13, 1956,* in which Popham proclaimed that "a social revolution with profound implications for domestic accord and world leadership confronts this country today." Popham stressed the dramatic legal and social adjustments which lay before the South, the tensions which had arisen and the necessity which the South faced of "coming to terms." Many southern leaders, Popham said, had reached the conclusion that integration was inevitable but he warned that "vengeance is directed at liberal and modern voices in much of the Deep South."

This, as Popham and Catledge were to concede, was overly optimistic. Just eighteen months ahead lay Little Rock and all that followed. For that Popham blamed (and was always to blame) President Eisenhower's failure to vigorously carry out the court's 1954 decision.

Popham sat in the Reed Hotel on a chilly day in December 1978 and looked back to 1954: "Eisenhower could have done it. There would have been no trouble. The power structure was ready to do anything for him. Any committee he wanted to form would have carried it out. It was his fault that the trouble followed. He didn't understand anything. He was more southern than we southerners. He grew up in Kansas and the border states. We had eight years of drifting. That was what we had to pay."

As the mood in the South went ugly and the national press turned its attention south of the Mason-Dixon line a stream of reporters knocked at Popham's door. It was standard procedure. First, check with Popham, then go on to the crisis wherever it was. Popham and the-South-as-Popham-saw-it began to be reflected a hundred times over in newspapers outside *The New York Times*, in the news maga-

---

*The "Report on the South" shared front-page space March 13, 1956, with a story headlined "Margaret Truman to Wed News Man." It was the announcement by former President Truman in Kansas City that his daughter was to wed E. C. Daniel, *Times* managing editor-to-be in April.

zines, in television and radio. To not a few reporters Popham didn't just cover the South—he *was* the South.

The road to *Sullivan* v. *The New York Times* and *Connor* v. *The New York Times* had opened. But those who were traveling it did not yet know where it would take them.

30

"It was *a Revolution"*

JOHN POPHAM'S MARCH 13, 1956, "Report on the South" warned against placing too much emphasis on what he called "mob violence" and "emotional outbursts by the leaders of either [black or white] race."

But the South was marching to a different beat than that for which Popham, his moderate liberals and *The New York Times* had hoped. The beat could be plainly heard even before *The Times'* study was completed. Peter Kihss was compelled to break off working on Popham's report and rush to Tuscaloosa, Alabama, where a twenty-six-year-old black student named Autherine Lucy had been enrolled at the University of Alabama, the first of her race.

There had been two days of cross burnings, ink spattering, car rocking, firecracker throwing and chants of "Keep 'Bama white!" and "Hey, hey, ho, ho, Autherine's gotta go!" by the time Kihss appeared on the campus a little before 8:30 A.M. on the bright cool Monday morning of February 6, 1956.

It was a scene that would become familiar with the years—a crowd, many too old to be students, standing outside the building where Miss Lucy was to have her first class of the day, Confederate flags flying from cars, anti-Negro chants and Miss Lucy, protected by highway policemen, barely making it into her geography lesson. By noon Kihss found her under siege, a crowd of four hundred students and outsiders milling around Graves Hall, attention centered on a gray-haired black, H. N. Guinn, who had driven Miss Lucy to Tuscaloosa from Birmingham, sixty miles away. When Kihss went up to Guinn the crowd closed in, starting to shove. "I'm talking to this gentleman," said Kihss, beanpole-thin, tall, studious, quiet-mannered, with very thick glasses, shoving a shover back. "He called that nigger a gentleman!" someone shouted. "Nigger lover! Communist!" the crowd chanted. That made Kihss angry. He was of Baltic descent and a profound anti-Communist. He found a police captain who agreed that Mr. Guinn best be removed from the scene quickly.

"Somebody started throwing eggs," Kihss recalled. "One spattered

Mr. Guinn with an omelet. Two eggs hit me. The courageous individuals who flung them must have been a long, long way back, for the eggs slid off my jacket to the pavement before breaking."

When a police car arrived to take Guinn away the crowd rushed in. "Assuming reporting did not call for complete detachment at such a point," Kihss said, "I slammed several with my right forearm. I trust I made an impression on two faces with a straight-arm."

Once Guinn was rescued Kihss turned, faced the crowd and said:

"If anybody wants to start something, let's go. I'm a reporter from *The New York Times* and I have gotten a wonderful impression of the University of Alabama. Now I'll be glad to take on the whole student body, two at a time."

No one took up Kihss' offer and he walked away through the crowd to find that police had spirited Miss Lucy out of Graves Hall and back to Birmingham. A bit later university trustees expelled her from the university for "her own safety" and that of the other students. Each element of what was to become the evolving agony of the Civil Rights struggle was present that cool bright Monday morning, the courageous black seeking to exercise her constitutional rights, the faint-hearted authorities, the reluctant and hostile police, the bullyboys working themselves up to violence with ranting, shouting and six-packs, *The Times* reporter on the scene recording the conflict, lending a little help to a victim of the mob's anger and himself becoming the metaphor of the enemy, "outside agitator," "troublemaker," "Commie," "lying northern newsman," blamed by his presence for the trouble, an alien entering a perceived paradise to disrupt, to destroy, to malign "the southern way of life."

Here were taken the first steps on the road to *Sullivan* v. *The New York Times.* More were quickly to follow. A year later in the Little Rock crisis *The Times'* education editor, Dr. Benjamin Fine, was on the scene at Central High School. State militia warned that he would be arrested for "inciting to violence" if he insisted on interviewing high school students.

"You better get out unless you want your head broken," an elderly well-dressed man yelled.

"Have you been to Moscow lately?" shouted a middle-aged woman.

A husky man in white shirt stepped out of the crowd: "I think we ought to turn our backs on that man working for the New York nigger papers."

"You gotta nigger wife?" called a waitress in a Little Rock tavern. Fine did not reply.

"Are you a Jew?" she asked.

"Yes," said Fine.

Other reporters managed to get Dr. Fine away from the trouble spot.

They felt he did not understand the personal danger he was in. Fine was a scholarly man who had never seen a riot in his life.

Claude Sitton

Within a year Popham gave up his southern reporting to become managing editor of the *Chattanooga Times,* and a new *Times* man, Claude Sitton, a lean thirty-two-year-old, raised on a Georgia farm, veteran of merchant marine and U.S. naval service in World War II, tough, courageous, plunged into coverage of what he was later to concede was nothing less than a revolution, a twenty-four-hour a-day job, constantly on the move, occasionally under gunfire, often threatened with his life, canny, cool with the kind of nerve which can calculate the odds on entering a dark, dirty red-neck crossroads with the precision of an electronic computer.

The South which Sitton was to cover was as dangerous a place as a reporter could find. Sitton was to endure six years of guerrilla warfare unscathed, worn to the bone, combat-wise, building an expertise no one in America could match.

"It *was* a revolution," he conceded long afterwards, hesitating in his judgment. "I didn't like the word at the time. But sure. It was a revolution and it is amazing we got through it with as little bloodshed as we did."

With the passage of time it is almost impossible to reconstruct Sitton's coverage of the South day by day, month by month, year by year. It is like putting together the history of a war. Nor is there any way of estimating the distance he was to travel. If Popham covered 50,000 miles a year Sitton doubled it. The action was too fast for driving. The "Green Hornet," the car which had carried Popham so far and so wide, was retired. Sometimes it had waited six weeks at the Atlanta airport for Sitton to get back from Alabama or Mississippi or Arkansas.

Sitton had come to *The Times* almost accidentally as a copyreader in October 1957. But his assignment to the South was no accident. It was the product of Turner Catledge's "southern strategy." Whatever initial misreading of the mood Catledge had gotten in his native Philadelphia, Mississippi, he knew that the transition to equality in race relations; equality in education; equality at the polls; equality in employment—all of this meant a revolution in the South. It would be, he felt confident, the greatest undertaking which American society would accomplish in his day and he was determined that *The Times* should report it with the depth, insight and style necessary to bring its full import to the nation. He believed, as he told Arthur Sulzberger, that "the unfolding race-relations drama was the biggest sociological story in American history." He conceded that he had been "overly optimistic" in the early months after the Supreme Court decision. "We had underestimated the resistance of the average southerner to integration," he recalled, "and the capacity of southern politicians to stir those deeply held prejudices and fears." It was a mistake he was not to repeat.

Catledge was certain that the story could best be covered by southern reporters, skilled in the folkways, talking the language, possessing the accents, reporters who were experienced and sophisticated, men who could put the social revolution into the context of the whole nation.

In Sitton he believed—rightly—that he had found a worthy successor to Popham, although Sitton could not have been more different in personality. In place of Popham's flow of Tidewater talk Sitton was flinty. He spoke no more than necessary. He lacked the courtly grace of Popham. He was always running, to catch a plane, to get to the scene of a riot, to get to the nearest telephone, to beat out a story on his typewriter, sometimes to save his life. "Christ!" he once recalled, "the times I'd get back into Atlanta on the last plane at midnight and there'd be a call and I was out again at 3:30 A.M." He knew every piney-woods charter-plane service in the South. There wasn't a back country airstrip (sometimes it was a cow pasture) that he hadn't landed on to be off and running to wherever hell had broken loose.

It was a time, as Marshall Frady, another fine reporter of the South, was to write, when "the very air seemed more vivid with some brilliant fever of super-reality. Goodness and courage and evil and justice had then, however briefly, a marvelously clear certainty and palpability."

The Civil Rights struggle would forge for *The New York Times* an unequaled band of reporters, almost all of southern heritage, although there would be exceptions like David Halberstam, born in Winsted, Connecticut, who got his baptism of fire in Nashville in 1960. Again and again these men were to endanger their lives gathering the news but little or no flavor of this would make the pages of *The New York Times.* Turner Catledge had an inflexible rule: reporters were on the scene to write and report what happened to others; not to write about themselves. Only when a man was wounded, jailed or in some inextricable manner became part of the event would Catledge permit the briefest mention.

These men were to form, in large measure, the cadre of a skilled, physically courageous, battle-trained staff which would go on to cover for *The Times* the street conflicts in the northern Civil Rights struggle, the campus violence, the Vietnam demonstrations, the widening and bitter action which marked the rising tensions and new politics of the sixties and the seventies. No other newspaper, no other media possessed anything comparable, and as other newspapers, magazines and television networks moved into the field they patterned themselves after *The*

Times, and learned from men like Popham and Sitton the rules of engagement, the value system of the struggle.

Sitton's background read like a typical southern middle-class résumé. His father was a railroad man who in Depression years was conductor on a freight train. One day he was uncoupling a car with a load of hides for a shoe factory when he caught his arm on a projecting nail and was hurled to the tracks, breaking his back. With his liability settlement he bought a small farm near Conyers, Georgia, where Sitton grew up. Sitton's grandfather had been a prosperous millowner in northwest South Carolina. The grandfather and two great-uncles served in the Civil War. Sitton's great-grandfather was a well-to-do landowner, a tax collector under the Confederacy, the owner of sixty slaves. Sitton's mother was the daughter of a Methodist circuit rider in northwest Georgia and a schoolteacher, a woman of strong moral principle, and she was to have great influence on Sitton. He was brought up to believe in *fairness, decency, right* and *wrong.* There was no color line in these principles. Like all white southern youngsters of the time Sitton had black playmates to the age of puberty. He worked with blacks on the family farm and an old black named Gus taught him how to follow a mule, how to get the mule to work, how to plow a straight furrow. In his high school years he worked for the Rogers food chain and sold groceries to blacks and white alike. "I learned a lot from that," he remembered, "I got to know people." One of the things he learned was that the world was not divided into good whites and bad blacks. Goodness and badness knew no race.

So, Sitton was later to say, he did not grow up in a typical southern middle-class family. He grew up in an *atypical* family. In those days the litmus test was whether you were for or against Gene Talmadge, the red-gallused racist governor of Georgia. The Sittons were against Talmadge. Sitton's mother didn't think Talmadge was respectable and she didn't like his opinions on race. That was Sitton's view. And remained his view.

When Sitton went into the Navy he saw the blacks as people. "I believed in treating them as individuals," he said. "I didn't have that crusading zeal. But I believed in basic fairness."

This was the ideological baggage which Sitton brought to his task of covering the southern revolution. It would not much change in the six dangerous years which were to follow and he would retain a simplicity, a frankness, a directness which gave him a prismatic view of the South, one which would always differ from the clichés, the politically oriented or emotional reporting which marked much of the struggle. There were few heroes in Sitton's catalogue. He had seen the actors close up and too clearly. He knew their faults, their vanities, their idiosyncrasies, their power plays. He put Medgar Evers, Mississippi NAACP director, above almost everyone, above Martin Luther King. "I don't want to take anything away from King," he said. "No one could have activated the whites—and the blacks—the way he did and, of course, they killed King, too, in the end."

But Evers, he said, was totally fearless and totally honest. That, of course, was why he was killed.

Sitton was at Tuscaloosa on the evening of June 11, 1963, where George Wallace had been "standing in the schoolhouse door" at the University of Alabama. There was an extraordinary crush of reporters, many of whom had not covered a southern story before. They congregated in Sitton's room to learn what had happened. Some reporters and Ed Guthman of the Justice Department were relaxing in the pool. Nick Katzenbach was sitting on the veranda. A good many reporters had broken out the little bottles of liquor which were what you bought in Alabama in those days. At this point word came that Medgar Evers had been shot. Sitton was on the way to the airport in minutes with Karl Fleming of *Newsweek.* They flew to Jackson, Mississippi, and Sitton wrote one of the most moving stories ever to come from his typewriter.

Evers had been killed by a sniper as he walked from the carport into his home. The bullet hit him just below the right shoulder blade.

"The slug crashed through a front window of the home, penetrated an interior wall, ricocheted off a refrigerator and struck a coffee pot," Sitton wrote. "The battered bullet was found beneath a watermelon on a kitchen cabinet.

"Mr. Evers staggered to the doorway, his keys in his hand, and collapsed near the steps. His wife, Myrlie, and three children rushed to the door.

"The screaming of the children, 'Daddy! Daddy! Daddy!' awoke a neighbor."

Sitton had great respect for John Lewis ("a very decent, very brave man, very practical") and Andrew Young. ("I don't think King could have made it without Young. He read about King in *The New York Times* and came down and joined him.")

But the man of men who moved Sitton was one whose name never made a headline. "I'll tell you who my real hero was," Sitton once said. "He was E. W. Steptoe of Amite County in southwestern Mississippi."

Mr. Steptoe was a black farmer and his son was the only registered black voter in Amite County when Sitton first met him in October 1961. He lived in a tar-paper house fifteen miles from a little town called Liberty, where a black named Howard Lee, active in voter registration, was shot dead at high noon in the town square in the view of dozens of townspeople. The man who killed Lee lived across the road from Steptoe. All this was known. There were few secrets in this backwoods of Mississippi. Feeling was so high that those participating in the voter registration could go out only at night. As a child, in the pattern of southern race relations, Steptoe and the man across the road had played together. The day Sitton called, Steptoe greeted him with a broad smile. "I'm proud to see y'all," Steptoe said. "I know I've got a few minutes to live while you all are here."

"His nickname was 'Easy,' " Sitton recalled. "He was the president of the Amite County NAACP. Now that's the kind of guy I respect. He had more courage than anyone I ever knew."

Steptoe had a 240-acre farm and five children. He sent them all to college—and died peacefully in his bed at home.

Under Fire

For many southern reporters the events of Sunday, June 30, 1962, at Oxford, Mississippi, when James Meredith was escorted to the Ole Miss campus to register, were the most desperate they lived through. Not all lived through that night. Two were killed, a French correspondent named Paul Guihard, and a bystander named Ray Gunter. "They didn't like his red beard and his red hair," Sitton said of Guihard. "They took him behind a tree and executed him." That night Sitton was compelled to huddle beneath a car to escape gunfire. He never was able to understand Mississippi's Governor Ross Barnett. President Kennedy once said he thought Barnett had lost his mind. Sitton called him "an odd duck." He recalled how Barnett once permitted a trusty at the Parchman state prison farm to go back to Oklahoma with two guards to get a stud horse which he promised would do wonders for the mares at the prison farm. Then he persuaded the guards to let him stay over a night to "see my mother." When next heard from he was out West with a woman who was definitely not his mother. Reporters asked Ross Barnett about this. He said, "Well, if you can't trust a trusty who can you trust?"

There were not many jokes being told about Ross Barnett on that June 30. Fred Powledge, who joined *The Times* a year later, was working the story for the *Atlanta Journal.* He got slugged early in the action when someone asked him where he was from and he said he was a reporter from Atlanta. "You're a goddamn nigger lover," the questioner said, slamming Powledge. A friend got Powledge away.

Most of the action was on a grassy oval in the center of the campus. The Lyceum, the Ole Miss administration building, was at the head of the oval. A gate through which reporters gained access to the oval was opposite. There was a burst of rifle fire and Powledge took refuge in Sitton's car, which was parked at about midway on the oval. Clouds of tear gas drifted down. He rolled up the windows and turned on the radio just in time to hear President Kennedy talking about the Meredith case, quietly and calmly (the President didn't know hell had broken loose), speaking of Mississippi's honor "won on the field of battle and the gridiron." The fighting came closer and Powledge started the car and roared away. Then he saw a gang at the gate.

"I'm a pacifist," Powledge said. "But I put my foot on the accelerator and pushed it to the floor. I was really prepared to do the cowcatcher act with them and fight it out later in court. But at the last moment they dodged out of my way."

For Sitton it was hard to pick worst cases—there were so many. There was the time he was in Louisiana in August 1961 covering a governor's campaign. Among the candidates was a man named William Rainach. "Earl Long once said Willie wants to live back in the jungle and eat coconuts and scratch lice," Sitton said. Sitton was covering a Rainach meeting in a Louisiana back-country town when Rainach spotted him and told the crowd, "You got a man from *The New York Times* sitting right here. A nigger lover." Rainach went into a violent attack. Even Sitton had never heard such a thing. He was trapped. The moment Rainach stopped he expected the mob to lynch him.

"But," he said, still surprised after all the years, "it didn't happen. Maybe Rainach went too far. Maybe they were just plumb flattered at having *The New York Times* in their little town. When Rainach got through talking more people came up and shook my hand than his."

Once he was in McComb, Mississippi. The Freedom Riders were coming in and he and Sam Fentress of *Time* magazine were sitting in the cafeteria of the bus station as a Greyhound bus from Baton Rouge pulled up and six blacks from Southern University and Louisiana State got out. One was a basketball star, big, lithe, tall. When they walked into the cafeteria the rednecks rose up and the place exploded. As Sitton watched in astonishment the basketball star leaped over a chest-high glass ticket booth, dance-stepped down a lunch counter the length of the room, never disturbing a plate, touched ground, then hop-scotched from tabletop to tabletop and plunged out the screen door without opening it. Fentress and Sitton, bug-eyed, expected the mob to turn on them at any minute.

"But," said Sitton, "we had on our London Fog coats and wool hats and we just sat there. The rednecks thought we were FBI."

Actually the FBI were two blocks down the street and after it was over had to come to Sitton for a fill-in.

Working under these conditions Sitton quickly got battle-wise. He became famous for a tiny notebook made by tearing an ordinary one into halves which he could conceal in the palm of his hand. He never took notes where anyone could see him.

"Actually," he said much later, "that was a damn myth. You don't use notebooks for Christ's sake on things like this. You just jot down a few words on any kind of scrap of paper."

But Sitton admitted that when it got very rough "you'd take off your coat and take off your shirt. Stomp it in the dirt, get it good and dirty with maybe a tear or two; put it back on and leave the last few buttons unbuttoned. Then go and sit down on the courthouse lawn and stick a straw in your teeth."

Or as Powledge remembered one time in Birmingham: He and Sitton and a couple of others had sat down to a good steak dinner at the Tutweiler Hotel when they heard sirens. "It seemed like we never did have a chance to get a good meal," Powledge said. They raced off and found that the house of Arthur Shore, a black leader, had been dynamited. The police wouldn't let them get close to the scene. Then, Fred recalled, "we heard machine-gun fire. Or I will always swear it was machine-gun fire. Claude and I flopped and I didn't raise my head to find out. Anyway it was rapid fire over our heads and we did the low crawl up a gutter. It was a tough night for us but it was tougher for Arthur Shore. He lost half his house."

That was the day that Hedrick Smith, later to be Moscow correspondent of *The Times,* had a talk with Bull Connor. Connor asked Smith where he was from. *"The New York Times,"* Smith replied. "Boy," said Connor, "I got a suit against your paper and you are going to be working for me." "What about a raise?" Smith replied.

At the moment when Sitton and Powledge were inching up a gutter under machine-gun fire Smith was trying to find a telephone booth to dictate his story and that of Sitton to New York. An improvised tank belonging to the Birmingham Police Department rumbled into view, zigzagging from one side of the street to the other. Smith, long-legged, built like a varsity football end, had to run out of the tank's path, finally ducking into a telephone booth and starting to dictate as the tank clattered past.

When the Birmingham situation eased a bit a report came in of bad trouble at Gadsden, Alabama. Smith rented a car and drove north through the night, arriving at Gadsden about 3 A.M. He found a black doctor treating a score of blacks, many of them badly hurt from a ferocious beating by sheriff's deputies or state troopers. He went to the sheriff's office to find out what they had to say. Al Lingo, head of the state troopers, was there. The sheriff said not much was going on. Smith asked what he meant—he had seen a score of people badly hurt.

Suddenly Lingo spoke up:

"Hey, Smith, where are your buddies? You didn't make the mistake of coming up to this town all alone did you?"

Smith was alone and he felt a lot more alone as Lingo's beedy eyes bored into his.

"Don't worry," he said, "they'll be here soon." He hoped he was right. When Smith went to Russia and traveled the backlands of Siberia, thousands of miles from any other foreigner, in situations where an "accident" by the Soviet plainclothes police could easily have been contrived, he often thought of his Civil Rights days in the South. He had joined *The Times* on July 9, 1962, his birthday, after spending his childhood in the South as an Army brat, to become, he hoped, a diplomatic correspondent in Washington. Within a week he found himself back South covering Civil Rights and didn't have a day off for three months.

As Powledge said, it was war—war with no rules and not always was it clear who was the enemy nor where he was.

During the long Albany, Georgia, struggle in 1961–62 it seemed that the police always knew in advance what was going to happen. The newsmen stayed in the Holiday Inn. It was, the reporters agreed, a hell of a place, telephones in the bathrooms, heat lamps and $7.00 a night, which was a good price in that day. The desk clerks sized you up. If they decided you were a reporter you got a front room upstairs to make it easier for the police to keep track. They sat in squad cars outside and watched for the reporters to burst out on the run. The police information was so good the reporters felt certain their phones were tapped. They suspected one reporter of being a spy but never were able to prove it. Once Pat Watters of the *Atlanta Constitution* was telephoning a column to Atlanta. When he finished, the third man on the line shouted, "You son of a bitch!"

Again and again the newsmen were beaten, wounded, sometimes killed. But the danger was never so great as to the black voter-registration workers, the white northern youngsters who went south for Mississippi Summer, their local supporters who had to live day and night in a sea of hate. To them newsmen like Sitton were a lifeline. There was hardly a SNCC worker in the early days who did not carry Sitton's Atlanta telephone number on a scrap of paper or engraved in his mind. Night after night telephone calls would follow him over the South from his answering service, from the national desk of *The Times* in New York, from young people in threat of their lives. Sitton would take the calls quickly, laconically, efficiently. Where were they, who were they, what was the nearest town. Then he would call back the local sheriff, the mayor, the police chief, the highway patrol. It became almost a routine. Sitton would bluntly tell them that so-and-so was the son or daughter of a very well-known family. "If a hair of her head is touched," he would say, "there will be hell to pay. You will have all the newspapers in the U.S.A. down there." Usually that was enough to give some protection to the endangered youngster.

Sitton never talked much about this side of his work (and he saw it as part of his work, just as getting the names and addresses straight was part of his work) and if he was asked about it in later years he would shrug it off. But there was one occasion that fixed itself even in his nondramatic mind. He was in New Orleans and he always liked being able to spend a night there. It was safe and relaxed and like a furlough from the front lines. He was asleep on September 6, 1962, in his room at the Roosevelt Hotel when, as always, the telephone rang. It was a young man named Ralph Allen of SNCC, a twenty-two-year-old student from Trinity College, Melrose, Massachusetts. He had called Sitton's answering service and gotten his number in New Orleans.

"Where are you?" Sitton asked.

"Lying on the floor," Allen replied. "They're firing at the house."

"No," said Sitton, "I mean where are you calling from."

Allen was calling from the town of Dawson, in Terrell County, Georgia. He said there was a gang of whites outside, firing into the house with buckshot. One of the SNCC youngsters was bleeding from wounds.

"Well," said Sitton, "have you called the doctor?"

No, Allen replied.

"Have you called the FBI?" Sitton asked.

No, Allen said.

"Have you called the police?" he asked.

No, was the reply.

"Well, what are you calling me for?" said Sitton a little testily.

"We thought you could do something about it."

Sitton sighed. "O.K.," he said, "I'll come over."

"So," he recalled, "I went out to the damn airport and caught the plane for Georgia."

But, first, of course, he called Sheriff Z.T. Mathews in Dawson and said he was on his way over and he was going to report what happened in *The New York Times*.

Philadelphia

But, there was no way of saving all the lives. There was no way Sitton or anyone could save the lives of the three SNCC youngsters, Michael Schwerner, James Chaney and Andrew Goodman, murdered Sunday, June 21, 1964, near Philadelphia, Mississippi, Turner Catledge's home town. Catledge later said that when he heard of the Philadelphia slayings he knew just who had done it. He could see it happen. He could see the red necks of the killers and hear them bragging about it afterward. He didn't mean he knew the actual men but he knew the types and knew them well.

Of course, Sitton was on the story immediately and, as so often, he was accompanied by his friend Karl Fleming. The two arrived Monday, June 22, the day after the three young men had been reported missing.

Sitton and Fleming headed for the Courthouse, where they interviewed Sheriff Lawrence Rainey, a bulky, slack-faced man, and his chief deputy, Cecil Price, more bulky, with black receding hair and a baby face. Ultimately Rainey and Price were to be among the seventeen men indicted in the Schwerner killings, Rainey to be acquitted, Price to be convicted and sentenced to six years in prison.

When Sitton and Fleming emerged in the rotunda of the courthouse they encountered a group headed by Clarence Mitchell, a local insurance man. "A huge man, his face so red it looked like it was going to explode," Karl Fleming remembered, "shouted, 'Get outa town you nigger-loving bastards. Get out right this minute or something is going to happen to you.' "

It was an ugly situation but Sitton thought he knew how to meet it. He had seen a sign in the town square over a hardware store that said TURNER and he knew the business was run by a relative of Turner Catledge's, a member, as Popham would have said, of the "local power structure."

"Come on across the street a moment," Claude said to Fleming. The two walked to the store, followed by members of the courthouse mob.

Sitton introduced himself to the proprietor, saying that Turner Catledge had suggested that he drop in. Mr. Turner listened warily. Sitton explained the situation, said that he and Fleming were just there to do the job, not to stir up trouble, and perhaps a word from Mr. Turner would ease the situation.

"It's like this," said Mr. Turner, slowly and emphasizing each word. "If you wuz a nigra and were laying out there and that bunch was kicking the hell out of you I wouldn't go out and help them. But you are just stirring up trouble here and I don't care if they stomp the hell out of you."

(When Sitton next saw Catledge he told him that he was a very influential man around the world—but not in his home town.)

Ordinarily Claude dressed very neatly, Brooks Brothers suits, rep ties, brown cordovan shoes, horn-rimmed glasses. Now he and Fleming decided they must try to fade into the background. They bought denim shirts, jeans, clodhopper shoes and a bottle of Clorox, bleached the clothes, put them on and went back to Philadelphia. Half a block from the courthouse they heard a shout from one redneck to another: "Here come those fuckin' nigra-lovin' reporters!" (They did not know that the adult male population of Philadelphia had been organized into one of the most effective Klan outfits in the South; not a person or car could get near the downtown section without being spotted by lookouts.)*

When the Philadelphia story finally quieted down Sitton and Fleming drove to Jackson and went to dinner at Le Fleur's restaurant, a favorite of the Jackson elite, decorated with murals of antebellum life, scenes, as Fleming recalled, of "happy niggers and patrician white folks."

Sitton was half hysterical from fatigue. They were living in a world where there was no refuge; no white person who could be depended on; no one, at least no one who they knew, who was on their side; in constant fear of someone kicking in the motel door at night, of being set up, of being run down on the highway. Fleming remembered going to a beer joint a couple of doors from the police station at Albany, Georgia, with a policeman. The newsmen ordered beer, the officer buttermilk. "How come you are drinking buttermilk?" Sitton asked. "Well," the policeman replied. "They's two things I really like to do. One is to drink buttermilk and the other is to kick the shit outa nigras and the same thing goes for reporters."

Now Sitton and Fleming sat in the smart restaurant, white table-cloths, candles, the dull glow of silver, well-dressed people, polite black waiters in white jackets. Claude asked for dessert. "Make it a baked alaska," he told the waiter. "With a flaming cross."

"Yes, sir," said the man, bowing his head. Presently the waiter returned bearing the baked alaska, the flaming cross illuminating the formal dining room. Conversation ceased and every eye followed the cross to the table where the reporters sat. The waiter placed it in front of Sitton with a flourish. Sitton sat with dazed eyes. Fleming could not help noticing that the cross had been made of two Popsicle sticks tied together. They watched as the cross finally flickered out, called the waiter, paid their bill and left.

For years the managing editor's home town frightened *Times* reporters. Roy Reed, a low-pressure Arkansan, born in Hot Springs, determined from the age of eight to become a novelist, joined *The Times* January 1, 1965, after learning how to cover the Civil Rights struggle on the *Arkansas Gazette* and went into Philadelphia June 21, 1966, with Martin Luther King after the shooting of James Meredith.

---

*Florence Mars, a Philadelphia woman who lived through the whole nightmare, wrote an exhaustively researched account of Philadelphia, its people and the hysteria which overcame them. She was encouraged by Turner Catledge, who wrote a foreword for her book. Because of Florence Mars' courage and forthrightness she suffered severe economic losses, was personally shunned and even jailed. Later, with Philadelphia's emergence from trauma, she became a folk hero. More than 700 copies of her book were sold in Philadelphia in the first six months after publication. (Florence Mars, *Witness in Philadelphia*, Louisiana State University Press, Baton Rouge, La., 1977)

"That was my most frightening moment of the whole Civil Rights movement," Reed recalled. "Philadelphia was a scary place. I never spent much time there."

King went into Philadelphia with twenty of his followers and, joined by 150 local blacks, started from Independence Quarters, the black residential section, on a two-mile walk to the courthouse square.

As they emerged from the black section a truck roared down the narrow street, almost hitting a CBS cameraman named Perez and injuring a black youngster. As the marchers passed the jail a fire hose sprayed them. Residents lined the streets and cars drove back and forth, the drivers cursing and shaking their fists.

When the group reached the courthouse lawn their way was barred by Deputy Sheriff Cecil Price and his deputies.

"Everybody knew Cecil Price had helped kill the three Civil Rights workers two years before," Reed recalled (Price was one of the first to be named in the federal indictments but had not yet been tried and convicted). "King and Price stood face to face for a few minutes, Price staring at King, King staring at Price. Somebody threw some cherry bombs and everyone thought it was pistol shots."

Reed looked around him. The courthouse seemed very ominous. The marchers were surrounded by angry whites. He looked up and felt totally vulnerable. They stood in the middle of the square. From the second-story window of any building a rifleman could have killed King (the memory of John Kennedy and Dallas was fresh in mind).

"King was smart," Reed said. "He didn't spend very long on his prayer."

King said, "In this county Andrew Goodman, James Chaney and Michael Schwerner were murdered. I believe in my heart that the murderers are somewhere around me at this moment. . . . I want them to know that we are not afraid. If they killed three of us they will have to kill all of us."

Cecil Price stood ten feet away as King spoke.

The marchers turned back toward the black section. Assault followed assault. King's marshals were picked off and beaten. A white girl marcher was seized by white bullies. They grabbed her legs. Her companions grabbed her arms and gradually pulled her onto a truck and safety. "I thought she would be pulled apart," Reed admitted. He took off his necktie, hid his notebook in his pocket and tried to mingle in the crowd. Sometimes "mingling" worked and sometimes not. Sitton remembered once when he was in the White River delta in Arkansas, covering a Faubus meeting. "Two big white bastards came after me," Sitton recalled. "One shoved me from one side, the other from the other. They asked if I was a newspaperman. I said I was. Where from, they asked. I said, 'The New York Times' in my best south Georgia accent. They thought that was such a comically improbable thing they burst out laughing and left me alone."

The Reporters

Many reporters, including Gene Roberts, who came to *The Times* in 1965, remembered Bogalusa, Louisiana, as the most dangerous story they were to cover. Roberts, born in Pikeville, North Carolina, near Goldsboro, was the son of a teacher of religion who founded a weekly paper which owed much of its success to a personal "shucks and nubbins" column called "Ramblin' Rural Wayne," a collection of farmers' reminiscences and crop talk in Wayne County. Gene's grandfather had been a tough segregationist but Gene's feelings were given form when he was twelve and tried to save the life of a black boy who fell in the river. Gene and his cousins dove and brought the boy up. Gene ran to a neighbor's for an ambulance. In his excitement he did not specify the boy was black. A "white" ambulance came, refused to take the child to a hospital and drove away, leaving the body on the riverbank. "So I kind of saw the excesses of segregation at an early age," Roberts recalled.

At Bogalusa, Roberts and several other newsmen were invited by the Grand Titan of the Klan, dressed in red boots, red hood and white robe, to attend a Klan rally at Crossroads, Mississippi. As the newsmen made their way through screaming women and children to a platform set up in a cow pasture the loudspeaker announced, "Will the sergeant at arms please collect the firearms from the White Knights?" (The White Knights were the tough, compact group that had organized Philadelphia.)

Soon the crowd started shouting against the newsmen. The reporters tried to escape across a field but their path was cut off by four or five men with knives. When they returned to the platform a little old lady, a "Klan Knightingale," that is, a member of the female auxiliary, tried to sell them chances on a Mustang being raffled by the KKK. Finally, the Grand Titan got on his walkie-talkie and broadcast, "Titan to Klaxon Three—need flying wedge for seven people." Instantly fifteen Klansmen in flowing robes appeared, formed a V and got the newsmen out.

Not long after Roberts succeeded Sitton as chief southern correspondent he went to Newton, seat of Baker County about forty miles from Albany, Georgia, to cover desegregation of the school. More than five hundred southern counties had been desegregated but not Baker, a lowland county, very poor, much of the land in hunting preserves owned by northerners.

Newton was a town of five hundred, the kind of place, as Roberts remembered, where "by seven in the morning people start sitting on the stoops of the stores with wine bottles in brown paper bags." He went to the school and found a Civil Rights worker named Charles Sherrod escorting a black girl into class. As Sherrod approached the school a wine drinker took a revolver from his pocket, extracted five cartridges, twirled the chamber with the one remaining cartridge, pointed the pistol at Sherrod's head and clicked the trigger. Sherrod did not flinch. Then the fellow and his companions came toward Roberts, who retreated into the courtroom. As he approached it every door and window slammed shut and Roberts found himself surrounded by rednecks.

A man named Fred Miller, of the Community Relations Service, 280 pounds, Georgian, built like a fullback and the most effective Civil Rights worker Roberts ever knew, entered the courthouse and found Roberts, a small compact man, backed against the wall. As Miller crossed the corridor his jacket caught in the water fountain and he exclaimed in a loud voice, "Cripes! I better not do that again or I'll knock my pistol loose." The crowd scattered at mention of the (nonexistent) pistol. Miller hustled Roberts out to the little country church that was the staging area for school integration. Here Roberts found Sherrod, collapsed on a church pew. He had gone through Russian roulette without batting an eye. Now he had fainted.

A few weeks later Roberts went back to Newton after reading in the paper that the town had been flooded and Main Street was under seven feet of water. The sheriff was perfectly hospitable and took him for a motorboat ride up and down Main Street. He was up for election but told Roberts, "I don' 'spect I will do too good." "You mean you are going to be defeated?" Roberts asked. "Yep," he said, "I 'spect I will." "Why's that?" "Well," the sheriff said, "once you shoot a nigger they never forget it." "And have you done that?" Roberts asked. "Well," said the man, "yes. I got me my first one in '47, and the second in '48 and, let me see, I don't rightly remember when I got my third."

He was believed, Roberts discovered, to have been involved in the deaths of six to eight blacks. The Civil Rights Division of the Justice Department had been unable to nail him but the NAACP filed Civil Rights suits for damages in each of the deaths. Soon he was involved in so many lawsuits his legal fees ran to $20,000 or $25,000. The only way he could get the money to pay the lawyers was through speed traps. But his victims had to be white. The blacks had no money. This aroused the whites. They teamed up with the blacks and beat him in the election.

Only one or two of the dozen remarkable young men who covered the revolution in the South remained on *The Times* by 1979—the others were gone, scattered to the winds, many of them like Roberts, Sitton and Walter Rugaber now editors of fine newspapers, possibly the most expensive hemorrhage of talent *The New York Times* had ever experienced. One of those who went on to cover the Carter campaign and presidency and resigned only in 1979 was Jim Wooten, born in Detroit of Appalachian emigrants, his father an itinerant Presbyterian minister, himself, as he described it, "an errant and erratic pastor," baptizing, marrying and burying in the hills of Tennessee until he got an annulment of vows, started a backwoods paper of his own, got a job on the Huntsville, Alabama, paper and "cursed all the time I had wasted." For Wooten, reporting, the tough, dangerous, perpetually exciting southern reporting, was "just love." Like so many he was brought to *The Times* by Scotty Reston. He covered the George Wallace campaign of 1968 and then took over the Atlanta bureau. It was late in the Civil Rights story now but this was a story that never seemed to end. With Roy Reed and Tom Johnson, a senior *Times* black reporter, Wooten covered the last big school integration battle in Mississippi in January 1971.

Early one morning Wooten, a tall handsome man who had gone to Bethel College, Kentucky, on a basketball scholarship, left the Admiral Benbow Motel in Jackson about 4:30 A.M. and drove down the Natchez Trace parkway toward Woodville, Mississippi, a lumber town of 3,000 on the western border of Mississippi.

Wooten found the usual red-brick courthouse in the center square, surrounded by confederate statutes with a World War I cannon on the steps. At the school only one little white girl and her brother had showed up; all the rest of the white children had been sent to the newly founded "seg" academy; the girl and her brother were two little white faces among the blacks. Wooten asked the girl why she was there and she said, "My daddy didn't have no money." It was a case of integration by poverty. The father was a logger and Wooten decided to look him up.

At the lumberyard a woman told Wooten the man wasn't there and that if Wooten knew what was good for him he wouldn't be either. Three young punks came in and snarled, "Get your ass outa town or we'll whup yah." They stood between Wooten and the door. As he backed into a corner he noticed a barrel beside the counter filled with ax handles. On impulse he picked one up and the punks stepped back. He was frightened to death but he put on a front. "If one of you tries to come close I'm going to lay this across your head," he said, walking quietly to the door. He dropped the ax handle, jumped into his car and drove off. Then he made a mistake. He decided to visit a black mortician who was the local head of the NAACP. He found the man's home, a neat well-tended house with a newly seeded lawn, parked his car and rang the doorbell. No answer. He rang again. No answer. Then a car screeched up with the three punks. Wooten leaped to his own car, whipped over the neat new lawn, jumped a small ditch and raced through town at sixty miles an hour out to the highway.

It was beginning to get dusk and he had to call New York and get off his story. He stopped at a general store but leaped back into his car when he saw his pursuers. He drove down the highway at eighty miles an hour, trying to compose his story in his head. He hated driving, hated driving fast, had been afraid of fast driving since a high school accident. But there was no alternative. It was almost dark when he spotted a doctor's office in a crossroads village. He swung in, switched off his lights and entered the office. He asked the nurse if he could use the telephone. Dr. Montgomery, an elderly, cantankerous man, asked what was going on. Wooten told him. The doctor grunted, went out, drove Wooten's car behind his office, turned off the front lights and announced, "There's a telephone in my magnificent operating room." He led Wooten into a bare room equipped with a plain operating table. "Now you've got to have a typewriter," the doctor said. Over Wooten's protests he and the nurse lugged in an ancient Underwood. Wooten called his office, reported in, wrote a few paragraphs on the Underwood, called back and dictated his lead and the body of the story off the cuff. In half an hour the story was in New York and he had met the deadline.

Now Dr. Montgomery broke out a bottle of bourbon, poured two large slugs in white inch-thick coffee mugs and, as Wooten recalled, "we got slightly stewed." Wooten asked the doctor if he read *The New York Times.* The doctor snorted. "I wouldn't read that commie rag!" It wasn't for love of *The New York Times* he had lent Wooten a hand. It was because "those damn punks are just white trash." The doctor believed in justice and fair play.

Wooten had long since learned that the die-hard segregationists had identified *The New York Times* as the enemy. It stood for all they hated —for the changes that had come into their lives, for poverty and barrenness, for frustration, for the puncturing of the illusory dream which they had lived by, for, in fact, all of the myths which they had created to try to save their shattered self-image.

Wooten had seen the recalcitrant opponents of desegregation focus their hatred on *The New York Times* as the metaphor of the enemy, "that no good commie-pinko-jew-northern paper trying to fuck up our hallowed land."

Not only the rednecks lived by this metaphor. So did members of the upper class, some of the business people, some of the intellectuals for they, too, felt threatened by the turbulence which had come into their lives and they, too, grasped with equal fear for a symbol on which to focus their hate.

Even years after the tensions had died; after Birmingham had shed its old image; after integration became a peaceful way of southern life; after the deaths and the suffering and the agony began to assume the burnished façade of legends, the spit and venom of "commie-pinko-jew" smoldered on even in Chattanooga and was spread by word of mouth against Mr. Ochs' original creation, the *Chattanooga Times,* compromising its efforts to preach commonsense and progress and lingering in the city's bloodstream like a sulfa-resistant strain of gonorrhea.

It was, as Powledge had said, a war, a guerrilla war. Or, as Sitton conceded, a revolution, and there was no changing the story or the conditions under which it had to be reported. You simply went back to it day after day and night after night, covering it as best you could and Sitton became very, very good, the best there was although for reasons which no one in his profession could understand, despite his years on the firing line, the brilliance of his reporting, the relentless honesty of his writing, the sheer clarity of his interpretation he was never to win the top Establishment honor of his profession, a Pulitzer prize. But this did not reflect upon him. It reflected on the judges of the Pulitzers.

It was out of these tensions, emotions, fear, dangers, cowardice and courage, vision and blindness that the route to *Sullivan* v. *The New York Times* was paved, a path that led to the case and then on beyond it with consequences which would change permanently the powers and abilities of *The Times* and other newspapers to carry out their First Amendment functions.

31

"Fear and Hatred Grip Birmingham"

*T*HE SOUTH where Adolph S. Ochs had been born and spent his formative years had changed so much by 1960 he would have had difficulty recognizing it. The changes were particularly striking in the "New South," the borderland with which he was so familiar, Tennessee, North Carolina, the Piedmont area of South Carolina, the contiguous parts of Georgia and Alabama, the industrial South, not the plantation South, the boom towns of Chattanooga, Birmingham, Charlotte and Atlanta where manufacturing, distributive and extractive industries were king—textiles, coal, steel, railroads and over-the-road trucking, huge complexes of flat-roofed supply and processing centers. No magnolias, no darkie songs, no crinolines. Much of it still Klan country.

Here something entirely new to the South burst into being in the winter of 1960, specifically, at 4 P.M. on February 1, 1960, at the F. W. Woolworth lunch counter in Greensboro, North Carolina—the first black sit-in. Within days sit-ins began to spread from one end of the non-cotton South to the other, to Charlotte, to Raleigh, to Rockhill, South Carolina, to Orangeburg, South Carolina, to Nashville, Tennessee. The black youngsters had never heard of sit-ins before, although they had been tried briefly and unsuccessfully in the North by the NAACP, just after World War II in Chicago and Kansas City.

The sit-ins were a phenomena as strange and unexpected to *The Times* as they were to the organized black movement and the southern Establishment. It was a week before Claude Sitton got onto the story with the sit-ins in Charlotte and Raleigh. Before this much of the Rights action had been inspired by whites and was largely confined to the courts. Now the blacks took action into their hands. They challenged segregation openly and in the marketplace. This was social-economic protest of a dramatic kind and this, as Sitton was to say, was its significance. It was simple, easy to organize, hard to stop, carried on by young blacks with politeness and patience. To halt them merchants closed their stores and police dragged nonresisting young people out of fast-food shops and department stores. Older blacks stood on the sidelines but they cheered the young people. The protest gave blacks a sense of dignity. Within a week the movement was leapfrogging across the South, more action than Sitton could cover single-handedly. *The Times* began to send in additional reporters and by the first of March I had been drawn into the coverage, reporting from Nashville, Raleigh and Orangeburg, South Carolina. On April 1, 1960, I went South on an extended swing to examine in greater depth a contrasting group of cities—Nashville, Baton Rouge and Birmingham.

Birmingham was known as a hard-rock center of resistance to integration. It was dominated publicly by a man named Theophilus Eugene Connor, a former radio announcer now police commissioner who listed his name in the Birmingham telephone directory as "Bull" Connor from his days as a sports broadcaster. Connor laid down the dictum, so it was said, that "we're not goin' to have white folks and nigras segregatin' together in this man's town." He was popularly reputed to have asserted, "Damn the law—down here we make our own law."

American Johannesburg

On the evening of April 1, I checked into a motel at Montgomery, Alabama, and that weekend the sit-in wave hit Birmingham. Ten black students went, two by two, to five downtown Birmingham stores. In each they made small purchases and sat at the lunch counter. All were arrested and held for eighteen hours on trespassing charges before making bail. In the next seventy-two hours three black ministers, the Reverend Fred L. Shuttlesworth, the Reverend Charles Billups and the Reverend C. Herbert Oliver and two students, one white, one black, were arrested. All were charged with vagrancy. In addition, the white student, Thomas Reeves, and one of the ministers, the Reverend Oliver, were charged with "intimidating a witness."

On April 5 the *Alabama Journal* published a story about an advertisement that had appeared March 29 in *The New York Times* captioned "Heed Their Rising Voices." The ad quoted from a *New York Times* editorial of March 19 which said, "The growing movement of peaceful mass demonstrations by Negroes is something new in the South, something understandable. . . . Let Congress heed their rising voices for they will be heard." The ad solicited funds for Martin Luther King and was signed by a list of notables including Mrs. Eleanor Roosevelt, Mrs. Ralph Bunche and Norman Thomas. It was signed, as well, by a group of southern ministers including several blacks from Alabama.

Grover Hall, editor of the *Montgomery Advertiser,* called the advertisement "lies, lies, lies—and possibly willful ones" and demanded that *The Times* disassociate itself from "a slanderous lie." A day or two later Alabama Secretary of State Bettye Frink proposed prosecution of the ad's sponsors for "falsifying the State of Alabama with lies" and said she would gladly swear out warrants if she could figure out what charge could be brought. Attorney General MacDonald Gallion said he was considering legal action.

The proposed legal action sounded far-fetched to me. The advertisement named no names and its text was vague if somewhat melodramatic. Much more significant seemed to be the news that the sit-ins had hit the bastion of Birmingham.

I spent the ensuing days in Birmingham taking a firsthand look. I had been warned by Sitton that Birmingham was touchy ground and one of the first persons to whom I talked told me that "Birmingham is no place for irresponsible reporting."

"Be careful of what you say and who you mention," he said. "Lives are at stake."

It was a message I had heard in other countries but never in the United States.

One newspaperman told me, "Birmingham is going to blow one of these days and when that happens that's one story I don't want to be around to cover," and I was surprised to hear the head of a local college apologizing, "I'm ashamed to have to talk to you off-the-record. It is not for myself. But these are not ordinary times. The dangers are very real and people up North must realize that."

By this time I realized that Birmingham was no ordinary story and I quickly compiled a list of horrors—beatings, police raids, floggings, cross burnings, assaults, bombings (dynamite seemed to be as common as six-packs), attacks on synagogues, terror, wiretapping, mail interception, suspicion of even worse, grist for a dispatch published under the headline "Fear and Hatred Grip Birmingham," in which I wrote:

> Every channel of communication, every medium of mutual interest, every reasoned approach, every inch of middle ground has been fragmented by the emotional dynamite of racism, enforced by the whip, the razor, the gun, the bomb, the torch, the club, the knife, the mob, the police and many branches of the state's apparatus.

One black called Birmingham "the Johannesburg of America." I found that those blacks and whites with whom I met preferred to meet inconspicuously in the evening. Some simply would not talk to me. I had checked in at Birmingham's ancient but pleasant Tutweiler Hotel and before I had gotten a whiff of the atmosphere used the hotel phone. But I soon realized that I had stumbled into a part of the United States where I had to apply the conspiratorial rules of reporting I had practiced for years in the Soviet Union.

Before I left Birmingham, batting out my story on a long night-plane trip to New York, I had learned enough to write:

In Birmingham neither blacks or whites talk freely. A pastor carefully closes the door before he speaks. A Negro keeps a weather eye on the sidewalk outside his house. A lawyer talks in the Aesopian language of conspiracy [this was the ineffable Charles Morgan, Jr., not yet having assumed his role of national champion of Civil Rights]. Telephones are tapped—or there is fear of tapping. Mail has been intercepted and opened. Sometimes, it does not reach its destination. The eavesdropper, the informer, the spy has become a fact of life.

And I added a paragraph out of my Russian experience:

To one long accustomed to the sickening atmosphere of Moscow in the Stalin days the aura of the community which once prided itself as the "Magic City" of the South is only too familiar. To one who knew Hitler's storm troop Germany it would seem even more familiar.

Those were strong words. Looking back over two decades they sound too strong. To *The Times'* editors in April 1960 they *were* too strong. The words were edited out and never printed. But as the tragedy of Birmingham evolved over the next three years I often thought my original judgment had been right.

Libel

The reaction in Birmingham was violent. Both newspapers, the *Birmingham Post-Herald* and the *Birmingham News*, attacked *The Times* and its correspondent. John Temple Graves, editorial columnist, set the tone:

This almost total lie. . . . This throwback to tooth-and-claw hate . . . purveyor of prejudgment, malice and hate . . . letting Mr. Salisbury foam at the mouth. . . . It is a form of race hate. . . . Hatred of the South, engendered by racial emotions. . . . There is nothing, by and large, of which Birmingham and the South can be more proud than the behavior of its police and its people . . . our much-mooted Police Commissioner Connor—tough as ever but determined to be fair. . . .

On May 6, 1960, the three city commissioners of Birmingham, Theophilus Eugene Connor, James Morgan and J. T. Waggoner, filed suit for libel against *The Times* and against myself individually. In each case damages of $500,000 was asked, a total of $1,500,000. On May 31, 1960, the three city commissioners of the town of Bessemer, an industrial enclave where Birmingham's steel mills were located, filed identical libel suits, asking $500,000 each, bringing the total to $3,-000,000. On July 20, 1960, a Birmingham city detective named Joe Lindsey brought a similar action asking for $150,000.

Simultaneously, April 26, libel action was initiated against *The Times* in connection with the March 29 advertisement for Martin Luther King. Each of the three city commissioners of Montgomery,

Alabama, sued, asking $500,000 apiece. Governor John Patterson of Alabama sued for $1,000,000 and a former Montgomery commissioner for $500,000, a total of $3,000,000.

In all *The Times* faced $6,150,000 in libel actions in the state of Alabama and I faced $1,500,000. As Louis Loeb, *The Times'* counsel, was to recall, "In all the years I have practiced law nothing had ever arisen that was more worrisome. Nothing scared me more than this litigation."

Loeb encountered a new shock when he sought to arrange Alabama counsel for *The Times*. Lawyers, like banks, have "correspondent" firms in other cities to whom they turn for collaboration on local cases. But when Loeb telephoned the extremely proper Birmingham law firm with which Lord, Day and Lord had long maintained association he suffered a blow not unlike that which he was to inflict a few years later on Punch Sulzberger in the Pentagon case. The Birmingham firm declined very politely but very definitely to represent *The Times*. A conflict of interest, they said, although what that conflict was Loeb was never to learn. He tried two more top-drawer firms with the same result. The message came through clear and direct: *The Times* was too hot for Establishment Birmingham firms to handle.

But just as Lord, Day and Lord's refusal to take the Pentagon case led *The Times* to the tough and successful combination of Cahill Gordon, Floyd Abrams and Alexander Bickel, so the refusal of blue-ribbon Birmingham firms to deal with *The Times* proved to be a blessing.

Loeb's partner, Tom Daly, had defended *The Reader's Digest* in Birmingham against a libel suit brought by former Governor James "Kissin' Jim" Folsom. Folsom's lawyer was a man named Roderick Beddow, and Daly had developed a high regard for his ability. In the extremity, Loeb approached the firm of Beddow, Embry & Beddow, a litigating office with a large criminal law practice and many black clients. As Cecil Roberts, a clear-eyed woman who over the years was to lead Birmingham's long struggle to emerge from the swamp, once said, "They were the kind of lawyers who took black clients and got them life sentences instead of the death penalty."

Beddow and his associate T. Eric Embry (later to become a justice of the Alabama State Supreme Court) moved with vigor, skill and imagination. "They jumped in lock, stock and barrel," Loeb recalled. "They worked like beavers, and their judgment and advice was sound."

Every bit of their expertise was needed. Immediately the pressure began to build up against anyone suspected of association with *The Times'* story—local newspapermen, lonely defenders of Civil Rights, clergymen, black and white, educators. Lawyers for the Birmingham commissioners demanded a list of all persons I talked with and when

they could not get it subpoenaed the telephone records of the Tutweiler Hotel.§

Then, August 29, 1960, a grand jury was convened in Bessemer to
investigate, it was announced, the conditions described in *The Times'*
article. Before that grand jury was paraded almost every person I had
met or telephoned from the hotel (but not Bull Connor, whom I had
telephoned several times and failed to reach). My careless use of the
phone brought tribulation to a dozen people who had had the courage
to talk with me. Birmingham newsmen who had met me found themselves in jeopardy of their jobs. Blacks got threats of arrest—or worse.
Educators encountered difficulty with their trustees, clergy with their
vestrymen.

One of those with whom I had talked through a long evening behind
carefully drawn curtains in his home was Robert Hughes, a slim young
Methodist minister who had been quietly working to ease racial problems in Birmingham for two years as a representative of the Alabama
Council on Human Relations. He documented case after case of beatings, intimidation, police violence, gang terrorism. Now he was subpoenaed to appear before the Bessemer Grand Jury and bring the
records of his organization. He was quite prepared to testify but not
to submit his records and thereby expose those who had helped him,
who had been helped by him and who had made contributions to him.
He met the same trouble *The New York Times* had encountered. He
could find no lawyer to defend him. Finally, Charles Morgan, Jr.,
stepped into the breech and with his partner, Jim Shores, mounted a
whirlwind campaign, rushing the case all the way to the U.S. Supreme
Court but that did not keep Hughes from spending a four-day Labor
Day weekend in Bessemer jail for contempt of court and being suspended by his ecclesiastical superiors, the North Alabama Conference
of the Methodist Church, a suspension that was lifted two days later
when Hughes was permitted to go as a missionary to Southern
Rhodesia, an assignment he had long coveted but had been denied on
health grounds. Now anything that would take him a long way from
Birmingham was okay.

The Bessemer Grand Jury, having, as it said, found no factual basis
for my report on Birmingham, on September 6, 1960, indicted me on
forty-two counts of criminal libel. It was the first indictment on such
a charge in Alabama in at least a quarter century and no direct precedent for the action could be uncovered by legal researchers. Each count
carried a penalty of $500 or six months in jail or both—for a possible
total of $21,000 in fines and twenty-one years in jail or both.

The Bessemer indictment had a scissors effect. If I appeared in

§See Notes section.

Alabama to testify in the Birmingham civil libel action I could be arrested on the Bessemer criminal libel counts. If I went to Bessemer to defend myself on the criminal charges I would be subject to service in the civil action.

This, as was quickly evident, was at least one objective of the Alabama actions—to keep reporters out of the South, to "chill" their reporting of Civil Rights cases, to make a newspaper or a TV network or a news magazine question the usefulness of sending a reporter into a southern state to cover a Rights controversy and to make them think twice about reporting the facts, harsh and raw as they often were. As the *Chicago Tribune* said editorially September 27, 1960:

> If those [cases] are allowed to stand, there is real danger that editors will be discouraged from sending reporters to explore conditions around the country. . . . The Alabama cases against The New York Times are of great significance for these reasons. We have no hesitation in saying that these are the most important challenges to freedom of information to have arisen in many years.

Nothing like this had been tried in the South or anywhere in the United States. It was a new and in the initial phase an effective tactic. *New York Times* reporters were instructed, on the advice of counsel, not to enter the state of Alabama. *The Times* was fighting Alabama's jurisdiction in the cases; it did not want any *Times* person available in the state upon whom service could be made. Effectively, it closed Alabama to *New York Times* reporters and compelled the newspaper to depend on press agency accounts.

"Boy, did I cuss you out," Sitton recalled years later. "Your damn stories kept me out of Alabama for over a year."

Reality

Loeb was quick to learn that he was up against conditions which he had never expected to encounter in the United States; conditions which seemed to him more like he might have found in a dictatorship.

"What happened down there [was] really astounding," he said later, "when you consider it took place in the latter half of the twentieth century."

When he went to Alabama with some witnesses for preliminary examinations he was advised by Embry not to stay in Birmingham or Montgomery. He and his party were put up incognito in a motel on the highway between the two cities. The rooms had been reserved under other names. During the trial in Montgomery, Beddow and Embry would take Loeb, Tom Daly and their associates to a restaurant and promptly vanish "on business." It was apparent they did not want to be seen in public with men from *The New York Times.* Four black ministers were named in the Montgomery case and they were represented by black lawyers. Embry instructed Loeb not to shake hands publicly with the blacks. The courtroom was segregated. One morning the black lawyers arrived early and sat in a section reserved for white lawyers. Nothing was said but after luncheon recess armed guards with pistols at their belts saw to it that the blacks took their proper places.

The judge who conducted the preliminary examination was Circuit Judge Walter B. Jones. Jones, an imposing, even rather handsome, man, born late in the nineteenth century, was the youngest son of Thomas Gude Jones, who served as governor of Alabama and then was named to the federal bench by Theodore Roosevelt at the suggestion, it was said, of Booker T. Washington, the famous black who founded the Tuskegee Institute. Although a conservative, Jones did not support the movement to disenfranchise blacks. He believed that if a Negro could afford to buy a first-class ticket he was entitled to ride first-class and if he could meet the property qualifications he was entitled to the vote. Jones was an imperious man with a small pointed beard and looked a bit like Lenin. His son, Walter B. Jones, went to the University of Alabama and graduated from law school. He was a member of the Sigma Alpha Epsilon fraternity, became its national president and wore his fraternity pin on his judicial robes as long as he occupied the bench.

Jones was described by a colleague as "queer as a three-dollar bill." Louis Loeb called him "a notorious pansy." Jones invited lawyers for both sides to his house for cocktails, taking them to see his study, the walls of which were covered from ceiling to floor with photographs of handsome young men, many of them nude. "God Almighty," Harding Bancroft exclaimed as he left the house. "What Tennessee Williams could do with this!"

Gossip in the Montgomery courthouse had it that Jones sat in with the Montgomery citizens who masterminded the "libel suit" strategy. Louis Loeb found "the whole thing very uncomfortable." He called Jones "very courteous and oily while sticking every knife into us that he could."

In Jones' courtroom Loeb saw something he had never seen before or expected to see again. On either end of the judge's gavel were pasted photographs of good-looking young boys. During the proceedings the judge spent much time turning his gavel end to end and contemplating the photographs.

The centennial of the Confederacy was being celebrated, and Montgomery, the old Confederate capital, was bedecked for the occasion. There were parades and ceremonials every day. To the amazement of Loeb and Bancroft half the jurors appeared in Confederate uniform, several with pistol holsters and pistols. Loeb and Bancroft hoped that the guns were only replicas. A Confederate flag stood in a stand behind Jones.

Under a glass top on the bench before him Jones kept a typewritten list of local attorneys who once supported a candidate who had the temerity to run against him. It was rare indeed for an attorney on that list to win a case in Jones' courtroom.

Jones made no effort to hide his extreme racist feelings. Once he observed, "The Fourteenth Amendment has no standing in this court-room." Needless to say *The Times* lost in Jones' court.

The two sets of cases, the Montgomery ones and the Birmingham ones, slowly moved up the judicial ladder. But life in Birmingham traveled on a faster track. Edward R. Murrow decided to do a special TV program on Birmingham which he proposed to call "The Johannes-burg of America." He and his producer, David Lowe, spent a week there in January 1961 and found a "grave defect" in my Birmingham reports—*conditions were much worse than I reported.* People tele-phoned them only from street-corner telephone booths, slipped anony-mous notes under hotel doors, made appointments to see them in parks, on street corners, in obscure lunchrooms, refused to come to the hotel except late at night, used only the side entrances. Murrow said he had not seen such an atmosphere except in Hitler's Berlin before World War II.

One year, one month and three days after my Birmingham story with its warning of the time bomb of violence ticking in the city's heart the *Birmingham News* on Monday, May 15, 1961, carried a double-truck headline:

Integrationist Group Continuing
Trip After Brutal Beatings Here
Mob Terror
Hits city on
Mother's Day.

The whole of page one was given over to stories and pictures of violence in Birmingham.

Across the top of page one under the caption "The People Are Asking, 'Where were the police?' " The *News* wrote:

> The City of Birmingham is normally a peaceful orderly place in which people are safe.
> Harrison Salisbury of the New York Times last year came to Birming-ham and wrote two articles about us which said, in substance, that "fear and hatred" stalked our streets.
> The Birmingham News and others promptly challenged this asser-tion. The News knows Birmingham people, as others know them, and they didn't fit this designation.

But yesterday, Sunday May 14, was a day which ought to be burned into Birmingham's conscience.

Fear and hatred did stalk Birmingham's streets yesterday.

It had happened almost precisely as my story of April 12, 1960, had predicted. And it went on happening. The trouble simmered during 1962. The next year brought George Wallace in as governor of Alabama and 1963 came to be known as the "year of Birmingham." *The Times* libel cases moved up and down court calendars but *Times* men had come back into Alabama. There was too much news to keep them out whatever the cost. Dr. Martin Luther King came to town and thousands of blacks went into the streets to demonstrate for their rights. This, Birmingham had never before seen. Almost immediately King was arrested and wrote his famous "Letter from the Birmingham City Jail."

Then on a cloudy Sunday, September 15, 1963, a bomb went off in the red-brick Sixteenth Street Baptist Church and four little girls, Cynthia Wesley, Denise McNair, Carol Robertson and Addie Mae Collins, none older than fourteen, all black, died.

The next day at the weekly luncheon of the Young Men's Business Club, Charles Morgan, Jr., spoke:

"Who threw that bomb? Was it a Negro or a white? The answer should be 'We all did it.' . . . We are ten years of lawless preachments. . . . We are a mass of intolerance and bigotry. . . . Who is guilty? Each of us."

As Morgan left the meeting the carillon atop the Protective Life Building played "Dixie." It was one o'clock. Every hour on the hour the carillon played "Dixie."

Neither Morgan nor any of those who heard the carillon that day could be certain of the future. But out of the emotional fire storm set off by the tragedy, the hatred and conflict began to dissolve and when I went back to the city in 1975 I didn't recognize the town, physically or spiritually. The power structure had changed almost entirely. County Commissioner Ben Erdeich said, "There's no Bull Connor any more and if there was one around he wouldn't last long." It was far from heaven but the heavy pall of smog no longer hung over the statue of Vulcan on Red Mountain nor did the acrid scent of racism dominate the community. I agreed with the cool words of Bessie Estell, a black high school principal who had just been named Birmingham's Woman of the Year, that the city had come a long way. As I flew out of Birmingham I riffled through some of the Chamber of Commerce literature. They were writing about the past (in order to glorify the present) and my eye caught a phrase: "A New York writer said of Birmingham in 1960: 'Every inch of middle ground has been fragmented by the emotional dynamite of racism.' " Well, I thought, they didn't use my name but I recognized my words and had to admit that I never thought to see the day when my $3,150,000 "libel" would be drawn upon by Birmingham to tell the story of what it once had been and how far it had now traveled.

Verdict

Not until January 6, 1964, did Alabama reach the Supreme Court. After many permutations the case which was argued before the court was that of Montgomery Commissioner L. B. Sullivan against *The Times.* Columbia Law Professor Herbert Wechsler (later to be considered for the same role in the Pentagon cases) argued for *The Times* and on March 9, 1964, Justice Brennan read the court's decision. As M. R. Nachman, Jr., the lawyer who represented Sullivan, was to say, "I had confidently predicted that the only way the court could decide against me was to change one hundred years or more of libel law." There were those who thought Nachman exaggerated his chances of winning but no one challenged his description of what the court had done. It had by a vote of six to three decided:

"The constitutional guarantees require, we think, a federal rule that prohibits a public official from recovering damages for a defamatory falsehood relating to his official conduct unless he proves that the statement was made with 'actual malice,' that is with knowledge that it was false or with reckless disregard of whether it was false or not."

The court noted that officials are protected in their official conduct against libel actions by ordinary citizens. Critics of official conduct, said the court, must have the same immunity.

"We conclude," said Brennan, "that such a privilege is required by the First and Fourteenth amendments."

The court declared that the position of the Alabama courts in the case against *The New York Times* struck "at the very center of the constitutionally protected area of free expression."

"We hold," wrote Brennan, "that such a proposition may not constitutionally be utilized to establish that an otherwise impersonal attack on government operations was a libel of an official responsible for those operations."

The verdict could not have been more far-reaching. By March of 1964 the total of libel actions outstanding against newspapers, news magazines, television networks and other public media had reached nearly $300 million. Actions had been filed in southern states from Florida to Texas. Editors and publishers could not send a reporter or a photographer into these states without putting themselves at risk. Had the Supreme Court's verdict gone in the other direction the burden of censorship and official intimidation might well have enabled the "southern judicial strategy" to prolong lawlessness as a final barrier against the revolution in Civil Rights.

But even without the Sullivan case *The Times* and the face-the-facts dispatches of the newspaper's southern reporters had brought to the people an image, an impression, a panorama of a kind of conduct which American society would not tolerate in mid-twentieth century. *Times* reporters and their expertise had become the standard which the rest of the press, print and electronic, had adopted. The insights of Catledge, of Daniel, of Popham, of Sitton and the rest had given the lead and the country had followed. Catledge's concept of the "Great Revolution" and the role *The Times* must play in it had been fulfilled and in so doing the pattern of American life had changed. Many a battle for Civil Rights lay ahead, particularly in the North, but the country had come to grips with *Brown* v. *The Board of Education.* Of the ultimate outcome there could be no doubt.

It was six months later that the Birmingham case finally went to trial in U.S. District Court before Judge H. H. Grooms. After a day of legal skirmishing only one case was left, that of Theophilus Eugene Connor. Despite the U.S. Supreme Court verdict in the Sullivan case, that of Connor was not automatically thrown out. It was heard before Judge Grooms and not without a few echoes of the old Birmingham. The forty-two-count criminal libel indictment against me was still standing in Bessemer. Beddow and Embry worked out a stipulation providing immunity on the Bessemer indictment while I was in Birmingham to testify in the Connor case. Suddenly word came to Judge Grooms that sheriff's deputies from Bessemer were on their way to arrest me. Grooms ordered federal marshals to surround the courtroom and advised the Bessemer district attorney that he would hold him in contempt if there was any interference while I was testifying or during a reasonable time to get out of town. Reluctantly the Bessemer deputies turned back. Not until I was safely on the plane to New York did Loeb and Daly tell me why they had been so careful to stay at my side, day and night, while we were in Birmingham.

A jury gave Connor a $40,000 award. *Two years later* the matter was finally put to rest. The Fifth Circuit Court of Appeals ruled August 4, 1966, that under the Sullivan rule Connor could not recover unless he could show "reckless disregard for the truth."

We [do not] intend to intimate, said the court, that The Times and Salisbury have merely followed the minimum course of conduct necessary to shield themselves from libel actions. On the contrary, they have exhibited a high standard of reporting practices. Salisbury did contact persons representing different viewpoints and made a conscientious effort to interview Connor and others.

There is no evidence that he misquoted his sources or gave the information acquired from them a different slant than intended as is so often done. The Times . . . did not hesitate to publish Connor's demand for a retraction . . . and publish a statement which would reflect views contrary to those voiced by Mr. Salisbury. Clearly these are not the actions of a sensation-seeking publication or of careless and shoddy reporting.

This was the contribution of Alabama to the rights of the American press. By invoking the libel laws to inhibit free reporting the Alabama officials produced the opposite effect—they enabled the courts to broaden and redefine the powerful privileges of the press in dealing with public officials. This placed almost—not quite—but almost full power in the hands of the press to report at will on the conduct of government officers, short only of malice, and it made clear that malice would be defined with narrowness. It stripped Connor and the whole range of southern officials of the ability to intimidate the press through the power of the purse and the libel law.

Placing the Pentagon Papers ruling and *Sullivan* back to back a careful analyst could see that there were few matters, indeed, which were likely to resist the probing powers of the press if the will to probe was present. Sullivan liberated the newspapers as never before and the combination of Sullivan and Pentagon was greater than the sum of its parts.

Thomas I. Emerson, Lines Professor of Law at Yale, the noted specialist on the First Amendment, called Sullivan a watershed case in the evolution of twentieth-century American doctrine. But he felt the Pentagon case was "probably more important." He put it alongside that of John Peter Zenger, on which the basic American freedom of the press rested.

Out of the crucible of Bull Connor, the sit-ins, the thrust of southern blacks to win the rights guaranteed by *Brown* v. *The Board of Education,* the determination of Turner Catledge to present the full and dramatic story of the "Great Revolution" in the South; out of the turmoil of a nation riven by the Vietnam war had been forged the instruments which soon would expose what John Dean later was to call "a cancer—within—close to the presidency, that's growing."

32

The Passion of
A. M. Rosenthal

A YEAR HAD PASSED since the Pentagon Papers, a year of expansion for *The Times,* a year of growing confidence for its publisher and for managing editor Abe Rosenthal. Rosenthal had emerged from the Pentagon Papers struggle in a mood of triumph. On the day of the Supreme Court ruling he had proudly worn his "Free *The Times* 22" button, an in-house joke relating the twenty-two-named defendants to the numerous cases of the turbulent 1960s (the Chicago Eight, the Minnesota Six, the North Carolina Fourteen, etc.).

"We had won a smashing victory," Rosenthal recalled. "That was my initial reaction." But gradually his elation began to erode. True, the court had upheld *The Times.* True, when Pentagon was put back to back with *Sullivan* the courts had affirmed tremendous powers for the press in carrying out First Amendment responsibilities. But there was a negative as well. There was something grudging about the Pentagon decision. Some of the language of the individual opinions held a tone of menace. Justice White practically invited the government to bring criminal action against *The Times.* And the Nixon Administration had begun to utilize a threatening procedure against reporters. It was issuing subpoenas compelling them to testify before grand juries and courts, producing their notes and private records, a process which seemed to Rosenthal and his colleagues a clear violation of First Amendment rights. The tactic was being employed by the Justice Department in delicate, tension-laden situations involving the violence in northern cities, in antiwar and Civil Rights causes. The case of Earl Caldwell, a *New York Times* reporter in San Francisco, was particularly to the point. Caldwell had been summoned to testify and submit his notes to a grand jury investigating the Black Panthers in Oakland. He refused on grounds that his communications were privileged and if divulged would destroy his ability to maintain his sources and cover Black Panther stories. *The Times* had won the case in the Ninth U.S. Circuit in California (and this decision had been an important fact in Judge Gurfein's reasoning in the Pentagon case) but the government had appealed to the U.S. Supreme Court. Much depended on how the high court would rule.*

And there were those who continued to insist it would have been better to have avoided the Pentagon court case entirely by printing the Papers in one solid block.

Rosenthal did not agree but it was pressed into his consciousness that the Pentagon victory was by no means the whole story. Nixon and Agnew had succeeded in stirring up an antipress mood in the countryside and, Rosenthal felt, a struggle was in progress, not just between *The Times* and the administration, but between the press as a whole and some of the Judiciary and the Bar, supported by a broad segment of the public, which simply did not believe in or support the concept of a free press as incorporated in the First Amendment and did not understand the emerging role of the press as the public's first defense against big government, big bureaucracy and those enormous complexes into which power in contemporary America had flowed.

These were not things which Rosenthal had really thought through. He possessed a mind that was touched much more sharply by emotions than by concepts but, instinctively, he understood that the press had moved onto new ground, it was playing a new role and in this role it was opposed by forces of great strength—both the government and the courts. The conflict had not been resolved by the Pentagon Papers or by the Alabama cases. It was still in progress.

"My sense of elation at the Pentagon victory was very sharp," Rosenthal said later, "but it did not last very long."

His feeling about the triumph had been diminished by another factor and again it was one which he had not initially sensed. The Pentagon Papers had changed the course of history and yet they had been almost lost to sight in the great court battle. No account of Vietnam could ever be written without these building blocks. Rosenthal saw the papers as a great sea chest. You opened the lid and here were compartments, one marked Truman, one marked Eisenhower, one marked Kennedy and a fourth labeled Johnson. You took one out and immediately you understood the contrast between what the Presidents did and what they said. None of them knew how his moves were going to affect history. But when you examined the boxes you saw what they did, what they thought they did and what really happened. You realized that each was leading the United States from one war to another, from one kind of a war to a different kind of war. Each

---

*The Supreme Court overruled the Sixth Circuit in the Caldwell case in June 1972, shortly after Watergate broke. It was the first in a succession of court rulings that began to chip away at the broad interpretations of the First Amendment that had culminated in the Pentagon Papers decision.

discovered that one war had failed and started another. "But nobody ever told us," Rosenthal was to say. "Nobody told us that they had lost one war and that was why they were starting another. It took a long time to learn that and that was the lesson which lay in the Pentagon Papers."

This, of course, was almost identical with Ellsberg's view and was in itself evidence in support of Ellsberg's feeling (and probably Kissinger's) that the Papers had a magic quality. Read them and you emerged opposed to the war. But the public had not read the papers. They had read, instead, about the legal battle, the Supreme Court case.

Ellsberg and Rosenthal had discussed the Papers at an accidental encounter in the winter of 1971–72 in Philadelphia, where Rosenthal received an award from the Associated Press Managing Editors for the Pentagon story. He ran into Dan and his wife, Pat. They had never met and now they had a long talk in Dan's room, Dan telling Rosenthal for the first time the story of his relationship with Sheehan and how the story had come about. Abe remembered it years later as "a very moving experience" and said he had been deeply touched by the Ellsbergs, particularly by Pat. Ellsberg remembered Rosenthal, a very emotional man, being moved to tears. (At the same Philadelphia meeting Abe met John Mitchell for the first time. Mitchell said, "You ought to share that prize with me.")

The Columbia Bust

For all this, the spring of 1972 was a quiet time for Rosenthal in what had been a turbulent life, a time when he could reflect a bit on where he had gotten. He had had dreams when he first came back to New York that he would stay on the city desk for only three years and pile up enough credit so that he could ask for the London bureau or the Paris bureau and *The Times* would give it to him. He had dreamed too of being a writing editor, of dividing his time between his desk and his typewriter, but that hadn't worked and, in fact, his major experiment in writing had left such deep scars, on himself, on relations with several associates and with important elements of the community (particularly young people), that he never tried anything like it again.

This story was a spectacularly melodramatic account of the Columbia University "bust" the night of April 29, 1968, when New York police violently ejected students who had been sitting in campus buildings. Rosenthal had attended the opening of *Hair* that night and came back to *The Times* to find that Police Commissioner Howard Leary had tipped off Nat Goldstein, his good friend and circulation manager of *The Times*, that he was going to bust Columbia. Leary told Goldstein he was going in at 1 A.M. Goldstein pleaded with him to go at 11 P.M. so *The Times* could make the story in its second edition but

Leary said, "Sorry, Nat, but we want to do this after Harlem has gone to bed." Leary gave Goldstein a ride to Columbia where Rosenthal found them. The anger of the students shocked Rosenthal. They were calling the police motherfuckers. They called President Grayson Kirk and Vice President David Truman motherfuckers. They called Abe a motherfucker. The devastation of Kirk's office appalled Rosenthal, the way books had been thrown around. Anyone who knew Rosenthal knew that it was the books that did it even though later he was to insist that the sight of the broken books did not arouse him as much as the "angry and authoritarian" attitude of the students for, as he was to add, "as a Jew, authoritarianism scares me." (As a teen-ager Rosenthal often spent his Saturdays going from one discount bookstore to another trying to decide which books to buy with the $1.50 or $2.00 he had saved. After his marriage the most precious possession in his Greenwich Village apartment was his collection of Heritage Press reprints of the classics.)

Rosenthal stayed at Columbia all night, and "witnessed such anger as I had never seen." His own response was angry, too, and he wanted to express his feelings in the way which was natural for him by writing a story. But a problem arose. Clifton Daniel telephoned early in the morning. His father had died during the night and he had to leave immediately for Zebulon, N.C. . Rosenthal, still seething, told Daniel about Columbia. Daniel recalled telling Rosenthal to keep his personal emotion out of the story. "I urge you in the strongest terms," Daniel recalled saying, "not to write and not to print that story." He told Rosenthal that he was catching a plane in 30 minutes; that Rosenthal would be in charge in his absence. "I was very upset about it," Daniel said years later, an echo of his disturbance coming into his voice as he spoke. Rosenthal had a different recollection: "Daniel didn't forbid me to write that Columbia piece. No assistant managing editor who is ordered not to write a piece then goes ahead and writes a piece."

Whatever the exact exchange, Rosenthal sat down and wrote a bold, emotional account which, years later, he described as "not a conformist piece." He felt he had seen terrible things and must bear witness.

"It was 4:30 in the morning," Rosenthal wrote, "and the president of the university leaned against the wall of the room that had been his office. He passed a hand over his face. 'My God,' he said, 'how could human beings do a thing like this.' "

(Years later, Kirk had no recollection of having seen Rosenthal at Columbia that night; perhaps passage of time had eroded his memory or possibly he had left before Rosenthal arrived on the scene.)

Rosenthal described Kirk wandering about his devastated office, the students being led away in manacles singing "We Shall Overcome" and a policeman picking up a book from the floor, saying "The whole world

is in these books. How could they do this to these books?" The images Rosenthal evoked were to linger long in the minds of his readers.*
Having written his story, Rosenthal was not entirely certain what to do. He showed it to me, explaining how strongly he felt. But it was not a problem which I was in a position to resolve for him. Finally he took the responsibility himself and ordered it into the paper. It ran on page one May 1, 1968, and the repercussions were considerable. Rosenthal's superiors were less than pleased. Columbia students picketed Punch Sulzberger's Fifth Avenue apartment house and Rosenthal acquired an aura of rightism, particularly so far as young people were concerned, which was not to leave him.

Roots

The role into which he had thrust himself plagued Rosenthal; he simply could not comprehend the distance between his generation and that of the 1960s although he, in fact, had been the child of radicalism. Few signs of this were still visible. He was in the 1960s the image of a good Jewish boy on the make, his hair closecropped, wearing the same thick-lensed, horn-rimmed glasses to shield his gray-green eyes he had worn since he was nine, just beginning to move from Harry Rothman suits off the rack to Brooks Brothers (Gay Talese would, for years, lecture Rosenthal on his clothes: "You must dress properly," Talese would say. "You are the *editor* of *The New York Times,* you must dress like the editor of *The New York Times*"). This was advice Rosenthal never really was able to absorb; his suits became better-cut but, as he said, "I never had a made-suit in my life"; his glasses became a bit larger and the rims more narrow. By the mid-seventies he had let his barber fashion an attractive, square-cut hair styling, blown-dry, his hair still thick, inky-black with hardly a trace of gray; but his shirttails continued to work out of his belt and his tie more often than not was skewed. He weighed 151 pounds and stood 5 feet 9½ or 10 inches tall. No longer did he resemble the youngster of whom his school teacher once said: "Close one eye and you'll look like a needle."

Abe's father had been a farmer near Bobruisk in Byelorussia like his father before him. His name was Harry Shipiatsky. Exactly why he changed it to Rosenthal his son never understood, possibly on the advice of an uncle in London, where he stopped en route to America before World War I. The uncle's name was Rosenthal and he may have

---

*When the Archibald Cox report on the Columbia riot was made public it minimized damage to Kirk's office, saying "There was no substantial vandalism." Rosenthal wrote Cox an indignant letter, insisting damage of $5,000 had been done. (Personal interview, A. M. Rosenthal, 10/8/79; Archibald Cox, *Report of Fact-Finding Commission on Columbia Disturbances,* New York City, 1968, pp. 108–109.)

thought Shipiatsky sounded "too foreign." As a little boy Abe remembered people coming to visit from Bobruisk and they would say, "Oh, that's Abram Shipiatsky's grandson." Abe's father was the first of the family to arrive in the western hemisphere. He went to Canada, where he joined a communal farm group, a true commune, founded on the principles of utopian socialism. By the time Abe was born in Sault Ste. Marie, Ontario, May 2, 1922, his father had become a fur trader and trapper. Every year he went into the bush where he bought and traded furs, sending them to his brother Michael in New York. The furs often got lost en route and Abe's mother became suspicious. She thought too many furs were being lost but whether that meant Abe's uncle Michael was finagling Abe never knew.

His father's ambition for Abe was that he might become a forester. Harry Shipiatsky was a powerful man, big-muscled, gentle, strong, a man with a temperament (as his son would be), a storyteller, adventurous, brave. He had been the only real farmer on the commune, the only one who knew how to plow, how to sow the seed, and the others, strong on socialist doctrine but weak on practice had drifted away. That was when Abe's father turned to furs. He was one of seven brothers and he helped them all leave Russia. He loved to tell stories, some about his own father who spent more time in the synagogue than he did on the farm. Harry Shipiatsky was not a religious man, not a religious Jew. He was a progressive, an advanced thinker. True, he had his first-born son circumcised but when the infant screamed and began to turn blue he handed the child to a friend, grabbed the *mohel*, the religious officiant, by the neck and did not relax his grip until the baby quieted. If anything had happened to Abe he would have strangled the *mohel* with his own hands. Abe was not taken to the synagogue, did not go to Hebrew school, had no bar mitzvah, was not brought up as a religious Jew. He called himself an atheist as did his father, married a Catholic woman, Ann Marie Burke, and their three sons were raised outside organized faith. But as Abe was to say, he always considered himself Jewish because he was perceived as Jewish.

Of course, it was infinitely more complex than this. In fact there was an echo of "Abie's Irish Rose" in the romance of Ann Marie Burke and Abe Rosenthal.

"I was a little Irish Catholic girl and he was a good Jewish boy," Ann remembered. "I know he says that he is an atheist. But he really isn't. When we decided to get married I went to my priest at St. Catherine of Sienna on East Sixty-Sixth Street. I told him about Abe, how he was an atheist and all. The priest was a marvelous young man, about thirty, I wish I could remember his name. Anyway he said that Abe didn't sound like an atheist to him; he sounded like a deeply religious man. He wanted to see Abe and talk to him."

Ann and Abe had to be married secretly because Abe's mother was still alive. She would have felt betrayed, Ann said. "It was a tremendous sacrifice for Abe and it went against everything he believed in."

The priest did meet with Abe and Ann. There were long forms to fill out, lots of questions, including the question of bringing up the children in the Catholic faith. When the priest came to that question he read very fast and said, "Of course, you will raise the children as Catholics, won't you?" And before Abe or Ann could speak he wrote down "yes" and hurried to the next question.

So Abe and Ann were married at St. Catherine of Sienna with only Ann's mother and father and sister present. Three days later, March 12, 1949, they had a civil ceremony at the Warwick Hotel with their friends and family present, Bernard Kalb, Abe's best friend on *The Times*, and Bob Shiffer, Abe's best friend from school, as his attendants, and Ann's sister, Kathleen Burke, and a friend named Gloria Wasserman as her attendants.

As for the children, when the three boys, John, and Andrew and Danny, came along Ann was determined not to have a divided family, not to raise three little Catholic boys for Abe, and so, while she continued to go to mass and to confession, the boys were raised ecumenically, exposed to almost any religion you could name, and, as young adults, Ann thought, they had religious feelings each in his own way. John was a sort of a Buddhist, Andrew had gone through a Shinto ceremony in Japan at the age of four or five. Danny married a Jewish girl but they had a civil ceremony—at her request, not his.

Abe's first memory was of a dog named Jack, leader of his father's team of huskies, the dog team that carried him on his fur-trading expeditions. The lead dog was always called Jack and Abe remembered being put on Jack's back and sliding off. He enjoyed that. The dogs were supposed to be kept in the backyard but one day when a Polish emigrant came to the house Jack was in the front yard and the Pole stepped over him. The dog bit the Pole and he went to court. The judge said the dog should not have been in the front yard but on the other hand no foreigner should step over a Canadian subject. He dismissed the case.

Abe remembered his father as a dashing man. When he stripped his shirt sleeves back and made a muscle it stood out like iron. His father liked to gamble now and then but was terrified lest his wife learn of it. Abe remembered going to the Coney Island boardwalk with his father, who dressed in style and wore a Panama hat. Soon his father was attracted by a hustler playing the shell game and before he was through he had lost $60, a tremendous sum, possibly two weeks' wages. Harry looked little Abe square in the eyes and said, "Look, sonny, one thing. You must never tell your mother." Abe didn't.

As Abe grew older he took a special pride in his childhood connection with the frontier, with the wilderness, the Canadian bush, even though it was a connection which existed more in the stories that were told to him than in reality. It was a hideaway inside his city-street youth, a special secret to which he clung, seldom shared with others, and which could not be guessed at when he reached adulthood, a thorough product of growing up in New York. In that private world Abe's father held a special place, a man who seemed to walk out of Jack London, a man with wide shoulders, a wide view of the world, like London a Socialist, but the kind of a Socialist who could tell tall tales and gamble away two weeks' salary on the Coney Island boardwalk.

Abe was never to come to grips with the wilderness himself. In 1947 when he and Bernie Kalb were sharing an apartment at the Hotel des Artistes they took a trip west in Abe's old Plymouth, a car which he had christened "Mr. Toad." The idea was to return to Abe's birthplace at Sault Ste. Marie. They got to Michigan, to Mackinac island, to Niagara Falls but for some reason never arrived in Sault Ste. Marie. Abe didn't go West again until after he became managing editor of *The Times* when *Times* national reporters and editors like Gene Roberts, David Jones and Wallace Turner introduced him to New Mexico, Jackson Hole, Yellowstone, the Pacific Northwest and Alaska. He made no pretense of an affinity for the back country, dressing in jeans, but they were city-cut jeans with saddle-stitched pockets, and conducting himself on Alaska's north slope as the tough, hard-nosed endlessly questioning reporter which he was—not the Jewish Jack London for which his father had hoped.

In New York, Abe's father got a job as a house painter and the family lived in the "Amalgamated," a cooperative housing project on Van Cortlandt Parkway in the Bronx sponsored by the Amalgamated Clothing Worker's Union, a strongly Socialist trade union, headed by Sidney Hillman and made up of Russian-Jewish emigrants. Harry Shipiatsky had hated his job, hated the big city, longed for the outdoors, the bush, the farming and the idealism of his youth. He was badly injured in a fall from a painting scaffold, lived on two or three years as a semi-invalid, and died when Abe was two months shy of his thirteenth birthday.

No one was evicted from the "Amalgamated" for lack of money. You put your savings in and stayed as long as you lived. Abe's family stayed on after his father's death, gradually moving into smaller apartments. The rent was $30 a month. Abe had five sisters, all older than himself, and he grew up surrounded by adoring women. His oldest sister died of pneumonia before Abe's father. She had gotten off the subway at the Mosholu Parkway station in the North Bronx, about a mile from the "Amalgamated." It was a cold winter night and, as Abe remembered, a degenerate had exposed himself, frightening her so she ran the whole mile, arriving home drenched in perspiration, caught pneumonia and died.

Despite this tragedy Abe was to recall his childhood as sheer happiness. He loved his sisters and they loved him as only a boy, youngest in a large family of girls, can be loved. Later he was to say, "I like women. I like women very much. I get along best with them. I grew up with them, my five sisters and myself." When, as it happened, after he became metropolitan editor and managing editor, there were complaints that his policies were not free of male chauvinism, when cases flared up about treatment of women on the paper, Abe found them hard to accept. He thought of himself as secure and at home in a woman's world and could not understand when the women in the city room reacted so differently. It was something that he often talked about and he felt hurt and misunderstood. When *The Times* in 1979 agreed to the settlement of the discrimination complaint brought by women staff members, Rosenthal irritated several friends by insisting that the settlement represented "a great victory" for *The Times*. When his friends pointed out that the settlement was an admission of fault, Rosenthal did not agree. Later he insisted to a friend that "I have done more about women and blacks than anyone on the paper."

Abe's father left a few thousand dollars when he died and the family was not impoverished. Abe got a Saturday job as a stock boy in Russek's fur-coat department for $3.00 a day but did not remember having any other job until he began to work on the school paper at City College. He never thought of being poor. He lived in the local public library and took home armloads of books. His sister, Ruth, seven years older than he, became a member of the Young Communist League in the early 1930s. She was very much like Abe, dynamic, very intelligent, a natural leader. She fell in love with, and in 1937 married, a man named George Watt, who had been won over for the Young Communists by a schoolmate at New Utrecht High School named Joe Clark, later to be Moscow correspondent and foreign editor of the *Daily Worker*. Soon Watt went off to Spain as a member of the Abraham Lincoln Brigade, fighting through the Civil War, a man of bravery, written about by Ernest Hemingway and Herbert Matthews, rising to the post of commissar of the Lincoln Brigade. The Spanish war was *the* event of Rosenthal's youth and although he was a young Socialist (at least in inclinations) while Ruth and Watt were Young Communists, Watt was Abe's hero just as Ruth was his heroine no matter how they argued about politics.

"God, how I admired that man!" Rosenthal said years later. "He was my hero."

The Spanish war, as Rosenthal said, was the cause for "all of us and

George went to Spain and fought. We all hated Carney [William Carney, *New York Times* correspondent who covered the Franco forces]; Matthews [who covered the Loyalists] was our hero. This was long before I came to *The Times,* of course. I so admired Watt and others like him. The Americans who put their lives on the line fighting fascism. The communism of these young people was almost a joke. It just expressed their anti-fascism."

Watt was almost the last American out of Spain, falling ill of typhoid and barely making the last train from Catalonia. He got back to the United States in January 1939. A year later Ruth gave birth to a son, Danny, and died within two weeks. Abe was prostrate at his sister's funeral, a Communist Party service at the Y.C.L. offices in the *Daily Worker* building on Twelfth Street. He never got over the fact that on his last real visit with his sister they had quarrelled violently over politics and then almost before he knew it she was gone. It was one of a succession of tragedies that took all but one of Rosenthal's sisters and his mother not long after he became metropolitan editor of *The Times.*

Temperament

Over the years the managing editors of *The Times* had been a disparate lot. Mr. Ochs' editor, the peerless Carr Van Anda, had been a severe, almost a private person who kept even Mr. Ochs at arms' length. Frederick Birchall was outgoing but felt more comfortable as a correspondent. Edwin L. (Jimmy) James was, in fact, an eternal boulevardier, letting his subeditors handle the staff. Catledge was the most gregarious, possessed a keen sense of news and a keener sense of institutional politics until the final years of his career. Daniel, a professional journalist to his fingertips, lacked the talent of making *The Times* staff his own.

These editors shared a common characteristic. They were reined-in, outwardly composed even in moments of great tension, skilled at dissembling their feelings. They did not bleed easily and if they suffered qualms over their role, they hid them away in some secret place.

Not so A. M. Rosenthal. He fought and bled and shouted and cried and agonized in public. When he came back from Tokyo the city room, which had drowsed away for decades, became a scene of melodrama, crisis succeeding crisis, played out before an audience of participants, Rosenthal's fellow editors and the staff which he directed.

He was a restless, uneasy man and he communicated his moods with the readiness of a Toscanini. One thing obsessed him. After years of coping with the problems of a psychotic Indian subcontinent, an ideologically obsessed Poland and an enigmatic Japan he could not identify the sources of the turbulence of America in the 1960s. The attitudes of the young, the blacks, Women's Liberation drove him up the wall, particularly the attitudes of the young.

He found it reflected not only on the political scene, in national politics; the 1968 Democratic National Convention deeply disturbed him with its violence; he was as concerned to see that young reporters on *The Times* sympathized with the demonstrators as he was by the vicious acts of the Chicago police, probably more so. It seemed to him that the young people in the city room were not as happy as they had been in his day. Rosenthal recalled his early days on *The Times* as sheer joy (which was not true at all—moments of enormous misery had punctuated his whole career). He remembered saying to Ann when they were stationed in India and he was wandering around the country, which to him was like a modern Arabian nights—this is incredible! Here we are in India, living in this lovely house, traveling wherever we want, writing for *The New York Times* and *I get paid for it.* That was the incredible part. He was being paid and was still being paid to do what he enjoyed more than anything in the world.

Of course, there were times when he looked at life more realistically. It had taken him ten years to achieve his ambition of going abroad. He thought he was going to make it in 1948 when he was sent to Paris for the United Nations General Assembly meeting but Cy Sulzberger did not warm up. One of Abe's friends told him Cy had said, "One Jew in Paris is enough."* Sulzberger had a bit of advice for Rosenthal if he wanted to be assigned abroad: "Stay single." But Abe was head over heels in love with his wife-to-be Ann Burke, a *Times* secretary (she had been the first *Times* copy girl to be hired in World War II, and antedated Abe on *The Times* by two years) who had wangled her way to Paris to be with him for the U.N. meeting. Thirty years later Ann's eyes sparkled over the weeks she and Abe had in Paris together. But Abe had taken Cy's remark about staying single with terrible seriousness. "It was traumatic," Ann remembered. "Abe got sick every time the question of going abroad came up." He and Ann even publicly announced in December 1948 that their engagement had been broken off in hope this might improve his chances for a foreign assignment. (It didn't, so they went ahead and got married in March 1949.)

Abe, as he now fully understood, hadn't been handed his *Times'* job as a wonderful present. He had been a good college correspondent from City College. One day Kitty Telsch, the Columbia University college

---

*Dan Schorr, a stringer for *The Times* in the Low Countries, recalled asking Cy for a staff job in 1952 and being told "we have too many Jews in Europe." (Personal interview, Schorr, 5/30/79) Sulzberger did not recall these references. He said he formed a negative opinion of Rosenthal because of a row Rosenthal got into with his Paris hotel over some missing travelers' checks. He thought Rosenthal somewhat naïve and lacking language qualifications. (C. L. Sulzberger, letter to author, 5/31/79)

correspondent, dropped her handbag, and a reporter's police card fell out. Abe was enraged. Kitty had a police card and he didn't. He then and there determined to get on staff. But there was trouble because he couldn't pass the physical. That had been the nadir of his life except for his sister Ruth's death; but he got on the staff as a "temporary," a temporary who somehow became permanent after four or five years. As Rosenthal looked back on his career he remembered the words of David Joseph, the city editor who had hired him. Mr. Joseph was a severe man, a man of great reserve who wore black-vested suits and a gold watch chain across the vest from which dangled a yellowing elk's tooth. (Soon after Ben Welles, son of Sumner, joined the paper in 1938 Mr. Joseph called Welles over and asked: "What was your name before it was changed to Welles?") There had been a party for Mr. Joseph in the Belasco Room of Sardi's and Abe thanked him for the opportunity he had gotten. Mr. Joseph replied: "Don't ever say thank you. None of those young people should say thank you. I never did anything for them." And that, Abe now thought, was right. He had gotten his job not by the magnanimity of Mr. Joseph but because he was a good college correspondent and he had gone abroad because he had been a fine reporter on the United Nations and he had gotten to be city editor because he was an able correspondent. It had taken him a long time to see it, but life wasn't a sweepstakes. He hadn't held a lucky ticket. He had fought and struggled and that was why he now was managing editor of *The Times.* There wasn't any Santa Claus.

Jewishness

And there was the question of his Jewishness. This had not been important to Abe when he was growing up. He hadn't gone to *kader,* he hadn't learned Yiddish or studied Hebrew, he had not gone to the synagogue. He remembered that when he went to the Mayo Clinic in Rochester, Minnesota, he was 17 years old and the year was 1940. He had been in great pain in walking and had been operated on at the Hospital for Joint Diseases in New York. It had been a traumatic experience, the operation was a failure, he was in a ward with fifty to sixty other men, in a cast from his neck to his toes. It was, he imagined, like being in hell, the stench, the screams, the dying. He was certain he must have cancer or tuberculosis. He thought he would soon be dead. His youngest sister, Ann, called the Mayo Clinic and they agreed to examine him. He got a "charity fare" railroad ticket. Every time he presented it he was ashamed. He had just enough money to get to Rochester and he paid for the first examination with $60 in cash. The Mayo Clinic diagnosed his case as osteomyelitis. He was put in a room with three other patients. Everyone was cheerful. For the first time in his life he saw how the ill should be treated. A surgeon operated on him for seventeen or eighteen hours and said he was going to be all right. One day a pretty young nurse came into his room and asked: "Are you a Hebrew?" No one had ever asked him a question like that. "Yes," he said. "Well," said the little nurse, "you're the first Hebrew I've ever met." Later when he got about on his crutches he found signs on the doors identifying the patients as Catholic, Protestant, Hebrew or whatever.

But it wasn't that way on *The Times,* no need for any signs. Abe was a Hebrew and he had a very Jewish name—Abraham Rosenthal. Actually, his name was Abraham Michael Rosenthal, an unlikely name for a youngster of Jewish origin even if his father was an atheist. Of course, the Michael was an anglicization. His name was really Mikl. When Abe came to *The Times* he knew he was going to have trouble. He knew from his fellow reporters that *The Times* didn't like Jewish-sounding by-lines. There had, in fact, been talk in his family about changing his name to Michael Rosenthal. There were two or three Abraham Rosenthals in the family and his sister Ruth suggested that he use the name Michael but Abe didn't want to. He had never had a by-line in *The Times* and the question was still open when he wrote a story about the battleship *New York.* It was a page-one story and that meant it had to carry a by-line. Abe knew that would present a problem. There were several Abes on the paper but their given names were never signed. Abe wanted his by-line but he was certain *The Times* would not stand for "Abraham Rosenthal" on page one. As he was leaving the city room that evening he passed the mailboxes where reporters got their mail. Under each box was the reporter's name. His name was listed as: Rosenthal, Abraham. Quietly he penciled in an "M" after the Abraham. Next morning his story appeared under the signature A. M. Rosenthal and that was the way it was to be.* Of course, this was not the end of the matter. He noticed that the bullpen didn't like his name signed to United Nations stories about Palestine. Once he had an eight-column banner story on Israel. It appeared without signature. He appealed to Lew Jordan, then foreign editor. "Don't get sore," Jordan said. "I wanted a by-line but 'they' took it off." Who was "they," Abe ruminated. It was always "they" who did these things. "They" were nervous about too much Jewish emphasis. "They" had been nervous about his naming his good friend Arthur Gelb as his chief assistant. But who "they" were Abe could never quite understand.

---

*"I taught my boys to recite that story by heart," Rosenthal once said. The story began: The Battleship New York, sixth of her name arrived yesterday, 31 months and four battles out of home port. Rosenthal quoted Captain Grayson D. Carter as shouting: "New York! My God! I love it!" This was a sentiment Rosenthal shared and often repeated. (*New York Times,* 10/20/45; personal interview, A. M. Rosenthal, 4/26/79)

Abe had never gotten over the reaction to Arthur Gelb, a lanky Damon to his shorter Pythias, the two so close that they became a fused personality Abe-'n-Artie, Arthur constantly jackknifed at Abe's ear, whispering urgent somethings, obsessed with time (running out) and distance (to be covered before the next deadline, the next birthday, the next meeting of the Pulitzer judges or of the Times Board of Directors), collaborating to abandon the grey idiom of the city room, banishing serious budgetary discussions, encomiums of Robert Moses, analyses of school curricula, hallmarks of *The Times'* sedate and concerned journalism. And, as Artie recalled with total joy, opening up a whole new world.

"We'll create it all," he remembered Abe telling him in breathless excitement. "We'll do everything we want. We'll do a big story on the homosexuals in New York." That, said Gelb, is an old story. "Not to me," Rosenthal replied. The year was 1963 and Abe had just come back to New York and discovered Third Avenue. They assigned *The Times'* veteran Paris man, Robert Doty, to do homosexuals. He thought it was a crazy idea but he did it. It was a sensation and Abe-'n-Artie were off and running, exploring the new world for *Times* readers, a world of live-in male-female relationships; of "cooping" police officers (sleeping off their hours in parked squad cars); of drugs and bizarre sex murders; of theatrical and other sensations (Doctor Feel-Good, Doctor "X"); of 38 witnesses who did not budge when murder was done, a world in which it seemed there was no subject *The Times* would not touch, illuminate, and, said some, exploit.

"Every story became a discussion," Gelb remembered. "Everyone in the city room was talking in one corner or another. In those years the city room was probably the most stimulating place in the city. Maybe in the whole country."

There were wild quarrels. Once Rosenthal walked out of *The Times* building at edition time he was so angry at Ted Bernstein, the bullpen editor, the man more responsible than anyone else for his getting his job. But never in the recollection of Abe-'n-Artie did *they* quarrel—disagree a bit, yes; quarrel, never. Only once in all the years since they came to the paper in 1944 could Gelb remember getting angry, really angry with Abe. That had been over J. D. Salinger's banana story, the ending of it. Gelb had gotten so mad he finally said: "I'm bigger than you." He picked Rosenthal up and threw him down. But those were days when Rosenthal still hoped to become a foreign correspondent and Gelb's ambition was to succeed Brooks Atkinson as *Times* drama critic.

But if the two men did not quarrel this was hardly true so far as others were concerned. Abe had warned Arthur that what they were going to do would cause talk "and make enemies." He was right. Nor was the talk and enmity confined to *The Times*. Nothing in the early career of Abe-'n-Artie matched the violence of their relationship with John Lindsay, first a passionate love affair, then an equally passionate denouement, one which left scars on both sides (Mary Lindsay once said Abe-'n-Artie had kept her husband from the Presidency). Scotty Reston, an old pro at politics, simply declared that Abe-'n-Artie had lacked balance in the Lindsay connection.

The Young

Abe's exercise in self-analysis did not leave him entirely satisfied. There were other questions that bothered him. He still couldn't understand the younger generation. Why were so many of them dissatisfied, so many of them miserable? Of course, some probably shouldn't be in the newspaper business at all. But why did so many good reporters leave —Halberstam, Dick Reeves, Gay Talese? Halberstam . . . he was the one who seemed to bother Abe most. Abe came back to Halberstam again and again. Why did Halberstam hate *The Times* so much? Why did he hate Abe? By this time Abe's tendency to identify with *The Times* had become almost total; any blow, any criticism of *The Times* was perceived as a blow or a criticism of himself. Why, he thought, when he was city editor, he had become Halberstam's rabbi, his adviser, he had protected him on the paper. Why had Halberstam changed so much?

It did not occur to Rosenthal that the passion with which Halberstam criticized Rosenthal, his public rebukes at annual assemblages of reporters under the auspices of the magazine *MORE*, Halberstam's not infrequent lectures on the failings which he perceived in Rosenthal's editorship delivered to members of the Sulzberger family at chance encounters, sprang from the same source as that of Abe's own, that is, a fierce love and dedication to *The New York Times* as an institution, a possessiveness almost as strong as Rosenthal's own.

These were the kinds of thoughts which ran through Rosenthal's mind but they were not urgent preoccupations, not the kind of compulsions which turned his life inside out, causing his brows to darken, his face to heat with blood and his pacing to begin, the pacing in and out of his office, back and forth, back and forth, as in the hours of Saturday, June 12, 1971, before the story of the Pentagon Papers went to press.

A year had passed and Rosenthal's worries were more distant, less pressing. He still hadn't really come to grips with the question of *The Times* Washington bureau but there seemed no special urgency there. Max Frankel had been Reston's choice, not Rosenthal's, but he and Frankel got on well enough. Given the past history of the Washington bureau it was not a question on which Rosenthal was in any hurry to act.

33

The Washington Problem

MAX FRANKEL had taken over the Washington bureau of *The New York Times* at the time of the inauguration of Richard Nixon, January 20, 1969, and his job had not been made easy by the antagonism of the President and his staff, an antagonism which had increased as a result of the Pentagon Papers.

Frankel, like Rosenthal, had gotten onto the paper as campus correspondent, Abe from City College, Frankel, a bit later, from Columbia. Frankel was able, ambitious, young and he moved upward quickly and easily under the stewardship of his mentor and career idol, Scotty Reston.

Frankel's great interest lay in diplomatic reporting and this had been a saving grace during the Nixon years. Nixon's diplomacy was spectacular and Kissinger maintained special relations with diplomatic correspondents, particularly men like Frankel and Reston of *The Times*, so that despite Nixon's hostility they were able to provide *Times'* readers with informed reports on the evolution of détente with the Soviet Union, the breakthrough with the People's Republic of China, negotiations in the Middle East and the progress of talks with Hanoi although Kissinger guarded the secret of his private meetings with Le Duc Tho so well that neither Frankel nor Reston got a hint; nor for that matter, despite Reston's coincidental presence in China, of Kissinger's first visit to Peking.

Frankel had become Washington bureau chief after the broiling intrigue and power struggle within *The Times'* upper echelon during the 1960s, which was commemorated by Gay Talese. And while by 1972 that struggle had long been over, its deep wounds and permutations continued to affect relationships among *Times'* editors and correspondents.

Frankel, for example, had been named to his post by Reston, the putative winner of the power struggle. In fact, as Talese closed *The Kingdom and the Power*, he described Reston as clearly on top. He seemed to have *The Times* firmly under control and ahead loomed an era of sweetness and light.

But things hadn't quite worked out that way and now Rosenthal, who had been an opponent of Reston in the 1960's quarrels, was very much to the fore, secure in his post as managing editor and this could not but exercise influence on the relationship of Frankel and Rosenthal. The two men seemed to work quite well together but below the surface lay strong competitive influences—and these inevitably would play a role in the events just ahead.

As Clauswitz might have said, the struggle between the New York and Washington power bases was now going forward by other means, as, indeed, it had since the early days of the paper. Mr. Ochs' great editor Carr Van Anda and *The Times'* bureau chief of those days, Richard V. Oulahan, had been competitors. So had Arthur Krock and Edwin L. James.

Rivalry

When Turner Catledge became managing editor and James Reston assumed the post of Washington bureau chief, the lines for further competition were laid. Each was extraordinarily able, ambitious, close to and highly regarded by Arthur Sulzberger, whose friendships with the men had been cemented during World War II. Each took long trips to war zones with the publisher, Reston to Russia, Catledge to the Pacific. For years after their 1943 trip to Moscow Reston addressed Sulzberger as "Mr. Gus" and Sulzberger called Reston "Pectoh." The Gus came from *gospodin* ("Mr." in Russian; "Pectoh" is the way Reston is written in Cyrillic). Catledge and Reston possessed attractive personalities and formidable political skills: Catledge's honed in the hill country of Mississippi and back-office drinking rooms of the U.S. Senate and Reston's bred in his Scots ancestry and refined by the wisdom of his wife, Sally. The two men maintained a wary, knowing and often witty balance. Each understood what the other was about, and their rivalry was far from destructive.

This equilibrium began to be disturbed with the emergence of Orvil Dryfoos as publisher in 1961. Reston was closer to Dryfoos and to his wife, Marian, than was Catledge, but Dryfoos' tenure was cut short by his sudden death in June of 1963.

Now, with the emergence of Punch as publisher the advantage went to Catledge. He, alone of the higher executives of *The Times*, had a warm and close association with Punch, one that went back a good many years. Both had had broken marriages, both enjoyed a quiet drink. They spent many evenings together. Reston seemed austere to Punch.

It was clearly a time for change. Catledge moved up to the post of executive editor and was succeeded by his long-time protégé Clifton Daniel. Lester Markel, founder of *The Times* Sunday edition and doyen of *Times* editors, was elevated to an advisory role and Catledge assumed responsibility for the Sunday paper as well as the daily. Reston, in Washington, turned over the bureau to his brilliant protégé Tom Wicker and assumed the role of *éminence grise.* Rosenthal was brought in by Catledge as city editor and given the rather grandiloquent title of "metropolitan editor."

Rosenthal had not been eager to take the city desk. His ambition, as he was to recall many times, had been to write a column on foreign affairs and, in fact, he had just been negotiating with John Oakes, editorial page director, to become a columnist at the time Turner Catledge arrived in Tokyo in late spring of 1962. Abe loved foreign reporting, had become very good at it, had devoted his professional life to it, having been assigned in 1946 to *The Times'* United Nations bureau at Lake Success. He had spent little or no time as a street reporter, knew nothing of Washington, had never been an executive and his only editing experience had been on the City College paper. He liked being a foreign correspondent, liked the freedom from bureaucracy, liked being his own man, loved writing and had a marvelous touch. He had written nearly a hundred pieces for *The New York Times Magazine.* No one had written so many for the notoriously finicky Lester Markel and no one was to match Rosenthal's mark. Dan Schorr, then with CBS, remembered walking in on Abe in the Hotel Bristol in Warsaw in 1958. Abe, one leg up on his desk, a cigar in his mouth, went on typing as he and Schorr talked. Finally Schorr asked what he was writing. A piece for the Sunday magazine, Rosenthal said. "I hate you!" Schorr burst out. "To be so relaxed—and writing a Sunday magazine piece."

Just before Catledge arrived in Tokyo Oakes rejected Rosenthal's plea for a foreign affairs column and offered him a place on the editorial board. Abe refused that. He did not prize anonymity. What he wanted was a platform of his own. Catledge and his wife, Abby, were staying at Frank Lloyd Wright's old Imperial Hotel. When Abe and his wife, Ann, arrived to meet them Abby wasn't dressed so while Ann waited for Abby, Abe and Catledge went into the coffee bar. Almost immediately Turner asked, "Are you happy here?" Abe spilled his coffee. He was happy in Tokyo, almost as happy as he had ever been on a foreign assignment (not *quite* as happy as when he was in India—always to remain his most pleasant foreign memory), and he knew that Catledge hadn't asked because he was worried about Rosenthal's happiness but because he had some proposition in mind and Rosenthal was not certain it would be something he would like. Catledge continued, "How would you like to be city editor?" quickly adding that the job actually would be that of "Metropolitan Editor." Catledge was great at coining new titles, titles which seemed to enhance or expand in some way the previous dimensions of the job.* "Turner," Abe responded, "you've forgotten who I am. You are looking for someone else. I've given sixteen of my last eighteen years to foreign affairs." Rosenthal told Catledge that he wanted to be a columnist but later when the two were together in India word came that Russell Baker had been named columnist and Catledge said, "See, there isn't any spot there for you."

Catledge went back to the United States without getting Rosenthal's agreement but he told Ted Bernstein, chief of the *Times* bullpen, an old friend and admirer of Abe and the one who had put the idea of Rosenthal's appointment into Catledge's mind, that he was going to talk Abe into the job. That year Abe's sister Ann died of cancer and he flew back to New York, his leg in a cast. He had torn his knee in a fall in a Japanese restaurant. The question of the city editorship was still open. He held long discussions with his friends and, in fact, consulted very widely, talking, among others, with Teddy White, whom he then did not know at all well. White got the impression that Abe thought the city desk was somehow demeaning, not consistent with his rank as a foreign correspondent. White urged Abe to take the job. He said New York was the greatest story in the world and it just wasn't being covered. Clifton Daniel, not yet managing editor of *The Times*, but clearly marked as Catledge's successor, said, "Take it. It's what you ought to do."

Coup

And so, ultimately, Rosenthal had come back to New York in the summer of 1963, stirred up a whirlwind, stirred up excitement, made a great splash, a truly great splash, and then, finally, almost lost his job, or so he thought. This was in consequence of an attempt by Catledge, Daniel, and Rosenthal to install Abe's protégé and dear friend James Greenfield as chief of the Washington bureau of *The Times*, replacing Tom Wicker.

The effort had failed spectacularly, disastrously and publicly because at the last moment, after Punch Sulzberger had given his blessing, Scotty Reston turned the publisher around with the argument that the game was not worth the candle, that it would blow up the Washington bureau, the staff would leave en masse (possibly, although this was never to be confirmed, suggesting that even he, Reston, might find *The Times* no longer a comfortable place to work), that whatever the cost in public scandal of "reversing the verdict," as the Chinese would say,

*When he named me national editor of *The Times* in February 1962 he invented the title "Director of National Correspondence," in part because another man, Ray O'Neill, already held the post of national editor, and in part because he thought his new title sounded flossier.

it was small compared to that which would come from going ahead.

Sulzberger, deeply troubled, had accepted Reston's arguments and called the deal off.

The melodrama of these events could not help color relationships within the paper for years to come and even after the Pentagon Papers this continued to be true. The print of those tensions lay near the surface of Rosenthal's consciousness. He had, after all, played devil's assistant in the scenario concocted by Catledge, Greenfield was *his* friend, had been brought on the paper by him, was vetted by him for the Washington post (Greenfield, an extremely agreeable, socially presentable man, had been a *Time* magazine correspondent in India, where he and Abe became acquainted) and Abe thought he had blown his career with *The Times*. He had had a fearsome row with Reston and although he went to Sulzberger and presented an emotional *mea culpa* he expected that he would have to resign. But Sulzberger had him out to his house the weekend after the failed coup and said that he expected Rosenthal to stay with the paper and that his career was open-ended.

Still, the memory cut harshly into Rosenthal's psyche and years later his friends would remark that despite his enormous success he still inwardly seemed to fear that something might go wrong and, in a flash, he could lose it all and be out in the street. One of his closest friends felt that Rosenthal's greatest worry after becoming managing editor of *The Times* was the fear that he would be fired.

Reston

Reston's prestige on *The Times* had never been higher than it was after he torpedoed the Washington coup. Inevitably he came into New York in the spring of 1968, taking over Catledge's title of executive editor. Wicker became associate editor and a columnist, and Frankel took over the Washington bureau. Reston's mandate was to reestablish peace and quiet; no more scandals; no more page-one stories; no more hysterics; no rocking the boat; let the dust settle. "I don't want to see anything about *The Times* in public print for a year," Punch told Reston. Reston gave his word that the lid would stay on. Later there were many who tried to explain why Reston had not really done well as executive editor; why the exciting promise he had brought to the job was not fulfilled; why he did not display in New York his golden touch with young reporters and editors; why his efforts to improve *The Times* made little imprint; why his tenure was marked neither by striking innovations nor great scoops; why he was unable to halt the hemorrhage of brilliant young writers, men like David Halberstam, Gay Talese, Anthony Lukas, leaving the paper; why his program for internships; for sabbatical leaves; for special status and new concepts to keep the best of the younger reporters from being lured away to books, TV, magazines never happened; why he stayed only 13 months.

The answer was complex. Reston was fifty-eight when he came into New York. He had been forty-two when he set Washington afire with his new bureau. Now he refused to give up his column, commuting a day or two to Washington each week in order to maintain it (inevitably the column went into a slump). He faced two ways, to New York and to Washington. This was too much for any man. Nor did he abandon his role as an informal consultant to powerful men in Washington and elsewhere. He had purchased the *Vineyard Gazette*, the remarkable Martha's Vineyard weekly of Henry Beetle Hough, just before being named executive editor, and this presented him with piddling but endless problems. Nor, perhaps, was Reston's soft-shoe, shirt-sleeves, antibureaucratic, no-chain-of-command style adapted to so large an enterprise.

But there was another factor. Reston had given a hostage to fortune. He had pledged to keep *The Times* out of the news columns for a year of rest and rehabilitation.

It never was to be made clear exactly how Reston had envisaged Rosenthal's role on the paper. Reston had a strong affinity for men whom he himself had "discovered" and brought along and he had a Ty Cobb nose for talent. Rosenthal was not one of "Scotty's boys" like Tom Wicker, Tony Lewis or Max Frankel; had never worked in Washington; his style was not Reston's style. Reston was a Glasgow lad transplanted to Ohio but he had a liking for button-down-collar reporters, a bit tweedy, a bit Ivy League (they didn't have to *be* Ivy League but they had to *look* Ivy League). Rosenthal didn't look Ivy League; he didn't act Ivy League; he looked very much what he was: a bright and ambitious young man out of City College who had clawed his way up by smartness, energy and ambition and who now was going to defend his turf with every ability he had.

Whatever Reston's ultimate intentions, he came into total collision with Rosenthal within days of taking over in New York. He met with him one evening to outline his plans, his news concepts, his schemes for creating an elite corps of correspondents. They would be based in New York; they would be on call for service around the world; or anywhere in the country. They would be well paid. They would have special privileges. This would enable *The Times* to meet the lure of any competition. It would give it access to the very best of the talented generations emerging from Harvard and Radcliffe and Princeton and would ensure that the paper could handle the new challenges in reporting and analyzing complex social, political and technological phenomena. It would put *The Times* in a category by itself and keep it there.

The elite corps (of course, Reston didn't use that word) would even—and this was startling in terms of the spare *Times* city room where everyone sat together, row on row of reporters, platoons of editors, no insignia of rank or privilege—have small offices of their own, secretaries or shared secretarial services. They would have sabbatical years off for writing their books; special arrangements whereby they would move in and out of *Times* assignments. Dream jobs they would be, and Reston was certain that this, in the late 1960s, would enable *The Times* to create and maintain a staff superior to that possessed by any news medium, print or electronic, and it would enable him to replicate in New York the miracle of his 1950s Washington bureau.

There were other components of Reston's plans—the free and easy movement of reporters from one staff to another, the ending of compartmentalization which gave editors proprietorial control over their men. If it seemed creative Reston would take a top political man and send him to the World Series; or assign an art critic to the Republican Convention. Ideas tumbled out of Reston's brain like wheat from a harvester.

As Reston talked Rosenthal grew more and more silent; a flushed look came over his face, the veins pounded at his temples. Finally he burst out. Enough! He was not going to preside over a second-class city room! He would not serve under a system in which he did not control his own men. He would not have *his* staff working alongside Reston's chosen few. It was impossible. Intolerable. It was a two-class society that Reston proposed and he would have no part of it. If this was what Reston had come to New York to do, he, Rosenthal, would get out. His resignation was available at any time. It would be on Reston's desk in the morning.

Reston had never heard anything like this in his life, as he told me when we met at his desk at 8:30 A.M. the following morning. The flow of words, the hyperbole, the rage boiling higher and higher. Finally Reston found himself trying to calm Rosenthal, trying to still the outpouring, trying somehow to help this man, whom he had hoped to make his partner in the new order, regain control over himself. But the torrent did not halt until Reston said, well, of course, if that is the way you feel I will have to review my plans. He did not have to say more. Rosenthal knew that he had won; and Reston knew it too. The only way he could go forward with his ideas was, he thought, at the cost of Rosenthal's resignation, and he had given his pledge to Sulzberger of a year of quietude.* So Reston gave another hostage to fate, a hostage which ensured that his tenure as executive editor would not be long and would not be successful. For Reston was too wise not to know and Rosenthal was too sensitive not to understand that if Rosenthal could veto Reston's plans it was Rosenthal not Reston who really held the reigns of power.

Listening to Reston's troubled account that morning I offered a few words of sympathy but inwardly made a note that the outcome of Reston's executive editorship had probably been determined by that single encounter. There was no way, I felt, in which Reston could regain command of the situation. Nor did I feel that there was room on *The Times* for two visions of the future. Only one could prevail and it seemed certain that it would be Rosenthal's. Rosenthal, on balance, was the tougher man. When the chips were down he was prepared to put his body, his future on the line. Of course, no one on *The Times* would talk publicly in these blunt terms but the fact was that Rosenthal had demonstrated that he had more balls than Reston. This primitive analysis had proved to be true. Rosenthal not only had won this seminal showdown with Reston but he went on and on and by 1969 Reston had gracefully turned over direction of the paper to Rosenthal and gone back to Washington, to his column, to his vice presidency of *The Times*.

Rosenthal had become managing editor, he brought back his friend Jimmy Greenfield from a job with Westinghouse Broadcasting and installed him as foreign editor. Or, rather, he had persuaded Punch to telephone Greenfield and offer him the foreign editorship. Greenfield said, "I'm glad you called. Of course, I'll come."

It was for Rosenthal a sweet, sweet victory. But even in June of 1972 it was not quite complete. Rosenthal was boss of the daily paper but not of the Sunday paper, still an independent entity under Markel's long-time right-hand man and loyal assistant, Dan Schwartz. And there was the Washington bureau. Somehow, the Washington bureau had eluded Rosenthal. Not that he felt a sense of urgency but Washington lingered in his mind as an unresolved question, one with which eventually he would have to deal.

*Ten years later the conversation had left no mark on Rosenthal's recollection. (Personal interview, Rosenthal, 10/9/79) Reston had not forgotten it. (Personal interview, Reston, 12/5/79)

34

The Smoking Pistol

*I*N JUNE OF 1972 neither Abe Rosenthal nor Max Frankel had any way of knowing what plans and strategy Mr. Nixon might be contemplating although both were perfectly aware that the President's hostility toward the press and, specifically, toward *The Times* had by no means diminished.

Much later Rosenthal was to conclude that Mr. Nixon's antagonism probably would have been just about as high even if there had never been a Pentagon case. But externally there were no signs of what he had in mind with the possible exception of the legal action which was going forward against Daniel Ellsberg and his friend Anthony Russo. The case had been subjected to delay after delay and endless grand jury proceedings but had finally come to trial in Los Angeles in June. It was, of course, recessed on the weekend of June 17–18 but jury selection was under way.

The Washington bureau, which had been put together by Frankel, building on the base of an excellent staff assembled under his predecessor Tom Wicker, was a good one, possibly not the equal of Reston's creation of twenty years earlier, but excellently qualified, many of the men and women with academic backgrounds in their fields of specialization. They were reporters who had been trained in the complexities of modern government. They knew the bureaucracy and the bureaucrats, the process of legislation, the law and the administrative byways of the regulatory agencies.

Many were veterans of *The Times'* extraordinary coverage of the Civil Rights struggle in the South. Among this number was a young reporter named Walter Rugaber, thirty-two years old, born in Macon, Georgia, a southern city which Walter was to describe as "never having been burned, neither by General Sherman nor its own carelessness," one which preserved the old residential pattern of "white" streets, interlaced by "black" streets or alleys. Rugaber treasured a snapshot of himself at the age of six on a mule belonging to a black who worked for Rugaber's father, riding the mule with the child of the workman. He described himself as having "no special views" on blacks, "nothing preachy," he just felt they were entitled to be treated like anyone else. He reported the Albany, Georgia, struggle, covered the Birmingham, Alabama, church bombing and the death of the four little girls and was proud of a story he wrote about another black youngster who was killed that day, a paper carrier named Virgil Wade, just thirteen, who was set upon as he was riding a bicycle, as Rugaber said, "by a gang of white punks and shot and killed—killed just because he was black and happened to be in their path." Two teen-agers were arrested in the shooting: both were Boy Scouts.

Rugaber came to work for *The Times* in Atlanta in 1967 and was transferred into Washington in January 1969 where he was given a chance to cover the Nixon White House, sharing the beat with Robert Semple, a low-profile, efficient newsman who grew up in Grosse Point, Michigan, went to Andover, graduated from Yale in 1959, taught school for a bit, spent a year getting his master's degree at Berkeley and at twenty-five came to Washington determined to get a job with *The Times*. He kept pounding at Scotty Reston's door, bothering him, he later thought, more than he should have, but it paid off. He joined *The Times* in 1963 and covered Nixon's 1968 campaign. He got along well with the Nixon people, particularly men like Patrick Buchanan and Ray Price, the Nixon speech writers. He didn't do so well with the Californians, Haldeman and Ziegler, but he didn't do badly either. He was himself a button-down-collar kind of man, a registered Republican in a bureau largely peopled by Democrats, and he was determined to do an objective job. His instincts were for the Nixon people, he mixed easily with them and it was no accident that he had been picked for what the editors of *The Times* knew was bound to be a difficult assignment. Semple took great interest in domestic issues, particularly the new welfare programs being developed by people like Pat Moynihan, and he got to know John Ehrlichman, Leonard Garment, Moynihan and others working on these programs quite intimately.

Covering the White House

Rugaber remembered Semple saying to him as they started out on the Nixon White House that they were lucky—they would be able to cover it fairly because they were young enough not to have grown up during the Jerry Voorhis and Helen Gahagan Douglas campaigns, the Hiss case, the Checkers speech or even the Nixon 1962 governorship campaign in California when passions had been so high.

"So," Semple said with sincerity and a little earnestness, "we can look at this man dispassionately and do a good job."

It didn't turn out exactly that way. Semple noticed that while he had gotten to know the Nixon people in the campaign it didn't pay off. "The Nixon people became kind of secretive," he recalled, "and you

couldn't get beyond a certain point with them." Rugaber found the
White House no fun. Staff members didn't return his telephone calls
(this was long before Pentagon), only a few would mix socially with
newsmen, and if they did, as William Safire quickly discovered, they
got into trouble—Safire's phone was tapped because of his association
with correspondents, including those of *The Times.* Rugaber admitted
he found covering the White House under Nixon "just dreadful." Ron
Ziegler was almost the only man who would talk with him.

Semple succeeded better. He developed a respect and even affection
for Ehrlichman, whom he considered the most humane of Nixon's
intimates, and was shocked and unbelieving when evidence of Ehrlichman's involvement in the "White House horrors" began to accumu-
late. He discovered that when he wrote stories about policy disagreements or policy failures his relations became very prickly and Ziegler
once admitted that word had gone out to cut him off. "When there
was a bite or an edge in your copy," Semple recalled, "they were quick
to let you know."

When the Pentagon Papers came out he got the cold shoulder. He
remembered that even George Schultz "gave me a dirty look" and Al
Haig glared at him and said, "What have you guys done?" For a period
he was simply frozen out (as Nixon had told his associates he wanted
The Times frozen out). There was a two-month period in which he
could not see Ehrlichman.

Max Frankel's only access to the White House was through Semple.
If Frankel wanted to talk to Ehrlichman it had to be arranged by
Semple; Frankel never did talk to Haldeman and his only conversation
with Nixon during the presidency was in Peking on the 1972 trip, an
event which Frankel covered with style and which was to win him a
Pulitzer Prize in 1973. Frankel and the other *Times* men did what they
could to establish better relations; they invited Nixon cabinet members
to staff luncheons; their views were presented to *The Times'* readers
and, as Frankel recalled, "we bent over backwards trying to cultivate
Nixon." The results were slim.

Not that *The Times* was treated with much more hostility than the
rest of what Vice President Spiro Agnew had dubbed the "elitist
eastern establishment press" (words written for him by Safire). Mr.
Nixon's White House was antagonistic to the press across the board.
Mr. Nixon was sincerely and totally convinced that the press had drawn
up its tents around him and laid siege. He did not believe any "strok-
ing" would change this situation and he read the Pentagon Papers affair
as confirmation of this deeply held view. He regarded himself and the
press as engaged in all-out combat and it was this philosophy which
encouraged him to send Agnew out tilting at the press and network
television (one of the first things Semple learned about the White

House was that Cronkite and the *Today Show* mattered a lot more than *The New York Times* and the *Washington Post*). There were many in the press then (and later) who felt that Mr. Nixon had serious designs upon the sanctity of the First Amendment and that he hoped to mobilize public opinion against the press, utilizing the Ellsberg case, a congressional inquiry into the Pentagon Papers, the subpoena powers of the Justice Department to that end. A careful reading of Mr. Nixon's discussions with his associates Haldeman, Ehrlichman and Kissinger largely supported that view. But Mr. Nixon displayed a distinct ambivalence. While he did not bother to conceal his hostility toward *The New York Times* he regarded the press, particularly when associated with a congressional investigating body, such as the House Un-American Activities Committee, as an especially effective medium for his purposes. In fact, he preferred this to the courts and, again and again, in talks with his colleagues emphasized that the Hiss case had demonstrated that enemies should be hauled before a hostile committee, interrogated and, meanwhile, be subjected to extensive damaging press "leaks." He was eager to avoid further court confrontations; didn't want the Justice Department to bring a case against *The New York Times;* reacted negatively whenever the subject of grand jury investigation of Neil Sheehan was mentioned, and this attitude probably caused the Boston Grand Jury, which was investigating the Pentagon Papers, to wither on the vine and die away. Mr. Nixon had hoped as late as autumn, 1971, that hearings might be held by the House Un-American Activities Committee, or possibly the House Armed Services Committee, but these possibilities drained away and by June 1972 he was concentrating on his reelection campaign. He was hesitant about initiating large-scale antimedia enterprises during an election. When columnist Jack Anderson published several extremely embarrassing stories in December 1971 revealing that the Joint Chiefs of Staff had a spy in the White House who passed to them copies of Henry Kissinger's secret National Security Council papers Mr. Nixon instructed his aides, particularly Kissinger, to play the incident down but promised "we'll prosecute Anderson et al. after the election." "Tell our people including Laird," Mr. Nixon instructed, "lay off Anderson now." At the same time he instructed Vice President Agnew to explore the feasibility of an official secrets act and make recommendations to the President. This order was given January 18, 1972. The question of an official secrets act, with severe penalties on the British and Canadian lines, had been in Mr. Nixon's mind since the publication of the Pentagon Papers.

Mr. Nixon's inner attitudes toward the press were not known to Max Frankel or Abe Rosenthal in June 1972 but nothing about them would have come as a surprise. Mr. Nixon's hostility was ingrained and, if anything, the editors may have somewhat exaggerated it, not perceiving that the President's views on the press were not at all simplistic. It was not, as many of them felt, a matter of "him or us"; Mr. Nixon regarded the press as an extraordinary instrument to be employed for his own ends; he also regarded it as a dangerous, hostile conspiracy which had sought to destroy him since his entry into California politics in 1946.

Watergate

At 2:30 A.M., Saturday, June 17, 1972, the Washington, D.C., police arrested five men in the Democratic National Committee Headquarters in the Watergate complex (where former Attorney General John Mitchell, head of the Committee for the Reelection of the President, popularly known by the acronym of CREEP, maintained his pleasant $350,000 duplex apartment). The men, carrying two 35-mm. cameras, electronic gear, a walkie-talkie, lock picks, small tear-gas guns and miniaturized bugging devices, were charged with burglary.

They identified themselves as Bernard L. Barker, Frank A. Sturgis, Virgilio R. Gonzalez and Eugenio R. Martinez, all of Miami, and James W. McCord, Jr., of Washington. The arrests occurred too late to make the Saturday newspapers, but Alfred E. Lewis, who had covered the police beat for thirty-five years for the *Washington Post*, was quickly onto the story, visited the scene of the break-in, talked with the arresting officers and put together the essential details—five well-dressed men, well supplied with money, most of it in sequential $100 bills, no ordinary burglars these.

Lewis was a classic police reporter. He did not write stories, he telephoned his information to the rewrite desk. For years he did not even have a typewriter in his police headquarters cubbyhole. Before Saturday was over the *Post* had eight men on the story, a local story, handled by the city desk with city-desk staff men. Among the eight were two young reporters named Carl Bernstein and Bob Woodward. Woodward covered the court hearing that afternoon for the five and learned that McCord was a former CIA man. Bernstein found that the other four had been involved in anti-Castro action and were believed to have CIA connections. It was a good story and the *Post* played it on page one Sunday, June 18, under the signature of Alfred E. Lewis. On Sunday the Associated Press discovered that McCord was "security coordinator" for CREEP and in Tuesday's paper Woodward, with the help of another *Post* police reporter named Eugene Bachinski, presented a story that linked Howard E. Hunt to the Watergate suspects and identified him as a "White House consultant" working for Charles W. Colson, Mr. Nixon's special counsel, known "as one of the original backroom boys."

Watergate had started.

No Alarm Bells

No alarm bells rang at *The New York Times* on Saturday, June 17. Not many members of the forty-man Washington bureau worked on Saturdays. It was an assignment everyone tried to avoid. They wanted to be away for the weekend, to their houses in the West Virginia hills, the Blue Ridge of Virginia, the eastern Maryland shore, or by mid-June to Martha's Vineyard or Nantucket where half the staff spent the summer along with their Georgetown colleagues from the government and the New York and Cambridge politico-intellectual establishment. Nothing was more un-chic than to stay in grubby Nixonian Washington over a weekend at any time from June 15 to September 15. *Nobody* worth knowing possibly could be in town. Even if you were a Nixonian you didn't stay in Washington. You were off to Bay Biscayne or San Clemente or Camp David for what Mr. Nixon and Ron Ziegler invariably insisted were *working* weekends. As one of the few *Times* men in Washington known for street-style hustle was to say, "The bureau was middle-aged, middle-class, affluent. Nobody wanted to work on weekends and nobody wanted to work on a police story. Damn few had ever been street reporters. They didn't know the mechanics and didn't want to." In this they did not differ from their colleagues of the national press corps. One Washington correspondent said, "If the national staff of the *Washington Post* had handled it the *Post* wouldn't have gotten the story. Even if it had been men like David Broder and Haynes Johnson [two of the finest political reporters in the country] I don't think they would have picked it up."

The situation had not radically changed since Arthur Krock, having gone to Washington in 1932 to take over *The Times* bureau, wrote Arthur Sulzberger privately about the Washington correspondent corps, "It is a sub-calibre group—lazy, sycophantic, the ways of local rooms forgotten, often stupid, devoted to the 'huddle' instead of original research in the quest for news, intent on radio appearances and Gridiron dinners . . . no breadth of outlook . . . this newspaper world folds upon itself and most of its members look inward."

Or, as James Naughton, a tough and able professional from Cleveland who came to *The Times* in 1969 after covering the Civil Rights struggle on ghetto streets and who went on to heads-up coverage of the Erwin inquiry and the impeachment hearings, later said, "The *Times* bureau was made up of well-established men who were not inclined to drop everything, their home life, their wives and children and hang onto a story night after night no matter how late or how much effort it took. There were no hungry young reporters in *The Times* Washington bureau in 1972."

Nor did *The Times* have a "local" staff in Washington. If something broke in the streets of the capital, if a senator was arrested for drunken driving, if a congressman was found splashing about in the Lincoln reflecting pool with an "exotic" dancer, *The Times* got the news from local Washington newsmen on a "string" basis, that is, after taking care of their own city desk, the reporters would fill in *The Times* on what happened.

That was the way *The Times* handled the start of Watergate, and a young beginner, a copy boy, not even a news assistant, was assigned that weekend to look into the story.

By Monday morning that changed. Tad Szulc, the keenest cloak-and-dagger man on the *Times'* staff, moved in on the story. It was, he was sure, *his* kind of story; these were *his* kind of Cubans; and he quickly tied Bernard L. Barker to the Bay of Pigs. Szulc didn't happen to know the arrested quartet but he had friends who did know them, and *The Times'* editors, troubled by a somewhat uncomfortable news problem, breathed a sigh of relief. It was going to be all right. Szulc understood this kind of thing, was good at it and, even though it came at a moment when his relations with *The Times* were not at their best (he was soon to resign and embark on a career of books and free-lance articles), there wasn't much doubt that he would quickly get to the bottom of whatever had happened at Watergate. Szulc, not noted for modesty, shared this view. He was confident that somehow the Bay of Pigs was involved, somehow the CIA, conspiratorial ideas revolved in his mind and when the name of Howard Hunt surfaced it looked as though Szulc had it made. After all he had known Hunt from the Cuba days, but unfortunately Hunt vanished (he had run to cover in Los Angeles) and Szulc couldn't find him. He did get the first interview with Bernard L. Barker, and Barker said some suggestive things. But the Szulc line began to peter out. He had a story a day for about a week, exploiting the anti-Castro link, but the trail didn't lead anywhere.

Later there were to be many who said *The Times* did not recognize the Watergate story; that it simply did not assign proper manpower; that the editors played down the stories that the reporters brought in, or killed them for lack of sound sourcing, but that was after the fact, and looking back at the reporting in the early phase of Watergate the comparative headlines in *The Times* and the *Post* did not sustain this view. James Reston, who always liked to describe himself as a "scoop artist," never accepted the "down-play" view.

"You could hardly miss what had happened," he said in later years. "It was like being hit on the head with a baseball bat. It was obviously not a two-bit burglary. I don't agree with the view that people thought Nixon was not involved. They did think so but no one thought that the trail could be followed so high or so far."

That, in Reston's opinion, may have been why everyone was slow in getting onto the story. "The *Post* didn't jump on the story. It wasn't jumping hard when it assigned Woodward and Bernstein, two comparatively inexperienced men from its local staff. Just the opposite," he said. "It was as if *The Times* had assigned a couple of district men from the city desk in New York."

Walter Rugaber

Walter Rugaber was detached from his White House beat and assigned to Watergate. From the moment McCord had been identified as chief of security for CREEP there was no doubt in Rugaber's mind that Watergate was a Nixon operation. How to prove it was another question. Rugaber was convinced that Szulc was in a blind alley. Curiously, Szulc's stubborn belief that Watergate was a CIA Cuban anti-Castro operation was the cover story which Nixon hit upon on Thursday after Watergate, June 22. The President's "theory" and Szulc's theory matched 100 percent. There was only one thing wrong: neither had a foundation in fact.

"I didn't believe that for a minute," Rugaber recalled. "Of course, I didn't know how far up the line it went but from the moment McCord was identified I was confident it could not be anything but a Nixon operation."

Rugaber moved in hard and on Monday, June 26, a week and two days after the break-in, he published a 3,000-word wrap-up which cast aside the Cuban scenario and pointed suspicion directly at the White House and Mr. Nixon's campaign associates.

Pondering how to develop the story, Rugaber had come to several conclusions. He did not believe that the Cuban-CIA line led anywhere. He did not believe that anything was to be gotten out of the White House or Nixon's associates (except by luck). They simply were not going to talk.

"The idea crossed my mind," Rugaber recalled, "that what we needed was incontrovertible proof of what was going on—if something was going on—between the White House and these people."

The link, he felt, had to be discovered in contacts that the five arrested men had made. A link must exist in the form of records, financial statements, deposit slips, something impersonal, something incontrovertible. The way to find it, he concluded, was to learn every possible thing about the five men: where they had come from; who they were; what their connections were; who were their associates. And the place to find this out was not Washington. In Washington he might spend half a lifetime chasing false trails or drilling dry holes. The men, four of them, came from Miami. The place to find out was Miami.*

Rugaber acted on his theory and went to Miami, but while he could (as Szulc had) discover a good deal about the four men from the Cuban colony this was not going to give him the "incontrovertible proof" that he was after. That proof, he concluded, probably lay beyond the reach of a newspaper reporter. What was needed was the power of subpoena, the ability to get into the records, the cash flow, the credit arrangements. Rugaber knew that the four men had to have bank accounts, they had to have telephones, they had to use checks, maintain charge accounts, carry credit cards. Somehow he had to intercept the computerized web which surrounded the lives of the four burglars. If he could get into that web he should quickly know if the men had a White House connection.

It chanced to be election year in Miami. Richard E. Gerstein, state's attorney for Dade County (Greater Miami), a handsome, popular prosecutor, six feet five in his stocking feet, a World War II bomber pilot, was running for his fifth term. Rugaber went to Gerstein with his problem. There was, he told Gerstein, at least a remote possibility that the Watergate plot had been hatched in Miami right in Gerstein's back yard. The investigation, of course, was being handled in Washington but it wasn't getting anywhere. Now, if Rugaber's suspicion was correct, and this was, in fact, a Miami crime, it would be very much in Gerstein's interest to investigate. The prosecutor conceded that Rugaber made a lot of sense and decided, then and there, to launch a quiet inquiry. It was, of course, understood from the start that he would not object if, as it were, Rugaber looked over his shoulder. Rugaber then sat down with Martin Dardis, Gerstein's chief investigator, shared with him such information as he had been able to dig up and Martin began to issue subpoenas for the paper chain.

In Washington, Watergate had come to a dead end. Howard L. Hunt had returned July 7 and provided a one-day sensation but the story then died like a Fourth of July skyrocket, leaving a few flickers in its train.

The city editor of the *Washington Post* sent Bernstein back to his customary beat, Virginia politics (it was the second time he had done

---

*Rugaber's June 26 story reflected this approach. He had already checked the airlines and discovered that Barker and his associates came to Washington from Miami via Eastern Airlines, paying for the tickets with Barker's American Express card. And he had found that funds from the Banco Internacional S.A., of Mexico City, had found their way into Barker's bank account in Miami. In this and in Rugaber's dealings with Richard Gerstein, the Greater Miami District Attorney, he was greatly assisted by *The Times* Miami correspondent, George Volsky, who had long been on close terms with Gerstein. (Rugaber, *New York Times*, 6/26/72; personal interview, Wally Turner, 4/16/79)

it; the first time Bernstein had won a brief reprieve; now it looked as if the city editor was prepared to make it stick). Woodward had a lot of time off owed him and July 22 he went on a vacation to Lake Michigan.*

The story was drifting out to nowhere in Washington but Rugaber's efforts in Miami were paying off and on July 25 he was able to report on page one of *The New York Times* that fifteen telephone calls had been made between March 15 and June 15 from Barker's phones in Miami to G. Gordon Liddy's office in the White House. A couple of days earlier *Newsday* had revealed that Liddy had been fired from CREEP for refusing to answer FBI questions about Watergate. It had been established that Liddy had worked for Ehrlichman.

The day Rugaber's story appeared in *The Times* Bernstein was pulled off Virginia politics. He was never to go back. Bernstein got on the telephone and, not without some difficulty (Rugaber did not reveal his source in his story), located Gerstein and Dardis. Dardis confirmed Rugaber's story and said he had subpoenaed Barker's bank records and had found some deposits which originated in Mexico. He made a date to show Bernstein what he had found on Monday, July 31. That Monday morning as Bernstein boarded his plane for Miami he picked up *The Times.* It carried a three-column page-one headline, a Rugaber story from Mexico City reporting that $89,000 in Barker's bank account had been traced to four Mexico City cashier's checks.

From the Miami airport Bernstein telephoned his city editor and proposed that he follow Rugaber to Mexico City but his editor suggested that he stay in Miami for a day and see what he could find out. One of Bernstein's most frustrating days followed. He spent most of it sitting in the district attorney's office waiting to see Gerstein and Dardis. Bernstein did not know about Rugaber's arrangements but it was clear neither man was in a hurry to receive him. It was after 6 P.M. when Bernstein worried his way in to see Dardis and worried out of him the data on five checks that had been deposited in the Barker account. Four were the Mexican checks that Rugaber had described. The fifth, for $25,000, was drawn on the First Bank and Trust Company, of Boca Raton, Florida, in the name of Kenneth H. Dahlberg. Before the 9:30 P.M. deadline for the *Post*'s second edition Woodward (back from his vacation) and Bernstein had tracked Dahlberg to Minneapolis, learned

---

*Later there were rumors that Howard Simons, the *Post*'s managing editor, was considering firing Bernstein for an accumulation of "crimes and misdemeanors," largely chargeable to his temperament. (Personal interview, Turner, 4/14/79) Bernstein never believed that. "There is no question that I was at loggerheads with management from time to time and I know I sometimes sent them up a tree," Bernstein recalled, "but it was never my perception that I was near getting fired." (Personal interview, Bernstein, 4/19/79)

that the $25,000 check represented money which Dahlberg had collected as chairman of the Republican Midwest Finance Committee and that the check had been turned over either to Hugh W. Sloan, Jr., treasurer of CREEP, or to Maurice Stans, Mr. Nixon's former Secretary of Commerce and chairman of the CREEP finance committee. It was a superb job of investigative reporting.

So there it was. Republican campaign funds flowing directly into the bank accounts of the Watergate burglars. A bull's-eye.

Rugaber returned to Miami on the morning of August 1. He found a call waiting for him from Bob Phelps on the Washington bureau desk. The *Post* that morning had traced the Dahlberg check, located Dahlberg, wrapped up the story. It was the first real breakthrough on Watergate. Rugaber later said, "In retrospect what I did on the checks I wish I hadn't done. I had the Mexican checks and I leaped onto a plane and raced to Mexico City to track them down. Dardis had promised to guard the fifth check with his life."

What he should have done, Rugaber conceded, was to have told Phelps about the fifth check and let other *Times* men work on it during his absence of three or four days in Mexico City. This, Rugaber always was to believe, was the single most significant story of Watergate. Certainly the most significant of the early period. It linked Nixon money to the financing of Watergate. The $25,000 was a campaign contribution by Duane Andreas, a wealthy Minneapolis grain man, friend and financial supporter of Hubert Humphrey who had decided to play it safe and provide money to Nixon without Humphrey's knowledge. Naturally. The money went to Dahlberg. He passed it to CREEP. CREEP gave it to G. Gordon Liddy. Liddy gave it (through Hunt or directly) to Barker and it was laundered through his bank account. It was, as Rugaber said, the smoking pistol, the precise bit of irrefutable fiscal evidence, the link in the paper chain which he had been certain would connect the burglars with the White House. It was his own evidence, turned up through his own ingenuity and his own persuasiveness. And he missed it. It was a mistake which he never forgave himself. He felt like a quarterback who has set the scene for a quick touchdown pass short of end zone. It worked perfectly. The opposition was faked out of position. But the ball was hurled straight into the hands of an opponent who ran the length of the field for a touchdown.

There were those who later were to say that it was this erratic twist, this specific misfiring of a remarkably well-calculated and conceived plan, this rabbit play by the wonderfully dogged, never-say-die, young *Post* reporters, Woodward and Bernstein, which, in final analysis, gave to the *Post* a well-earned, well-deserved edge in the incredibly intense competition for the Watergate story.

The Dahlberg check was a spectacular chapter in what became the nation's greatest political melodrama. As weeks and months passed *The Times* and the *Post* again and again were to come up with shattering scoops, remarkable reporting. So would other reporters and newspapers. But as Barry Sussman, the *Post*'s city editor, said to Woodward as he finished the Dahlberg story, "We've never had a story like this before." That was true or almost true and it was to color Watergate coverage thence forward.

35

"You Will Just Have to Believe Me"

A MAN WHOM MANY of his peers regarded as the best investigative correspondent in the world went to work in the Washington bureau of *The New York Times* two weeks before Watergate, Seymour Hersh, a Vesuvius of a reporter, a man so volatile, so hyperkinetic, so quick of mind and body, so tenacious, so cajoling, so telephonic (he seemed to have been born with a receiver at his ear) so greater than life-size that during his working hours from 9 A.M. to midnight persons within hearing range found themselves transfixed by the mini-dramas played out over his telephone.

Sy Hersh, loose-jointed, disarrayed, a walk-on from *The Front Page,* was thirty-four years old in 1972. He had won the Pulitzer Prize two years before for what some called the greatest reporting achievement of the Vietnam epoch, the story of Lieutenant William Calley and the My Lai massacre. He had gotten that story as a free-lance journalist, working for himself, by himself, totally on his own, no boss, no fringe benefits. He had taken the whisper of a news item and clawed his way into the story, had done it by persistence, not a little guile and some old-fashioned blarney. He had flown from one end of the country to another, often not knowing whom he needed to see or where he could be found. He worked for days with no results. He had taken wild chances, made lucky guesses and come up with the biggest scandal of a scandalous war. A few months later he approached Max Frankel, the new *Times* Washington chief, for a job. They lunched and Frankel said he was "very flattered" at the idea of Hersh coming to *The Times* but somehow it hadn't happened.

A year later Hersh, still free-lancing, had a chance to get into North Vietnam and wanted to sign up *The Times* for his stories. *The Times* had bought his My Lai series but hadn't used the first of them. Rosenthal wanted to check Sy's quotes from a GI named Paul Meadlo, wanted one of his reporters, John Corry, to meet Meadlo and Sy and Abe got into a hassle. "Okay," Sy remembered saying. "You want to meet Meadlo? Well, he's in New York. Try and find him." He hung up on Rosenthal. Later the matter was smoothed over a bit but Hersh's introduction to Rosenthal didn't seem promising.

Now early in 1972 Hersh came into *The Times* office to sell his Hanoi stories to foreign editor James Greenfield, who agreed to take them and then said, "Come on in and meet Abe." The two went into Rosenthal's office and Rosenthal said, "Why haven't you ever come in for a job?" Hersh explained he had talked to Frankel and nothing came of it. Now there was a pleasant conversation and after Hersh came back from Vietnam he went to work for *The Times,* reporting for duty in the Washington bureau just before Watergate.

Hersh did not arrive at *The Times* empty-handed. He brought with him a series of stories on which he was already working, stories for the most part originating in the Pentagon, in the Vietnam war, the most important being an exposé of General John D. Lavelle and the secret bombing of North Vietnam. The first of the Lavelle stories appeared two days before Watergate. Tenacious as a terrier, Hersh was not going to give the stories up, having worked hard on them and being convinced that the secret air strikes were Nixon's way of getting around the bombing halt. During the early phase of Watergate Hersh had a story almost every day on the secret strikes and the story continued into autumn when congressional hearings were held.

When Watergate broke, the obvious move was to turn Hersh loose —a superinvestigative story, a superinvestigative reporter. But life is not so logical. Frankel tried to arouse Hersh's interest but had no success. The fact was Hersh was not convinced that Watergate, in the words of one of his associates, "was going to fly."

Hersh was not a team player. He didn't like stories other reporters were working on. Anthony Lewis called Hersh "a nervous badger" and David Halberstam cited him as "America's greatest national resource." But Gloria Emerson probably put it best. She said simply that Hersh was "a disturber of the peace," the peace of his friends, the peace of his competitors, the peace of those he was investigating and most of all the peace of complacent citizens and complacent government. Hersh was not a man of tact or social amenity and Clifton Daniel once asked a little plaintively if Sy had only that one sweater with the holes in it. Sy didn't know for certain and probably had never noticed the holes. Sy was a twin and Gloria Emerson's fancy was that somehow he had gotten the brains, the liver, the heart and the energy for two people.

"I didn't want to do Watergate," Hersh recalled. "I would pick up the *Washington Post.* There would be an eight-column headline all about wrongdoing, lots of wrongdoing, and it would mention eight people I'd never heard of before."

Hits and Misses

Perhaps, Hersh said later, it was a sense of self-protection. He didn't have any sources on Watergate, he wasn't convinced the story was really there and he had the impression Frankel wasn't convinced either. "Maybe Kissinger told him there was nothing to the story," he mused later, "and I didn't know myself." Hersh may have been right about Frankel's skepticism. Kissinger was Frankel's most valued source and his judgment would have been persuasive but Max could not recall having heard anything from him in the early phase of Watergate. Later Kissinger told him that Watergate was not so important that it should be permitted to sap the President's energies and divert him from important foreign affairs matters. R. W. Apple remembered saying to Max at the time of the Republican National Convention in late July, "I guess I'll go and talk to Maurice Stans [the finance chairman of CREEP]" and Frankel replying, "You've got a fixation on Watergate. That story is dead."

John Crewdson recalled going out for a drink one day with Sy and Frankel. Hersh was just back from Sweden, where he had gone in late September to cover the release by Hanoi of three American airmen and he simply had no interest in Watergate. Crewdson was a "hungry young man," a classic example of the type which was said not to exist in the Washington bureau. A protégé of the *Times'* Pulitzer Prize-winning senior investigative reporter Wallace Turner, who found him at Berkeley and got him on as a news assistant in New York and later in Washington, Crewdson went to work for *The Times* in 1970 and, being young, born in 1945, totally a postwar product, and endlessly energetic, was out on the Washington streets covering demonstrations and riots from the moment he joined the staff. In autumn 1971 he went to Oxford for a year, having been given a $3,000 interest-free loan by *The Times*. He thought he might return to academic life but a year in England satisfied him that he was a reporter and he landed in Washington on Sunday, June 18, 1972, to read "this funny story on page one of the Washington *Post* about the break-in." He set about to find a place to live but was called in on Wednesday, June 21, assigned to Watergate and never left the story, emerging two years later a professional investigative reporter of skill, as lively as Bernstein or Woodward, having put his name to half a dozen first-flight exclusives and author-to-be of a rapidly growing file of major exposés.

Crewdson, small, nervous, wiry, warm, was low man on the Washington totem pole on the evening he joined Frankel and Hersh for a drink but there wasn't much that he missed and it was obvious to him that Hersh was not, for the time being, going to move into Watergate.

Crewdson believed there was little *The Times* could have done in the first months that would have made a great difference to the final outcome of Watergate. He was a realist; he liked good reporting as well as any man who did it superlatively but he believed that Watergate was decided not by the press, not by Woodward and Bernstein, not by the achievements of *The Times,* people like Rugaber, like a good man named Bob Smith, like himself and ultimately like Hersh. The make-or-break factors, in his opinion, were Judge John J. Sirica, the letter to Sirica from James McCord, released March 23, 1973, and, soon thereafter, the decision of John Dean to go to the prosecutors.

There was another factor which affected *The Times.* It should not have played a role. But it did. The Pentagon break-in occurred in the week that a proposal was made to Frankel by Punch Sulzberger that he take over the Sunday editorship. This was a critical career break for Frankel. It placed him in the number two news position on *The Times,* a post from which he might well be named executive editor (although at that moment the paper had no executive editor, Punch having sworn after his not entirely happy results with Catledge and Reston to scratch the position from his table of organization). The arrangement was that Frankel would take the Sunday job January 1. This meant that 1972 would be the last (as well as the first) occasion in which he would be the senior *Times* man on the national political conventions and the presidential campaign. He was eager to make the most of this opportunity. His mind was filled with sugar-plum dreams, ideas for improving the Sunday edition, for reorganizing the famous News-of-the-Week-in-Review, hardly changed since Lester Markel invented it in the 1930s, and for giving a new look to the somewhat jaded *New York Times Magazine.* He would want to assemble new personnel, to learn the Mycenaean cipher in which the affairs of this vast news machine were encoded, and devise means for putting his personal stamp on one of the most original and successful components of *The Times.* These were not small affairs and it was natural that they took precedence in Frankel's mind over a story about which he had many uncertainties. One member of Frankel's staff felt that the typical reaction in the bureau when Woodward and Bernstein broke a story was "It can't be true. How could they know that? It's a lot of poppycock." He did not think Frankel's judgment differed. As Frankel put it later, "They were writing stuff that we couldn't have gotten into *The Times.* Judged by what they printed we couldn't feel they had a solid hold on the story, particularly when they broke the Haldeman story." The Haldeman story, a Woodward-Bernstein exclusive linking H. R. Haldeman to control of the CREEP fund for political espionage and sabotage, was published October 25, 1972, the eve of the election. It was instantly denied by the White House. In fact, as developments were to show, the *Post*'s story was essentially correct but the information had not been presented to the Watergate grand jury by Hugh Sloan, the former CREEP treasurer, as the story stated. Of all the stories put together by the young reporters this was the only one to misfire seriously and it misfired on a technicality, not on its essential truth.

But Frankel had touched a critical point. *Times'* style and *Times'* tradition did create difficulties. It is in the nature of investigative reporting that the reporter often learns more than he is able to attribute to quotable sources. People tell him things that they do not wish traced back. The reporter can put two and two together but he cannot spell out the arithmetic in his story. *Times* editors and copyreaders worried about such stories, sometimes rejected them, often held them up for rechecking and rewriting. (The same thing, of course, happened at the *Post.*)

Then there was a question of psychology. One editor who worked at that time in both Washington and New York was convinced that "nobody really thought it was a story—just a cheap low-level crime of some kind. There was no perception in either Washington or New York of what it added up to."

This was an overstatement but what street-wise reporter Bill Kovach discovered was not.* Kovach was called down from Boston in the first week of Watergate to give the Washington bureau a hand. The bureau had still not gotten anyone into the Watergate hotel where the burglars had stayed. They wanted to interview the maids on the seventh floor but did not, he recalled, know how to go about it. Kovach went to the Watergate, checked in as being from the Massachusetts Tool & Die Co., said he was a little superstitious, could he have a room on the seventh floor, got a room next to that which the Plumbers had occupied, came back to the bureau, handed over the key and said there it was.

Lawrence O'Brien, the Democratic National Chairman whom Kovach knew from Boston, was giving information to the *Washington Post.* There were few newspapermen whom O'Brien did not know or assume that he knew, a more accessible man did not exist in Washington. Kovach went to O'Brien and said, "For Christ's sake quit passing all your stuff to the *Post.* You need *The Times* with you too." O'Brien said, "Honest to Christ—they have never called me." Kovach arranged for a *Times* man to see O'Brien that afternoon. Three days later he checked O'Brien. No one from *The Times* had called.

"How in hell," Kovach later said, "could they cover investigative news like that?"

Then there was the story of Alfred Baldwin III. Baldwin was a

*In 1979 Kovach was named operational chief of *The Times* Washington bureau.

former FBI agent who had monitored the bug placed in the Democratic Headquarters at Watergate. He had a wealth of detail about Watergate and other Plumbers' operations. Many reporters knew about Baldwin, knew that he had a good story, knew that he was talking to the government, knew that he lived in Hamden, Connecticut. Woodward and Bernstein had talked to Baldwin's lawyers but had been put off by suggestions that Baldwin wanted to sell his story. *The Times* knew of Baldwin and Robert Phelps of the Washington bureau passed word to New York, urging that a hard-nosed reporter be assigned to Baldwin, to sit on his doorstep until he appeared. New York sent a regional reporter named Larry Fellows to locate Baldwin. He went to Baldwin's house, knocked at the door, no one answered and he went about his other duties. At Washington's urging he was sent back a second time, but when, once again, no one was home, Fellows was not instructed to pursue the story further. Two or three days later, on October 5, Jack Nelson and Ron Ostrow of the *Los Angeles Times* published Baldwin's firsthand account of the Watergate affair. *The Los Angeles Times* had scooped both *The Post* and *The Times.* It was the first big one for *The Los Angeles Times* on Watergate.

Later there were so many postmortems about *The Times* and Watergate that you could pick your explanation off a tree. A favorite with Rosenthal in New York was what he called "the three-hundred-mile gap," the notion that because three-hundred miles separated Washington and New York communications broke down. This hardly seemed valid. The distance between Washington and New York was constant. It had never before kept *The Times* Washington bureau from doing a superlative job. Historically there had always been differences between *The Times'* chiefs in Washington and New York but no problems of "communications," personal animosity or rivalry had handicapped *The Times* in covering a big Washington story before and no hard evidence ever turned up to indicate that this happened on Watergate. There were technical and personnel problems. The Washington bureau in early summer of 1972 was massing its resources for the 1972 political conventions and elections. Gene Roberts, *The Times'* veteran of the southern Civil Rights and Vietnam stories, was now national editor. Watergate came under his jurisdiction but that summer he was privately negotiating for a job with the Knight newspapers, as managing editor of the *Philadelphia Inquirer,* a post he took up in September. Like Frankel, Roberts' mind was not sharply focused on Watergate.

Rosenthal was to assume basic responsibility for *The Times'* performance on Watergate. "As the editor," he said, "I can't assign the blame to anyone but myself. I was the managing editor sitting in my big fat office. I was terrified at what was taking place."

The management of the paper was in New York, not Washington, he pointed out. The paper was in the middle of a transition period. What should have been done, he thought, was to put together an investigative team in New York and send it into Washington.

"Our base," he said later on, "is not in Washington. It is in New York. To do the big story in Washington we would have had to transfer our base to Washington."

But that hardly seemed realistic. Assembling a cadre of investigative reporters in New York and transferring them cold into Washington, a city of infinite personal networks, cozyness, compartments within compartments, would not have solved the problem. *The Times* had first-class men available in Washington. Some like Rugaber, Crewdson and Bob Smith did excellent work from the start (Smith resigned in the autumn of 1972 to return to Yale and take a law degree). Others like Hersh could have been put on the story. Kovach could have been recruited. There was never a genuine lack of manpower. Semple, who worked in the White House, remembered going to talk to John Mitchell just after July 1, the day Mitchell resigned as head of CREEP, Mitchell contending that it was because of his wife Martha's illness. Semple knew Mitchell well and liked him. Now he found himself talking to a rather shattered man. "Had I had my wits about me," Semple was to say later, "I should have wondered what had happened to cause this. Mitchell was a strong man." This stuck in the back of Semple's mind, worrying him a bit, but his focus was on the election campaign, and he carried on with normal coverage of the White House and men like Crewdson were thankful that he did. They could still go to him for background on who was who, the names that kept popping up, guidance on relationships and rivalries. "If Semple had played hardball at the White House," Crewdson said later, "we would have been in the same box as the *Washington Post.* He kept the line open and that was very important."

Later Semple was to blame himself, saying that he should have understood earlier what was going on but he didn't and not until the James McCord letter did he begin to understand how serious it all was. By that time he was out of Washington, transferred to New York to work on the national desk.

What was lacking in this, lacking in the consciousness of many editors and even in reporters like Hersh, was a sense of dimension. Later it was easy to see it all and see how clear and consistent was the Nixon White House, to see how the paranoia, the secret apparatus, the extralegal tactics, the wiretapping and all that went with it escalated into burglary and unlawful conduct. Anyone who had possessed even a clue to Mr. Nixon's private discussions about the Pentagon Papers, his technique for dealing with that and other crises would have moved with all possible force on Watergate. Every element of Watergate had been present in the days before and after the Pentagon Papers. The same individuals who carried out Watergate had tried their hands earlier with the Ellsberg break-in and other plots, conceived and executed or conceived and not executed. The Pentagon Papers were a dress rehearsal for Watergate.

But the signals of Pentagon had not been clearly read, had not been understood and integrated into the thinking of *The Times'* editors. Woodward and Bernstein leaped on the story not because they had some knowledge of how things worked or were working inside the White House (they knew nothing about the White House) but with the simple ferocity of eager reporters, following a trail, oblivious to where it led. They were *out to get a story,* acting on the most basic reporter's instinct. There was nothing philosophical about what they did. They had no communications problems, no logistics problems. They were not thunder-struck if the trail led them to the doorsteps of the high and mighty. They did not mind working until midnight or 3 A.M., telephoning and telephoning and telephoning, calling on one cold prospect after another at whatever hour they had available. They did not ring the doorbell once and consider the assignment fulfilled. They acted as Hersh did on My Lai and a hundred other stories; as Crewdson was learning to act; as Rugaber had acted in cutting into the Miami paper trail.

But this was not an easy lesson for some newsmen to get into their bloodstream. In part this difficulty may have flowed from an ingrained respect for their country, the belief instilled almost from birth of reverence for the President, the associations with Washington, Jefferson and Lincoln. As Semple was to say, "It was hard to believe that a national administration, a President, would stoop to something like this. Maybe there was a belief all around that it just couldn't have happened."

The Tapes

Something like that must have been at work in *The New York Times.* No other explanation fits some of the attitudes taken and conclusions drawn.

The habit grew up in *The Times* Washington bureau as the Watergate story went on and on for the group working on it to assemble at 10 or 11 A.M. every morning to review the prospects. One day in December 1972 a *Times* photographer named Mike Lien poked his head into the room. He stood for a while, listening to the discussion, then said he had something to report. He spent a lot of time with the police and Secret Service men on his job and off-time he frequently joined them for a drink.

"You know," he said, a little diffidently (there was a measurable difference in status in the Washington bureau between correspondents and photographers except for the senior *Times* photographer, George Tames, of whom it was said he had taken pictures of every President since Warren G. Harding), "I was talking with some of my Secret Service friends last night. We were out drinking together. And they told me something interesting. They said the President has a whole taping apparatus in the Oval Office. It's run by the Secret Service. They tape everything that goes on there."

The reporters had looked up from the long yellow legal pads on which they were jotting down their notes for the day, their shared impressions, their assignments, possible leads, checks on stories published by the *Washington Post* and other papers.

There was a moment of silence. No one offered a comment.

"Well," said Lien, a little embarrassed, "it sounded kind of interesting and I thought you might want to know."

"Thanks a lot," someone said, and then the reporters and editors went back to their discussion, their plans, their strategies.

"These were men," said one of those present that day, "who had not yet arrived at the belief that a man like John Mitchell could lie."

Lien's curious story about the taping system in the Oval Office faded away in their minds where it had only the most peripheral lodging, never to be acted on, not again to be recalled until that Monday, July 16, 1973, when Alexander Butterfield, a former deputy assistant to President Nixon, testified publicly before the Ervin committee that the President maintained "voice-activated listening devices in the Oval Office."* By this time Lien was dead, victim of an automobile accident.

Daniel

The day after Nixon was reelected in November 1972 Frankel went to New York to prepare for taking over as Sunday editor. Clifton Daniel, former managing editor who had become associate editor after Rosenthal took over the managing editorship, took on the assignment of Washington bureau chief. For a while the two men commuted to their new jobs, Daniel flying to Washington from New York, Frankel flying from Washington to New York.

The Washington bureau of *The Times* historically did not react easily to a change of command and the shift from Frankel to Daniel proved no exception. Daniel was not well known in Washington, had never worked there and had not been in direct charge of a news

---

*Philip Geyelin, editorial page editor of the *Washington Post*, thought "voice-activated" were the two most important words of Watergate and wrote an editorial to that effect. His point: Nixon could not now contend the tape wasn't switched on and had failed to record critical conversations. (Personal interview, Geyelin, 4/19/79)

operation for two or three years. To many in Washington he was an outsider, known only for his role in the ill-fated effort to depose Wicker several years previously.

Daniel, however, contrary to the assumption of some Washington correspondents, was a professional and during his brief tenure in Washington came to win high regard and genuine affection. One of the first and in some ways most surprising of Daniel's achievements was to forge a warm and close bond with Hersh, the total loner, the man who ate editors alive.

There were probably several reasons why Hersh finally moved onto the Watergate story. Professional pride, for one. He had stood aloof during summer and much of autumn but it was increasingly plain that Watergate was not going to go away; that it was likely to be the great story of the era, certainly in Washington; and it was impossible for a man of Hersh's competitive instincts not to get into it.

The skillful and sympathetic approach of Daniel played a role. Hersh had not gotten along with Frankel—no fireworks, simply a lack of compatibility. Nor was Hersh exactly Reston's style of reporter although as time went on even Reston began to take a fancy to his chutzpah.

In the end a totally extraneous circumstance helped to propell Hersh into Watergate. In late autumn he heard that a man named Andrew St. George, a free-lance writer who had often written about Castro and who had close contacts with the anti-Castro colony in Miami, was circulating the outline of a book which he proposed to write in collaboration with Frank Sturgis, one of the four Miami men involved in Watergate. This titillated Hersh's fancy. About the time Daniel came to Washington Hersh began to investigate the Sturgis story and soon, with Daniel's encouragement, having made contact with St. George, was in touch with Sturgis himself.

By December 1972 Hersh was hooked on Watergate, and by New Year's Day had produced a three-part series that, in the final event, was consolidated into one long story which appeared in *The Times* January 14, 1973. Hersh revealed that four Watergate defendants were still receiving financial support; that CREEP had paid them out of $900,-000 in 1972 campaign funds; that the Republicans had undercover agents in both the Muskie and McGovern campaign organizations and, most important, that John Mitchell knew what was going on and was aware of the Watergate break-in. The last item was the kicker, and this, in Hersh's memory, led to some delay in publishing because of threat of a libel action by Mitchell. But in the end the story was published, including the Mitchell part. There had been trouble in both New York and Washington over the sourcing, it was not as clear and complete as *The Times* liked, but Hersh remembered telling the editors that "at some point you will just have to believe me and trust me. A number of guys had told me about the story." *The Times* did trust Hersh. It published the story. At long last the great investigative story and the great investigative reporter had been linked. They would stay together for the duration of Watergate.

36

The Age of the Hippopotami

J AMES NAUGHTON, a laconic man with a devil's instinct for practical jokes (he once smuggled a ewe into the hotel room of a bucolic colleague, then smuggled its cost into his *Times'* expense account; he appeared at a Ford press conference wearing a giant chicken's head and complained that "your campaign puts me in a fowl mood"), was working on the *Cleveland Plain Dealer* in 1968 when Gene Roberts, *The New York Times* Atlanta correspondent, came North to report racial violence in Cleveland. *The Times Magazine* wanted Roberts to do an article on Carl Stokes, the new black mayor, but Roberts was leaving for an assignment in Vietnam and recommended Naughton, whom he had met on the Cleveland streets. Naughton wrote the piece and it was published, no questions, no rewrite, the first draft straight into print. Naughton had no idea that this was unusual and when he was asked to do another article promptly wrote it and it, too, was accepted, no questions, no rewrite. This happened four times in a row and Naughton thought that was the way the *Times Magazine* operated (often the magazine required three or four rewrites and it rejected half the articles it commissioned). Then he got an offer to work in *The Times* Washington bureau and instantly accepted it.

By 1972 Naughton was covering national politics and had been assigned to George McGovern's presidential campaign. McGovern mentioned Watergate only occasionally but late in the campaign he made a major speech about it, so late that political writers regarded the speech as an act of desperation but Naughton felt it was lucky he made it, at least McGovern put himself on record. Although Naughton was distanced from Watergate by the constant travel of the campaign he suspected there was a good possibility that it might be traced back to Nixon and the White House.

When Nixon defeated McGovern in November, Naughton was out of an assignment. Traditionally the reporter who covered as candidate went on to the White House when his man won. When his man lost it was another matter and within a week or so Naughton got his new post—he would be covering Congress instead of the President. Naughton told Robert Semple he didn't envy him the White House beat. All Semple could look forward to was covering the President while he, Naughton, could look forward to the story of Nixon's impeachment. As Naughton later conceded he did not have total confidence that impeachment would come about but it seemed like a good long shot.

Naughton went on to report the Erwin committee and the House Judiciary Committee proceedings which led to the recommendation of impeachment, and, in the end, to Nixon's resignation, effective at noon, Friday, August 9, 1974. It was the story of a lifetime.

When Naughton made his declaration the Watergate exposé did not appear to be in very healthy shape. It had become increasingly difficult for reporters to pry out new revelations as the autumn weeks wore down to the November election. In fact, for the first time a bit of puffing had appeared in the Woodward and Bernstein reporting, particularly in their exclusive October 10 on the dirty campaign tricks of Donald Segretti* and former *Post* reporter Ken Clawson, then working for the White House and now exposed as author of the infamous "Canuk letter" which was used against Senator Edward Muskie in the 1972 New Hampshire primary campaign.†

The Woodward and Bernstein story declared that at least fifty undercover Nixon operatives had been engaged in a nationwide campaign of dirty tricks against the Democrats. The story provoked a powerful reaction from the White House, which claimed the *Post* was throwing mud in the final weeks of the election.

The *Post,* competitive though it was, was somewhat relieved when *The Times* published an exclusive by Rugaber on October 18, 1972, confirming, in effect, the Segretti story and tying him to the White House, revealing that he had made innumerable telephone calls to White House aide Dwight Chapin. *The Times* had gotten the story when a stringer walked into a small Southern California telephone office, asked for a copy of Segretti's telephone calls and the clerk obligingly duplicated the list and handed it over without blinking an eye. Rugaber's story confirmed the Segretti connection with the White House but evidence of "at least fifty undercover operatives" never surfaced.

What had begun to happen, although the reporters and editors didn't quite understand it, was that they were reaching the outer limits of their investigatory abilities, lacking the subpoena powers of the

Times reporter Bob Smith got a tip on this story in July from a contact in the Justice Department. He wasn't where he could take notes but memorized the name by repeating to himself "Segretti, Spaghetti" over and over. *The Times* did not follow up the tip.

†The letter was designed to turn voters of French-Canadian origin in the New Hampshire primary by falsely accusing Muskie of referring to them as "Canucks."

courts and the Congress. Not even the advent of *The Times'* redoubtable Sy Hersh stirred up a great storm. Hersh's comprehensive story of January 14, 1973, laid the basis for future big exclusives but, in fact, Watergate had hit a patch of dead water from which it would not emerge until March and the letter from James McCord to Judge John J. Sirica charging that political pressure had been applied to cause the Watergate defendants to plead guilty, that there had been failure to identify others involved in the plot and false insinuations spread that it was a CIA scheme. He asked to talk privately with Sirica for fear of retaliatory measures against him and his family.

The McCord letter heated the limping scandal to incandescence. Actually, the elaborate cover-up within the White House had begun to come apart although no one on the outside, none of the investigative reporters or their editors would realize this until much later.

Now the conjunction of the McCord letter, the disclosures of the L. Patrick Gray nomination hearings and the accelerating Senate investigation under Senator Sam Erwin began to give the story a momentum which even reporters like Woodward, Bernstein, Hersh and Jack Nelson of the *Los Angeles Times* found hard to keep up with.

For the sixteen months which were to pass before Richard Nixon's resignation it was to be the Legislative and Judicial branches of the government that made the pace on Watergate. This was not entirely perceived either by the public or the press. By this time the romantic image of Woodward and Bernstein, the attractive, endlessly energetic reporters, two young Davids pitted against the Goliath of the White House, had captured popular and professional imagination.

"The attraction of the two young police reporters bringing down the President was irresistible," Rugaber was to say much later. "And they *did* do a hell of a job."

Rugaber was right. The legend of Woodward and Bernstein, solidly based on fact and achievement, was fully formed by this time. It would not be demolished in the future no matter how much good reporting was done by Hersh and the others. It did not require best-selling books or superb motion pictures to create it. The reporters and their work had done it.

The Investigative Reporters

Young John Crewdson, learning investigative mechanics in the fastest league, soon began to reach maturity. In June of 1973, tracking a persisting rumor that somewhere in the Nixon Administration a plan had been conceived for what was called "selective domestic assassination," Crewdson flew to Indianapolis with another *Times* reporter named Chris Lydon. There they confronted in his comfortable law offices Tom Charles Huston, one-time security adviser to Mr. Nixon and author of what became notorious as the "Huston plan" for domestic security—bugging, mail covers, surveillance. The reporters braced him with the rumors about "selective assassination." "That's ridiculous," said Huston, and pulled out the plan he had submitted to the White House, going over it point by point. He was right. There was nothing in it about domestic assassination. Crewdson asked if he could have a copy to "set the record straight" and Huston obliged. Crewdson and Lydon hurried back to Washington with a major revelation. A bit later a friend of Crewdson's in the FBI put the full FBI file on Segretti in a briefcase, walked out of the building and turned it over to the *Times* reporter. And through those weeks, bit by bit, Crewdson obtained the names of all seventeen reporters and officials who had been wiretapped by the FBI, many at the suggestion of Henry Kissinger.

In normal times these stories might have won Crewdson a Pulitzer Prize. But this was no normal year, the stories were mere grist for the Watergate mill and the Pulitzer Prize was won by the *Washington Post*. As had been the case with *The Times* and the Pentagon Papers, the prize went to the *Post* as an institution rather than to Woodward and Bernstein, and, just as many on *The Times* felt Neil Sheehan should have gotten the prize for the Pentagon Papers, so many felt the *Post*'s prize should have gone to the young reporters. The fact was the *Post* almost missed the prize; it had been passed over in the preliminary judging, and had not the McCord and Dean disclosures suddenly put the story front and center the Pulitzer judges once again might have missed the boat.

There was on April 8, 1973, a dinner that symbolized the new balance of forces. It brought together for the first time the *Post*'s young pride, Woodward and Bernstein, and *The Times'* Sy Hersh. This dinner of champions was arranged by David Obst, a literary agent who had sold the My Lai story for Hersh and was then acting as agent for Woodward and Bernstein (he was also Ellsberg's agent and later was to become a vice president of Simon & Schuster).

The group met at Hersh's house for drinks and went on to a Chinese restaurant called the Shanghai on the Lee Highway in Virginia. Chinese food was one of Hersh's passions. The reporters joined in airing their gripes about the *Post* and *The Times*, their hang-ups and their coups. They expressed themselves freely about the men in the White House, the subjects of their exposés and their investigations. There was talk of war criminals but very little of heroes.

In the course of the evening Hersh put on record his philosophy about investigative journalism. Speaking of Henry Kissinger, Hersh said, "I'd really love to get that son-of-bitch. I know him from way before Watergate. But he'll get no cheap shots from me—either I get him hard with facts, solid information, evidence, the truth or I don't touch him."*

Hersh's words spoke for the three of them. They were the hardest-hitting reporters in the world. They went up against the big ones. But they were not tainted by the morals of the men about whom they wrote. No dirty tricks, no corner-cutting. Just the truth. The truth was more devastating than anything.

It did not really matter now whether *The New York Times* was to print a string of Watergate exclusives—that Hersh, as he said, "got very hot" that spring and broke the story of the White House wiretaps, the Dwight Chapin resignation, John Mitchell's trip to the grand jury, the secret Cambodian bombing, and the very basic fact that the cover-up was not so much triggered by Watergate as by fear that other "White House horrors" would be exposed—or that Woodward and Bernstein would on April 19 publish a story quoting Magruder as saying that Mitchell and Dean had approved the Watergate operation.

To be sure, the newspaper competition went on, deadly and serious to its participants, and Clifton Daniel was always to remember the night of April 18, 1973, "as the worst I ever spent in my newspaper career." That evening he was at dinner at the British Embassy in Washington when he got a telephone call. The *Washington Post* was out with an eight-column banner—Magruder spills the whole story, or words to that effect. It filled half of page one. Daniel went back to the dinner table, sat quietly a few moments until dessert was finished, then excused himself and raced to the *Times* office. He found a pick-up staff trying to get the facts but it was apparent that unless they reached Magruder they could not match the *Post.* For some reason R. W. Apple, nominally covering the White House, was trying to put together a story. Half a dozen other reporters were calling over town, an endless and fruitless series of telephone calls. "They didn't have the right numbers," Daniel said. They never got to anyone who could confirm the *Post*'s detail and wound up with something which did little more than quote from Woodward and Bernstein. "It was a lousy story," Daniel remembered. "I'll never forget it." But, typically, that same night *The Times* had its own lesser exclusive, Hersh reporting that Attorney General Kleindienst had disqualified himself from handling Watergate because three or more of his colleagues might be indicted and John Dean was ready to implicate others in the cover-up. Not a bad night for the two fiercely competitive newspapers.

There is something about the nature of newspapers that causes

---

*In 1979 Hersh was to leave *The New York Times* to write a book about Kissinger. He had hoped to get a leave of absence to do the project but Rosenthal refused, giving Hersh no option but to quit.

reporters and editors to see things small rather than large; to concentrate on the breaking story rather than long-range implications; to focus their attention on getting a story first and ahead of "the opposition" rather than sitting back, thinking through the philosophical implications of the event and then publishing conclusions. It used to be said before consumerism made the simile archaic that yesterday's newspaper was "what you wrapped dead fish in."

In going back over the Watergate record it is clear that the press, in fact, played its assigned role. It was the alarm crier, the night watchman, the sentry at post, the lookout on the hill. It spotted something wrong, something terribly wrong, and reported it to the country, which had no other way of knowing that anything untoward had happened. It alerted the public, it triggered the investigatory agencies of the independent arms of government, of the Legislative and Judicial branches, and under impetus of competitive reporting in the classic tradition roused the country to what Dean was to call "the cancer" in the Executive Branch.

But for the most part neither at the time nor later did the editors see themselves in these roles. Rather, they felt and acted as competitors in a paper chase which led into the White House. They did not halt to draw sociological lessons nor did they often stop to compose essays in political science because, in fact, that was not their primary function. Their function was to dig out the facts as rapidly and accurately as possible, exercising as much ingenuity and energy as they possessed. Once the facts were presented it was the duty of others, the public and their sworn representatives, to take such action as was necessary.

This was why during the Watergate days it would have been hard if not impossible to find among those concerned with the reporting any discussion of the broadened powers which now lay in the hands of the press, thanks to the court decisions in the Pentagon Papers case, in *Sullivan* and in *Connor*.

When Clifton Daniel invited a group of twenty senior members of the Washington staff of *The New York Times* to dinner at the pleasant house just off Foxhall Road where he and his wife, Margaret Truman Daniel, lived to discuss the work of the bureau with Seymour Topping, assistant managing editor, in September of 1973, there was no one present who talked of the theory of American Government, of changes in the American Establishment, of the legal rights of the press, of the constitutional privileges of the White House.

What was discussed was Watergate and the fact that for all the efforts of the bureau (and the record had been sparkling since the spring of 1973) it was still perceived by the public and, more significantly, in the belief of bureau members, by management in New York as doing a second-class job.

It did not matter whether this was actually what the public thought; nor, in fact, the image held by Rosenthal (although this had been his perception in an earlier period)—it was the way the bureau felt that it was seen and, as Topping was to explain, he had come to Washington "to try to get the monkey of Watergate off the bureau's back."

Bill Kovach, by this time news editor in Washington, talked to many of the writers before they went to Daniel's house. He was anxious that those at the meeting discuss substance and get away from what he called "the Watergate syndrome," the feeling of the reporters that whatever they did, New York thought they had come in second.

"Actually," Kovach said, "the bureau was really very much on top of the story."*

Daniel served a fine dinner, a catered meal. The Daniels were not much given to home cooking and any that was done was usually done by Clifton.

"What I remember best about the evening," Crewdson said later, "was the wine. It was terrific, a very good red Bordeaux."

That was almost the only good thing about the meeting. Naughton spoke and made his points well. He said he had never belonged to an organization that was Number Two and he was sick and tired of hearing that *The Times* was Number Two on Watergate. He no longer thought that it was possible for the bureau to prove to New York that it was Number One. The New York attitude was ingrained. It was probably historical and institutional. He felt that *The Times* had a fine Washington bureau and, in Clifton Daniel, a fine chief. Later he was to pay tribute to Daniel for maintaining the bureau's morale under excessively difficult conditions. "He was caught in the middle," Naughton said, "and he swallowed a lot of frustration without ever letting the men in the bureau know."

But after Naughton's remarks the meeting degenerated into anger, personalities, and complaints that the New York editors were insisting on levels of sourcing impossible under realistic conditions, that nitpicking had replaced editing, that the bureau was not trusted.

Finally Kovach said, "I'm not going to listen to any more of this bullshit. Everyone is excusing himself for what he did and blaming the other guy. It's time to get onto something new and quit wallowing in the past."

He walked out and the meeting dribbled to a bathetic close. (Hersh did not attend the dinner. It wasn't his style.)

---

*About this time Reston told some of the men working on Watergate that if it was up to him he would take them on the last Atlantic passage of the *France* (which had just been announced) as a reward for their hard work and good job. (Personal interview, Naughton, 3/30/79) This was hardly the attitude in New York.

This was hardly what might have been expected from as expert a group of newsmen as could be assembled in one room. But it was symptomatic of what competitive strain and internal stress had brought to a finely tuned reporting team.

Significance

There was not to be found in such moods (or the equivalent mood of editors in New York, where, as Rosenthal recollected, "I'd come in in the morning and start screaming") the detachment required for analysis of what was actually happening: that the *Washington Post* and *The New York Times* were fulfilling the functions specifically enumerated in the First Amendment and confirmed in landmark Supreme Court decisions. This process was going forward despite the fact that investigative reporters had penetrated the core of the American system, the White House, the office of the Chief Executive, that of the presidency itself and the President's nearest and closest associates.

Not in the history of the American state had this occurred. The petty quarreling, backbiting, faultfinding, the nerve-jangling competition for deadlines and stories was a small price to pay. The founders of the American Constitution had not specified that a charter of freedom, a charter of press responsibility was something light and without burden. It would not have occurred to them to state that the price of liberty was pain and anguish. This was in their bones. It did not have to be expressed because that was the way they had won their freedom. To them the anxieties of the staff of *The New York Times,* for example, would have seemed trivial indeed.

The truth was that neither the *Post* nor *The Times* gave much thought to the Founding Fathers. It is doubtful that Woodward or Bernstein were conscious of Judge Gurfein's words about "a cantankerous press, an obstinate press, a ubiquitous press" even as they acted into life the principles he had committed to paper in his decision of Saturday, June 19, 1971. Nor is it likely that Rosenthal thought much about the cloak of protective security which had been thrown over the press by the decision of Justice Brennan in the Sullivan case.

Not infrequently, as Watergate roared toward conclusion, the White House raised the threat of legal action against the press; there were repeated warnings of libel suits that would be brought against newspapers that published one story or another. But not one libel case was actually brought. The grounds had been cut from under the President and his intimates by the language of *Sullivan* and *Connor.* As U.S. Circuit Judge Thornberg wrote in *Connor,* "While verification of the facts remains an important reporting standard a reporter . . . may rely on statements made by a single source even though they reflect only one side of the story without fear of libel prosecution by a Public official." No Watergate story by *The Times* or the *Post* was published on the basis of a single source. Always two, three or even more were obtained.

Again and again Mr. Nixon raised or tried to raise the shield of "national security" to protect one hideous secret or another. It did not work. The Pentagon case had shorn him of credibility as far as "national security" was concerned—and would have shredded that protection even further had the truth of Nixon "security," as exposed in these pages, been publicly known.

As Floyd Abrams, years later assessing the implications of the Pentagon case, was to say, "It demonstrated that other societal interests, or the impingement on other societal interests do not pose enough threat to cause prior restraint. National security claims could not prevail against the greater claims of the press."

In Abrams' view the Pentagon case and subsequent Supreme Court rulings created what he called a "de facto" prohibition against prior restraint.*

To one man there was a short straight line that connected the Pentagon Papers with Watergate. This was Benjamin Bradlee, executive editor of the *Washington Post.*

"I've often said," he declared some years after Watergate, "that Watergate was decided when Kay Graham said that night 'Go ahead and print it.' "

He referred to the decision of Mrs. Graham over the protests of the lawyers for the *Post* to publish the Pentagon Papers after *The Times* had been halted by Judge Gurfein's order of prior restraint.

The Pentagon Papers to Bradlee's mind was the critical case, critical for the *Post* in assuming its full First Amendment responsibilities, critical for Watergate.

"It was of enormous importance for the *Post,*" he said. "It was the first time the *Post* decided to risk its assets in a bold and worthy cause. The *Post* could have said, shit, let *The Times* do it."

And, he could have added, *The Times* might have said in the Pentagon case, as *its* lawyers advised, no, we'll not publish unless the government gives us permission. Had *The Times* taken that decision in the Pentagon Papers it surely would not have gone forward to fight toe to toe with the *Post* for the facts of Watergate. Just as, in Bradlee's opinion, had the *Post* stepped back from publishing the Pentagon Papers until *The Times'* case was decided it would not have taken the broader and bolder challenge of Watergate.

---

*Abrams' remarks were made before U.S. District Judge Robert W. Warren in Madison, Wis., enjoined the *Progressive Magazine* in 1979 from publishing an article on the hydrogen bomb.

"Pentagon," said Bradlee, "had a most important effect on our development."

Bradlee did not believe that any other paper would have done what *The Times* did and what the *Post* did, except, possibly and aberrationally, the *Chicago Tribune* at the peak of the eccentric career of Colonel Robert R. McCormick.

"You know," Bradlee said, "I never agree with Abe Rosenthal on anything. But Abe is quoted as saying there are only two papers and then there is the rest of the press. Well, I didn't say it but I think I agree with him. We have benefited each other and I think the other papers too. I just can't think of any other papers around the country that would have done it."

The question would remain open as to whether without the press Watergate would have been exposed and the Nixon Administration brought to its dismal ending.

Historical precedent offered no real clues. Only one President of the United States had been impeached, Andrew Johnson in the angry, tortured aftermath of the Civil War. In this enterprise the press, the northern, partisan, bitter Republican press, served as lackey to the arrogant Republican Congress.

There was one other partial precedent—what might be called the posthumous impeachment of President Harding, the inquiry into Teapot Dome and the scandals which came after his death and which, had Harding still been living and in office, might have brought him down. Two newspapers played an exemplary role in the post-Harding investigations, the Pulitzer journals, the then surviving *World* in New York and the *St. Louis Post-Dispatch.*

Paul Anderson, the Washington correspondent of the *St. Louis Post-Dispatch,* took so prominent a part in that investigation that he was often credited with having brought about the exposure of Albert Fall, Sinclair and the rest of the "Ohio gang." He won a Pulitzer Prize but Anderson was not really an independent investigative reporter. He was at the side of Senator Tom Walsh of Montana, chairman of the Senate investigation. Anderson's wit, his knowledge of the Washington political scene, was of great value to Walsh's examination of witnesses, but the investigation that brought down Harding's men was carried on by Walsh's Senate staff.

Thus, in neither of the two historic cases could a direct parallel be drawn. There had not, to repeat the words of Barry Sussman, the *Post*'s city editor, ever been "a story like this before" and it moved like a Greek tragedy to Mr. Nixon's resignation, his tearful farewell to his White House staff and his departure for the last time by helicopter from the White House lawn. But he left behind him a multitude of unanswered questions and one concerned the press—specifically, *The New York Times.*

The role of the press had been redefined by Watergate, by the Pentagon Papers, by the decisions of the courts in the Alabama cases, by the new but scarcely tested function of the nation's journalists as surrogates of the public in monitoring the new hippopotami which now strewed the landscape—the bureaucracies which had burgeoned beyond human imagination, the imperial presidency, the military-industrial complex, the intelligence community, the welfare state, the supranational corporations, the aggregates of power, vested influence and pervasive authority in whose presence the ordinary citizen was little more than an intelligent pygmy.

After Watergate where would destiny lead *The New York Times,* the press, the country? There had been a tidal shift in power relationships. The American presidency had been diminished. Congress now stood supreme. The courts were stronger than ever. The press had assumed a new function. Did it possess the resources, the imagination, the vision and the courage of the responsibility thrust upon it?

37

Five Cents a Copy

*I*N THE AUTUMN OF 1977 Cyrus L. Sulzberger, nephew of Arthur and Iphigene Sulzberger, first cousin of Punch, was at the age of sixty-five approaching retirement from *The Times* after nearly forty years of work on the family's newspaper. It was a gloomy autumn, a gloomy time for Cy. He was a compulsive reporter and had been since he cut his teeth with the *Pittsburgh Press* during the Depression, just out of Harvard, bold as the March wind, dressed as a bum, living in flophouses, writing a notable series for his editor, Ed Leach, on what the breadline was like in 1933.

Cy, handsome, audacious, intelligent, had hoped to become a poet when he emerged from Harvard. His most precious possession of those years was a magnificent Salvador Dali which he had bought for $300. By late 1977 he was a sad, bitter man, no poet, the Dali sold,* his newspaper career coming to an end, his Marina, the Greek imp whom he had romantically married during World War II, tragically dead and his ambition to become editor of his uncle's newspaper long turned to dust. He was a stiff, proud man, partially deaf, plagued by gout, who had become more and more difficult with the passage of years and frustration of hopes. In 1977 he lived and worked in almost total isolation from his associates on *The Times,* on crusty terms with his relatives, with the exception of his incomparable aunt Iphigene, whose heart encompassed every member of her extraordinarily extended family, no matter how grumpy.

From the beginning Cy had been arrogant. He did not come to work on *The Times* when he finished Harvard because, as he often said, "I'll never ask my uncle for a job." This was not because of bad feeling.

---

*Cy bought the Dali at the Carnegie International Show in Pittsburgh which he covered (because the art critic was drunk) for the *Pittsburgh Press* in 1934. He paid for it on the installment plan, $12.50 a week from a $25 a week salary. He had to sell it in 1939 because he was broke and in debt. In 1945, when he came back to the United States, the purchaser, Thomas J. Watson, Sr., permitted Cy to buy it back from him. He finally sold the Dali in 1975 for $150,000 to buy a Paris apartment. (Letter, C. L. Sulzberger to author, 5/9/79)

Arthur Sulzberger had been surrogate for Cy's father, who died when Cy was six. It was simply Cy's posture. First he would become a newspaperman, first he would demonstrate his ability, and then, if his uncle wished, he would consider a career on *The Times*, this actually being his fierce ambition.

Cy was a natural newsman, prototype of the contemporary investigative reporter. In the years in which he worked under Lyle C. Wilson, chief of the United Press in Washington, he broke one exclusive after another, covering the labor beat, establishing intimate relations with men like John L. Lewis and the Reuther brothers, laying close lines to New Deal insiders like Tommy Corcoran and Benjamin Cohen, driving Harry Hopkins wild with his questions, never hesitating to call Eleanor Roosevelt or the head of U.S. Steel at any time of night. For a man who fancied himself a poet he had a deaf ear for prose, but as a terrier in digging facts he was cut of the stuff which fashioned a Sy Hersh, a Carl Bernstein, a Bob Woodward.

Had Cy been born into the generation of Mississippi Summer, Vietnam and Watergate he would have matched stories with the best of the best. That was the kind of reporter he made of himself before coming to *The Times*, a "scoop artist" in Reston's best sense of the word, a digger, a man with colossal effrontery, brash, brilliant.

The Bernstein Charges

In autumn 1977 the young Cy Sulzberger had long since vanished and the older Cy, a year after Marina's unexpected death, was melancholy. Two years earlier he had proposed his immediate retirement (he was thinking then of living in Ireland) but impulsively changed his mind and now approached compulsory retirement at sixty-five with unalloyed bitterness; he felt retirement was arbitrary and prejudicial; an exception should have been made; he was neurotically concerned about money.

In September of 1977 he had been, as he often was at that season of the year, staying at his villa on the Greek island of Spetsais. From the time of his marriage to Marina, Greece had been the lodestone of their life, she because it was her birthplace and she came from a family deeply engaged in Greek political and cultural life, and he because of Marina and because since his first days in Europe in 1937 he had been strongly drawn to and attached to Greece and the Balkans.

One afternoon in late September, Cy got a telephone call from the United States. At the other end of the line was just such an outrageous young reporter as Cy himself had been forty years before, Carl Bernstein, calling around the world, calling, calling, calling regardless of time, regardless of distance, regardless of person, trying to track down a story.

Later Cy was to suggest that he wasn't fully alert when he talked to Bernstein. To a friend who had sat beside him in the old UP Washington office on the seventh floor of the National Press Building and listened to him telephone Madame Perkins at 2 A.M. or get John L. Lewis out of bed at 3 A.M. to pry out an exclusive, Cy's words had an ironic flavor.

Bernstein was working on a story about connections between the CIA and newsmen. He did not yet know exactly what he would do with his piece (he had left the *Washington Post* after Watergate) and he told Cy it might appear in the *Columbia Journalism Review.* He had some questions to put to Cy. He had been told (by sources within the CIA, as it transpired) that Cy had such close ties that he was listed as what the CIA called "an asset" and that he had carried out specific tasks for the agency. Bernstein told Cy he had been told (also by CIA sources) that Arthur Hays Sulzberger had an understanding whereby *Times'* "cover" from 1950 to 1966 was provided to "about ten CIA operatives." Bernstein said he had been told that Cy and his uncle Arthur had signed what he called "secrecy" agreements with the CIA. Such documents, usually called "nondisclosure" statements, constituted a pledge by the signatory not to reveal information privately disclosed by the CIA.

Bernstein's charges appeared in *Rolling Stone,* October 20, 1977. Cy had told Bernstein he thought his uncle had signed a nondisclosure statement and that he might have, too, but denied any nonprofessional conduct.* He cited the locus of Bernstein's article with sarcasm. He had not known, he said, that *Rolling Stone* had a connection with Columbia.

But sarcasm was no real reply. Bernstein had the best of credentials, no one could challenge him as an investigative reporter. It was obvious that he had approached this matter with a keen sense of responsibility and full deployment of his reportorial skills.

The editors of *The Times,* Punch Sulzberger, his mother, Iphigene, and the family were distressed. Denials were issued, explanations were offered, Cy tried to persuade James Goodale to file a libel action on behalf of himself and *The Times.* But the essential question would not go away. Had the leading newspaper of the United States (and the world) been for many years in some sort of partnership with the CIA? Had the man who had served as chief European correspondent from late in World War II to 1955 and as *The Times'* commentator on foreign affairs a secret relationship with the CIA? It was not good enough to say that the image of the CIA had changed from its early, almost romantic, beginnings; that the agency was established by men

---

*Cy later told me he had signed "some kind of a release." (Letter to author, 11/17/77)

who were close and intimate friends of senior *Times'* personnel; that the dangers of the cold war validated many things which post-Vietnam, post-Watergate America found nonacceptable.

The Times had itself set the standards for reporting and editorial objectivity. If *The Times* and other newspapers were to fulfill their difficult and controversial task as watchdogs for the public; if they were to probe into a secret, lie-infested war; if they were to place before the nation the tough, unsavory facts of race conflict and inequality in the South (and the North); if they were to dig, dig, dig until they had dug out the dirty reality of Watergate, they must themselves face the same standards which they set for others. There could be no skeletons in the attic; no undercover deals; no double-talk.

Keeping It Straight

In later years, after he had become executive editor, Abe Rosenthal liked to say that his main ambition was "to keep *The Times* straight." By that he meant, essentially, to keep the faith, keep faith with the ideals, principles and practices of *The Times* despite changes in the world, changes in society, technology and of taste. What he felt important was that while incorporating into *The Times* the gadgetry of computers, electronics and photo composition; while constructing a new economic platform to support an automated infrastructure; while confecting rich soufflés for young readers turned off by the tastes of Krock and Catledge he would maintain the traditions that had made *The Times;* made it and made it great; objectivity of the news, catholicity in its selection, decency, goodwill, honesty—a paper you wanted to read, must read, and a paper you could trust.

There was nothing new about this. It had been Arthur Sulzberger's goal when Mr. Ochs' mantle fell on his shoulders. In fact, so important was his feeling for continuity that he put aside projects for change already under way before Mr. Ochs died in 1935. He postponed, for example, the abandonment of the rotogravure section for a whole year because he did not wish anyone to think that with Mr. Ochs' death he was out to change *The Times.* It was Turner Catledge's boast that he had transformed *The Times* from a paper as stylistically indifferent as a Sears Roebuck catalogue without a reader noticing that it was no longer the good, gray *Times.* (Rosenthal considered that he had done the same thing!) The reading type of *The Times* was gradually increased from 6 point to 8.5 point, with hardly a reader understanding why the paper had become so much easier to read.

Gradualness was not exactly Rosenthal's style but he saw himself as the inheritor of *The Times'* traditions and these he would defend to the last, no matter that some of his critics called him the chief despoiler of *The Times'* virtues.

In no field was Rosenthal more vigilant than that of maintaining the purity of the news columns. Nothing sent him more quickly into one of his famous tantrums than something that he perceived as an effort to pervert the paper; to slant its news stories; to turn *The Times* to some subversive, self-serving or venial end. To him the paper was like Caesar's wife. When his suspicion was aroused he became Othello.

In Rosenthal's vigilance he was at one with Arthur Hays Sulzberger although Rosenthal's demons were, perhaps, somewhat different. Arthur Hays Sulzberger's first great battle to "keep *The Times* straight" (an expression he would have abhorred; he was an elegant man and stylish in his English usage) began in the mid-1930s and arose from the unionization and radicalization touched off by the Great Depression and Mr. Roosevelt's New Deal. Unions were not exactly Arthur Sulzberger's long suit but he was prepared to deal fairly with them. Mr. Ochs had always run a union shop, was proud of his membership in the Typographers Union and unions had never troubled *The Times.* But the typographers, the printers, the linotypers, the pressmen were craft unions, among the oldest in industry. What the New Deal brought was the American Newspaper Guild, a union of writers and white-collar workers, organized in New York by the famous radical columnist of the *World* and *World-Telegram,* Heywood Broun. The American Communist Party, active, feisty and omnipresent in the New York of the thirties, played a major role in the guild.

Arthur Sulzberger could grit his teeth and put up with a union of his editorial employees; he could grit them harder and deal with a union in which Communist influence was known and strong. But he was not then or ever prepared to turn over his staff to the control of an outside influence. In his first public statement to *The Times'* staff on the guild he said, "The management has never sought to know whether this or that person was affiliated with the guild any more than it has inquired into the individual's church membership or political party adherence."

Later he was to change this position as far as Communist Party membership was concerned but in general this was to remain his basic philosophy. But he was adamantly opposed to a closed union shop for news and editorial workers, contending that it would not be possible to maintain the purity of the news and the objectivity of reporting and editing if newsmen were compelled to belong to an organization that took political positions, strong positions, often far to the left. For many years it was well known that Arthur Sulzberger was not prepared to take a strike on *The Times* on any issue other than that of the closed shop in the news department. On that he was adamant.

These were years of political passions, many of them symbolized by the Spanish civil war. The city room of *The Times* was violently divided over this cause; there was a "Catholic" faction which backed Generalissimo Franco and William Carney, who reported from Nationalist Spain, and a "liberal" faction which supported Herbert L. Matthews, who reported the Loyalist side. It was literally true that, quite probably at the instruction of Edwin L. James, the somewhat remote managing editor, himself a Catholic, the members of the "Catholic" bullpen edited the two reporters with a ruler, trying each night to give them a roughly equal number of inches; that night after night the "play" story changed, one night the Nationalists, the next the Loyalists, with little regard for the story's overall importance. The air rang with charges that Carney was a "fascist," that Matthews was a "communist."* These absurdities troubled Sulzberger but not so seriously as the possibility that a halter might be placed on his staff by a militant union. He knew both *The Times'* correspondents in Spain personally. He knew that Carney was not a fascist but a devout Catholic who permitted his feelings to color his reporting. He had known Matthews from the time he came to work for Frederick Birchall in the 1920s as private secretary; had known him when he was accused of being a fascist for the enthusiasm with which he covered Mussolini's invasion of Ethiopia. He knew that the campaign against Matthews had been orchestrated to some extent by the very conservative (at that time) Roman Catholic Archdiocese of Brooklyn and supported by many Catholic readers of *The Times.* He regarded all this as a nuisance and he was sensitive to its economic implications but it never caused him to doubt his judgment of his men. Matthews was to remain a respected member of *The Times'* staff although before his retirement in 1967 he managed to inspire another and even greater controversy with his reporting on Fidel Castro.

The outbreak of World War II was to bring to Arthur Hays Sulzberger another concern over the independence and objectivity of his staff. There were in 1939 a number of non-Americans on *The Times'* staff abroad. In part this was a legacy of the Ochs day. Partly because Americans with expertise, for instance, in Central Europe or the Middle East were scarce and partly because foreigners could be hired more cheaply, *The Times* traditionally had many non-American foreign correspondents, particularly Englishmen. Not long after the outbreak of the war Sulzberger learned that a number of these correspondents had

---

*Matthews preserved the originals of the cables he filed from Spain. Robert L. Barber, a student at Princeton, made an exhaustive study of Matthews' dispatches as written and as published in *The Times* for a bachelorian thesis in 1971. This meticulous study leaves no doubt that the editing of Matthews' work was seriously biased. No comparable study seems to have been made of Carney's dispatches. (Robert L. Barber, *The Politics of Journalism*, April 1971, unpublished thesis)

connections with MI-6, the British intelligence agency.* He was very angry. Despite his strong pro-English sympathies he told Scotty Reston that he would never again hire a foreign national as a correspondent; they could not serve two masters. The danger to the news report was too great. Scotty, born in Scotland, took a cooler, canny, Caledonian view. "You're going to have to hire foreigners," he said. "Even *The Times* can't afford American correspondents in every part of the world."

Arthur Sulzberger regarded any intelligence link with his staff as a grave matter. He was a patriotic man, had served in World War I and felt, as one of his associates said, that *The Times* was not only a *public* institution but an *American* institution. He was prepared to help his country in almost any way. During World War II *The Times* repeatedly withheld information which it felt should not be published in the national interest even though censorship did not require this. But this did not mean Sulzberger was prepared to turn *The Times* into an adjunct of the American Government. When Colonel William Donovan set up the OSS in 1942 he came to Sulzberger with a proposal that *The Times* and its staff be placed at the disposal of American intelligence. He wanted *Times* correspondents to double in brass, reporting not only to *The Times* but to the OSS; to carry out intelligence tasks where possible as part of the war effort. Sulzberger refused. Even in wartime he was not willing to compromise the integrity of *The Times'* staff.

Cy Sulzberger

By the end of World War II Arthur Sulzberger had an intimate personal grasp of the cadre of men who comprised the foreign staff of *The Times.* They were perhaps not quite so brilliant at writing as were the Homer Bigarts, the Allen Raymonds, the Joe Barnes, Walter Kerrs and Jeff Parsons of the *Herald-Tribune* but they were, for the most part, young vigorous correspondents, quick to respond to the news and capable in dealing with it—men like William H. Lawrence (later to become famous as a political reporter), Drew Middleton in Germany, Gladwin Hill with the Air Force, Clifton Daniel, Brooks Atkinson, a converted drama critic who was to re-convert, Raymond "Pete" Daniell, and veterans like Harold Callender and Arnaldo Cortesi, a formidable lineup, capable of coping with any eventuality. None had built a better record than Sulzberger's own nephew Cy. Cy had gone to Europe in 1938 after publishing a warm, readable book called *Sit Down*

*In the memory of one *Times* staff man leaks to British intelligence through *The Times* continued after U.S. entry into the war. (Personal interview, Hanson Baldwin, 4/23/79)

with John L. Lewis, probably the best piece of writing ever to come from his typewriter. He had been compelled to leave UP in Washington, which felt Cy's book too sympathetic to the left-wing villain, as Lewis was then perceived, to permit Cy to meet UP's standards of objectivity. Cy had gone to Europe, burying himself in the Balkans, saturating himself in the languages, culture and complex politics, supporting himself by writing for the London papers, packing in background, building up contacts. He was sure World War II would come and convinced that, like World War I, it would start in the Balkans. Hardly an American correspondent ventured beyond Vienna except for an occasional weekend of wine and women in Budapest. Cy set about to establish himself as an authority, certain this would be money in his pocket. Thirty years later in Sofia, Bucharest and particularly in Belgrade, he still possessed friends who had known him in the days when they were all students, revolutionaries and poor as only Balkan students can be poor. Cy may not have been as radical as they but there was nothing he enjoyed more than tossing a brick through the window of the comfortable and the complacent.

Cy was in Sofia when Munich broke in 1938 and got an urgent cable to meet his uncle in London. Arthur Sulzberger wanted his nephew on *The Times* then and there. Cy refused. He felt he had an obligation to Lord Beaverbrook for whom he was working but he agreed that when war did break out he would join *The Times* and meantime he would go back to the Balkans, set up a network of string correspondents for *The Times* and establish a communications system.

On September 1, 1939, the day Hitler marched into Poland, Frederick Birchall called Cy from Berlin. He was in Bucharest. "Well, laddie," said Birchall, "the time has come."

By the end of the war Cy had a long string of firsts. He was the first *Times* man back into Russia after Hitler's attack (in a fit of pique *The Times* had abandoned coverage of Moscow during the Russo-Finnish war) and his first dispatch brought what some thought was incredibly naïve and others remarkably sophisticated news—word that Russians wore shoes, a metaphor for the fact that they still had the means to carry on in the fierce and difficult war. Cy had reported out of Turkey, having been driven from the Balkans by the Germans, leaving behind his beautiful Marina (but broadcasting his dispatches over Ankara radio, spelling out the difficult words, *M* for Marina, *L* for love, which she miraculously intercepted in starving Athens, inspiring her to make a dangerous journey across the Nazi lines to join Cy, they getting married in Cairo in 1942). He had reported the rise and fall of the desert war, Rommel, Montgomery and Alexander; had fought the censors and the red tape until the British put a king's X on his passport and it took him three months to get the redoubtable Mrs. Ruth Shipley of the State Department to permit him back into the Middle East.

There in Cairo he had met with Vlado Dedijer, recuperating from wounds in a military hospital, learned the story of the young Yugoslav radicals with whom he had drunk slivovitz in the cafés of Belgrade. The story Vlado told was the epic of Tito's partisans and Cy's dispatch occupied more than two pages in *The New York Times* of December 22, 1943. It was the first story of the Yugoslav partisan war behind the German lines, an enormous scoop, and at a single stroke it established Tito as the force to contend with in Yugoslavia, gave him a world reputation, cast the Chetnik movement of Mihailovich into doubt. It was, in a word, a political event of the first water.

But in a personal sense it was a tale of tragedy. Of the students with whom Cy sat in the Belgrade cafes only one, Vlado Dedijer, was still alive and he had hung for weeks at the edge of death with a bullet in his brain. Cy wrote of sitting in the cafés with Dedijer, with Ivan Ribar, Jr., with Mira Popova, with Vlado's wife, Olga, with Slobodan Principe, tobacco smoke clouding the air, gypsies striking their tambourines. He told of the deaths of each of his friends; of Principe, dead of German bullet wounds and typhus in late 1943; Popova, captured by the Chetniks, turned over to the Italians and executed; Ribar, killed by a German bomb together with a British liaison officer; and finally Olga, who had once danced like a flame to the music of the cymbalon, her shoulder torn off by German shrapnel, no medication, nine days staggering with the partisans over mountain trails, her arm amputated on an open field where gray and black magpies picked the thinly sown seeds, refusing a heart stimulant, sinking to her death, buried in flinty soil in a shallow hole dug with knives. Vlado, himself terribly wounded, took her revolver as a memento. It lay by his side in the Cairo hospital bed as he talked to Cy. It was the best story Cy had ever written, the best story he was ever to write.*

In 1944 Cy had joined Eisenhower for D-Day in France and from that time forward covered the European war, SHAEF, the entry into Paris, the whole glory and glitter of the war's end.

Edwin L. James was still managing editor of *The Times*. He had been Mr. Ochs' choice and, naturally, Arthur Sulzberger was thinking of the future and a possible successor. Cy felt that he was entitled to consideration and his uncle did not discourage him although a realist would have been bound to list Cy's name third, below those of Turner

*Later Cy and Vlado were to quarrel violently over Cy's postwar writing. But with Marina's death, Vlado, half ill, wrote Cy a letter of reconciliation. He knew the deep sorrow Marina's loss had brought to his wartime comrade. (Personal interview, Dedijer, 4/17/79)

Catledge of whom Arthur Sulzberger was very fond and Scotty Reston, the endlessly energetic, appealing, ambitious young Scot who had informed Sulzberger confidentially and confidently that his aspiration was one of the top management roles in *The Times.*

Still, of the three, Cy was *family* and a great favorite of his uncle's. There was in their relationship an inner affection which grew out of Arthur's role as surrogate father. He was proud of Cy, proud of the way he had succeeded during the war and Cy had rounded off the edges of his relationship with his uncle, feeling he had demonstrated that he was a newspaperman in his own right, regardless or in spite of his name. He had made his own way and in his self-confidence it is not likely that he saw in Catledge or Reston competitors whom he could not outdistance.

Cy's confidence was not a matter of airy projection. His uncle recognized his nephew's abilities in making him chief European correspondent in 1944. He was to be not only chief European correspondent with the right and duty to travel anywhere in Europe (or the world, should he so desire); cover any story which was his fancy but was given supervisory authority over the European correspondents; a job which met Cy's immediate aspirations and raised his expectations for the future; an assignment which more or less made him boss of his peers among *Times* correspondents, enabled him (within some limits) to pick and assign correspondents and placed him inevitably in conflict with managing editor James and ultimately with the man Sulzberger had chosen as James' Number One assistant, Turner Catledge, a politician to his fingertips, blessed with a soft-shoe, southern style, and sitting 3,000 miles closer to Sulzberger than Cy, who in the twenty years to follow was in constant motion, crisscrossing Europe, often girdling the globe several times a year.

If the CIA had tried to invent a journalist who would be eternally useful to its intelligence arm it could not have created a better one than Cyrus Leo Sulzberger. (Maurice Delarue of *Le Monde* called him "this Prince of journalism.") But the mere fact that he existed, the fact that he controlled a network of correspondents, a pool of information which could rival or exceed in quality that of the fledgling American Secret Service did not mean that he or the information pool was necessarily any more available to the CIA than it was to anyone else who could afford the price which in those times was five cents a copy.

38

"The Paris Workings"

O N DECEMBER 31, 1913, the "Great Magister," Aleister Crowley, a
practitioner of the black arts, magico-sexual rituals, a latter-day
Nicodemus and guru, began what his followers later came to call "The
Paris Workings."

Crowley, an Englishman, of extravagant sexual eccentricity, was a
believer in ancient magic, fertility rites, pseudo-religious sexual rituals,
mumbo-jumbo, perversions and opium. He depended on his sexual
magic, one way or another, to provide him with funds, of which he was
in perennial need since he devoted his life to sexual visions, sexual
explorations, sexual rites and writings—by the time of his death he had
written almost a hundred volumes, recounting in minute detail every
sensation experienced by his private parts or perceived by his cerebel-
lum and calibrating each nervous twitch with cabalistic symbols.

The "workings" of December 31, 1913, and twenty-three "workings" which followed each few days until February 12, 1914, were
recorded in the linguistic code which characterized Crowley's cult and
would today be of interest only to collectors of erotica were it not for
the identity of one of the participants. Crowley began the proceedings
which, in his mind, were designed to evoke the gods Jupiter and
Mercury, "by receiving the sacrament" from a certain priest "A.B."
A.B. was Walter Duranty who had on December 1, 1913, that is just
thirty days previously, been hired by Wythe Williams as a member of
the staff of *The New York Times* bureau in Paris on a promise that he
would get a story for *The Times* about an airplane that could fly upside
down.

Duranty was a young Englishman, born in Liverpool (not the Isle of
Man as he sometimes romanticized) who had attended, it was said,
Harrow and gone on to Cambridge. Crowley was his close friend. After
the homosexual act the Priest A.B. painted a magical symbol of the god
Mercury, called a pentacle. Another partner named Victor Neuburg
danced what was called "the Banishing Ritual of the Pentagram" and
Crowley flogged Neuburg on the buttocks, cut a cross over his heart
and bound a chain around his forehead. The two men engaged in

another homosexual act, Crowley being the passive partner, and together chanted a Latin verse composed by Duranty: "Magician is joined with magician: Hermes King of the Rod, appear, bringing the unspeakable word." It was not an entirely successful "working" since Neuburg did not reach sexual climax.

Another "working" occurred on New Year's Day, 1914. This was said to have been more successful. A third occurred January 3, 1914. More Latin verses written by Duranty were chanted:

"Every drop of semen which Hermes sheds is a world. . . . People upon the worlds are like maggots upon an apple. . . . All worlds are excreta, they represent wasted semen. Therefore all is blasphemy."

A fourth "working" was held in the home of Crowley's mistress, or more properly, one of Crowley's many, many mistresses, Jane Cheron, who was at the time living with Duranty, later sometimes described as his wife. Duranty was an active participant with Crowley in this ceremony.

In later years Duranty was to put Aleister Crowley and himself into a rather bad novel and he wrote in fictional terms of his addiction to opium and the terrors of breaking the habit. Whether he was an addict is not certain but he told women he had been during his long and painful convalescence after losing a leg in 1924 in the wreck of the Paris-LeHavre express. He described the symptoms of opium addiction in his novel: "You get caught, and your feet are stuck in the glue, and your lovely and fanciful dreams change suddenly to nightmare."

To the end of his days he talked of opium and the pipe; how he smuggled opium into Moscow from London; how he brought it with him to the United States. He talked lightly of black magic and Magister Crowley and said "I don't believe in magic but I'm not sure that I disbelieve it." He told a young woman in Russia that he "didn't believe in anything but wouldn't it be funny if all the magicians went to heaven?"

As late as 1979 there were those who remembered Duranty's passion for rituals. "I never heard him talk of Crowley," an old associate said. "But if it had anything to do with orgies he would have liked that."

Once Duranty attended an "immurement." There was a party of young Russians, Duranty among them; much to drink; opium to smoke and sex of many varieties. The evening was climaxed by immuring a young couple in a wall. How long the couple was confined within the wall was never made clear but the combination of sex, opium, drink and diversity was very much to Duranty's taste.

Duranty to his last days possessed an extraordinary attraction for women. It was great before he lost his leg and greater after the loss for reasons which his friends thought could only be found in Krafft-Ebing. Jane Gunther, who met him as a friend of her husband, John, in 1947 counted Duranty the most captivating man she had ever seen. "He had a kind of magic," she remembered. "He could make you laugh. An evening with him was like an evening with no one else." In those days Duranty's female companion was Marjorie Worthington, divorced wife of William Seabrook, writer of bizarre books, a friend if not an acolyte of Crowley, a professed cannibal whose gastronomical quirk was once called by the *Montgomery* (Alabama) *Advertiser* "this incredibly sordid affair." Whether Seabrook was a cannibal or pretended to be one for the sake of the headlines there was no doubt that what attracted him to Mrs. Worthington was her pleasure in letting him keep her in chains. Since childhood Seabrook had possessed a passion for chaining, locking up and whipping the female objects of his desire. Duranty was a close friend of Seabrook's and in due course became an even closer one of Marjorie Worthington's. By this time Mrs. Worthington, an ample lady with a little girl's voice, had left Seabrook (then confined to Bloomingdale's sanatorium as a chronic alcoholic) and become even more ample. The vision of her in chains being whipped by the cannibalistic Seabrook sent John and Jane Gunther into paroxysms of laughter.

Duranty to Russia

Walter Duranty was to work for *The New York Times* from December 1, 1913, to April 1, 1934, a total of twenty-one years, and to continue for another eleven years on a retainer basis, although not, in fact, making a substantial contribution to *The Times* after 1940. He was one of the best-known correspondents in the world and the best known ever to write from the Soviet Union. He was also the most controversial man ever to serve on the staff of *The Times,* a controversy which opened in 1922, the year after Duranty went to Russia, and which never was to end. As late as 1979 Joseph Alsop was still fulminating that "Duranty was a great KGB agent and lying like a trooper." Not one of the critics of Duranty (so far as research could disclose) ever bothered to examine the nature of the man, his motivation or the likelihood that the "KGB" (which did not exist in Duranty's period in Russia; in 1921 it was Lenin's Cheka; it would change in 1936 to the NKVD and the MVD and then, much, much later, to the KGB) would have placed in its employ an acolyte of the Great Magister, one of the great lady's men of his generation, a calculating careerist, a man whose private god (if he had one) was surely Machiavelli rather than Marx.*

The fact is that controversy embraced Duranty long before he went

---

*Bizarre sexual habits did not preclude recruitment by the Soviet secret police as witness the case of Burgess and Maclean. However, Burgess and Maclean were devout Communists from their Cambridge days. Duranty was assumed by the public to be a liberal or radical. Privately, he left no doubt he was a conservative egocentric.

to Russia. His bureau chief at the end of World War I was a reliable and respected correspondent named Charles A. Selden. He wrote *Times* managing editor Carr Van Anda April 9, 1919, raising a "very embarrassing factor." Selden wanted to be postwar Paris chief but he refused to do so if Duranty was to be attached to the bureau. It had been all right, he said, during the war when Duranty was at the front (where he did well) and visited Paris only occasionally. But Selden regarded him as "most unreliable and tricky" and he simply would not work with him. Richard V. Oulahan, the senior *Times* correspondent, resident in Washington but in Paris for the peace conference, "fully agrees with me in this matter," Selden reported.

It was this circumstance that probably propelled Duranty in the direction of Moscow. He was sent in 1919 to the Baltic to cover news coming out of Russia, most of it wildly unreliable, partisan and exaggerated. His record in the Baltic was hardly outstanding but he went into Russia in 1921. He was instantly scooped by Floyd Gibbons, a famous *Chicago Tribune* correspondent who wore a black patch over a lost eye, on the terrible famine, which brought in Herbert Hoover and the American Relief mission. Within a year Van Anda was complaining privately that Duranty's reports were "completely different" from those from correspondents outside Russia—not necessarily a negative since the outside reports were malicious, malevolent and seldom factual.

"A Test of the News"

It was the persistent publication of the "Riga rumors" that caused Walter Lippmann and Charles Merz to compile their famous study "A Test of the News," published in *The New Republic* of August 4, 1920, revealing that on ninety-one occasions between November 1917 and November 1919 *The Times* reported that the Bolshevik regime had fallen or was about to fall. Fourteen times the collapse of the Bolsheviks was said to be in progress, four times Lenin and Trotsky were reported as preparing to flee, three times they had already fled, twice Lenin was reported to be retiring, once he had been killed and three times he had been thrown into prison.

The news reports, Lippmann and Merz concluded, had been dominated by the hopes of the editors of *The Times* [for failure of the Soviet regime] and, in general, "the news about Russia is a case of seeing not what was, but what men wished to see. The chief censor and the chief propagandists were hope and fear in the minds of reporters and editors."

This was a severe indictment, as severe as any that had been directed at *The Times* in the past or would be in the future and there is no question that it was seriously taken by both Mr. Ochs and Carr Van Anda.

But the appointment of Duranty as Moscow correspondent did not seem to Van Anda to have resolved the problem. His concern about Duranty was evoked by the reporting by Duranty on the trial of a Roman Catholic priest named Butskevich who was executed by the Bolshevik regime. Duranty appeared to accept without question the Bolshevik version. It was this kind of reporting by Duranty which, over the years, was to stimulate angry controversy surpassing anything which later arose over Herbert Matthews or any other *Times* reporting including my trip to and reporting from Hanoi during the Vietnam war. By 1923 Duranty was being called a "pro-Bolshevik correspondent" by an ad hoc Committee on Soviet Propaganda.

Whatever the case—"pro-Bolshevik" or, as careful examination of the evidence would suggest, "cynical man-on-the-make"—Duranty's dispatches through the 1920s and into the 1930s saw Soviet Russia through lenses which, if not rosy, were certainly soft focus, no hard edges, no dark underbelly. The Soviet which he painted was a little like Prohibition as pictured by Herbert Hoover, "an experiment noble in intent." He was quick to defend Stalin and to provide a rationale for the rude measures of the thick-fingered Georgian dictator. Twice Duranty had exclusive interviews with Stalin. If a positive image of the Soviet Union began to emerge in America despite the anti-Soviet propaganda and "red scares" of the 1920s it was painted by Duranty and printed in *The New York Times*. One of Duranty's friends of those years was to say later, "Duranty cast his lot with Stalin early on. He picked him as a winner and stayed with him."

As William H. Stoneman of the *Chicago Daily News* put it, "He was simply amoral without any deep convictions about the rights and wrongs of Communism." His colleague William Henry Chamberlain said, "He decided that the Communists were going to survive their troubles and that it was his job as a correspondent to back them, especially since he had no particular scruples about the dirty things they were doing."

Duranty presented to Adolph S. Ochs in a letter written from Le-Havre, where he lay recuperating from the amputation of his leg, in December 1924 as good a statement of his early view on Russia as was to survive:

> Behind the facade of Communism, the quarrels and confusion it produces inside Russia and abroad, there is all the fret and turmoil of a great young nation, newly freed from Tsarism and feudalism which stifled it before. I am convinced that many of the Bolsheviks themselves feel this though perhaps obscurely and are honestly trying to do their best for their country and its people, despite the wild economic theories to which they are attached.
>
> Because I am so convinced and because I am trying to put forward

this aspect of Russia I may sometimes make the mistake of appearing even sympathetic towards their efforts without giving sufficient thought to the impression it may create in America.

If this is the case, I hope you will forgive me and believe that I have done and will intend to do my utmost best to give The Times an accurate and as far as possible unprejudiced picture of Russian life and events.

No more staunch antagonist of communism could have been found than Mr. Ochs and Duranty's words made sense to him.

Duranty's philosophy would hardly have satisfied strident critics of the Bolshevik regime in the United States and their representatives on *The Times*. If Van Anda was often dissatisfied with Duranty the same was true of his successors Frederick Birchall and Edwin L. James.

There was on *The Times* a group that was even more dissatisfied. This included the gentle, scholarly and philosophical Simeon Strunsky, for many years the writer of an unsigned column on the editorial page, a staunch anti-Bolshevik, and, even more important, Joseph Shaplen, a prominent member of Russia's Socialist Revolutionary Party, the most principled of all opponents of the Bolsheviks going back to the early days of Vladimir Lenin.

These men saw Duranty as little more than a press agent not only for the Bolsheviks but for the worst Bolshevik of all, Stalin.

The struggle over Duranty was, to some extent, a reflection of the struggle in the United States over the Russian question, and by 1930 it had begun to concern Frederick Birchall, Mr. Ochs and Arthur Hays Sulzberger, now paying more and more attention to the editorial concerns of the newspaper.

Duranty had acquired a full-fledged claque and anti-claque. Each Duranty dispatch produced critical mail. Each absence of Duranty from the paper (he made trip after trip to Berlin, supposedly for the purpose of having his artificial leg and a spare repaired) brought questions from pro-Duranty-ites who were certain he was being suppressed. Feelings ran so high Birchall and James developed standard letters of reply to the pro and con groups. It was in this period that the phrase "Uptown Daily Worker" was coined by the anti-Duranty-ites to categorize *The New York Times*. The anti-Soviet bloc paid no heed to the staunch anti-Communist editorial stance of *The Times* or the anti-Bolshevik articles produced by Strunsky, Shaplen and others. It was war to the end. By 1930 Birchall was suggesting that Shaplen replace Duranty in Moscow, and Simeon Strunsky in a private survey of Duranty's dispatches on Stalin's collectivization drive reported in white-glove words, "It should be possible to maintain a more objective attitude to official claims or official figures."

In the autumn of 1931 and into the cruel winter of 1932 and the slow spring, the worst famine to hit Russia since that of 1921 struck the Ukraine and lower Volga in the wake of Stalin's forced collectivization. Tens of millions suffered, millions died, cannibalism was not infrequent. Reports eddied out of Russia about the catastrophe. Duranty did not report it. On March 9, 1932, he advised New York "to the best of my knowledge there is no famine anywhere although partial crop failures [occurred in] some regions." Stoneman and Ralph Barnes did report the famine. They got a tip on it from Eugene Lyons, the United Press correspondent. Lyons' secretary, Natalia Petrovna Shiroshikh,* had spotted a small item in the newspaper *Molot* of Rostov-on-Don and Lyons cabled the news to UP. Lyons did not go to the Ukraine or the Kuban, nor did Duranty or any of the other Moscow correspondents. Stoneman and Barnes traveled extensively in the famine areas until arrested by the Soviet police and sent back to Moscow, where they mailed their dispatches to Berlin to escape the censorship.

One month and twenty-one days after knocking down the famine story Duranty was awarded the Pulitzer Prize for reporting from Russia but before the year was out he was subjected to the most ferocious attack of his career by editor Abraham Kohan of the Jewish *Daily Forward,* an attack so strident that Duranty vainly urged *The Times* to bring action against the *Forward* and the *Chicago Tribune,* which reprinted the *Forward*'s allegations. Not until April 23, 1933, did Duranty finally go to the Ukraine to investigate the starvation. He had failed to report one of the greatest of Stalin's crimes, one of the most important stories of the decade.

On August 16, 1933, Birchall offered his conclusion to James that Duranty "doesn't want to be anybody's Moscow correspondent but to do as he pleases while maintaining a string upon us." James advised Arthur Sulzberger August 23, "I think it is very difficult to escape the conclusion that Mr. Duranty is not now and probably does not intend to be in the future a good Moscow correspondent." Ochs on August 28 regretfully recorded that "we have given Mr. Duranty the widest latitude because of our confidence in his integrity, and his alertness and ability to send us authentic news. There have been indications for some time past that he is relaxing in his attitudes to his duties and not keeping us fully informed."

As a matter of fact as early as September 16, 1931, Duranty had proposed that he give up his Moscow post and go on a part-time basis. His best-selling book, *I Write as I Please,* was about to appear. He was

*Later Natalia Petrovna Rene. She became Moscow correspondent for INS during World War II and later one of the leading authorities on Soviet ballet, writing many books on the subject by the time of her death in 1975.

the sensation of the American lecture circuit. He had begun to find covering Moscow a bore and the "eternal worry about every trifling detail" was too much. Duranty made a triumphal visit to the United States, accompanying Maxim Litvinov on his mission to negotiate U.S.-Soviet diplomatic relations, a cause which Duranty's dispatches had unquestionably advanced, and then insisted on retiring as Moscow correspondent as of April 1, 1934, although agreeing, for an annual retainer of $5,000, to spend three or four months a year in Russia working for *The Times*.

It is difficult to argue with James' view that Duranty no longer intended to be a good Moscow correspondent. He was repeatedly faulted on his interpretations of the Stalin purge trials; he consistently denied reports from Menshevik and Socialist Revolutionary sources in New York which later turned out to be accurate. He was replaced as permanent correspondent by Harold Denny, a run-of-the-mill man who never became a serious target for the anti-Soviet bloc although Max Eastman did write one sound critique of Denny's reporting of the Bukharin trial which produced an extraordinary but fortunately unpublished rebuttal by Denny insisting that "most of us believe that beneath all the improbabilities if not falsehoods of the last trial there was a substratum of truth."

Duranty's judgment on Russia did not improve. He spent more and more time on the lecture trail in America, basking in the company of adoring ladies, visiting in Palm Beach and becoming a habitué of the "21" Club. If he had ever been bothered by the ideological quarrels conducted in his name there was no sign of it in his mood and life-style, neither of which related to the proletarian cause. His judgment about Russian affairs grew no better. In April 1939 he chanced to be in Moscow and reported the resignation of Maxim Litvinov as Foreign Minister, an event which he attributed to Litvinov's health, angrily rejecting any suggestion that it boded ill for negotiations then in progress for a mutual defense pact among Russia, England and France. His bad judgment persisted after the signing of the Hitler-Stalin pact in August 1939. On his last trip to Moscow in 1940 he bet a fellow correspondent $100 that the pact would endure, saying "Hitler and Stalin aren't that crazy."*

---

*Duranty died October 4, 1957, in Orlando, Florida, shortly after marrying a Mrs. Enwright, the last of his ladies, with whom he had been living for some time. He had long since run through all of his funds and in a pathetic letter to Arthur Hays Sulzberger in August appealed for a pension. Sulzberger sent him his personal check for $2,500 September 5, 1957. (*Times'* archives)

Lessons

The case of Walter Duranty, in many ways, typified the manner in which Mr. Ochs managed "his business," that is, *The Times*. Mr. Ochs knew that coverage of Russia and the Soviet Union was of paramount importance to *The Times* and its readership after World War I. His decision to send a man to Moscow probably was stimulated in part by the critical Lippmann-Merz study. The selection of Duranty was accidental and possibly dictated by the fact that he was not liked by his Paris colleagues. Duranty's sexual fantasies were not known to Mr. Ochs. His Victorian principles would not have permitted him to retain such a man on his family newspaper. Edwin L. James, who worked with Duranty in Paris and who treasured boulevard gossip, could hardly have been unaware of Duranty's peccadilloes but never mentioned them. From early in his Moscow career *The Times'* editors knew that Duranty was not, in all respects, a satisfactory correspondent but they knew also that he was a brilliant man; they were not bothered by propaganda that he was a Communist agent but by practical evidence that he was not always an accurate and diligent newspaperman; they knew Duranty well enough to know he was nobody's agent but his own; they also knew him well enough to know that he was not always punctilious in checking stories and that he became increasingly nonchalant and confident of his infallibility. The last thing that any of them, Mr. Ochs, his young son-in-law Arthur, his fine editors Van Anda, Birchall and James, would have tolerated was a Stalinist propagandist and there was a powerful group of subeditors and writers on *The Times* who were quick to challenge any such propaganda (although equally assiduous in disseminating their own).

The Duranty experience, the Matthews-Carney conflict over the Spanish Civil War, the roiling battle over left-wing Guild control of the news staff—these challenges to the objectivity of *The Times'* columns toughened and strengthened Arthur Hays Sulzberger in his dedication to the purity of *The Times'* reporting in the post-war era, in the period of the rise of McCarthyism, the threats to the paper posed by the Eastland inquiry into communism on *The Times* and loose talk of 100 Communists on *The Times,* allegations which paralleled Joseph McCarthy's infamous list of seventy-two active Communists in the State Department.

It was out of the *Sturm und Drang* of these struggles to "keep *The Times* straight," in Rosenthal's words, that the issue of the CIA was to be met.

39

"The Voice of a Free Press"

TWENTY-FIVE YEARS AFTER the events it was still almost impossible to capture the painful texture of the passage of *The Times* through the McCarthy period. It had become fashionable to think of the era in terms of heroes, of Edward R. Murrow standing up to McCarthy in his CBS special, of gruff old Joseph Welch, counsel in the Army hearings, of brave witnesses, of the Hollywood Ten, of Lillian Hellman and Arthur Miller. The memory had dribbled away of a thousand little people, suddenly in peril of their reputations, their jobs; of men who saw great institutions facing wanton destruction, men who knew their decisions would determine far more than their personal fate.

The name of McCarthy is only a label for an epoch. There were many McCarthys and there was a bit of McCarthy in everyone, including some who emerged with the mantle of hero. There were men who struggled with the McCarthy within them and put it down. Not all the victims were individuals and the deepest wounds were to our national being, wounds which a quarter century later still lay half hidden, half healed.

The men who went through the period on *The New York Times*, the men at the top like Turner Catledge, Charles Merz of the editorial page, General Greenbaum, Arthur Sulzberger's personal counsel and closest friend, and Louis Loeb, lawyer for *The Times*, were unanimous in calling these days, and particularly the witch-hunting Eastland investigation of *The Times*, Arthur Sulzberger's finest hour, his great test, the moment when he stood firm for the principles of *The Times*, for integrity of the news and of the gatherers of the news and they were as one in describing the experience as the most difficult they had known. There was in it not only peril to the newspaper to which they were dedicated but the pain of personal tragedy, friendships broken, images cracked, careers destroyed. It was not like the Stalin period in Russia but the scent was there.

No account can capture the full flavor. In the archives of *The Times* stand drawer after drawer labeled "Communism," endless records, daily reports, memoranda, interviews, correspondence, interrogatories and recommendations which constitute a yellowing pulp-paper testimonial to the struggles of conscience set off by paranoia and demagogy.

Arthur Sulzberger was by every definition a man of the center. He and Iphigene had made a trip to Russia in 1929 and the country left an indelible mark on his consciousness, a land of grayness, of crushed spirit, fear and despond. He wrote a long account of his impressions and when I read it twenty-five years later on returning from Moscow myself I thought it conveyed the essence of what went wrong between the revolutionary dream of 1917 and the emergence of Stalin's iron regime.

Sulzberger had a second look at Russia during World War II on an American Red Cross mission. He came to respect Russia's war sacrifices but his conviction that Moscow was following a policy hostile to American interests deepened.

In a memorandum which he wrote at the end of 1944 he expressed concern over postwar security. He saw Russia as the danger. "Russia," he said, "is a burnt child and, I fear, a brutal youth. She has her specific problems and she will continue to express herself and to follow her own dictates up to the time that we are either prepared to fight her or to put economic screws on her."

With the end of World War II, Arthur Sulzberger's worry deepened. He wrote Merz from London October 26, 1951:

"As you know, I have been saying for some time that my three fears were: first, Russia; second, the rearmament of Germany in order to protect ourselves against Russia, and three, ourselves. And by that I meant what we do, what attitude we would take once we and our allies were fully armed. That fear becomes more real if we continue to emphasize a 'D-Day' (let us say, the year 1954, as being the time at which we expect to be fully armed)."

Arthur Sulzberger's fear of the Soviet and of Communism was not to diminish. He argued for several years with Merz over an editorial that had been drafted—but not published—in the mid-1950s by Otto Tolischus, an extremely conservative member of the editorial board, about Russia's broken promises. The editorial was so long it would have occupied the whole *Times* editorial space, very harsh and listing every pledge which, in Tolischus' opinion, had been broken by Stalin. As late as 1960 Arthur Sulzberger was proposing that the editorial be exhumed and published. Merz wrote a long, patient rejoinder, pointing out that the editorial had become outdated; that it dealt solely with Stalin, now dead seven years, and that it hardly was germane to Khrushchev's policies and would "puzzle and confuse our readers and be interpreted by many of them as a deliberate effort to sabotage the [Eisenhower-Khrushchev] Summit Conference." To which Merz received the reply, "I guess you're right about the Russian piece now but don't throw it away because we're going to have to use it sooner or later."

This then was the philosophy of Arthur Sulzberger, a man with a passionate devotion to the integrity of his newspaper, hardly a man who would knowingly cherish on his staff elements which would propel *The Times* or influence its readers in the direction of Marxism or its latter-day manifestations.

McCarthyism

The virus that came to be known as McCarthyism had appeared within *The Times* itself long before McCarthy. Elements of it could be seen in the bitter quarrels over Duranty and Matthews in the 1930s and in the internal feud between Communist and anti-Communist factions in the Newspaper Guild in the 1930s and 1940s.

And a clear harbinger emerged improbably in a campaign launched by Arthur Krock against the content of *The New York Times Book Review,* which he believed to be infected by Communist influence. In 1947 and 1948 Krock repeatedly wrote Arthur Sulzberger about "pin-kos [who] get into the *Book Review.*" He cited Henry Steele Commager's review of John Gunther's *Inside U.S.A.* and John Kenneth Galbraith's review of a Twentieth Century Fund study of American resources. He characterized a review by Arthur Schlesinger, Jr., of a book by Harold Stassen as filled with "young pinko doctrines" and was outraged at a review by Justin O'Brien of a work by Jean-Paul Sartre. He entered what he called a "personal complaint" at a Commager review of Robert Sherwood's *Roosevelt and Hopkins.* There is no evidence that Krock's complaints caused Lester Markel, who was in charge of the *Review,* to drop reviewers like Henry Steele Commager, John Kenneth Galbraith or Arthur Schlesinger, Jr., but the *Book Review* and its "leftist slant" was to become a McCarthyite theme.

Arthur Sulzberger despised McCarthy and his methods. As one of Eisenhower's earliest backers, nothing made him more uncomfortable than the general's association with the McCarthy wing of the party.

"Much as I dislike some of the company you've been keeping of late," Sulzberger wrote Eisenhower August 18, 1952, "I recognize the existence of certain political necessities. I am hoping, however, that before long you can make a statement that [makes] clear that the Old Guard has not swallowed you.

"And finally, if you would cut yourself loose affirmatively from McCarthy, I think the heart of the world would rise up to you. And it would be you talking and you're the fellow we want to hear."

Eisenhower toyed with the idea of repudiating McCarthy but did not. He endorsed McCarthy's reelection to the Senate, permitted McCarthy to travel with him on a campaign swing across Wisconsin and deleted from a speech in Milwaukee a paragraph of endorsement for his old chief, General George Marshall, who had become a McCarthy target. William H. Lawrence, *The Times'* tough and accurate political reporter, was told that the paragraph had been written for Eisenhower by Arthur Sulzberger himself.

Sulzberger did not turn against Eisenhower despite his disappointment, nor did he relinquish his opposition to McCarthy. Before McCarthy's death on May 2, 1957, *The Times* had published between fifty and sixty editorials dealing with the McCarthyite hysteria.*

Sulzberger was aware that *The Times* offered a tempting target for McCarthy. Report after report reached him that the senator was preparing to sizzle *The Times* over the coals of his investigatory cookstove. He was not deterred. At the end of 1953 he received confidential information that McCarthy had selected as a principal victim Scotty Reston, based, of course, not on that doughty Scotsman's proven capitalist and antitotalitarian bias but upon one of the usual "sworn statements" from a "Communist" or "ex-Communist" informer.

There is no way now of knowing what may have lain behind this report but Reston, on December 25, 1952, had published answers from Josef Stalin to a series of questions he had submitted by cable.

Arthur Sulzberger was disturbed because he had not been consulted in advance and he felt Reston had given Stalin a propaganda bonus. Reston and Arthur Krock, who had approved the venture, agreed they should have told Sulzberger in advance but strongly supported the basic idea, enlisting Charles Bohlen, the State Department's Soviet specialist, in their cause. When Sulzberger remained unconvinced Reston finally wrote the publisher:

"It is true—and in the present atmosphere of the country inevitable —that such inquiries will produce a storm of criticism. . . . It is also true that the easy course is not to submit such questions or get involved in such controversies. But it seems to me that, if we are—as I believe we must—to live by the noble precepts of your speech at the Waldorf the other night [in which Sulzberger defended the role of the free press] we must continue to search for the answers to fundamental questions. . . . If we are in the business of watching and enquiring about the course of events in the camp of the enemy, why should we not question there as we question in every other capital in the world."

Sulzberger finally conceded that some good might come out of the Stalin questions, although he wrote Reston, "I am one of those who

---

*When news of McCarthy's death came Merz telephoned Sulzberger. "I don't think we need an editorial on this," Arthur Sulzberger said. "I had arrived at the same decision myself," Merz rejoined. His feeling was "why dignify the bastard; let him pass from the scene without more attention." (Personal interview, Merz, 3/14/70)

automatically and instinctively distrust everything, and I mean everything, that Stalin *says."*

Despite hatred for Stalin, distrust of the Soviet regime, revulsion toward Communists, Arthur Sulzberger did not waver on McCarthyism. He did not say one thing in public and do another in private. His support of Eisenhower did not mean that he was willing to tolerate the isolationist wing of the Republican Party.

Within six weeks of receiving the confidential tip that McCarthy was planning to make Reston the spearpoint of an attack on *The Times* the publisher was congratulating Merz on a strong anti-McCarthy editorial called "Playing With Fire" and urging him to "keep pounding McCarthy and everything we call McCarthyism." He pointed out that it was not only McCarthy who wore that label.

"I would be quite prepared to see us do it as strongly as we opposed the Bricker Amendment," Sulzberger wrote. "I thought that series of editorials was excellent and I know that they had an impact.

"Let's keep slugging!" he told Merz.

Eastland

Perhaps it was because of Arthur Sulzberger's bold and consistent stand against McCarthy; perhaps it was because of a "tough guy" camaraderie which developed between McCarthy and *The Times'* rugged political correspondent William H. Lawrence; perhaps it was chance but McCarthy never was to attack *The Times.* That cause was taken in hand by Senator James O. Eastland from Catledge's native Mississippi, or, more accurately, by Julian G. Sourwine, counsel to Eastland's Senate Security subcommittee. Eastland and Catledge had never been close but Catledge tried to find what was behind the senator's investigation and turn it off if possible. But he got nothing more from Eastland than an afternoon of catfish drawl, Mississippi pleasantries and bland denials that *The Times* was his target. Reston made a similar effort to draw out Sourwine but established only that it was Sourwine who was the sparkplug of the committee, not Eastland. Sourwine, like Eastland, was full of assurances that *The Times* was not the target of the committee.

This, of course, was not true. The committee was already toying with *The Times,* cat and mouse, on the basis of testimony given by a witness who had been a Communist, a psychiatric patient, a member of the New York Newspaper Guild, and who contended that *The Times* had on its staff "well over 100 dues-paying" Communist Party members, a figure he later increased to "126 in the Sunday department alone" and still later, reduced to three—two commercial department clerks and one news department clerk who had long since been fired. In giving *Times* reporter Gladwin Hill the names of the three men he explained that his earlier figures had been "estimates" based on having once heard that Communists on *The Times* could round up five hundred votes for the party ticket. He had calculated membership on a rough ratio of one Communist to ten votes. Of such slender reeds the Eastland committee began to construct its house of straw.*

Sulzberger had long been concerned over the possibility that Communists might work themselves into sensitive news positions in *The Times.* He was totally confident that his editors could maintain the objectivity of *The Times* but he wanted no one on the news staff with ties to alien ideologies or alien powers. He was as adamant on this as he had been on the question of a Newspaper Guild monopoly of *Times'* personnel or use of *The Times* by the British or the wartime American intelligence agencies.

The question had bothered him long before the McCarthys and the Eastlands appeared on the scene. His early conviction that membership in a political party, including the Communist Party, was a private matter had evaporated. *The Times* in an editorial in 1948 entitled "We Have a Right to Know," discussing the testimony of a witness before the House Un-American Activities Committee who refused to say whether he was a Communist, declared:

"If a man belongs to the Communist Party, or the Democratic Party or the Republican Party, he should be willing to say so. . . . Only the vicious hide behind the sheets. Iron curtains are equally to be distrusted. We, as citizens, have a right to know those who are behind them."

A few months later he wrote his friend General Lucius D. Clay, then commander in chief in Berlin (these were the days of the Berlin blockade):

"Of course, I would not employ a reporter or an editor whom I knew to be a Communist and I believe I would dismiss one from The Times if he were presently employed and I learned that he was a Party member. . . . I asked my associates yesterday what their views would be if we suddenly found ourselves at war with Russia. They agreed instantly that all of these persons, plus those who were even suspect, would be out. Then I asked them if a state of peace existed now. . . . I wish you, with your intimate contacts, were here to help us on this one."

The line which Arthur Sulzberger drew in the letter to Clay and the position taken in the editorial "We Have a Right to Know" did not

---

*The witness, a man named Harvey Matusow, ultimately recanted most of the testimony he had given as a professional witness in Communist investigations and was sentenced to five years for perjury. (*Times'* archives, Will Lissner memorandum, 3/14/69)

differ greatly from the expressed attitude of the Eastland committee. Both positions were vigorously anti-Communist but while the Eastland committee and McCarthy sought to sow general distrust and hatred of the press, Arthur Sulzberger was fighting to preserve the press and protect it against contamination. He expected his editors to guard vigilantly against tainting of the news and he expected them to keep a sharp eye on news pertaining to communism or the Soviet Union. When I was sent as correspondent to Moscow in January 1949, as the McCarthy tensions were building up, Sulzberger took pains to make certain that the dispatches of the new man from Moscow were carefully scrutinized by a veteran *Times* reporter, Will Lissner, a dedicated anti-Communist and Soviet economics specialist, a wise precaution as it turned out because charges of pro-Soviet bias were quick to arise, both within *The Times* (General Adler and Lester Markel took a lead in this) and outside *The Times* among the anti-Communist claque to whom the dateline Moscow was enough to raise suspicion. Lissner was able to report no signs of Communist bias in the new man's report; quite the reverse.

"It would be impossible for me to overstate what a high standard of honesty and objectivity Sulzberger expected of his reporters," Catledge once said. "He was acutely aware of the trust that millions of people put in *The Times*, and he expected every reporter to live up to that trust, just as he himself tried determinedly to do."

The year of 1955 was as difficult a year as Arthur Sulzberger was to experience. Catledge and Loeb set about the task of interviewing every *Times* editorial employee who had been named in one way or another as a possible Communist (as it transpired the Eastland committee's main source of names was the raw unevaluated files of the FBI).* Two men were fired and one resigned under pressure. In each case the criteria was failure to cooperate in discussing past Communist Party membership. Sulzberger had not finally resolved in his mind what he would do with Fifth Amendment cases but he did know that the bottom line for maintaining management confidence was a frank statement by the employee of his relationship with the Communist Party. (Of twenty-five subpoenas issued by the Eastland committee for *Times* employees Catledge and Loeb interviewed all but two; among them they found not one current member of the party and only six who had ever belonged.)

Careful investigation in later years by Lissner disclosed that in 1932

---

*Two important *Times* executives, Amory Bradford and Harding Bancroft, had been personal friends of Alger Hiss. This fact was certainly known to the Eastland committee but no point was ever made of it. (Personal interview, Bradford, 10/28/78)

there were exactly two Communists on the staff of *The New York Times,* both long gone before Eastland entered the picture. In 1934 a Communist Party nucleus was formed on *The Times* made up of three people, none of them news personnel. In the late 1930s a cell meeting attracted no more than seventy persons, including friends of members. Almost all the party members were from the mechanical and commercial departments. By the early forties the cell began to shrink and was smaller than those at the *Herald-Tribune* or *Time* magazine. By the late forties or early fifties only thirty party members remained on *The Times,* not one in the news or editorial departments. Over a period of twenty years, according to Lissner's calculations, not more than fifty employees of the news-editorial departments had ever been party members. Members tended quickly to resign or be fired for failure to do their jobs properly.

The number of employees at *The Times* grew from 1930 to 1950 from 3,000 to 4,000. The agony that the paper went through in 1955 arose from a trivial number of men, a fraction of a fraction of a percent. And *not one was an active member of the party.*

Arthur Sulzberger did not find it easy to resolve his views on the Fifth Amendment. He discharged a financial copyreader who took the Fifth before the Eastland committee in July 1955, declaring, "It is my opinion that as a member of *The New York Times'* staff it was your duty to answer the questions put to you by the committee and that your refusal to do so has ended your usefulness as a reporter." A month later he was proposing to his colleagues that all employees being hired for "sensitive" departments, that is news, Sunday and editorial, be questioned as to whether they were members of the Communist Party. He did not propose to employ present party members but he did not wish to bar former members—necessarily. He felt that membership "should properly cast some doubt upon the general good judgment of the individual involved."

The Times' Stand

As the end of 1955 approached Arthur Sulzberger drafted a lengthy position paper which he proposed to circulate to his employees. On the Fifth Amendment he said that it "stands as a refuge for any man who feels the need of such protection but nowhere is it written that a person who invokes it—thereby casting suspicion upon himself—is entitled to work in a sensitive department of this newspaper. Such a position requires frankness on the issue of communism on the part of the individual who holds it. The responsibility inherent in the First Amendment is in conflict with the right to plead the Fifth. On The New York Times it will result in dismissal if invoked by a member of our news, Sunday or editorial departments."

He expressed his belief that former party members should testify fully about their associates and other party members but said *The Times* would judge each man's case individually.

This draft was never issued. John Oakes, then on the editorial board, urged further thinking on the question. He feared it would freeze *The Times'* position and make it seem that the paper had knuckled under to Eastland. Oakes urged that Sulzberger handle each case on its merits and make no declaration of Fifth Amendment policy. Catledge had equally deep concerns. So did Merz.

The draft of Sulzberger's statement included a quotation from the declaration of *Times* editor Charles R. Miller when he appeared before the Senate committee in 1915 to testify against the allegations of British ownership of *The Times:*

"I can see no ethical, moral or legal right that you have to put many of the questions you put to me today. Inquisitorial proceedings of this kind would have a very marked tendency . . . to reduce the press of the United States to the level of the press of some of the Central European empires, the press that has been known as the reptile press, that crawls on its belly every day . . . to the Government Officials and Ministers to know what it may say or shall say, to receive its orders . . ."

It was the spirit of Miller's declaration which was to illuminate Arthur Sulzberger's final and definitive statement.

After a searching of conscience and lengthy discussions with Arthur Sulzberger, Charles Merz invited the publisher and his closest associates to the tenth-floor editorial offices. "I think," Merz said, "this is a case in which we can use our own strength." To an audience of Arthur Sulzberger, General Adler, Orvil Dryfoos and Amory Bradford he read aloud an editorial which he had composed and titled "The Voice of a Free Press." Before Merz had reached the final lines there were tears in the eyes of all present. Sulzberger approved the editorial without change. The Eastland committee was opening its hearings in Washington the next day. Bradford was detailed to go to Washington and observe the proceedings. If it was clear that *The Times* was the target of the committee's attack he would telephone Dryfoos and Dryfoos would order the editorial published. Bradford went to Washington. By the end of the day it was obvious that the committee had aimed its barrels at *The Times.* He telephoned Dryfoos and the editorial was published January 5, 1956.§

This editorial, in the opinion of Mr. Merz, was the most important piece of prose to which he ever set his hand; the most important declaration of *The Times* in his period and that of Arthur Sulzberger.

§See Notes section.

There were those who believed it was even more historic; that it was the most important statement of faith by *The Times* since Mr. Ochs' original determination to publish the news "without fear or favor." It had a powerful effect on the country. It was reprinted in every significant newspaper of the United States and abroad. Television was not so pervasive in those days but the words of the editorial were recorded by the national networks. More than 3,500 letters poured into *The Times*, most of them of congratulation.* It came as an inspiration to those forces in the nation which were beginning to demand an end to the lies of McCarthy and his imitators. As time went on "The Voice of a Free Press" came to be accepted as the basic modern statement of freedom of the press and of the dedication of *The New York Times* to its principles.

"The Voice of a Free Press" was reprinted again and again in many formats and for years a reproduction hung on the wall of the tenth-floor reception room of the editorial department of *The Times*, a quiet Gothic nook of fumed oak. Then in one of the spells of remodeling through which *The Times* constantly passed, the room vanished and with it the declaration of principle that had hung upon the wall.

---

* *The Times* received 677 letters on the Eastland hearings on *The Times*, 484 favorable, 162 negative, 31 neutral. (*Times'* archives, memo to Dryfoos, 2/28/56)

40

The Gumshoe Agents

*J*ULIUS OCHS ADLER and Allen Dulles were classmates at Princeton, class of 1918, good friends in college, good friends all their lives. Adler, who had been brought up almost like a son to Adolph S. Ochs, nourished natural hopes to succeed his uncle as publisher of *The New York Times.* He took his displacement by Arthur Hays Sulzberger with good spirit and for years occupied a big office at the east end of the fourteenth-floor executive suite at *The Times,* handling business matters while Arthur Sulzberger sat at the west end, putting most of his attention on editorial matters. Adler called Sulzberger "Sulz"; Sulzberger called Adler "Julie."

Adler went to France with the AEF in 1917, a company commander in the 79th Division, and ended the war with the rank of major. He saw service in World War II in the Pacific with General MacArthur. Once it was reported that Adler was at the verge of death after a heart attack. An editorial was prepared for *The Times* but it turned out to be a mistake; Adler was being flown to Walter Reed Hospital in Washington for a gall-bladder operation. He emerged from World War II a major general, a no-nonsense patriot, an ardent anti-Communist, sometimes coming on like an American Colonel Blimp but with an inner warmth which made him dear to his children despite the fact that, as a close friend once said, "he treated his family as he would his regiment in battle."

Adler cherished his military associations, stayed on the reserve list, went to Washington on military missions and often was tapped for committees dealing with defense matters. He vastly admired Allen Dulles for his notable intelligence activities in Switzerland during World War I and World War II and after World War II when Allen went into the CIA the relationship grew closer. Adler fancied himself as something of an ombudsman on *The Times,* watching the work of correspondents (Sulzberger made a point of knowing personally the principal foreign and Washington correspondents, inviting them to lunch at *The Times* when they were in New York and bringing them as guests at his Hillandale estate; Adler's acquaintance with the staff was more remote), often pointing out dispatches which he felt brought "comfort to the enemy." The enemy, of course, was the Soviet Union. He sometimes argued about *Times'* editorials but not often since these were the personal province of Sulzberger. He was not much of a traveler but he enjoyed meeting with the great, and in 1951 he went to England to negotiate with Winston Churchill for *The Times'* rights to publication of his memoirs and put down a meticulous account of Churchill's remarks, including the assertion that if he were Prime Minister he would bomb China and clamp a naval blockade on the China coast. Churchill declared that if he could get U.S. agreement he would send an ultimatum to Russia, telling the Kremlin that unless it yielded to our demands (specifics not stated) we would atom-bomb twenty or thirty Russian cities. Churchill was sure the Russians would reject the ultimatum but by the time the third city was wiped out would meet "our terms."

This was too much even for Adler. He told Churchill he did not think the United States would consent to "such a form of preventive war."

Adler was proud of his association with Douglas MacArthur, who told him soon after the Churchill meeting that Churchill was the one political leader to his taste. MacArthur's arguments for bombing China differed not a whit from Churchill's. He did not, however, share Churchill's concern over the Soviet threat.

Later in this year Adler jotted down some thoughts about his philosophy which he passed on to his three children, Julius, Bobbie and Nancy. He expressed a firm belief in God which he found "synonymous to me with Conscience"; and an equally firm belief in the principles of the Declaration of Independence and the Constitution, particularly the Bill of Rights.

"If," he wrote, "the masters of the Kremlin would acquaint themselves with and then uphold these fundamental rights, I am confident the horrible threat of World War III could no longer hover over mankind. Together with the peoples of Russia and of the other captive states, we could carry on our normal lives in peace and tranquility."

The Gruson Affair

On the first or second of June 1954, General Adler dined in Washington with his friend Allen Dulles. In the course of a pleasant evening Dulles told his classmate that the situation in Guatemala was very delicate and that he and his brother, Foster, would feel more comfortable if Sydney Gruson, the *Times* correspondent in Mexico City, were not to cover the story. Dulles did not tell Adler exactly what was up in Guatemala but rumors of a coup against the leftist regime of Colonel Jacob Arbenz were widely circulating.

Gruson, an able and personable correspondent who joined *The Times* in London during the war, had been devoting a great deal of attention to the Guatemalan story. By chance he had returned briefly to Mexico City to attend to some personal business (he owned five race horses at the Mexico City track) before going back to Guatemala for the coup—if it came off.

On the evening of June 3, Emanuel Freedman, *Times* foreign editor, telephoned Gruson and told him to remain in Mexico City. Freedman said *The Times* had received information indicating that there might be a "Mexican angle" in connection with the rumored coup. Since another *Times* man, Paul Kennedy, had now arrived in Guatemala, Gruson was to sit tight and await developments.

Gruson was indignant. He had spent two and a half years watching the Guatemalan story, he could think of no possible way in which Mexico might be embroiled and he did not wish to be left out of the action. He made his views clear to Freedman but Freedman would not budge. He had been told by Turner Catledge to pass the instructions to Gruson and that was that.

What neither Gruson nor Freedman knew, and what was not to work its way to the surface for many, many years, was that Allen Dulles had told General Adler that the CIA had information which caused them to be concerned about Gruson's political reliability. He told Adler that Gruson traveled on a British passport that had been issued in Warsaw; that his wife, Flora Lewis, an extremely active and talented correspondent in her own right, traveled on Gruson's passport; that Gruson was born in Ireland (which was about the only true thing that Dulles said); and that the agency was so disturbed over "Gruson's leanings" that it wanted him out of Central America while the coup was on. Many, many years later Robert Amory, long-retired deputy director of CIA for Intelligence, disclosed that the source of suspicions about the Grusons was Frank Wisner, late Director of Plans (dirty tricks, including Guatemala). "He was absolutely paranoid about the Grusons," Amory said. "You have to use that word. Wisner was absolutely sure they were agents, particularly Mrs. Gruson."

Adler, who had earlier concluded that Gruson was a possibly dangerous "radical," promptly passed Dulles' tip to Arthur Sulzberger, who, in turn, ordered Gruson held in Mexico City and invented the cover story that Mexico might be involved in the coup.

Gruson was far too good a reporter not to sense a red herring. Before returning to Mexico City he had written a series of stories which had infuriated the U.S. ambassador to Guatemala, John E. Peurify, who (unknown to Gruson or any but a narrow circle within the State Department and the CIA) was one of the architects of the forthcoming coup. The CIA had been making secret preparations to overthrow

Arbenz for some time, judging him a dangerous radical who, in their belief, would open the way for communism and the establishment of a Soviet sphere of influence in Central America. The vehicle for the coup was to be a group of exiled anti-Arbenz politicians. Bases had been established in adjoining Salvador and Honduras and at the famous *finca* of Retalhuleu ninety miles from Guatemala City, later to be used in the Bay of Pigs operation.

An enormous stir had been created by the arrival at a Guatemalan port of a shipment of arms bought by Arbenz from Czechoslovakia and delivered by a Swedish freighter. The State Department denounced the action as a "development of gravity." Gruson reported meticulously on the arms shipment but he also said that the U.S. denunciation had tended to unite Guatemalans around Arbenz and had been, in effect, counterproductive to U.S. interests.

It was this, as was later to be disclosed, and the fact that Gruson was reporting the story as he saw it that angered Peurify. He vented his rage to Gruson and to other American correspondents. Of course, what Gruson did not know and what was carefully concealed from both the American and Guatemalan public, was that on May 15 the National Security Council in Washington, acting at the initiative of Allen Dulles, had decided to use the excuse of the arms shipment to trigger the anti-Arbenz coup. Just as Gruson was reporting on the counterproductivity of U.S. policy Peurify and his intelligence aides were activating the long-planned operation for the overthrow of Arbenz.

In retrospect it was totally apparent why the Dulles brothers wanted Gruson out of Guatemala and why they did not hesitate to employ slanderous and duplicitous means to persuade Arthur Sulzberger to keep him from the operational zone. Gruson was too good a reporter. He knew too much. He was too capable of uncovering the truth. Neither Allen Dulles nor his brother wanted a man like that on the scene as the CIA was attempting by clandestine and illegal actions, totally in violation of all treaty obligations of the United States and of international law, to overthrow the peaceful if somewhat uncomfortable government of a small neighboring country.

The coup was carried out with skill and celerity June 16, the "rebels" having been given the use of three old American B–26 bombers which were flown off the airstrip at the Retalhuleu *finca.* (One of the participants in the operation was the later-to-become-famous Howard Hunt; the characters in these dramas seemed to repeat themselves again and again like an old Pearl White movie serial.)

From the beginning of the Gruson affair Arthur Sulzberger showed distinct uneasiness. This was not the kind of thing *The Times* did. He acted because, as presented by Allen Dulles, it sounded like a national emergency. But the information provided to Adler was thin and when Sulzberger talked to Dulles it didn't seem to possess much substance. Still, Sulzberger was a patriot as was General Adler; if the national security was at stake he could not see himself not being a good soldier. But he began to press Dulles for details—politely, sympathetically but persistently. The coup had not yet occurred but he wanted to know what it was that *really* motivated Dulles. If Gruson was a security risk, he, the publisher, should be given the information; if not . . . At the same time Gruson was importuning Freedman. He did not want to miss the fireworks. His Guatemalan visa ran out June 10; he had left his clothes and his typewriter behind in Guatemala City—when could he get back?

Arthur Sulzberger's persistence put Dulles in a bind. The fact was he didn't have any derogatory information about Gruson. The problem Allen and Foster Dulles had with Gruson was the same that many people around the world had with *New York Times* reporters. They *knew* too much; they were too good at finding things out; they couldn't be suborned or fooled, or utilized. It was the trouble Nixon was to have with *The Times* over the Pentagon Papers. *The Times* men *knew* too much, it came up again and again.

At first Dulles temporized. He put Sulzberger off with scanty details about Gruson's background, details which simply didn't match the real Gruson. When Sulzberger pressed for more, offering to come to Washington and talk to him, or to meet him at a place of his own choosing, Dulles back-pedaled. The coup still hadn't come off. It was not a time for him to talk. He saw General Adler again at the Princeton class reunion and gave him "one or two thoughts which might be of some use." But he was back-pedaling hard. He assured Sulzberger he hadn't intended to bring any pressure to bear; that he simply wanted to be helpful; that he wanted to present to Sulzberger "some considerations which might not otherwise have been brought to your attention." And he had no plan for coming to New York and made no offer to meet with Sulzberger.

Dulles wrote that letter the day before the coup. By the time Sulzberger got it he thought he could understand somewhat better the background of the affair. But he was far from satisfied. He returned to the attack, pointing out that Dulles had told Adler and himself that he had "some disquieting reports" about a member of *The Times'* staff; Sulzberger had agreed to hold Gruson out of Guatemala "because of my respect for your judgment and Foster's." He wasn't going to argue about the request. But it was not fair to either *The Times* or Gruson to let the issue hang. What did Dulles have on

Gruson? Sulzberger revealed that in the past there had been two examples of individuals on *The Times* whose loyalty had been questioned, that in one case the charges had been denied and he had been convinced they were not founded; in the other there had been "admission of early association but an attestation of reform years ago." Both men were at work on *The Times* and Sulzberger had utmost confidence in them.

Now, he made plain to Dulles, it was time to tell him what his case was. Dulles began to squirm. He really didn't think there was anything more he could say. He felt apprehension, he said, that "a man having his particular nationality, background and connections should be representing you at a particular place at a particular juncture." He appreciated what Sulzberger had done. But that was that. He had no information to pass on, no recommendation to make.

Arthur Sulzberger began to suspect he had been used. He went back to the case once more, trying to ferret out some supporting detail from Dulles. The correspondence grew more formal. Finally, Dulles said he really didn't have anything additional but if Sulzberger wanted to see the data personally he would send it up by messenger. In the end (because he had been ordered to bed by his doctor) Arthur Sulzberger sent his nephew Cy down to Washington and when he received Cy's report he wrote again to Dulles, closing the correspondence with a statement that "My judgment, formed on the basis of our experience with the man and on Cy's report to me of what he learned, is that he is a good newspaperman who happened upon some stories which the people reporting to you did not like because they did not want them published."

It was, perhaps, a salutary experience. It left a bad taste in Arthur Sulzberger's mouth and reinforced the lesson which he got again and again that when someone complained about *The New York Times* or one of its reporters it was not because *The Times* was wrong but because *The Times* or its reporter had published the truth. The truth was very uncomfortable for many people, including some officials of the U.S. Government.

It was years before all the circumstances of the Gruson episode were sorted out but, like the excellent reporter he was, about a week before Arthur Sulzberger finally closed his difficult correspondence with Dulles, Gruson had written back to New York a fairly accurate reconstruction of what had happened. He told of Peurify's anger over his dispatches and, putting two and two together, concluded that Peurify and the State Department had put the quarantine on him because they did not want him around when they staged their coup. Gruson was only then released from the holding pattern in Mexico City and went on to pursue a successful career with *The Times,* by 1979 having moved up to the post of vice-chairman of *The Times Co.* *

"A Stinking Pie"

If, as seems evident, Arthur Sulzberger was disturbed by the specious manner in which Allen Dulles interfered with *The Times* in Guatemala there was more to come. Turner Catledge had gone to Europe in July, even before the Gruson matter had been finally laid to rest. He had not been abroad for four years and he found many changes. One of the most disturbing was in Germany. Sometimes it seemed that half the men on a news story were trench-coated agents right out of *The Third Man,* equipped with press credentials from American newspapers and press services, some genuine, others fake. These men spent half their time investigating each other and the few legitimate correspondents in Germany. The rest of the time they seemed to be involved in plots and activities so nebulous it was difficult to tell what lay behind them. But murder was not uncommon; blackmail was almost customary; surveillance and phone tapping were the order of the day.

Catledge got most of these details from *The Times'* resident correspondent M. S. Handler, a serious, rather old-fashioned man with a powerful sense of morality and a sure feeling for professional proprieties. He was extremely disturbed by the situation, felt it was against U.S. interests. Whatever the origins it had degenerated into an expensive and dangerous game of cops-and-robbers. It was beginning to interfere with legitimate news coverage Handler found that if he were so much as to call on a new or unconventional source the operatives were onto him in a minute, bothering him about who he talked to, bothering his sources.

Catledge was outraged by the activities of what he called "the gumshoe" agents of the CIA, the State Department and other government agencies.

"They seem to feel that it is part of their duty," he wrote Sulzberger, "to investigate newspaper people and the sources of their information." He said that any time Handler wrote a story off the beaten path "he can count on a dragnet being put out to find out where he got it."

Handler told Catledge that he had been approached by the CIA to spy on other newspapermen. He had, of course, refused, but this was not true of all newspapermen. Some had "rather readily joined in this

---

*Within the CIA the impression was to linger for years that the transfer of Gruson out of Mexico City and to eastern Europe shortly after the Guatemalan affair resulted from agency intervention at the time of the coup. This was not true but the agency felt that resentment by Gruson and other important *Times* personnel persisted as a consequence of the Gruson case. (Freedom of Information Act documents, Col. Stanley Grogan to Deputy Director CIA, 10/1/65)

sort of business hoping to get, in return, certain sources of inside information."

Catledge instructed Handler to put together all the information he had for one or more stories and wrote Sulzberger so he would know what was going on. "I know you will say," Catledge wrote, "that under the circumstances our cue is to resort to characteristic courage and to look with wary eyes and listen with wary ears to any reports that might come to us affecting adversely our own paper."

He warned Sulzberger that if word got out that Handler was doing the story he would be the subject of an investigation. "This investigation fever," Catledge said, "seems to have spread like wildfire in a complex purpose which is security, self-advancement and stupidity mixed in one stinking pie. I certainly think we ought to print something about it when we are able to give chapter and verse."

Arthur Sulzberger took a personal interest in the story but little got into print. A highly sanitized version of Catledge's "stinking pie" appeared in *The Times* September 29, 1954, combined with and subordinated to a story on German policy. It was so buried that not one reader in a hundred would have noted a sentence in which Handler reported that "various security agencies have compiled dossiers on United States reporters" and that some American reporters were giving U.S. agencies a wide berth because of a "severe case of spy hunting." Handler, an economics graduate of the University of Chicago in its great days of the 1920s, was one of the most sophisticated and skilled correspondents of *The Times'* post-war European staff. But he had a notable defect. He was wonderful at telling a story across the table but had fiendish difficulty in putting it through his typewriter. He returned to the United States in the 1960s, developed a remarkable relationship with Malcolm X, wrote some notable stories about him and then drifted off to limbo in the vast *Times* city room, finally to retire, misunderstood and badly misused by Abe Rosenthal.

CIA Pressures

The CIA, "the Agency" or "the Company," as its operatives liked to call it, was rolling by 1954. It had in a sense come of age with the Guatemala coup and the earlier Mossadegh affair. It had demonstrated its ability to impose an American pattern on the course of events, to achieve "by other means" the objectives of American policy. After Guatemala, the White House, the State Department, particularly Foster Dulles, even the military had to sit up and take notice. The Agency was not just playing clandestine games. It was now a prime mover. It was throwing its weight around and that was apparent in Germany in the summer of 1954. What was also apparent was that the CIA had begun to swing its weight in the press, in newspaper circles, in the media. It had succeeded in pulling a top-ranking *Times* correspondent off his job in order, as it thought, to ensure the success of the Guatemala coup. It was all over the map in Germany, using newsmen as "cover," dressing up its agents as reporters for nonexistent or little-known news agencies, infiltrating the ranks of legitimate correspondents, twisting them to its purpose. It was intimidating sources of the news, intimidating or trying to intimidate correspondents who were not playing its game. Old Agency hands would say later that the Agency had no interest in influencing *American* news coverage; that all it wanted to do was to influence *foreign* coverage in order to advance American policy. But in the summer of 1954 anyone who could put two and two together could see that this was not true; it was not even an acceptable euphemism. The Agency had influenced American reporting and *New York Times* reporting on Guatemala and it was trying to influence American reporting and *Times* reporting out of Germany; moreover it was hardly putting a fig leaf over these efforts. They were up front where knowledgeable newsmen could see them. They had practically been forced down the throat of Arthur Sulzberger, like it or not. And he was not liking it very well.

Catledge had hardly gotten off his letter to Sulzberger when the Otto John affair broke. The Otto John affair was exceedingly embarrassing for the CIA and for Allen Dulles personally.

Dr. Otto John was head of West Germany's Counter-Intelligence organization. He had the closest connection with U.S. intelligence and with Allen Dulles although Dulles' main reliance in West Germany had come to be another intelligence group, the Gehlen organization, originally put together for Hitler but after the war placed at the service of the United States. John vanished into East Germany July 20. It was, as one commentator said, as though J. Edgar Hoover had suddenly taken off for Moscow. What the repercussions might be no one in the CIA knew. It could be that just as the Agency was reaping the returns of the Guatemalan coup it might be dealt an irreparable blow by John's revelations. The Agency was particularly upset by reports that Otto John had "defected" to East Germany. The CIA version was that he had been the victim of an East German plot, that he had been kidnaped into the East.

The trouble with the CIA version was that it was not true. Tad Szulc, always into hugger-mugger, had accurately reported the John affair on page one of *The Times*. Handler had done the same thing from Bonn and had turned up the unpleasant fact that John and the CIA's bought-and-paid-for Gehlen organization had been engaged in bitter competition (probably accounting for some of the Third Man episodes in Berlin, some of the random killings).

It was a critical moment and the CIA started a massive counter-propaganda offensive, calling in Washington correspondents, planting stories, urging them to carry "their" version of what happened. Joseph and Stewart Alsop published several articles giving the Agency's account.

The pressures came to the attention of Scotty Reston and he raised the question directly with New York—what was *The Times* going to do about this kind of thing?

It was not, he noted, entirely a new problem. For a long time "we have been conscious of the difficulty of reporting information which has to do with the activities of our own secret service agents [CIA] here and abroad."

Since, Reston noted, we were in a form of warfare with the Communist world it had not been too difficult to ignore information which would have been valuable to the enemy. "Thus," he said, "we left out a great deal of what we knew about U.S. intervention in Guatemala [Reston was not fully informed about Dulles' hand in the Gruson case but knew the general outline] and in a variety of other cases involving the capture of some of our agents and the shooting down of some of our planes over Communist territory."

The captured agents to whom Reston referred were hapless former Russian and Ukrainian nationals who were being parachuted into the Soviet Union in one of the most reckless of CIA operations; the agents were all lost, all of them, either killed in descent or immediately captured and executed. Thirty years later it was impossible to conceive what caused the Agency to launch the program. The planes that were shot down were another matter. They were intelligence planes deliberately flown along the borders of or into the Soviet Union. Periodically they were shot down by Soviet gunners and the United States raised a great outcry, pretending that the planes had mistaken their way, strayed inadvertently into Russia or had not even been overflying the Soviet Union.

Reston pointed out that in such cases U.S. officials were willing to take responsibility for their statements and that *The Times* published these statements although, as he implied, *The Times* knew the statements were not true.

But up to this point, Reston said, what *The Times* had been asked to do, as in the case of Guatemala, was to leave things out of the paper.

Now a totally new question had been raised by the CIA. It was asking *The Times* to go beyond omission and "publish speculative articles which may or may not be based on correct premises and to do so on our own authority without any attribution to them or anybody else in this government."

The question had arisen with special force, he said, in the Otto John case. The CIA was "very embarrassed." It was "furious" about Tad

Szulc. It was "upset" by *The Times'* dispatches from Bonn. Now it had set about to "counteract" *The Times'* stories (and the truth). It had tried to foist off on *The Times* its version of the John affair but would not take responsibility for the statement and Reston had instructed his bureau not to carry the CIA material since it contradicted *The Times'* own information. The CIA had then come forward with what it called a "projection" of how the Russians were likely to "exploit" Dr. John. But here again they refused to take responsibility for totally speculative material.

The problem for *The Times,* Reston noted, was that the CIA was extremely persistent. If they could not persuade one *Times* man to carry a story they would try a second; if he refused they would try a third. If they could not get *The Times* to carry a story they would feed it to the AP and the UPI. If a news agency carried it then the New York desk of *The Times* was likely to ask the Washington bureau for the story. In fact, that had happened on the John story. After the bureau turned it down the CIA gave it to the UP. New York saw it on the UP wire and asked the Washington bureau for it. In Reston's absence the story was picked up by a deskman and appeared in *The Times.*

The question, said Reston, was a serious one: "Whether *The Times* wishes to make its columns available for the publication of unattributed speculative articles which we would not normally publish but which might be very useful to the Government. I am against this but it is obviously a policy question beyond my authority to decide."

Reston said he thought if uniform policy could be determined by *The Times* and everyone advised what the policy was the issue could be handled with a minimum of fuss.

So there it was, fair and square. Should *The Times* subvert the truth for the benefit of the CIA or not? There was no hesitation in Arthur Sulzberger's response. He was in full support of the position argued by Reston. "We cannot permit ourselves," he said, "knowingly to pull chestnuts out of the fire even for our own Government or any administrative Agency of it if we know in advance that the chestnuts are no good."

The Times, he said, was prepared to print any statement made by the government if they permitted themselves to be quoted and "we will do this whether we believe them or not." However, if the government wanted something run without attribution "then we must impose our own judgment as to whether or not it is true and use the story only if we believe it is true."

He conceded that there were occasions "when the Government is entitled to ask us not to use a particular story" but those occasions, he added, no doubt with Guatemala very much in mind, "should be few indeed and they should not be assented to lightly." In every such case, he said, the information should be transmitted to New York, together with who it was that wanted to suppress the news. New York would make the decision.

He distributed his letter to the top operational executives of the paper and to the line editors as well, so that there might, as Reston suggested, be no confusion between the various desks as to what *Times'* policy was.

By this time it was fully apparent to Arthur Sulzberger and to his chief editors that the task of steering an objective news course through the treacherous waters churned up by the cold war and the interaction of Soviet and American clandestine operations was not an easy one and would require all the diligence of which *The Times* was capable. Indeed, the situation had already become more complex and curious than Catledge or Arthur Sulzberger could have imagined.

41

The Arrangement

MANY MORE THINGS were happening at *The Times* in the 1950s than Arthur Sulzberger ever was to know. Some of them had to do with the CIA and others probably didn't but were born of inner hysteria created by the cold war, the suspicions it fostered, the sickly imaginations of people and, of course, years later when revelations about the CIA began to bubble to the surface, it could be seen that the suspicions were not entirely unjustified; possibly the wrong individuals were suspected; possibly incidents were misinterpreted but it became plain that, witting or not, there was a CIA presence on *The Times* and there were CIA efforts to suborn individuals on the paper.

Many of the cases were to remain enigmatic. Take, for example, that of George Leiber, a Belgian, a brilliant man, possessor of several languages, very European, a man who had lived in Kenya and South Africa and who wound up working in *The Times'* wire room in the late 1940s.

Leiber was a loner, he was studious, he read a lot, he kept to himself and after Radio Free Europe was started he began to moonlight evenings at RFE. He was not a reporter or an editor. His job on *The Times* was that of a technician, a copy handler, transmitting stories on the teleprinters, tearing copy off the machines and forwarding it to the editors. He was liked by his associates and twenty-five years after his death (he died at thirty-five of a brain tumor) he was remembered by some with affection. After a few years in *The Times'* wire room Leiber left to work full-time as a writer and editor at Radio Free Europe. After he went to work for RFE he used to drop back to *The Times* and gossip with his friends.

The first job Gay Talese had at *The Times* was in the wire room and when he came to write *The Kingdom and the Power* he devoted a line or two to "a quiet clerk in the telegraph room" who was on the payroll, unknown to *The Times,* of the CIA. That was all. There the matter lay despite a demand by Nat Hentoff of the *Village Voice,* writing in the *Columbia Journalism Review,* for more facts.

Who was George Leiber and what was he doing in *The Times'* wire room? Was he, as Talese seemed to insinuate, keeping his eyes out for anything that might interest the CIA? Certainly from the Agency viewpoint the wire room was a marvelous checkpoint to keep track of what was known, what was unknown, what was suspected and what was not suspected by the world's most responsible news machine. Here the news flowed in not only from *The Times'* own correspondents but from all the news agencies of the world—1,500,000 words a day. Possibly more important to an intelligence agency, through the wire room passed all the service traffic of *The Times*—orders to correspondents, messages in single copies for the eyes only of the publisher or managing editor, tips on rumors, off-the-record information on situations, advance notice on presidential statements, confidential assessments of Stalin's health or the political stability of the French Cabinet. A treasure trove for the CIA or the KGB.

The question of the role of George Leiber, as it happened, was not original with Talese. It had been raised earlier, at the time Talese was working in the wire room, by another *Times* man named George Anderson Cicero, an excitable and unbalanced individual who ultimately committed suicide. He suffered delusions of persecution and went to *Times'* management, claiming that Leiber was persecuting him and worked for the CIA. He went to the American Newspaper Guild with the same story. Then he changed his version and claimed Leiber was a Communist. The men who worked with Leiber and Cicero never took the matter seriously although *The Times'* management investigated the affair.

One of those who worked with both men said in 1979, "We never had any reason to think Leiber was CIA. He left us and became an editor and writer at RFE." Well, whatever Leiber was doing in *The Times'* wire room (if he was doing anything untoward the chances are his colleagues would have spotted it; deviations from the norm in newspapers are remarkably easy to detect) the fact was that in Leiber's part-time moonlighting for RFE he was working for the CIA because, while this was not known to Leiber's comrades in the wire room, RFE was a CIA subsidiary.

It was these shadowy games that made the task of tracking down CIA connections inside *The New York Times* (and any institution, for that matter) so difficult. The connections were by definition clandestine. The CIA was, after all, a secret agency. It did not conduct its business in the open. But enough had been painfully dredged to the surface by the late 1970s to make clear that latter-day protestations by old-boy CIA executives that they kept their hands off *The Times* because it was "too precious," as one of them said, bore little resemblance to reality.

Wayne Phillips

In the spring of 1952 Wayne Phillips was twenty-five years old, married, with two children, a graduate student at Columbia's Russian Institute, just assigned to night rewrite after being a copy clerk on the foreign desk of *The New York Times*. He was a young man in a hurry and his ambition, as it had been since he had interviewed a man named Geroid Robinson while working for the *Denver Post*, was to go to Moscow as a newspaper correspondent, preferably for *The New York Times*.

Robinson was one of the leading American experts on Russia, particularly on Russian peasant life, a man of such high scholarly standards that he was the despair of graduate students unable to meet his impossible demands. He was also one of the first Russian specialists to join OSS, and when CIA emerged in the postwar period Robinson was one of its staunchest pillars.

Inspired by Robinson, encouraged by two Columbia men at the University of Denver, Phillips applied and was admitted to the Columbia Russian Institute. He got a night job at *The Times* to support himself and his family.

Wayne was bright, hard-working, attractive. Soon he advanced to the night rewrite bank, a remarkable collection of young reporters. Max Frankel sat next to Phillips. Frankel was doing his M.A. in political science at Columbia. Next to him sat Tad Szulc, not yet having donned his cloak and dagger. Arthur Gelb, later to become Brooks Atkinson's choice as successor to himself as drama critic and still later Rosenthal's right-hand man, was another. So was George Barrett, who became a senior editor on the metropolitan staff, and Richard Amper, a fine political reporter who suffered an early death.

No one was in doubt as to Phillips' ambition. Between telephone calls and hurried stories of disasters he was constantly reading or writing Russian. He got a free-lance job working on a Soviet *Who's Who* (financed, although there was no way in which Wayne might have known this, by the CIA), he was always in need of money. He and Frankel sat side by side, Phillips boning away on his Russian, Frankel on his political science. A man named Frank Adams was city editor of *The Times*, a quiet man whose greatest pleasure was the office bridge game after "good night" had been given to the day-side reporters. He took a fondness for Phillips. He knew he was having difficulty making ends meet, that his family life was not too comfortable, that he was dying to go to Russia. Adams said nothing to encourage Phillips but he kept a close eye on him. And once Phillips remembered Harry

Schwartz,* *The Times'* resident specialist in Soviet affairs, talking to him about his Russian ambitions, drawing him out on his knowledge and aptitudes.

One day in early June of 1952 Phillips got a telephone call from a man who gave his name as Richard A. Suter. He said he was a graduate of the Russian Institute and a friend of Geroid Robinson and he wanted to talk with Phillips. The men met at the College Inn, a coffee shop on Broadway between 112th and 113th Streets. Suter told Phillips "You'll know me by a red rose in my lapel." He asked Wayne whether he would like to work for "a government agency." He did not mention the CIA but Wayne understood by the aura of cloak and dagger that this was what was involved. Nothing was said about subversive or secret work. Years later Phillips would say that he assumed what was involved was research and study of Soviet materials. Phillips said he certainly was interested and Suter said, well, okay, we will send you an application form. In a week or so the form arrived in Phillips' mailbox. He filled it out June 10, 1952, and sent it back to Washington, where with the normal bureaucratic delay it was stamped "received July 8, 1952" and on that same day the CIA opened a file on Phillips.

Nothing now happened for many months. Phillips had no recollection of telephone calls or contact from Suter nor did the CIA files, which years later he received through a Freedom of Information request, disclose any additions to the file on Wayne Phillips until in February 11, 1953, the CIA began a security check of his background, which was to go forward for months. The request for a security check said that it was intended to assign Phillips to the "SR division," that is, Soviet Russian division, and that he was to be "absorbed in (   ) program." The meaning of this heavily censored passage was never to become entirely clear but the application was stamped "For Covert Employment."

Whatever may have become the intention of the CIA, Phillips went about his work. He told no one about his CIA interview and men like Arthur Gelb and Tad Szulc on the rewrite bank in later years had no recollection of anything unusual in Phillips' conduct. Like all of them, he worked to the limit of his energies. There was great esprit de corps on the rewrite bank. The members thought that they were the best rewrite team that had ever been assembled. Phillips' relations with

*Schwartz, a graduate of the Columbia Russian Institute, worked for OSS and after the war joined the faculty of Syracuse University. He contributed free-lance articles on Soviet economy to *The Times* and eventually was taken on *The Times'* staff as a Soviet specialist, joining the editorial board, where he remained until retiring in 1979. He had close contact with the CIA, and when Robert Amory, one of Dulles' top assistants, took over the Agency's economic section he frequently consulted with Schwartz. (Personal interview, Amory, 4/23/79)

Frank Adams burgeoned and Adams came to regard him as something of a protégé. Phillips completed his master's thesis on "Lenin and the Origins of the Third International."

All this time security checks of Phillips were going on, the details of which were revealed in dim outline in the documents Phillips recovered from the CIA and FBI. The file showed that he "had admitted" membership in the American Newspaper Guild (which he had joined when he went to work for the *Denver Post*) and that he "admitted attending Communist Party meetings" which he had, in a sense, since as a reporter in Denver he had covered several Communist front meetings. Eventually, as he later learned, his Columbia thesis entered that file as well as a 3,000-word feature story he had done for the *Denver Post.* It was all grist for the security mill.

Apparently Phillips passed the security hurdles because on August 23, 1953, the CIA bureaucrats sent a request to employ Phillips up through channels, presumably for Allen Dulles' approval although that was not specified nor was it indicated what position Phillips would fill.

It had been fourteen months since Suter made the original contact when in early September 1953 the telephone rang on Phillips' desk. It was Suter. Could he come down to Washington for a meeting with himself and another man? Phillips took the train and met the CIA men on the second floor of a steak house named Marty Lafal's at Eighteenth and H streets. Years later he was to discover that this place was a favorite with CIA men who worked at an office at 850 Nineteenth Street N.W., just around the corner.

The meal was good, a good steak, and Phillips, whose budget did not afford many steaks, was impressed. The conversation was impressive too. The men seemed to like Phillips and their talk was big league. If Phillips accepted the Agency's proposal they had news for him. They could arrange with *The Times* to send him to Moscow as correspondent and they would pay him $100 a week over and above his *Times* salary. They were ready to deposit it in any bank he chose.

This was heavy talk to a man whose most intense ambition was to go to Moscow and who was perpetually short of money. Phillips remembered saying immediately he'd like the money, please, deposited in a U.S. bank. Then he got a grip on himself. He had never heard of a deal like this—"were there any other correspondents who had such an arrangement?"

"Oh, yes," Phillips recalled the men saying. "We have a regular working arrangement with the publisher of *The Times,* Mr. Sulzberger. There are other correspondents who have the same deal and we can guarantee that you'll be sent to Moscow."

Phillips went back to New York his mind in a whirl. He had accepted the offer on the spot. When he ultimately retrieved his CIA file there was no mention of that, no mention of the meeting at the Washington steak house or the College Inn coffee shop either.

Once in New York Phillips began to think and the more he thought the more he worried. How did he know the men he was dealing with were really CIA? How did he know that they were not covert KGB agents? He was in no position to check their credentials. Maybe he was being led down a garden path. Finally, he did something which only a young newspaperman would do. One night he sat down at his typewriter on the third floor of the big *Times* city room, took out a sheet of *Times* stationery, inserted it in the machine and wrote a personal letter to Allen Dulles explaining how he had been contacted, the names of the men, the proposition they had put to him. How about it, Mr. Dulles, he said in effect—are these your men? Is this on the legit or is somebody taking me for a ride?

He got a quick answer. Within the week Suter called from Washington. "Forget it," he said. "You've gone in the front door when we tried to make the arrangements through the back door." This was the end of it. Phillips got in the mail a $17 refund of his round-trip railroad fare to Washington. A few weeks later a man with CIA credentials came to the city room and asked for Phillips. He told Phillips that the men who made the offer to him had the authority to make it. That was all the CIA man had to say; he knew nothing about it himself; he was merely the bearer of a message.

This ended the story of Wayne Phillips and the CIA until years later when he obtained the sanitized files and gave the outline of what had happened to John Crewdson, *The Times* reporter who was then digging into the story of the CIA relationship with the media, including *The Times.*

By one of those twists of fate which often appear in life Phillips later came close to going to Moscow on the up-and-up, in the ordinary way, as a legitimate *Times* correspondent, making it on the strength of his ability and eagerness for the assignment.

Turner Catledge had begun to take an interest in him. Phillips had told Catledge that he was going to the Russian Institute, had learned the Russian language and that his ambition was the Moscow post.

In the autumn of 1954 Clifton Daniel had been sent to Moscow to replace me. I was finally back in New York after five long years in the Soviet Union. Catledge had taken over the management of *The Times'* European correspondents, having eased Cy Sulzberger out of his post as chief European correspondent. Catledge had had great trouble locating a nominee to replace me until Daniel unexpectedly volunteered. Now, with Stalin dead and Khrushchev moving to the fore, there was a surge of news out of Russia and the Russians indicated they might permit *The Times* to have a second man in Moscow. Catledge thought he had in Phillips a good prospect. There was one drawback—Phillips had a wife and three children, one an infant, just born. Nonetheless Catledge decided to prepare Phillips for Moscow.

But hardly was the decision made when Phillips' wife tragically developed cancer. It was out of the question to send him under the circumstances.

Twice more proposals were made to send Phillips to Moscow but family complications made it impossible and eventually Phillips left *The Times* for public relations work.

The secret manipulations of the CIA to get "its own man" into Moscow as *The Times* correspondent were not to come to the surface during Arthur Sulzberger's lifetime. Nor did energetic and exhaustive research in the files of *The Times* and the memories of surviving editors and reporters turn up evidence to support the bland assertion of Richard Suter of "an arrangement with Sulzberger." Suter was long dead before the inquiry started and Phillips' reclaimed CIA files neither included a report of Suter's original interviews nor a record of Phillips' letter to Allen Dulles and any action Dulles took in response thereto.*

But Phillips was left with a feeling that there might have been something behind Suter's declaration, particularly in view of the fact that the CIA man sent to see him in the city room said the approach was authorized. Long after the affair Phillips retained a belief that there might, indeed, have been some *Times* correspondents who had accepted the $100-a-week offer. He remembered several years after the Suter matter spending an evening with some *Times* foreign correspondents. The subject happened to be Russia and there was a conversation that lasted far into the night. Out of that talk he emerged with the feeling that one of the men in the room (by this time no longer serving abroad) might once have been a $100-a-week man for CIA. But this was only a subjective reaction. Not the kind of check you could put in the bank.

'Company' Connections

Turner Catledge in later years searched his mind for evidence to support the assertion made to Phillips by Suter of a standing "arrangement" between Arthur Sulzberger and the CIA that would enable the Agency to use *The Times* with Sulzberger's permission as "cover" for Agency employees. He could come up with nothing to support the

---

*The Phillips case was the subject of extended discussion between myself and a high-ranking CIA official who repeatedly promised to run down all the facts, particularly the basis for assertions of an "arrangement with Sulzberger." After many months he produced no facts whatever. Instead he lamely suggested a Freedom of Information action which he conceded would not necessarily produce the information. Phillips filed such an action in 1979 but had received no response as this book went to press.

statement and said that had he learned of such an agreement he would have "broken it up."

Catledge did, however, have a persisting recollection that the Agency had on at least one occasion attempted to utilize *The Times* as cover. He had a clear memory of being called to Arthur Sulzberger's office one day when a man from the CIA came to Sulzberger with a proposal to put a CIA man under *Times'* cover. He could not recollect the precise date, the name of the CIA man or the details but he was certain that the effort had been made. "We turned him down," Catledge said. "I remember that clearly."

It was Catledge's impression that this was not the only occasion on which the Agency requested the use of *Times'* cover for an agent. "Periodically," he said, "people would come to us, sometimes in the government, sometimes not, and they would ask *Times'* credentials for one thing or another. The publisher was utterly opposed to this and we did not permit it."

Catledge's testimony cut directly across the notion that the Agency had an ongoing agreement whereby it could send men out with *Times'* credentials. The idea of such a formal agreement did not jibe with the conduct and philosophy of Arthur Sulzberger as reflected through the eyes of his intimates. Nor did it conform to the impressions of many high-ranking members of the CIA, those still within the Agency and those in retirement. It was true, they agreed with almost full unanimity, that the CIA did have understandings with various organizations, business, academic institutions, and quite certainly with some elements in the media. But they did not think it plausible that this would exist with *The Times.* There were too many alternate kinds of cover, they said. Why should the Agency want *Times'* cover in western Europe or Latin America, one high executive said. There was all kinds of cover available without dragging in *The New York Times. The Times* was in "too precious a category" to be used like that. Now, he went on, if we could have put our own man into Peking or Moscow that might have been a different thing. But even then, he believed, it probably would have been regarded as too dangerous to compromise an organization like *The Times.* In this period of the late 1940s and the early 1950s, it should be remembered, for practical purposes the CIA *did not exist* as far as the Soviet Union was concerned—no station chief; no apparatus; nothing but adolescent, costly and tragic attempts to use former Soviet nationals. The only "inside" intelligence coming out of Russia was either from diplomats of other countries or from not-very-skilled U.S. military attachés whose method of finding out what was happening was to go off in pairs on such railroad trips as were permitted and count freight cars, railroad sidings and telegraph poles.

The last thing I would ever expect to find in the CIA archives, said one man who had been close to the top in those days, is a piece of paper with Allen Dulles' name and Arthur Sulzberger's name on it saying, "Whereas, the party of the first part agrees to furnish *Times'* cover for 'X' number of agents, etc. . . . It just isn't sensible" this man said. "A written agreement would be counterproductive. It is not enforceable and it is highly embarrassing if revealed." This former CIA executive spoke with personal knowledge of such arrangements. He said that the understanding could be negotiated only at the very top level. If it involved Arthur Sulzberger on one side it had to involve Allen Dulles on the other. Even if an understanding, oral or written, was agreed to, there remained serious problems in activating it. It wasn't, he said, like hiring someone to work for the Ford Motor Company. You had to have great flexibility. How many hours and how many days and how many weeks would the man work for the Agency? How many for the company that provided cover? How would the division of time and division of reimbursement be arranged? How would personnel shifts and transfers be worked out? The questions might sound trivial but in a bureaucracy they were real.

On the other hand Richard Bissell, who succeeded Frank Wisner, the wizard of the Agency who seemed to have had intimate relationships with almost everyone in the media world and who was ultimately to take his own life, would not renounce the possibility that *Times* men had been used on an individual basis and on a case-by-case arrangement. Bissell, who left the Agency after the Bay of Pigs disaster, was close to Wisner and privy to some of his arrangements but by no means to all. No one in the Agency then or later pretended to have knowledge of all the balls Wisner kept in the air, all the kites he flew, all the understandings he had.

But, as Bissell noted, the occasional use of a correspondent in a particular circumstance was far different from a long-term contractual arrangement with a man who was going overseas for a period of years. It was far different from a continuing arrangement at the top to provide cover.

"There was an allegation made," Bissell said, "of an arrangement by Arthur Sulzberger to place CIA agents in *The Times* organization. Now, I have no knowledge of that. It is conceivable that I might have known about something like that in the past, but, to be perfectly honest, I have no recollection of it now."

Bissell pointed out that there were, in fact, documented cases in which the CIA did employ journalistic cover. "But I am not aware," he said, "of any enduring arrangement between Allen Dulles and Arthur Sulzberger. Maybe there might be some example of an occasional use. But I feel that there was not likely to have been an instance of a man going abroad for a tour of duty of some long standing ostensibly for *The New York Times* but actually as an Agency employee."

John McCone, who headed the CIA under John Kennedy, recalled that he had once decided to "examine the interface between *The Times* and the CIA." He had discussed the matter with Arthur Krock, who had not seemed to know of any relationship, and he, McCone, did not believe that a covert relationship existed. Richard Helms, who headed the Agency under Richard Nixon, said he just didn't know. Cord Meyer, an ex-Agency official who was active in setting up the CIA program with cultural organizations, students and educators in the late 1940s and 1950s, said there was an informal "relationship of cooperation between *The Times* and the Agency in the fifties and sixties but now it's all gotten screwed up by Mr. [Sy] Hersh [*The Times* investigative reporter] and people like that." He said he knew nothing about a covert relation between *The Times* and the CIA. Lyman Kirkpatrick, whom many believed would have headed the Agency had he not suffered an attack of poliomyelitis in the early fifties, offered a severely circumscribed disclaimer. "I was never personally present at any meeting between Allen and Arthur Sulzberger at which such an arrangement was discussed," he said. "I don't think that Arthur would have done anything that went beyond normal warm relations, certainly nothing that would compromise or endanger his correspondents, nothing like espionage or anything like that. But I can't give you a categorical denial."

A Congressional investigator who carefully examined interconnections between the Agency and the press reported that he had been able to discover no permanent on-going contractual arrangements between the Agency and *staff* members of *The New York Times*. This did not cover "string" correspondents. He found a number of correspondents of string status who worked on a regular salaried basis for CIA. "Of course," he said, "I could have missed someone but it is not likely."

"Arthur Sulzberger was a very patriotic man," James Reston recalled. "He would agree to one-shot things when he felt it was in the government's need—something like the Gruson affair. But he would not have agreed to any continuing arrangement."

Despite the fact that men like Reston, Turner Catledge, Clifton Daniel, John Oakes, Harding Bancroft, Amory Bradford, myself, Iphigene Sulzberger, Punch Sulzberger and his sisters felt that a secret arrangement with the CIA was not compatible with Arthur Sulzberger's philosophy; despite the fact that no evidence of an agreement or staff assignments flowing from it could be found in *The Times'* records, there remained no way of proving a negative. The absence of a document or documents, the absence of hirings or discharges that would fit a pattern of Agency involvement did not prove the case. In Arthur Sulzberger's personal files there existed confidential documents mentioning the CIA but nothing about any "arrangement." He kept a careful record, for example, of the Gruson case but the manner in which he handled it did not suggest that Sulzberger was in the habit of making clandestine arrangements with the CIA—just the opposite. The correspondence between Sulzberger and Dulles bore no suggestion that they had dealt with matters of this kind before or, in fact, that they were used to dealing with each other in any way. The truth was that they were not close and never had been; the closest association Dulles had on *The Times* was with Adler. When correspondents in Washington had a social evening with Dulles, as they did once or so a year, they invariably sent a report to Sulzberger, who carefully had it filed as a "confidential document" in a brown paper envelope. Usually he would write a note to Reston or Krock saying the report was interesting but it gave him more respect than ever for his own correspondents because he had read it all previously and in better detail in his own newspaper.

These were not the communications of a man who had in a clandestine fashion placed his newspaper at the service of his country's secret intelligence agency.* Not that he was hostile to the Agency. He believed the CIA was dedicated to America's best interests and he had the same cause at heart. But he did not feel that news and intelligence made a good mixture.

In January of 1949, after I had been hired by *The Times* to go to Moscow as correspondent, Arthur Sulzberger spent several days escorting me about *The Times* (which I hardly knew at that time, knowing only Turner Catledge, Cy Sulzberger, assistant managing editor Theodore Bernstein and foreign editor Emanuel Freedman). Arthur Sulzberger wanted me to know *The Times* and obviously he wanted as well, to know me, going off to Moscow at the nadir of Soviet-American relations, a moment when talk of war was common. In the last conversation we were to have before my departure for Moscow he spoke of something which had obviously been on his mind and which he was a little hesitant about bringing up. "You know," he said, "it's possible that you may be approached by our intelligence people [I don't think he used the words CIA]. I just want you to know that you should feel under no obligation to do anything for them." I thanked him for his guidance. He then added that "in fact, we would be happier if you didn't."

---

*Allen Dulles' correspondence at Princeton University's Firestone Library does not suggest intimacy between himself and Arthur Sulzberger nor between himself and Cyrus Sulzberger. Letters exchanged by Arthur Krock and Dulles, Arthur Krock and John McCone, Arthur Krock and Frank Wisner, held at Firestone, indicate a considerably closer friendship. (Nancy Bressler, Firestone Library, 7/26/79)

At the time I thought it was a sensible thing for him to say; I had had no experience with the CIA, although in later years on the rare occasions when I returned from Moscow (in 1953 and 1954) I would get a telephone call from Colonel Stanley Grogan, Allen Dulles' press officer, and be invited down to luncheon with Dulles and an interesting and literate discussion of Soviet questions, particularly those which had arisen after the death of Josef Stalin.

It seemed to me in 1949 that Sulzberger was reflecting the reality of the world. He did not want to put his foot down and say "No" to contact with intelligence people but he left the plain indication that he would be much happier if I stayed clear. Which I did.

Only much much later in the atmosphere of closest scrutiny of relationships between the CIA and the media did it occur to me, as it did to others, that, in fact, Arthur Sulzberger was acquiescing in an intelligence contact if, for some reason, I thought it advisable.

While it is possible to put his words in this context I do not think that was in his mind. I took it at the time, and still take it, as a quiet word of advice to steer clear. It does not seem likely that a man who offered this guidance to a new correspondent going into the very heart of "enemy" territory was a man who had a secret deal with Allen Dulles. On the basis of such testimony the verdict on an "arrangement" between Sulzberger and Dulles clearly was that old Scotch one —"Not proven."

For all this the evidence was inescapable that there had been on the staff of *The Times* in the postwar period men with connections to the CIA—men in low places and some in higher places. The story of *Times'* ties to the Agency was subjected to intensive investigation by myself and others. Some facts were to be established, others could not be proved in a legal sense, and others probably will never be dug out.

42

The CIA and
The Times

*W*HEN CY SULZBERGER began to rebuild *The Times* foreign staff after World War II it was natural that he would turn to men whom he had met and worked with, particularly correspondents whom he had known during the war, men from the Middle East, the Balkans and Russia. Thus, Meyer S. Handler, whom he had come to like and respect in Moscow, where Handler worked for the United Press, was taken onto *The Times* and sent to Yugoslavia to report on the efforts of the Yugoslav Communists to establish a brand of Marxism which in almost every way was the reverse of what was done in Russia. Handler hated Stalinist Russia and was delighted with a chance to report on Tito's "upside-down" communism.

Another wartime friend whom Cy placed on *The Times* was Sam Pope Brewer, a serious, modest man, not at all loquacious, who had covered the Middle East for the *Chicago Tribune* while Cy was covering it for *The Times.* Cy thought Brewer very promising and wanted to send him to Latin America but there was a hitch. Sam had worked for OSS during the war. There was no secret about this. It was known to the *Tribune* and to his colleagues. Many newsmen had such roles during the war, particularly in the Middle East. Farnsworth Fowle, an old friend of Cy and Sam in Turkey (later Fowle was also hired by Cy for *The Times*), remembered meeting a newly arrived news-agency man during the war in Istanbul. After a few drinks the man said, "I've got to meet a fellow named Fowle. I've been told to hire him for undercover work." Fowle identified himself and politely declined to become a double agent.

As Cy recalled it he told Sam that before he could work for *The Times* he had to end his intelligence activities. "I made him swear he had broken all his ties," Cy said. "That was a must." But there is no real evidence Sam did sever his connections. In fact he probably maintained them to the end of his life and this was how he came to play a clandestine role in the spy case of Guy Burgess, Donald Maclean and Harold G. "Kim" Philby.

Burgess, Maclean and Philby were for many years members of the

English diplomatic service while simultaneously spying for the Russians. It was Philby who tipped Maclean that MI-5, the English counterintelligence branch, was on his trail, enabling Maclean and Burgess to escape from London May 25, 1951, and make their way to Moscow. Philby, number two in the British Embassy in Washington at the time, had already aroused the suspicion of General W. Bedell Smith and Allen Dulles of the CIA. When Burgess and Maclean made their getaway Smith's suspicions solidified and he insisted that Philby leave Washington, which he did, returning to London in July 1951.

Philby resigned from the Foreign Office but not from the Secret Service. Philby was an intelligence officer using the British Foreign Service as cover. The Secret Service subjected him to intensive interrogation, ostensibly clearing him of connection with the spy ring in 1952. Although Philby had been "cleared" he remained under secret surveillance. The top figures in British and U.S. intelligence felt that given his tether Philby might well commit a misstep which would provide evidence of his links to the Russians.

Sam Brewer was an old friend of Philby's. They had covered the Franco side in the Spanish Civil War, Brewer for the *Chicago Tribune,* Philby for the *London Times.* Philby, a Communist from Cambridge days, went to the Fascist side in Spain to obtain "coloration" for his role as a Soviet spy. He had already been recruited by the Russians. He won a reputation in Spain as an anti-Communist and as a brave reporter. He was the only survivor of a bomb that hit a touring car in which he, Edward J. Neill of the Associated Press and two other correspondents were riding near Teruel in 1938.

The world of foreign correspondents, diplomats and intelligence agents is parochial. They trade in the same kind of goods, move from one capital to another, frequent the same bars, go to the same cocktail parties, have the same interests. They know each other. They talk shop together. Not every correspondent knows whether the diplomat whom he has met in Paris, Bangkok and Istanbul is in intelligence nor does the diplomat know whether the correspondent is. But they all know men who are in intelligence and who are diplomats or correspondents.

So it was not surprising that the paths of Brewer and Philby would cross and recross and that Cy's path would cross both of theirs. Eleanor Carolyn Kearns, whom Brewer would marry in 1948, was part of this world, too. Sam had met her in Istanbul during World War II where she worked for OWI and she stayed on in Turkey after the war, possibly in some minor intelligence role.

Brewer and Philby saw each other only occasionally. It was not necessarily a close friendship, but like most bonds between foreign correspondents it endured.

Sam Brewer was in Spain when the Burgess-Maclean case broke

into the open in May of 1951. He was just coming through a crisis. The Franco Government had withdrawn his credentials and threatened to expel him because of his articles about corruption in the regime. *The Times,* naturally, backed Brewer to the hilt and the Madrid Government permitted him to stay. Brewer was doing competent work for *The Times* and Arthur and Cyrus Sulzberger agreed that Brewer would remain in Madrid for at least another six months. Spain was not to be given the impression that *The Times* was susceptible to blackmail.

The Brewer Case

On Monday, May 28, 1951, *within hours* of the alert to British security officers that Maclean and Burgess had vanished (by disappearing on Friday evening, May 25, they had given themselves the whole English weekend, nearly three days headway on any pursuit) a CIA representative named Alfred Corning Clark* paid a hurried call on Arthur Sulzberger with a highly unusual proposal, so unusual that Sulzberger sent him down to the third floor to meet with managing editor E. L. James and assistant managing editor Catledge.

Clark wanted *The Times* to give Brewer an immediate leave of absence to work for the CIA, a three-year tour of duty at pay of $10,000 a year plus $2,000 in overseas allowance. The proposal put up the backs of both *Times* editors. They had no interest in placing *Times* men at the service of U.S. intelligence agencies. James wrote a semi-sarcastic memo to Sulzberger opposing the CIA proposal in toto. James and Catledge were extremely suspicious of the CIA's motivation in wanting to take on Brewer "at this particular moment." James probably was alluding to Brewer's Spanish troubles. Neither he nor Catledge had any knowledge of the Burgess-Maclean case, which would not break into public view until June 6, 1951; nor could they have known of Bedell Smith's suspicions of Philby; nor any connection between Brewer and Philby; nor of connections between Brewer and the CIA. But James was too good a newspaperman not to smell a rat, although he didn't know what kind of rat it was. While Clark insisted he had not been in touch with Brewer, James was skeptical.

These considerations, however, were secondary to the objection in

---

*Alfred Corning Clark was the great grandson of Edward Clark of Cooperstown, New York, founder of the Singer Sewing Machine Co. He served for several years as CIA "case officer," assigned to *The New York Times,* among other large corporations. He died September 29, 1961 of, it was said in his *Times* obituary, "natural causes," 13 days after marrying his sixth wife, Alicja Darr Furdan. A colleague who served with him in the New York office of CIA described him as "mortally afraid of women." He dressed in nondescript old clothes to try and avoid feminine attention, an objective which he signally failed to achieve. (*New York Times,* Sept. 30, 1961)

principle of James and Catledge. The CIA wanted it both ways; it wanted Brewer to work under cover on an intelligence assignment and it wanted him to come back to *The Times* after it was through with him.

"That," said James, "would leave him a *New York Times* man, that would leave our tag on his shirttail all the time and if, as sometimes happens, he got into a jam by doing secret service work for the government, there is a good chance that it would reflect not only on his future but on other of our correspondents."

James could see nothing in the proposal for *The Times* except headaches. "I would hate to see us do this in the first instance because it would be too likely to lead to similar requests concerning other men," said James. "Mr. Catledge concurs in this memorandum."

To which Arthur Sulzberger responded in a crisp note to James, "Please note and advise Mr. Catledge that I have turned down that proposal which concerned Mr. Brewer."*

That was the end of that—or was it? In all probability it wasn't even the beginning. Confirmation of Brewer's CIA connections did not come until 1977 after his retirement from *The Times* and his death. But earlier some of Brewer's colleagues had developed a suspicion or two. Newsmen know how newsmen respond in given situations. They are quick to detect a false note—questions which don't quite track, nuances in handling stories, higher-than-normal anxiety levels. Brewer was a placid individual on the surface but sometimes he displayed a nervousness that did not match the news pattern.

Clifton Daniel happened to go to Spain in the spring of 1951 with a friend for a vacation. They stayed at the Ritz and almost every evening Brewer came over for a drink. It was at the height of his row with the Franco authorities. He was threatened with expulsion, an unpleasant but hardly unusual situation, but he lived in terror that the government might arrest or kidnap him. He had sent his wife, Eleanor, and their daughter, Ann, to France, to Saint-Jean-de-Luz and moved in with an American Embassy official so that he might be, he said, safe from arrest at night. Daniel thought Sam overreacted, that somehow he was "too close" to the embassy, and later on was to wonder whether

---

*Government requests for the "loan" of *Times* personnel for intelligence or quasi-intelligence posts were not uncommon in the postwar period. Almost invariably they were turned down by Arthur Sulzberger, sometimes even without reference to the correspondent involved. A request for Drew Middleton's services was rejected late in 1947. (*Times'* archives, Middleton to Sulzberger, 11/3/47) After much arm-twisting Sulzberger permitted Shepard Stone, number two to Lester Markel in the Sunday department, to work for Gen. Lucius Clay in Berlin on a "temporary basis" which became permanent when Stone went to the newly organized Ford Foundation after completing his work with Clay. Such examples were rare. (*Times'* archives)

Brewer's alarm stemmed from journalistic concerns or Agency concerns.

After being "cleared" in his security investigation Philby returned to Spain briefly for the London *Sunday Observer*. Whether Brewer saw him then is not certain. But in 1956, after a series of odd jobs, Philby came back to the Middle East, this time for the *Observer* and the London *Economist*. Whether he knew it or not he was being watched by both British and U.S. intelligence for some move that might give him away. Sam Brewer and his wife were now in Beirut, where Sam was serving as *Times* correspondent after a tour of duty in Latin America. Sam was away from Beirut on assignment but he had told Eleanor to watch out for his old pal. She did. On September 12, 1956, she met him in the bar of the St. Georges Hotel, had a drink and introduced him to her friends. From that day forward Philby, Eleanor and Sam Brewer were inseparable. Later there were those like Kermit Roosevelt who, with James Angleton, had warned Allen Dulles in 1951 of their suspicion that Philby was the "third man" who seemed skeptical that Sam could have held a "watching brief" on Philby for CIA. But a CIA man who was in Beirut at that time said "we were all instructed to watch Philby."

While the intimacy of the Brewers and Philby may have been propitious in intelligence terms it was unpropitious on a personal level. Within a year Eleanor and Kim had fallen in love, and after Eleanor obtained a Mexican divorce in 1958 she and Philby were married. Brewer stayed for a while in Beirut and the divorce did not entirely disrupt the relations of the trio. Sam always denied as apocryphal a story that when Philby told him he and Eleanor wanted to get married his response was, "You mean that you are asking my wife's hand in marriage?" But the relations of the trio were never very conventional.

January of 1963 was a time of growing tension for Philby. He knew his pursuers were closing in. Always a heavy drinker, he now drank "ferociously" one old friend said. January 21, as Eric Downton, the London *Daily Telegraph* correspondent in Beirut, recalled, Kim and Eleanor dined at his house, Philby drinking very hard. Before the evening was over he gave Eleanor a karate chop, stunning her. As she dozed Downton and Philby talked late into the night—about the Spanish Civil War, about Cambridge and somehow Philby gave Downton the impression that he was really very left wing.

Two days later the Philbys were invited to dinner at the home of Glen Balfour-Paul, first secretary at the British Embassy, and his wife, old friends. Kim never showed up. He had vanished—to Moscow as it later would transpire. Eleanor, badly shaken, telephoned an intelligence friend in the British Embassy and the hunt was on. But it was a private hunt. Not a word was to leak publicly of Philby's disappearance for weeks.

By one of the many apparent coincidences that marked the Philby-Brewer story, Lise Wangel, a close friend of Sam and Eleanor, whom Sam would marry in 1965, arrived in Beirut Saturday morning, January 24, the morning after Philby's disappearance. She came to visit Ann and Eleanor and hoped to meet Philby, the extraordinarily charming man of whom she had heard so much. That was not to be. She had missed him by a dozen hours. Eleanor said her husband had vanished but warned Lise to say nothing to other correspondents if they asked about him (as they did) when they had a drink on the St. Georges terrace. Lise, with whom Eleanor later was to stay both before and after going to Moscow to join Philby, became convinced that Eleanor knew nothing of Philby's spying for the Russians. "Eleanor drank a lot," she recalled. "She spoke very frankly. I don't think she could have concealed that."

As to Sam's knowledge, that was a different matter. He certainly knew something, Lise conceded. She remembered him saying that Philby "doesn't look at things in the same vein that I did." She thought Sam felt "there were some Commie instincts" in Philby. That Sam knew Philby was a Soviet agent she could not say. But now Sam did something that aroused strong suspicion of his role. He was no longer stationed in Beirut, having been transferred back to New York to become a member of *The Times'* staff covering the United Nations. *The Times* was midway into the Long Strike of 1962–63. Sam had vacation time coming; there really was nothing for him to do in New York and suddenly he flew off to Beirut, ostensibly because he was worried about his daughter, Annie. Although no public announcement had been made about Philby (nor would word leak out until March 3, 1963), Sam, of course, knew he had vanished, believed that he had gone to Moscow and put it out that he was fearful Eleanor would join Philby, taking Annie and Philby's two children, who were with her.

Eleanor did not entirely accept Sam's explanation. He had already been to Washington to check out Philby and she thought he "probably knew more about the case than most people in Beirut." Sam's colleagues in Beirut thought he knew a great deal. Nothing had yet appeared in the press and Eleanor kept insisting that Philby had gone to Yemen, where he had spent a good deal of time since the revolution and civil war a year before. In the gossipy atmosphere of Beirut, Sam's movements attracted attention. He made the rounds of Philby's hangouts, the Hotel Normandy, where Philby had a mail drop, the St. Georges Club, not far from the hotel, a couple of Lebanese restaurants that Philby enjoyed. He spent some time with the CIA station chief at the American Embassy, a man well regarded by the correspondents.

He had a splendid villa but his children swore it was haunted. There were bad jokes about the spook's place being spooked. Brewer saw an old friend named Sam Souki, a successful Lebanese public relations man who had been a correspondent in Cairo for UPI and *Newsweek,* a personable man reputed to have connections with the CIA. He visited Abu Sayd Abu Reech, long employed by *Time* magazine, who had close relations with the U.S. Embassy and CIA.

There was a coup in Iraq on February 8 and many Beirut journalists expected Philby to turn up there. He did not but one afternoon Sam Brewer was sitting with the correspondents on the St. Georges terrace. The talk went to the closing of the Syrian frontier. No one could remember the name of an obscure village, the last village on the Lebanese side before you came to the Syrian checkpoint. "Oh," Sam intervened, "you mean so-and-so." One of those present was amazed —and suspicious. Either Sam had a remarkable memory or he had been checking out the border points through which some believed Philby had secretly passed. This newsman remembered rumors that the Americans were so enraged that Philby had given them the slip that they had a team of picked agents en route to Beirut, intending to shanghai Philby, if necessary, and take him back for interrogation. Feeling between the British and American intelligence groups, he said, was intense. "I even think that the Brits tried to make a case on Sam Brewer as an American Philby," he said. There were some on *The Times* whose suspicions of Brewer's intelligence connection were reinforced at this time. Daniel noted that Brewer seemed to have a special nose for espionage and undercover activity. Peter Kihss remembered that no one had such excellent intelligence sources as Brewer, and Farnsworth Fowle, who had known him from the beginning, agreed. Nonetheless, Fowle refused to believe that Brewer had a link to the CIA. One correspondent who had known Brewer for many years, all during his United Nations days, hesitated a long, long time over the question of Brewer and the CIA, finally observing that he just could not say, that is, "not for certain." Besides, he went on, Sam was now dead. Why talk about it? It was a good enough point. Brewer was liked and respected by his colleagues; they felt that whatever he might have done for the CIA he had tried to meet his journalistic responsibilities. Yet, the truth was that Brewer had never during his years on *The Times* achieved the level of work which Cy Sulzberger had expected and, examining Brewer's private news memoranda, his response to stories and events, his replies to messages from the foreign desk, a critic could not but wonder whether he was totally independent and objective as a correspondent. The question might not have arisen, perhaps, if the Agency connection had not existed. But knowing the connection it seemed almost certain that a potentially first-class journalist had tailed off to second rank because he tried to serve two masters.

Stringers

The examples of Sydney Gruson, Wayne Phillips and Sam Pope Brewer do not exhaust the CIA's interventions or attempted interventions with *The New York Times*. Other staff correspondents were recruited by the Agency or had Agency connections before being hired by *The Times*. The names of several of these men have been published by *The Times*. Others have not because the cases are not susceptible to public proof. And the CIA had ties to men and women who served *The Times* as "string" correspondents in many parts of the world. A "string" correspondent is a reporter who (usually) works for a local newspaper and sends news to *The Times* on the side as a part-time job. The association with *The Times* is often as important for reasons of local prestige as it is for financial rewards. A stringer may work for *The Times* over a long period of years. *The Times* has no real control over such individuals, who are, in essence, private contractors. They are hired at long range and often are only occasionally seen by a *Times* correspondent who happens to turn up in their obscure country or city. It was *Times'* policy not knowingly to employ such an individual if he had intelligence ties but, in practical terms, such connections often did exist, not only with U.S. agencies but with the other intelligence agencies. On one occasion after World War II a *Times* string correspondent in Ankara, a distinguished local newsman named Aslan Humbaraci, opted for the Soviet side to the embarrassment of Cy Sulzberger, who had hired him. And there was the equivocal case of Ali Mehravari, for many years a stringer for *The Times* (and for Reuters) in Tehran. In the early 1970s the English Queen Mother was passing through Tehran and at the British Embassy Mehravari was honored with the award of an O.B.E. As Tehran gossips put it, "He must have done something in the past to deserve it."

Humbaraci was not the first stringer hired by Cy to opt for the other side. There was the tragic case of Ralph Parker, a distinguished English correspondent of *The Times* of London. Cy met Parker in Belgrade before the war and hired him to file to *The New York Times* from Belgrade. Parker's wife was killed by a German bomb in the Nazi invasion of Yugoslavia, a stunning blow to Parker. He was then assigned by the *London Times* to Moscow. Cy again hired him to represent *The New York Times*, which he did until 1944 when the connection was severed because of Parker's growing Soviet bias. He had fallen in love with and married his beautiful but erratic Russian secretary, Valentina, who swung him swiftly and sharply to the Communist viewpoint. He wound up his career as correspondent of the London

Communist Party paper, the *Daily Worker.* His old friends, including George Kennan, who had known him in Prague, retained an affection for Parker although distressed by his ideological turnabout.

Probably the best-known CIA string correspondent of *The Times* was Henry Pleasants, station chief in Germany, who for several years served as *The Times'* music correspondent. He was a distinguished musicologist and received a $15 a month retainer from *The Times.* He had risen to $25 a month when he was let go about 1954 after *The Times'* music department finally became aware that Pleasants was doubling in brass.

What the encounters between *The Times* and the CIA demonstrated was that there did not seem to be an "understanding" whereby the CIA could employ *The Times* for cover, as an Agency source long after the event had declared. Nor did the denials of the highest Agency officials that they would never have stooped to tamper with *Times'* personnel, *The Times* being "too precious" and there being no real need on the part of the Agency to draw on *Times'* personnel, hold up. The evidence showed that, in fact, the Agency did seek to recruit, to pervert, to draw upon *Times'* personnel when it thought this would serve its purpose; that intentional or not, these Agency efforts did influence, dilute or otherwise wound *The Times'*s news-gathering process by affecting the judgment of *Times* men who had CIA connections.

That the Agency's efforts did not influence or affect *The Times* in a broad sense was not because of self-imposed restraint or rules adopted by the Agency. The Agency stuck its hand into *The Times* when it thought this served its purpose. The protection to *The Times* came from the resistance of *Times* editors to intervention from the outside from whatever source. The response of James and Catledge to the CIA for the "lend-lease" of Sam Pope Brewer was a spontaneous negative. Nor was there any hesitation by Arthur Sulzberger. Arthur Sulzberger was a rigorously principled man. He felt it his duty to listen to his government whether in the person of the CIA, the State Department or the White House. He was willing, within reason, to respond—as he did in the Gruson case. But he was not going to put *The Times* and its reputation in jeopardy for anyone.

The documented conduct of Sulzberger, James and Catledge in the Brewer case added force to Catledge's assertion many years later that if he had ever seen a sign of an "arrangement" between Arthur Sulzberger and the CIA he would have "broken it up."

Argus

One day in June of 1958, Walter Sullivan, science editor of *The New York Times,* walked into the office of Richard Porter, chief of the panel on rockets and satellites of the National Academy of Science for the

International Geophysical Year, in the General Electric Building, at Fifty-first Street and Lexington Avenue in New York, and without saying a word slipped a piece of paper on Porter's desk. On the paper, Sullivan, a slim, angular man whose body seemed to be constructed entirely of sinew and tendon after a lifetime of ascending the Himalayas, crossing Greenland glaciers, trekking the wastelands of Australia and canoeing the wilderness of Hudson's Bay, had typed the word "Argus." Below it was a date, the location, height and yield of a series of nuclear blasts which the United States was preparing to set off in outer space.

Sullivan's friend was both horrified and amused.

"I can't tell you not to print it," he said. "But I can say this—if you do, the operation will never take place."

A day or so before this Hanson Baldwin, military editor of *The Times,* had asked Sullivan for a few moments in private. He had learned of a forthcoming experiment called "Argus" which was to be conducted in the loneliest spot in the South Atlantic, equidistant from Antarctica, South Africa and Cape Horn. Nuclear bombs were to be carried by multistage rockets three hundred miles into outer space and exploded to see if this would create a thin but intense shell of radiation around the earth which would disrupt radio communications and make it impossible to obtain radar echoes from incoming missiles.

The project was of intense scientific interest and of great potential military importance. Baldwin had obtained his information in a manner which put no barrier on immediate publication but he was troubled at publicizing the experiment before it was carried out and he wanted Sullivan's opinion. That was why Sullivan put the typed piece of paper before his scientific friend.

Baldwin and Sullivan by all ethical considerations were free to publish a story of enormous interest and importance. However, they quickly concluded that they would not publish prior to the carrying out of the experiment. Within an hour of Sullivan's meeting with Porter, William H. Godel, security chief of the Pentagon's Advanced Research Projects Agency, was on the telephone to Sullivan. Sullivan told him to relax. *The Times* had decided to hold the story until the experiment took place.

The experimental firing occurred July 31, 1958. It was the understanding of Baldwin and Sullivan that an announcement would be made immediately and they would then be free to publish. But nothing happened, although scientists all over the world quickly detected the effects of the test, began international inquiries and prepared scientific papers which, in a guarded way, discussed the results. Some of this material was presented at the American Astronautical Society meetings in New York in December. The Russians, of course, had detected the experiment at their observation stations, and scientists around the world were rapidly analyzing what had happened. Still the government would not release the story, although Sullivan and Baldwin put continuous pressure on the authorities. Sullivan telephoned scientists around the world and demonstrated how simple it was to put all the facts together without consulting U.S. sources. Still the secrecy lid was maintained. The experiment had been carried out under the auspices of the International Geophysical Year, an international experimental collaboration under which all parties were obligated to tell the others the results of such experiments. Scientists inside and outside the government demanded that the test be announced. Finally Baldwin and Sullivan learned that the government was preparing a limited announcement. They decided on March 16, 1959, they could wait no longer. Up to this point no one at *The Times,* no editor, no other newsman, shared the knowledge possessed by Baldwin and Sullivan. By March 18 they had their articles assembled. They placed the articles and their reasoning before Arthur Sulzberger, Orvil Dryfoos and Turner Catledge.

Sulzberger did not object to publication but said, "I do not want to do anything that is going to do the country harm." Sullivan suggested that he inform the White House as a courtesy. Sulzberger agreed but added, "If the White House phones and says the story will do serious damage we are not going to print it."

The story was set into type; photographs, diagrams, background material was assembled. The layout was made. Sullivan telephoned the White House, explained the situation and said he would await a return call.

With the story placed in the paper, the pages allotted, Sullivan and Baldwin walked up Eighth Avenue and Forty-seventh Street to Barbetta's restaurant. They had a drink and ordered dinner. The office was instructed to telephone if a call came in from the White House. They waited. None came. The presses rolled and on March 19 the story of the Argus experiment was presented to the world.

It was, *Times* men agreed, a characteristic example of what *The Times* regarded as journalistic responsibility. The story was held up not because of pressure or interference by the government or the White House but because responsible journalists on *The Times* believed this action was in the overall interest of science and the country. It was published at a moment when *The Times'* writers and editors knew that there was no logical reason for further restraint. Every reasonable precaution had been taken. There was not the faintest doubt that the Soviet knew as much as *The Times.* The only barrier to publication had been the bureaucratic blockade, the refusal of government officials to move, to release to the people of the United States the information which it was their privilege and prerogative to share.

This conduct of *The Times* in a case of genuine as opposed to political pretense of security was so typical as hardly to cause comment within the paper itself. No one had been surprised when in 1945 the government had turned to *The Times* and its science writer, William L. Laurence, obtained his special services after letting Arthur Sulzberger in on the secret and commissioned him the official reporter to record and witness the atom-bomb story for the world. The government knew that *The Times* and Laurence were to be trusted; Sulzberger and Laurence knew that they could take the government's bona fides in good faith. In later years, of course, these bona fides began to lose value.

The Argus story was not the only one in which the judgment of *The Times* was exercised, independent of government recommendation or involvement, in the interest of what was regarded as national security. When *Times* men suggested at the time of the Pentagon story that they were more competent than the government to judge such issues they were not indulging in bombast. They knew. They had been there. Their actions had been responsible, not self-serving, as government decisions tended to be.

U-2

On May 1, 1960, Francis Powers, a contract employee of the CIA, was shot down in his U-2 spy plane near Sverdlovsk in the Soviet Union. The incident created a world sensation. When President Eisenhower took personal responsibility for the overflight Premier Khrushchev withdrew an invitation for Eisenhower to visit Russia and a severe dent was put in relations between the superpowers.

The moment the announcement of the U-2 came through Hanson Baldwin wrote for *The Times* a comprehensive account of the plane, details of how it had been developed, the work that had gone into it in the so-called skunk factory, the experimental laboratory of Lockheed Aircraft, which had designed the plane at the direction and order of the CIA. Baldwin had needed only to sit down at his typewriter and write the story because he had known of the existence of the U-2 for more than two years.* Baldwin, an old Navy man and Annapolis graduate, did not have many Air Force sources because he was regarded as partial to the Navy. But he had one friend who told him about the project.

Not only had Baldwin heard of the plane and its extraordinary characteristics, he had seen one on an airfield in Germany and instantly recognized it despite a crude effort to distract his attention. Once he

*Arthur Krock also possessed knowledge of the U-2 flights long in advance of May 1960. (Arthur Krock, *Memoirs,* New York, 1968, p. 181)

had the details of the story he went to Allen Dulles and told him what he knew. Dulles confirmed Baldwin's facts. He said that the Russians had known about the U-2 overflights almost from the beginning but had decided not to protest because they did not possess weapons capable of shooting down the U-2s and so long as the United States did not make public the fact of the overflights Dulles felt the Russians would remain silent. This, in fact, was what happened.

Baldwin said that he would not damage U.S. interests by putting his story into print but that the instant a hint of the spy plane found its way to public knowledge he would break the full and detailed account. Dulles thought that fair enough. When the U-2 story broke Baldwin's informed account was a worldwide scoop.

Baldwin had no regrets over holding up the story. It was true that had he published when he first heard of the U-2 the diplomatic crisis which was touched off in May 1960 would not have occurred but it was equally true that the crisis would not have emerged had Eisenhower thought to suspend the U-2 flights in view of his upcoming trip to Russia. Baldwin's responsibility in the U-2 crisis seemed attenuated to say the least. He had not bothered to consult his editors, secure in the knowledge that his judgment was sound and would not conflict with theirs. There is no reason to think he was mistaken. His conduct was consistent with that which he displayed on the Argus story. When he revealed his knowledge of the U-2, no one on *The Times* took him to task. Had he consulted in advance with Arthur Sulzberger or the editors their reaction would have been the same as his own.

In the case of the U-2, as in the case of Argus (and earlier with "Atomic Bill" Laurence's story of the A-bomb), the *Times* men were dealing with genuine, quantified military and security secrets; not history; not politics; not propaganda. They demonstrated that they understood the difference. That was what responsible journalism as defined by *The Times* was about. That was not journalism as it was defined by many in the government and surely not by the CIA and by its sublime activist, the late Frank Wisner, who boasted of having "a mighty Wurlitzer" at his command, a great media organ made up in part of bought-and-paid-for newspapers, news agencies and radio chains around the world, in part of undercover agents in scores of countries masquerading as newsmen, and in part of legitimate newsmen, cajoled or subverted, to play a role in the "organ" or other intelligence activity of the Agency, and in part, of course, of patriotic men of the Fourth Estate like Joe Alsop, who considered it his duty and his obligation to assist his country and its objectives by helping an agency run and operated almost entirely by his friends. Alsop was not, of course, the only journalist who took that view.

43

"What is this CIA?"

D URING TURNER CATLEDGE'S DAYS as managing editor of *The New York Times* he held a conference in his office at the southwest corner of the city room at 4:30 each weekday afternoon to discuss with his principal editors the news of the day and decide what stories to play on page one.

On September 2, 1965, Nathaniel Gerstenzang, deputizing for foreign editor Sydney Gruson, who was absent, reported a curious item from Singapore. Lee Kuan Yew, the Prime Minister, had made a speech about an incident five years earlier in which two CIA agents had been arrested. He said he had rejected a $3,300,000 bribe from the CIA for their release and demanded $33 million instead but eventually had freed the men without payment.

The State Department denied the story. Now Lee had produced a letter by Secretary of State Rusk apologizing for the incident.

Catledge expressed astonishment—how could such a thing happen? What was going on with the CIA? Didn't anyone have control over it?

These were good questions, fundamental questions. They had been germinating in Catledge's mind for a long, long time, possibly since 1954 when Meyer Handler had opened his eyes to the Third Man games being played by trench-coated agents in Germany, possibly even before that on the occasion in 1951 when the CIA had come to solicit Sam Brewer's services. Catledge's concern had been magnified by the Bay of Pigs episode in 1961 and the slow but steady accretion of rumors about Agency operations.

The Lee Kuan Yew story triggered a strong reaction in Catledge which was not diminished when it became apparent that the episode had been touched off when a lie-detector apparatus brought in by a CIA agent to test a local operative blew a fuse in a Singapore hotel. Actually, although this would not emerge until later, the caper was part of a CIA attempt to set up its own agent network in Singapore, which was, under the CIA's arrangement with the British Secret Service, "British territory." The British soon would be turning autonomy over to Lee and the CIA had decided to get in on the ground floor with its own organization. Many intelligence specialists believed that the CIA agents had been "blown" by their British associates to teach them a lesson about poaching on the other fellow's preserve.

Whatever lay behind the Singapore episode Catledge's questions were to lead to the first serious effort to investigate the CIA since the Agency had been spawned as the postwar successor to the OSS. American secret intelligence had been born in World War II. Not until September of 1965 had any agency, public or private, made an effort to analyze its overall performance, evaluate its achievements, expose its faults. True, there had been extensive debate after World War II before President Truman agreed to establish a Central Intelligence Agency but this debate had been largely theoretical. The U.S. had had no peacetime experience in intelligence. Before World War II intelligence was regarded as unnecessary and un-American, typically "European," basically dangerous to and unnecessary for a democracy.

There had been, of course, a crash inquiry into CIA by the Kennedy Administration after the Bay of Pigs. But little of the findings had reached the public. To the ordinary American the CIA was one more acronym, sometimes blamed for policy disasters, sometimes praised for successes—the overthrow of Mossadegh and Arbentz—but basically an enigma. What was true of the public was largely true of the press and of Congress.

By September 3, 1965, Catledge had determined to conduct a major *Times'* inquiry into the CIA, its activities, its policies, its objectives, the manner in which it was directed, the way it responded, or did not respond, to government control.

The CIA Project

"What is this CIA?" Catledge asked. "For God's sake let's find out what they are doing. They are endangering all of us."

To be sure *The Times* had conducted surveys of other government operations, the State Department, the Defense establishment, in the past but it had done nothing quite like the CIA inquiry. The CIA investigation was to be, although Catledge and the participants had no way of perceiving this, a pattern setter for the future, the first big venture by *The Times* into the new journalism of the late sixties and seventies, the investigative reporting which was to give the profession a new face and a new role in the power structure of the country.

The first steps toward setting up the CIA project went forward September 4 and by September 15 questionnaires were dispatched to *Times* overseas correspondents, some by mail, some carried by *Times* men traveling abroad because, as the memo said, "of the sensitivity" of the subject, a not very subtle hint that the questions might fall into the hands of CIA or other intelligence agents. Tom Wicker came up from Washington and met with Catledge, Daniel, foreign editor Gruson and myself. Wicker was placed in charge of the project and Daniel remembered telling him that if "you do a good job on this you will probably win a Pulitzer." This was not to be; the Pulitzer did not go to Wicker and the team that worked with him in Washington, but *The Times'* story was a close contender in the 1967 awards. This was not the only award *The Times* was to lose out on in 1967. *The Times* failed with a second example of the new journalism when the decision of the 1967 jury to grant the prize in foreign correspondence to me for my dispatches from Hanoi in December 1966 behind the Vietnamese lines was overturned by a one-vote margin in the advisory board, made up of senior editors and publishers. The advisory board's decision was sustained by a one-vote margin among the Columbia University trustees, where the question was raised. Later Catledge was to call the CIA and Hanoi stories the landmark journalistic achievements of his term as managing editor of *The Times.*

Every *Times* correspondent who might have had contact with or knowledge of CIA operations was enlisted to share his experience and the Washington team set about interviewing Agency chiefs, former Agency heads, knowledgeable senators and congressmen, ex-Presidents Truman and Eisenhower, high White House aides, generals, admirals and military spokesmen, any source which might cast significant light on the nature of "this CIA," as Catledge had put it. The Washington staff did not talk with President Johnson, who wanted to stay clear of the issue; nor did it talk with the CIA head, Admiral William F. Raborn, for the same reason.

It was recognized that the CIA was bound to know of the enterprise and, outside of initial caution in distributing questionnaires, no particular security precautions were undertaken. This "dangerous enterprise," as some Agency men dubbed the questionnaire, was drafted by Tom Wicker. It asked *Times* men to describe operations of the CIA as they had observed them and to evaluate the Agency's performance in terms of U.S. national and foreign policy interests. It asked for anecdotal materials, descriptions of the style of CIA enterprises, reports on successful and unsuccessful operations, a rating of the caliber of CIA personnel and whether they worked in cooperation or competition with other U.S. representatives and whether, in fact, as specified by the President, U.S. ambassadors effectively controlled the CIA. The *Times* men were invited to sum up "gains, setbacks, benefits and risks for U.S. policy arising out of CIA activities."

James Angleton, chief of CIA counterintelligence, later was to boast that his operatives within *The New York Times* came to him with copies of the questionnaire even before responding to it. They warned him, he said, that *The Times* was about to disembowel the CIA. He regarded *The Times'* enterprise with dark suspicion. Angleton said privately that he had his own men on *The Times,* men whom he could meet on street corners, men who weren't on his payroll but to whom he provided expense money. Never, he said, had he gone to *Times'* management about this. He just took the people he wanted and got what he wanted. Whether that was true or a secret operative's brag there was no way of knowing, but Angleton did, of course, count men on *The Times* as his friends, present or past. John Oakes had known him in the X-2 group of OSS during the war as a "a very spooky quiet kind of guy" but had not seen much of him since. Ben Welles regarded Angleton as a "good friend." They, too, had worked together in X-2 for OSS and had remained close. Welles was thought by many of his colleagues to be remarkably intimate with the CIA. Walter Sullivan, *The Times'* science specialist, went to Yale with Angleton. In fact Sullivan, McGeorge Bundy and Angleton were on the board of the Yale *Literary Magazine* together, Sullivan and Bundy being the literary conservatives and Angleton the radical who sponsored an appearance of Ezra Pound. Pound showed up in what Sullivan recalled as a priest's hat and a monkish gown that swept the floor, a presence that so embarrassed Sullivan he wanted to run away. It was a measure of the difference in two men's value systems that forty years later Angleton indignantly rejected Sullivan's description. Pound, he said, wore an Italian artist's black hat and a flowing velvet cape. Moreover, Angleton had no recollection of his unromantic classmate Walter Sullivan. John Oakes, however, he remembered very well since, of course, they had been colleagues in X-2. They had worked together in London under the direction of James R. Murphy, a Wall Street lawyer and friend of Donovan's, and John had gone on to Paris and Germany, where he worked with Allen Dulles while Angleton went to his beloved Italy. Ben Welles of *The Times* had been Oakes' assistant.

Angleton's long, close and wide friendship among men on *The Times* did nothing to quell his anxiety about the *Times'* inquiry. The message to *Times* men asking questions about the CIA (he recalled it as a telegram rather than what it was, in fact, a letter) was phrased, he thought, precisely as if it had been drafted by the KGB. He called the language of the inquiry "EEI," that is, he said, "the essential elements of intelligence"* and he felt it betrayed the hand of Soviet operatives.

---

*The initials "EEI" are understood in intelligence circles to stand for "the essential elements of information," a standard phrase probably originating in military terminology, meaning the ABC's of a situation, an organization or an individual; in other words, the who, what, why, where, when and how of newspaper usage. Apparently Angleton was under the impression that only intelligence agents sought such basics.

It told him, he said, a lot about the nature of those who were conducting the survey. To Angleton *The Times* posed a direct threat to the Agency and he made no secret of his concern. Whether, as he was to hint, he was able to "cool" the response of some *Times* correspondents to the questions is beyond the ability of latter-day research to establish. This was certainly Angleton's hope and that of other Agency men. It was true that not all *Times* men were forthcoming in their contributions to the series but this was not unusual. Some men conscientiously and carefully responded; others were superficial and about ten of the roughly forty *Times* men who received the questionnaire did not bother to reply. That this pattern was affected by Angleton or other CIA operatives with inside connections to *Times* men cannot be established. A *Times* man in one large European *Times* bureau recalled later that there seemed to be a notable lack of enthusiasm on the part of some of his colleagues to the questionnaire. Who knows? The fact was that regardless of any chill administered by Angleton the replies flooded back from abroad. If they didn't cover everything they covered enough to provide an extraordinarily illuminating pattern.

Opposition

But Agency-generated opposition to *The Times'* project soon manifested itself. One center of this was Paris, where Ambassador Charles Bohlen was described as having "hit the roof." He was determined, one *Times* correspondent reported, "to keep us from upsetting the applecart." He was no more disturbed than Cy Sulzberger, who added his own strong dissent. (Years later Cy said he could recall neither the survey nor his dissent.) Bohlen had long been a staunch CIA supporter and Sulzberger, of course, was the man on *The Times* who had been closest to the CIA since its founding. In his constant traveling to every corner of the earth Cy never missed calling on the Agency chief in every country he visited, whether he saw the ambassador or not. The station chief in Paris traditionally became one of his close friends.

The Times' survey moved forward with customary *Times* grandeur and stately rhythm, memo after memo, interview after interview, *Times* men traveling across the country, searching out sources, probing tips on Agency enterprises. John Finney, who had known John McCone since his chairmanship of the Atomic Energy Commission, journeyed to Los Angeles and the two men swam back and forth in McCone's magnificent swimming pool, McCone doing a comfortable breast stroke and Finney relaxing on his back with the sun in his eyes as McCone discussed the Agency's problems in frank terms.

One day Secretary of State Dean Rusk telephoned Punch Sulzberger, only a couple of years into his role at the head of *The Times.* Punch knew the CIA study was under way but not much more and had the call routed to Catledge's office. The three men, Rusk, Catledge and Sulzberger, talked on Catledge's squawk box. Rusk expressed himself as deeply upset. He declared *The Times'* material might damage U.S. global intelligence efforts, expose agents, alarm allies, encourage enemies, harm the national interest and undermine national security. He stopped short of asking that *The Times* kill the story—but barely. Catledge did not take Rusk's words at full value. He had the feeling that one thing that disturbed Rusk was not U.S. security but his own security. He was afraid of what he might learn if *The Times* published what it knew because so often the CIA had left the State Department in the dark. *The Times'* revelations, Catledge felt, might embarrass Rusk more than they did the country.

Rusk and Catledge were southerners, Rusk from Georgia, Catledge from Mississippi, both Presbyterians, both raised in the churchy ways of the rural South, and so when Dean made his pitch he concluded by saying to Turner, "As my revered father, the Presbyterian preacher, would have said, I hope you'll give this prayerful consideration." To which Catledge responded, "Well, Dean, as my sainted Presbyterian mother would have said, we will let God help us to find the way."

Catledge recognized that *The Times* was dealing with a sensitive issue. He certainly did not wish *The Times* to endanger a U.S. secret agent or disturb the security of the country. On the other hand he was totally, stubbornly and sincerely certain that *The Times* must go ahead and he had Punch Sulzberger's full support. He came to Clifton Daniel with the problem. Daniel recalled suggesting that when the piece was completed *The Times* could let the CIA take a look at it—if they had objections the objections could be considered for what they were worth. Some informal initiative along this line was made but didn't get far. *The Times* was not eager to have the Agency looking over its shoulder and the Agency didn't want to put itself in the position of saying "yes" or "no," and thus place its imprimatur on the finished product.

No one on *The Times* knew that the Agency was scared out of its wits; that it feared *The Times* might write the CIA's death warrant.

On October 1, 1965, less than a month after *The Times'* project was set in motion by Catledge (the time lag did not speak too well for the Agency's vaunted ability to penetrate *The Times* and learn quickly what it had under way) a memorandum was drafted for Richard Helms, then deputy director, by Colonel Stanley Grogan, the seemingly easygoing, unflappable ex-Army officer who had for so long served as the CIA's liaison with the media, first under Allen Dulles, then under McCone and now under Raborn. It was couched in terms of hysteria.

Grogan headed his memorandum:

"Subject: NEW YORK TIMES Threat to Safety of the Nation"

Grogan gave the impression that the country was tottering on the brink. The "damage to national security could be immense," wrote Grogan. "The CIA is the first line of the defense of the Nation." He suggested that the consequence of *The Times'* study might be that President Johnson and Congress would join to take action against the CIA "to lessen the threat to their prestige, political power and judgments" which publication of the truth—or as much of the truth as *The Times* could lay hands on—would present.

Grogan conceded that *The Times* had a perfect legal right to undertake the survey and publish what it wished. But, he said:

"It also has a responsibility for the security of the Nation and to the people of the United States and to the Free World. It should not give to the Communist and other anti-United States nations grist for their propaganda mills."

Grogan noted that not only was the Washington bureau of *The Times* engaged in the CIA survey but also New York editors like Catledge, Daniel, Salisbury and Gruson. He was especially concerned because Gruson "is said to have resented alleged CIA actions that resulted in his transfer to Eastern Europe" from Mexico.* Grogan pointed out that Hanson Baldwin, military editor of *The Times,* was extremely knowledgeable about the CIA and "not favorably impressed with some of the Agency personnel with whom he has come in contact" and that Daniel "is said to have doubts of the Agency's competence." Grogan was bothered that men like editorial page director John Oakes, editorial board member Harry Schwartz and myself "know a great deal about CIA and its methods."

Grogan proposed action "NOW" and he capitalized the word to stress his anxiety. He suggested "defensive action in the Field" be undertaken to thwart efforts by *The Times* to learn about CIA operations abroad. And he recommended "positive action stateside without delay."

He proposed a direct effort to counteract the activity of what he called "the New York group" of *The Times.* "To create a preventive atmosphere it would seem wise for the Agency's heaviest weapons to be employed in talking to the New York editors," he said, suggesting that both Raborn and Helms take on the task. He thought one of them

---

*Neither Gruson nor anyone on *The Times* connected Gruson's transfer from Mexico to the CIA. Gruson had been negotiating for a post in Washington or Europe long before the CIA intervention to get him out of the way of the Guatemalan coup. Grogan's remarks sounded as though someone in the CIA had a guilty conscience. Or possibly Grogan picked up the impression from an old friend in the New York office of *The Times,* Marshall Newton, an assistant city editor and one-time Army officer. Grogan's impression was shared by others and years later the notion still persisted among old Agency hands.

might make a personal call on Arthur Hays Sulzberger.

"The President of the United States," said Grogan, "may well consider the advisability of his calling Arthur Hays Sulzberger to point out that the safety of the Nation could be seriously damaged by the Times and request that for security reasons the copy be checked by the White House well in advance of publication."*

This kind of alarm flashed through the Agency and while not all of Grogan's proposals were carried through (Dean Rusk's call to Punch was apparently the White House substitute for Grogan's proposal of an approach by Lyndon Johnson to Arthur Hays Sulzberger) the alert defensive posture which he laid out was, in fact, the essence of the line which the Agency was to take.

Viewed through the prism of years the Agency's reaction sounded like a scream from outer space. There was in the minds of these men total identification of the Agency with the country's security. It was, in Grogan's words, the "first line of defense." Any question about the CIA's conduct was interpreted by Angleton as the equivalent of enemy action, as dangerous as a maneuver by the KGB to penetrate the CIA and frustrate its purposes. *Any* intervention, *any* questions, *any* attempt to probe what the CIA was doing, how it operated, what its intentions might be was seen as hostile, dangerous and frightening, capable of destroying the Agency. There were in the response of these men not only elements of frightening insecurity but an astonishing *hauteur*, total certainty that what they did was not to be questioned, that they were endowed with a higher purpose, a superior knowledge, a supreme objective which was not to be questioned. This was, in fact, the ultimate elitism. Nothing could have been more prescient than Catledge's sure, instinctive question: "What is this CIA?" Catledge had asked the right question. But if he and *The Times* were to get the right answer it would not be thanks to the CIA. The Agency would employ every means at its disposal—and these were formidable means —to thwart and frustrate *The Times,* to overawe the paper and its editors, if necessary, to overwhelm them with the sophisticated views of high and influential personages, to divert them with "friendly guidance," to make certain that the paper did not discover the truth. Once again—as had happened so often and was to happen so frequently— it was *the truth* that the CIA feared above all things, truth was what was so "frightening" in the Agency's words, the truth could destroy the Agency, its men felt; the truth must be avoided at all cost.

It was beyond the imagination of *The Times'* editors and reporters engaged in the CIA project to conceive of such a psychosis as was manifest in the personality of many men within the CIA. In the light

*Grogan's memo turned up in response to a FOIA request by me.

of later events this would not seem so remarkable. But in terms of 1965 and 1966 the CIA was a tabula rasa to most journalists.

Catledge may not have known much about the CIA but he was an old Washington hand. He had learned government in the "educational" precincts of Senate hideaways where he imbibed branch water and bourbon with past masters like Senator Pat Harrison of Mississippi and Vice President John N. Garner of Texas. He might not know the CIA but he knew how political bodies were buried, how bureaucrats manipulated the machinery of government and the press. He was a canny man and he had grown up in the alphabetical soup of the New Deal. To him the initials CIA did not seem so different from PWA, SEC, FHA, FDIC, NRA and the rest. He knew the bureaucratic mind and the bureaucratic process. When the Dean Rusks and the Chip Bohlens weighed in he recognized the pressure tactics of government men. He was a professional at coping with that and when he hit upon the idea of bringing in John McCone he was not concerned with national security but with the security of *The New York Times*. Catledge, as he had said before and after the Bay of Pigs, and was to say again, thought he could assess national security as well as an alphabetical agency man even if the initials did spell CIA. But he was too wise to let himself be trapped into giving CIA a stick with which to beat *The New York Times*.

As Catledge was to say, "Any newspaperman is liable to error and when fifty or one hundred newspapermen file stories from around the world on an espionage agency the possibilities of error are very high indeed. It is better to correct errors before you make them than to apologize for them afterward. In this case there was the risk that the CIA would use one error to attack the entire series. Obviously there was the risk the government would lie or distort the facts in order to protect itself."

McCone

A first draft of the CIA survey—five articles, each 3,000 to 4,000 words long, roughed out of hundreds of hours of interviews and scores of memos; more than twenty *Times* foreign correspondents had contributed and there had been fifty or more detailed interviews with high officials and former officials—was completed in mid-December 1965. The rough draft was discussed at a meeting in New York of Wicker, Frankel, Daniel and myself and extensive revisions were undertaken, for the most part, organizational, to get the material into sharper focus. The bottom line, as Wicker pointed out, was "whether in the long run the vast and increasing reliance of the government on clandestine, illicit and [in any other activity] immoral and demeaning tactics harms us more than benefits us." And there was the question of who, in the end, was going to have, as Wicker expressed it, "the *will*" to control the CIA. By the end of January 1966 the articles had been put into publishable form. Daniel felt the stories were "very good."

"They contain a lot of information I never knew before," he said. "They present very clearly what is involved in the issue of appointing a congressional committee to oversee the CIA. While the series contains a lot of new material, it does not seem to me to unduly expose the CIA."

This was the text (with some small further editing revisions) which was submitted to McCone February 7, 1966. McCone had come east for a meeting at Princeton and was staying at the Waldorf Towers. He had agreed, at the request of John Finney, to have a look at the material.

Later some were to contend that because *The Times* permitted McCone to read the draft articles, the CIA, in effect, exercised censorship over the series. Nothing was farther from the fact. McCone certainly consulted the CIA about the series; he read the articles carefully and submitted to *The Times* a list of points. Then, it was up to *The Times*. Few of McCone's questions dealt with matters of great substance. He objected to a statement that the CIA station chief's house in Lagos was larger and more impressive than that of the ambassador. The Lagos item stayed in. He objected to a reference to laser beams being focused on windows to intercept conversations. The reference to the technique stayed in; the word "laser" went out. He was bothered by the explicitness of a description of a Chinese Nationalist band operating on the Chinese Communist border in Burma. The reference stayed with minor editing. He protested publication of an estimate of the CIA budget at "a little more than $500 million" of a total intelligence budget of $3 billion; the figure stayed. *The Times* estimated CIA had 6,600 operatives abroad; he said there were only 2,200; both numbers were used in the series. He objected to the use of the word "terrorism" as a CIA tool; the word came out. He objected to quotations from Presidents Truman and Kennedy criticizing the CIA; the quotations ran. He wanted a reference to Colonel Nasser's "management consultant" (Kermit Roosevelt) deleted; it stayed. He felt a reference to CIA opposition to Prince Sihanouk was too strong; it was slightly modified. He objected to descriptions of General Phouimi in Laos and Diem in Vietnam as CIA choices; the references remained.* A description of CIA involvement in the Congo was rephrased in line with his views. A description of Mustafa Amin, a Cairo editor then on trial for alleged CIA ties, was softened. Objections to

---

*Actually, the story overstated the role of the CIA in relationship to Diem.

references to CIA ties to the magazine *Encounter* and the Congress for Cultural Freedom were overridden. A reference to Admiral Raborn's relationship to the Dominican crisis was revised when McCone noted that the coup occurred the day Raborn took office. He opposed but reluctantly accepted a mention of CIA support of MIT's Center of International Studies and was unhappy about a phrase that drew a parallel between the CIA and the KGB. One of McCone's strongest objections was against revelation of the CIA relationship to Radio Free Europe and Radio Liberty. The question was put to Turner Catledge, who said the reference must stand.

My response on receiving McCone's criticisms was:

"I fully agree with Tom Wicker that no very serious problems are involved in meeting most of the objections which he raises. A certain number of them I think we should ignore. Several can be handled by simple rewording, qualification, etc., and only one or two involve really prickly points."

The memo went on in similar vein: "Points 1 to 4 can be handled with minor editing . . . so far as point 5 is concerned let our language stand . . . on point 6 we should correct our reference to get the dates accurate . . . on point 6A I am not impressed with Mr. McCone's argument. I think our language can stand . . . on point 6C I think our version of the situation is substantially correct . . . on point 9 this is merely a quibble . . . on point 16 I would ignore . . . on point 18 I think we can fuzz our language a little bit . . . on point 19 perhaps we ought to discuss it somewhat with McCone . . ." And so on.

This detail, if tedious, faithfully reflects the back-and-forth between McCone and the editors of *The Times.* The process took time. It was not until the first week in April that I was able to advise Clifton Daniel that the "final edited version of the CIA series" was in hand. McCone's intervention had not weakened the series; it had reinforced it because his views had been tested and the stories rechecked and strengthened in the light of his observations. Weak points had been dropped, sources had been scrupulously reexamined; errors eliminated and conclusions fortified. (Only one factual error was brought against the series as published; in discussing CIA funding of the magazine *Encounter* the article mistakenly said *Encounter* had editions in France and Germany.)

My memo to Daniel noted that every point raised by McCone had been carefully considered and that never "in my history with *The New York Times* has a series of articles been prepared with such great care." Catledge recommended publication to Punch Sulzberger April 19, 1966, and on April 25 *The Times* printed the first story under a headline "CIA: Maker of Policy or Tool." To illustrate the article *The Times* reprinted a *New Yorker* cartoon showing a volcano erupting against a Southeast Asian background. The cutline read, "The CIA did it. Pass it along."

And that was that. But not quite. For the first time an exhaustive and critical analysis of the CIA had been published. The picture it painted was not all black. It gave CIA credit for achievements as well as raising questions about failures, drawbacks and, most of all, its overweening thrust for power, the lack of control by its directors, by the government, by the White House, by *anyone.* It said, in effect, that so far the nation had not been seriously damaged but it was time to consider the consequences if the CIA continued to move forward in the pattern described in *The Times'* series. It had taken *The Times* nearly seven months to accomplish its investigation. To some this seemed an inordinate length of time but this was *The Times'* style and this was what lent *The Times* its reputation. If the subject was important—and the Pentagon Papers and the CIA were preeminently important—*The Times* was prepared to invest unstintingly to accomplish the task with distinction and penetration. But this did not still the critics. Dean Rusk lunched at *The Times* a month after the CIA series had been published. He was still upset, still opposed to publication, still thought *The Times* had acted badly, had acted wrongly and, as was his custom, stated his views with considerable force. He was concerned with "giving comfort to the enemy." Arthur Sulzberger the next day wrote Rusk acknowledging the serious responsibility which *The Times* took upon itself when publishing something like the CIA series but reminded the Secretary of State this problem was not unique. "It is," Sulzberger wrote, "one that confronts us always and it's probably the most serious matter that we have to face during periods of stress." It was clear that Arthur Sulzberger did not believe that fear of comforting the enemy meant that Americans should not know the truth about themselves and the agencies of their government. The "comfort to your enemy" argument was a familiar one, often raised by government in the face of unpleasant truths.* A few days after the CIA series Tom Wicker encountered a ranking CIA official at a cocktail party who accosted him loudly, drunkenly and abusively, shouting that Wicker should be proud. His name was being mentioned by Moscow radio. Later the CIA man apologized but his reaction was almost Pavlovian and was a direct product of the hard-line cold-warism which permeated the CIA.

McCone took a more sophisticated view. He made no secret of his belief that the series should not under any circumstances be published, with or without the changes which he had recom-

---

*It was violently raised by government public relations men in response to my Hanoi articles.

mended. He lunched with Catledge and several *Times* editors and expressed this view. Why, asked Catledge, did McCone and the Agency people object so strongly? Much of what *The Times* had published had already appeared in print in one place or another. Much of it was in the public domain.

"Yes," McCone said, as he recalled years later, "but in fact it was published by Jack Anderson in his column or in some book by a writer nobody knows and we didn't worry about that. But now when it comes out in *The New York Times* it is like the State Department issuing a White Paper."

"Well, then, John," Catledge said with a twinkle, "what you are saying is that we shouldn't publish it because we are so good."

"Exactly," McCone said.

Publications

McCone's point was valid. Publication in *The Times* put the question of the CIA, its role and its performance on the national agenda.* It did not result in the cataclysm envisaged by Grogan but it did bring home to the public and to Congress the fact that the CIA was not just a collection of initials. It was an entity which played a national and an international role and it would bear a close watch and closer examination. The fact was that *The Times'* inquiry aided national security rather than impairing it and would have aided the national well-being more profoundly if it had examined with greater care some areas which it virtually ignored, notably domestic operations of the CIA. Several memoranda by *Times* men touched on domestic operations but in a way that revealed no sensitivity to the question and the series contained hardly a mention of domestic matters outside of the MIT involvement, the use of foundations as a conduit for CIA funds and revelations of the use by CIA of wholly owned "proprietaries," business concerns like Air America and others. There was hardly a mention of CIA relations with newspapers or newspapermen, although, here too, the question was touched on peripherally in some memos. This information simply didn't strike the correspondents or the editors (including myself) as of vital consequence. The actual ingredients of the famous Penkovsky case were not exposed, that is, the fact that Penkovsky was a British client, not an American one (having been rebuffed by the CIA in the first instance) nor was there a suggestion that his famous "Papers," a sup-

---

The Times articles focused on the problem of responsibility for CIA operations and of bringing the Agency under effective control. It expressed doubt that a congressional oversight committee, such as came to exist, could monitor the Agency effectively and emphasized that there must be Executive will to control the Agency if it was not to maintain a largely freewheeling course. The principal effect of the series was to stimulate serious discussion in Congress of the CIA problem.

posed memoir of his work as a spy in Moscow for the USA, were a CIA concoction. There was no mention of the Agency's interference with Gruson in Guatemala although Gruson's memorandum gave an accurate summary of the incident (of course, Gruson didn't know that the matter had been handled on the high level of Arthur Sulzberger and Allen Dulles); there was not much on the Bay of Pigs; nothing on efforts to assassinate Castro; nothing on the U.S.-CIA role in the plot to overthrow Diem.*

Alongside these omissions were important revelations and even juicy tidbits which were quickly to be forgotten—a line about using satellites to pick up conversations by Moscow Politburo members using telephones in their cars, a "revelation" which was to occur all over again when Jack Anderson in 1971 found it in the suppressed diplomatic volume of the Pentagon Papers, an Anderson item which typically produced wild charges of "revealing" CIA secrets that had been no secret for at least five years to an alert newspaper reader.

There was one more chapter to *The Times'* CIA series. *The Times'* publication had produced excitement among book publishers. Half a dozen wanted to make a contract. Negotiations were going forward when, one day in early May, Tom Wicker was called to the telephone while lunching in San Francisco with his good friend *Times* correspondent Wallace Turner at Bardelli's restaurant. It was New York telling him that a decision had been made: no CIA book. No explanation either. But, of course, it wasn't long before Tom discovered what had happened. The CIA's hysterical antagonism to what McCone had called a "white book" had not diminished. Richard Helms, deputy director, and Tracy Barnes, his number one assistant, had come to New York and had met with Punch Sulzberger, Ivan Veit, Harding Bancroft and Turner Catledge about the proposed book. Their argument was simple: newspaper publication had been bad enough; if the series appeared in book form it would be much worse; there would be a permanent, easily accessible record. They simply didn't want such a record made available. Punch thought this was reasonable. *The Times* was a newspaper, not a book publisher (this was before *The Times* had its own book subsidiary) and so it was agreed. No book. Which may well be the reason that memory of *The Times'* CIA exposé quickly faded in many minds, including those of some who later were to track their way across the same trail, rediscovering many things about the CIA which *The Times* had earlier brought to light and why some who never bothered to examine the facts supposed that what *The Times* published was an Agency-sanitized version rather than a critical examination that

---

*The lack of mention of Gruson and other newspaper-CIA connections reflected Catledge's long-standing bias against mentioning reporters in the news.

terrorized what by 1966 had become a hermetic apparatus exercising secret, almost hypnotic, influence in the inner recesses of American power, unseen, uncontrolled, unresponsive, undirected, unknown to the people whose taxes supported its wildest fancies.*

*Many writers on CIA credit the now-defunct *Ramparts* magazine for the first major exposé of CIA. This is not correct. *Ramparts* in its April 1966 issue published an article about a Michigan State University "Vietnam Project" funded by the CIA. A year later it published a very important article exposing the CIA funding of the National Student Association. *The Times'* series was the first and for years the only extended newspaper examination of the CIA.

44

The Year of Intelligence

*W*ITH RICHARD NIXON'S DEPARTURE from the White House August 9, 1974, the obvious question facing the press and the country was: What next?

The initiative and resources of the media had played a critical role in Watergate but it was not certain how the press would utilize its new-found responsibilities or, indeed, whether it was prepared and capable of acting as a responsible surrogate of the public.

To *The New York Times* and, especially, to A. M. Rosenthal the path seemed plain. Secrecy and deceit had lain at the core of Watergate as it had in the Pentagon Papers. A great deal had been made public concerning the covert agencies of the government, the CIA, the FBI, the NSA; a great deal had been learned of abuse of power by secret agencies and the abuse of these agencies by those in high office. Much more was suspected and Watergate had shown that protestations of innocence and good conduct were rarely worth the paper they were typed on.

It was as though Sy Hersh had been born for this moment; as though he could not wait for the end of Watergate and the advent of the Ford presidency to throw himself into the CIA story. His battered desk in the *Times'* Washington office was stuffed with CIA materials. He had been collecting them for years, long before he came to *The Times:* interviews, clippings, congressional hearings, carbon copies of old stories, the raw data *The Times* had used in its 1966 CIA investigation, sheets torn from foreign newspapers, notebooks with the scribblings of a hundred interviews, the debris of a reporter always too much on the run to sort out the paper, but there it was, an investigator's dream, the raw materials of a dozen smash stories just waiting to be fleshed out, and, most precious of all, his scribbled memo pads and notebooks with the telephone numbers of the men in the Agency, out of the Agency, favorable to the Agency, critical of the Agency, those who would tell a little, those who might be jollied into talking, those who could be counted on for the last critical details, the tools of the best investigative reporter in the business.

If Rosenthal had been a bit uncomfortable with the Pentagon Papers, if he had had difficulty in coming to grips with Watergate, there seemed to be nothing to hold him back on the CIA. He did not harbor an old-boy affinity for the Agency. Rosenthal was a staunch, sometimes it would seem almost an evangelical, anti-Communist, his opinion fixed, as far as he could recall, at the time of the Stalin-Hitler pact in 1939, and powerfully reinforced by Poland. Poland was his first and only Communist country and his views on communism would have commended him to any cold-warist in the Agency, but he liked to describe himself as "anti-Communist, anti-fascist, anti-authoritarian" and he had a low tolerance for those who violated the democratic norms, the CIA included. Sy Hersh took him to meet William Colby in the fall of 1974. Abe's only visit to the CIA's heralded headquarters at Langley. They talked for twenty minutes or so, Abe telling Colby that he was very anti-Communist. Then Rosenthal said, "How come every time I come across the CIA I find they are on the side of the fingernail pullers?" Well, Mr. Rosenthal, Colby replied in his quiet, reasonable way, his blue eyes focused on Rosenthal's grey-green eyes, you know we are only a function, a function of what the President wants, what a given President wants. Sometimes we are on the side of the democratic forces, sometimes we are on the other side. When Sy and Abe emerged, when they walked past the statue of Nathan Hale and the stars for the CIA men lost in action "to the enemy," those with names and those eternally nameless, Rosenthal was shaken; the cold words, the cold blue eyes of Colby had shaken him.

Abe had wanted to go to Poland in order to experience life in a Marxist country at firsthand but he found it depressing and he didn't share the exhilaration of his predecessor, Sydney Gruson. Gruson had loved Poland and the Poles, had gotten to know almost everyone worth knowing and had written extraordinary articles at the time of the Polish October in 1956 when it was nip-and-tuck whether the Soviets and the Poles would go to war. As Russian tanks rumbled toward Warsaw the Poles had used Gruson as their channel of communications to the West.* Seldom had a *Times* reporter written such dispatches, and they played a role, many thought, in staying Khrushchev's hand and should have, but did not, win Gruson a Pulitzer. Rosenthal liked to put down Gruson on Poland, particularly on his Polish friendships, insisting that Gruson's Poland had been only six Jewish intellectuals and that they

---

*There was another Polish line open to the West. Marguerite Higgins of the *Herald-Tribune* knew some people on *Tribuna Ludy,* the Warsaw Communist paper. She held an open phone from Warsaw to her Washington apartment during much of the crisis. Robert Amory, CIA chief of intelligence, listened in. (Personal interview, Amory, 8/19/79)

had all disappeared by the time Rosenthal left. To Abe, Poland was a grim and sometimes terrifying place, and when he was expelled for writing several articles which gave uncanny insight into the thought, problems and mood of Party Secretary Gomulka (who, amazingly, Rosenthal never met) he was angry but hardly upset. His articles won him a Pulitzer, which he deserved fair and square, although there would always be some who said that Rosenthal really won Gruson's Polish Pulitzer, the one the judges had overlooked two years before.

Rosenthal's experience crystallized his anti-communism, which had not been so important to him before Poland but was to be much more important thereafter. Jack Chancellor remembered Rosenthal's arrival in Vienna after being expelled from Warsaw.

"He was pissed off," Chancellor said. "I said, 'But you got thrown out for the best of possible reasons.' 'Yes,' Abe said. 'But the fuckers threw me out. They threw out *The New York Times!*' "

The grounds on which Rosenthal's expulsion from Poland was ordered were that he had been probing too deeply into Poland's political scene.

Rosenthal, Chancellor thought, was pleased at the reason he was thrown out but outraged that the Poles should inhibit *The Times* in covering Poland. And, as he noted, Abe's stories about Gomulka were human in their quality, vignettes of a trouble-haunted man, not political or polemic. Jack was inclined to see Rosenthal as essentially apolitical. But Abe didn't think that was true. He came in later days to describe himself as a "bleeding-heart conservative," strong for civil liberties, sour on taxes, sour on "the liberal camp." Rosenthal's close friend, William F. Buckley, founder with Rosenthal of an eight-man marching-and-chowder society which they sometimes called the "Abe-Rosenthal-for-President Club," and sometimes the "Boys' Club," spoke of Rosenthal with awe as a "terrific anti-Communist." Richard Clurman, another friend and club member, felt that Abe's political roots lay in the cold war. He thought, too, that the emotional impact of witnessing the Columbia University "bust" on the night of April 29–30, 1968, had powerfully moved Rosenthal toward conservatism.

Actually, like that of every talented person, Rosenthal's philosophy was too complex to be described in cold-war clichés or the embroidered vocabulary of the *National Review.* There lingered within him not a few response syndromes of his youth. On the night in 1968 when Robert Kennedy was assassinated Rosenthal heard the news in a bar where he was drinking with his close friend, Andrew Fisher, then a vice-president of *The Times.* Abe broke down and wept and Fisher remembered walking up the street with him, tears flowing from Rosenthal's eyes. At middle-age he still counted the Abraham Lincoln Brigade that fought in Spain for the Loyalists a band of heroes, "the original political naïfs, fighting fascism." FDR had been for Abe, and still was a bright star. In childhood he had had two disparate idols, Abraham Lincoln (a hero of his father's) and Percy Bysshe Shelley. No man reflecting such attitudinal congeries could be easily categorized and Rosenthal betrayed no ideological bias when he encouraged Hersh to turn loose his talents on the CIA.

Hersh

The first fruit of Sy's effort was a spectacular exposé of the role of the CIA in the coup which overthrew Allende in Chile, tying together the CIA, ITT and the White House. Bits and pieces of the story had floated around the edges of Watergate. Sy had looked at them but, as he conceded, in the end it was "a story that just walked in." It walked in and its publication in October 1974 made a big splash, notice to the world that *The Times* was still up to speed, that the momentum of Watergate had not faded.

But the next Hersh story on the CIA did not walk in. This was one on which Sy had been collecting material for years; it was what his desk was full of, the domestic operations of the CIA. It had long become apparent that the CIA had systematically violated its charter forbidding domestic operations. Some of this evidence had surfaced in the original *Times'* CIA exposé of April 1966.

But what Sy was into was something far more extensive, far more serious, far more critical to American life, far more criminal than the rather adolescent games the Agency had been playing in the world of academia. What Sy was into was basic violation of civil liberties of Americans, of U.S. citizens in their homeland, in their own homes and home life, their professional and business occupations, in that heart of the American contract, the Bill of Rights.

Sy's story, headlined "Huge CIA Operation Reported in U.S. Against Anti-War Forces, Other Dissidents in Nixon Years," was published in *The Times* December 22, 1974, a Sunday. It proved to be the single most influential story published about the CIA, led to three far-reaching official investigations of the Agency, and a national self-examination into the political and ethical values which the CIA epitomized. It produced a major realignment in governmental and congressional oversight procedures and placed upon the national agenda (where it still rests) the underlying issue of whether there did, in fact, exist any method in the modern technological state whereby a suprabureaucratic and covert elite could be controlled, could be prevented in the end, from turning upon its presumed masters in a cannibalistic process in which the controlled devoured the controllers and ultimately the total culture in which both existed.*

It raised the question of not just how can we bring the CIA under control (which had been Catledge's question) but can we permit the CIA to exist?

Hersh revealed that the CIA had conducted a "massive" and totally illegal domestic intelligence program. The targets were not foreign spies but American citizens, ordinary citizens who had violated no law, committed no crime, indulged in no espionage, knew no spies, belonged to no subversive organizations, Americans totally dedicated to their country, its laws, its ideals but deeply convinced that its leaders and policies were carrying the nation into the swamp. The CIA, of course, held no responsibility for, no oversight privilege over, no legal authority to inquire into any domestic activities, subversive or not subversive, not even, should it exist, a native American revolutionary movement; it was only chartered, only legally authorized to operate in the foreign field, to undertake foreign assignments, to investigate foreign action. Its targets lay beyond the shores of the U.S., crimes at home fell within the jurisdiction of the police, the sheriffs, the state troopers, the revenue agents, the FBI, etc., not the CIA.

Hersh revealed that the CIA had set up what it called Operation Chaos, which had compiled dossiers on 10,000† or more U.S. citizens, for twenty years had opened mail on a colossal scale, tapped wires and intercepted, with the aid of the National Security Agency's electronic talents, hundreds of thousands if not millions of private communications, broken into private homes and offices almost as a matter of routine. The CIA, it quickly appeared, was the biggest burglar, the biggest eavesdropper in the world, outdoing its domestic partner, the FBI. It was difficult for one like myself, who was familiar with and had lived under the omnipresent surveillance of the KGB, to detect much difference between Operation Chaos and business-as-usual within Soviet society. The ultimate triumph of the dialectic seemed to be approaching: antithesis was approaching synthesis; the harder CIA fought KGB the more alike they became.

*This process, of course, was far advanced in the Soviet Union. Before World War I, Leon Trotsky had predicted that under Lenin the party cadres would take over from rank-and-file members; the Central Committee would take over from the cadres; then a dictator would replace the Central Committee. All that had happened and now the dictator's secret police was virtually triumphant over the dictator.
†The CIA repeatedly rejected the word "massive" in connection with its operations against American citizens. The adjective gave an exaggerated image, they said. Ultimately it transpired that instead of 10,000 dossiers on American citizens, as Hersh reported, the real total was 300,000.

Colby

Now occurred something curiously disturbing in the Washington press, almost unbelievable after three years of the Pentagon Papers and Watergate. *Nothing* happened. The journalists of Washington did not hone in on the CIA; did not rush to verify and expand the findings of Hersh and *The Times*. Instead word circulated in Georgetown that Hersh had put *The Times* out on a limb. Ben Bradlee of the *Washington Post* had said, so the gossip went, that Sy's story was overwritten and underresearched. This was a cheap shot but it was fairly typical of Washington reaction. Oh, yes, the CIA had undoubtedly done some domestic things—but not really on the scale Sy reported. The story was just too exaggerated to be believed. So the comments went. Why any horror should have aroused skepticism in post-Watergate Washington was hard to fathom; but it was true that Hersh possessed a certain arrogance and Rosenthal was neither known nor admired by the Washington press corps. Hersh was hardly shaken. For one thing a friend had talked to James Schlesinger, who headed the CIA from January to April 1973 and initiated the wholesale housecleaning from which the Agency was to resonate for years, and Schlesinger said the situation was worse than Sy depicted. And David Wise, the dean of CIA investigators, passed word to Hersh that he had a source who said Sy's figure on the number of Americans on whom dossiers were kept "is on the short side."

What the press skeptics did not know (but should have guessed) was that Sy's story had not only been carefully and conservatively written, the buzz word "massive" having been approved by Rosenthal in consultation with Larry Hauck of *The Times* bullpen. Hersh had discussed and confirmed the general outlines of the dispatch with CIA Director William Colby Friday morning, December 20, 1974, before publishing it.

True, as Colby revealed later, he sought to persuade Hersh that the operation was not "massive"; he emphasized that orders to cease these activities had been issued in 1973; he contended that the only reason CIA infiltrated the antiwar movement was concern that it might have been supported or manipulated by some foreign government, a thesis which no intelligence officer with the wit of a six-year-old would have tolerated for a minute.

Actually, what Sy had plunged into was what had become known within the CIA as "the family jewels," a Top Secret list of CIA atrocities, that is, CIA activities in violation of its charter and of the law, including assassination plots, political initiatives and illegal and unauthorized domestic operations. The family jewels, so christened by Colby, had been assembled under a directive of May 9, 1973, drafted by Colby and signed by Schlesinger. The 683-page report was regarded by the Agency as so sensitive that it had not been communicated to either Nixon or Ford.

Later, there was to be so much commotion about the Hersh story and the "family jewels" that Colby's enemies in and around the Agency were to make the absurd charge that he was a "Soviet mole" bent on destruction of the CIA. But this was interesting only as a measure of the intensity of emotion which the Hersh story produced. For if, on the outside, in Georgetown circles, there was toward Sy's revelations insouciance and simulated *ennui* (and even subordination of journalistic responsibility to personal pique) there was nothing like this inside the CIA, inside the government.

Colby understood the seriousness of the report, as did President Ford. Colby and Ford were immediately in touch even though Ford was flying that Sunday aboard *Air Force One* for a skiing Christmas at Vail, Colorado, and Ford issued a statement echoing Colby's assurances that all illegal practices and programs had been halted under the 1973 directive.

But the matter hardly rested there. Colby prepared for Ford a report based on the "family jewels," itemizing the assassinations, the assassination plots and the other scandals and sent it forward within forty-eight hours. He used the occasion to insist on the resignation of James Angleton, the remarkable "ultraconspiratorial," in Colby's phrase, CIA director of counterintelligence whose removal he had long advocated.

By this time the world, specifically the Communist world, was perceived by Angleton, in his phrase, as a "wilderness of mirrors" in which almost everything assumed the shape of its opposite. Thus, Malenkov not Khrushchev, was the author of the famous "secret" de-Stalinization speech; the Tito-Stalin breech was a fake; the Sino-Soviet conflict was an exercise in disinformation; Rumania was a toady of Moscow, not a dissident; Khrushchev was not ousted, he retired to his country estate and ran things from there, etc.

"A press and political fire storm immediately erupted," Colby recalled. "The charge that the Agency had engaged in domestic spying, the inference that it had become a Gestapo, proved the fatal spark."

The discharge of Angleton and resignation of several aides gave legitimacy in many minds to the Hersh charges; if the CIA was not guilty it would not have fired its director of counterintelligence. President Ford took a similar view and on January 4, 1975, named a commission headed by Vice President Rockefeller to investigate the CIA. In part, of course, Mr. Ford was hoping to contain the fire storm but the tactic did not work. Congress moved in and after Colby, on January 15, 1975, essentially confirmed the Hersh story before a Senate committee it was apparent, as Colby said, that "The Year of Intelligence" in Washington had begun. It was to be a year of almost continuous testimony by Colby and Richard Helms, his predecessor, Helms returning time and again from Iran where he was ambassador, to testify before one committee or another. Again and again CIA witnesses would attempt to explain why their domestic surveillance was not "massive," as *The Times* said. But each attempt simply confirmed or expanded what *The Times* had reported.

Ford

Sy's story had been confined to domestic operations of the CIA. He had heard, as had almost every literate newsman, that the CIA had not scrupled at the use of assassination to "destabilize" a hostile regime or eliminate an enemy of the United States. Talk of such operations was commonplace in Africa, Asia, Latin America, even in the U.S.A. But tangibles were hard to come by. Rumor had fed on rumor until hardly a leader in the world could die without stories of CIA involvement. Kennedy assassination bugs had theorized that the CIA had some role in Dallas. A CIA hand in the deaths of Lumumba, Sukarno, Trujillo and others had been speculated. Lyndon Johnson had talked openly about the CIA running a "Murder, Inc." in the Caribbean and playing a role in the deaths of Trujillo and Ngo Dinh Diem. But there was no hard evidence.*

Clifton Daniel had established a warm and easy relationship with President Ford. Ford had lunched with the *Times* Washington bureau while Vice President and in a typically hospitable gesture (not without a natural eye to politics) Ford invited the editors of *The Times* to a "return" luncheon at the White House.

Daniel and Scotty Reston represented *The Times'* Washington office, and Punch Sulzberger, A. M. Rosenthal, John Oakes, Tom Wicker and Max Frankel came down from New York. The editors ate with Ford in the second-floor family dining room. Ford was accompanied by Ron Nissen, his press secretary, and two aides, the economist Alan Greenspan and Robert A. Goodwin.

It was an amiable occasion and nothing of import was said by Ford until Rosenthal raised the question of the Rockefeller commission to investigate the CIA. He suggested that the commission seemed to be somewhat pro-CIA and he wondered why—was the commission supposed to protect the CIA or was the case against the CIA so bad that a sympathetic commission was needed to give the report credibility.

---

*The Church committee discovered that Helms had drawn up a 125-page report for Johnson relating to allegations of a CIA "Murder, Inc." in the Caribbean. Inside the front cover Helms had a single page of "talking notes." Only the "talking notes" were given to LBJ, not the bound report. (Personal interview, F.A.O. Schwartz, Jr., 4/4/79)

Ford said that the charter of the commission and its membership had been done carefully to ensure that it stayed within the parameters of domestic CIA activities. He didn't want the commission getting into foreign operations because they were "a cesspool." Revelations, he said, "will ruin the U.S. image around the world," ruin the reputation of every President since Truman and shock the American public. These operations included everything, even assassinations of foreign political leaders.

Then, said one of the *Times* men, Mr. President, you oppose a congressional inquiry into the CIA. Not at all, Mr. Ford rejoined; in fact, I not only do not oppose it but I would be in favor of a joint congressional inquiry. He said that he had brought Dick Helms in and told him that the Justice Department would get a record of all charges made against him. In a word, Helms had been put on warning that he faced possible criminal prosecution. Mr. Ford specifically put the information about Helms off the record. The warning to Helms of possible criminal prosecution may well have had much to do with the high state of nerves which Helms displayed as inquiry succeeded inquiry, culminating in an episode when he shouted out at Daniel Schorr in April, on emerging from a lengthy Rockefeller commission hearing "You son-of-a-bitch! You killer! You cocksucker! Killer Schorr! Killer!"

Ford wound up the luncheon with a rather conventional plea for the $300 million he had asked of Congress to wind down Cambodia, a final appropriation which he was not to get.

The *Times* men emerged from the White House in a state of shock. They had hardly believed their ears when Ford started talking about assassinations by the CIA, not just one assassination but killings that went back years, killings that, he implied, had been approved or acquiesced in by Eisenhower, Kennedy, Johnson and Nixon, Allen Dulles and all the directors of the CIA since.

Wicker had been totally astonished. He was certain Ford expected them to use the information, that whatever his reasons, Ford wanted it out. But it was an uncanny thing for a President to do, first to tell a group of newsmen that he had set up the Rockefeller commission in such a way that it would not touch on such matters as assassinations and then to spill the beans to the press. As Wicker was to note, Ford had been around Washington too long not to understand what he was doing. If the technique seemed bizarre, the intent seemed clear enough.

Rosenthal shared Wicker's view but said he was not experienced in Washington and wasn't sure how these things were handled. The two were for publishing the information or at least following through on it. It seemed plain to them that the President had not put a hold on what he said. True, he had put the Helms bit off the record but by so doing implied that the other material was not off the record.

There ensued a classic *Times'* argument. Reston and Oakes strongly opposed publication. They believed that the President considered the conversation off the record, otherwise he would not have spoken so freely and easily. To publish, in their opinion, was to violate a confidence. Frankel had to catch a plane to New York and did not participate. Daniel felt that the ground rules of the previous luncheon applied, that is, that it was off the record. Punch Sulzberger said, "Well, this is a question where you guys are the authorities. You'll have to decide."

Finally, over Wicker's objection, Daniel called Nissen and to no one's surprise the press secretary said the talk was off the record.

The editors were uncomfortable about the decision but in different ways and for different reasons. Wicker was openly and angrily disturbed. He thought the policy of silence was self-imposed and not in the public interest. He strongly pondered the idea of breaking the story in his column but decided against it because it wasn't a decision which he ought to make unilaterally. Daniel was disturbed because he felt that he owed it to Sy Hersh to fill him in. He told Sy he could not tell him what had happened but that Sy would probably learn of it soon. Daniel believed Ford was going to make the information public but felt that his hands had been tied. Reston was annoyed with his colleagues for raising such a fuss; Oakes was bothered but felt the decision correct; Rosenthal felt frustrated but acted out the role of a good soldier; Frankel put himself apart from the argument; Punch felt it was an editor's question and stood aside.

The matter rested there—or rather it did not rest, it simmered. Inevitable rumors spread to a narrow circle in Washington. But only the *Times* men knew that the President had expressed himself in favor of a congressional inquiry into the CIA, which was the key, a clear signal that, one way or another, he wanted the information out. There were reports that he had told some old friends on the hill about Colby's "family jewels," which, of course, was the list from which he had drawn his information about the assassinations.

Sy Hersh was too good a reporter not to hear echoes of this but, restive as he was, he was held off by Daniel, who tried to steer the delicate course of directing Sy's attention toward the assassination subject without breaching the confidence of the President. It was not easy to do and he was not successful at it. Rosenthal tried the same thing. He telephoned Sy and said, "Keep on working." "On what?" Sy asked. "Never mind," Rosenthal said. "Keep working." Sy realized that something was being communicated to him but couldn't figure out what it was.

There was not long to wait. One of those who had heard reports about the luncheon was Dan Schorr, then at the peak of his investigative activity into the CIA for CBS. Schorr didn't have the whole conversation (in fact, this is the first time that all the details have been published) but by February 28 he had put enough together to go on CBS *Evening News* with a report that Ford had warned "associates" that if the CIA investigation went far enough it would "uncover several assassinations of foreign officials involving the CIA." That blew it. The assassination genie was out of the bottle and Ford directed the Rockefeller commission to investigate although he did not make public their findings, leaving it to the Church committee to develop the details of "an Executive Action" unit, a "Health Alteration Committee" and the like. It looked very much as though what Ford had actually wanted was, as he had said, a congressional inquiry into the assassinations, that is, a Democratic-sponsored inquiry, presumably feeling that the subject was too hot for his own Rockefeller commission to handle, that too many Republican oxen would be gored.

Whatever the President's motivation the story did come out; the inquiry into the CIA rolled forward, only slightly impeded by what some newspapermen felt were pantywaist objections and semantic arguments among the inner circle of *Times* editors.

45

Project Jennifer

IF THE ASSASSINATION GAMBIT was one which was bound to surface sooner rather than later, another CIA issue, much more serious in principle, was moving toward denouncement.

This was Project Jennifer, the building of the *Glomar Explorer*, a remarkable deep-oceanic recovery vessel, ostensibly for Howard Hughes by Global Marine, Inc., at a cost of possibly $350 million, possibly $500 million, but actually for the CIA to be used, it was later insisted, in an attempt to recover an eighteen-year-old Soviet submarine sunk in the Pacific Ocean in 1968.

In late autumn of 1973 with Watergate still boiling, Sy Hersh picked up a tip about "this crazy scheme" by the CIA to recover, as he understood it, Soviet ICBMs, fired from Central Asia on test courses into the Pacific Ocean. Sy didn't know a lot about the project. He knew it involved an enormous barge and a tender but he had never heard the name Glomar, Global Marine or Howard Hughes in connection with it. Sy's source had called it by the CIA code name Project Jennifer.

Hersh had made only a few checks when he got a call from Colby, who had heard of and been concerned about Sy's inquiries for almost a month. Unknown to Sy, Colby had conferred repeatedly with CIA associates on how to handle the matter, had consulted with Henry Kissinger, now Secretary of State, and had called Clifton Daniel, Hersh's superior, and warned him that he had to talk with Sy urgently.[*] Colby arranged to stop by *The New York Times* office at 3:30 P.M., February 1, 1974, on his way to Capitol Hill to deliver some materials which the Watergate Committee had requested. Sy asked Bob Phelps, the chief Washington editor, to sit in and when Colby arrived in his long black limousine he was ushered up to the eighth floor and into

---

[*] By no means all of Colby's associates favored his direct approach to Hersh. Henry Kissinger was opposed. He "thought I was crazy," Colby told the late Fred Buzhardt, White House counsel. Kissinger was involved at every step of Colby's effort to contain the *Glomar* story. He made at least two telephone calls to *The New York Times*, one to Punch Sulzberger, one to Clifton Daniel. (Personal interview, Colby, 7/17/79; FOIA documents on *Glomar*)

Phelps' brush-closet office. In the conversation Sy and Colby kept dancing around the story, Sy hinting that he knew a lot but Phelps' impression (a correct one) was that Hersh didn't have the details, not enough to go with a story. There was no word about a sunken Soviet submarine.

Colby did not conceal his concern. He said it was a matter of extraordinary national security and asked Hersh not to write anything and, indeed, not even to mention the project to anyone. Hersh responded that neither he nor Phelps had authority to make a deal to withhold the story but added, "There's no way I am going to be worrying about that story for the next six months or a year. There is too much going on with Watergate." He said that when he did go back to work on the story he would call Colby.*

Much, much later Sy conceded that he could understand why Colby thought a deal had been struck. Project Jennifer retreated to the back of Sy's mind, although he did tell Bill Kovach, who took over the Washington desk in March, about the story. Kovach urged him not to neglect it, but with all that was happening on Watergate, Sy didn't return to Jennifer. Despite Sy's assurances Colby continued to worry and when he chanced to lunch in New York February 20, 1974, with Punch Sulzberger and the New York editors he took Punch aside after lunch, told him of Jennifer and Sy Hersh and, as he later was to tell General Brent Scowcroft, then deputy to Henry Kissinger, "Sulzberger . . . was great. He was delighted to be trusted. I made the point it is not just printing. It is talking that can hurt us as bad."

So the matter ended for a time but it was a recollection of Sy's having kept faith with him on *Glomar* that played a role in Colby's frank talk with Hersh December 22 about the "family jewels."

First Break

Several stories about *Glomar* had appeared in print but attracted no attention. Some were published by the *Philadelphia Inquirer,* about the building of the ship by the Sun Shipbuilding yards at Chester, some on the Pacific Coast, one or two in the *Honolulu Advertiser.* Because they identified the ship as a Howard Hughes vessel and its mission as exploring ocean-floor minerals the stories raised no dust. None hinted at a CIA connection. The cover was working. Sy knew nothing about these stories. Nor did he know that his colleague John Crewdson had been working on a tip about *Glomar.* Crewdson heard in the summer of 1974 that Charles Colson, now out of the White House, had been

*Colby's notes recorded the impression that *The Times* would not be going back to work on the story for two or three months. (FOIA documents, Colby memo, Feb. 21, 1974)

talking about a CIA "spook ship" called the *Glomar Explorer* which had been built at the Sun Shipbuilding yards. As White House labor liaison officer Colson had negotiated clearances with labor unions for its construction. Crewdson put together a good deal of technical data but nothing to break the CIA cover story that it was a Hughes enterprise. He had never heard of Project Jennifer and had no knowledge that Hersh possessed any information about it.

Neither Hersh nor Crewdson knew that there had been a burglary June 5, 1974, at the Los Angeles office of Summa Corporation, the Hughes organization for which the spook ship had been built, nor did they know that valuable documents had been stolen, two footlockers full,* in fact, nor that the burglars had tried to extract $1 million in ransom from Summa for their return. (These facts had been suppressed by the police.)

Jim Phelan, a free-lance writer who specialized in Hughes affairs and who had been working closely with Wallace Turner, *The Times* senior investigative reporter, a long-time specialist on Hughes, and San Francisco bureau chief, heard of the burglary when it happened. The police report was routine and he put it out of his mind as one more detail in the endless demonology that surrounded the name of Hughes.† Neither Phelan nor Turner had ever heard of Project Jennifer but Turner knew Crewdson had been looking into a CIA angle in connection with *Glomar Explorer.* Turner didn't think there could be a connection between Hughes and the CIA.

In early February 1975 Phelan got a tip that the Summa burglary had involved secret papers, a ransom attempt, a CIA connection (but nothing about *Glomar* or Project Jennifer). After checking and consultation with Turner, Phelan set about to prepare a story for *The Times.* He was working on his piece when the early-bird Saturday edition of the *Los Angeles Times* appeared, a little after noon on Friday, February 7. It carried a double-truck headline in letters four-inches high: "U.S. Reported After Russ Sub."

There it was—*Glomar Explorer* had burst into print, a CIA project,

*Colby reported the number as four. (William Colby, *Honorable Men,* New York, 1978, p. 414)

†Phelan had heard even before the Summa burglary that *Glomar* was tied to CIA but had no sources with which to check his tip. Later in the year he happened to run into Hersh in Washington and put a question to him on the fly about *Glomar* being a CIA operation. Hersh, busy on another story, gave him a blank stare and later Phelan deduced Hersh didn't know what he was talking about. Phelan bumped into Hersh again just after *Glomar* broke. "Nobody seems to have known about *Glomar* in advance," Sy said. "I did," Phelan replied. "I had a tip that *Glomar* was CIA." "Did you tell anyone?" Sy asked. "Yes," Phelan replied. "I told you." (Personal interview, Phelan, 6/17/79) The CIA had known since June 24, 1974, that Phelan had connected *Glomar* and CIA. (FOIA memo, Feb. 19, 1975, p. 3)

built in Summa Corporation's name, designed to raise a Soviet sub from the ocean floor, secret papers telling all about it stolen from the Summa office the prior June 5. It was a sketchy story, very sketchy indeed. It had the submarine in the Atlantic, not the Pacific. It didn't call it Project Jennifer. It didn't tell much—but it did blow the CIA cover and it confirmed to anyone who had a bit of background what the CIA had been up to.

After consultation with Turner, Phelan filed a spot news story on the robbery of the Summa office and two ransom demands. He included a paragraph saying that the *Los Angeles Times* had reported that among the stolen papers was "a contract to help salvage a sunken Russian submarine." He said it was not clear whether the *Glomar Explorer* had carried out this operation. The story ran under a three-column headline on page twenty-three of a replate of the late *Times* edition of Saturday, February 8, 1975.*

The angle about the Soviet submarine was played down because neither Phelan nor Turner had been able to get independent confirmation and Turner had concluded the *Los Angeles Times* was wrong. Phelan did a more detailed story which ran in *The Times* Sunday, February 9, but dropped mention of the submarine.

What had happened was that the *Los Angeles Times*, getting a tip that *The New York Times* was preparing a story on the Summa burglary, scurried around, found out more than Phelan and Turner knew (even though some details were wrong or absent), threw a story together and rushed it into print.

It was this action by the *Los Angeles Times*, a purely competitive response to what it had heard another newspaper was doing, that set off the train of circumstances which quickly was to put *Glomar Explorer* on front pages around the world.

The Colby Campaign

The *Los Angeles Times* had gone to press with its story—but the papers were just beginning to roll out—when the CIA went into action, having learned of the story, apparently through Hughes employees in the Summa office. Carl Duckett, the CIA's deputy director of science and technology, telephoned Dr. Franklin Murphy, chairman of the board of the Times Mirror Corporation. Murphy served on the U.S. Intelligence Advisory Board and the men knew each other.

---

*Colby later was to claim he got *The Times* to bury this story on page thirty of its first edition and kill it in subsequent editions. His memory misled him. Because of the three-hour time differential to the Pacific Coast Phelan's story missed the first edition of *The Times* and ran only in a replate of the late city edition. (Colby, *Honorable Men*, p. 415)

Murphy had heard of *Glomar* as a member of the advisory board but, of course, had never spoken to the *Los Angeles Times* about it. He told Duckett he had nothing to do with what *The Times* published and that he should speak to the editor, William F. Thomas. "A matter of this kind is entirely in the hands of the editor," he said.

Duckett telephoned Thomas, who told him the story was already on the press. Duckett said he would like to send to Thomas a CIA representative who would tell him "anything [he] wanted to know." The CIA did not ask Thomas to kill the story but felt that once Thomas knew the facts he would act at his own initiative. Thomas moved the story off page one in later editions, putting it on page eighteen where it became almost invisible, hidden in the interior forest of the *Los Angeles Times'* advertising pages. Later, the CIA was to quote Thomas as regretting the publication of the story and saying that he would have killed it had he known of the CIA objection earlier. A CIA memo said Thomas was keeping his reporters on the story but promised to "exercise the full authority of his position to keep the results from ending up in the *Los Angeles Times*"—language which sounded more like that of a CIA bureaucrat than a newspaperman. One CIA communication from Los Angeles to Washington assured headquarters that Thomas agreed that in the future he would publish only "white DOMP" on Glomar. "DOMP" was a CIA cryptonym for propaganda. "White" meant material officially released; "black" was material made up by the CIA but attributed to some other source. DOMP was not a household word, even in the CIA. Colby claimed he hadn't heard it and didn't know what it meant.

The reports of the Los Angeles CIA representative to Washington made it appear that Thomas was groveling about, trying to please the CIA. In fact, Thomas, like a good newspaperman, listened politely to the CIA, agreed to hold back the story for the time being (on a promise that he would be advised if anyone else was releasing it), kept his reporters at work and cultivated the CIA to get additional data on the story. Thomas was in constant contact with Jack Nelson, his investigative reporter in Washington who was also in touch with Colby. All in all, the *Los Angeles Times* did very well on the story. The CIA's internal reports on *Glomar* provided a lesson in the manner in which bureaucratic paper work distorted the facts. The memos were larded with fly-blown compliments to Colby, supposedly uttered by various newsmen, more likely invented by toadying Agency hands.

After *Glomar* broke nationally, Thomas explained that even if the CIA had not intervened he would have moved the story inside in later editions. *The Times* often displayed flamboyant first-edition headlines to compete with the afternoon Hearst *Herald-Examiner*. These stories tended to vanish inside for the home-delivered morning editions. Despite Thomas' conversation with the CIA the *Glomar* story was placed on the *Los Angeles Times-Washington Post* syndicate wire and delivered around the country to other newspapers, a good many of which published it and UPI also carried the story.

The Los Angeles publication sent Hersh into a frenzy. When he called Turner on the West Coast his words tumbled together so as to be almost unintelligible. He hadn't known, he said, that Summa Corporation was Hughes and he arranged to fly to Los Angeles immediately. Crewdson gave him the materials he had put together about *Glomar.* Before he left Washington Sy called Colby and said he was back on the story. "You've been first-class about this thing for a long time," Colby said. "It is not a question of being good. I am a citizen, too," Hersh replied. (Later Sy was embarrassed by this remark; he didn't like anything that undercut his image as a tough, 'bad ass' reporter.)

It was not long before Sy had put together a detailed account of what the CIA had done. He showed it to Turner, who shook his head. He told Sy that *The Times* wouldn't publish it. For a while Turner was right. Colby had embarked on a desperate campaign to keep the project from surfacing. He called one editor and publisher after another, sometimes when he learned they were working on the story, sometimes before they had even heard of it, and asked them to hold off on grounds of national security contending CIA needed time to make another pass at lifting the submarine. He made three calls to Punch Sulzberger, once saying, "I hate to bug you on this," to which Punch replied, "You do not bug me ever." Colby responded, "That's for damn sure!" His first call came on Saturday morning, February 8, the day *The Times* ran the story on the Summa office burglary and *Glomar.* The story didn't appear in the edition of *The Times* that had been delivered to Punch in Stamford and some confusion ensued. Colby asked Sulzberger if it "might be possible to cool it down a little" and Sulzberger promised to look into it. Colby called Monday, February 10, to thank Sulzberger, who said, "I very gently passed on the word and I think everyone understands." Colby called again the next day, telling Sulzberger he had talked to Hersh, and that the *Los Angeles Times* "is closing it off. . . . I just wanted to tip you and I will get out of it," Colby told the publisher. Punch said, "Good, I have it."

Colby was taking no chances with *The Times.* The whole CIA network had been alerted. Sy could hardly make a telephone call or a swing to the West Coast or East Coast without Colby getting an immediate report. On February 25, Clifton Daniel telephoned Colby and asked for a date at Langley. Colby gave him an appointment at 4 P.M., February 27. Colby alerted Kissinger and the CIA hierarchy and prepared some arguments for a last-ditch struggle to contain the story. Daniel specified that Hersh and Bill Kovach would accompany him.

On the way to Langley, Hersh speculated on what kind of a reception they would get. Daniel remembered telling him that they would get red-carpet treatment and when the guard at the entrance took one look and waved them through he said, "What did I tell you, Sy?" But there was nothing hospitable in the demeanor of the young aide who escorted them to Colby's office. The four crowded into a small interior elevator and from his flushed face and angry look it was apparent that the escort felt himself in the presence of the enemy. "The hostility was palpable," Kovach recalled. "Obviously, he felt Sy was the incarnation of evil." "This twenty-eight-year-old was giving me the staring hard-ass number," Hersh remembered. "I guess he was trying to lay bad vibes on me."

In the director's office, Colby, as always, was cool and downbeat. He had Carl Duckett on hand to go over the scientific and intelligence importance of *Glomar*. There were facts and figures and some gory details of the recovery of bodies of Soviet submariners and how careful *Glomar* had been to take photographs of the bodies, not only stills but motion pictures in black and white and in color, ultimately to be turned over to the Russians. The rationale for this was not exactly clear but when Sy's story was published this detail was included.

What emerged from this discussion, essentially, was an agreement. *The Times* would not publish the story unless advised by the CIA that the proposed second pass at the sub by *Glomar* was completed or aborted or until someone else published. In return the CIA promised to advise *The Times* on all three points, particularly if it heard someone else was breaking the story. Neither Hersh nor Kovach liked this but Daniel felt it was fair. He was not empowered to make a deal but would recommend it to his superiors in New York. The arrangement was approved by Rosenthal and Daniel notified Colby by letter March 3.

Duckett, in a memo for the files, emphasized that the meeting was "totally friendly" and thought Daniel was "at least 50–50" on the story. He described the *Times* men as "impressed by the Hughes patriotism pitch." Clifton Daniel shook hands on leaving, a fact Duckett found worthy of recording and quoted him as saying that "regardless of where we come out [*Glomar*] is a great accomplishment." Positive as Duckett had described the meeting, it was decided to have Kissinger call Punch Sulzberger to nail it down. Duckett would have been slightly less sanguine had he known that he had gotten off to a bad start by introducing himself as having been born halfway between Zebulon, North Carolina (Daniel's hometown) and Johnson City, Tennessee (Kovach's hometown). The *Times* men felt this a cornball con; that

Duckett wanted to show that they were all good old boys, which they were not.

Sulzberger had told Rosenthal of his several calls from Colby but knowing that Sy was working night and day to put the story together Abe said nothing to Hersh. After Daniel's letter to Colby on March 3, Rosenthal sent Hersh a memo saying that *Glomar* was an ongoing military operation and he was going to hold the story until (a) the CIA completed another try at the submarine, (b) until they abandoned the attempt or (c) until someone else broke the story. Hersh responded in a three-page memo, the essence of which was, okay, so this was an ongoing operation—what about the Vietnam war, wasn't that an ongoing military operation when you published the Pentagon Papers? Abe came back saying he had a "feeling in his stomach" about *Glomar* and he was going to hold the story for the time being. Hersh rejoined that he thought something else had upset Abe's digestion.

Working day and night, Colby succeeded in sewing up most of the major news outlets, always leaving the decision to the editor or publisher, but each time emphasizing that others had already agreed to hold back—the *Los Angeles Times, The New York Times,* etc. Before he was through he had tied up the *Washington Star, Washington Post, Time, Newsweek,* the three networks, *Parade* and National Public Broadcasting.

Glomar Published

Tom Wicker heard of the story on the morning of March 18. He had a call from Charles Morgan, Jr., the Civil Rights lawyer, who, improbably, had heard a tape on which Colson was talking about the *Glomar* project.* Morgan had been trying to get the story published, had talked with Crewdson and other reporters, and knew *The Times* was holding up Sy's story.

Morgan caught Wicker's interest instantly. Wicker was still simmering over the Ford luncheon. He went to Rosenthal, who told him the story was being held on security grounds and offered to give him a fill-in. Wicker declined the offer, telling Abe that "depending on circumstances" he might write about it in his column and did not want to be privy to off-the-record information. Wicker then saw Punch Sulzberger, who told Wicker that he was in a quandary about the story,

---

*The tape was made by Colson at the time he was defending himself on the Watergate charges. Later the private investigator who made the tape for Colson got in touch with Morgan, then with the American Civil Liberties Union and extremely active in 1974 in the cause of bringing impeachment proceedings against Nixon. (Personal interview, Morgan, 6/25/79)

wasn't at all sure *The Times* had made the right decision and was going to talk to Rosenthal and see whether they should not reconsider.

Wicker had to leave for Detroit to do a television show. In the studio he heard a news program quoting *The Times* on *Glomar*. Gosh, Wicker thought, I really got them to break the story. He was very pleased.

What Wicker did not know was that among those activated by Morgan was the columnist Jack Anderson. Anderson had checked the story out and despite arguments from Colby had decided to publish. He called Sy Hersh and told him he planned to go on the air with it at 9 P.M. on the Mutual Broadcasting System radio program from Washington. Sy alerted Clifton Daniel. After the meeting with Colby, Daniel had persuaded Hersh to rewrite the story and had edited it to have it ready for publication. Rosenthal decided to get the story into *The Times'* first edition. Instantly the air was filled with excitement, telephone calls from copy editors from New York to Washington and Washington to New York. Sy, not adverse to a little hazing, asked Rosenthal, "Why should we run it now? It still involves national security. We didn't run it before—why should we do it now just because Anderson does it?" Rosenthal wasn't in a mood for banter. "Aw, shut up, Sy," he said and publication roared forward.* In the midst of this Hersh got a frantic call from Anderson. "Jesus!" Anderson said, "Is this story all right?" "I'll stake my reputation on it," Sy said. After calling a naval officer whom Sy suggested could affirm that no real question of national security was involved Anderson broadcast the item.

It had been more like the scenario of a Mack Sennett comedy than a sophisticated journalistic enterprise but, one way or another, *Glomar* finally made it onto page one of *The New York Times*. The implications of this remained to be analyzed.

*Months later Rosenthal was reading excerpts of William Colby's *Honorable Men* in *Esquire* and came to Colby's description of his meeting with Hersh in January 1974. Hersh happened to be standing outside Rosenthal's office. Rosenthal said: "Sy, come here. I want to read you something." He read the passage and said, "In other words you had this story for a year before it broke." "Yeh," Sy said. "And then you complained when I held it up?" "Yeh," Sy said. "So," recalled Rosenthal, "I chased him back into his office, hitting him over the head with *Esquire*, all the way." (Personal interviews, A. M. Rosenthal, 8/9/79; Hersh, 10/27/79)

46

A Quiver of Questions

*W*HAT COLBY HAD called the Year of Intelligence, the year of CIA exposés, left in its train a quiver of sharp and not easily answered questions. The editors of *The Times*, Abe Rosenthal, foremost, felt that *The Times* had given a fine account of itself, had measured up well to the intimately linked consequences of Watergate—the enormous expansion of the power of the press and the widening of its responsibility, its role as servant of and surrogate of the public.

Ben Bradlee of the *Washington Post* in his offhand way expressed a similar sentiment. It seemed to him that the press had done pretty well. Of course there were thousands of things that should be done and not all of them were being done; there had been lots of confusion, lots of right turns on the wrong road and wrong turns on the right road.

"But all in all," he said, "I think that we have been right. After Watergate a lot of people were arguing that what we needed was a period of peace and quiet, that we had rocked the boat enough, and they were saying, oh, you are out to make a Watergate out of everything. But that's not right. We haven't. We've missed some but there is a lot we haven't missed."

Bradlee's conclusion was too comfortable. The performance of the press in the Year of Intelligence reminded some of that of a half-trained colt, speedy, intelligent but skittish on the track, quick to shy and uncertain of staying the course.

The Times had shown resource and muscle on the Allende exposé and on domestic activity of the CIA but it had tied its own hands on President Ford's assassination revelations and it had played on-again, off-again finnegan on *Glomar Explorer*. The Washington press, and the *Washington Post*, particularly on the CIA domestic story, still demonstrated a preference for the "official view."

Glomar raised serious questions. True, *Glomar* was an enormously complex story involving both intelligence and far-out technology. In some ways it resembled the U-2 story, which *The Times* stayed away from on Allen Dulles' argument that while the Russians knew about it they had decided not to make a public protest (having no ability to shoot down the U-2s) as long as the Americans kept their mouths shut. The possibility that the U-2 flights might ultimately produce a diplomatic disaster—as they did—did not enter the minds of Hanson Baldwin or Arthur Krock, the *Times* men who knew of U-2. Nor did Baldwin or Krock see a contradiction in the fact that the Russians knew the operation was in progress and could "blow it" anytime they desired while the American public was funding it in ignorance.

In the case of *Glomar,* Colby lobbied to keep the story out of the press on grounds that it was an ongoing operation; that CIA wanted cover for "one last chance" to raise the missing part of the submarine; and that it was in the national interest that the press go along.

This argument was maintained, even intensified, after the cover was destroyed by the *Los Angeles Times,* after the *Los Angeles Times'* story had been distributed all over the country and after *The New York Times* had carried its own first tentative story. If the KGB had not yet heard of *Glomar* they now knew; even the most stupid Soviet intelligence organization was bound, like a score of U.S. editors, to spot the story and begin working on it. The situation constituted a virtual rerun of the Bay of Pigs after Paul Kennedy's story in *The New York Times* of January 10, 1961. *Glomar* might not yet be a household word to the U.S. public but it was to the Russians, just as the Bay of Pigs had been to Castro. In his effort to keep *Glomar* out of the papers Colby didn't contend that the Russians didn't know about the operation; he claimed that publicity might cause them to send a naval squadron to the scene; that armed conflict might break out. This melodramatic scenario hardly seemed plausible because under maritime law anyone was entitled to recover a sunken vessel; the U.S. had full legal right to raise a Russian submarine if it could and the Russians could recover any American hulk they had a fancy for. Both nations had long adhered to this code of the sea. But if there was a real chance that the Russians might threaten armed combat with the U.S. over the eighteen-year-old submarine this, it would seem, was a powerful argument for letting the public know what the CIA had gotten us into before the balloon went up.

What, in retrospect, seemed most disturbing was that despite recent past history—U-2, the Bay of Pigs, Nixon's claim of national security in Watergate—editors and publishers up and down the line, including those of *The New York Times,* accepted Colby's argument. Not one challenged Colby's assertion that the CIA's cover hadn't *really* been blown by the *Los Angeles Times* story.

The critical flaw in the response of *The New York Times* editors was that the history of the U-2, the Bay of Pigs, and the others, had left so faint a tracing on their minds. Once again was displayed a lack of historicism; a failure to consult precedent; an impulse to react positively and even appreciatively to a call, a request, a suggestion of a Colby, a Kissinger.

Colby's Motivation

For, when it came to the bottom line, why did Colby want to keep *Glomar* out of the headlines? Hersh had known, *The Times* had known and Colby conceded that Russian trawlers had appeared on the site within two or three days of the time *Glomar* began to work. How could there have been doubt in Russian minds as to the business of *Glomar?* Nor could there have been genuine hope by the CIA that the Russians would not spot *Glomar* and its accompanying vessels immediately. They were too vast, a ship the length of two football fields; a barge even larger; Soviet satellite coverage was bound to spot and locate the expedition instantly. This was not the kind of thing that could be sneaked out on a dark night into the Atlantic or Pacific oceans. Not with today's scientific technology. (But years later Colby still resisted this reasoning. He insisted that the Russian trawlers had not figured out what *Glomar Explorer* was doing even after they had seen it at work and he contended that there was no sign the Russians spotted the *Los Angeles Times'* and *New York Times'* stories in February 1975. "There was no visible sign," he said. He did not explain how he was so certain of this but possibly he based himself on NSA monitoring of Soviet signals traffic.)

An inquisitive person, a Sy Hersh, an Abe Rosenthal, was bound to ask, what was the game? What was it that Colby was trying to protect? Was it, as Hersh strongly suspected, a fear that *Glomar* would be perceived as a half-billion-dollar boondoggle? Had the intelligence achievement been less than a dazzling technological triumph? Was, as some later suggested, sour grapes involved on the part of Navy men (probably Sy's sources) who did not like the enormous gouge in Naval appropriations that had been carved out by *Glomar?*

These were the questions that should have zipped through editorial minds but there was little evidence that they had. Later there were critics who contended the whole thing was a hype by Colby and the CIA, a way of getting superpublicity and counteracting the terrible beating the CIA was taking on Watergate, on domestic intelligence and the rest. But when documents relating to Colby's efforts to suppress *Glomar* became available under the Freedom of Information Act they did not bear this out. Colby's effort to keep the lid on began too far back, back in early January 1974. His effort had been consistent; the internal memos and the internal transcripts did not support the theory of hype.

Another hypothesis was advanced later—that the story of *Glomar* and the submarine was an elaborate cover, that the real function of *Glomar* was something quite different, to recover, some said, Soviet missile structures from the ocean floor after they had been fired on the test courses, to enable the CIA to examine them and establish the state of the Soviet art. But, as one knowledgeable specialist was to point out, *Glomar* wasn't needed for this; the Navy possessed much simpler and cheaper pressurized cabs and remote-control apparatus that did the job very nicely. No need for spending hundreds of millions and devising hoists capable of lifting nearly fifteen million pounds of deadweight. Of course, there was Charles Morgan's suspicion that *Glomar* was designed not to lift objects from the ocean floor but to plant objects there, nuclear launching pads, for example, and secret nuclear missiles aimed at the Soviet. But specialists rejected this theory as well. The idea didn't make military sense. The Navy's nuclear-powered submarines provided a much better launching mechanism. Or could *Glomar* be used for installing a subsurface detection system, one which would make it impossible for Soviet submarines to move without U.S. detection? The technology experts ruled out that. The U.S. already had had for a long, long time a subsurface detection system that ran from Iceland to Norway. It hadn't taken *Glomar Explorer* to install that.

But the possibility that a hypersecret use of *Glomar* existed could not be put aside—except—except for what happened later, after the hullabaloo was over. *Glomar* didn't just quietly vanish into the entrails of CIA. Instead, it became a highly visible white elephant, no longer, it seemed, of use to the CIA. It was put up for auction but no one wanted to buy it even at a low knock-down price. Late in 1978 a consortium in which Lockheed, Standard Oil of Indiana and Royal Dutch Shell participated was formed with the intention of trying to use *Glomar* for oil or mineral exploration.

But this was only an interim solution. *Glomar* had little value to anyone in the configuration in which it had been constructed. It could, however, be modified for ocean drilling—at a cost of $100 million or more. It could be used in exploring the great continental shelves which lie beyond the reach of conventional drilling. An experimental international ocean-exploration program had been in existence for several years, based at Woods Hole, Massachusetts. It had been using *Glomar Challenger, Explorer*'s predecessor. The international group included the Soviet Union, which contributed $1 million a year to the work. Now plans were drawn to convert *Glomar* for use in a new international ocean-bed program. Thus, the possibility arose that the Soviet (whose fancied outrage at *Glomar* lay at the core of Colby's pitch to keep the story out of the papers) soon would be associated as an active, financial and scientific partner in the use of the mystery ship.

The argument might be raised that there had been no way for the editors of *The New York Times* to conceive of these questions in advance but one glaring omission had marked *The Times'* editorial process. At no point did the editors turn to *The Times'* science specialists for an evaluation of the CIA's claims for *Glomar*. The chance that *The Times'* science staff could have provided invaluable guidance was very high. Once *Glomar* went public Walter Sullivan, *The Times'* renaissance science editor, was invited to join a high-level committee to consider what use might now be made of the ship.*

The Issues

There was widespread discomfort among *Times* editors—and within the press generally—over their role in *Glomar*. Tom Wicker stated the concerns with some eloquence—the unanimity with which Establishment newspapers, individually, agreed to Colby's appeal; the evidence that the press did tend toward a monolithic unity, a unity which belied the suggestion that it was "anti-government, anti-security, anti-conservative or 'pro-leftist.'"

There was the troublesome argument that Sy Hersh raised the night *The Times* decided to carry the *Glomar* story. If national security had really been at stake how did Jack Anderson's report change the issue? Was it not possible, as Anderson had suggested, that by suppressing the story the press was just trying to prove "how patriotic and responsible we are, that we are not against the Establishment, the government, that we are not all gadflies?" In other words, was nonpublication just a matter of cosmetics, an attempt to respond to those who felt the press had gone too far in Watergate and the Pentagon Papers?

Wicker asked about the public interest—wasn't it valid to examine the utility of spending more on *Glomar* than President Ford was requesting for a last-ditch effort in Cambodia? What if the CIA's actions produced a Soviet counterresponse, possibly a technological riposte? What about the linkage of Hughes and the CIA? Charles B. Seib, the *Washington Post's* press critic, concluded that "the media's brief, self-imposed gag rule and the subsequent rush to publication was hasty, confused, error-ridden journalism." It was difficult to dispute his judgment, as difficult as it was not to dispute the judgment of the Pulitzer judges who failed to honor Hersh's remarkable reporting on the CIA. The omission marked one of the rare years when *The Times* won no Pulitzers at all.

Not until the CIA made available under the Freedom of Information act a mass of documents concerning Colby's efforts to suppress the *Glomar* story did it become possible to assess the complex factors that motivated him. One was his genuine concern that publicity would, in

---

*Sullivan turned down the invitation. Both he and Rosenthal felt it might handicap his freedom in writing about *Glomar*. (Personal interview, Sullivan, 6/22/79)

some manner, abort the intelligence mission of *Glomar*. That mission, it was clear from his private comments to members of CIA, the intelligence community, Kissinger and General Scowcroft, was still in progress. Whether it was actually the raising of a second part of the Soviet submarine sunk in the Pacific was not so clear; nor, in fact, was it clear that a Soviet submarine sunk in the Pacific was the target; the possibility remained that it could have been a submarine in the Atlantic, as the first *Los Angeles Times'* story asserted.*

Exactly why Colby felt the operation had not been blown by the *Los Angeles Times'* and *New York Times'* stories remained murky. But some of his comments seemed to imply a tacit understanding with the Russians that would be violated by publicity. Several times it was suggested that he let a story be published that the operation had already been completed. This would throw the Russians off the trail. For reasons which the FOIA documents did not make clear, Colby did not buy this approach.†

Colby had a possibly more important concern. He was in the midst of a struggle to preserve the CIA's existence, dangerously threatened by Watergate, Nixon, and a stream of unsavory revelations. He was determined to use Glomar to repair CIA's reputation. He laid down strict rules. Neither he nor his deputy directors were permitted to tell lies about *Glomar* (no such ground rules applied to lower employees). They were not permitted to use "no comment" as a response to inquiries from Congress but some latitude could be invoked with the press.‡ As Colby spelled it out, "It is important not to get into boxes wherein

*Colby insisted that calm summer weather was necessary to carry out the second phase of the *Glomar* operation. As late as 1979 he said that the six-week lid which he kept on *Glomar* served no practical purpose since he had to keep *Glomar* under cover until summer for further operations. But the area in which the Soviet submarine sank in the Pacific was quiet both winter and summer. (Personal interview, Colby, 7/19/79)

†The curious detail of the photographs and films taken by CIA in black-and-white and color of the *Glomar* operation may, in some manner, relate to all this. Colby told Hersh that they were to be turned over to the Russians at the end of the operation. It was Hersh's understanding that the films would show that the CIA had treated the bodies of the Soviet submariners with respect. But later on Colby was vague as to whether the pictures had ever been given to the Russians, didn't think they had and suggested that this was a matter for the State Department. (Personal interview, Colby, 7/19/79) This curious and unexplained detail plus Colby's statements again and again to editors and reporters that it was just as important "not to talk" about Glomar as it was not to publish and identical statements made by Colby in private conversations with Kissinger and other security officials raised the possibility of some totally deniable "understanding" with the Russians.

‡Despite this the morning after *Glomar* broke the White House decided that the government's response would be "No comment." This, Colby said, was agreed upon after he recalled that Khrushchev blamed the U-2 crisis not on the overflight but upon President Eisenhower's acknowledging responsibility for the action. (Personal interview, Colby, 7/19/79)

statements might be made which could subsequently be shown to be false—the Watergate syndrome."

Moreover, Colby specified that "realizing the actions of senior press officials in respecting the security of important programs [i.e. *Glomar*], without concurring in nefarious dealings, we must accept their willingness to abide by National Security guidelines, as long as there is no suspicion of concealment of such nefarious doings, nor must we impugn their integrity or diligence in surfacing wrongdoing. Thus, disclosures made in covers to press representatives cannot later be denied."

What Colby was attempting, as he told General Scowcraft on March 14 and March 17, 1975, was to run "the weirdest conspiracy" to keep *Glomar* out of print. He was persuading one paper after another to hold its information from the public and even going to AP or UPI, telling them about the story and asking them, in effect, to join the conspiracy. By March 14, he could say to Scowcroft "We are in a situation right now where we don't give a damn how many Americans know about it."

Three days later he told Scowcroft it was like *The Perils of Pauline* but he still thought he had a fighting chance of controlling the date when the story would be made public.

In the end, of course, *Glomar* did go public March 18, not to Colby's great surprise. He had known it was an odds-on gamble. But he felt in the end it had paid off. It had bought the Agency six weeks in time and it had dramatically improved the Agency's credibility.

Second Thoughts

At first Rosenthal defended *The Times'* handling of *Glomar*. "The advantage of publishing it immediately did not outweigh," he said, "the disadvantage of writing about a military operation of some importance." But as time went by he became more and more dubious and finally was to confess in a memo to Punch Sulzberger a year later, "I think frankly Colby used us on the Soviet submarine story." Sulzberger shared this feeling. By this time *The Times* was engaged in a vigorous effort to compel the CIA to divulge connections which might have existed in the past between the paper and the agency, between employees of the paper, including string correspondents, and the Agency.

The endeavor had, for practical purposes, begun November 25, 1973, when William Colby lunched with James Reston and other *Times* correspondents in Washington. Over lunch Reston asked Colby whether anyone now on *The Times* worked with the CIA. Colby assured Reston that no one now did—making perfectly plain that the denial applied only to the current moment; it did not go to the past; nor were details spelled out. It was a denial which had plenty of crevices in it.

The question of CIA-*Times* links bothered Rosenthal. He had, as he was later to say, been somewhat naïve about the CIA. He had stayed away from it himself. To be sure, he had gotten to know some CIA men overseas, one of them, Peer Da Silva, becoming quite a good friend. Da Silva was in Vienna when Abe arrived after being expelled from Warsaw. Abe later saw him in Korea and when Da Silva retired from the CIA he helped get his book published by The New York Times' book company.* Abe had avoided the CIA when he was in Poland and was glad that he had when at the time of his expulsion the Poles made an effort to link him with a high Polish intelligence agent named Pavel Monat, who had defected from Warsaw to the U.S.A. via Vienna about four months earlier. After he got to Vienna, Abe wrote an exclusive story about the Monat case, the first public mention. His information, he said later, came from various intelligence sources.

Abe was to treasure a delicious memory of Vienna, the CIA and the KGB. John MacCormac, *The Times'* staff man in Vienna, invited Abe to a party in the magnificent Empire flat he occupied on the Ringstrasse. Abe was talking to a friendly Russian and asked the man what he did. The Russian pointed across the room to an American and said, "My job here for the Soviet Union is the same as his job for your side." The man to whom the Russian pointed was the CIA station chief in Vienna. Before the evening was over Rosenthal realized that half the guests were spies for one country or another; it was a veritable feast of spooks.

Despite the omnipresence of spooks Rosenthal never really thought of them employing the press or newsmen in intelligence tasks. He was, he said later, just naïve. "I always believed that no correspondent would touch that stuff and then along came Sy Freidin," he said. Freidin was an old friend who worked for the *Herald-Tribune* and had been named as having worked for the CIA in the past. When Abe was in India, he remembered, the correspondent corps was extremely small. He was positive that there had been no CIA infiltration there.

"I just couldn't believe that the CIA would trade off the press," Rosenthal was to recall. "I couldn't believe that about the CIA. That was a basic mistake on my part. I had never believed it could be."

Abe's misjudgment about the CIA had come from his own peripheral experiences.

In Poland he had once gone out to Yasna Gora, headquarters of the Warsaw Pact. He told a polite Soviet aide that he wanted to see the commanding general. The aide said the commander was busy. Abe said, O.K., we'll drive around, do some sightseeing and be back in a couple of hours. Another aide brought word that the general would be

---

*Abe helped another old CIA friend get a book published by *The Times'* book subsidiary. This was Harry Rositzke, a CIA specialist in Soviet affairs, with whom Abe got acquainted when Rositzke had a tour of duty in India. (Personal interview, Manny Geltman, 8/16/79)

busy all day. So Abe responded, well, never mind. We'll spend the night at the hotel and come back in the morning. A third aide now appeared and said very firmly that the general would be busy for the rest of the month.

A couple of days later Abe was having a cup of coffee in the embassy snack bar when the local CIA man came in. "Where've you been?" the CIA man asked, all curiosity. "You mean, Sam," Abe said, "you don't know?" "What do you mean I don't know?" the CIA man replied. "Well," said Abe, "it's this way, Sam, if you're not cleared for this kind of thing then I can't say anything." Abe let the CIA man stew for a half hour then looked him up in his embassy office behind the steel-grilled doors. "Look, Sam," Abe said. "I'm not cleared for anything. I just wanted to let you know how it feels."

Once in Karachi, Abe bumped into Allen Dulles, who was on an inspection trip. Dulles gave him an appointment two days later in New Delhi. Abe arrived at Dulles' office to find every spook in the embassy (there were only five or six) waiting to see the boss. As he was ushered in he could see them looking at each other and read their thoughts: "Is he one of us?" He spent thirty or forty minutes with Dulles and came out. The spooks were still there. Abe put a knowing smile on his face and walked away.

Now by late 1975 and early 1976 Rosenthal was totally convinced that the CIA had left dirty paw prints on the media. He was determined to get to the bottom of this and thought the first step was to explore the CIA's relationship with *The Times*. On January 30, 1976, Rosenthal renewed his urgings to Punch Sulzberger to make every effort to expose any connections between the Agency and *The Times*. George Bush now headed the CIA and when he came to lunch February 4, 1976, in New York at *The Times* Punch raised the question and a formal demand was once more submitted for a full list of *New York Times*' staff men and string correspondents with CIA connections. Bush was most pleasant and full of assurances of cooperation but the results were nil. Three weeks later he wrote Punch refusing the request and a bit later a similar request initiated in Washington by Clifton Daniel was turned down.

Back and forth the matter went, Rosenthal trying to persuade *The Times* to sue for the information under the Freedom of Information Act and Sulzberger directing to Bush a new formal request in which he said, "We must have assurances that CIA has no agreement or understanding and will have no agreement or understanding with any of our employees or stringers to act for the CIA, to assist the CIA or perform services for the CIA." On October 6, 1976, George Bush once again refused to release the information.

47

Self-Analysis

T HE YEAR OF 1976 was one of major change at *The Times*. The CIA and the responsibility of *The Times* to itself and its readers was far from the only question on the minds of Rosenthal and Sulzberger. Despite the extraordinary run of news that had started with the Pentagon Papers, continued through Watergate, the Nixon resignation, Ford and the CIA, the economics of *The Times* had weakened. Costs climbed up and up. Circulation held at a fixed point. Advertising income hit a plateau. The Times Corporation was healthier than ever —the subsidiary operations were booming—but *The Times'* newspaper was rocking along just above red ink. The situation worried Punch, worried his vice presidents. A healthy, profitable *Times* must be the heart of the corporation. If *The Times* slid into red ink there would be cutbacks, quality would drop, the whole enterprise would sag. There was no crisis but it was not hard to envisage one on the horizon. New York City's economy was suffering and *The Times* was by no means as strong as it should have been in the suburbs. Only belatedly was it getting into the new cold-print computerized technology.

From the moment he had become publisher Punch had felt it uneconomic and inefficient that *The Times,* in effect, constituted two newspapers—the daily and the Sunday, each with its own editor, its own staff. True, the Sunday staff was minuscule compared to the daily. True, the Sunday paper for the most part was written by the daily staff. Still it seemed to his orderly mind untidy and wasteful. Now one wintry February day he arrived early on the fourteenth floor of *The Times* building, walked into Sydney Gruson's office and said he had decided to consolidate the two staffs under a single direction. It would save a lot of money, he thought, and help with the red ink. Despite his ill luck with two previous executive editors, Catledge and Reston, he was going to name a third and he had made up his mind that it would be Rosenthal.

After discussion Sulzberger modified his plan a bit. He decided to ask both Rosenthal and Frankel, then Sunday editor, to submit projects for combined operations. He did not tell Rosenthal and Frankel specifically but it was implicit that the man with the best plan would win the jackpot.

The Florida presidential primary was coming up in March and Abe went down to the Four Ambassadors in Miami. He saw a bit of campaigning, met Senator Henry Jackson and Governor George Wallace and then holed up and batted out a thirty-page draft plan on an office portable he had brought from New York. He came back, had his secretary retype the thirty pages and gave it to Punch. A few days later Punch said he was going ahead with it—but he said nothing about the executive editorship. On April 2, the day before they were to leave for the Gridiron dinner in Washington, he said to Abe, "Well, I'm offering you the job." "Oh," said Abe, "then I'll take it."

So Abe, who had fought and schemed and scrambled for every job he had gotten on *The Times,* felt he had been handed the job he had wanted most of all. He never had asked for it, would not have thought of asking and hadn't supposed that it would come his way. But come it did and with it problems of consolidating the two staffs (the savings actually were piddling); getting in his own men to run things (Max Frankel and Jack Rosenthal, who had headed the Sunday department and the magazine went to the editorial page); naming Seymour Topping managing editor and Arthur Gelb deputy managing editor.

There had, in the end, been plenty of trauma over the changes. Frankel hadn't wanted to become chief of the editorial page. Jack Rosenthal hadn't wanted to become his deputy. Topping hadn't wanted to be managing editor (he had hoped to succeed Oakes on the editorial page). Rosenthal long ago had promised that when Dan Schwartz retired as Sunday editor he would see that Arthur Gelb got the job. That had not happened; Frankel had been given the spot. Then Rosenthal had promised Gelb that he would make him managing editor and now that did not happen either. There were many rough edges in the transition but nothing like the creative tension that built up as the task of the redesign of *The Times* got under way, as fundamental a change as had been undertaken since Adolph Ochs refounded the paper in 1896. The redesign, the four-section paper, like every change in *The Times,* had been discussed and discussed for years. The chief proponent of the idea (and his arguments were bluntly economic) was Walter Mattson, a tall, angular production man who had come to wield more and more influence on the business side of the paper and who in 1979 at 47, was to be named president of The New York Times Company, that is, operating chief of The Times conglomerate.* He

---

*In the aftermath of Mattson's appointment, *The Times* lost the services of one of its most brilliant executives. James Goodale, who led the paper's fight in the great legal battle of the Pentagon Papers, resigned his post as vice-chairman and general counsel,

described himself in *Who's Who* as a "Communications Company executive," a phrase that hardly endeared him to old-fashioned *Times'* editors and reporters. Like his personal hero, Adolph Ochs, Mattson got into newspapering as a printer, setting type and wrapping papers in his uncle's weekly, published near Pittsburgh, when he was in eighth grade. Before he was out of college he held a card in the Typographer's Union and was setting type on the Portland, Maine, *Press-Herald.* Later he got a degree in accounting, went into Democratic politics in the state of Maine, published his own weekly, got a graduate degree in engineering, worked as an advertising man and newspaper consultant, finally joining *The Times* with some reluctance, in 1960, taking time off from *The Times* for studies in advanced management at the Harvard Business School. There was no one on *The Times* quite like Mattson, with his tough, pragmatic, shirtsleeves approach tempered by academic studies. The no-nonsense practicality of Mattson's mind and his dollar-and-cents arguments, presented in the plain-speaking tradition of his Swedish ancestors, did not always commend him to his colleagues. Rosenthal had great respect for Mattson's technical abilities but he didn't like his proposals for changes in the content and makeup of *The Times.* However, confronted with compelling economic arguments, he threw himself with his habitual creative violence into the task of changing *The Times.*

The original idea of Mattson had been simply to create a section that would entice food advertising. He wanted a conventional mix of cookbook recipes and household hints. How to bake a chocolate cake and remove wine stains from the tablecloth. Instead, Rosenthal cannibalized *New York* magazine. "We swallowed *New York,*" Rosenthal recalled. "I'll steal any idea from anybody if it's not nailed down."

And he did. As Clay Felker was to say (having left *New York* magazine for *Esquire* by that time), "You've created a fifty-cent daily magazine." This was true. Mimi Sheraton on corned-beef sandwiches, Craig Claiborne all over the paper, John Leonard every week on his Jungian couch, pop culture to a fare-thee-well, an instant success except to veteran *Times'* readers who complained that they hadn't been able to consume the paper before—and now look what *The Times* had done to them! And there were those who criticized the new incarnation saying that *The Times* must now invent another section and label it "News." To this Abe's answer was that the new sections had given the paper a financial floor that made its position virtually unassailable, and this at a moment when the *News* and the *Post* were floundering. Now, unlike any other paper in the country, *The Times* could and did throw

---

and returned to private law practice with the firm of Debevoise, Plimpton, Lyons and Gates.

$30,000 a month, maybe $50,000 a month, over and above salaries and staff into covering the fall of Iran, the money was there, no strain. Abe could maintain forty correspondents in Europe without looking over his shoulder at the auditors and he had created more newspaper excitement than New York had seen since the days of Frank Munsey. To a colleague who had told Rosenthal the day he became managing editor that, unlike all his predecessors, he would be the first managing editor of *The Times* whose most serious problem would be economic, Rosenthal presented *"The New New York Times"* (he hated the phrase) as not a bad solution.

With this going on it was hardly surprising that the question of the CIA would not again become acute until the autumn of 1977, not until Carl Bernstein published his *Rolling Stone* article with its allegations about Cy Sulzberger and Arthur Hays Sulzberger. Now *The Times'* effort to extract the information from the CIA went back into high gear. The internal paper chain of *The Times* was peppered with memoranda. Max Frankel demanded the fullest disclosure of all past CIA connections of *The Times,* volunteering that "I once had a conversation with Allen Dulles about my travels in Siberia." Cy Sulzberger backed up his denial of the Bernstein charges with a communication to general counsel James Goodale, proposing legal action to compel Bernstein to disclose his sources. "The public is entitled," Cy said, "to be in a position where it can judge whether the charges are true or false." But once again the CIA refused to budge.

Rosenthal decided to try a new approach—*The Times* would investigate itself (as well as the rest of the press). There had been piecemeal attempts at this but nothing on the scale now launched.

"I couldn't just laugh it off," Rosenthal said. "There were just too many reports. I could not rest until we got it all out on the table."

He assigned John Crewdson to the story, assisted by Joseph B. Treaster. "I got John on the story," Rosenthal said. "He had no fish to fry. No interest in covering up any tracks. He did very careful work. He was not going to overlook anyone. He wouldn't tell me what he was doing but he wasn't going to go easy on anyone."

Rosenthal was proud of the Crewdson series, which began publication on Christmas Day, 1977, and continued for three days. It was the most comprehensive examination of the relationship between the CIA and the press which had been published and the most careful and complete examination which a newspaper had attempted of itself. "We printed everything we could establish," Rosenthal said. "I think we got everything since World War II and most important we showed our deep journalistic intent."

The last words were the most important—"deep journalistic intent."

This constituted recognition of a premise that many in the press had not yet understood. If *The New York Times* was to go forward in the role of public monitor, if it was to subject high public figures, great government agencies, important institutions and corporate bodies to searching scrutiny it could do no less than subject itself to the same surgical process. The Crewdson investigation constituted a forward step toward realization of this intent. It named *Times* correspondents and stringers who had possessed ties to the Agency. It revealed that in the case of Wayne Phillips the Agency had deliberately sought to recruit a *Times* man for its staff and had openly boasted of a connection with Arthur Hays Sulzberger that would have permitted the CIA to place Phillips in Moscow.

But it left unresolved the major allegations of the Bernstein article —the question of what relationship, if any, had existed between the Agency and the two Sulzbergers. This question continued to echo in the corridors of *The Times,* the subject of gossip, of speculation, of frustration.

48

The Two Cultures

*L*IKE A MANGY DOG, the CIA seemed to come back again and again to squat on the doorstep of *The New York Times.*

Harriet Ann Phillippi, acting for *Rolling Stone* under the Freedom of Information Act in 1977 compelled the CIA to make public documents pertaining to Colby's effort to suppress *Glomar.* The documents were released with names deleted. Thus, in reporting Colby's conversations with Punch Sulzberger the CIA identified him only as "E–1." Under pressure of the Phillippi litigation, the CIA in January 1978 asked Sulzberger if it could release his name.

The CIA had refused for four years to release the names of *Times* men who had a connection with the Agency. Now it was asking Punch whether he objected to the release of his own name! The request was accompanied by strong hints that he probably would prefer not to in which case the Agency would fight for his privacy rights in the courts. The transcripts showed that the CIA secretly and without permission had transcribed Sulzberger's conversations.

To Punch it was a case of "mine enemy delivered unto my arms." He fired back a letter to Admiral Stanfield Turner, CIA chief under President Carter, saying he had no objection whatever to the release of his name but he had strong objections to "the apparent recording by the CIA, without my knowledge or consent, of several of my conversations."

He pointed out that the CIA seemed to be guilty of duplicitous policy (he tactfully called it "an apparent discrepancy in . . . treatment") by refusing his requests for documents concerning CIA relationships with *The Times* or *Times* personnel on the grounds it could not release any names. Punch suggested that the CIA inquire of these individuals, as they were doing with him, and see if they objected to release of the information. He asked the CIA to hand over the materials *The Times* had sought, deleting only names of individuals who refused their consent.

The CIA refused. It was, said general counsel Anthony A. Lapham, protecting its own interests; this had nothing to do with the rights of individuals. Lapham said the transcripts of Punch's conversations were not recordings but a stenographer's report. [They contained clear internal evidence of recording.] He asked "as a matter of curiosity" whether *The Times* didn't sometimes record or monitor telephone conversations, a red herring that testified to the lack of concern the CIA had to its own violations of statute. Punch replied that *The Times,* as a matter of policy, did not monitor or record telephone conversations without knowledge of the parties on the line.

But there, astonishingly and embarrassingly, the matter ended. The obvious next step was to bring a lawsuit under the Freedom of Information Act demanding the release of the information that the CIA continued to hold secret. That step was not taken and no clear reason could be discerned as to why it was not. It was true that after the long tug-of-war Punch didn't really care whether he knew or not. But Rosenthal took the opposite position. More strongly than ever he felt the search for truth must be pursued to the end; whatever might be disclosed must be disclosed and let the world judge. He was confident that *The Times* could stand on the logic of the situation whatever it might be and that this was better than a lingering scent of scandal.

So the case rested. As far as *The Times* had been able to determine from a well-intentioned search of its own records they contained no evidence, pro or con, that bore on the charges of a CIA connection. The files of Arthur Sulzberger, of Turner Catledge and of corporate records had been searched. Those of Cy Sulzberger were kept in Paris and were not available for examination. Crewdson had done all he could think of to ferret the information out of the Agency, talking to every past or present Agency man who he thought might possess a clue. It was a tough unrewarding task. Agency men did not talk. This was their discipline. Nor had he been able to break the case by intensive interviews and investigation of members of *The Times.* Crewdson did not exclude anyone from his list of possible CIA links—not Punch Sulzberger, not Abe Rosenthal, not Scotty Reston, John Oakes, Cy Sulzberger, Harding Bancroft, Sydney Gruson, Clifton Daniel, myself; nor those long dead, such as the late foreign editor Emanuel Freedman, Arthur Krock, General Adler, Arthur Hays Sulzberger and Lester Markel.

To all intents and purposes it was a dead end. One thing kept Crewdson going. He had found one source within the CIA, a "Mr. K.," whose credentials lent weight to his words and who encouraged him to persevere. There existed, Mr. K. told Crewdson, good grounds to keep at the hunt. Mr. K. was morally certain that one man still on *The Times,* still active, possessed the secret that Crewdson was looking for. But this gem of information proved most frustrating of all. Crewdson could not locate "Mr. X," as he began to think of the CIA contact within *The Times*. He braced several *Times* men whom he thought the description might fit but got angry denials. Still, out of those denials he formed his own hypothesis—of who Mr. X was—but as long as the CIA and Mr. X stayed silent Crewdson had no means of proving his hunch.

So the enigma remained, a "dirty little secret," it could be said, but a "dirty little secret" no longer of substantive importance. Arthur Hays Sulzberger had died in 1968, Cy Sulzberger had retired at the end of 1977. None of those whose names had been turned up in the investigative search remained on the paper. Most were dead. Careful examination of *Times'* reporting and editorial policies for the past two decades made it obvious that in no way could the CIA be influencing news or editorial positions.* No one could exclude the chance that the CIA had had a correspondent here, a stringer there, a bookkeeper, a chauffeur or a wire-room attendant who was keeping an eye out for them. But it was plain in the public and private attitudes of the men who edited *The Times*, developed its policies and controlled, in so far as anyone controlled its news coverage and play, that they were fiercely independent. One had only to read the editorials of *The Times* under the stewardship of John Oakes and Max Frankel to see that no CIA ghost was peeking over their shoulders. One had only to look at the vigor with which Edwin L. James, Turner Catledge, Clifton Daniel and Abe Rosenthal pursued the news about the CIA, the way in which they rebuffed interference in the editorial process by any outsider, to understand that the chase after Mr. X was a chase on a trail long since cold, a thrust into the vanished past.

The Brave Easterners

What really was more important than whether a piece of paper might turn up in the files of *The Times* or the CIA was an understanding of the personal relationships of the men who made the CIA, the men who dominated it in the postwar period and into the early 1950s, and the men who made up *The New York Times* in those days. They were for the most part men of the same social and geographic circle, precisely those whom Agnew was to excoriate as the "eastern elite" (although not all were actually easterners nor elites), the "brave easterners," as Stewart Alsop, who knew them all, was to call them in a book written in 1968. They had gone, by and large, to the same schools, Groton, again and again, Groton; they had married into each other's families; they were Yale and Harvard and Princeton, only occasionally Columbia; they were New York, Boston, Washington; Massachusetts,

---

*Except, of course, for specific efforts chronicled herein: *Glomar*, U–2, the Arbenz coup in Guatemala, the 1966 *Times'* survey of the CIA, etc.

Pennsylvania and Virginia; they were lawyers and bankers and business-men and journalists. They were General Adler and Allen Dulles; Ben Welles and Walter Sullivan and James Angleton; they were John Oakes and his brother, George, who was in the Agency for a while and then left, so it was said, to go on walking tours in England and write travel books until his tragic death in 1965; they were Kim Roosevelt, the CIA man who pulled off the Mossadegh coup and Sam Pope Brewer and Kennett Love; they were James Reston and his deputy in the Washington bureau until he left in 1962, Wallace Carroll, and Carroll's intimate friend, Richard Helms, with whom he had worked in prewar UPI days in Europe; they were all the correspondents who had been wined and dined and flattered by Allen Dulles and Frank Wisner and Des FitzGerald (Frankie's father) and Tracy Barnes—Reston, Daniel, Frankel, Drew Middleton and myself; they were Cy Sulzberger and Frank Wisner and the Bob Joyces and Allen Dulleses and Helmses and Colbys and station chiefs all over the world. They knew each other, they stayed at each other's houses, they drank together and dined together and golfed together and traveled together and talked together and they knew each other's secrets—a lot of them anyway.

Cord Meyer, the CIA man who had started out as a World Federalist, probably put it best when he said that there had been in those early days a "relationship of cooperation between *The Times* and the Agency, a relationship of trust between the CIA and *Times* correspondents," a useful relationship for all, one which he thought had been totally discreet.

There was an intimacy about this which had its roots not only in cultural and social identity but in a common view of the world, the role of the United States, the nature of the Communist peril. So many of these men had come through World War II together, they had fought the Nazis and the Japanese and they emerged from the war with a shared opinion that the Soviet Union and the Communists represented a continuation of the same danger. Stalin had replaced Hitler, and to them, to Arthur Sulzberger, for example, Stalin and what he stood for seemed an even graver threat. These men had worked together through World War II, now they went on working together against what they perceived as a new and more dangerous enemy. Again and again Agency men and correspondents of the period would recall their friendships; they would smile in a reminiscent way, remembering evenings in Rome, adventures in Cairo, shared segments of danger, girls, drinks and, of course, a shared purpose. Robert Amory, who was one of Allen Dulles' stalwarts, remembered talking about this at a latter-day intelligence seminar at the Woodrow Wilson Center. It was a familiar exercise. In the days when he handled Soviet economics for CIA, Amory used to assemble Agency men and academic economists at the

Princeton Gun Club and they would argue the figures. "The British could never understand about this," Amory recalled. "We would go over our figures with the scholars. They would make useful contributions and go back to their classes and they could lecture more knowledgeably about economics and politics and we went back to Langley having tested our thinking against that of the best of the non-Agency experts. I don't see anything morally corrupt about this."

Now at the new post-Watergate seminar Amory was talking about those days, about the luncheons at which Allen Dulles met and talked with correspondents like myself who had come back from Moscow or the Middle East; about the dinners that he gave at the Alibi Club in Washington for the CBS correspondents after their annual year-end roundup of the news, first the CBS men going on the air to the nation and then assembling at the Alibi Club as Dulles' guests, consuming a fairly decent dinner, drinking some wine and talking until 2 A.M. about the news-behind-the-news.

"Everyone had a good time," Amory said, "and maybe everyone learned something. It was a totally mutually beneficient arrangement."

(Another Agency man thought the Alibi Club meetings were a disaster; that the correspondents came to think Allen Dulles had assembled them for pep talks on loyalty; but that was another thing.)

One participant at the intelligence seminar was Sy Hersh. He listened to Amory's remarks and, as Amory remembered it, said, "Okay. In those days you were all gentlemen. That's no longer true. Now you are a bunch of shits."

Hersh's remark was characteristically vivid just as Amory's were characteristically nostalgic. Each contained an essential truth. Certainly there had been non-gentlemen and roughnecks in the old CIA, the silent man with the faint Mafia look whose name you didn't quite catch at Dulles' stylish lunches, the one who sat a bit sullenly, made no remarks and seemed a little uncomfortable with the finger bowls. But today those men were the common denominators of the Agency. If the ethnics had not yet taken over they were on the way. Porcellian and Skull and Bones were on the way out. And the reporters and editors played a rougher game, too. They were no longer all in this together and the contrast between the present and the vanished past constituted a distorting lens. To the old-boy network it seemed that those who wrote today about the Agency had it all wrong; to those who wrote today about the Agency it seemed that the old boys and their relationships were all wrong. It was a gulf which was not likely to be bridged.

The frames of reference were out of alignment. Miles Copeland, very much a spokesman for the Old School, could write in warm approval that an Agency station chief would go out of his way to spend "long hours in the company of leading American and British columnists . . . giving them large amounts of confidential information and his interpretations of it "because he knew that the President, the Secretary of State and even the CIA director "will read, believe and be impressed by a report from Cy Sulzberger, Arnaud de Borchgrave or Stewart Alsop." Or as an old Agency man put it with regard to Cy Sulzberger, "I think the relationship with Cy was like that with the Alsop brothers. We checked our judgments. I might talk with Joe [Alsop] and share my confidential information on Soviet steel production and if he had just been in Moscow he would give me his judgment on the Politburo."

Now this had changed. It was precisely the Sulzbergers, the de Borchgraves and the Alsops who were the targets of the new investigative journalists. Carl Bernstein in *Rolling Stone* published the allegation that Cy Sulzberger had based a column about Soviet spies on a "handout" from Dick Helms, then head of CIA. *MORE* magazine elaborated on this by bringing Howard Hunt of the Plumbers into the picture. As Hunt later was to claim, he had been asked by Helms to prepare the material for Cy. "Dick had this 'sweetheart' arrangement with Cy," Hunt was to say. He said he went to the Soviet Russia desk of CIA, talked to the counterespionage people, got the materials, a list of KGB men serving abroad under diplomatic cover, turned it over to Helms, who gave it to Cy, who published it in his column of September 11, 1967, under the headline "Where the Spies Are." *MORE* said Cy published the information virtually verbatim. Cy denied this. Certainly, he said, he got the information from Helms. He had asked him to assemble it one day when they were having lunch and Helms several days later sent him a "listing of names of a great many people and I think I used a great many of the names." But the column was Cy's, written by him, containing his own conclusions. There was another series of columns which Cy wrote, these from Saigon in April 1966. They were headlined "The Bonze Age in Vietnam" and dealt with an uprising of Buddhists against Premier Ky, a powerful movement which had swept Saigon, Hue and Danang, forcing Ky to agree to hold a constitutional convention that summer. Cy asserted there was a covert link between the Buddhists and the Vietcong and that the rising was part of a plot to overthrow Ky, oust the Americans and install a Vietcong-Buddhist coalition. This version of events—totally at odds with what was reported by correspondents on the spot—was given to Cy, on the assertion of Neil Sheehan, by Gordon L. Jorgensen, CIA station chief. After it was published Sheehan and other correspondents bombarded the CIA with demands for evidence in support of Cy's columns. But the CIA offered none. In Sheehan's opinion, Cy had been taken by the Agency, falling for the story because he was not familiar with the local scene, trusted the CIA and didn't check the information.

The "revelation" of the source of Cy's columns was hardly sensational nor was the source reprehensible. At worst Cy might have been criticized for naïveté, for accepting a distorted picture of events in Saigon or of overhasty processing of a list of alleged Soviet spies. He had written scores and scores of columns based on this kind of information. So had his colleagues. The CIA was almost always regarded by correspondents as better informed, less tendentious, less propagandistic than political ambassadors or even career diplomats. The Agency men usually had been on the job longer, knew more about the scene and were more willing to share their information, expecting, of course, some information in exchange. Trade-in-secrets, as Max Frankel so eloquently noted in his deposition in the Pentagon Papers case, was the name of the game.

Trade-in-secrets . . . There was hardly an old CIA station chief who did not remember Cy Sulzberger with warmth and pleasure. "How's Cy?" was the first thing they asked when you called them at their retirement homes in Georgetown or Virginia or Vermont or Rhode Island. "Give him my best." "You know," Robert Amory recalled, "we had very close relationships. Cy and (Ambassador) Chip Bohlen and I always had a talk in Paris. We even had a codename for Cy. In the cables, I think, I was Barwent and he was something like Fidelis (the faithful)."

Of course, Amory reminisced, Cy wasn't the only one. There was Joe Alsop and the men on the *Herald-Tribune* and the "CBS man in very deep cover in Paris." Amory used to ride around the Place de la Concorde with the CBS man on his motorbike, leaning an ear close to the correspondent's mouth so that he could pick up the conversation. It was a very tight establishment, a *bruderbund,* as Amory remembered. "Cy was a very stimulating man who could get a lot out of you," a CIA man long stationed in Paris recalled. "Each of us used to try to get the most out of each other. We met every month or so. We went over the whole story. Of course we shared information. He protected his sources and, of course, I knew he wrote a memo of each conversation so I had to be careful what I said. He always wanted to get more out of me than I got out of him. All my relations with *Times* men were the same. I would swear that they did not have any connection with the Agency and I would have known—I would certainly have known —at that time."

Frank Wisner

Frank Wisner was the key to a great many things, a brilliant, compulsive man, a talker, he was as hooked to the telephone as Sy Hersh would be later on, a man of enormous charm, imagination, conviction that anything, *anything* could be achieved and that he could achieve it. In the early days he held the job of CIA chief of operations, clandestine operations, that is, and he knew everyone. There were few whom he knew better and more closely than Cy Sulzberger: Cy and his remarkable Marina, Frank and his wife, Polly, who was to marry Clayton Fritchey after Frank's suicide, the Wisners staying with the Sulzbergers in Paris, the Sulzbergers staying with the Wisners in Washington, Marina writing Polly from the ends of the earth, Frank calling Cy more often than either of them could count.

With that kind of a relationship, said a man who had been at Wisner's side in those days, why should there have been anything formal? What was the need of it?

"I can guess a bit as to the nature of Cy's relationship with Wisner," he said. "I knew Frank extremely well. I knew how his mind worked. First of all Frank and Allen made it their business to talk with journalists and other well-informed people and they were willing to talk to them about substantive things, giving them information for the purpose of getting information in return. That was the above-the-board thing, the Alibi Club dinners, the lunches, the things like that."

Then, he said, there was what was going on under the table and he would not necessarily know about that. There were Frank's calls to Cy and other journalists, trying to get them to go easy on some piece of news or "to put something into perspective."

"Now," said Wisner's associate, "was Wisner trying to influence people on what they would report? No. I don't think so. Government officials all the time are trying to get journalists to publish things in a friendly way. Frank would warn his friends about things he thought were threatening security and he made efforts to see that a certain treatment of a particular topic not be published—or be published. Frank knew the Grahams [Phil and Katherine of the *Washington Post*] very well. He knew everyone. He knew Scotty well. He worked that way. That's about all I can say on this."

This man simply did not believe Wisner or Sulzberger could have been party to a formal arrangement whereby someone would be sent overseas for an extended stay, ostensibly for *The Times* but actually for the CIA. But he would not rule out the possibility that Wisner might persuade *The Times* to send someone to a particular area to look into a particular situation at a particular time. "As far as Cy is concerned," he said, "considering what he gave Cy how in hell could Cy have refused to do a favor for Wisner? There's no way Cy could have turned him down."

"There were all kinds of things which Frank did," he said. "He could say to someone if you're going into Czechoslovakia keep your eyes open and come back and tell me about X. I know he did it. I don't know it for a fact but it would have been natural for him to say that to Cy or others."

The view of Wisner's associate was consistent with that of a man who had been at Dulles' right hand. "In no way could Cy have been on the payroll. There could have been no formality," he said. "Now I don't mean that if he had gotten into a hot spot in Turkey that the CIA guy there wouldn't have gotten him on a military plane and flown him out to Athens. He probably would have. But that's something different."

To John Maury, an old Agency hand, specialist in Soviet affairs since doing duty at Murmansk in World War II, a man who wound up handling CIA relations with Congress and later acting as congressional liaison for the Defense Department under Melvin Laird, much of the debate about the CIA and the press seemed an argument of the deaf, neither side getting the other's point. For six years he served as station chief in Athens. Every time Cy Sulzberger went to Greece, and that was quite often, the two lunched and had a long talk. He thought that he usually got more than he gave. But he saw nothing in the conversations that was wrong in intent or context, these were meetings which were useful to both sides.

But when Maury turned to the atmosphere of those days, an atmosphere which permeated the Agency and which, he believed, contributed enormously to the problems of the contemporary CIA, the recollection was sometimes disturbing. In the cold war years, he said, the whole idea was *to go forward!* Everything could be done, everything would be done. There were pep talks and sanctimonious speeches. There were people who were dealing with Allen Dulles and acting on implications, on hints, on words unspoken. They were overselling what could be done by covert means and Allen Dulles was telling his men, "Well, you can figure out a way to handle that"; or, "I don't have to spell it out"; or, "You can imagine what that means." Never putting it on paper. Never on paper, not actually giving a word of command, but pointing a way and, as Maury said, the Agency was still paying for that although he had finally concluded that in most cases the trail led back to the White House, that the White House was the worst offender, wanting results yet not wanting to know how they would be achieved, creating an atmosphere of permissiveness. In this, he thought, most of the "atrocities," not all of which he necessarily thought were atrocities at all, had their origin, and to suppose that this always represented the Agency acting on its own was to misread the past. Its conduct was a product of the thought and the atmosphere of the times.

He could well imagine a group of eager-beaver young men recruiting for the Agency who might come to an eager beaver on *The New York Times* and try to sign him up and promise that they could send him to Moscow because they had a deal with Arthur Sulzberger that enabled them to do this.* This could have come out of thin air—but again, he conceded, it might not have. There were different levels and different outfits within the Agency and everything was compartmented and designed that way and nobody, not Wisner, certainly, and not Allen Dulles, ever knew everything that was going on and that was the way it was intended to be.

So it went, the explanations of the Agency men and while some might be taken with a grain of salt the picture that they painted was a consistent picture, a picture in which the last thing in the world that might be important was a piece of paper with terms and specifications written on it. An Agency man who was a close friend of Wisner's and who went to Harvard with Cy Sulzberger contemplated the problem of trying to establish a negative in the relationship between *The Times* and the Agency and sighed. "That is like trying to prove that right-wing Republicans in Congress in 1865 were not responsible for the assassination of Abraham Lincoln," he said.

"But," he said, "you know in those days people, everybody, anybody, was gung ho for the Agency. You asked them and they did it."

He pointed to the pitfall of the historian—the pitfall of judging matters by pieces of paper in the Agency files. He described the experience of Phil Geyelin of the *Washington Post,* who found himself named as a CIA "source" and a resource and God-knows-what-all in the Agency files.

"When one sees reports of what one has said," he added, "this is sometimes surprising."

But even to get to see those bits of paper was extraordinarily difficult. Phil Geyelin got to see his because his lawyer, Joe Califano, muscled George Bush when Bush was head of the CIA. Geyelin had taken a leave of absence from *The Wall Street Journal* in 1950 during the Korean war and had worked for the CIA for eleven months. Innuendos were spread (and some were published) that he had worked for the Agency before and perhaps still did while editor of the editorial page of the *Washington Post.* He and Califano spent two days at Langley going over what the CIA had in its files. He found hundreds of memos on conversations he had had with CIA men, some of whom he knew were CIA, some of whom he suspected were CIA and some of whom he had never known were CIA. Again and again he was described as "a reliable source," a "CIA resource" and even as a "willing collaborator." What did that mean? he asked. "Oh," said an Agency man, "Just

---

*The trouble with this thesis was that the Wayne Phillips case was not an isolated one; a parallel case came to light at CBS where a correspondent named Sam Jaffe was given an identical pitch by CIA recruiters; if Jaffe would sign up with the CIA they would guarantee to get him into Moscow for CBS.

that you are somebody who was willing to talk to CIA. It is not suggesting that you work for us." "It was real government make-work," Phil said. "All these reports were being sent back to Washington and they were very incriminating, the language they used"—all but one memorandum from a station chief to whom Geyelin once talked when he was planning to go to Poland. The chief sent a cable to Washington suggesting that they set up Geyelin, make a proposal to him to find out certain things. But Geyelin refused and his refusal was in the record. As a matter of fact he never even went to Poland. This was the kind of trash that Geyelin uncovered and he was certain there must be similar information in CIA records about practically every American foreign correspondent. While Geyelin had managed to see his own file it was still under CIA lock and key and even the allegations about him, which were entered in the Pike committee's record of its CIA investigation, were also sealed.

So Geyelin felt he was damned if he did and damned if he didn't. If the CIA kept the record secret the aura of suspicion would continue; if he managed to pry it loose it was written in such a way as to blacken his name. Finally he managed to get a letter from George Bush certifying that he had no connection with the Agency, he was clean as a hound's tooth. But this was not easy. The Agency said that if they did it for him they would have to do it for many others. In other words if the Agency corrected one mistake, cleared one reputation, it would have to admit many mistakes and clear many records. Better not to clear anyone's reputation—this might make difficulties for the CIA. While this might seem to some a callous and immoral position it was consistent with the practice of secret agencies. The KGB, for example, had made many "mistakes" in the Stalin period, mistakes which had cost the lives of millions of innocent people. The Soviet security agencies had been extremely reluctant to correct these "mistakes." Nothing could be done, of course, about the lives lost, but slowly over many years it had issued documents to survivors and heirs saying that investigation showed that Citizen X was not, after all, guilty of "crimes against the people." But it tried to keep these little "corrections" private; no public notice; that might lead to "misunderstandings"; better not to stir the ashes of old fires.

Except where exceptional pressure had been brought the CIA fought tooth and nail to maintain the inviolability of its records, heedless of the fact that this aspersed the good name of most American journalists who worked abroad during the first three decades after the war and many, many others. The fact that this fed into the hands of the Communist propaganda organs which for years had charged that U.S. newsmen acted as agents of American intelligence just as Soviet correspondents acted as agents of the KGB moved the CIA not at all.

A man who had spent his whole Agency career in the field of Soviet intelligence uttered another warning. Remember, he said, a memorandum is proof only of what a particular man wants it to say. Just because the memo is there does not mean that what it describes actually happened. There might or might not be a memorandum in the Agency file which said that Arthur Sulzberger agreed to such-and-such or that Cy Sulzberger agreed to so-and-so and that X, Y and Z on *The New York Times* promised to do something that the Agency wanted. But who knows the reality of this? Who knows whether X, Y or Z actually promised to do anything? If you hunted enough in the Agency files, he thought, you could find anything—literally anything—proving that one was or was not a tool, assistant or helpmeet of the CIA. And if the memo was not there now it could be put there tomorrow or taken out the next day. "I don't think," he said, "that anyone knows everything Frank Wisner did on some dark night." Or that if Wisner had not killed himself in the grip of clinical depression in 1965 even he could have remembered it all.

The Witting

There was beyond all this what William Colby called the question of the "two cultures," using the term in the sense Charles Snow had used it to delineate the world of science and the rest of the world, the world of nonscientists, of scholars, politicians and ordinary citizens. There were two cultures, the intelligence culture and the nonintelligence culture and while they used the same language they gave different meanings to the same words. Each possessed a set of values and they divided personal relationships into different compartments. The condition was epitomized by the terms "witting" and "nonwitting." To the Agency a "witting" individual was a man of their world, he knew the language, the code words, the customs, the recognition symbols. The "unwitting" was out in the cold, unaware of what went on around him, ignorant of the elite conceptions that guided the closed circle of intelligence. One of the earliest *Ramparts* reports about CIA and its connections talked about people who were "witty" and those who were not, a sign to any Agency man that the author of the piece was not among the "witting." To be "witting" was to belong to the club. To talk the language. To understand the high signs. To know the fraternity grip.

The unwashed did not know when they dined with Dulles that they were being "debriefed." They did not know that if they had a good friend in the Agency he might classify them as "assets." They did not know, as Geyelin did not know, that when he had a drink with Mr. Smith in a bar in Beirut his words would wind up on a cabled memorandum in the Agency files. They did not know, as I did not know, that when I telephoned my old friend Colonel Stanley Grogan to ask if he could get me a figure on the current estimate of Soviet troops on the Chinese frontier that I was being "briefed."

"Well," said Bill Colby, a patient man who had been through a lot and who never raised his voice, "there you are. It's two cultures, two languages and one side doesn't know what the other is talking about."

Colby thought this had been brought out pretty clearly in the Church committee hearings on the press and the CIA; the language seemed to be shared in common but it wasn't. He was asked what he thought an Agency man meant when he talked about a "special relationship," a phrase which the Agency's Mr. K. had used over and over again to describe what went on between *The Times* and the CIA. James Angleton, the saturnine, cryptic CIA chief of counterintelligence, had been asked the same question. Angleton was quite harsh about it. "It is not a word of the art," he said, by which he meant it was not a special intelligence term. "I would not use it myself." Now Colby supported Angleton's view. "I don't think," he said, "that the fellow knows what he's talking about. I really don't."

49

The Special Relationship

*T*HE CIA DID NOT spring full-born from the head of OSS. First OSS was dissolved, a period of confusion ensued and then something called the Central Intelligence Group was set up in 1946 and in 1947 it became the Central Intelligence Agency, that is, the CIA.

Lieutenant General Hoyt Vandenberg, nephew of Senator Vandenberg and an Air Force commander during World War II, headed the CIG during most of its sixteen months of existence, a hectic period. The cold war was getting under way. Stalin had tested President Truman's mettle in Iran, Winston Churchill made his Iron Curtain speech at Fulton, Missouri, and not a few generals were warning that we would have to use the A-bomb "to stop the Russians."

A week before Christmas in December 1946, General Vandenberg wrote Arthur Sulzberger a letter telling him about the new Central Intelligence Group. He described its mission as coordinating "all activities of the Government involved in obtaining and analyzing information about foreign countries which this country needs for its national security." He expressed hope that Mr. Sulzberger would be willing to render "assistance in accomplishing our assigned task" and said he was sending a representative to see the publisher and explain the program of the CIG.

It was, perhaps, typical of the confusion of the times that this letter did not reach Arthur Sulzberger for fifty-six days, not as it might be thought in contemporary times because of poor mail delivery but because Vandenberg had entrusted his communication to an aide to be "safe-handed" from Washington to New York. For some unknown reason it did not reach the fourteenth floor of *The New York Times* until February 11, hardly an auspicious omen for a newborn intelligence agency.

Arthur Sulzberger responded immediately. He wrote Vandenberg that "you and your representatives will always meet with the fullest cooperation from all of us here at *The New York Times*" and suggested that "until the machinery is established, all inquiries be addressed directly to me."

Vandenberg deputized James Ramsey Hunt, Jr., his newly appointed New York representative, to meet with Sulzberger. John Oakes, just out of OSS, just settling in at *The Times* to work under Lester Markel, telephoned Sulzberger giving him Hunt's name, and accompanied Hunt to the meeting with the publisher. (Thirty years later Oakes was to have no recollection of the incident; that of Hunt was quite vivid.)

What Vandenberg wanted was access to "FYI," For Your Information material, private reports and letters that *Times* correspondents sent to their editors filling them in on situations that could not be reported: a still maturing political crisis; spicy corridor gossip; background on developing events; postmortems; memoranda to be used by New York writers in locally written stories; guidance to editors; information useful in evaluating the trend of events, particularly in countries under censorship, such as the U.S.S.R. and the evolving Soviet bloc. It was information that could be priceless to an intelligence organization, especially a new one with many gaps in its coverage. *Times* men were almost uniformly competent; the pool of information that the paper gathered was incomparable. John Bross, a very skilled, very experienced CIA official, now retired, offered the opinion that through the 1950s and perhaps later *Times* (and other American) correspondents were presenting a more accurate and informed picture of conditions in eastern Europe than the Agency's. In fact, he attributed the Agency's failure on the ouster of the Shah in Iran in 1979 to the divorce of the CIA from outside people, especially the press, to the rigidity of bureaucratic minds that lacked the cross-fertilization of politically uninhibited outsiders, particularly newsmen.

The Times correspondents sent their reports back to New York by returning friends, travelers, diplomats going to Paris or London or New York, but most often they used the diplomatic pouches of the State Department. The correspondence came back by pouch to Washington. There the State Department turned it over to *The Times,* either to the Washington bureau or, more usually, to New York by ordinary mail.

What Hunt had been sent to negotiate was a look at this material and an arrangement for getting that look. This, as Hunt recalled years later, was quickly and efficiently done. It was his recollection that Arthur Sulzberger designated John Oakes as liaison with the CIG and that Hunt, in turn, designated his associate Alfred Corning Clark as liaison with *The New York Times.* Oakes, thirty years later, had no recollection of an arrangement and believed that Hunt's version must be mistaken. Clark was dead but some of his associates confirmed that he did, indeed, serve as "case officer" for *The New York Times,* handling contacts over an extended period. It was Clark, it should be recalled, who approached Arthur Sulzberger in 1951 asking for the release of Sam Pope Brewer for a CIA assignment.

Hunt was not involved directly in subsequent dealings but it was his recollection that Clark did obtain information from *The Times,* particularly from Moscow, which Hunt routinely transmitted to Washington. Long before Hunt left his New York post (he was a close friend of Allen Dulles and went to Washington in the early fifties and then to Paris, where he stayed through 1958 in charge of clandestine operations) the arrangement started to run down. The rationale for it had begun to vanish, the Agency had its own men in the field, they talked to correspondents in the foreign capitals, they had their own liaison with the embassies, got what they needed on the spot, no need for a special apparatus and, Hunt said, it just died a natural death.*

Hunt's mission was not merely to obtain access to confidential *Times'* information. The CIG was interested in talking to *Times* men when they came back from assignment abroad and this, too, was set up. In fact, the procedure became so conventional, so cut and dried, that after a while it came to be regarded as completely normal and bureaucratic. The contact for this for many, many years was Emanuel Freedman, *The Times* foreign editor, now dead. The same CIA case officer who had handled these contacts since the early 1950s was still on duty in New York, still handling the same chores in 1979. He had been in the New York office for thirty years, but didn't want his name mentioned because he thought it might bring danger to his family. For years his relationship with *The Times* had been almost totally open, no secrecy on either side, and the CIA New York man got to know many *Times* correspondents and editors quite well although always on a business basis.

But what might have seemed purely a matter of convenience, a small favor to a new government organization dedicated to helping defend the United States against its enemies, could take on different coloration in practice. Should a correspondent in an Iron Curtain capital send private memoranda to his editor in New York and should the secret police in Moscow or Warsaw or Bucharest discover the fact they might bring a charge against the correspondent of violating censorship. They might even throw him out. But they would hardly go further (unless they had simply been given an order to make up a case against the

---

*Hunt died in December 1979 at the age of 70. He spent 23 years with the Agency after a war-time career in Naval intelligence. He became chief of covert activities for the CIG with Offices in New York in December 1946. In 1951 he went to Washington as special assistant for clandestine activities to Allen Dulles; in 1954 he became senior CIA representative in Paris; in 1959 he returned to Washington, serving as chief of operations, that is, clandestine affairs, and later as deputy chief of counterintelligence. When he retired in 1969 he was given the CIA's Intelligence Medal of Merit. He was for many, many years one of the Agency's most senior and highly regarded officers. (*New York Times,* 12/11/79)

reporter with any materials that came to hand). But if the KGB had discovered that Correspondent S was sending back confidential letters to his colleagues in New York via the diplomatic pouch and that these "confidential letters" were winding up in the hands of the CIG or the CIA—that would be quite another matter; that, in the definition of Soviet law would be espionage; and the penalty for that was death.

It is not to be supposed that such considerations entered the mind of Jim Hunt, fresh out of U.S. Navy intelligence and new in his job as CIG representative in New York, and it surely could not have occurred to Arthur Sulzberger. There was nothing he was less likely to do than put his correspondents or his newspaper in jeopardy. It can only be supposed that when Cy Sulzberger asked me, for example, to write him as often as I could, say, every few weeks or once a month, and fill him in on what I could not put in stories, could not put through the Moscow censorship, he never thought that he might be putting into jeopardy a very old friend and a very new correspondent of *The New York Times* in Moscow. The information would be valuable to him in his understanding of the Soviet Union, his insight in writing about Soviet affairs and possibly might tip him to some stories.

The critical point, however, was that under the arrangement with CIG these letters from the correspondents in Moscow and other sensitive capitals ended up not only on the desks of *Times* men. They ended up in the hands of the intelligence agency; they ended there without the knowledge of the men who wrote the letters.*

Now, if the question even was discussed it probably was argued that the danger of a leak to the Russians was virtually nonexistent. But an Agency man recalled many years later, "Those were the days when sometimes the KGB managed to have an undercover man in the U.S. Embassy in Moscow but the CIA didn't." That was supposed to be a joke but it was a joke with the hard crust of truth about it.

It would seem many years later that this arrangement must have been the origin of what that latter-day Agency man, that Mr. K., with his troubling lack of proper intelligence language called "the special relationship" between *The Times* and the CIA and possibly of the Carl Bernstein report in *Rolling Stone*.

But it did not seem likely that the total content of the relationship could be recaptured. There was, for example, the stubborn insistence of Mr. K who originally told John Crewdson that there was alive, well and active on *The New York Times* as late as December 1977 a man who knew the whole story of the Agency's relationship, a man who had been promised "eternal secrecy," Mr. X, in other words.

*Two retired Agency men in 1979 recalled having seen at least some of my private Moscow correspondence.

Mr. K. insisted that Mr. X acted as a "clearing house" for Agency matters. When the Agency Director came to lunch at *The Times,* he said, he and another Agency man would sit outside, and after lunch they would follow up on specifics with *"The New York Times* guy," that is, Mr. X. That sounded very solid and convincing until Times records were checked and disclosed that Allen Dulles had never lunched or dined at *The Times* while director of CIA and John McCone had been at *The Times* only once, on June 29, 1964.

And the New York Agency man who had been the case officer for *The Times* for more than 20 years insisted that no Mr. X existed or had ever existed. The Agency's contacts had been with a variety of individuals, not with a single man. Had there been a Mr. X he would have known him, he would have had to know him and, indeed, it would have vastly simplified his work. He was never aware of "a general understanding" with *The Times* for collaboration with the Agency and would have had to be aware had there been one.

It was his belief that *The Times,* unlike some employers, for instance, the Luce organization with which he was very familiar, or possibly the *Wall Street Journal* or the late *Herald-Tribune,* or CBS felt that it was up to the individual employee to do what he wished; to cooperate with the Agency or not to cooperate. There was never in his experience pressure from *Times'* management for a correspondent or editor to have anything to do with the Agency.

On the other hand, he admitted, the Agency never dealt with employees without first getting an overall OK from management. He supposed this must have applied to *The Times* as it did to a dozen great corporations with which he dealt. He said that he had over the years heard "from chitchat and the gossip of persons with long memories" that certain, as he called them, "original relationships" had grown up abroad between *Times* men and Agency men, relationships which he thought probably should not have grown up, as far as the best interests of both sides were concerned.

As to his own contacts, he said, he thought *Times'* management didn't want to know and didn't know about them. It wanted to be informed only on what he called "something major."

"Something Major"

Perhaps it was "something major" that brought Joseph Bryan, III, of Richmond, Virginia, to New York in the winter of 1951 to consult with Arthur Hays Sulzberger. Cy Sulzberger had written his uncle from Paris in mid-January to tell him Bryan was coming "to see you about something very important." Cy marked his letter "PERSONAL AND CONFIDENTIAL" and warned his uncle that he must be sure to see Bryan no matter how busy he was and that the matter "involved is one for *you only* and cannot be delegated to anybody else in the office." Arthur Sulzberger assured Cy he would see Bryan and "solve the mystery." In due course Bryan turned up.

Bryan, a well-known writer who had contributed to the *Saturday Evening Post, Colliers* and other magazines, spent several years working for the CIA. Neither then nor now was there any secret about that but the subject of his conversation with the two Sulzbergers left no specific impression on Bryan's mind.

Bryan considered himself a good friend of Cy's, particularly in the years 1949, 1950 and 1951. While he did not have a precise recollection he was certain that he would have been talking to Arthur Sulzberger about cooperation with the Agency, seeking his help on something, possibly use of the resources of *The Times*, perhaps the reference facilities of the paper, something like that. He was meeting with four or five people a day on such matters in those times and it was hard to recall individual instances. *The Times*, in his recollection, was always very cooperative. He was a close friend of Arthur Krock and often saw him in Washington on affairs of this kind. His talk with Arthur Sulzberger, he felt, would have had to deal with getting his cooperation, getting him to make something available to the CIA.

That was not the way Cy remembered it. He thought Bryan had come to Europe to circulate among correspondents and get them to sign nondisclosure statements so they could be given access to secret CIA materials. It was his recollection that Bryan called on him in the course of this swing. Cy remembered telling Bryan that he wasn't empowered to sign such a piece of paper and sent him to his uncle in New York. Bryan did, in fact, meet with Arthur Sulzberger, Cy said, but he did not know the outcome.*

But Bryan could not confirm Cy's memory. In fact, he said, "I don't know what he's talking about. If I went to see Cy I went to get information from him; not to give it to him. Why should I go around Europe with nondisclosure statements? It doesn't make any sense."

Bryan apologized for his bad memory. He wished he could recall more exactly what he had talked about with Arthur Sulzberger, for whom he had great respect, but he couldn't. He wasn't trying to fudge. He just drew a blank.

So there it was, as so often happened in trying to get to the heart of long-ago matters; two honorable men; two sets of memories—what conclusion could be drawn? One was obvious. There had been plenty of back-and-forth between *The Times* and the Agency in the old days but what could be pinned down did not support a theory of an across-

---

*Cy's recollection about signing or not signing "a piece of paper" varied from time to time.

the-board contractual bilateral relationship. The more that was uncovered the more it sounded like ad hoc, hit-or-miss contacts. This view was strongly supported by a congressional investigator of the CIA. This man had the opportunity of processing and reviewing a large number of CIA files dealing with Agency relations with the media.

The files were sanitized, in a sense, that is, actual names were not specified, but to a man like the investigator with sophisticated knowledge of the press it was not difficult to put two and two together. In his examination he did not find a case of an "operational" relationship between a *Times* man and the CIA, that is, the case of a man who was tasked by the Agency and paid for the tasks. He was not talking about stringers. There were *Times* stringers on the Agency payroll. Of course, he conceded, he might have missed a few *Times* staff men. What he did find were "cozy" relationships, relationships of friendship with Frank Wisner or Dick Helms. And one more thing. The Agency did maintain a relationship with at least one person on each major paper, a person whom they could contact when they were running an operation in Berlin or Bangkok, so the paper could be put on the alert and not be misled by DOMP, that is propaganda or phony news stories, put out by the agency.

But, said the congressional investigator, his examination of CIA information had disclosed a significant deviation from the norm so far as *The Times* was concerned. He had not been able to identify a top level executive at *The Times* who served as the official "clearing agent." He concluded that unlike at CBS, the late *Herald-Tribune*, the Luce publications, such an individual did not exist at *The Times*. His chief aide in the congressional inquiry who had made an even closer examination of CIA materials and practices agreed with his assessment. But both conceded that there was no way ever of being certain that the CIA had disclosed the full extent of its relations.

Again and again Agency and ex-Agency people cited one man who, they felt, could put the matter at rest, certainly so far as Cy Sulzberger was concerned. This was Helms. "He is the only living man who could say with certainty," said one retired CIA man who knew both of them well. The relationship of Helms and Cy had been so long, so close, so enduring. Just how close was emphasized by Cy's diary notation of March 1972. He lunched with Helms in Washington at that time and recorded Helms as saying: "You know I tell you just about everything."* But Helms flatly refused to resolve the question. Given three opportunities to do so he said he had no records, did not know how to help and doubted that anyone still alive knew about it. He liked Cy. He couldn't remember any connection but Cy traveled all over the

---

*Sulzberger, *Postscript with a Chinese Accent*, New York, pp. 69–70.

world and he just didn't know what his relations were. Cy was a good friend of his and he thought Cy was pissed off at him. "I know that kind of leaves it like a dead duck in the water but I don't know what else to say." He apologized for being so equivocal but said he didn't know what else to say.*

What more there was between the CIA and *The Times* could only be guessed at. Whether there had been winks or nods over the occasional assignment of a correspondent to Timbuktu or the hiring of a low-level clerk could not be established until or unless the CIA finally opened its files, for of course all of this, the CIA initiative by General Vandenberg and what followed, was brought to light not through the aid or assistance of the CIA. The CIA was still jealously protecting its dirty little secrets. What has been presented in these pages has been the product of painstaking inquiries carried on over a period of several years and of physical search of *Times'* archives, a search that led from floor to floor, from cupboard to cupboard, from one obscure dustbin to another, even to the fifteenth floor of *The Times,* a kingdom of eaves and skylights, the abandoned debris of sixty years of newspaper publishing, a giant grandmother's attic whose existence was known to only a handful of *Times* workers.

The special relationship . . . What, after all, did the Agency man mean by that? Well, it would appear, something like the special relationship between England and America, something like the special relationship in the founding days of the British Secret Service and the CIA, not necessarily a contract, something more than that and something less, an understanding of service to the country.

There was nothing out of the ordinary about this at the time. The Agency seems to have had the same kind of understanding with most, if not all, of the major media, arrangements established, like that at *The Times,* very early on, in fact, even before there was an Agency, when it was just the Central Intelligence Group. Those with Jock Whitney and the *Herald-Tribune* and William Paley of CBS were especially close. Richard Salant was long to remember that when he took over CBS News in 1961 one of the first calls on a private tie-line

---

*Helms, of course, fully understood the implications of his refusal to make a flat denial of CIA connections with Cy. He differentiated his response from that which he gave regarding Arthur Sulzberger. Of Arthur Sulzberger he said simply and firmly: "I don't know of any CIA connections." (Personal conversations, Helms, 4/23/79; 5/4/79; 7/19/79) During the Church committee inquiry into the CIA, Helms was asked in an unpublished interrogatory about providing material to C. L. Sulzberger, and specifically about Cy's column on KGB members. Helms confirmed that he had, in fact, provided this material. He was not asked about any other past association of the Agency with Cy.

was from the New York CIA representative expressing hope that things would go along just as they had with Salant's predecessor, Sig Mickelson. Salant briefly and forcefully enlightened the Agency man that a new day had dawned.*

A new day dawned for *The Times* as well and the memory of the old faded away so that the only record of it was, in the end, a dim recollection in a few minds, a bit of paper here and there—and whatever massive print-outs might someday spew forth from the Agency, because as one thoughtful Agency man said, "The way things are everything is going to come out, sooner or later, it will all come out and everything will be published and someone will get it in a Freedom of Information action."

What was important about the "dirty little secret," in the end, was its total irrelevance to *The New New York Times*. What was relevant to the new paper was the changing face of the country, the changing balance of the power structure, the way *The Times* would measure up to the challenge of the present and the future, whether it was going now, with the new technology, to fulfill Orvil Dryfoos' frustrated dream of becoming a truly national paper on the pattern of *The Wall Street Journal*, whether it would be able with electronics, automation, photo composition, push-button layout and makeup to produce editions that would serve other regions of the country, not just the northeast triangle.

These were the questions which revolved in Punch Sulzberger's mind as he pushed toward the twentieth year of stewardship of his grandfather's remarkable creation. Walter Mattson, with his pragmatism and Harvard business school expertise had pushed the paper to the leading edge of the state of the art, now it would be seen whether an economic basis could be found for the national experiment.

For the more distant future the fate of *The Times* rested in the hands of The Thirteen, the thirteen great-grandchildren of Adolph Ochs. Three of the Thirteen were working on *The Times* in 1979, Arthur Ochs Sulzberger, Jr., 28, son of Punch by his first wife; Stephan Golden, 32, son of Ruth Holmberg by her first husband; and Bobby Dryfoos, 34, Marian's son. Michael Golden, Steve's brother, 30, was working on the *Chattanooga Times*, and Danny Cohen has been learning the TV business in Orlando, Florida.

It was too early to say what roles each of The Thirteen would play

---

*The man who called Salant was the same case officer assigned to *The Times*. At CBS the Agency had an arrangement to look at CBS "outtakes" of film, unused segments, roughly similar to *The Times'* FYI materials. Mickelson recalled that "we sold film to anyone in those days, we made a lot of money out of CIA." (Personal interview, Mickelson, 10/27/79)

but, in spirit, they seemed remarkably attuned to the goals and ideals which so long had marked *The Times*. Young Arthur, a brisk and able Washington correspondent, put his greatest emphasis on *The Times* newspaper, its reporting and editing. He could not imagine a *Times* which did not possess the dedication it had shown since Mr. Ochs' day to objective and independent reporting. He had, he confessed, little interest in "soft" news and features, the kind of materials which made the new sections so successful. But if they were needed to provide financial underpinning for *Times'* hard news coverage—fine. The financial security of *The Times* must be secured so that it could continue in the great tradition. He thought he and his cousins were as one on that. To him the most compelling problem the paper faced was attracting and developing new young reporters and editors, men and women to take the places held by Rosenthal and his staff as they moved on. "I'm a journalist," he said with his father's easy grin. When he said it there seemed no doubt that in his vocabulary there was no higher vocation.

Steve Golden, working on *Times'* business and production problems in New York, spoke in terms almost identical with those of his cousin. "The big problem," he said, "is to identify people to do these things and then let them do them. I am sure that we are going to make the decisions so that 50 to 75 years from now we are going to be doing what *The New York Times* is doing today and doing it under the same ownership and direction. In my family we have always stressed quality and excellence."

Steve spoke of the social responsibility of *The Times*, much greater, he thought, than that of most corporations. "We can't," he said, "present one view on the editorial page and do something else in our organization."

Both young men talked like true grandsons of their incomparable grandmother, Iphigene. They did not believe their cousins held views that differed much from theirs.

Abe Rosenthal was restlessly struggling in 1979 with the problem that had possessed him since the ill-fated coup of 1968, the problem of the Washington bureau. This problem had lain at the heart of *The Times'* agony over Watergate and it held the key to whether *The Times* was to regain that prestige (and readership) lost to the *Post* in Watergate days. Before Watergate *The Times* had been first in Washington; now it was not. In 1979 Rosenthal was to try yet another approach. Hedrick Smith had been named Washington bureau chief in 1976, coincident with the election of Jimmy Carter. But Smith's tenure, to Rosenthal's mind, had not been satisfactory and so in the spring of 1979, after thrashing about, public arguments between Smith and Rosenthal, rumors and snippety items in the press, Rosenthal announced a new setup for Washington—Smith to be chief correspondent but the bureau functions, the news functions, the management side, to be taken over by Bill Kovach, the tough, straight-talking, no-nonsense, editor whom many colleagues thought the most competent man on a desk and the most competent man on the street *The Times* had had for many years. David Halberstam, who claimed credit for getting Kovach on the paper, a frequent critic of Rosenthal's editorship, called it "the best appointment on *The Times* in fifteen years."

But even the Kovach appointment did not satisfy Rosenthal's restless psyche. He was talking of still other moves, of possibly taking a small apartment in Washington himself, of dividing his time between New York and Washington, of trying for once in his life to get a feel of the capital, an experience which his reporting career had denied him. Going to the scene, he thought, should narrow that geographical and psychological gap which he still thought constituted a handicap to *The Times.* Washington, he had concluded, was where so much of the news was; it was ever more important with the country so large, its functions so centralized; *The Times* must be first and best from Washington as it had in the past but had not been during his editorship.

Washington . . . it was a code that Rosenthal had not yet broken and he was determined to do it. He had built a good newspaper. Of that he was confident. He had kept it straight. Of that he was certain. But he was not satisfied. He knew that he was not liked by many people, including many people on the paper, people in the city room. He knew that his tenure had been marked by quarrels and feuds and rows. In the winter and early spring of 1979 he had been in the hospital and recuperating at home for six weeks. He had injured his knee in an accident at home; his legs had always, it seemed, been vulnerable. He had a long painful operation and a painful recuperation in Lenox Hill Hospital, in a room next to Prince Sihanouk's. Punch Sulzberger had been in New York Hospital, too, at the same time, flat on his bed with a painful back which, in the end, he would conclude was, as his doctor insisted, largely psychosomatic in origin, a product of stress and strain in his personal and professional life that few except close associates would have suspected behind his easy, low-key, throw-away style. Some amateur Freudians in *The Times'* city room wondered whether there could be a connection between the publisher's back and Rosenthal's knee; those who knew the two realized that this could not be.

When Abe came back to work he carried a heavy cane and felt he looked quite wicked with his big black stick and he thought perhaps people saw him as the image of evil, stumping through the city room. One day a copyreader stopped him and they started to talk. He asked the copyreader why people reacted the way they did, some liked him, some didn't, some people wrote awful things about him. The copy-reader said he thought it was because Rosenthal was an agent of change, he had changed the paper and he had changed people, he had changed reporters and editors and the whole atmosphere of the city room, and what he was doing made people angry. And, said the copy-reader, of course, you have your own polarized style. You are either benign and loving or wrathful and threatening.

Rosenthal felt that the copyreader's analysis was not unrealistic. He knew some said there was no humanity in the city room; that it was too big; a place of numbers; of slots; of cubicles and electronics; that people were changed like parts in a machine. He did not believe this. Did not agree with it. But he knew there were those who thought this. And, as he said, he was intelligent enough to know that it couldn't all be other people's fault. When he had come back from Tokyo and taken over the metro desk and the first criticism began, the days of the "cabal," a loose grouping of reporters and editors who used to meet and air gripes and resentments over the new regime of Abe 'n Artie, Abe and his alter ego, Arthur Gelb, a steam valve for the pressures that built up (but which Abe mistakenly thought was a plot to undermine his authority) in the shouting and hullabaloo that marked that period, Rosenthal had let it be known how hurt he was. And since then it had gone on and on. If, as he said, the bull didn't bleed you didn't throw darts at it.

The paper had never passed through such a period, he felt; the competitive threats from the electronic media had been enormous. The whole production process had been transformed, the methods of composition, the look of the city room, even the typewriters had been replaced by viewing consoles. There had been an astonishing turbulence in society, turmoil on the paper, the country had gone through crisis after crisis and there were, he felt, many people who hated him. Lately he had been subjected to such a barrage from the Murdoch press. Of course, he conceded, he had expressed himself about Ruppert Murdoch, had said in an interview in *Esquire* magazine that he hoped Murdoch would be out of town in a couple of years. But still—the way Murdoch had mobilized his *Post* and his *Voice* and his *New York* to print nasty stories about him—he found it shocking.

He was not, he granted, a passive person. He involved himself in everything. There was a Yiddish word for it—*kuchlefel,* the ladle. That was him. He was the *kuchlefel* always stirring up the pot. But he was amazed at the violence of reactions against him. He had changed people's work habits, their desks, their assignments, and people resented it. He could understand the need for an image of personalized hate. And he understood that he was such an image. It had begun a long time ago. Even before the Columbia bust. A friend of his from

Columbia and a friend of his friend had come to him one evening at the apartment and said, Abe, we have concluded that you are going to become the target of the student left. The media is the most tempting target they have. *The Times* is the most tempting target of the media and you personify that media and that target. And it had happened like that. *Just like that.*

Abe tried and tried to recollect which of his friends had displayed such prescience. Finally he concluded that it might have been Arnold Beichman, a one-time *Christian Science Monitor* foreign correspondent who in 1968 was taking graduate work at Columbia and later joined the faculty of the University of British Columbia.* But Beichman said he wasn't the source of the warning; moreover, he didn't think the idea had any merit; he knew Mark Rudd and the students who led the Columbia sit-in; he was convinced the uprising had been spontaneous and that none of the radicals had targeted Rosenthal, *The Times* or anything else. "The whole thing was unpremeditated. Like the fall of the Bastille," Beichman said. "I discount the conspiracy theory entirely." But Rosenthal wasn't entirely convinced by this. Even a decade later he was still bothered, still upset, still basically disturbed by the young people of the 1960s. When in the summer of 1979 *The Times* ran a retrospective and reflective series of articles on the tenth anniversary of Woodstock he had been angered by some of the reporting; he still could not believe that principles were involved in Woodstock and that the young people sought to inject into their lives new and noninstitutional values and symbols. He insisted on *The Times'* material being reworked and rewritten.

And he was writhing over a major discrimination complaint filed against *The Times* by its black employees and, particularly a devastating affidavit submitted by Roger Wilkins, the most distinguished black journalist on *The Times,* a member of the editorial board who had given up his editorial position to work for Rosenthal, writing analyses of urban affairs. The relationship with Wilkins had not worked out (Wilkins quit *The Times* in October 1979) and when Rosenthal discussed the complaint of the blacks his face paled and he began to pace his office. "I do not think we are guilty of racial discrimination," he said, "and I don't think they will be able to prove it in a thousand years."

At first he called it "a kind of social blackmail." Then he reconsid-

---

*Beichman got a mention in Crewdson's series on the CIA and the press. A former CIA man recalled Beichman publishing a story which the CIA had embellished about a Soviet diplomat named Alexander Kaznecheyev who defected to the U.S. Embassy in Rangoon, Burma. Beichman conceded he wasn't certain what the source of his information had been. (*New York Times,* 12/25/77)

ered: "Blackmail is the wrong word. It's a First Amendment problem: We are going to be forced to testify against our own staff. Have to get up in Court and testify under oath: What do you think about this person? That person? Because they are a woman or a black. I see *The Times* as a victim. We are political targets."

These issues exaggerated the contradictions within Rosenthal's personality. He did not believe he was, as he knew some young reporters had suggested, a mean person. He was irritable, yes. But not mean. He pushed for things. Pushed hard. When he had become editor he thought he could still be one of the boys and go to Sardi's with the reporters after the paper came out. He was wrong. He thought the attitudes toward himself were unjust and he fought back hard. And one thing he had never done. He had no hit list as some of his critics contended. He didn't reward his friends or punish his enemies. When Bill Buckley got into trouble with the SEC Abe played it straight, page-one, hardball reporting.

But this was small talk, personal talk. Not what really counted. What really was important, he felt, was the emerging struggle between the courts and the press. The battle lines had shifted. The White House was fighting to regain the power it had lost to Congress and Congress was fighting to hold its power. The courts had turned on the press. This was the great story of the moment and this was the struggle that would determine the future of the press and its ability to carry out First Amendment functions. The courts, Rosenthal had concluded, were the strongest totalitarian element in our society. One of his reporters named Myron Farber had done an investigative article on a New Jersey physician and the doctor had been brought to trial. This had produced a tremendous explosion. The New Jersey judge had ordered Farber to produce his notes in court and when he refused Farber was put in jail. Both Farber and *The Times* had been cited for contempt of court. *The Times* had fought the case, James Goodale battling like a bulldog, and Rosenthal urging him on, but, in the end, the case was lost and Rosenthal was badly shaken. He had little or no experience of courts as a reporter. He was shocked at the way everyone had to defer to the judges, the rights the courts arrogated to themselves, the way lawyers and everyone else had to kowtow, the absolute and arbitrary power wielded by the courts. (He did not attempt to correlate this feeling with his enthusiasm over the Supreme Court verdict *in favor* of *The Times* in the Watergate case.) He had visited Farber in jail and the experience had moved him. It was the first time he had ever been inside a prison. The courts today, he was coming to believe, were Nixon's revenge. The press was living through times in which it was going to lose some battles. This was inevitable. The courts and the law—it was the most important thing in which Rosenthal was now engaged. (Some of his

friends thought he was *too* engaged.) He had personally intervened on
the question of *The Times'* editorial stand on the case of the *Progressive*
magazine in which the government in the spring of 1979 had won an
order of prior restraint against publication of an article about the
H-bomb. He had gone to the publisher and had gone to Max Frankel
and he took credit for turning *The Times'* position from one of cautionary words into forthright support of the First Amendment rights of the
Progressive.

Now, one afternoon in 1979 Rosenthal stood, as he so often did, at the
reading stand outside his office, his elbows resting on an unread file of
the *Washington Post,* and gazed out over the city room which was his
joy and his despair, *his* city room as he had thought of it since 1963,
and asked once again: "Why do people hate me so?" This was no
put-on, no role-playing. It was a *cri de coeur* from as contradictory a
personality as contemporary journalism could boast. He knew that
people *did* hate him and that some of those who did were at that
moment within his field of vision. And while, in a measure, he could
understand such feelings he could not accept them for, in a paradox
which many of his friends, most of his associates, and surely all of his
enemies did not perceive, Rosenthal's psyche was founded on love.
What neither he nor those around him really grasped was the swiftness
with which love, that capricious and untidy emotion, could change at
the flicker of an eye, a perceived tonality of speech, a physical gesture;
could change from milky, almost maudlin affection into Othello's paranoia, suspicion, fear and hate.

By every measure Rosenthal *had made it.* He was executive editor
of *The New York Times,* earning a salary of $150,000 a year, possessed
options to buy 20,000 to 30,000 shares of *New York Times* common
stock, some at favorable prices, some not, owned and occupied with his
loyal wife, Ann, an eight-room penthouse apartment on Central Park
West which gave him a front-row seat on the New York skyline. No
other editor, not even his rival Ben Bradlee of the *Washington Post,*
could challenge his eminence. Like it or not, and Abe Rosenthal certainly liked *this,* the editor of *The Times* was automatically the most
powerful editor in the United States. No one in his birthplace of Sault
Ste. Marie had reached such heights.*

There were bubbling moments when he looked on this scene, stand-

---

*Some residents of Sault Ste. Marie contended that their native son, Phil Esposito,
National Hockey League scoring champion, earning nearly $300,000 annually, was
their most famous product. They pointed out that Esposito's picture was even sold at
hockey stadiums in Moscow, and that he drew huge crowds to shopping centers on
personal appearances.

ing beside the pillar where he had put up a poster of his heroine, Beverly Sills, and shouted: "I love this paper!," when he was ready to throw his arms around anyone within reach, even instigators of what he felt were those unfair and terrible women's and black discrimination actions, just so they were part of this incredible world of his emotion, *The New York Times,* his pride, his love, his life.

But there were other moments when the faceless image of "they" haunted his mind.

He had begun to attend more and more meetings, more and more seminars, more and more conferences on the question of the First Amendment. It was the only thing he made speeches about. He liked to tell about the reporter behind the Iron Curtain who interviewed an official on questions of the day; he took careful notes; he wrote a story; then he took his notes and burned them and flushed them down the toilet. He was afraid the police would come to his house, search it, find the notes and arrest him. It was, he told his audiences, a story about himself, about the days when he was a reporter in Poland two decades ago. And, he said, it was getting that way in the United States. Well, not exactly, of course. But it was getting more like it than many people realized.

These were dangerous forces, dangerous to *The Times.* He conceded that he identified himself with *The Times.* Almost totally. That had not been true before. Now it was. But, he felt, you could not be a great editor of a great newspaper without consuming yourself.

He spoke not in the words, not in the mood in which Adolph Ochs had written his manifesto for *The Times* in 1896 but it was clear that he believed that during the term of his editorship *The Times* would continue to be guided as it had in the past by Ochs' pledge to publish the news to the best of its ability without fear or favor.

Sources

NO GREAT AMERICAN INSTITUTION HAS been more written about and less studied than *The New York Times*. Not one critical work of magnitude or seriousness has ever been undertaken and only one book about *The New York Times* has been written in more than a quarter century, Gay Talese's *The Kingdom and the Power*, a wonderfully readable account of *Times* men, their personalities, intrigues and power struggles.

Thus, curiously, for an institution which once (but no longer) advertised itself as *the* newspaper of record, the archive to which generations of statesmen and scholars turned for the chronicle of their days, there are only a handful of printed sources.

The body, soul and heart of this book come from hundreds of interviews conducted over a period of more than a dozen years, interviews with every individual on *The Times* who played a significant role in the contemporary epoch (and many who did not) and interviews with figures in government and out who participated in or had knowledge of the events and issues that comprise the fabric and texture of *Without Fear or Favor*.

At the heart of this study lie the Pentagon Papers. The Pentagon affair, as the reader quickly discovers, is presented as a metaphor of the transformation of Adolph S. Ochs' Victorian *New York Times* into a late twentieth-century institution headed by his grandson, Arthur Ochs (Punch) Sulzberger. It symbolizes the metamorphosis of *The Times* from a newspaper which recorded the action to one which has become, like it or not, a very considerable part of the action. This, I submit, came about not through the will of any single man or group of men, but through the evolution of American society and its institutions.

The reconstruction of the Pentagon case as presented here required hundreds of hours of interviewing, interviewing men on *The Times*, formerly on *The Times*, editors and reporters of other newspapers, men of government and formerly of government, including the principal personages of the Nixon Administration, members of the bar and of the Judiciary.

This was necessary if the full dimensions of the Pentagon affair were to be revealed. One document, John Ehrlichman's notes in clear, bold handwriting of every meeting that Mr. Nixon had in the White House, beginning Tuesday, June 15, 1971, through May 2, 1973, which dealt with the Pentagon Papers and their repercussions, more than 150 pages of notes, admirably concise, well-organized, occasionally utilizing a stylized Greek-symbol shorthand, offered remarkable insight into the Nixon White House. It is doubtful that Mr. Nixon's tapes, when and if they are finally made available, will more fully expose the inner fraud of his effort to suppress the Pentagon documents, the hollowness of his claim of "national security." The notes etch the roles of each of Mr. Nixon's men, the parts played by Henry Kissinger, H. R. Haldeman and Ehrlichman in the drama of deceit which was to lead inevitably from the Pentagon Papers to Watergate to Mr. Nixon's downfall.

The final acts of Pentagon were played in the federal courtrooms and Mr. Ehrlichman's notes provide clues by which can be illuminated the manner in which Mr. Nixon and his aides sought to employ the government's security apparatus in an effort to crush the press and destroy the First Amendment. It is a story more chilling than anyone on the outside could have imagined.

No single person, no judge, no lawyer, certainly no editor on *The Times* nor even, it is likely, any one person in the government entirely understood all that was going on. To many of those deeply involved in the Pentagon affair the evidence adduced in these pages will come with surprise and shock. Almost ten years after the event many details presented here had hitherto remained hidden, obscure, secret, largely unsuspected and even, in some cases, still sheltered by *in camera* court proceedings and sealed records.

Because this book, inevitably, focuses on the interaction between *The Times* and government and the sociopolitical changes flowing from that interaction, the sources which have been drawn upon cover a very broad range, including almost every official of the Nixon Administration who had either a role in or knowledge of the Pentagon Papers case and Watergate. Among those consulted were: former President Nixon, H. R. Haldeman, John Ehrlichman, Henry Kissinger, John Dean, Charles Colson, Howard Hunt, Egil Krogh, Alexander Butterfield, General Al Haig, John Mitchell, Ron Ziegler, Herb Klein, Tom Huston, John Scali, Pat Buchanan, Bryce Harlow, Richard G. Kleindienst, former Ambassador Kenneth Rush, Steve Bull, former Ambassador William Macomber, William Safire, former Senator Hugh Scott, former Secretary of State William Rogers, former Secretary of Defense Melvin Laird and Lyndon K. (Mert) Allin of the Nixon White House staff.

Mr. Nixon responded to several inquiries which clarified certain aspects of the Pentagon affair. John Ehrlichman was helpful in reconstructing chronology and assessing the ambience of the White House during the Pentagon-Watergate period. Others whose assistance was particularly valuable were John Mitchell, H. R. Haldeman, Pat Buchanan, William Safire and Herb Klein.

Central to the examination of the Pentagon Papers was the evidence of Neil Sheehan, who brought the story to *The Times,* and of Daniel Ellsberg, self-appointed custodian of the Papers. Both Sheehan and Ellsberg made themselves available over several years for repeated interviews. My account draws heavily on their recollections. Each individual who played a role in the Papers was interviewed, most importantly, Federal Judges Murray Gurfein and Gerhard A. Gesell, who heard the cases of *The New York Times* and the *Washington Post,* former Solicitor General Erwin S. Griswold, who argued the cases for the government in the Supreme Court (and also in the U.S. Court of Appeals for the District of Columbia), former Assistant Attorney General Robert Mardian, U.S. Prosecutors Whitney North Seymour and Michael

Hess of the Southern District of New York, Floyd Abrams and William Hegarty of Cahill Gordon, and the late Alexander Bickel, all three counsel to *The Times,* James Goodale, general counsel of *The Times,* Harding Bancroft, former executive vice president of *The Times,* Herbert Brownell and the late Louis Loeb of Lord, Day and Lord, formerly chief counsel to *The Times.*

Among those who provided special insight on the Pentagon matter mention must be made of Lieutenant General Robert W. Pursley, Ret., who served successively as military aide to Secretaries of Defense Robert McNamara, Clark Clifford and Melvin Laird. Pursley had a unique intimacy with the Pentagon Papers project and the interrelationships of the Defense Secretaries and the White House, particularly the McNamara-Johnson relationship, that of Walt Rostow, the Clifford-Johnson relationship, and finally, the extraordinarily complex relations among Melvin Laird, Mr. Nixon and his White House group, especially Henry Kissinger and Al Haig. Leslie Gelb, who directed the Pentagon study, was helpful as was Morton Halperin, McNamara's first choice to head the Pentagon project. Halperin possessed unusual understanding of the Nixon-Kissinger Administration through his role as an aide to Kissinger. It was Halperin who directed my attention to the Ehrlichman notes, which had been made available to the House Judiciary Committee in its impeachment hearings.

Others consulted in the Pentagon case included Paul Warnke, McGeorge Bundy, William Bundy, Marcus Raskin, Richard Falk, Richard Barnett, Walt W. Rostow, Winston Lord, General Robert Gard, former Secretary of State Dean Rusk, Helmut Sonnenfelt, Dan Henkin and, of course, former Secretaries McNamara, Clifford and Laird.

All of *The Times* personnel involved in Pentagon were interviewed, including James Reston, A. M. Rosenthal, Max Frankel, Tom Wicker, publisher Arthur Ochs Sulzberger, Sydney Gruson, Clifton Daniel, John Oakes, Ivan Veit, Dan Schwartz, Ned Kenworthy, Anthony Lewis, Seymour Topping, Bill Kovach, James Greenfield, Jerry Gold, Al Siegal, Larry Hauck, Hedrick Smith, Richard Mooney, Muriel Stokes, Bob Rosenthal, Robert Phelps and Robert Semple.

Katherine Graham, Ben Bradlee, George Wilson, Chalmers Roberts, and Donald Graham of the *Washington Post* and Ben Bagdikian, formerly of the *Post,* provided essential details. So did many others, including Priscilla McMillan, Howard Zinn, Lloyd Shearer, Roger Wilkins, Whitney Ellsworth, Homer Bigart, Malcolm Browne, David Wise, James Thomson, Jerry Wiesner, Senator William Fulbright and, particularly, David Halberstam.

The account of the Pentagon Papers in the courts draws not only on the recollection of the participants but on the full court records, including the *in camera* documents now largely but still not entirely released by order of Judge Gesell. The Freedom of Information action for release of the *in camera* material was brought privately by Anthony Lewis.

Each major segment of *Without Fear or Favor* has been constructed upon a palimpsest of interviews, supplemented by whatever other source materials could be found. The account of the Bay of Pigs, for example, is based on extended interviews with Turner Catledge, Clifton Daniel, Tad Szulc, Richard Dudman, David Kraslow, Peter Kihss, Theodore Bernstein, Lewis Jordan,

Herbert Matthews and the archives of *The Times;* that of the Ngo Diem Dinh affair on consultation with former Ambassador Henry Cabot Lodge, William Colby, Richard Helms, Robert Shaplen, Charles Mohr, William Lambert, Wallace Turner, Howard Hunt, Pat Buchanan and Tom Huston.

The chapter on Amory Bradford and the long strike is founded upon extensive interviews with Bradford, Bradford's own personal papers, interviews with Dr. George Cardin, Marian Dryfoos, Andrew Fisher, Punch Sulzberger and Turner Catledge.

The chapter on Walter Duranty draws upon materials from *The Times'* archives, extended examination of the voluminous writings of Aleister Crowley, interviews and information from one-time associates and friends of Duranty, including William Stoneman, George Kennan, Henry Shapiro, Parker F. Enwright, Beth Bigelow, Robin Kinkead, Jane Gunther. I wish to acknowledge special assistance from Sally Taylor, who is completing a study of Walter Duranty, and Allen Johnson, who has spent many years working on a Duranty biography.

The chapters on the Civil Rights struggle are based upon interviews with John N. Popham, Claude Sitton, Ruth Holmberg, Fred Powledge, Peter Kihss, Ray Jenkins, Hedrick Smith, Turner Catledge, Clifton Daniel, Gene Roberts, Karl Fleming, James Wooten, Walter Rugaber, Roy Reed, Gay Talese, Louis Loeb (and the Louis Loeb oral history in *The Times'* archives), Harding Bancroft, Tom Daly, T. Eric Embry and Cecil Roberts. I am indebted to the research of Florence Mars of Philadelphia, Mississippi, and to Robert Gorley, archivist, Birmingham City Library (and his study of Birmingham in the Civil Rights years). I have drawn upon my own experiences in Birmingham and in the Connor case. Jeff Norrell kindly let me see research on Southern Civil Rights reporting which he did for a graduation thesis at the University of Virginia.

The chapter on Mollie Parnis' party is based on her recollections and those of her guests, including Henry Kissinger. The materials on Communists and *The Times* and the Eastland inquiry are drawn from *The Times'* archives and from interviews with the late Louis Loeb, General Greenbaum and Charles Merz. Will Lissner was of special assistance. Materials on Herbert Matthews were provided by himself, by Merz, by *The Times'* archives, and the Princeton graduation thesis on Matthews of Robert L. Barber.

The principal sources on Watergate were Max Frankel, A. M. Rosenthal, Clifton Daniel, Seymour Topping, Bill Kovach, James Naughton, James Wooten, Gene Roberts, Robert Semple, David Jones, Jack Rosenthal, Russell Baker, James Reston, Robert Phelps, Tad Szulc, R. W. Apple, Seymour Hersh, John Crewdson, Roger Wilkins, Walter Rugaber, Carl Bernstein, Robert Woodward, Philip Geyelin and Ben Bradlee.

Considerable new material on the CIA was discovered, as indicated in the text, in *The Times'* archives. Sources within *The Times* included A. M. Rosenthal, Turner Catledge, Clifton Daniel, Harding Bancroft, James Goodale, Sydney Gruson, C. L. Sulzberger, Arthur Ochs Sulzberger, Iphigene Sulzberger, John Oakes, Peter Kihss, Flora Lewis, Andrew Fisher, Tom Wicker, Wallace Carroll, Drew Middleton, Hanson Baldwin, Will Lissner, Anthony Lewis, Seymour Hersh, Wallace Turner, Gloria Emerson, John

Crewdson, Joseph B. Treaster, John Finney, Ben Welles and Harry Schwartz. Cy Sulzberger was endlessly patient in responding to inquiries.

I am particularly indebted to Carl Bernstein and former CIA Directors William Colby, John McCone and Richard Helms and to many CIA officials (more past than present), including J. M. Knoche, Joseph Bryan, III, Seymour Bolten, James Hunt, John Bross, James R. Murphy, Robert Amory, Frank Snepp, Harry Rositzke, James Angleton, Donald Jamieson, Howard Hunt, John M. Maury, Stephen Millett, Cord Meyer, Lyman Kirkpatrick, Richard Bissell, Alfred C. Ulmer, Jr., and others who provided important information but chose to remain anonymous.

Wayne Phillips was the principal source on the incident involving himself, supplemented by materials from John Crewdson, Turner Catledge and *The Times'* archives. The story of Sam Pope Brewer has been pieced together from materials in *The Times'* archives, from Agency sources, including Kermit Roosevelt, old friends of Brewer on *The Times,* including Farnesworth Fowle, Clifton Daniel, and Peter Kihss and Eric Downton of the *Vancouver Sun.* Brewer's widow, Lise Brewer, kindly provided some background. Anne S. Wells, manuscript librarian, University of Mississippi, was helpful in checking the Catledge papers held there.

The *Glomar Explorer* story is based on materials from A. M. Rosenthal, Seymour Hersh, John Crewdson, William Colby, Wallace Turner, James Phelan, Arthur Ochs Sulzberger, James Goodale, Clifton Daniel, Tom Wicker, Bill Kovach and materials released under a Freedom of Information action.

The account of Argus derives from Walter Sullivan and Hanson Baldwin, the U-2 account from Baldwin and Robert Amory. Arthur Krock mentions his prior knowledge of U-2 in his *Memoirs.*

Several archivists were of assistance, none more than Chester Lewis of *The Times.* Richard Jacobs of the National Archives provided professional guidance and Nancy Bressler of the Firestone Library, Princeton University, checked the archives of Arthur Krock and Allen Dulles. Linda Amster, chief of research for *The Times,* was, as always, endlessly helpful. So was Paul Greenfeter, *Times* librarian.

Since so much of this book is based on interviews and oral sources the so-called "Watergate rule" has been applied as far as humanly possible—that is, no statement has been made unless it has been confirmed by two or more independent sources. This qualification has been rigorously imposed on the delicate and controversial aspects of the Pentagon Papers, Watergate and the CIA sections.

This book had its beginning in a lengthy series of talks (interview is too formal a word) with Iphigene Sulzberger in 1968. Mrs. Sulzberger was at that time, as she was to be for a number of years, engaged in writing the memoir of her childhood years in New York, reminiscences of her father, Adolph S. Ochs, early impressions of *The New York Times,* of growing up *in* and *of* her father's newspaper, a charming series of vignettes in which she was assisted by her granddaughter, Susan Dryfoos. She published it privately in 1979.

Iphigene Sulzberger's remarkable memory of detail, clear and candid views of herself, her family, *The Times,* its editors and the role of a newspaper have done much to shape my understanding of the Ochs-Sulzberger tradition.

Without Fear or Favor is not, as is apparent to the reader, an "institutional" book. It is the author's book and only the author's. No one on *The Times* saw it in advance; nor did anyone on *The Times* possess a power of veto; any faults must be placed at my door. I have sought to examine *The Times* with that same absence of fear or favor to which Mr. Ochs dedicated his newspaper. If there be bias in this book let me confess publicly a bias toward Iphigene Sulzberger, that remarkable inheritor of the Ochs' newspaper genius and progenitor of those into whose hands Mr. Ochs' heritage is now entrusted.

Iphigene Sulzberger made no effort to influence these pages in any way. She is too good a newspaperwoman for that. Once she said, a little shyly, "Be kind." I am afraid this is not a "kind" book; but I hope it is not unkind.

Members of the Ochs-Sulzberger family have given many hours to interviews and inquiries and I am most indebted to Arthur Ochs (Punch) Sulzberger and his sister, Ruth Sulzberger Holmberg. The whole of *The Times'* archives has been at my disposal but it must be recorded that the archives are far from complete and there are great gaps. Most papers of Mr. Birchall have vanished; Mr. Ochs destroyed many of his own; those of Mr. James are incomplete; only a handful of those of Mr. Dryfoos have been preserved.

Among the older generation of *Times* people those whose interviews were valuable were the late General Edward Greenbaum, the late Louis Loeb, the late Arthur Krock, the late Herbert L. Matthews, the late editor in chief Charles Merz, former editors Turner Catledge and Clifton Daniel, former editorial page director John Oakes, James Reston and George Wood, Harding Bancroft, Ivan Veit, Amory Bradford and Andrew Fisher.

Among contemporaries no one was more generous than executive editor A. M. Rosenthal, who spent scores of hours in interviews over a period of several years. The range of *Times* reporters and editors, past and present, who lent a hand is too broad to recount in full. Let me mention Seymour Topping, Arthur Gelb, John Pomfret, Walter Mattson, Charlotte Curtis, Roger Wilkins, Walter Sullivan, Wallace Turner, Arthur O. Sulzberger, Jr., Steve Golden, Julius Adler, Nathan Goldstein, Irvin S. Taubkin and David Schneiderman. Nancy Finn helped with many details. Ruth Strauss typed the manuscript with great care.

The paucity of printed works on *The Times* has been noted. Before Talese there was Meyer Berger's *The Story of the New York Times,* commissioned for the paper's one hundredth anniversary in 1951. Before that there was a slender commissioned *History of the New York Times 1851–1921* written by Elmer Davis in 1921. Gerald W. Johnson wrote a commissioned biography of Adolph S. Ochs called *An Honorable Titan,* published in 1946. And that is it.

There have been a handful of biographies of *Times* editors, *Raymond of The Times,* a study of Henry Jarvis Raymond, founder of *The Times,* published in 1951 by Francis Brown, editor for many years of *The New York Times Book Review,* and *Mr. Miller of "The Times,"* by F. Fraser Bond, 1931. Charles Miller was the editor and one of the owners of *The Times* when Mr. Ochs purchased the paper. He continued as editor until his death in 1921.

Personal memoirs have been published by several *Times* editors, notably

Turner Catledge's *My Life and The New York Times,* Arthur Krock's *Memoirs: Sixty Years on The Firing Line,* Herbert L. Matthews' *A World in Revolution, A Newspaperman's Memoir,* 1971, *A Long Row of Candles* and other works by C. L. Sulzberger.

Times correspondents and reporters, of course, have written prolifically about stories, countries and situations in which they have been professionally involved. The list is far too long to recite here but some volumes that should be noted are David Halberstam's *The Making of a Quagmire* (on Vietnam), William H. Lawrence's *Six Presidents, Too Many Wars,* John Herber's *No Thank You, Mr. President* (on the Nixon White House), Tom Wicker's *On Press,* James Reston's *The Artillery of The Press* and the author's *Moscow Journal: The End of Stalin.*

Two disparate books give special insights into *The Times.* Ruth Adler's *A Day in the Life of The New York Times,* 1971, records *The Times'* day of February 28, 1969. It is now a monument to an epoch which has passed, the epoch of hot type, linotype composition, lead, old-fashioned printers and pre-electronic newspapering. Chris Argyris' *Behind the Front Page,* 1974, is a pseudonymous report of his psycho-management sessions with *Times* editors.

Outside of ephemeral newspaper and magazine pieces, published materials on the Pentagon Papers are rare. The basic document is *The Pentagon Papers,* published in 1971 by Times Books and Bantam with an Introduction by Neil Sheehan. Sanford J. Ungar of the *Washington Post* published *The Papers and the Papers* in 1975, an excellent but preliminary study, handicapped by lack of knowledge as to how *The Times* came to publish the Papers and ignorance of what went on within the Nixon Administration. Peter Schrag's *Test of Loyalty,* 1974, focused on Daniel Ellsberg and the Ellsberg trial.

The best and most serious study of the Bay of Pigs is that by Peter H. Wyden, *Bay of Pigs: The Untold Story,* 1979. Tad Szulc recorded the episode as he saw it in *How I Got That Story,* 1967, and in *The Cuban Invasion* (with Karl Meyer), 1962. The standard accounts are in Arthur Schlesinger, Jr.'s, *A Thousand Days,* Theodore Sorensen's *Kennedy* and Robert Kennedy's *Thirteen Days.*

The literature on Vietnam is so extensive that it cannot be dealt with in this context except to note that no satisfactory study of the relationship of correspondents, their dispatches and reporting on the war has yet been made. Perhaps the subject is simply too large and too amorphous. The study by Peter Braestrup, a former *New York Times* and *Washington Post* correspondent, is exhaustive but reflects an extraordinary pro-government, anti-press bias. Nor is Phillip Knightley's once-over-lightly on Vietnam reporting in *The First Casualty* more satisfactory although his conclusion that Vietnam was "better covered than other wars" may, on balance, hold true.

Almost all the participants in Watergate have written books or are in the process of doing so—President Nixon, H. R. Haldeman, John Ehrlichman, John Dean, Charles W. Colson, Howard Hunt, Jeb Stuart Magruder, John Mitchell and Henry Kissinger. Each in its way is useful when collated with the public record of the Erwin committee and the House Judiciary Impeachment hearings. So are the works by Judge Sirica and Prosecutor Leon Jaworski.

Two other works are essential, the classic Woodward and Bernstein *All the President's Men,* which captures the excitement and the drama of the *chase,* and J. Anthony Lukas' *Nightmare: The Underside of the Nixon Years,* the basic source book for Watergate.

Shockingly, there exists today no good overall study of the Civil Rights movement in the South of the 1950s and 1960s. There are individual studies of brilliance and insight, Charles Morgan, Jr.'s, two autobiographical books, *A Time to Speak* and *One Man, One Voice* among them. Nothing is likely to surpass Richard Kluger's *Simple Justice* in its analysis of *Brown* v. *the Board of Education,* but no one has attempted the epic (impossible?) task of telling the story outside the courtroom, the South as it existed in the flesh in the years before and after Brown, the dramatic, dangerous and optimistic epic of America reported day-by-day by correspondents of *The New York Times.* Howell Raines, now a *Times* correspondent based in Atlanta, has come closest in *My Soul is Rested,* 1977, taped interviews with blacks and whites involved in the struggle.

There has been a torrent of CIA books but the first, *The Invisible Government,* by David Wise and Thomas B. Ross, 1965, is still basic. Others that are valuable are William Colby's *Honorable Men,* 1977, Philip Agee's *Inside the Company,* 1975, Miles Copeland's *The Game of Nations,* 1969, Victor Marchetti and John D. Marks' *The Cult of Intelligence,* 1974, Frank Snepp's *Decent Interval,* 1978, Thomas Power's *The Man Who Kept the Secrets,* 1979.

None of these books is in any way satisfactory in illuminating the critical "interface," as John McCone once called it, between press and CIA. But taken together they go far toward destroying the myth that contacts between the Agency and newsmen were low level, marginal, insignificant, trivial. No scholar, no journalist, no political scientist has yet tackled the critical question of the extent to which the news process has been bent, twisted or thwarted by the CIA.

All of these mentioned works and many, many more have been used to fill in the framework of *Without Fear or Favor.*

This study is fully sourced and footnoted. An annotated copy of the manuscript is available in the author's hands and another will be placed in *The New York Times'* archives for reference purposes. Source notes have been omitted only for the purpose of accelerating the publication process. I have tried to indicate textually the source of all important details. In almost every instance quoted and attributed statements were made to the author by the subject.

Notes

page 33

Arthur Hays Sulzberger had a gift for self-analysis. On December 15, 1959, he wrote the following memorandum to himself:

"I'm getting a bit worried about my political views these days. I'm growing too conservative and while it would be utterly wrong to say that I'm anti-labor, there is no denying the fact that our strike of last year profoundly affected me. Some fifty negative votes taken among a small minority of one union cast more than 15,000 persons out of work and kept them out for three weeks just before Christmas. I would charge the Democrats with that sin more than the Republicans, and yet instinctively I count myself a Democrat. I hope my ballot may again be counted in its columns but not too soon. If Rockefeller runs next year, I should like to support him against all comers of all parties. If he does not run, I would at this time like to support Stevenson. I wonder how I'll stick to this?" (*Times'* archives)

page 36

This is an educated guess. Ellsberg would never say more than that he kept the papers in the "apartment of a relative." He had two relatives in Cambridge that year, Patricia's stepmother, Idella Marx, and a half brother, Spencer, who later moved into the Ellsberg apartment at No. 10 Hilliard Street. Both were subpoenaed in the grand jury investigations of Ellsberg, Mrs. Marx in Boston, Spencer in Los Angeles. The FBI claimed it had found a note in Ellsberg's garbage can saying "Material being kept at Spencer's place." Mrs. Marx's apartment was just down Brattle Street from the Ellsberg's. The fact is that Ellsberg had materials stashed in a great many places. One rumor was that a set was hidden in a culvert in a small Vermont village but had to be removed when a heavy truck broke through the culvert. Ellsberg said this was just an exciting legend. (Personal interviews, Whitney Ellsworth, 11/2/78; Priscilla McMillan, 11/16/78; Ellsberg, 1/14/79) In truth the incident didn't happen in Vermont, there was no culvert, there was no truck and it didn't basically involve the Pentagon Papers. What happened was this: Ellsberg gave a large quantity of documents to a friend for safekeeping. The friend thought these were the Pentagon Papers but, in fact, the bulk were other documents (although the Pentagon Papers were included). After *The Times'* publication the friend decided they were no longer important and buried them in an embankment beside a road. A hurricane struck the area and the embankment collapsed. Highway bulldozers cleared away the debris, using it for landfill. Ellsberg and his friend learned where the earth was dumped but were never able to recover the documents, some of which were the only copies Ellsberg possessed. (Personal interview, Ellsberg, 1/19/79) Ellsberg had documents stashed all over the country. After *The Times* published the Papers David Obst, Ellsberg's friend and then literary agent, flew coast-to-coast picking up papers from caches in New York and California. He retrieved Ellsberg's footlocker from the Bekins warehouse in Los Angeles literally forty-five minutes before FBI agents appeared (according to a memo from David Young to H. R. Haldeman which turned up in the Watergate inquiry). (Personal interview, Obst, 4/20/79) Later, in violation of a ruling by Judge William M. Byrne during Ellsberg's trial, the FBI seized a number of Ellsberg's boxes in the warehouse but returned them when they found they contained mostly old books and his Marine uniforms. (Sanford Ungar, *The Papers and The Papers*, New York, 1975, p. 288)

page 60

At a meeting of the American Historical Association in Atlanta in 1975 Dean Rusk proposed an investigation of the Pentagon project. He said later that there might have been "a political conspiracy inside the Government against a sitting President"; there were all kinds of "murky questions here." He cited an interview given by Leslie Gelb to BBC which suggested the project might have been designed to prepare a campaign document for LBJ or Robert Kennedy. (Personal interview, Rusk, 10/1/78; Gelb in Michael Charlton and Anthony Moncrieff, *Many Reasons Why*, London, 1978, p. 170) Walt Rostow raised somewhat the same questions, contending Gelb did not have access to Rusk's papers, White House papers and possibly not even McNamara's papers. (Personal interview, Rostow, 9/28/78) Rostow was mistaken. Gelb had access to everything in the Pentagon, to all State Department materials he wished (with Rusk's approval), to CIA files, all the National Security Council files and a certain amount of White House material but not, as Rostow noted, to memos of LBJ's Tuesday luncheons where many decisions were made. (Moncrieff, p. 171) McNamara commented that he was "absolutely amazed" Rusk would suggest the study might have been designed to support Robert Kennedy's Presidential candidacy. (Personal interview, McNamara, 1/16/78) Morton Halperin felt there could have been no Robert Kennedy connection. He said the study took on a shape of its own, McNamara never interfering because he didn't want to "taint the raw material." (Personal interview, Halperin, 10/6/78) Neither Paul Warnke nor General Robert Gard, McNamara's liaison on the study, gave any credence to the Robert Kennedy or "conspiracy" hypotheses. Both said McNamara instructed them to keep hands off the study, let the historians do their work and avoid any influence on their conclusions. (Personal interviews, Warnke, 1/28/78; Gard, 10/12/78) Arthur Schlesinger, Jr., working on his monumental study *Robert Kennedy and His Times* found no evidence to support Rusk's suspicions. (Personal interview, Schlesinger, 11/14/78)

page 122

Publication of the Yalta texts did not quiet the political clamor. It went on and on. On March 17, 1955, the day *The Times* published the Yalta texts, it carried a story by Harry Schwartz on a discussion between Stalin and Roosevelt on the subject of Jews. The passage in the Papers quoted Stalin as talking about the problem of Soviet Jews. The Jews raised difficult questions. The Jews did not like the special settlement which had been created for them in Birobijan, in eastern Siberia. They drifted away. They were traders, Stalin thought, rather than industrial workers. Roosevelt broke in to say that he, Roosevelt, was a Zionist and to inquire whether Stalin was. Stalin said he was a Zionist "in principle" but he recognized what he called the "difficulty of the matter." Schwartz noted that a line of asterisks preceded Stalin's remarks and suggested the discussion might have been initiated by someone else. Arthur Hays Sulzberger was in London at the time and his curiosity was piqued by the Stalin-Roosevelt exchange. Catledge investigated and cabled the publisher that at the Yalta plenary session Feb. 10, 1945, Stalin asked Roosevelt whether he intended to make any concessions to King Ibn Saud of Saudi Arabia.

"Following believed to be direct quote in original," Catledge continued: "President replied that there was only one concession he thought he might offer and that was to give him [Ibn Saud] the six million Jews in the United States."

Catledge added that in the margin of the original copy of the Papers was a notation in the handwriting of Undersecretary of State Walter Bedell Smith saying, "Delete this. It is not pertinent history." Catledge added that Dulles asked that the reference be deleted for the same reason. (Personal interview, Reston, 12/12/78; Cable, Catledge to Arthur Hays Sulzberger, 3/23/55; *The Yalta Myths*, Arthur G. Theoharis; Yalta Documents, DOS 1945) Two years later Arthur Hays Sulzberger was still troubled by a charge that *The Times* had "suppressed" a segment of the Yalta Papers dealing with Palestine in order to curry favor with the Zionists and supporters of Israel. (*Times'* archives, Arthur Hays Sulzberger memo, 4/17/57)

page 128

Mr. Reick came to *The Times* from James Gordon Bennett's *Herald.* Bennett, then in Paris, summoned Reick to France in 1906, kept him waiting three or four days, then received him. Reick said, "I thought you were in a hurry to see me." Bennett replied, "I just wanted you to see that the *Herald* could come out without you." To which Reick replied, "Very well, I think I'll make my absence permanent." He resigned on the spot and Mr. Ochs hired him effective January 1, 1907. Mr. Ochs offered him 10 percent of the stock in *The Times.* Reick and Ochs did not hit it off well and when he left after three years he turned the stock back to the treasury. Reick's successor was the famous Carr Van Anda. (Personal interview, Iphigene Ochs Sulzberger, 6/5/70)

page 157

The *Miami Herald* was probably the first U.S. newspaper to learn of the invasion plan. The CIA set up a Cuban training camp near Homestead, thirty miles south of Miami. In August 1960 some Florida youngsters, having heard drill commands and shouting of the trainees over a loudspeaker on the drill grounds (which were surrounded by a wove-wire fence), tossed some firecrackers into the compound. The Cubans roared out, firing carbines, and wounded a youngster in the head. The police arrested three Cubans but the district attorney did not prosecute because of intervention by the State Department.

The *Herald* heard of this and asked David Kraslow, its Washington reporter, what was going on. Kraslow found out almost all of the story, largely because a feud had erupted between FBI Director J. Edgar Hoover and Allen Dulles. Hoover claimed (correctly) that the training activity was in violation of the Neutrality Act, which he and his agents had sworn to uphold. This was one reason why much of the operation was moved to Guatemala. Kraslow wrote the story but his editors could not decide what to do with it. Finally, they sent Kraslow and Ed Lahey, chief of the Knight newspapers' Washington bureau, to see Allen Dulles. Dulles said the story would be harmful to "the national interest" and the *Herald* suppressed it. The paper did, however, continue to watch developments. (Personal interview, Dave Kraslow, 11/17/78) On January 11 (the day after Paul Kennedy's story on Retalhuleu appeared in *The New York Times*) the *Herald* published a story on the airlift from Miami to Retalhuleu, noting that the story had been withheld for more than two months but was now being printed because U.S. aid to "anti-Castro fighters in Guatemala was first revealed elsewhere." In April, after the Szulc story, the *Herald* again began to write about the project. (Aronson, *The Press and the Cold War*, p. 158; personal interview, Dave Kraslow, 11/17/78)

page 175

Melodrama also attended Arthur Hays Sulzberger's assumption of the role of publisher after Mr. Ochs' death April 8, 1935. Mr. Ochs had not designated his successor. The control stock was left to his daughter, Iphigene, through the mechanism of the Ochs Trust of which there were three trustees, Iphigene Sulzberger, her husband, Arthur, and her cousin Colonel Julius Adler, whom many had considered the heir apparent although Mr. Ochs had told Iphigene, "If I had picked a son-in-law to my taste I could not have done better." (Personal interview, Iphigene Ochs Sulzberger, 1/14/69) General Edward S. Greenbaum, the closest friend of the Sulzbergers and their legal counsel, recalled meeting for four evenings in a row in the house on Eightieth Street where the Sulzbergers then lived to decide what to do. Arthur and Iphigene, holding two of the three trustee votes, controlled the situation. It was a question of tactics. Finally, in Greenbaum's recollection, Iphigene said to the two men, "You are just stupid—both of you. You've been talking for three nights and you haven't decided anything. Now, listen to me! Tomorrow morning we are going down to *The Times* and I am going to sit in Papa's chair and Arthur is going to sit in the room with me. Then the next morning we are going down early and we'll do the same thing. And then the morning after that I'll be a little late and the first thing you know I won't come in at all and

Arthur'll just be sitting in the publisher's chair." At first Arthur objected but in the end they did just that. (Personal interviews, Greenbaum, 10/15/69; 1/21/69) Iphigene never remembered it exactly like this. She thought she may have suggested that Arthur just go and take her father's chair and office but not that she go with him. She was the one who had to tell her cousin Julie of the decision that there was going to be one boss and that it was going to be Arthur. He took it like a gentleman, she recalled, although he was very disappointed, but he promised that "you can count on me to do my part." Iphigene said that she thought Arthur much better qualified to be publisher. "He was a more able man, less conservative and, besides, he was my husband." (Personal interview, Iphigene Ochs Sulzberger, 1/14/69)

page 207

Greene had been alerted two or three days earlier that *The New York Times* was working on "some god-awful powerful project" which seemed to have a connection with the Pentagon. He had checked carefully with Pentagon intelligence, the CIA and the FBI but could find no one who had a clue to what the story might be. Nor did he get any useful information from Henkin that evening. After *The Times'* first edition hit the street the *News* editors telephoned him a brief summary. Greene then wrote a story, using as his principal source a reference book, the size of an encyclopedia volume, which had been prepared for the use of the Republican National Committee by Felix Cotten, an INS reporter. It was called "The Story of Vietnam" and was made up entirely of page-one stories from *The New York Times* and reports by *Times* columnists. "Half the stuff in the Pentagon Papers," Greene recalled, "had already appeared on page one of *The Times.*" (Personal interview, Jerry Greene, 1/19/79)

page 223

No story about the Pentagon Papers had been carried by AP or UPI on Saturday night, June 12, nor did any network broadcast a report about the Papers. This situation prevailed until Sunday evening when UPI finally sent out a report for Monday A.M. publication. Sunday night David Brinkley led with the story on NBC-TV; CBS-TV led with the birth of nontuplets in Australia, three of whom had already died. It did not mention the Papers. (Personal interview, Allin, 9/15/78) Deskman Jerry Gold and Neil Sheehan listened to the Sunday night network news broadcasts and heard nothing about the Papers. They kicked their wastebaskets in anger and thought the series was a failure. Somehow they missed the Brinkley newscast. (Personal interview, Bob Rosenthal, 7/19/77) AP didn't carry a Pentagon story until its Monday P.M. cycle. *Time* and *Newsweek* had an hour or two Saturday evening to catch their Monday editions but did not bother. (Ed Diamond, *New York* magazine, 8/16/71)

page 243

Mardian, whose memory was not notable for accuracy, recalled no call from Mitchell to Brownell in his presence at the Mitchell Watergate apartment on Monday evening but felt certain it could not have been made on Sunday since when he arrived in his office at the Justice Department early Monday there was no message from Mitchell or the White House pertaining to the Pentagon Papers. Had there been interest he was certain he would have found an alert on his desk when he came in that morning. (Personal interview, Mardian, 3/26/79) Kenneth Rush, then U.S. Ambassador to Germany, chanced to accompany Kissinger to his 6 P.M. meeting with Mr. Nixon and then went on to John Mitchell's to dine at about 7 P.M. He did not recall becoming involved in any White House discussions concerning *The Times*. He talked to Mr. Nixon about secret negotiations on a new Berlin agreement and left the Oval Office before Kissinger. He didn't recall meeting Mardian at the Mitchell apartment (although Mardian remembered him). He thought Mitchell filled him in during the evening about the Pentagon Papers. Later, in December 1972, Rush was to be Mr. Nixon's choice to succeed Rogers as Secretary of State, an appointment Mr. Nixon was never to make. (Personal interview, Kenneth Rush, 3/31/79) Mitchell remembered talking with Rush that evening about the new four-power agreement in Germany. "We were using a little back-channel communication to keep it out of the State Department," he said. It was his strong recollection that Henry Kissinger joined them after dinner and that the conversation went on to the Pentagon Papers. (Personal interview, Mitchell, 4/24/79) At first Kissinger wasn't certain whether he was there but finally concluded he probably did drop in after dinner. He couldn't remember whether the Pentagon Papers were touched on but conceded that they might have been. He was certain that he had had a number of long and detailed discussions of the German question with Rush and Mitchell because, for reasons he did not specify, the matter was being kept away from the State Department and the department was not being filled in. (Personal interviews, Kissinger, 6/4/79; 6/13/79)

page 248

Iphigene Sulzberger recalled sixty years later that she and her mother were traveling in Germany at the outbreak of World War I. Iphigene had just graduated from Barnard and her father planned to join them on an around-the-world trip. She and her mother had to make their way across the German frontier to Holland and then to England from which they sailed Aug. 15, 1914, two weeks after the outbreak of war, for New York. As she remembered she was quite pro-German. She had taken European history courses from Professor W. M. Sloane, who had a rather German viewpoint. Her opinion was further influenced by her travel in Germany, her admiration for German culture and social legislation and a German boy friend whom she met on the ship coming back to New York. Her sympathy for the German side did not long endure or influence her father, who was so pro-British he got anonymous letters asking why he didn't change his name to John Bull. (Iphigene Ochs Sulzberger to Doris Faber, unpublished MSS, pp. 139 et seq)

page 275

The text of Lodge's last talk with Diem, a telephone conversation at 4:30 P.M. the day of the coup, was published in the Pentagon Papers and supported the view that the U.S. had no complicity in the Diem assassination. Lodge told Diem: "I am worried about your physical safety. I have a report that those in charge of the current activity offer you and your brother safe conduct out of the country if you resign. Had you heard this? Diem: No. (and then after a pause) You have my telephone number. Lodge: Yes. If I can do anything for your physical safety please call me. Diem: I am trying to re-establish order." (Pentagon Papers, Quadrangle Edition, New York, 1971, p. 238) Lodge said he offered Diem safety under the aegis of the United States and "was prepared to give him asylum in my house, to help him enter a new government as a ceremonial figure or to leave the country." (Lodge, *The Storm Has Many Eyes,* New York, 1973, p. 210) Robert Shaplen, *The New Yorker* correspondent who conducted an extensive inquiry into the coup, concluded (as did the Pentagon Papers) that the United States knew of the coup and encouraged it but had not desired nor acquiesed in Diem's murder. The U.S. plan, Shaplen said, was to fly Diem out of the country. (Robert Shaplen, *The Lost Revolution,* New York, 1965, pp. 211–12) Much of Shaplen's information came from Lou Conein.

page 277

Charles Mohr, *Time* magazine correspondent in Saigon, had just quit *Time* in a celebrated dispute over the rewriting and distortion of his copy, and arrived back in Vietnam for *The New York Times* the day the Diem brothers were killed. He recalled that Mert Perry of *Time* had heard the shooting which inaugurated the coup during siesta time, November 1. He jumped into a taxi and raced to "CIA row" where Conein had a house. He found Conein and a group of CIA men angrily conferring on the terrace. He tried to talk to Conein but Conein said, "Gee, I can't talk to you now. I've got to go." Conein dashed off to join the generals who had launched the coup. Conein obviously had not had advance word on the timing. (Personal interview, Mohr, 1/31/79) Conein was considerably indebted to the Nixon Administration. His CIA contract was about to be terminated in the summer of 1971 but the Nixon Administration found him a place in Bureau of Narcotics, a predecessor of the Federal Drug Enforcement Agency. In the circumstances it seems unlikely Conein would have withheld a "smoking pistol" had he possessed one.

page 285

The essence of Frankel's affidavit follows:

The Government's unprecedented challenge to The Times in the case of the Pentagon papers, I am convinced, cannot be understood, or decided, without an appreciation of the manner in which a small and specialized corps of reporters and a few hundred American officials regularly make use of so-called classified, secret, and top secret information and documentation. It is a cooperative, competitive, antagonistic and arcane relationship. I have learned, over the years, that it mystifies even experienced professionals in many fields, including those with Government experience, and including the most astute politicians and attorneys.

Without the use of "secrets" that I shall attempt to explain in this affidavit, there could be no adequate diplomatic, military and political reporting of the kind our people take for granted, either abroad or in Washington and there could be no mature system of communication between the Government and the people. That is one reason why the sudden complaint by one party to these regular dealings strikes us as monstrous and hypocritical—unless it is essentially perfunctory, for the purpose of retaining some discipline over the Federal bureaucracy.

I know how strange all this must sound. We have been taught, particularly in the past generation of spy scares and Cold War, to think of secrets as *secrets* —varying in their "sensitivity" but uniformly essential to the private conduct of diplomatic and military affairs and somehow detrimental to the national interest if prematurely disclosed. By the standards of official Washington— Government and press alike—this is an antiquated, quaint and romantic view. For practically everything that our Government does, plans, thinks, hears and contemplates in the realms of foreign policy is stamped and treated as secret —and then unraveled by that same Government, by the Congress and by the press in one continuing round of professional and social contacts and cooperative and competitive exchanges of information

The governmental, political and personal interests of the participants are inseparable in this process. Presidents make "secret" decisions only to reveal them for the purposes of frightening an adversary nation, wooing a friendly electorate, protecting their reputations. The military services conduct "secret" research in weaponry only to reveal it for the purpose of enhancing their budgets, appearing superior or inferior to a foreign army, gaining the vote of a congressman or the favor of a contractor. The Navy uses secret information to run down the weaponry of the Air Force. The Army passes on secret information to prove its superiority to the Marine Corps. High officials of the Government reveal secrets in the search for support of their policies, or to help sabotage the plans and policies of rival departments. Middle-rank officials of government reveal secrets so as to attract the attention of their superiors or to lobby against the orders of those superiors. Though not the only vehicle for this traffic in secrets—the Congress is always eager to provide a forum—the press is probably the most important.

In the field of foreign affairs, only rarely does our Government give full public information to the press for the direct purpose of simply informing the people. For the most part, the press obtains significant information bearing on foreign policy only because it has managed to make itself a party to confidential materials, and of value in transmitting these materials from government to other branches and offices of government as well as to the public at large. This is why the press has been wisely and correctly called The Fourth Branch of Government.

I remember during my first month in Washington, in 1961, how President Kennedy tried to demonstrate his "toughness" toward the Communists after they built the Berlin wall by having relayed to me some direct quotations of his best arguments to Foreign Minister Gromyko. We were permitted to quote from this conversation and did so. Nevertheless, the record of the conversation was then, and remains today, a "secret."

I remember a year later, at the height of the Cuban missile crises, a State Department official concluding that it would surely be in the country's interest to demonstrate the perfidy of the same Mr. Gromyko as he denied any knowledge of those missiles in another talk with the President;

the official returned within the hour and let me take verbatim notes of the Kennedy-Gromyko transcript—providing only that I would not use direct quotations. We printed the conversation between the President and the Foreign Minister in the third person, even though the record probably remains a "secret."

I remember President Johnson standing beside me, waist-deep in his Texas swimming pool, recounting for more than an hour his conversation the day before, in 1967, with Prime Minister Kosygin of the Soviet Union at Glassboro, New Jersey, for my "background" information, and subsequent though not immediate use in print, with a few special off-the-record sidelights that remain confidential.

I remember Secretary of State Dean Rusk telling me at my first private meeting with him in 1961 that Laos is not worth the life of a single Kansas farm boy and that the SEATO treaty, which he would later invoke so elaborately in defense of the intervention in Vietnam, was a useless instrument that should be retained only because it would cause too much diplomatic difficulty to abolish it.

Similar dealings with high officials continue to this day.

We have printed stories of high officials of this Administration berating their colleagues and challenging even the President's judgment about Soviet activities in Cuba last year.

We have printed official explanations of why American intelligence gathering was delayed while the Russians moved missiles toward the Suez Canal last year.

These random recollections are offered here not as a systematic collection of secrets made known to me for many, usually self-evident (and often self-serving) reasons. Respect for sources and for many of the secrets prevents a truly detailed accounting, even for this urgent purpose. But I hope I have begun to convey the very loose and special way in which "classified" information and documentation is regularly employed by our government. Its purpose is not to amuse or flatter a reporter whom many may have come to trust, but variously to impress him with their stewardship of the country, to solicit specific publicity, to push out diplomatically useful information without official responsibility, and, occasionally, even to explain and illustrate a policy that can be publicly described in only the vaguest terms.

This is the coin of our business and of the officials with whom we regularly deal. In almost every case, it is secret information and much of the time, it is top secret. But the good reporter in Washington, in Saigon, or at the United Nations, gains access to such information and such sources because they wish to use him for *loyal* purposes of government while he wishes to use *them* to learn what he can in the service of his readers. Learning always to trust each other to some extent, and never to trust each other fully—for their purposes are often contradictory or downright antagonistic—the reporter and the official trespass regularly, customarily, easily and unself-consciously (even unconsciously) through what they both know to be official "secrets." The reporter knows always to protect his sources and is expected to protect military secrets about troop movements and the like. He also learns to cross-check his information and to nurse it until an insight or story has turned ripe. The official knows, if he wishes to preserve this valuable channel and outlet, to protect his credibility and the deeper purpose that he is trying to serve.

I turn now in an attempt to explain, from a reporter's point of view, the several ways in which "classified" information figures in our relations with government. The Government's complaint against The Times in the present case comes with ill-grace because Government itself has regularly and consistently, over the decades, violated the conditions it suddenly seeks to impose upon us—in three distinct ways:

First, it is our regular partner in the informal but customary traffic in secret information, without even the pretense of legal or formal "declassification." Presumably, many of the "secrets" I cited above, and all the "secret" documents and pieces of information that form the basis of the many newspaper stories that are attached hereto, remain "secret" in their official designation.

Second, the Government and its officials regularly and customarily engage in a kind of ad hoc, de facto "declassification" that normally has no bearing whatever on considerations of the national interest. To promote a political, personal, bureaucratic or even commercial interest, incumbent officials and officials who return to civilian life are constantly revealing the secrets entrusted to them. They use them to barter with the Congress or the press, to curry favor with foreign governments and officials from whom they seek information in return. They use them freely, and with a startling record of impunity, in their memoirs and other writings.

Third, the Government and its officials regularly and routinely misuse and abuse the "classification" of information, either by imposing secrecy where none is justified or by retaining it long after the justification has become invalid, for simple reasons of political or bureaucratic convenience. To hide mistakes of judgment, to protect reputations of individuals, to cover up the loss and waste of funds, almost everything in government is kept secret for a time and, in the foreign policy field, classified as "secret" and "sensitive" beyond any rule of law or reason. Every minor official can testify to this fact.

Obviously, there is need for some secrecy in foreign and military affairs. Considerations of security and tactical flexibility require it, though usually for only brief periods of time. The Government seeks with secrets not only to protect against enemies but also to serve the friendship of allies. Virtually every mature reporter respects that necessity and protects secrets and confidences that plainly serve it.

Some of the best examples of the regular traffic I describe may be found in the Pentagon papers that the Government asks us not to publish. The uses of top secret information by our Government in deliberate leaks to the press for the purposes of influencing public opinion are recorded, cited and commented upon in several places of the study. Also cited and analyzed are numerous examples of how the Government tried to control the release of such secret information so as to have it appear at a desired time, or in a desired publication, or in a deliberately loud or soft manner for maximum or minimum impact, as desired.

page 294

Two courses of action were open to the government. The *Post* maintained offices in New York and the case could have been combined with that against *The Times* in New York. However, the action was filed against the *Post* in Washington late Friday. It was Seymour's belief that the Washington venue was chosen by Mardian because he and Mitchell did not like the way Seymour was conducting the case in New York and wanted Mardian to handle it in Washington. Mardian denied this. (Personal interview, Mardian, 2/15/79) The Washington case was assigned to Federal District Judge Gerhard A. Gesell, who heard it with remarkable celerity. The hearing opened at a little after 6 P.M. and Gesell's 600-word decision refusing the government's request for an injunction was read at 8:05 P.M. while Gurfein was still hearing *The Times'* case. Some lawyers thought Gesell's prompt and forthright action might have encouraged Gurfein to take a similar stand. Mardian conceded years later he was not pleased with Seymour's performance but denied this had anything to do with bringing the *Post* action in Washington. "We brought suits in New York, in Washington, in Boston, in St. Louis—wherever the newspapers were published," Mardian recalled. "Actually it would have been much better from our standpoint if the *Post* case had been handled in New York. Everyone knew that the federal courts in Washington were the most liberal in the country." (Personal interview, Mardian, 2/15/79)

page 296

Secretary of State Rogers selected Macomber as a witness because, as he recalled later, "he was the best-organized and persuasive man with broad experience whom we had." He was, in Rogers' opinion, an ideal witness, not a career Foreign Service officer but a man of experience and a man who had had no connection with the Pentagon Papers, which Rogers regarded as a plus. (Personal interview, Rogers, 3/6/79) "They wanted a senior spokesman," Macomber recalled. "I fitted that description." He still felt years later that the case was a reasonable one to adjudicate but confessed "for what it is worth, the more I read, the less reason I saw for the case." (Personal interview, Macomber, 3/1/79)

Macomber, according to Ehrlichman's notes, had been, in Mr. Nixon's words, "got ready" for his testimony by John Scali, a former wire-service correspondent who left a job with ABC to join the Nixon Administration. After doing back-room propaganda chores Scali became Nixon's representative to the United Nations. In what manner Scali got Macomber "ready" Mr. Nixon did not specify but he felt it qualified Scali to help in the administration's "PR campaign" after the Supreme Court upheld the right of *The New York Times* to publish the Pentagon Papers. (House Judiciary Committee, Appendix III, p. 117) Macomber had no memory of consultation with Scali. He could not recall having even met Scali prior to Scali's becoming Ambassador to the United Nations. (Personal interview, Macomber, 3/1/79) Scali had a vague impression he might have talked to Macomber at the time of the Pentagon Papers but no recollection as to why. (Personal interview, Scali, 3/7/79)

page 331

The quarrel on June 29 specifically concerned Mr. Hoover's determination to discipline Charles Brennan, FBI chief of Domestic Intelligence, for having interrogated Louis Marx, Ellsberg's father-in-law, without Hoover's permission. Brennan had forwarded to Hoover a proposal to interrogate Marx. He received it back with a notation by Hoover which he mistook for approval and undertook the interrogation. Too late an aide noted that Hoover had disapproved. But the deed was done and Hoover reacted with customary anger, believing he had been defied. Mr. Nixon mistakenly thought the Brennan incident would cause such fallout that he could rid himself of Hoover and put his own man in. He was mistaken. The White House believed that because Marx and Hoover were close friends Hoover would never conduct a thorough inquiry into Ellsberg. The truth was that Marx was only a casual acquaintence of Hoover's. They had lunched once or twice at Dinty Moore's in New York, met at public dinners at the Waldorf, shared mutual friends and Hoover always replied with warmth to Marx's Christmas gifts of toys to distribute to children. One theory of Hoover's overreaction in the Brennan affair was that Mardian had been in direct contact with Brennan as had the White House. Hoover, ever jealous of outside interference, cracked down on Brennan as a lesson to his men and to the White House. (Personal interview, Ellsberg, 1/19/79)

page 340

In the end even Ellsberg was puzzled by exactly what had gone on in Cambridge, particularly when John Kenneth Galbraith told him that his son, Jamie, then at Harvard, had seen the Papers at Quincy House long before *The Times* published them. But Jamie Galbraith was no part of a "second Ellsberg ring." He happened to have a friend who worked in a Harvard Square copying shop. One day "an MIT professor" came in and wanted a rush job on a box of secret documents he was using, he said, in a history of the Vietnam war. The friend brought some pages back to Quincy House and showed them to Jamie. The young men were much interested—the documents bore names like Mac Bundy and Walt Rostow. The "MIT professor," of course, was Ellsberg himself, as Jamie discovered when *The Times* published the documents. Jamie used to exchange winks during the weeks that followed when he chanced to encounter the young woman who ran the copying shop. The FBI was all over Cambridge but for some reason never found out that her shop copied any of the papers. Ellsberg was amazed at this. He had thought the FBI had located all the many copying spots he had used. (Personal interviews, Ellsberg, 4/1/79; Jamie Galbraith, 3/31/78; John Kenneth Galbraith, 3/16/79)

page 383

In 1977 the discovery was accidentally made of thousands of files stored in an abandoned firehouse near the Birmingham City Hall among which were stenographic reports, recordings and secret information obtained by police agents and others during the Bull Connor regime. The discovery made by city archivists revealed that Connor routinely kept under surveillance figures in the

Civil Rights movement, newsmen and others. The police had arrangements whereby they were informed of the arrival of newsmen from the outside and/or others whom they might wish to keep an eye (and ear) on. They had the cooperation of at least one local newsman as well as hotel clerks and others. Most of the records related to the period after 1960 but there was reason to believe the program had its origin considerably earlier. In many cases these records provided the only documentation of meetings of Civil Rights groups. They served in this manner the same historical function as the records of the Okhrana, the Czar's police, did for the Russian Revolutionary movement. (Personal interview, Robert Gorley, Birmingham archivist, 4/6/79)

page 475

The editorial said:

"We do not question the right or the propriety of an investigation of the press by any agency of Congress. The press is not sacrosanct. It is as properly subject to Congressional inquiry as any other institution in American life. It is the inescapable responsibility of Congress, however, to make certain that any such inquiry be conducted in good faith and not motivated by ulterior purpose.

"A few employees of this newspaper who have appeared before the Eastland subcommittee have pleaded the Fifth Amendment. A few others have testified to membership in the Communist party over periods terminating at various dates in the past. So far as we are aware, no present member of the Communist party has been found among the more than four thousand employees on our rolls.

"The policy of this newspaper with regard to the employment of Communist party members has been stated many times and may be stated here again. We would not knowingly employ a Communist party member in the news or editorial departments of this paper, because we would not trust his ability to report the news objectively or to comment on it honestly, and the discovery of present Communist party membership on the part of such an employee would lead to his immediate dismissal.

"In the case of those employees who have testified to some Communist association in the past, or who have pleaded the Fifth Amendment for reasons of their own, it will be our policy to judge each case on its merits, in the light of each individual's responsibilities in our organization and of the degree to which his relations with this newspaper entitle him to possess our confidence.

"We may say this, however. We do not believe in the doctrine of irredeemable sin. We think it possible to atone through good performance for past error, and we have tried to supply the security and favorable working conditions which should exist in a democracy and which should encourage men who were once misled to reconsider and to reshape their political thinking. . . .

"It is our business to decide whom we shall employ and not employ. We do not propose to hand over that function to the Eastland subcommittee. Nor do we propose to permit the Eastland subcommittee, or any other agency outside this office, to determine in any way the policies of this newspaper. . . .

"It seems to us . . . that The Times has been singled out for this attack precisely because of the vigor of its opposition to many of the things for which Mr. Eastland, his colleague Mr. Jenner and the subcommittee's counsel stand —that is, because we have condemned segregation in the Southern schools; because we have challenged the high-handed and abusive methods employed by various Congressional committees; because we have denounced McCarthyism and all its works; because we have attacked the narrow and bigoted restrictions of the McCarran Immigration Act; because we have criticized a 'security system' which conceals the accuser from his victim; because we have insisted that the true spirit of American democracy demands a scrupulous respect for the rights of even the lowliest individual and a high standard of fair play. . . .

"This newspaper will continue to determine its own policies. It will continue to condemn discrimination whether in the South or in the North. It will continue to defend civil liberties. It will continue to enlist goodwill against prejudice and confidence against fear. . . .

"Our faith is strong that long after Senator Eastland and his present subcommittee are forgotten, long after segregation has lost its final battle in the South, long after all that was known as McCarthyism is a dim unwelcome memory, long after the last Congressional committee has learned that it cannot tamper successfully with a free press, The New York Times will still be speaking for the men who make it, and only for the men who make it, and speaking, without fear or favor, the truth as it sees it."

Index

ABC, 238, 547,
Abrams, Floyd, and Pentagon Papers, 238, 246–7, 255–6, 259, 260, 283, 315–16, 330, 445; in District Court, 289–91, 297, 300, 312
Abzug, Bella, 49–51
Acheson, Dean, 81, 91, 341
Adams, Frank, 152n, 491, 493
Adler, Julius, 66, 115, 176, 252n, 473, 477–8, 566; Dulles and Gruson, 478, 481
Adler Trust, 115
Agence France-Presse, 7
Agnew, Spiro, 51n, 95, 224, 416, 417
Air Force, 75
Alabama: libel suits vs. *Times* (see also titles), 381–90; race relations, 359, 367–8, 379–90, 415; University of, 359–60, 364
Alabama Journal, 379
Albany, Ga., 368, 371
Alejos, Roberto, 143
Alexander, James W., 102, 103, 105n
Allen, Ralph, 369
Allen, Richard V., 278
Allende, 532, 549
Allin, Lyndon K. (Mort), 231–2, 262–3
Alsop, Joseph, 87, 94, 460, 486, 513, 568, 569
Alsop, Stewart, 122–3, 186, 486, 565, 568
American Astronautical Society, 510
American Bar Association, 335
American Political Science Association, 23, 76–7
Amin, Mustafa, 523
Amper, Richard, 491
Amory, Robert, 479, 492n, 566–7, 569
Anderson, Jack, 417, 526, 527, 548, 553
Anderson, Paul, 446
Andreas, Duane, 424
Angleton, James, 93, 505, 516–18, 521, 535, 566, 575

AP, 7, 41
Apple, R. W., 428, 441
Arbenz, Jacob, 143, 149, 478, 480
Argus, 509–12, 513
Atomic weapons, 510–12, 513
Argyris (Chris) study of *Times,* 64–5, 67–9, 93
Arkansas, 352–3, 360–1
Arkansas Gazette, 371
Arnold and Porter, 172n
Ashmore, Harry, 356
Associated Press Managing Editors, 393
Atkinson, Brooks, 454, 491
Atlanta Journal, 365
Austin, Anthony, 23, 24, 42–3, 214

Bachinski, Eugene, 118
Bagdikian, Ben, 292, 293
Baker, Mimi (Mrs. Russell), 226
Baker, Russell, 226, 409
Baldwin, Alfred, III, 430–1
Baldwin, Hanson W., 45, 510–13 *passim,* 520, 550
Balfour-Paul, Glen, 505
Ball, George, 190, 284
Bancroft, Harding, 66, 126, 473n, 527; Alabama suits vs. *Times,* 385–6; Pentagon Papers, 136, 171–2, 185, 186, 205; Pentagon Papers and government action, 239–46 *passim,* 260, 290, 298, 300, 324; security and "Top Spook" episode, 316–18
Barber, Robert L., 453n
Barker, Bernard L., 420, 422n, 423, 424
Barnes, Joe, 454
Barnes, Ralph, 464
Barnes, Tracy, 158, 527, 566
Barnet, Richard J., 74, 87
Barnett, Ross, 365
Barrett, George, 491
Bartlett, Charles, 123n, 152

615